THE COLLECTED LETTERS OF
WILLIAM MORRIS

VOLUME I

EDITED BY NORMAN KELVIN

THE COLLECTED LETTERS OF

William Morris

VOLUME I
1848-1880

PRINCETON UNIVERSITY PRESS

PUBLICATION OF THIS BOOK HAS BEEN AIDED BY A GRANT FROM
THE ANDREW W. MELLON FUND OF PRINCETON UNIVERSITY PRESS

CLOTHBOUND EDITIONS OF PRINCETON UNIVERSITY PRESS BOOKS
ARE PRINTED ON ACID-FREE PAPER, AND BINDING MATERIALS ARE
CHOSEN FOR STRENGTH AND DURABILITY

THE PREPARATION OF THIS VOLUME WAS MADE POSSIBLE (IN PART) BY A
GRANT FROM THE PROGRAM FOR EDITIONS OF THE NATIONAL ENDOWMENT
FOR THE HUMANITIES, AN INDEPENDENT FEDERAL AGENCY.

LIBRARY OF CONGRESS CATALOGING IN PUBLICATION DATA

MORRIS, WILLIAM, 1834–1896.
THE COLLECTED LETTERS OF WILLIAM MORRIS.

INCLUDES INDEXES.   CONTENTS: V. 1. 1848–1880.
1. MORRIS, WILLIAM, 1834–1896—CORRESPONDENCE.
2. AUTHORS, ENGLISH—19TH CENTURY—CORRESPONDENCE.
3. ARTISTS—ENGLAND—CORRESPONDENCE.
4. SOCIALISTS—ENGLAND—CORRESPONDENCE.
I. KELVIN, NORMAN. II. TITLE.
PR5083.A4 1983   821'.8 [B]   82-47604
ISBN 0-691-06501-2 (V. 1)   AACR2

TO PHYLLIS, ELIZABETH, AND JANE,
AND THE MEMORY OF MY FATHER

CONTENTS

LIST OF ILLUSTRATIONS

LIST OF ILLUSTRATIONS

SCOPE OF THIS EDITION

THE COLLECTED LETTERS OF WILLIAM MORRIS comprises some 2,400 documents. Approximately 1,500 of them have not been previously published, and others have not hitherto been published in full. We do not know what fraction of the total of Morris's letters has been preserved, but all those known to survive, after an extensive search, have been included. They are arranged in one chronological sequence, with personal, business, formal, and public correspondence mixed together as in daily life. Each volume contains two indexes: one listing all correspondents and the pages on which letters to them appear; and the other a general subject index.

EDITORIAL PRACTICES

Transcription

FOR MOST of the letters, the text has been taken from the holograph original. In cases where the only extant source is a printed text (notably Mackail's 1899 biography), the letter or whatever part of it was quoted is reprinted here.

Inevitably, the translation of a holographic document to the printed page introduces some distortion of the original. Certain visual cues are lost: in particular, the end of a handwritten line may indicate the completion of a sentence even though a period is not used; space left between sentences may signify the sense of a new paragraph whether or not a new line is started or an indentation appears; a sentence may contain interpolated or crossed-out material indicating the writer's second thoughts. These features appear often in Morris's letters. My ideal has been to remain completely faithful to the text, but the realities of putting into print documents which were in no way intended for posterity have forced me to adopt certain conventions for the sake of readability with which the reader will want to be familiar.

Morris did not always divide his letters into formal paragraphs. Conventional paragraphing is here when it has seemed likely, from the spacing between sentences, that he intended some sort of break in the thought.

To have attempted to preserve the spaces as Morris had them would have been an enterprise doomed to frustration because of the different arrangement of words on the printed page and the regularity imposed by type; to have printed the body of the letter as a single unparagraphed block, although in some ways a good representation of the appearance of the holograph letter, would have been as much a departure from the spirit of the original as the introduction of formal paragraphs. I have therefore chosen, among admittedly unsatisfactory alternatives, to promote ease of reading by paragraphing.

Material crossed out by Morris, but still readable and representing a variation from what he finally wrote, is given in angle brackets. False starts in spelling, however, are not shown.

Occasionally I have expanded a word that Morris abbreviated, interpolated a clarifying word, or added *sic* to avoid confusion. In all such cases the added material is enclosed in square brackets. Question marks in square brackets indicate uncertainty in reading the preceding word. Most of the time Morris's handwriting is perfectly legible.

Dates and addresses have been placed at the upper right. When a date, or any part of one, has been supplied by the editor, it is given in square brackets. A question mark indicates that the suggested date is a plausible one only. When there is no question mark, the bracketed date is offered with confidence, since it was arrived at through internal evidence, cross-reference, or other compelling information. Letters that could be assigned only approximate dates have been placed in best-guess chronological order.

Apart from these liberties, Morris's words stand as they were written. Misspellings, run-on sentences, most abbreviated words, idiosyncratic punctuation and capitalization, occasional obscure passages or apparent slips of the pen are by and large not the subjects of editorial notation except as noted above, in the belief that the reader will prefer to work things out or ponder the ambiguities as Morris's actual correspondents may have had to do. In the publication of historical evidence there is no reason for the editor to come between the document and the reader except insofar as the translation from the original medium to print poses problems that must be solved typographically.

Annotation

A note giving the location of the holograph manuscript, or the published source if the original letter no longer survives, will be found following each letter. Previous publication in biographical or critical works, not including short excerpts, is also noted. The other notes then follow. I try to give useful, and sometimes new information about Morris's correspondents, the people and things he mentions, his work, and his connections with the events of the time, without overwhelming the letters themselves. In the case of well-known figures, for whom full biographies and other studies are readily available, a brief identification is given on first appearance, and thereafter such details are added as throw light on the letter at hand. For lesser-known figures, about whom information is harder to come by, a somewhat longer biographical account is provided at first mention. Cross-references from later references back to the first note are given when it has seemed particularly useful to do so, but in general readers should use the indexes to locate information. I should also mention that the notes occasionally provide comment on a peculiarity in the text.

The letters collected here are the fruits of fifteen years of searching. There may be others not yet found. Any letters that come to light too late for publication in chronological order will be included in an appendix to the last volume of this edition.

Manuscript Locations

Morris's letters are located in about 140 libraries and private collections in several countries. In Great Britain the main repository is the British Library, which holds the May Morris and Robert Steele bequests, the papers of George Bernard Shaw, John Burns, and Sidney Cockerell, and the Ashley Collection. The Library also holds, as one might expect, scattered Morris letters in the correspondence of other individuals. In the William Morris Gallery at Walthamstow, London, is another major group of letters, including those to Morris's mother and sister Emma, to Charles Faulkner, and to J. Bruce Glasier, the last an important part of Morris's socialist correspondence. There are significant holdings also in the library of the Victoria and Albert Museum and in the Bodleian Library, Oxford. A few letters are also to be found in the college libraries in Oxford. The Society of Antiquaries, London, Trustees of the Morris estate, have acquired the letters to E. W. B. Nicholson. There are also several letters in, among others, each of the following archives: the Fitzwilliam Museum, Cambridge, the Hammersmith Public Library; Kings College and Jesus College, Cambridge; Exeter College, Oxford; Transport House; The British Library of Political and Economic Science at the London School of Economics; the Manchester Public Libraries; the Public Record Office; the National Library of Scotland; the University of Sheffield; and the Birmingham Public Libraries.

The correspondence between Morris and George Howard, ninth earl of Carlisle, is located in the Castle Howard Archives, and contains the most important group of Morris's letters to survive among family papers.

Other archives in Europe notable for Morris holdings are the National Library of Iceland, the repository of most of the letters to Eiríkr Magnússon; and the International Institute of Social History, Amsterdam, which houses the papers of the Socialist League, including the correspondence between Morris and Andreas Scheu.

In the United States, the main institutional collections are at the Humanities Research Center, University of Texas, Austin, where many of the letters to Louisa Baldwin, Aglaia Coronio, Charles Fairfax Murray, and Emery Walker are located; Harvard University, the repository of letters to Charles Eliot Norton and Robert Thomson; Duke University, which has acquired the important series of letters to Thomas Wardle; the Pierpont Morgan Library, recently enriched by the gift of the collection of John M. Crawford, Jr.; and the Huntington Library, where letters to Sidney Cockerell, and others pertaining to the Society for the Protection of Ancient Buildings, may be found. There are significant numbers of letters also at Columbia University, including those to Emma Lazarus; at Princeton, which has obtained the Troxell Collection of Rossetti's correspondence; and at Yale, where letters to Rowley, Shaw, and W. J. Linton are located. There are Morris letters also in the Fales Library at New York University; in the libraries of the University of California at Los Angeles, Ohio State University, the University of Kansas, and Syracuse University; and in the Berg Collection and the Manuscript Division of the New York Public Library.

Among private holdings, the most extensive collection is that of Sanford and Helen Berger, whose Morris archive, impressive in all categories, includes the largest number of letters in private hands. Many other collectors have contributed to these volumes, as will be evident from the listing of manuscript locations. The generous cooperation of the institutions and individuals who have made this edition possible is detailed in the Acknowledgments.

PUBLICATION HISTORY

THE HISTORY of the previous publication of Morris's letters points to the need for the present work. About 685 letters were first given in full by May Morris, who incorporated them into the introductions to the twenty-four volumes of *The Collected Works*, published between 1910 and 1915, and into the two supplementary volumes, *William Morris: Artist, Writer,*

Socialist, published in 1936. Philip Henderson's pioneering *Letters of William Morris to His Family and Friends* (1950) included about 350 letters, many drawn from May Morris's introductions to *The Collected Works* and from J. W. Mackail's biography, *William Morris* (1899). Mackail is the only source for several of the letters, most importantly some of those to Georgiana Burne-Jones, Cormell Price, and F. S. Ellis. There were also a few letters printed in Georgiana Burne-Jones's *Memorials of Edward Burne-Jones* (1904). R. Page Arnot's *William Morris: The Man and the Myth* (1950) saw the first publication of the letters to J. L. Mahon; the *Labour Monthly* (1951) was the first to print many of those to the Rev. John Glasse; and in the *Socialist Review* (1928) appeared some of those to Andreas Scheu. An unpublished dissertation by Ney Lannes McMinn (1928), "The Letters of William Morris to the Press (1868-1895)" included most, though not all, of Morris's letters in this category. Several biographies of Morris, notably the first edition of E. P. Thompson's *William Morris: Romantic to Revolutionary* (1955) and Philip Henderson's *William Morris: His Life, Work and Friends* (1967) drew on unpublished letters. Richard L. Harris's "William Morris, Eiríkr Magnússon, and Iceland," *Victorian Poetry* (1975) brought to light a number of previously unknown letters to Magnússon. Other letters, singly and in small groups, have been the subjects of brief notes and articles which are not listed here.

As stated earlier, the present edition includes approximately 1,500 letters never before published and others not previously published in full. The newly collected correspondence pertains mostly to Morris and Company, the Eastern Question Association, the Society for the Protection of Ancient Buildings, the translation of saga literature, socialism, the Kelmscott Press, and Morris's friendship with Aglaia Coronio. For almost any other nineteenth-century figure the range of new letters would comprise an impressive number of categories enriched, but in the case of Morris we may candidly lament the areas scanted, such as Pre-Raphaelitism, his friendships with Georgiana Burne-Jones and her sisters, and his relationships with contemporary poets and novelists. The biographical data suggest, for example, that there ought to have been more letters to Tennyson, Browning, and Rossetti, as well as a few to W. B. Yeats, but a diligent and focused search has turned up none but those which appear in this edition. Nevertheless, there are letters printed here for the first time that do add, specifically, to our knowledge of Morris's relations with Rossetti, Burne-Jones, Browning, Swinburne, and Gladstone. Of much importance, too, particularly in tracing the history of certain of Morris's relationships, is that about 500 letters in this edition are dated for the first time or bear dates that are corrections of those given in previous sources.

ACKNOWLEDGMENTS

THE DEBTS INCURRED in editing a work as extensive and complex as the present one make difficult and risk-laden the effort to acknowledge all help received, in the degree given. Those persons and institutions thanked here are the ones that are currently in mind because of their continued interest and their recent help, or because their names are apparent in the written record that my own correspondence files have become. Any neglect or oversight receives my apology and will be corrected in the later volumes.

I wish first of all to thank the Society of Antiquaries of London for permission to publish Morris's letters. Permission was granted by the Society as Trustees of the William Morris Estate.

A special sense of gratitude is gladly expressed to Sanford and Helen Berger, who have provided me with photocopies of all the Morris letters in their impressive collection, and have also made available both their hospitality and the entire range of their Morris material, much of it indispensable for the annotation of the letters. I am deeply indebted also to R.C.H. Briggs, the former Honorary Secretary of the William Morris Society, who has been an ever-present guide and support during my researches in England; to Professor Jerome H. Buckley, whose generous help in scholarly matters predates the beginning of this edition; to Dr. Gordon N. Ray, President of the John Simon Guggenheim Memorial Foundation, who has expressed enthusiasm for the project and generous interest in it.

Equal thanks are due and gladly given to John M. Crawford, Jr., who shared both his magnificent Morris collection and his knowledge of the world of institutions and persons interested in Morris; to A. R. Dufty, C.B.E, F.S.A, a friend of many years in both his official and unofficial capacities, who made available the important collection of the Society of Antiquaries, and whose hospitality at Kelmscott Manor and elsewhere made every stay in England a lesson in the way a professional activity can be made a human one; to Joseph R. Dunlap, Secretary of the William Morris Society in America, whose vast acquaintance with details of Morris's life and career, the location of Morris documents, and the names and whereabouts of Morris people was always at my disposal; to the Hon. George Howard, who made me welcome at Castle

Howard and permitted me to obtain copies of the letters in the Castle Howard Archives, the most important archive still in family hands.

My full thanks go also to W. E. Fredeman, whose contributions to Pre-Raphaelite studies have become indispensable, and who has been helpful in bringing letters to my attention, as well as generous in sharing those in his own collection. Richard L. Harris shared with me his important find of letters to Eiríkr Magnússon. The late Philip Henderson, pioneer in contemporary Morris studies and a man whose capacity for friendship matched the fine literary sensibilities he brought to editing Morris's letters and writing his biography, was a warm and gracious host whenever I was in England. Dan H. Laurence's own enormous undertaking as editor of the Shaw letters has never prevented him from writing to tell me of each and every Morris letter that has come to his attention. Kenneth A. Lohf, Head of the Special Collections Library at Columbia University, has generously communicated to me his discoveries made in the pursuit of his own interest in the Morris circle. My ex-colleague Christopher Mulvey took time from his own research in England to do crucial work in behalf of my project. Paul Needham, Curator of Printed Books in the Pierpont Morgan Library, shared with me his unparalleled knowledge of the books at one time in Morris's library and has made possible the annotation of letters concerning book and manuscript purchases by Morris. From Graham Parry, a fine scholar and a good friend, I have learned much about the Pre-Raphaelites and Morris's England. Carole Silver, Morris scholar and lecturer, over the years has been generous with her time and interest in the progress of this edition. Peter Stansky, distinguished scholar, is a friend from whom I have learned much about British political history and Morris's place in it. His readiness to answer queries has benefited every user of this book.

Thanks, too, to William S. Peterson, who has never failed to write in detail, informing me of archival discoveries made in pursuit of his own work on Morris. It is a pleasure, also, to thank Nicolas Barker for true generosity: for his willingness to share the results of his own scholarship before they were published.

I want also to record a debt of gratitude to R. Page Arnot, who gave me free access to the letters to J. L. Mahon. Karl Beckson not only recorded the location of all Morris material that he discovered during his own research, but conveyed the information to me in so full and organized a way as to do half the work for me. John and Gillian Beer, whose hospitality and friendship have made visits to Cambridge memorable, helped on many occasions to bring needed materials within reach.

ACKNOWLEDGMENTS

Alan Bell took the initiative and told me of letters in the National Library of Scotland. C. L. Cline made my visit to the Humanities Research Center of the University of Texas at Austin a fruitful and pleasant one. During my stay in Austin, David Farmer kindly helped to facilitate my access to the holdings in the Center. Elizabeth de Haas welcomed me at the Emery Walker House and has permitted me to use much important Morris material. Kenneth Goodwin, whose good will was constant, made available to me his extensive listing of locations of Morris manuscripts. Cecil Y. Lang early shared with me his knowledge as an editor of letters. E. V. Quinn, librarian at Balliol College, went out of his way to make Oxford accessible to my inquiries. Lance Thirkell offered me hospitality, permitted me to see family papers, and related family recollections, passed on to him, that reach back to Edward and Georgiana Burne-Jones and Morris himself. E. P. Thompson, author of the book that reestablished the political dimension of Morris's career, supported my efforts when I began and directed me to archives where Morris's political correspondence is to be found. F. H. Thompson, General Secretary of the Society of Antiquaries, patiently and cheerfully simplified the problems that arose in the course of my correspondence with the Society in their capacity as Trustees for the William Morris Estate. Martha Salmon Vogeler always found time in the course of her own research to alert me to Morris material that had come her way. Ray Watkinson has shared with me his Morris letters, his time, and his great knowledge of Morris and of the history of English design. Expending much time and effort, Lorraine Price made available to me the diaries of her grandfather, Cormell Price. My gratitude to her is very special.

Although I owe thanks to librarians and archivists in many institutions, and will express my gratitude in a moment, a special place in my acknowledgments must go to Norah C. Gillow, of the William Morris Gallery, and to Judith Oppenheimer, formerly Archivist of Castle Howard. In the final preparation of the typescript for Volume I each of the above-mentioned was generous with her time and interest beyond reasonable expectation, answering my many letters seeking missing details for annotations, invariably to good purpose and with cheerfulness and patience. Both have acquired thick files of correspondence with me in the last few years, and each file is a testimony to the aid they have given.

And for assistance beyond what one ordinarily expects, I wish to thank also the following librarians and archivists: Grímur Helgason (National Library of Iceland), Joyce Whalley (Victoria and Albert Museum), M.W.S. Schreuder and Gotz Langkau (International Institute of Social History), and Herbert Cahoon (Pierpont Morgan Library).

To Allen Mandelbaum and Lillian Feder, my thanks for courteously extending to me certain facilities at the Graduate Center of the City University, at a time when it was important that I have these facilities. I want to express, too, my appreciation to Morton M. Pavane, Director of the City College Office of the City University Research Foundation, and to Morris D. Silberberg, Dean of Faculty Relations of the City College. Editions of letters depend, for their progress, on large and steady funding. Through the many crises in that area, Morton Pavane helped with his knowledgeable advice and good cheer to keep this project from foundering. Dr. Silberberg, at a cliff-hanging moment, helped me, in his capacity as Acting Provost of City College, to know that I would be able to keep up my end of the production schedule for this volume.

I wish to offer special thanks to my colleagues in the English Department of the City College of New York. Their dedication to scholarship and teaching has created a community and a climate in which it is a privilege to work; and which, as a source of encouragement and stimulation, was one of the reasons for my embarking on this project in the first place. Moreover, the good will and forbearance of my colleagues, their patience with me in matters which I can only suspect required patience, involved as they were with their own writing, helped carry me through the curves and bends of days in which teaching and the *Letters* insisted, with equal reasonableness, on attention. To Saul N. Brody, chairman and friend, I owe thanks for all these reasons and for an interest in my work that translated into practical aid of the most essential kind.

I am grateful to Bernard Korman, friend of many years, for wise counsel. I am indebted also to Robert Lekachman, old and good friend, too, for patient listening and sharing of professional experience.

A Senior Fellowship from the National Endowment for Humanities enabled me to begin the necessary research in England near the beginning of this project, and more recently, support from the Endowment's Division of Research Grants has made it possible for me to bring this volume to completion. During the years between these grants, I received generous support from the John Simon Guggenheim Memorial Foundation and additional help from the American Council of Learned Societies, the American Philosophical Society, and the Research Foundation of the City University of New York. I am pleased and grateful to be able to acknowledge their support.

It is a pleasure to thank Kathleen A. Morales for her indefatigable and essential effort in behalf of this project, over several years. Her transcription of the bulk of the letters gave the work its first faint outline as a book. As she solved problem after problem that arose in transcribing, her role became that of research assistant, and in the latter capacity she became a stabilizing presence: her participation enabled the work to proceed with dependable regularity, and obstacles never became a reason for forward motion to cease.

A special category of gratitude must be reserved for Margaret Home Smith. In her capacity as research assistant, she made contributions of far greater extent and requiring much more professional initiative than her offical title indicates. Joining the project at a point of low ebb in its fortunes, when the typescript, files, and sundry notes were falling into alarming disarray because help had not been available in the previous few years, she worked with purpose and zeal to restore order and allow the annotating process to go forward again. Indeed, her own contribution to that process was of first importance, for it was she who amassed the information that enabled the second—and first substantive—round of note writing to begin. It is no exaggeration to say that she was, at a certain stage of the project, more an associate than an aide.

Gale Sigal, too, made contributions that required professional ability and participation far beyond that routinely expected of a research assistant. She too, has been more of an associate than an aide and has played an essential role in the third and final expansion of notes, locating needed information in background sources and preparing it in a manner that often required little rewording. Finally, she has helped with the difficult and complex task of bringing the typescript into conformity with the editorial principles as these finally emerged. It is a pleasure to include her name with those for whom my special gratitude is reserved.

To Tamara Pakes and Shelley Kleiman, I give warm thanks. Although their association with the *Letters* was brief, my thanks need not be curtailed. Tamara Pakes often returned from library research with information others had declared nonexistent. Shelley Kleiman, away from New York on her own business, located essential information at its source.

My thanks go also to Marjorie Sherwood of Princeton University Press. The vision and enthusiasm that informed her support of the work were essential to the process of publication.

For help with locating information and with proofreading the manuscript, my thanks to Gill Haroian-Guerin, Laura Jeffers, Veronica Makowsky, Steven Meyers and Michael Petty.

I wish to express my gratitude to the librarians, archivists, curators, and keepers, not previously mentioned, who extended courtesy and aid to me when I visited, and were generous with their time and interest in correspondence. They are G. E. Awdry (National Liberal Club), Wilfred Blunt (Watts Museum), Shirley Bury (Victoria and Albert Museum), Carole Cable (Humanities Research Center), Alexander E. Conway (William Andrews Clark Memorial Library), Nigel Cross (Royal Literary Fund), Clive E. Driver (the Philip H. & A.S.W. Rosenbach Foundation), Ellen S. Dunlap (Humanities Research Center), Elizabeth Ellem (King's College, Cambridge), John Fuller (Victoria and Albert Museum), John A. Gere (British Library), Rachel K. Grover (University of Toronto Library), Gene DeGruson (Kansas State College), Michael Halls (King's College Library, Cambridge), Tyrus G. Harmsen (Occidental College), J. P. Harthan (Victoria and Albert Museum), Jack W. Herring (Armstrong Browning Library), John Hopkins (Society of Antiquaries), David Jervis (British Library), Froda Jones (Jesus College, Cambridge), Alan Jutzi (Huntington Library), J. T. Killen (Jesus College, Cambridge), Donald King (Victoria and Albert Museum), Beverly Ruth Vander Kooy (State University of New York at Buffalo), Lionel Lambourne (Victoria and Albert Museum), Ronald MacDougall (University of Southern Maine), J. R. Maddicott (Exeter College, Oxford), J. Marks (British Library), David I. Masson (Brotherton Library, University of Leeds), G. Matheson (Rylands University Library of Manchester), James Moseley (St. Bride Printing Library), Barbara Morris (Sotheby and Co., formerly of the Victoria and Albert Museum), K. D. Murtova (Institute of Russian Literature), Frank Paluka (University of Iowa), Linda Parry (Victoria and Albert Museum), the Keeper and Staff of the Public Record Office, Brian Reade (Victoria and Albert Museum), Elizabeth G. Riely (Yale University Library), F. W. Roberts (Humanities Research Center), Florian J. Shasky (Stanford University), T. C. Skeat (British Library), H. M. Stanley (State University of New York at Cortland), Lola Szladits (The Berg Collection, New York Public Library), Frank Taylor (Rylands University Library of Manchester), James Thorpe and staff (Huntington Library), K. J. Wallace (British Library), Jan Ward (Armstrong Browning Library), M. Weaver (William Morris Gallery), James M. Wells (Newberry Library), Brooke Whiting (University of California at Los Angeles), Ian R. Willison (British Library), Paul Woudhuysen (Fitzwilliam Museum), and the members, not named here, of the staffs of the many libraries and archives who have helped in person or have corresponded with me, during the preparation of the edition.

Others who have shared with me their special knowledge in the many areas on which Morris's letters touch have earned my gratitude for their ready assistance. I am grateful to Chaim Abramsky, Gary L. Atho,

Douglas F. Bauer, Geoffrey Beard, Felicia Bonaparte, Florence Boos, Malcolm J. Bosse, Andrew Brown, Charles E. Brownell, Gail Buckland, Grace J. Calder, Joseph Campbell, Margaret Campbell, C. E. Carrington, J. V. Chapple, Morton N. Cohen, Dame Margaret Cole, Thomas Cullen, Monica Dance, John Dreyfus, E. M. Dring, Helen Eisenman, Richard Ellmann, Peter Emmett, Peter Faulkner, Richard J. Finneran; William Fishman, Penelope Fitzgerald, Paul Fussell, Marvin Gettleman, Chandler Grannis, Roger Lancelyn Green, Gordon S. Haight, Leo Hamalian, H. G. Harley, Michael Harrison, Rupert Hart-Davis, L. F. Hasker, William S. Henisch, A. B. Holiday, Robert Hosman, Marilyn Ibach, Fred Kaplan, Frederick Karl, Kumar and Valerie Krishna, Mary Lago, Robert Langbaum, John LeBourgeois, Eugene D. LeMire, Robert Leslie, Lady Elizabeth Longford, Roger Lovatt, Jeremy Maas, Lionel Madden, K. A. Manley, Ian MacDougell, Keith A. McKenzie, Paul Meier, Winifred A. Meyers, Liam Miller, Philip Miller, Annie Milsted, Henry Morris, Dan Murphy, William M. Murphy, James F. O'Gorman, Edward O'Shea, J.H.P. Pafford, Edmund Penning-Rowsell, Sir John Pope-Hennessy, John Ranlett, the late Sir Herbert Read, Diana J. Rendall, John D. Rosenberg, Andrew Rothstein, Nicholas A. Salerno, Michael J. Salevouris, Mark H. Samuels-Lasner, A. C. Sewter, Sotheby Parke Bernet Co., Jeffrey Spear, the late Lionel Stevenson, Susan Thompson, the late Geoffrey Tillotson, Michael Timko, Joel Wiener, John Wilson, Carl Woodring, and Senator Michael Yeats.

I wish also to express my thanks to the institutions, and my special gratitude to the individuals, who kindly made available copies of letters in their possession and gave permission to publish them in this edition. They are: Allegheny College Library; the Trustees of Amherst College; Elmer L. Andersen; the Society of Antiquaries, London; Paul Avrich; Balliol College, Oxford; Mrs. Freeman Bass; D. R. Bentham; D.M.H. Betts; Birmingham Public Libraries; Howard Blanke; Bodleian Library, Oxford; Museum of Fine Arts, Boston; Frederic G. Melcher Library, R. R. Bowker Company; John Brandon-Jones; the British Library Board; British Library of Political and Economic Science, London School of Economics; the Colbeck Collection, the Angeli-Dennis Papers, and the Penkill Papers in the Special Collections Division, University of British Columbia Library; Brown University Library; Bryn Mawr College Library, Gift of the Friends of the Library In Honor of Mary Peirce '12; J.P.T. Bury; Lafayette Butler; Department of Special Collections, Research Library, University of California, Los Angeles; University of California at Santa Barbara; William Andrews Clark Memorial Library, University of California, Los Angeles; the Syndics of the Cambridge University Library; Cambridge University Press; Castle Howard Archives; Special Collections Department, Honnold Library, Claremont Colleges; Special Collections, Miller Library, Colby College, Waterville, Maine; Special Collection, the Charles Leaming Tutt Library, Colorado College; Rare Book and Manuscript Library, Columbia University; Manuscript Division, Library of Congress; Cornell University Library; Royal Institute of Cornwall; Dartmouth College Library; Gene DeGruson Collection; the Collection of Derbyshire Museum Service; Estelle Doheny Collection of the Edward Laurence Doheny Memorial Library, St. John's Seminary, Camarillo, California; Trustees of the Thomas Hardy Memorial Collection in the Dorset County Museum, Dorchester; A. R. Dufty; Sir Thomas Wardle Papers, Perkins Library, Duke University; Edinburgh City Libraries; the Rector and Fellows of Exeter College, Oxford; Fabian Society, London; the Syndics of the Fitzwilliam Museum, Cambridge; Folger Shakespeare Library; Fondation Custodia (Coll. F. Lugt), Institut Néerlandais, Paris; Colin Franklin; John A. Gere; London Borough of Hammersmith Public Libraries; Houghton Library, Harvard University; Colonel James A. Heathcote, USAF; Huntington Library, San Marino, California; National Library of Iceland; University of Illinois Library at Urbana-Champaign; Lilly Library, Indiana University, Bloomington, Indiana; Institute for Russian Literature, Leningrad, U.S.S.R.; International Institute for Social History; Iowa State Education Association, Des Moines, Iowa; Iowa State Historical Department, Des Moines, Iowa; University of Iowa Libraries, Iowa City, Iowa; The Irving Archive, Theatre Museum, Victoria and Albert Museum; the Master and Fellows of Jesus College, Cambridge; Department of Special Collections, Spencer Library, University of Kansas; King's College Library, Cambridge; Herman W. Kapp; Albert S. Kerr; Kirklees Libraries and Museums Service; Labour Party Library; Thomas V. Lange: Brotherton Collection, University of Leeds; Eugene D. LeMire; Walter Leuba; Lockwood Memorial Library, State University of New York at Buffalo; Greater London Record Office, County Hall, London; University of London Library; Cudahy Memorial Library, Loyola University of Chicago; Department of Rare Books and Special Collections of the McGill University Libraries; David Jackson McWilliams; the Cultural Services Committee of Manchester Central Library; Lady Rosalie Mander; University Library, University of Massachusetts at Amherst; the Collection of Edith S. and John S. Mayfield, Bethesda, Maryland; Charles M. Monell; Jacks Collection of the Monterey Public Library; F. C. Morgan; Pierpont Morgan Library; Mitchell Library, Sydney, Australia; Henry W. and Albert A. Berg Collection, The New York Public Library, Astor, Lenox, and Tilden Foundations; Fales Library, New York University; Newberry Library, Chicago; Nottingham Record Office; Nuffield College, Oxford; Occidental College; Ohio State University Libraries; the late Norman Holmes Pearson; Historical Society of Pennsylvania; the Master and Fellows of Peterhouse, Cambridge; Carl H. Pforzheimer Library; Rare Book Department, The Free Library of Philadelphia; L.A.C. Price; Rare Books and Special Collections Department, Princeton University; Rossetti Collection of Janet Camp Troxell in Princeton University Library; the Public Record Office; Bernard Quaritch, Ltd.; University of Queensland Library; the Philip H. & A.S.W. Rosenbach Foundation, Philadelphia; Julia V. Rosenthal; Irving Rosenwater; John Rylands University Library of Manchester; St. Bride Printing Library; The Trustees of the National Library of Scotland; William H. Scheide; Collection of Stuart B. Schimmel; Scottish Record Office; Ella Strong Denison Library, Scripps College; Director of Libraries, City of Sheffield Libraries; University of Sheffield Library; John Shulman; The Principal and Fellows of Somerville College, Oxford; H. L. Spilstead; Department of Special Collections, Green Library, Stanford University; Norman H. Strouse Collection; John D. Swales; George Arents Research Library for Special Collections at Syracuse University; Taylor Institution Library, University of Oxford; Humanities Research Center, University of Texas, Austin; Alan G. Thomas; Metropolitan Toronto Library Board; Thomas Fisher Rare Book Library, University of Toronto; Trinity College, Cambridge; The Board of Trinity College, Dublin; Francis Fitz-Randolph Rare Book Room, Vassar College; the Victoria and Albert Museum Library; National Library of Wales; Michael L. Walker; John J. Walsdorf; William Morris Gallery, Walthamstow; Walthamstow Public Library; Wellesley College Library; the West Sussex County Archivist and the Governors of Dunford House; Henry Francis du Pont Winterthur Museum, Joseph Downs Manuscript Collection; The Osborn Collection, Yale University Library; Beinecke Rare Book and Manuscript Collection, Yale University Library; and Amy Yates and the late Arnold Yates.

Any acknowledgment of thanks must conclude with a word about the contribution of Judith May, my editor at Princeton University Press. A number of the editorial principles that have shaped the final text were formulated by her. Nearly every annotation has benefited from her styling. The introductory material as well as some notes underwent such extensive revision at her hands as to constitute joint authorship of the final wording. Her queries were relentless in demanding more or better information or the removal of ambiguity. Though the forest of tags that adorned the copyedited typescript when I first received it back from her caused my spirits to sink, the need to traverse that terrain again was finally for me an exercise in growth of awareness: growth of awareness, I do not hesitate to say, of the requirements of modern scholarly editing. To the extent that this edition falls short of the best modern practice in editing, the responsibility is mine. To the extent that it has incorporated the best current editorial practices, the credit is Judith May's. It is she who insisted that Morris's letters are, first of all, historical documents; she brought to the project a clear and consistent sense of the obligations of the editor to the reader and user of such documents. The hours she has devoted to the task, the patient but persistent guidance of the work from original manuscript to printed book are reasons not only for my gratitude but for that of all who will use this edition.

Custom dictates that one's family be acknowledged last, and the practice has the virtue of reserving the emphasis of a conclusion for those whose contribution is least easily described. My wife, Phyllis, shared the labors, the problems, and the solutions at every step of the way. With grace and a clear view, she accepted the permeation of our lives by a project that could not be confined to particular hours or days. My daughters, Jane and Elizabeth, have not known a time when this edition was not in progress. They would have every right to object to its intrusion into their lives, but they have, instead, developed the mildest of possible feelings toward William Morris. To say that the work could not have been accomplished without the support of my family is to say that their share in this book is to be recorded, not measured.

INTRODUCTION

THE STRONG, PERSISTENT THEMES in William Morris's letters are architecture and the decorative arts; work, its pleasures and to a lesser degree its problems; socialism, which, arguably, is a synthesis of his other interests; and in the last years of his life, the Kelmscott Press, which is even more a bringing together of earlier commitments and enthusiasms. Threaded through these themes is another subject—love and the lack of it: love of family and of friends, love that tries to redeem, even challenge in importance, the apparent absence of physical love in Morris's marriage.

When he left Oxford in 1856, Morris planned to follow architecture as a career, and though he abandoned the ambition, after a brief period in the office of G. E. Street, he never stopped thinking in architectural terms. This was literally so, for he believed, with Ruskin, that architecture was the mother of all the other arts. It was metaphorically true as well, for he saw the raising and decorating of buildings as the human continuation of nature's own business. For Morris, to decorate was to know a joy and pleasure akin to what Wordsworth felt when he looked at mountains and streams or apostrophized them in poetry (though Morris loved landscape too). It was to know the joy and pleasure that those who love others greatly know in human intimacy.

Taking architecture in its literal meaning only, the letters Morris devoted to this subject, or accented by passing allusions to it, are outnumbered only by those concerned with socialism. Perhaps more to the point, Morris is at his most fluent when he is defending an ancient building against the planned depredations, as he saw them, of the restorers. His many letters written in behalf of the Society for the Protection of Ancient Buildings—"Anti-Scrape"—are complemented by the letters written for Morris and Co. having to do with stained-glass windows and other decorative additions to buildings, and by letters to family and friends in which a report on a building he has seen is a way of letting them know what the pleasures he experienced really were on some journey undertaken for business, lecturing, or holiday. If we were to add to these groups the letters pertaining to the Kelmscott Press, arguing, as Morris believed, that the principles of good book design are the principles of good architecture, the letters that could then be said to discuss "architecture" would by a great margin be the largest number in this collection.

Architecture also occasioned a range of styles in Morris's writing, not merely a removal of the clumsiness that is present when he is writing against the grain—writing, that is, on a subject he would rather leave alone. In a letter to a newspaper, he argues eloquently that an ancient building is part of the fabric of history and must be preserved as such. In 1879, he corresponds with a number of people, urging them to protest the proposed restorations of St. Mark's, Venice. He moves through a range of tones and attitudes, from the formality with which he addresses Gladstone to the warm, expansive, and detailed account he provides Browning, a fellow poet, a friend, and a man who can be relied on to *see*. To Ruskin, whose support he assumes he will have, he is friendly, respectful, and soberly anxious. To Georgiana Burne-Jones, he exults in obtaining on a petition against the proposed St. Mark's restoration the signature of Disraeli, whom he had vilified two years earlier during the Eastern Question protest.

When English buildings need to be defended against the restorer, Morris is even more confident: concise and ironic directness, the mark of his style at its best, controls the tone. This is because letters written in behalf of English buildings reflect not so much his commitment to the idea that art is universal as his nontheoretical, intense Englishness, a fundamental trait of his character that must figure in any discussion of his activities, whether architecture, the decorative arts, poetry, book design, or socialism. The letters about English churches and other ancient buildings assume an air of wanting only what would be desired by any sensible person who knew the facts—the facts of history and of aesthetics that reveal the restorers to be arrogant blunderers. Irony is used sparingly but always to effect. The national characteristics of the English—the deplorable ones—are named. In denouncing the piling up of monuments in Westminster Abbey, Morris chides the English for their infatuation with themselves. In protesting the removal of the statues around the spire of St. Mary's, Oxford, he links the dons' alleged view of their function—to educate the sons of the middle class to become leaders of capitalism—with their massive indifference to the integrity of buildings and thus to history. Always, in writing about a building in danger of being restored, he is indignant, incredulous, amazed at the chicanery of some and the ignorance of others, impatient with complacency in all its manifestations. Even his despair, an underlying note in many of these letters, serves as an ironic challenge-to-combat, thrown down to architects, deans of cathedral chapters, building committees, and, by inference, the general public, who have to be roused from their

indifference and to be educated. This note of the educational impera-
tive—for Morris is a teacher, perhaps a teacher before all else in his
letters on public issues—anticipates the tone of the letters on socialism.
Indeed, it anticipates his view of socialist action, which came to be,
essentially, that socialists should teach.

Architecture, as a theme in the letters, leads directly to friendship.
Among Morris's few long and unbroken friendships, the one best rep-
resented in the surviving letters is that with Philip Webb. They met in
1856, in Street's office, where Morris had just been articled and Webb
was then chief clerk. In the letters, Webb is the friend with whom Mor-
ris is most often spontaneous and at ease. Only when writing to Webb,
among men, can he discuss novels and poetry without awkwardness or
self-conscious constraint. It is clear that Webb, unlike others, did not
make him feel that his extraordinary antimodernism in literary taste was
a failing. With Webb, too, Morris will initiate a discussion of literature,
whereas with others, notably George Bernard Shaw and even his be-
loved Georgiana Burne-Jones, he usually squirms before an apparent
request for an opinion, so that he ends up, defensively, merely finding
fault with the book or author about whom his view has been solicited,
and in no very profound or perceptive terms. Notable in this respect
are his strictures on Tolstoy in a letter to Georgiana Burne-Jones, 1888,
and his clumsy comments on Robert Louis Stevenson in one to G. B.
Shaw of 1886.

The warmth that Morris felt for Webb inspired an admixture of blunt
directness and graciousness. An example is the letter of August 27, 1894.
Webb had protested Morris's regularly sending him the sumptuous
Kelmscott Press books as gifts. Morris tells him the story of the traveler
in the American West who ordered chicken at his hotel, only to find
himself looking into the barrel of a derringer as the hotel clerk said:
"Stranger, you will not have chicken, you will have hash." Morris draws
the moral: "This story you seem to have forgotten. So I will apply it,
and say that you will have the Kelmscott books as they come out. In
short you will have hash because it would upset me very much if you
did not have a share in my 'larx.' . . . You see . . . I do the books
mainly for you and one or two others; . . . I tell you I *want* you to have
them & finally you *shall*."

But it is not only affection and eloquence that give the letters to Webb
their importance. These letters are the only ones written to a friend that
bridge in time Morris's early enthusiasm for architecture and his later
commitment to socialism. For among earliest friends, only Webb and
Charles Faulkner followed Morris into socialism in 1883 and then stayed
loyal as he left first the Social Democratic Federation and then the So-

cialist League, to come to rest finally in the Hammersmith Socialist Society. Since friendship, work, and socialism are among the main themes in Morris's letters, those to Webb are a strong, continuous, and bright thread in this collection, binding the early years to the later ones, indeed to Morris's last days.

In emphasizing their importance, I am not unmindful that I have not yet spoken of the family letters. The letters to Jane, Jenny, and May Morris ought to be given first consideration, it might be argued, since together they constitute the largest number, and many of them illuminate Morris's work and activities. There is a problem, however. Those among them of chief interest—the letters to Jane and Jenny Morris— have to be read in the light of new information about Morris's marriage and about the effects of Jenny's illness upon the household. In one sense, the letters to Jane Morris and to Jenny, because both wife and daughter were in different ways the cause of much anguish, and because Morris's protective love for Jenny—and sympathy for Jane—were two of the forms of affection elicited by the circumstances, can be regarded as the most revealing. In another, they are not revealing at all. What they "reveal" is Morris's ability to conceal much that is on his mind and much that he feels.

We know now not only that Jane Morris and D. G. Rossetti were lovers from 1867 or 1868 to 1875 but that Wilfrid Scawen Blunt, to whom we are indebted for some of the most acute observations of Morris in his last years, became Jane's lover about 1884, in part, he seems to imply, in order to be able to view himself as the successor of Rossetti, whom he admired as a poet. We know also that Jenny's illness wracked Jane Morris beyond endurance and that the strain between husband and wife during Jenny's worst periods was severe. But Morris's letters to Jane record only a bleakness of tone or a tender solicitude on unnamed grounds. If he ever made reference to the actual events that Blunt and Jane Morris record in some detail, the letters, or the particular passages, in which he did so have not survived.

Perhaps the absence of any letters to Jane Morris earlier than 1870 speaks of a crisis in the late 1860's and suggests strongly that letters of that period, and possibly earlier ones, were destroyed by her. However infrequently he may have been away from her between April 1859, when they were married, and 1870, there was almost a year of their engagement—the summer of 1858 to April 1859—and one year, as well, between their meeting and their engagement. With Morris in London for the better part of these two years, it would be an even stranger marriage than it appears to have been had there not been a fair amount of correspondence. None of it, if there was, seems to remain, however, and this contrasts with the survival of letters after 1870, when some kind of agreement was apparently reached between them, having as its main article that Jane could do as she pleased.

One of the earliest letters to her, dated December 3, 1870, seems to have been in reply to a despondent one: "As for living, dear," Morris writes, "people like you speak about don't know either what life or death means, except for one or two supreme moments of their lives, when something pierces through the crust of dullness and ignorance, and they act for the time as if they were sensitive people—For me I don't think people really want to die because of mental pain, that is if they are imaginative people; they want to live to see the play played out fairly—they have hopes that they are not conscious of—" Though he seems to refer to someone other than Jane, it is difficult to believe that the words affirming life are not meant for her, are not a response to something she had said or hinted about the state of her own feelings. It is hard, that is, not to see this letter as anticipating his later words, "Please dear Janey be happy," written to her from Iceland in 1871. Since Jane was then living at Kelmscott with Rossetti, it is possible that guilt— despite Morris's tacit acceptance of the situation—had made her ask her husband for something more than acceptance, perhaps for approval and encouragement. Another possibility is that Rossetti had begun to cause her unhappiness and that she had turned to Morris for consolation, as if he were merely a good friend. And except for this one poignant sentence, the letters to Jane from Iceland concentrate on saga literature: they deliberately avoid discussing what would be at best a bleak topic for Morris, however clear the understanding between him and his wife. Similarly, in letters from Florence in 1873, and from Wales in 1875, Morris only describes what he sees: he does not speculate on what Jane may be doing or feeling at home. He does not ask questions.

The most significant letters to Jane, with a view to our understanding her, are those that begin in the late 1870's and discuss, at first, Liberal Party politics. It may be that the end of her affair with Rossetti in 1875 lifted a weight from Morris and made him feel free to write to her. But whatever the cause, the fact is that he apparently assumes that she is informed about politics and able to share in his own analyses of events. That Jane was aware of the larger world, interested in it, and socially sophisticated by the 1870's, is suggested by her friendship with George and Rosalind Howard, who liked her and sought her company. Art, politics, and literature were the topics of conversation at the Howards' home at Naworth. Morris's letters to Jane of the late 1870's are evidence that he not only regarded her as a person of intelligence but that husband and wife had found in public affairs circumscribed common ground.

What was true of the 1870's, when Morris was active in the Eastern Question Association and in touch with the Liberal Party, remained true in the 1880's, when he became a socialist. Circumstantial reports, particularly G. B. Shaw's "Morris as I Knew Him," have created the view that Morris never discussed socialism with Jane. This is misleading. Although references to socialism occur more often in the letters to his daughters, the letters to Jane also seem to expect, through their tone and manner, a sympathetic and informed reader. It is in a letter to Jane that we get an account of the march of socialist and workingmen's organizations to Highgate Cemetery, March 18, 1884, to commemorate Karl Marx and the Paris Commune. Morris clearly enjoys writing this letter, and his narrative skill and eye for detail are much in evidence, from his reference to the march as "a religious function" to his description of himself: "I trudged all the way from Tottenham Court Rd. up to Highgate Cemetery (with a red-ribbon in my button-hole) at the tail of various banners and a very bad band." Another letter to Jane, dated December 18, 1884, describes the decisive meeting of the Social Democratic Federation in which Hyndman was outvoted on the motion to expel W. J. Clarke. The tone, manner, and details presume much familiarity on Jane's part with Morris's political associates and their relations with each other—indeed, greater knowledge than Morris seems to expect from some of the socialists with whom he met or corresponded regularly.

Nevertheless, there are fewer letters to Jane in the years of intense socialist activity—1883 through 1889—than there are in the Liberal period, also seven years. The reason for the rise and fall in the frequency of Morris's letters to Jane may be either that she destroyed or simply neglected to keep those of certain periods, or that when she was involved with a lover, Morris refrained from writing to her—refrained from intruding on her or simply had no heart to discuss anything with her on a regular basis. Thus, the letters increase in 1876, the year after Jane's affair with Rossetti ended. But then, in August 1883, about a year after Rossetti died, she was introduced to W. S. Blunt at Naworth Castle by Rosalind Howard, who deliberately brought them together. It is not clear exactly when Jane and Blunt became lovers, but her earliest surviving letter to him is dated July 6, 1884, and although its subject is prosaic enough—she asks him to write an article on Egypt ("as you are better acquainted with Egyptian matters than anyone else") for the socialist magazine *To-Day*—it ends: "When are you coming to see me again?" It is possible, therefore, that although she shared Morris's interest in socialism more than has ever been noticed by Morris's biographers, the whole socialist period was shadowed for him by the knowledge that Blunt and his wife were lovers. Morris's letters to Jane of that period may well need to be read in that light, as those from 1870 through 1875 require an awareness of Rossetti in the background.

As for the surviving letters to Jane of the 1890's, they are a mere handful, explained in part by Morris's traveling less as illness slowed him and in part by the replacement of socialism by printing as his major interest. What Blunt's influence is here, is not clear. In a diary entry for October 18, 1890, Blunt wrote: "I spent the day yesterday with Mrs. Morris, the last I fancy in a quite intimate way— She felt this and said it, and I did not contradict." But this was premature. Between that date and the summer of 1894 there was not only much intimate talk recorded in Blunt's diary, but on August 11, 1892, he noted: "We slept together, Mrs. M. and I, and she told me things about the past which explain much in regard to Rossetti. 'I never quite gave myself,' she said, 'as I do now.' "

Jane's continued desire for Blunt, whatever the decline in his ardor for her, is enough to explain the paucity of letters from Morris: either he wrote few to her or she kept few. But those that survive, by design or not, show a continuing and genuine sharing of interests with her. And Jane's letters to Blunt show what she presumably expressed to Morris as well: a keen interest in the Kelmscott Press (when Morris began printing Blunt's *Love Lyrics and Songs of Proteus*, she wrote to Blunt that the work went slowly "with *our* [italics mine] two men "but that "soon we shall take two more . . .").

Morris's last letters to Jane are about the Kelmscott Press. They are cheerful and warm and give brief progress reports on books being printed. They are also hurried in a way that suggests she will understand that he is busy, but contentedly so. The last surviving letter to her, written in early 1893, says: "Now this is a bad letter. . . . I can't write a good letter, so please accept the will for the deed my dear." In his earliest letters to her, he often seemed anxious that his desire that she be happy compensate for his inability to make her so. He concludes as he began.

The letters to Jenny and May Morris, taken together, undermine some received views about his correspondence with them. The letters to Jenny are not always marked by a special fondness. There is not always less affection expressed in the letters to May. It is true that there are more surviving letters to Jenny than to May, the result of Jenny's being often away in a nursing establishment after her first epileptic seizure in 1876. But what we must do is read these letters against the background of new information, or confirmation of old suspicions, namely, that Jane

Morris could not tolerate her ill daughter and that Morris's worries about Jenny and the possible effects of Jane's neglect were exacerbated by his knowledge of her effect on Jane.

For these reasons, Morris masks all his anxieties when he writes to Jenny, and bends his energies to be only cheerful and gentle. At first, he hardly succeeds: some of the letters to her of the late '70's and early '80's show nothing so much as his inability to find something to say. They are staccato and diffuse. But when she is grown, his tenderness finds its proper key. Many letters of the 1890's to Jenny are chatty, confidential; they allude to shared delights, and are sensitively aware always that Jenny misses him. He wants to protect her from the hurt not only of her illness but of her mother's inability to help her. The year 1892, for example, records a series of tender, caring letters to her. There is frequent correspondence between June and October; a particularly newsy, cheerful letter, dated August 12, ends (as do all the letters of that summer): "Best love darling, to you & Mother." It is hard to escape the conclusion that Morris, suspecting Blunt's affair with Jane (as Blunt surmised he did), was more concerned with its effect on Jenny than with any other meaning or consequence it might have had. It is Morris at his most selfless, doing in human relations, what he does best.

The first surviving letter to May Morris alone (one was sent jointly to the two sisters from Reykjavík in the summer of 1873) is dated March 21, 1876. The style and manner anticipate the gaiety and warmth that mark his letters to her as an adult, when she became his partner and companion, especially in the cause of socialism, the business of Morris and Co., and the Kelmscott Press.

In these letters, there are moments of candor—less noticeable in his letters to Jane or Jenny—about other people, including friends. About Mary De Morgan, who disapproved of socialism, Morris writes to May on April 1, 1885: "[She] came in and straightway fell to tackling us with her usual noise; but with rather more than her usual ignorance." This letter also reflects the oddly rough camaraderie between Morris and his younger daughter during the years of great socialist activity. The early months of 1885, when the Socialist League had just been founded, were a period of high optimism for Morris. The letters to May, written at this time, are hardly distinguishable in tone from those to the men with whom he corresponds about League affairs. As developments in the League begin to aggravate Morris, the letters to May become telegraphic and uninformative. She is too well versed in the controversies to need extended accounts of them, the letters seem at times to imply. At other times, they suggest that the air is thick with the factionalism Morris hates and that for this reason he will discuss nothing in particular; May is not one whom he will burden with his disillusionment or pessimism. In the background, too, is May's becoming a young woman, and her marriage to H. H. Sparling in 1890. Perhaps what we read in the letters to her after about 1885 is reticence: a feeling that to speak of his daughter's private life is to interfere, even as in the letters to Jane he avoids any reference to her life apart from him.

Of course, it is possible that May Morris, zealous and faithful preserver of the record of her father's life, made an exception of letters having to do with her own affairs and destroyed them. Her marriage lasted from June 14, 1890 to mid or late May, 1894. In this entire period, there are only two surviving letters to her, one dated June 20, 1890, and the other (which I have conjecturally dated), January 1893. The feebleness of this showing is grounds for suspecting that she destroyed letters from her father. She might have done so even if each of them contained only one obligatory paragraph inquiring after Harry or commenting innocuously about him. Although only Jenny, among family members, receives Morris's letters regularly during these years, even Jane does better than May: six letters to her, written between April 1890 and early 1893 (the date of the last) survive. That May Morris was determined to eliminate all evidence of her marriage, insofar as the proof existed on paper, is attested to by her use of ink eraser to remove from a guest book the name "Sparling" after her own.

The reason for noticing Morris's letters to Edward Burne-Jones only after those to Webb and family is that remarkably few have survived. From the earliest Oxford days, when Morris and he were fellow members of the Oxford Brotherhood, which included Cormell Price, W. Fulford, C. J. Faulkner, and R. W. Dixon and which stands in the record as Morris's first quest for a fellowship in art, Burne-Jones is usually designated as Morris's closest friend. It was with Burne-Jones that Morris started his career, when they shared rooms at 17 Red Lion Square on Morris's leaving Oxford for London in 1857; their intimacy was to be interrupted but never ended. Yet the scarcity of surviving letters stands in some contrapuntal relationship to the fact of lifelong friendship.

It is often explained that Morris regularly spent Sunday morning with the Burne-Joneses after they took The Grange, in Fulham, in 1867. But if this is the reason for the dearth of letters, how explain the very large number to Georgiana Burne-Jones that have survived, in part at least? And it cannot be argued that Morris probably added greetings to her husband in his letters to Georgiana, for if he did we would have to charge Mackail with systematically excising all hints of such harmless amenities: there is not a single reference to Edward Burne-Jones in all

Morris's letters to Georgiana Burne-Jones published by Mackail, or published by herself in the *Memorials*, or surviving elsewhere. If this is to be partly explained by Burne-Jones's frequent involvement with other women, it only brings us back to the question, why have so few letters to him come down to us?

Some possible answers are these. Burne-Jones was perhaps careless about preserving letters from Morris. During the 1880's, when socialist politics were central in his thought and feeling, Morris may have felt no impulse to write to someone who was on the one hand very close to him and, on the other, unsympathetic to his interests of the moment. Then, too, Burne-Jones, or Georgiana, may have destroyed some or even many letters from Morris to him; and their descendants—possibly even Mackail, their son-in-law and Morris's biographer—may have done away with some. But if the destruction of any significant number was the fate of letters between Morris and Burne-Jones, the question is again why? There is, so far, no single answer more satisfactory than any other.

The handful of letters we do have, however, are marked and distinguished by the intensity of the feeling they express. In November 1864, the Burne-Joneses' second child, Christopher Alvin, was born prematurely and died at the age of three weeks. Georgiana was ill with a fever. Morris himself was bedridden. Burne-Jones, dispirited, wrote to say that the plan for the two families to live together in Red House had to be abandoned, even though Webb had already designed a new wing and construction was to start in a few months.

> As to our palace of Art, I confess your letter was a blow to me at first, though hardly an unexpected one—in short—I cried; but I have got over it now. As to our being a miserable lot, old chap, speaking for myself I don't know, I refuse to make myself really unhappy for anything short of the loss of friends one cannot do without. Suppose in all these troubles you had given us the slip what the devil should I have done? I am sure I couldn't have had the heart to have gone on with the firm; all our jolly subjects would have gone to pot—it frightens me to think of Ned. . . . I need hardly tell you how I suffered for you in the worst of your troubles; on the Saturday I had begun a letter to you but it read so dismal (as indeed I felt little hope) that I burnt it.

Morris's need for friends, his dependence on Burne-Jones as a particular friend, his equation of friendship with cooperative effort in work, are patently the main themes of this letter (the death of the child and Burne-Jones's suffering are clearly secondary). The need for his friend is the theme again a few years later, in a scrap that has survived: "We seem to quarrel in speech now sometimes," Morris wrote on May 25, 1869, "but forgive me for I can't on any terms do without you." Other fragments give the positive side of this dependence: they talk about work, and they are open, intense, and enthusiastic, sometimes boyishly so, as when Morris writes in September 1895 about the planned Kelmscott Press edition of *Sigurd the Volsung*: "I am afire to see the new designs . . . as to the age that be blowed!" He thus touches also on a theme that Burne-Jones and he could agree upon, namely, that the arts are in decline—though the two men differed as to the reason.

It is of course wrong to draw too much attention to the pattern in the snippets of letters to Burne-Jones that Georgiana Burne-Jones, Mackail, or someone else decided could survive. Yet these fragments are not to be discounted or ignored. They show that Morris felt a pleasure and excitement, when sharing or contemplating sharing an activity with Burne-Jones, that is seldom, if ever, recorded elsewhere in his letters and which is, when it does occur in letters to others, usually inspired by a landscape or a memorable building rather than by anything directly to do with the person to whom he is writing.

Among letters to other friends, first in importance chronologically, if not in number, are those to Cormell Price. These letters, concentrated for the most part in 1855 and 1856, give the most detailed picture we have of Morris discovering himself to be an artist, first as a poet, then, he hopes, as a painter. Like the letters to Burne-Jones, they combine an intense feeling, indeed a special affection, for the recipient with an uncontained enthusiasm for the subject, which is not only poetry and painting, but architecture—the great cathedrals seen during a summer trip to France with Burne-Jones and Fulford. Indeed, the letters articulate the idea of the Oxford Brotherhood—that art takes its shape from communal fellowship—and they touch also on what was to be the second embodiment of the quest signified for Morris by the Brotherhood: the founding of the short-lived but important *Oxford and Cambridge Magazine*. These letters from France, moreover, anticipate the brilliant, precise, and strongly felt letters Morris was to write in behalf of the Society for the Protection of Ancient Buildings, for they interweave intense feeling with sharply observed detail and are alert, as well, to the threat (the alarm having been given by Ruskin) of the restorer. (Of the transept front of the church at Dreux Morris writes to Price on August 10, 1855: "very elaborately carved once, now very forlorn and battered, but [Deo gratias] not yet restored.") One wishes for more leters to Cormell Price, letters that must have been written, for Price's diaries suggest that the friendship was continuous, and the few, brief surviving notes of later years show that Morris's affection for Price never abated.

The surviving letters to D. G. Rossetti are also relatively few, and also suggest only part of the range of what must have been encompassed by the entire correspondence, one that began possibly in 1856, when Rossetti was for Morris a hero, mentor, and guide. But the first letter of any consequence that has survived is interesting for what it does not discuss. Dated April 16, 1874, written, that is, when the relationship between Rossetti and Jane Morris was causing Morris keen unhappiness, however much he was trying to accept it, the letter was sent to accompany Morris's share of the quarter's rent for Kelmscott Manor: "I send herewith the £17.10 to you, not knowing where else to send it since Kinch is dead. As to the future though, I will ask you to look upon me as off my share, & not to look upon me as shabby for that, since you have fairly taken to living at Kelmscott, which I suppose neither of us thought the other would do when we first began the joint possession of the house; for the rest I am too poor &, by compulsion of poverty, too busy to be able to use it much in any case, and am very glad if you find it useful & pleasant to you."

That Morris felt keen despair and defeat at this time, we know from his letters to Aglaia Coronio and Georgiana Burne-Jones. But the readiness to relinquish a house he actually loved may have had a special significance. He seems to be saying that if Jane Morris has decided to leave him altogether, to live openly with Rossetti in Kelmscott Manor as his wife or mistress, he, Morris, is willing to step out. Of course it did not come to this, perhaps because, as Jane Morris intimated to Blunt, she was never wholly content with her relationship with Rossetti; it was Rossetti who, that same year, 1874, gave up his share in the house (to be succeeded by F. S. Ellis as joint tenant with Morris). But the note of extreme passivity—the asking Rossetti not to look upon him as "shabby," alleging himself too poor and busy to use Kelmscott Manor "in any case"—seems the keynote of the entire relationship of Morris to Rossetti at this point.

Two letters to Rossetti concern the break-up of the Firm at the end of 1874. Morris writes evasively, choosing to ignore Rossetti's sympathy with Ford Madox Brown and P. P. Marshall, who were united in their sense of grievance against Morris. He writes also in apparent ignorance of Rossetti's intention to make over to Jane Morris his share of the settlement. It is as if a quarrel with Rossetti would have been too embarrassing or painful, a suggestion that is strong in the letter of the previous April concerning Kelmscott Manor. It is as if, indeed, to fracture a friendship or acknowledge its end is intolerable for Morris in a way that recognizing his wife's lack of love for him is not.

This seems borne out by his continuing to write to Rossetti, though it has also been conjectured that Rossetti, anxious for commissions from the reorganized Morris and Co., was equally concerned to avoid an open break. Then, too, there may have been a relaxation of the tension; Jane Morris told Blunt that her intimacy with Rossetti ended, as has been mentioned, in 1875. Whatever the explanation, two years later we find Morris writing to Rossetti with genuine affection, asking him to become a member of the executive committee of the Society for the Protection of Ancient Buildings: "Don't be afraid," he writes, " 'tis not political this time"—strongly suggesting that he had written earlier asking him to join the Eastern Question Association—"but an attempt to put a spoke in the wheel of the 'restorers' of ancient buildings who have so grieved my soul." We are reminded of the letters to Burne-Jones— Morris's eagerness to see a friend join him in a public venture is like the desire to link himself to another through work. And in October 1881, only a few months before Rossetti's death, Morris writes to thank him for an inscribed copy of *Ballad and Sonnets*, ignoring what he could hardly not have known: that many sonnets in the "House of Life" sequence were addressed to Jane Morris. To the very end, arguably, the pleasure he took in a friendly gesture was greater than the grief or anger he felt in his wife's not loving him. "I never loved him," she told Blunt, and it is as if Morris always knew this, learned early to accept it, and found that it was friendship, not sexual love, that he could not do without.

How to describe Morris's letters to Georgiana Burne-Jones and Aglaia Coronio is a problem caused by the lack of an answer to a basic question: whether there was physical intimacy between Morris and either or both of these women. Whatever the truth of the matter, there is no doubt, on the basis of the letters to both, that the relationship with Georgiana was the more important of the two for him. She was the woman to whom he addressed himself most openly and fully on all occasions, with whom he shared his interests and concerns, and not least his political ones. She was the woman, that is, whom he treated as a friend before all others.

The letters to Georgiana always indicate that they are part of a continuous exchange, either in writing or person. In the late 1870's, when his work for the E.Q.A. and S.P.A.B. marks his turning outward, the beginning of his wholehearted commitment to the public world, his letters to her record his embrace of these movements. He also writes to her of his pleasure in Icelandic sagas. Moreover, she, along with Philip Webb and occasionally Aglaia Coronio, is one of the handful of correspondents with whom he seems at ease when discussing nineteenth-century literature. It is, finally, in the letters to Georgiana that Morris tries to sort out his thoughts about political action and how it relates to his chief concern, the future of the arts. In a letter of January 1, 1881, a New Year's Day greeting sent after the E.Q.A. had ceased to exist but before Morris had broken with the Liberals and joined the Social Democratic Federation, he writes: "I try to join thoughts with you to-day in writing a word of hope for the new year, that it may do a good turn of work toward the abasement of the rich and the raising up of the poor, which is of all things most to be longed for, till people can at last rub out from their dictionaries altogether these dreadful words rich and poor." And writing to her in July, he makes the connections among nature, art, and history that characterize his thought at its best: "Certainly to take . . . trouble," he writes, "it is needful that a man should be touched with a real love of the earth, a worship of it, no less; and that is seldom felt except by very simple people, . . . You know the most refined and cultured people, both those of the old religions and these of the new vague ones, have a sort of Manichean hatred of the world (I use the word in its proper sense, the home of man). Such people must be both the enemies of beauty and the slaves of necessity, and true it is that they lead the world at present, and I believe will do till all that is old is gone, and history has become a book from which the pictures have been torn." By pictures he means here ancient buildings. In many ways, Morris is not a man of the nineteenth century. But in his awareness of history as a visual dimension of a building, he is— though he insists that a building, as an historical phenomenon, should persist rather than alter through a dialectic process or simple change. It is this insistence on keeping the past intact, its integrity unviolated, that is both the source of his creativity and the measure of its limits.

Those who would tear out the pictures from the book of history, that is, destroy ancient buildings, are the same as those who do not love the earth. Without reasoning through the logic of this, Morris has intimated that for him buildings are an extension of the processes of nature itself. By defining the world as "the home of man," he further argues implicitly that man as worshiper of earth is the decorator of earth with architectural monuments. Buildings continue nature's own process of self-adornment, and also remain as emblems and witnesses to the social drama of human communities—as emblems or "pictures," finally, of the spirit of human societies.

A letter that further extends and develops his synthetic vision, easy to overlook because of his casual manner, his avoidance of conscious or deliberate theorizing, was written in September of the same year. Here he links art and politics, for politics to Morris is the necessary instrument through which to express discontent with society when once the ideal fabric that should encompass both nature and society has been rent—when society has become discontinuous with nature and alien to it. "To do nothing but grumble and not to act—" he writes to Georgiana, "that is throwing away one's life: but I don't think that words on our cause that we have at heart do nothing but wound the air, . . . Of course if the thing is done egotistically 'tis bad so far; but that again, how to do it well or ill, is a matter of art like other things." The emphasis here is on language, and it was through language—as a lecturer and editor—that Morris acted politically. Thus a new note in the letters to Georgiana Burne-Jones is heard in the 1880's. Morris became involved, after 1882, almost on a daily basis at times, in the affairs first of the Social Democratic Federation and later of the Socialist League. Socialism had become his religion; and frequent argument, much of it, we can imagine, with Georgiana, had begun to mark his days. The tone and substance of the letters suggest that in conversation or correspondence with him Georgiana has become a brake to his enthusiasm and a voice of skepticism countering his faith. For example, in February 1886, he feels obliged to write: "If you had only suffered as I have from the apathy of the English lower classes (woe's me how low!) you would rejoice at their awakening, however ugly the forms it took. As to my capacity for leadership in this turmoil, believe me, I feel as humble as could be wished; yet after all it is my life, and the work of it, and I must do my best." Georgiana, it would seem, put Morris on the defensive in socialist matters, and forced him to examine his motives, his understanding, and his capabilities closely. These letters therefore form an important part of his political autobiography. They reflect the doubts about himself as a leader, but they reflect also his dogged determination to hope and work for the creation of human community and fellowship. This was, as he said, the work of his life—one might say the ordained work made clear to him by his religion.

Morris's letters to Aglaia Coronio suggest a relationship that both resembles—and contrasts with—his friendship with Georgiana Burne-Jones. Especially in the 1870's, he often confides in Aglaia. It would appear that they met at about the time *The Earthly Paradise* was published, and that she, taking the initiative, soon became a confidante and consolation to him, their friendship sustained by a mutual interest in poetry and the other arts and by her loyal sympathy in the matter of Jane Morris and Rossetti.

Thus in the first surviving letter to her, dated the end of April, 1870, he writes: "Ned says you want to know how to read Chaucer; I will bring you a vol: in my pocket, and with your leave will induct you into the mystery, wh: is not very deep after all. . . . I have done my review [of Rossetti's *Poems*, for *The Academy*] just this moment—ugh!" On October 8, 1872, he writes to her in Athens: "I have been backwards and forwards to Kelmscott a good deal this summer and autumn; but I shall not go there so often now as Gabriel is come there, and talks of staying there permanently." And on October 24 he asks: "When are you coming back again? You know how much I miss you so there is no need of talking of that anymore."

Another letter, which is not only frank about many things but gives us a glimpse of the complexity of his feelings for Jane, all mingled with what seems to be a confession of sexual inadequacy, was written on November 25, 1872: "When I said there was no cause for my feeling low, I meant that my friends had not changed at all towards me in any way and that there had been no quarrelling: and indeed I am afraid it comes from some cowardice or unmanliness in me. One thing wanting ought not to go for so much: nor indeed does it spoil my enjoyment of life always, as I have often told you: to have real friends and some sort of an aim in life is so much, that I ought still to think myself lucky: and often in my better moods I wonder what it is in me that throws me into such rage and despair at other times: I suspect, do you know, that some such moods would have come upon me at times even without this failure of mine." And whatever the "failure" was, if it was not sexual, he continues: "I am so glad to have Janey back again: her company is always pleasant and she is very kind & good to me." One reason that he is glad to have Jane back is that his communication with Georgiana has been interrupted and Aglaia has been away, "so that I have had nobody to talk to about things that have bothered me." All three are his friends, or rather, what equalizes all good relationships for him is the element of friendship, and it would seem, nothing else. But Rossetti is not a friend at this time, not a friend in the sense that Jane is, for Morris writes: "another quite selfish business is that Rossetti has set himself down at Kelmscott as if he never meant to go away; and not only does that keep me away from that harbour of refuge, (because it is really a farce our meeting when we can help it) but also he has all sorts of ways so unsympathetic with the sweet simple old place, that I feel his presence there as a kind of a slur on it."

His reference to Rossetti has a special significance here. It is only when writing to Aglaia that Morris, in the surviving letters, is able to express the anger or pain that Rossetti caused him. On November 25, 1872, he writes: "I know clearer now perhaps than then what a blessing & help last year's journey was to me; or what horrors it saved me from."

Similarly, but perhaps more curiously, it is when he writes to Aglaia

that Morris is able to confess that he misses Jane, even when he antici-
pates continued intimacy with Aglaia. On January, 23, 1873, he tells
Aglaia that he has taken Horrington House, where Jane and children
will chiefly reside when the family is in London. As for 26 Queen Square,
where the business of Morris and Co. will remain, he will keep his
study and a little bedroom there "and I daresay as time goes on I shall
live here a good deal," anticipating, possibly, an amicable and discreet
separation from Jane. Moreover, "I can always see anyone I want in
Queen Sq: quite safe from interruption: so in all ways it seems an ad-
vantage, does it not?" Yet, in a contradictory tone, one that suggests
that a hope for happiness with Jane could always be revived in him, he
writes on February 11 of the same year: "My own room [at Horrington
House] is particularly cheerful and pretty, and I can work in it with
much better heart than in the dingy room in Queen Sq:."

The letters to Aglaia continue to the last year of Morris's life, and
although they remain friendly, they become increasingly less suggestive
of intimacy. A postscript to one of February 17, 1880, reads: "I don't
come for the books: but I really am ashamed you should so load me
with presents & take such trouble for me." On June 7, 1880: "Janey
will be very glad to see you on Wednesday & I will call on you with
much pleasure on Friday." By the 1890's it would seem that the rela-
tionship with Aglaia had become somewhat one-sided, kept going, on
his part, out of fondness and a wish to avoid the unpleasantness of a
break. In 1891, he apologizes for not answering a number of her letters,
then writes: "Again, amidst one thing or other I forgot to keep a copy
of the *Glittering Plain*, and there is not a copy to be had for less than
about £4. However, promises must be kept, and I believe I can let you
have one of my own." It is not a very gallant letter. Moreover, when
contrasted with the letter to Philip Webb of August 1894 ("you will
have the Kelmscott books as they come out [for] I do the books mainly
for you and one or two others"), it would seem that the new pleasure
in the Kelmscott Press had deprived Aglaia of the special place she had
had among the friends dear to Morris.

Taken together, at no point do these letters to her suggest a great
passion. There is hardly the strength of feeling that is present in the
letters to Georgiana. Morris seems grateful for something: for sexual
intimacy? for kindness in the face of sexual failing? or perhaps only
because she was a good listener and was one of the few people to whom
he could confess unhappiness. That many letters to Aglaia have sur-
vived, so that they rival in number those to Georgiana, is probably a
testimony to Aglaia's careful preservation of every scrap received from

Morris. Nevertheless, bulk is always a measure of significance of some kind, and in this case it at least expresses the important place that Morris held in Aglaia's life.

Bulk also characterizes the surviving letters dealing with socialism. If we add letters to family and friends that refer to socialism, to correspondence with political associates and strangers, the sum dominates his correspondence in the '80's. That many of these letters have survived can be explained by assuming that the recipients recognized the importance of Morris's correspondence and were pleased to think of themselves as becoming part of the historical record.

But when the survival of so many letters on socialism has been explained by citing the interests of those to whom they were written, another reason requires equal emphasis. Between 1883 and 1889, Morris threw himself into socialism with a degree of energy new even for him. He helped finance *Justice*, and contributed to it. He was editor of *Commonweal*. He delivered nearly three hundred lectures, traveling throughout Britain to give them. In London, he attended frequent executive and other committee meetings, often presiding. All this went on simultaneously with his continued work for the S.P.A.B., his writing of poetry and prose romances (though this fell off during the years in question), his designing for Morris and Co., and his conducting of the business, which was a growing one. Moreover, his socialist activity was carried on, almost from the beginning, in an atmosphere of conflict, of disagreement over ways and, to some extent, theory and ideals. This internal strife is only a final item in the account of where Morris's time and energy went, but for the letters, it is an important one, for it generated much of the correspondence in which he was obliged to define and explain his views and his position.

What the strife was about is a large part of any discussion of Morris's socialism. Simply put, Morris early became convinced that socialists should stay out of Parliament, since they would only, once in, acquire middle-class values and tastes and be corrupted by power. For similar reasons, he was skeptical of the trades union movement. Many of the letters record Morris's struggles to maintain his position as British socialism moved toward a clear embrace of parliamentarism and the formation of the Independent Labor Party. The issue was one of those dividing Morris and H. M. Hyndman, and was at the heart subsequently of his disagreement with such figures as John Burns, Joseph Lane, and Belfort Bax, though, as the letters testify, the disagreement never permanently separated him from anyone, even from Hyndman if Hyndman's own testimony is accurate and if Morris's later willingness to make common cause with the Social Democratic Federation and publish in their journal means anything.

On the other side, Morris felt himself dogged by the anarchists, whom the parliamentarists—and Friedrich Engels—accused him of encouraging, but whose views he disavowed just as strenuously. The anarchists, at least, did not regard him as one of themselves, for it was they, finally, who wrested control of *Commonweal* and of the Socialist League from him in 1890, most of the parliamentarists having parted company with him long before.

What did Morris believe and how do the letters help us to understand this? It is not enough to assess his debt to Ruskin and to Marx and to see how their ideas combine in his thought. The letters show that insofar as he had thought out the mechanism of social change, he saw it for the immediate future as education—one might say, education alone. But how such a raising of consciousness in the working man would express itself in a political process Morris does not make clear. The goal, on the other hand, is explicit: the abolition of classes and of private property, the formation of a government that manages things rather than people, a state of society that can best be described as communism or, some would say, as anarchy. In addition, he seems, like Marx, to have thought of the Paris Commune as a model for socialist society, though he does not explain how the model will provide the England of the 1880's with a method for realizing the change.

Arguably, however, Morris does, in one way, consider method. At various times, as in the letters of 1888 to the Rev. George Bainton, he seems to regard state socialism as a probable, if undesirable, intermediate step, and such an acceptance can be viewed as an interest in process. But again, how is state socialism to be achieved if there is to be recourse neither to Parliament nor to the barricades? The question is finally not to be asked of Morris, unless one wishes to accept *News from Nowhere* as a commitment to armed conflict and thus as an answer. The issue—the method of social change—is raised here only to say that Morris is, as the letters abundantly show, political only in the sense that he recognizes that power exists and is functional, but not political in the sense that one who broods over or calculates the means of obtaining power is political.

Morris's concern is with a vision of the future, not with a mechanism for bringing a future society into being. He is thus in the last analysis a humanist concerned with values rather than a political theoretician interested in the manipulation of the instruments of change. And of all values none is more important to him than art: the making of it, and the enjoying of it. The psychological connection between the human desire for pleasure and the human desire to make or enjoy art is at the heart of Morris's socialism. Indeed, Morris seems to have defined man as an art-making and art-loving animal. "My belief is," he writes to George Bainton, in May 1888, "that the merely necessary labour, the labour that will supply us with food and shelter, will be a very light burden in the future, properly distributed as it will be; and that the greater part of the work we do will be done with pleasure, just as a poet writes a poem or an artist paints a picture." He concludes: human happiness consists "in the pleasurable exercise of our energies."

In the same letter, he describes the political structure of a future society in which the pleasurable exercise of our energies will be possible: "Civilization would mean the federalization of a variety of communities large and small, at one end of which would be the township and the local guild . . . and at the other some central body whose function would be almost entirely the guardianship of the *principles* of society. . . . But even this shadow of centralization would disappear when men gained the habit of looking reasonably at these matters." Also: "Between these two poles there would be various federations which would grow together or dissolve as convenience of place, climate, language, &c. dictated, and would dissolve peaceably when occasion prompted." (In the light of statements like this, it is easy to see why the parliamentarists said Morris encouraged anarchism.) As for how long it will take to bring about the desired state of things, and how to get from here to there, Morris, in a gross sense, does point to a mechanism, the class struggle: "I admit that this is a long way ahead," he writes: "the contest of classes is still going on, and we cannot help taking part in it." But the mechanism is only roughly described. What "contest of classes" means, whether it is to take place in Parliament, in the streets, or elsewhere is, again, not clear.

To this last question, Morris's letters on socialism taken together do, however, provide a partial answer though it must be said that the overview revealed is not very dramatic. There are times in the letters when Morris intimates an acceptance of the possibility of violence, but when he does he is prompted by mood rather than by ideology or doctrine. Just as often he envisions a near-anarchist future, described in the passage from the letter to Bainton already quoted, brought about, paradoxically, by what can only be called a mild and localized democratic process. Thus, in that same letter to Bainton, he writes: "State socialism will have to intervene between our present breakdown and communism; especially as I think there are signs it will come in the municipal rather than the imperial form; which I think a very good thing." Elections held for the London County Council and similar bodies are thus to be the initial step; that is, local parliamentarism, with all its factionalism, is to lead, through majority rule, to the abolition of Parliament. Faith in an aggregate of municipal councils coalescing into a loose national federation, all without coercion (which, needless to say, Morris detested), indicates nothing so much as a lack of interest in the use of political power, in the political process itself.

As already suggested, what Morris was concerned with was the future of art, or more precisely, the future of the human desire for it. His eyes were always on the society of the future, rather than on the road to it, because the need for social change was, along with the alleviation of misery, the need to enable people to gratify their natural desires. Chief among those desires, as Morris saw it, was the desire for art. Thus, in the very last year of his life, he wrote to an American journalist: "I have *not* changed my mind on Socialism. My view on the point of the relation between art and Socialism is as follows: Society at present is organized entirely for the benefit of the privileged classes, the working class being only considered in the arrangement as so much machinery." The whole world is caught up, he continues, in artificial poverty, "which . . . debars men of all classes from satisfying their rational desires. Rich men are in slavery to Philistinism, poor men to penury. . . . Before we can so much as hope for any art, we must be free from this artificial poverty. When we are thus free, in my opinion, the natural instincts of mankind toward incident and beauty will take their due place; we shall *want* art. . . ."

Morris's real concern, then, is with the way art and pleasure relate to instinct and reason. The concern is political insofar as he insists that these connections, desirable on their face, can be made only after society has been reorganized to permit the desire for art to express itself, and be gratified. Yet more important is his belief—best called genetic—that the desire for art is a natural one, biologically and psychologically based. The "wanting" of art and the gratifying of the want is as *primary* as pleasure-seeking in sex is for Freud. The desire for art is in no sense, for Morris, a sublimation of a drive for sexual or any other gratification. Moreover, for Morris it is *rational* to seek pleasure in art, and thus in the psychology he has adumbrated, the primary human instinct is always a constructive and life-enhancing one; never, indeed, is it in conflict with the needs of a rational society or with another part of the self. It is not hard to see why Morris courted disaster at the hands of those who made the acquisition of political power, and the exercise of it, the primary object of their own desire.

By 1890, Morris was ready for another move. His lack of enthusiasm for the emerging Labor Party had weakened his following within the main body of English socialists. At the same time the anarchists, whom he had been accused of unwittingly aiding but who knew perfectly well that he was not one of them, succeeded in ousting him from the editorship of *Commonweal*. Although he had grown weary of the position because of the conflicts within the Socialist League, and had no intention of trying to retain it, the ouster decided him. He left the League as he had left the Social Democratic Federation at the end of 1884. Again he took with him his intimates and close associates, even fewer in number this time, but more purely a personal following than ever before.

Once again he organized the saving remnant. He established what was called, simply, the Hammersmith Socialist Society, its name announcing its determination to be no more than a local group of like-minded persons, whatever readiness they might have to cooperate with others on a national scale.

The letters on socialism of this last period are relatively few. They record a reluctant acceptance of parliamentarism, of the emergent Labor Party, after the London Dock Strike of 1889. They witness Morris's decent support of the parliamentary candidacy of others—of John Burns in particular—in the immediate aftermath of the strike. He finally endorsed, they show, what he could not help to create. They are also punctuated, if infrequently, with vigorous affirmations of his faith in socialism as an idea, and in 1893 he was to join G. B. Shaw and H. M. Hyndman in drafting a Manifesto of English Socialists.

But socialism in whatever meaning it had for Morris or for the times, does not dominate the letters of the final years as it does those from 1883 to the end of the '80's. The surviving letters from 1890 through 1896 are chiefly about the Kelmscott Press, and a related activity, the building by Morris of his personal library of early printed books and medieval manuscripts. These were purchased, he told himself, so that they might serve as models for his own printing, but he purchased them also, the letters show, for the sheer pleasure they gave him.

His two main ventures of the '90's—the Hammersmith Socialist Society and the Kelmscott Press—connect. Friends like Emery Walker and associates like Catterson-Smith joined him in both. Moreover, it can be argued that one explanation of Morris's retreat (or advance) to the Hammersmith Socialist Society, after several years of political activity on a wider scale, was that he was driven there by the temperamental and intellectual traits that caused him stubbornly to focus on art. It was therefore time, the argument might continue, for another paradigmatic demonstration of art as a communal activity. There was no deliberate reasoning along such lines by Morris, who set out only to gratify a desire to print beautiful books. Yet he is surely an example, in this undertaking, of a person "wanting" art. Moreover, the guild-like enterprise he desired the Press to be, with himself as master printer, fits well with his personal vision of a socialist future.

But it is the craft and not the possible significance of the Press that is reflected in the letters. Their common theme is that something be done—or redone—to meet Morris's standards. The design of type, cutting of punches, making of decorative borders and illustrations, manufacture of paper and ink, and design of bindings are the subjects. In all these matters, Morris is the craftsman insisting on precision and on form appropriate to purpose. He is also at times the businessman, particularly in his dealings with Bernard Quaritch, publisher of many of the Kelmscott volumes (and of the Saga Library, a subject which occasionally intertwines with the correspondence about the Press). The letters to Quaritch, as well as those to Joseph Batchelor, manufacturer of paper, and to J. & J. Leighton, binders of the Kelmscott books, recall those to Thomas Wardle in the 1870's, when once before Morris had embarked on a new enterprise that required someone else to be his business associate, executor of a technical process, and partner in a creative venture all at once. And in this multiple relationship, it is always Morris who insists that the manufacturing process be attended with exhaustive care, that the resultant object, in this case a book, give pleasure.

It is interesting to note also that the letters on book and manuscript buying often show Morris in a double relationship with Quaritch and Leighton. He obtained money from Quaritch gained by the sale of Kelmscott Press books and returned the cash to him for rare books Quaritch obtained at auction. Accounts also had to be kept straight with Leighton, who bound the books of the Press for a fee but also purchased books at auction and sold them to Morris. The delight Morris took in these books, works like the Huntington Psalter and the Tiptoft Missal, was second in intensity—if second at all—only to what he felt when he had himself made something that gratified him. For Morris, pleasure in art had always meant both the pleasure of making, and the pleasure of enjoying what others had made.

The letters that deal strictly with the Press and are not about business are brisk, hastily written, often composed in a moment snatched from work. But they are buoyant and confident. Morris does not question the value of what he is doing, as he sometimes did when internal strife among socialists wearied him of political activity or when thoughts about philistine customers undermined his satisfaction in the work of the Firm. Writing to those who have joined him in producing the books of the Kelmscott Press, or to those who will receive them as gifts, he is writ-

[xlix]

ing to members of his last fellowship, to those who had joined him or encouraged him in his final effort to redeem the hopes first announced by the Oxford Brotherhood.

And if the Kelmscott Press realizes the early dream of beauty produced by communal effort, it testifies also to Morris's distinct role in the process: inspirer, organizer, and leader. He was everything in the affairs of the Press that he could not be in the party politics of the 1890's. Drawing on the very forms of the medieval scribe and early printer, he used history as a source of architectonic design—of the principles that for him should govern the making of a book, as well as of a house. (It is not surprising that the two chief objects of pleasure for him—a building and a book—were the products, in his view, of the same structuring rules.) He combined history and architecture in designing and producing books and thus realized at once two of his loves. In the enterprise, he also connected with other people in the manner he best could: through his need for their skill, cooperation, and presence, and through their need for his direction. In a way that Morris would insist was not at all paradoxical, there came out of this communal effort a beauty that we recognize as individual, the distinct and final achievement of Morris as artist, and as man.

Norman Kelvin
The City College of New York
May 1982

MORRIS CHRONOLOGY

BASED on "A Calendar of Principal Events in Morris's Life," May Morris, *William Morris: Artist, Writer, Socialist*, II (Oxford, 1936), 632-37; and on the letters in the present edition.

1834   Born, March 24, at Elm House, Walthamstow.

1840   Family moves to Woodford Hall, Walthamstow.

1847   Father dies.

1848   Goes to school at Marlborough. Family moves to Water House, Walthamstow.

1851   Leaves school at Christmas, after school rebellion in November.

1852   Reads with Dr. F. B. Guy, Forest School, Walthamstow. Matriculates at Exeter College, Oxford, in June. Plans to prepare for the Church.

1853   Goes to Oxford in January. Meets Edward Burne-Jones, C. J. Faulkner, R. W. Dixon, Harry Macdonald, and William Fulford. In rooms at Exeter College by December. During this and following year reads Ruskin's *Stones of Venice*, Carlyle's *Past and Present*, Thorp's *Northern Mythologies*, and Charlotte Yonge's *The Heir of Redclyffe*.

1854   Visits Belgium and Northern France in the summer, seeing the paintings of Memling and Van Eyck, and Amiens, Beauvais, and Rouen Cathedrals. Meets Cormell Price. Reads Ruskin's *Edinburgh Lectures* and becomes aware of the Pre-Raphaelites. Morris, Burne-Jones, and their circle plan a monastic brotherhood.

1855   Reads Chaucer and Malory. Makes second tour of France, accompanied by Burne-Jones and Fulford. Morris decides not to take orders, and to follow art as a career.

1856   Edits and finances the *Oxford and Cambridge Magazine*. Articled to G. E. Street, the architect, in whose Oxford office he meets

Philip Webb. Takes his B.A. degree. Moves to London with Street's office and shares rooms with Burne-Jones. Meets Rossetti and abandons architecture for painting by end of the year.

1857   Decorative work begins at 17 Red Lion Square. Frescoes in the Oxford Union painted, under leadership of Rossetti. Meets Jane Burden. Macmillan rejects *The Defence of Guenevere*.

1858   *The Defence of Guenevere* published by Bell and Daldy at Morris's own expense. With Faulkner and Webb, visits France again.

1859   Morris and Jane Burden married on April 26. Tour of France, Belgium, and the Rhineland. Philip Webb builds Red House, at Upton, Kent, for them.

1860   Morrises move into Red House. Edward Burne-Jones and Georgiana Macdonald married on June 9.

1861   Firm of Morris, Marshall, Faulkner and Co. founded. Jane Alice ("Jenny") born January 17. Morris begins writing stories for *The Earthly Paradise*.

1862   Mary ("May") Morris born March 25. Firm shows work at the Great Exhibition and is awarded two gold medals.

1864   Morris ill with rheumatic fever. The Burne-Joneses decide against sharing Red House, and the plan for a "Palace of Art" there is abandoned.

1865   Red House sold to a retired naval officer and Morris family moves to 26 Queen Square, London, where the Firm also sets up shop.

1866   *The Earthly Paradise* takes form. Morris visits France again, with Warington Taylor and William Fulford.

1867   *The Life and Death of Jason*, originally intended as a tale in *The Earthly Paradise*, published separately in January. Firm begins decoration of dining room at South Kensington Museum.

1868   *The Earthly Paradise*, Volume I, published in April. Morris begins studying Icelandic with Eiríkr Magnússon.

1869   "The Saga of Gunnlaug Worm-tongue" published in the *Fortnightly Review* (January). *The Story of Grettir the Strong* published in June. Morris takes his wife to Bad Ems for her health. Burne-Jones's breakdown, precipitated by affair with Mary Zambaco.

1870   Volumes II and III of *The Earthly Paradise* published. Transla-
        tion (with Magnússon) of *Volsunga Saga* published. Completes
        first illuminated manuscript, *A Book of Verse*, as gift for Geor-
        giana Burne-Jones. Meets Aglaia Coronio and begins long
        friendship and correspondence.

1871   Takes Kelmscott Manor, Lechlade, Gloucestershire, in joint
        tenancy with Rossetti in June. Rossetti and Jane Morris and
        children take up residence there. In July Morris leaves on first
        Icelandic trip, accompanied by Faulkner, Magnússon, and W. H.
        Evans. Makes an illuminated *Rubáiyát of Omar Khayyám* for
        Edward Burne-Jones. A second (on vellum), a gift for Geor-
        giana Burne-Jones, begun and completed following year.

1872   Morris family leaves Queen Square (Firm continues there) for
        Horrington House, Turnham Green. *Love is Enough* published.
        Rossetti suffers breakdown and attempts suicide.

1873   With Burne-Jones, visits Florence and Siena in spring. Second
        trip to Iceland in summer.

1874   Rossetti gives up his share of Kelmscott Manor. Morris takes
        family on trip to Belgium. In winter of 1874–75, begins illu-
        minated *Aeneid* on vellum.

1875   Morris, Marshall, Faulkner, and Co. dissolved and reestab-
        lished as Morris and Co., with Morris as single owner. Takes
        M.A. degree at Oxford. *Three Northern Love Stories* published.
        Begins experiments with dyeing, staying with Thomas War-
        dle, at Leek, for the purpose. Morris's translation of *The Aeneid*
        published.

1876   Becomes Treasurer of Eastern Question Association and be-
        gins first period of political activity. Appointed Examiner at
        School of Art, South Kensington. Jenny suffers first epileptic
        attack and becomes semi-invalid for the rest of her life. *Sigurd
        the Volsung* published.

1877   Gives first public lecture, "The Decorative Arts." Helps found
        the Society for the Protection of Ancient Buildings ("Anti-
        Scrape") and becomes its first secretary.

1878   Takes family on visit to Venice, Verona, and Padua in spring.
        Move to Kelmscott House, Hammersmith, on return. Morris
        begins tapestry weaving. Russo-Turkish war ends with Treaty

of San Stefano in March; after Congress of Berlin, June–July, EQA becomes inactive.

1879   Leads protest by S.P.A.B. against proposed restorations at St. Marks, Venice. Becomes treasurer of the National Liberal League. First meeting with H. M. Hyndman, founder in 1881 of the Democratic Federation.

1880   Firm decorates Throne Room at St. James's Palace.

1881   Merton Abbey works of Morris and Co. started.

1882   *Hopes and Fears for Art* (first collection of essays) published. Death of Rossetti on April 9.

1883   Joins Democratic Federation on January 13. Made Honorary Fellow of Exeter College on same day. Death of Karl Marx, March 14. High warp tapestry started at Merton Abbey works. Lecture, "Art and Democracy," sponsored by Russell Club and delivered in University Hall, Oxford, with Ruskin in chair, in November.

1884   Partially subsidizes *Justice*, organ of the Democratic Federation. *Chants for Socialists* and *A Summary of the Principles of Socialism* (with H. M. Hyndman) published. In dissension with Hyndman at end of year, and along with others resigns from Democratic Federation (renamed Social Democratic Federation in August).

1885   The Socialist League founded and *Commonweal* started with Morris as editor. Free speech demonstration, Dod Street, on September 20. Morris arrested (charge dismissed in court next day) when protesting sentencing of free speech demonstrators. *The Pilgrims of Hope* published in *Commonweal*, 1885-86.

1886   Demonstration of unemployed in Trafalgar Square, February 8 ("Black Monday"). *A Dream of John Ball* appears in *Commonweal*, 1886-87. *A Short Account of the Commune of Paris* (with E. Belfort Bax and Victor Dave) published.

1887   Morris's translation of the *Odyssey* published in April. *The Tables Turned; or Nupkins Awakened* produced at hall of Socialist League on October 15. Trafalgar Square demonstration attacked by police, November 13 ("Bloody Sunday"). Pall bearer at funeral of Alfred Linnell, who was fatally injured in demonstration.

1888   *Signs of Change*, second volume of lectures, published in May. Lectures on tapestry weaving at the first exhibition of the Arts and Crafts Exhibition Society. Attends the first Art Congress, held in Liverpool. *The House of the Wolfings* published in December. (Takes interest in its design and begins to consider the technique of printing.)

1889   Delegate at International Socialist Congress, July, in Paris, at which Second International is founded. London Dock Strike (August 14–September 14). *The Roots of the Mountains* published in November. Opens series of lectures at second exhibition of the Arts and Crafts Exhibition Society. Attends Art Congress in Edinburgh (November).

1890   Designs type, preparing to start the Kelmscott Press. *News from Nowhere* appears in *Commonweal*. Leaves Socialist League at end of year and forms Hammersmith Socialist Society.

1891   The Kelmscott Press begins printing in January; its first book, *The Story of the Glittering Plain*, issued in May. *Poems by the Way* and first volume of Saga Library published in October. Serious illness. Takes Jenny to France. Address on Pre-Raphaelites at Municipal Art Gallery, Birmingham, in October.

1892   Death of Tennyson on October 13. Morris mentioned as possible candidate for Laureateship. Reputedly declines to be considered. Elected Master of the Art Workers' Guild for the year. Principal Kelmscott Press books: *The Defence of Guenevere, The Golden Legend, The Recuyell of the Historyes of Troye.* Second volume of Saga Library published.

1893   Joint Manifesto of English Socialists drawn up by Morris, G. B. Shaw, and H. M. Hyndman. *Socialism: Its Growth and Outcome* (with E. Belfort Bax) published. Principal Kelmscott Press books: More's *Utopia, News from Nowhere.*

1894   Morris's mother dies at age of 90. Principal Kelmscott Press books: *The Wood Beyond the World*, Swinburne's *Atalanta in Calydon*, Keats's *Poems*, and Rossetti's *Sonnets and Lyrical Poems.*

1895   Goes to Rottingdean for his health. Death of Friedrich Engels in August. Kelmscott Press publishes *Beowulf* (Morris's translation) and *The Life and Death of Jason*. Purchases Huntingfield Psalter and Tiptoft Missal. Speaks at Sergius Stepniak's funeral.

1896 Kelmscott Press publishes *Chaucer* and *The Well at the World's End*. Sea voyage to Norway in attempt to restore health. Death of Morris, October 3.

1898 Death of Burne-Jones.

1900 Death of Ruskin.

1914 Death of Jane Morris.

1915 Death of Philip Webb.

1920 Death of Georgiana Burne-Jones.

1935 Death of Jenny Morris.

1938 Death of May Morris.

ABBREVIATIONS
OF MANUSCRIPT LOCATIONS

Andersen Coll.	Collection of Elmer L. Andersen
Bentham Coll.	Collection of D. R. Bentham
Berg	Henry W. and Albert A. Berg Collection, New York Public Library
Berger Coll.	Collection of Sanford and Helen Berger
Birmingham	Birmingham (England) Public Libraries
BL, Add. MSS.	British Library (British Museum), London, Additional Manuscripts
Bodleian	Bodleian Library, Oxford
Brown	Brown University Library, Providence, Rhode Island
Columbia	Rare Book and Manuscript Library, Columbia University, New York
Cornell	Cornell University Library, Ithaca, New York
DeGruson Coll.	Collection of Gene DeGruson
Doheny	Estelle Doheny Collection of the Edward Laurence Doheny Memorial Library, St. John's Seminary, Camarillo, California
Dunlap Coll.	Collection of Joseph Riggs Dunlap
Duke	Sir Thomas Wardle Papers, Perkins Library, Duke University, Durham, North Carolina
Exeter College	Exeter College, Oxford
Fitzwilliam	Fitzwilliam Museum, Cambridge
Folger	Folger Shakespeare Library, Washington, D.C.
Fredeman Coll.	Collection of William E. Fredeman
GLRO	Greater London Record Office, County Hall, London
Heathcote Papers	Family Papers of James A. Heathcote
Harvard	Houghton Library, Harvard University, Cambridge, Massachusetts

Horsfall	D. F. Skinner, "T. C. Horsfall, A Memoir" (unpublished typescript), property of Mrs. D. M. Betts
Howard Papers	Family Papers of George Howard, Castle Howard Archives, Castle Howard, Yorkshire
Huntington	Huntington Library and Art Gallery, San Marino, California
Iceland	National Library of Iceland, Reykjavík
Illinois	University of Illinois Library at Urbana-Champaign
Inst. Rus. Lit.	Institute of Russian Literature, Pushkin House, Leningrad
Iowa	Iowa State Education Association, Des Moines
Iowa State	Iowa State Historical Department, Division of Historical Museum and Archives, Des Moines
Jesus College	Jesus College, Cambridge
Lange Coll.	Collection of Thomas V. Lange
LC	Manuscript Division, Library of Congress, Washington, D.C.
Leuba Coll.	Collection of Walter Leuba
Lohf Coll.	Collection of Kenneth A. Lohf
LSE	British Library of Political and Economic Science, London School of Economics
McMinn Papers	McMinn Papers, Society of Antiquaries, London
Mander Coll.	Collection of Lady Rosalie Mander
Mayfield Coll.	Collection of Edith S. and John S. Mayfield
McGill	Department of Rare Books and Special Collections, McGill University Libraries, Montreal
McWilliams Coll.	Collection of David Jackson McWilliams
MFA	Museum of Fine Arts, Boston
Monell Coll.	Collection of Charles Monell
Monterey	Jacks Collection, Monterey Public Library, California
NLS	National Library of Scotland, Edinburgh
NLW	National Library of Wales, Aberystwyth
NYPL	Manuscript Division, New York Public Library

NYU	The Fales Library, Elmer Holmes Bobst Library, New York University, New York
Ohio	Ohio State University Libraries, Columbus
Pennsylvania	Historical Society of Pennsylvania, Philadelphia
Peterhouse	Master and Fellows of Peterhouse, Cambridge
Pforzheimer	Carl H. Pforzheimer Library, New York
PML	J. Pierpont Morgan Library, New York
Price Papers	Family Papers of Lorraine Price
Princeton T.	Rossetti Collection of Janet Camp Troxell, Princeton University Library, Princeton, New Jersey
PRO	Public Record Office, London
Ray Coll.	Collection of Gordon N. Ray
RLF	President and Council of the Royal Literary Fund, London
Rosenwater Coll.	Collection of Irving Rosenwater
Schimmel Coll.	Collection of S. B. Schimmel
Scripps	Ella Strong Denison Library, Scripps College, Claremont, California
Sheffield	City of Sheffield Library
Somerville	Principal and Fellows of Somerville College, Oxford
Spilstead Coll.	Collection of H. L. Spilstead
SRO	Scottish Record Office, Edinburgh
St. Bride	St. Bride Printing Library, London
SUNY, Buffalo	Lockwood Memorial Library, State University of New York, Buffalo
Swales Coll.	Collection of John D. Swales
Syracuse	George Arents Research Library for Special Collections, Syracuse University, Syracuse, New York
Trinity College	Trinity College Library, Cambridge
UBC: Angeli-Dennis, Colbeck, Penkill Papers	Angeli-Dennis Papers, Norman Colbeck Collection, and Penkill Papers in the Special Collections Division, University of British Columbia Library, Vancouver
UIowa	University of Iowa Libraries, Iowa City

UKansas	Department of Special Collections, Spencer Library, University of Kansas, Lawrence
ULondon	University of London Library, London
UMass	University Library, University of Massachusetts, Amherst
USheffield	University of Sheffield Library
V&A	Victoria and Albert Museum Library, London
Vassar	Francis FitzRandolph Rare Book Room, Vassar College Library, Poughkeepsie, New York
Walthamstow	William Morris Gallery, Walthamstow, London
Watkinson Coll.	Collection of Raymond Watkinson
Wellesley	Wellesley College Library, Wellesley, Massachusetts
West Sussex	West Sussex County Archives, Chichester
WPL	Walthamstow Public Library, London
Yale B.	Beinecke Rare Book and Manuscript Collection, Yale University, New Haven, Connecticut
Yale O.	Osborn Collection, Yale University Library, New Haven, Connecticut
Yates Coll.	Collection of the late Arnold Yates

ABBREVIATIONS
OF WORKS FREQUENTLY CITED

Anscombe and Gere	Isabelle Anscombe and Charlotte Gere, *Arts and Crafts in Britain and America* (New York: Rizzoli, 1978)
Bornand	Odette Bornand, ed., *The Diary of W. M. Rossetti, 1870-1873* (Oxford: Clarendon Press, 1977)
Broadhurst	Henry Broadhurst, *Henry Broadhurst, M.P. The Story of His Life* . . . (London: Hutchinson, 1901)
Buxton Forman	H. Buxton Forman, *The Books of William Morris* (1897; rpt., New York: Burt Franklin, 1969)
Callen	Anthea Callen, *Women Artists of the Arts and Crafts Movement, 1870-1914* (New York: Pantheon, 1979; London: Architectural Press, 1979)
Clark	Fiona Clark, *William Morris, Wallpapers and Chintzes* (New York: St. Martin's Press, 1973; London: Academy Editions, 1973)
Cobden-Sanderson	T. J. Cobden-Sanderson, *The Journals of T. J. Cobden-Sanderson*, 2 vols. (1926; rpt., New York: Burt Franklin, 1969)
Compton-Rickett	Arthur Compton-Rickett, *William Morris: A Study in Personality* (London: H. Jenkins, 1913)
Crow	Gerald Crow, *William Morris, Designer* (New York: Studio Publications, 1934; London: The Studio, 1934)
CW	William Morris, *Collected Works*, ed. May Morris, 24 vols. (1910-1915; rpt., New York: Russell and Russell, 1966. The Introductions to these volumes have been separately reissued as May Morris, *The Introductions to The Collected Works of William Morris*, 2 vols. (New York: Oriole Editions, 1973)
Doughty	Oswald Doughty, *A Victorian Romantic: Dante Gabriel Rossetti*, 2nd ed. (Oxford Univ. Press, 1963)
Doughty and Wahl	Oswald Doughty and J. R. Wahl, eds., *Letters of*

	Dante Gabriel Rossetti, 4 vols. (Oxford Univ. Press, 1965–1967)
Dunlap	Joseph R. Dunlap, *The Book That Never Was* (New York: Oriole Editions, 1971)
Fairbank	Alfred Fairbank, "A Note on the Manuscript Work of William Morris," in *The Story of Kormak* by W. Morris and E. Magnússon with an introduction by Grace J. Calder (London: William Morris Society, 1970)
Faulkner	Peter Faulkner, ed., *William Morris: The Critical Heritage* (London and New York: Routledge and Kegan Paul, 1973)
Fitzgerald	Penelope Fitzgerald, *Edward Burne-Jones* (London: Michael Joseph, 1975)
Girouard	Mark Girouard, *The Victorian Country House*, rev. ed. (New Haven, Conn.: Yale Univ. Press, 1979)
Harrison and Waters	Martin Harrison and Bill Waters, *Burne-Jones* (London: Barrie and Jenkins, 1973)
Henderson, *Letters*	Philip Henderson, ed., *The Letters of William Morris to His Family and Friends* (London: Longmans Green, 1950)
Henderson, *Life*	Philip Henderson, *William Morris: His Life, Work, and Friends* (London: Thames and Hudson, 1967)
LeMire	Eugene D. LeMire, ed., *The Unpublished Lectures of William Morris* (Detroit: Wayne State Univ. Press, 1969)
Lethaby	W. R. Lethaby, *Philip Webb and His Work* (Oxford Univ. Press, 1935; rpt., London: Raven Oak Press, 1980)
Lindsay	Jack Lindsay, *William Morris* (London: Constable, 1975)
Mackail	J. W. Mackail, *The Life of William Morris*, 2 vols. (London: Longmans Green, 1899)
Memorials	Georgiana Burne-Jones, *Memorials of Edward Burne-Jones*, 2 vols. (London: Macmillan, 1906)
MM	May Morris, ed., *William Morris, Artist, Writer, Socialist*, 2 vols. (1936; rpt., New York: Russell and Russell, 1966)

Morris, *Victorian Embroidery*	Barbara Morris, *Victorian Embroidery* (London: H. Jenkins, 1962)
Noyes	Alfred Noyes, *William Morris* (1926; rpt., New York: Benjamin Blum, 1971)
Parry	Linda Parry, *William Morris Textiles* (New York: Viking Press, 1983)
Robinson and Wildman	D. Robinson and S. Wildman, *Morris and Company in Cambridge* (Cambridge University Press, 1980)
Scott	*Autobiographical Notes of the Life of William Bell Scott . . . 1830-1882*, ed. W. Minto, 2 vols. (London: Osgood, McIlvaine and Co., 1892)
Seton-Watson, *Disraeli*	R. W. Seton-Watson, *Disraeli, Gladstone, and the Eastern Question* (London: Macmillan, 1935)
Sewter	A. Charles Sewter, *The Stained Glass of William Morris and His Circle*, 2 vols. (New Haven, Conn.: Yale Univ. Press, 1974-1975)
Sparling	H. Halliday Sparling, *The Kelmscott Press and William Morris Master-Craftsman* (1924; rpt., Folkestone: William Dawson and Sons, 1975).
Stirling	Anna M. W. Stirling, *William De Morgan and His Wife* (London: Butterworth; New York: Holt, 1922)
Surtees	Virginia Surtees, *The Paintings and Drawings of Dante Gabriel Rossetti (1828-1882): A Catalogue Raisonné* (Oxford: Clarendon Press, 1971)
E. P. Thompson	E. P. Thompson, *William Morris: Romantic to Revolutionary* (1st ed., London: Lawrence and Wishart, 1955; 2nd ed., London: Merlin Press, 1977, and New York: Pantheon, 1977). References are to the first edition unless otherwise indicated.
G. C. Thompson	George C. Thompson, *Public Opinion and Lord Beaconsfield*, 2 vols. (London: Macmillan, 1886)
P. Thompson	Paul Thompson, *The Work of William Morris* (1st ed., London: Heineman, 1967; 2nd ed., London: Quartet Books, 1977). References are to the first edition.

Troxell   Janet Camp Troxell, *Three Rossettis: Unpublished Letters to and from Dante Gabriel, Christina, William* (Cambridge, Mass.: Harvard Univ. Press, 1937)

Vallance   Aymer Vallance, *William Morris: His Art, His Writings and His Public Life* (London: George Bell and Sons, 1898)

THE COLLECTED LETTERS OF
WILLIAM MORRIS

VOLUME I

1 • TO EMMA MORRIS　　　　　　　　　　　　　　　Marlbro' College
　　　　　　　　　　　　　　　　　　　　　　　　　　Feast of All Saints
　　　　　　　　　　　　　　　　　　　　　　　　　　November 1, 1848

My dearest Emma[1]

I received your letter this morning and I am glad to hear that you like the new house[2] so much but you have not exactly described the situation of the house to my satisfaction. I can't understand which one you mean　it can't be the one that used to be Mrs. Clarke's, is it? Or is [it] the one next to it where whenever I passed there were sure to come up to the street gate a whole legion of greyhounds Scotch, English, and Italian, do you know the one I mean? It is not I know Mr. Farquharson's and least of all our old house; however in whatever place it is, you must write and describe the place exactly for I can't for the life of me understand where it it[3] is. Things go on much in the same way as usual　three new Prefects are going to be made in a few days, Today being a Saints day I am one to be chatechized in Evening Service today as I was also catechized last Sunday; these last two or three days it has been very misty and dark indeed, the gates are shut now at 5 o clock and the lamps are lighted at the same time. When you sent that letter with the money you said you would send me till Christmas postage stamps when I wanted them, will you be kind enough to send me about 7 I don't think I shall want any more till Christmas, after which time according to our agreement I shall have to get them myself. I think the winter is regularly coming on now, the trees are getting very bare indeed about here, it is now only 7 weeks to the Holidays, there I go again! just like me! always harping on the Holidays. I am sure you must think me a great fool to be always thinking about home always, but I really can't help it I don't think it is my fault for there are such a lot of things I want to do and say, and see, but I can't write any more now so best love to all and believe me dearest Emma

　　　　　　　　　　　　　　　Your most affectionate Brother
　　　　　　　　　　　　　　　W. Morris

MS: Walthamstow. Extract published: Mackail, I, 18.

[1] Emma Morris (b.1829?), Morris's eldest and favorite sister. According to one of her nieces, Effie Morris (see below), Emma married Joseph Oldham, her German tutor, at the age of 19, while Mackail gives the date of her marriage as 1850. He describes Oldham as curate at Walthamstow from 1845 to 1848 (I, 24). Morris had four brothers and three sisters in addition to Emma. Henrietta (1833-1902) never married, and late in life became a Roman Catholic. Isabella (1842-1923) married a naval officer, Archibald Gilmore, in 1860, and after forty years of marriage, trained as a nurse. Alice Mary (b.1846) married Reginald Gill, a banker, but was widowed soon afterward. The brothers were Hugh Stanley (1837-1911, known as Stanley), Thomas Rendall (1839-1884, known as Rendall), Arthur (b.1841), and Edgar Llewellyn (b.1844). Stanley became a prosperous farmer,

living near Southampton. Rendall attended a German university and later joined the Gordon Highlanders. Arthur had a military career which took him to India and China. Edgar, a businessman, became bankrupt and ended up working as a dyer at Merton Abbey. See letter dated November 7, 1958 from Effie Morris in the William Morris Gallery, Walthamstow, MSS 106-109.

² Water House, Walthamstow, London. The family had been living at Woodford Hall, on the edge of the Epping forest, since 1840. After the death of Morris's father in 1847, this residence became too large and difficult to manage. The move was made in the autumn of 1848.

³ For all anomalies that seem to be printer's errors, see Editorial Practices, pp. xi-xii.

2 • TO EMMA MORRIS   Marlbro College
                                                         March 19, 1849

My dearest Emma

On Friday I received your letter and I thought that it had been rather long in coming but I suppose it was just too late for the delivery on Thursday and at the college there is only one delivery and that is at 7 AM. however, it signifies very little indeed though I expect a letter tomorrow. I should think you would like to know all about the Confirmation so I will tell you as much as I can about it; the Bishop¹ came into the town on Friday afternoon   he staid at Mr. Wilkinson's² all the evening and slept there   we went into Chapel at 8 AM. all the candidates for confirmation sitting together near the Altar   the Bishop's charge was received by us all standing   it was about 20 minutes long, the Bishop himself is very tall and thin and he does not [look] very old though bald at the top of his head   his name is Dennison and he is of a high family; the Holy Communion was administered the next day (Sunday).   it [is] here administered on to every one ⟨separatly⟩ singly. I think respecting a certain thing that it would [do] to get a plain copy of the Communion plate (which is but half as much as the other) and make up the difference with smaller plates of different views about, do not you?

The new Surgeon is I think very generally liked   I myself like him very much, so far as I know of him he comes regularly every morning and evening to Chapel. I know Hayley very well. Last half and the half before he was Captain of my dormitory   I asked him about Mr. Capel and he knows him but it happens to be neither his *father* or *uncle* but his *brother* that lives with Mr. Capel. I hope very soon to get a *tremendous* long letter from you dear Emma but in the mean time I must say good bye for the present with my best love to all

                                    I remain dear Emma
                                    Your most affectionate Brother
                                    W. Morris

[4]

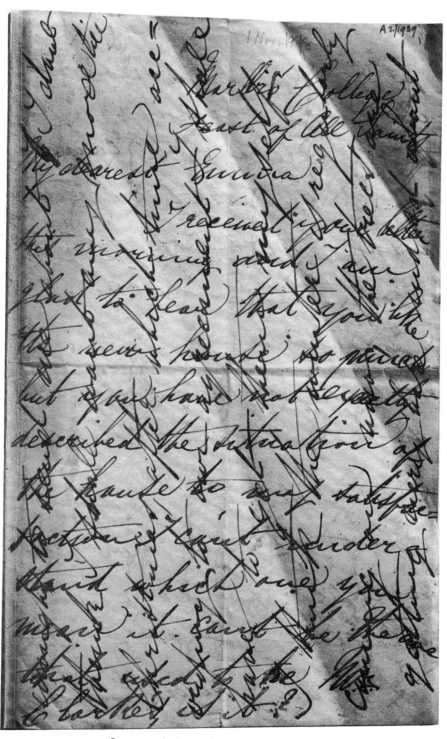

Letter no. 1, Morris's earliest known letter.

P.S. March 20th. Have just received your letter with 10s. and I want just to ask you something. James before I went gave me a rabbit and I asked him to sell the young ones for me which he said he would do for me.   do you think there was anything wrong in it   will you write and tell me if you think it so; (you need not tell anyone of it)   the reason I did it was to get a nice fishing rod   I did not like to ask Mamma to give me one and what with other things I did not think I should have enough to buy one otherwise; will you let this part of my letter be private and confidential dear Emma and again

Believe me

Your most affectionate Brother

W. Morris

MS: Walthamstow. Published: Henderson, *Letters*, 3-4.

  [1] Edward Denison (1801-1854), Bishop of Salisbury.

  [2] The Rev. Matthew Wilkinson, headmaster of Marlborough College from 1843 to 1851.

3 • To Emma Morris   Marlbro College
                                                      April 13, 1849

My dearest Emma
   I received your dear letter yesterday and I am glad you liked the anthem on Easter Tuesday. We here had the same anthem on Monday and Tuesday as on Sunday   it was the three first verses of the 72nd Psalm, In Jewry is God known, his name is great in Israel   At Salem is his tabernacle and his dwelling at Sion. There brake he the arrows of the bow, the sword, the shield, and the battle   I certainly thought it was very beautiful though I have never heard it in Cathedral and like you could not tell how they would sing it there; but a gentleman (one of the boys' fathers) said on the whole our choir sang better than at Salisbury Cathedral; Anyhow I thought it very beautiful. The first verse was sung by the whole the second began by one treble voice till at last the base took it up again gradually getting deeper and deeper then again the treble voice again then again the base   the third verse was sung entirely by base, not very loud but with that kind of emphasis which you would think befitting to such a subject. I almost think I liked it better than either of the other two   the only fault in the anthem seemed to to [sic] me that it was too short. On Monday I went to Silbury Hill which I think I have told you before is an artificial ⟨Hill⟩ hill made by the Britons   but first I went to a place called Abury[1] where there is a

Druidical circle and a Roman entrenchment both which encircle the town originally it is supposed that the stones were in this shape: first one large circle then a smaller one inside this and then one in the middle for an altar but a great many, in fact *most* of the stones have been removed so I could [not] tell this on Tuesday Morning I was told of this so I thought I would go there again, I did and then I was able to understand how they had been fixed; I think the biggest stone I could see had about 16 feet out of the ground in height and about 10 ft thick and 12 ft broad the circle and entrenchment altogether is about ½ a mile; at Abury I also saw a very old church the tower was very pretty indeed it had four little spires on it of the decorated order and there was a little Porch and inside the porch a beautiful Norman doorway loaded with mouldings the chancel was new and was paved with tesselated pavement this I saw through the window for I did not know where the sexton's house was, so of course I could not get the key, There was a pretty little Parsonage house close by the church. After we had done looking at the lions of Abury, which took us about ½ an hour we went through a *mud lane* down one or two water fields and *last* but not *least* through what they call here a *water meadow* up to our knees in water, now perhaps you do not know what a water meadow is as there are none of them in your part of the world So for your edification, I will tell you what a delectable affair a water meadow is to go through; in the first place you must fancy a field cut through with an infinity of small streams say about four feet wide each the people to whom the meadow belongs can turn these streams on and off when they like and at this time of the year they are on just before they put the fields up for mowing the grass being very long you cannot see the water till you are in the water and floundering in it except you are in[?] above the field. luckily the water had not been bog[?] when we went through it else we should have been up to our middles in mud, however perhaps now you can imagine a water meadow: after we had scrambled through this meadow we ascended Silbury Hill it is not very high but yet I should think it must have taken an immense long time to have got it together I brought away a little white snail shell as a memento of the place and have got it in my pocket book I came back at ½ past 5 the distance was altogether about 14 miles I had been out 3 hours ½ of course Monday and Tuesday were whole holidays. As [you] are going to send me the cheese perhaps you would set[?] Sarah to make me a good large cake, and I should also like some biscuits and will you also send me some paper and postage stamps also my silkworms eggs, and if you could get it an Italian pen box for that big box is too big for School. I am very sorry I was not at home with you at Easter but of

[7]

course that was not to be and it is no good either to you or to me to say any *horrid stale arguments* about being obliged to go to school for of course we know all about that. Give my best love dearest Emma to all.

And believe me,
Your most affectionate brother
William Morris

MS: Walthamstow. Published: Mackail, I, 22-24; Henderson, *Letters*, 4-6; Noyes, 11-12.

¹ Avebury.

4 • TO CORMELL PRICE

Clay Street
Walthamstow, Essex.
Tuesday in Holy Week
[April 3, 1855]

My dearest Crom¹

Yes, it's quite true, I ought to be ashamed of myself, I am ashamed of myself: I won't make any excuses: please forgive me. As the train went away from the station, I saw you standing in your scholar's gown, and looking for me. If I hadn't been on the other side, I think I should have got out of the window to say good-bye again . . . Ted² will shew something to criticise, or stop, I may as well write it for you myself; it is exceedingly seedy. Here it is.

> 'Twas in Church on Palm Sunday,
> Listening what the priest did say
> Of the kiss that did betray,
>
> That the thought did come to me,
> How the olives used to be
> Growing in Gethsemane.
>
> That the thoughts upon me came
> Of the lantern's steady flame,
> Of the softly whispered name.
>
> Of how kiss and words did sound
> While the olives stood around,
> While the robe lay on the ground.
>
> Then the words the Lord did speak
> And that kiss in Holy Week
> Dreams of many a kiss did make:

Lover's kiss beneath the moon,
With it sorrow cometh soon:
Juliet's within the tomb:

Angelico's in quiet light
'Mid the aureoles very bright
God is looking from the height.

There the monk his love doth meet:
Once he fell before her feet
Ere within the Abbey sweet

He, while music rose alway
From the Church, to God did pray
That his life might pass away.

There between the angel rows
With the light flame on his brows,
With his friend, the deacon goes:

Hand in hand they go together,
Loving hearts they go together
Where the Presence shineth ever.

Kiss upon the death-bed given,
Kiss on dying forehead given
When the soul goes up to Heaven.

Many thoughts beneath the sun
Thought together; Life is done,
Yet for ever love doth run.

Willow standing 'gainst the blue,
Where the light clouds come and go,
Mindeth me of kiss untrue.

Christ, thine awful cross is thrown
Round the whole world, and thy Sun
Woful kisses looks upon.

. . . .

Eastward slope the shadows now,
Very light the wind does blow,
Scarce it lifts the laurels low;

I cannot say the things I would,
I cannot think the things I would,
How the Cross at evening stood.

[9]

Very blue the sky above,
Very sweet the faint clouds move,
Yet I cannot think of love.[3]

There, dear, perhaps I ought to be ashamed of it, don't spare me. I have begun a good many other things, I don't know if I shall ever finish them, I shall have to show them to Ted and to you first: you know my failing. I have been in a horrible state of mind about my writing; for I seem to get more and more imbecile as I go on. Do you know, I don't know what to write to you about; there are no facts here to write about; I have no one to talk to, except to ask for things to eat and drink and clothe myself withal; I have read no new books since I saw you, in fact no books at all.

The other day I went 'a-brassing' near the Thames on the Essex side; I got two remarkable brasses and three or four others that were not remarkable: one was a Flemish brass of a knight, date 1370, very small; another a brass (very small, with the legend gone) of a priest in his shroud; I think there are only two other shrouded brasses in England. The Church that this last brass came from was I think one of the prettiest Churches (for a small village Church) that I have ever seen; the consecration crosses (some of them) were visible, red in a red circle; and there was some very pretty colouring on a corbel, in very good preservation: the parson of the parish shewed us over this Church; he was very civil and very, very dirty and snuffy, inexpressibly so, I can't give you an idea of his dirt and snuffiness.

TEXT: Mackail, I, 53-56. Published: Henderson, *Letters*, 6-8.

[1] This is the earliest letter surviving from Morris's years as an undergraduate at Exeter College, Oxford. Cormell Price (1836-1910) attended King Edward's School, Birmingham, and was a student at Brasenose. He later became headmaster of the United Services College, Westward Ho!, Devon, the model for the school in Rudyard Kipling's *Stalky & Co.* Morris and Price were lifelong friends, though the surviving letters are an unsatisfactory record of the fact. Price's diaries attest to regular and frequent meetings through the years. These unpublished diaries begin in 1856 and do not include the early Oxford diaries, which I have been unable to locate.

[2] Edward Burne-Jones (1833-1898), Morris's lifelong and intimate friend. Educated, as was Cormell Price, at King Edward's School, Birmingham, Burne-Jones entered Exeter College with Morris in January 1853. As a painter, illustrator, and designer, he collaborated with Morris in many enterprises, beginning with the *Oxford and Cambridge Magazine* (1856) and culminating in the books issued by the Kelmscott Press between 1891 and 1896, the last year of Morris's life. When Morris joined the Social Democratic Federation in 1883 Burne-Jones declined to follow him, but even during the years of Morris's most intense activity in behalf of socialism their friendship continued.

[3] One of the few poems not destroyed by Morris in 1858 when he burned all the early ones not included in *The Defence of Guenevere*, published that year. See Mackail, I, 52-56.

5 • TO CORMELL PRICE   [Clay Street
                                                            Walthamstow
                                                            April 1855]

It was not at sermon-time that I thought of the 'Kisses,' but as the second lesson was being read: you know the second lesson for Palm Sunday has in it the history of the Betrayal. I say, isn't *tomb* a very fair rhyme for *soon* by the way? the rhymes you call shady,[1] I should like to be able to defend: I think I could do it *viva voce* but can't by letter. . . . It is very foolish, but I have a tenderness for that thing, I was so happy writing it, which I did on Good Friday: it was a lovely day, with a soft warm wind instead of the bitter north east wind we had had for so long. For those bad rhymes, I don't like them, though perhaps I don't feel them hurt me so much as they seem to do you; they are makeshifts, dear Crom: it *is* incompetency; you see I must lose the thought, or sacrifice the rhyme to it, I had rather do the latter and take my chance about the music of it; perhaps I may be able in the course of time to rhyme better, if my stock of thoughts are not exhausted, and I sometimes think they mayn't all be gone for some time.[2]

I have read a little Shelley since I saw you last; I like it very much what I have read; 'The Skylark' was one: WHAT a gorgeous thing it is! utterly different to anything else I ever read: it makes one feel so different from anything else: I hope I shall be able to make you understand what I mean, for I am a sad muddle head: I mean that most beautiful poetry, and indeed almost all beautiful writing makes one feel sad, or indignant, or — do you understand, for I can't make it any clearer; but 'The Skylark' makes one feel happy only; I suppose because it is nearly all music, and that it doesn't bring up any thoughts of humanity: but I don't know either.

I am going a-brassing again some time soon: to Rochester and thereabouts, also to Stoke D'Abernon in Surrey.

TEXT: Mackail, I, 56-57. Published: Henderson, *Letters*, 8-9.

  [1] This refers to some criticism Price had made of the poem in letter no. 4.

  [2] Morris apparently enclosed two new poems. Mackail, who is the source of this information (I, 57-58), does not name them but writes of their "showing an influence that might not otherwise be suspected in him, that of Mrs. Browning."

6 • TO EMMA SHELTON MORRIS   Ex: Coll: Oxon.
                                                           Monday Evening
                                                           [May 28, 1855]

My dear Mother[1]

I enclose the receipt for D.G.C.[2] Dividend, signed: I hope its' all right; I think I can wait to invest it, or part of it till I come home; I suppose you can send it in to the banker's — I suppose by this time you have got the print all safe, at least I hope so; you see it is a kind of medieval family picture; and is [a] votive picture for the recovery of the little boy in the Virgins' arms, you must remember this, and take note that the child is *not* the young Christ, but as said. if it were the Divine Infant it would be poor, but is I think good enough as the figure of a sick child: the head of the family is a Senator of Basle; there seems to me something very truthful and beautiful in the heads and faces of the kneeling family, & though they might be mistaken in the way they showed their faith, yet doubtless they had it. —

How hot it has been these last two or three days! but it is cooler today — I have written several things since I was at home; nothing however of any length, a thing that I wish to do particularly, but I suppose I must wait till I can be quiet at home, and have about a weeks' continuous thinking which I can't get here; at all events not on one subject. —

I wrote to Stanley[3] some time ago — I am pretty much by myself these four days, as Edward Jones and my other chief crony[4] are gone up to London for the short vacation to see the Exhibition[5] and so forth. I will write to Henrietta[6] at Emma's — my best love to her and to all —

Your affectionate Son
William Morris

MS: Walthamstow.

[1] The daughter of a prosperous family, Emma Shelton had married the elder William Morris in 1826. Her family had "strongly developed musical tastes. . . . Emma Shelton's father, it is said, threw up everything for music" (Henderson, *Life*, p. 3).

[2] Devon Great Consols, a Devonshire copper mine, shares in which were the source of the Morris family's wealth. During the lifetime of William Morris senior, the holdings had risen in value to £200,000.

[3] Hugh Stanley, Morris's youngest brother.

[4] Cormell Price.

[5] The Royal Academy Exhibition, which had opened at the beginning of May. Here Morris first saw a picture by Ford Madox Brown, *The Last of England*, and a painting, as well as several drawings, by John Everett Millais. For these and other details of what was an important step in Morris's discovery of the Pre-Raphaelite painters, see *Memorials*, I, 110.

[6] Morris's second sister.

7 • TO CORMELL PRICE
Friday morning
Walthamstow
[July 6, 1855]

Dearest Crom,

What am I to say about your letter? for I was very glad to get a letter from you even though it brought such bad news; and you should not have said what you did say about Fulford,[1] for though I like him very much, and though he will without doubt be a very pleasant travelling companion, yet to me he is a very poor substitute for you.[2] . . . Please write as often as you can. I am so awfully glad to hear that you are writing something, do let me see anything you do, I am not at all afraid of it; I should think Trench's 'Study of Words'[3] would do very [well,] but that as it's a little bit old, it would perhaps be better to put it in the second or third number, rather than the first, but by all means write it; I have finished the tale I began last term and failed signally therein,[4] I am afraid that it won't do for the 'Brotherhood';[5] I am going to send it to Dixon[6] and Ted to look at, and see if it is altogether hopeless, will you look at it too? . . . If you remember, you were to review 'North and South'; are you thinking of it?[7]

As to Cambridge, it is rather a hole of a place, and can't compare for a moment with Oxford;[8] it is such a very different kind of place too, that one feels inclined to laugh, at least I do, when I think of it. I suppose by this time, Ted has told you all about it, and how we went to see Ely, which disappointed me somewhat, it is so horribly spoilt with very well meant restorations, as they facetiously term them; the bit of a hill that the Cathedral stands on is very jolly however, green fields and gardens and many trees, all dotted about with quaint old houses, and bits of the old conventual buildings; there are several gorgeous bits about the Church too, and outside happily it has been hardly touched, which makes the exterior much more beautiful and interesting than the interior.

I saw the Exhibition the other day and liked the Procession of Cimabue[9] better than I thought I should have done, as I said to Ted, I wish I hadn't seen Ruskin's Pamphlet[10] before seeing the picture, for I don't know now what effect his commendation may have had upon me. Millais's Picture[11] is indeed grand, how gorgeously the dawning is painted! I had been sitting up late the night before, and saw the dawn break, through the window in our hall, just as it might have been there, minus the smoke. There was a very sweet little picture by Collins[12] in the Octagon room, called 'The Good Harvest of '54,' did you notice it? I think Maclise's picture[13] about as bad as possible, fancy the brute spoiling one of the best scenes in your favourite comedy, don't you hate him therefore? I saw Dyce's[14] 'Christabel' and thought the face very sweet; but Ruskin says the face is a copy; certainly it doesn't help me at all to the understanding of Coleridge's Poem.

I saw that same day an impression of Albert Dürer's S. Hubert, and very nearly bought it but couldn't afford it, the same being 6 guineas; I think I should have done so though if I wasn't living in hope of getting a photograph of it; the photographs represent the engravings much better than I thought they did, looking very much like impressions whose paper is yellow by age, only somewhat darker: what a splendid engraving that S. Hubert is! O my word! so very, very gorgeous.

I bought some engravings from Fra Angelico's picture in the Louvre, I am afraid only pretty good; will you have them? they represent the picture fairly I think on the whole, only the loss of colour makes of course a most enormous difference, where the colour is so utterly lovely as in the original — well, I hope you will like them. I have just been doing them up into a parcel whose clumsiness is something absolutely glorious, it is so clumsy. O this steel pen! — tell me if they reach you safely. Well, good-bye. I have forgotten what else I had to say to you, though I know I had plenty.

Yours most lovingly,
Topsy.

TEXT: Mackail, I, 69-71. Published: Henderson, *Letters*, 9-10.

[1] William Fulford (1832-1897), a student at Pembroke College and one of the leaders of the "Birmingham colony," which included most of Morris's undergraduate friends. In February 1856, Fulford became editor of the *Oxford and Cambridge Magazine*, planned during the summer of 1855 by "The Brotherhood," as the Oxford group then began to call themselves. (Morris was the editor for the first issue. However, an entry in the diary of Margaret Price [sister of Cormell Price] for January 9, 1856 reads: "Morris does not like being Editor of the O. and C. Magazine, so gives Fulford £100 a year to be Editor." *Memorials*, I, 127.) The *Magazine* was published in twelve monthly numbers from January to December 1856 and is the subject of Morris's comments in this letter about projected reviews and articles. Though its title page read "Conducted by members of the two universities," it was wholly edited, and largely written, by Morris and his Oxford friends.

[2] Morris and Burne-Jones had planned a walking tour of Normandy in July. Price and Fulford were to accompany them, but Price had to withdraw, as this letter indicates.

[3] Richard Chenevix Trench (1807-1886), a philologist, whose *Study of Words*, published in 1851, popularized linguistics. No review of the book appeared in the *Oxford and Cambridge Magazine*.

[4] Probably *The Story of the Unknown Church*, which, despite Morris's denigration, appeared in the January number.

[5] The magazine had not yet been named, and "Brotherhood" was one of several titles being considered.

[6] Richard Watson Dixon (1833-1900), one of the Pembroke set, had been at school with Burne-Jones and Price in Birmingham. The *Oxford and Cambridge Magazine* originated in Dixon's suggestion to Morris that the Brotherhood publish a literary journal. Dixon, who took holy orders, was to officiate at the marriage of Morris and Jane Burden in April 1859; and it is possible that Morris's influence helped him in 1875 to obtain the curacy of Hayton, not far from Naworth (see letter no. 185). Dixon is chiefly remembered today as the friend who encouraged Gerard Manley Hopkins during his isolation and literary obscurity. He was also a poet, and in later life became Canon of Carlisle Cathedral and a Church historian.

[7] Price did not review *North and South* by Mrs. Gaskell. He did, however, write about Mrs. Gaskell's work, contributing a piece entitled "Lancashire and Mary Barton" to the July issue. His other reviews and articles were "Shakespeare's Minor Poems" (February); "Unhealthy Employments," co-authored with C. J. Faulkner (May); and "The Work of

Young Men in the Present Age" (September). See Buxton Forman, pp. 28-33 and also the *Wellesley Index*, II, 14-52.

⁸ At the invitation of Wilfred Heeley (1833-1875), an undergraduate in Trinity College, Morris and Burne-Jones had gone to Cambridge to discuss joint publication of the *Oxford and Cambridge Magazine*. Heeley contributed to the *Magazine* and later shared The Grange with the Burne-Joneses (1867-1868), went to India, returned an invalid, and died in 1875. See *Memorials*, passim.

⁹ Painted by Frederic Leighton and shown in 1855 at the Exhibition of the Royal Academy.

¹⁰ *The Academy Notes* for the Exhibition had been written by John Ruskin, already a commanding figure for Morris. Queen Victoria, possibly because of Ruskin's enthusiasm for Leighton's painting, purchased it. This was the making of Leighton's career.

¹¹ *The Rescue.*

¹² Charles Austin Collins (1828-1873).

¹³ The painting by Daniel Maclise (1806-1870) depicted the wrestling scene from *As You Like It*.

¹⁴ William Dyce (1806-1864), a painter and deeply religious High Churchman. He had visited Italy and had been influenced there by painters of the Nazarene School, who in some ways anticipated the Pre-Raphaelites.

8 • TO EMMA SHELTON MORRIS

La Tete du Boeuf
Abbeville, Picardy
⟨12.⟩ Midnight —
[July 20, 1855]

My dear Mother

We got here (to the Station at least) at half past 10 — We had a wet passage across but not at all a rough one; I was not ill, nor, was either of my friends; the rain went off before we got to Boulogne & it is a glorious night — the 5 o'clock train did not stop at Abbeville, so we had to wait till the 8.15. train wh: was a slow one; we went 3rd class, wh: is pleasant enough here.¹ We walked from the station to our inn though it was so late, & it is more than a mile & of course we knew nothing of the road; however we walked along a paved road with poplars on either side, till we came to the River Somme into wh: we nearly walked, but a railway porter showed us the way into the town, and at last by dint of asking the way, we found the Tete du Boeuf, wh: seems to be a good inn, we have got very good rooms at 6 francs. We caught a glimpse of the Big Church, it looks exceedingly splendid, a very mountain of wrought stone; I long for tomorrow morning: as far as we could see the country about the town is very pretty; but of course a beautiful starlight night does wonders — My best love to Emma & Joseph² Henrietta the boys & all of them —

Your aff: Son
William

MS: Walthamstow.

¹ Morris, Burne-Jones, and Fulford (see letter no. 7, n. 1) had started on July 19th on a tour of Normandy. Abbeville was their first stop.

² The Rev. Joseph Oldham and Morris's sister Emma were married in 1848 (or possibly 1850). See letter no. 1, n.1.

9 • To Emma Shelton Morris
Rouen. Hotel de France
⟨Saturday Evening.⟩
Sunday. July 29 [1855]

My dear Mother

I suppose you will be expecting to hear of me by this time, so here is a dull account of what we have been doing since we landed; Abbeville has a very fine Church, though very unfinished, and the town itself is very old and full of exceedingly good houses; we were all three in exstasies thereat; we left Abbeville about midday the next day (Friday) and got to Amiens in an hour or so, we stayed there till the next morning, being in the Church nearly all the time; my friends were utterly taken aback at the grandeur of the French Churches and have remained in that state ever since: well on the Saturday we went first by train to Clermont, and thence walked ⟨by?⟩ to Beauvais, (about 17 miles) we reached that town about 5 o clock in the evening having had a splendid walk through the lovely country, a very flower garden it is at this time of the year; I was rather knocked up by the walk, in consequence of having to wear my slippers, for the shoes I brought with me I could not wear at all: I think I like Beauvais Cathedral better than Amiens; the apse of Beauvais must be the finest in the world: well we stayed there till the Sunday Evening, when we went back to Clermont by diligence and got to Paris by ½ past 11 o'clock: we stayed at Paris Monday, Tuesday, and Wednesday; and saw there the Beaux Arts department of the Exhibition, which was very well worth seeing for the English pictures therein and for nothing else;¹ we stayed there about 7 hours on one day. We saw too the Picture Gallery in the Louvre; Notre Dame & some half dozen other Churches, including the Sainte Chapelle, & besides that, the Hotel de Cluny; nothing else, though we worked hard at sight seeing for at least 12 hours a day, doing a great deal of walking; I don't quite like Paris yet, though my friends are delighted with it: we left Paris on the Wednesday Evening, and got to Chartres about 10½ o'clock, and stayed there all the next day Thursday, enjoying ourselves immensely over its quaint streets and gorgeous Churches; on the Friday morning early, we took train back to Maintenon ('tis a very little way). From Maintenon to Dreux by a very quaint nondescript public conveyance, Dreux is a very quaint old town with a fine church: from Dreux to a place with an unpronounceable name Boueill, by the same conveyance; from Boueill to Evreux by a railway, it is only a half hour's ride, we had a very short time at Evreux to our grief for seeing the beautiful Cathedral there, and then had to go on by a similar nondescript conveyance to Louviers; by the way this same conveyance is a thing with an open coupée holding three, and a rotonde holding 4, it is drawn by one horse, and goes very slow I can tell you, but I can't tell you the name thereof. Louviers has a very rich, and beautiful, though (for France) small Church: well from Louviers we went for a few miles by omnibus to Louviers S. Pierre where we met the Rouen railway, and got to Rouen by 8½ P.M.   this was much better we thought than having to go back to Paris and lose a day in railway travelling; for we fairly enjoyed this journey (wh: took us in all about 15 hours and cost about 9s a piece) travelling through a most beautiful country, (no Lowland country I ever saw equals the valley in wh: Louviers lies) seeing too 3 picturesque old towns each with its lovely Church   it was quite delightful, I have seldom enjoyed a day so much; the railway took us little more than an hour in all. —

Well here we are in Rouen, glorious Rouen; yesterday we went about the Churches; mounted to the top of the view spire (360 ft.)   Such a view from there. Went all about the roof and Lantern of S. Ouen; heard vespers at Notre Dame, and finally after diner mounted Mont S. Catherine and wandered about there till it was quite dark. —

Well we have had a glorious time of it, working desperately hard; my two friends have been in a state of ecstasy since we landed, and for the matter of that so have I. The weather has been just what we could have wished: we hope to be able to stay out another fortnight. I musn't write any more or it will be over weight — Best love to all —

Your affectionate Son
William

(The pen is *very* bad)

MS: Walthamstow. Extract published: *CW*, I, xxxii.

[1] Fulford wrote: "conceive our delight to find no less than seven Pre-Raphaelite among the English pictures: three by Hunt, including the Light of the World, three by Millais, one by Collins." Quoted in Mackail, I, 72.

10 • TO EMMA SHELTON MORRIS
Hotel de France
Coutances, Normandy
August 7, 1855

My dear Mother

We left Rouen on the Wednesday morning, &, being disappointed of the Havre boat (wh: doesn't begin to run till later in the year went on foot to Caudebec, we had a glorious walk but it was rather too far perhaps for one day's tramp, being 25 miles, we were all three a good deal knocked up, (you know I have very bad shoes for walking or I could have done it easily) and we could not well walk the next day so we went by a diligence to Yvetot & by railway from Yvetot to Havre; and by the way as a rather remarkable fact, I might tell you that we paid the sum of one penny sterling for our ride from Caudebec, to Yvetot a distance of 10 miles; we slept at Havre the Thursday night, and went on the Friday morning to Caen by steamer over a very smooth sea; Caen is a fine place, but I was never the less disappointed therewith as I had heard so much of it but I was not disappointed with S. Etienne in that town, which is a splendid church; we left Caen on Saturday afternoon by diligence for Bayeux, slept there on Saturday Evening, and saw the Cathedral wh: is a very good one, and the tapestry on the Sunday; but as they were repairing the choir and transepts, we could not, in spite of our strenuous efforts get into that part of the Church much to our disgust; the tapestry is very quaint and rude, & very interesting. well on the Monday morning we went on to Coutances stopping an hour or two at S. Lo where there is a fine Church; the Cathedral here is one of the finest we have seen, built almost uniformly in a style like our Early English, very plain but very beautiful; there are two fine Churches here besides: the town is built mostly of granite, and lies up a steep hill overlooking a very pretty country, very English in its look, much like Clay Cross without the Chimneys. We go on tomorrow by diligence to Avranches from whence we shall see Mont. S. Michel, & there alas! alas! will end our French tour, for we shall go back to Granville on the Saturday evening, & start from Granville for Jersey on the Sunday morning (at 11 o'clock just when you are all in Church) and I suppose the Monday or Tuesday following will see me at Walthamstow, in a very seedy condition as to my clothes, for my coat is a beautiful russet brown where the sun has caught it, & my beautiful violet ribbon, had become so seedy that I was obliged to throw it away at Caudebec, and no words can describe the seediness of my dusty hat; then my shoes, O! my shoes! I was obliged to buy a pair of cloth boots at Paris, (boots like you wear, you know) because those shoes I took with me had made my corns so bad, well they were not good things to walk in, but they were the *only* things I could wear, and I hope they will hold together till I come home, but I don't think they will, they have been patched twice at the sides, and now the heels are coming off, and today I took them to a cobblers, there were 3 men and a boy there. I said when I had taken off my boot (in French of course) 'Can you mend my boot if you please' and made a face expecting what the answer would be, well they laid their heads together and presently they (or rather one of them) said, 'Monsieur we cannot mend it' — so I went away —

Well, I can't tell you when I shall be at home as I don't quite know whether we shall be obliged to sleep at Jersey or not, if I can find out before leaving Avranches I will write and tell you —

It is, I am happy to say, just dinner time, so good bye. Give my best love to all —

Your affectionate Son
William

MS: Walthamstow. Extract published: *CW*, I, xxxiv.

11 · To Cormell Price   Avranches, Normandy,
                                              August 10, 1855

Dearest Crom

I haven't quite forgotten you yet, though I have been so long writing, but the fact is, I am quite uncomfortable even now about writing a letter to you, for I don't know what to say; I suppose you won't be satisfied with the names merely of the places we have been to; and I scarcely think I can give you anything else. Why couldn't you come, Crom? O! the glories of the Churches we have seen! for we have seen the last of them now, we finished up with Mont S. Michel yesterday and are waiting here (which is a very beautiful place however) till Saturday evening or Sunday morning when we shall go back to Granville and take steamer for Jersey and Southampton. Crom, we have seen nine Cathedrals, and let me see how many non-Cathedral Churches; I must count them on my fingers; there, I think I have missed some but I have made out 24 all splendid Churches; some of them surpassing first-rate English Cathedrals.

I am glad that Fulford has lightened my load a little bit, by telling you what we did as far as Chartres: so I won't begin till after we left that place: Well, Crom, you must know that we had thought that we should be forced to go back to Paris to get to Rouen and that we should be obliged to go by railway all the way, which grew so distasteful to us after a bit, that we made efforts, and found that we could get across the country with very little railway indeed; so we went; I enjoyed the journey very much, and so did the others I think, though Ted's eyes were bad, as they have been all the time whenever the sun has been out: we went the greater part of the way in a queer little contrivance with one horse the greater part of the way. Behold our itinerary. We started from Chartres quite early (six o'clock) with drizzling rain that almost hid the spires of the Cathedral, how splendid they looked in the midst of it! but we were obliged to leave them, and the beautiful statues, and the stained glass, and the great, cliff-like buttresses, for quite a long time I'm afraid — so we went for about 20 miles by railroad to a place called Maintenon, where we mounted the quaint little conveyance and went off, with the rain still falling a little, through the beautiful country to Dreux, for a distance of about 17 miles; there was plenty to look at by the road, I almost think I like that part of the country better than any other part of the lovely country we have seen in France; so gloriously the trees are grouped, all manner of trees, but more especially the graceful poplars and aspens, of all kinds; and the hedgeless fields of grain, and beautiful herbs that they grow for forage whose names I don't know, the most beautiful fields I ever saw yet, looking as if they belonged to no man, as if they were planted not to be cut down in the end, and to be stored in barns and eaten by the cattle, but that rather they were planted for their beauty only, that they might grow always among the trees, mingled with the flowers, purple thistles, and blue corn-flowers, and red poppies, growing together with the corn round the roots of the fruit trees, in their shadows, and sweeping up to the brows of the long low hills till they reached the sky, changing sometimes into long fields of vines, or delicate, lush green forage; and they all looked as they would grow there for ever, as if they had always grown there, without change of seasons, knowing no other time than the early August. So we went on through this kind of country till we came to Dreux, and the rain had cleared up long before we reached it, and it was a bright sunny day. Some distance from Dreux the country changed very much into what I will tell you afterwards, but a great part of Picardy and the Isle of France seemed to be a good deal the same kind of country, and the land between Rouen and Caudebec, along the side of the Seine, was much like this, so much so, that I think I had it in my mind a good deal just now; perhaps it is even lovelier than this, the hills are much higher, but I scarcely think the flowers are so rich, or perhaps, when we went through it, the flowers had gone off a good deal. Well, we had to stop at Dreux about an hour and we saw the church there, a very good one, flamboyant mostly, but with an earlier apse very evilly used, and with a transept front very elaborately carved once, now very forlorn and battered, but (Deo gratias) not yet restored: there is a delightful old secular tower at Dreux too, and that is flamboyant also, with a roof like the side of a cliff, it is so steep. So we left Dreux, and set our faces as though we would go to Evreux; we were obliged to undergo about half an hour's ride in the railway before we got there, to my intense indignation. We had only a very short time to stay at Evreux, and even that short time we had to divide (alas! for our Lower Nature) between eating our dinner and gazing on the gorgeous Cathedral: it is an exceedingly lovely one, though not nearly so large as most of the Cathedrals we saw, the aisles are very rich flamboyant, with a great deal of light canopy work about them; the rest of the Church is earlier, the nave being Norman, and the choir fully developed early Gothic; though the transepts and lantern are flamboyant also by the way: there is a great deal of good stained glass about the Church. When we left Evreux we found that the country had changed altogether, getting much more hilly, almost as glorious in its way as the other land perhaps, but very different; for it is a succession of quite flat valleys surrounded on all sides by hills of very decent height with openings in them to let out the river, the valleys are very well wooded, and the fields a good deal like the other ones I have described, quite without hedges, and with fruit-trees growing all about them; so we kept going on, first winding up a long hill, then on a table land for a greater or less time, then down into the glorious lake-like valley, till at last we got to Louviers; there is a splendid church there, though it is not a large one; the outside has a kind of mask of the most gorgeous flamboyant (though late) thrown all over it, with such parapets and windows, it is so gorgeous and light, that I was utterly unprepared for the inside, and almost startled by it; so solemn it looked and calm after the fierce flamboyant of the outside; for all the interior, except the Chapels, is quite early Gothic and very beautiful; I have never, either before or since, been so much struck with the difference between the early and late Gothic, and by the greater nobleness of the former. So after we had looked at the Church for a little time we mounted the omnibus to go to the railway station where we were to take train to Rouen — it was about 5 miles I should think from Louviers to the station. What a glorious ride that was, with the sun, which was getting low by that time, striking all across the valley that Louviers lies in; I think that valley was the most glorious of all we saw that day, there was not much grain there, it was nearly all grass land and the trees, O! the trees! it was all like the country in a beautiful poem, in a beautiful Romance such as might make a background to Chaucer's Palamon and Arcite; how we could see the valley winding away along the side of the Eure a long way, under the hills: but we had to leave it and go to Rouen by a nasty, brimstone, noisy, shrieking railway train that cares not twopence for hill or valley, poplar tree or lime tree, corn poppy or blue cornflower, or purple thistle and purple vetch, white convolvulus, white clematis, or golden S. John's wort; that cares not twopence either for tower, or spire, or apse, or dome, till it will be as noisy and obtrusive under the spires of Chartres or the towers of Rouen, as it is [under] Versailles or the Dome of the Invalides; verily railways are ABOMINATIONS; and I think I have never fairly realised this fact till this our tour: fancy, Crom, all the roads (or nearly all) that come into Rouen dip down into the valley where it lies, from gorgeous hills which command the most splendid views of Rouen, but we, coming into Rouen by railway, crept into it in the most seedy way, seeing actually nothing at all of it till we were driving through the town in an omnibus.

I had some kind of misgivings that I might be disappointed with Rouen, after my remembrances of it from last year; but I wasn't a bit. O! what a place it is. I think Ted liked the Cathedral, on the whole, better than any other church we saw. We were disappointed in one thing, however, we had expected Vespers every afternoon, we found they were only sung in that diocese on Saturday and Sunday. And weren't they sung, just. O! my word! on the Sunday especially, when a great deal of the psalms were sung to the Peregrine tone, and then, didn't they sing the hymns!

I bought The Newcomes[1] at Rouen, Tauchnitz edition, it is a splendid book. Well Crom, I can't write any more, I am fairly run down; I am tired too, and have got to pack up as well, which is always somewhat of a bore; when I see you (which I hope will be soon) I will tell you about the rest. Ah me! if only you had been here, how I have longed for you! so very, very much. This is a seedy letter to send to such a fellow as you are, Crom, please forgive me, and be jolly when I see you. Shall I see you at Birmingham?

Your most loving
Topsy.

TEXT: Mackail, I, 73–78. Published: Henderson, *Letters*, 11–14.

[1] Thackeray's novel first appeared serially between 1853 and 1855 and was published in book form in London and Leipzig 1854–1855.

12 • To Cormell Price [Walthamstow
September 29, 1855]

I went to Malvern the day after I parted from you,[1] it is certainly a very splendid place, but very much spoiled by being made into a kind of tea gardens for idle people. The Abbey bells rang all the day for the fall of Sebastopol,[2] and when I went by railway to Clay Cross[3] the next day, they had hoisted flags up everywhere, particularly on the chimneys at Burton — at Chesterfield they had a flag upon the top of their particularly ugly twisted spire — at Clay Cross, by some strange delusion, they had hoisted all over the place the *Russian* tricolour (viz., horizontal stripes of blue, red, and white,) thinking, honest folks, that it was the French flag; they have no peal of bells at Clay Cross, only one bell of a singularly mild and chapelly nature, said bell was tolled by the patriotic inhabitants ALL day long, the effect of which I leave you to imagine. My life is going to become a burden to me, for I am going, (beginning from Tuesday next) to read for six hours a day at Livy, Ethics, &c. — please pity me.[4]

TEXT: Mackail, I, 82.

[1] A few days after returning from France, Morris went to Birmingham, where, with Burne-Jones, Fulford, Price, and Heeley, the *Oxford and Cambridge Magazine* was further discussed.

[2] On September 9, Sebastopol, besieged for eleven months during the Crimean War, fell to a final assault by British, French, and Turkish troops.

[3] The Oldhams (Morris's sister, Emma, and her husband, Joseph) were living at Clay Cross, Derbyshire.

[4] After the tour of France Morris decided to devote himself to art rather than pursue a career in the church as had been expected of him when he went to Oxford. Planning to take up architecture, he wanted to be finished with the university, and set himself to read for his Final Schools.

13 • TO CORMELL PRICE [Walthamstow
October 6, 1855]

Thank you very much for taking so much interest in me — but make your mind easy about my coming back next term, I am certainly coming back, though I should not have done so if it had not been for my Mother;[1] I don't think even if I get through Greats that I shall take my B.A., because they won't allow you not to sign the 39 Articles unless you declare that you are 'extra Ecclesiam Anglicanam' which I'm not, and don't intend to be, and I won't sign the 39 Articles.[2] Of course I should like to stay up at Oxford for a much longer time, but (I told you, didn't I?) I am going, if I can, to be an architect, and I am too old already and there is no time to lose, I MUST make haste, it would not do for me, dear Crom, even for the sake of being with you, to be a lazy, aimless, useless, dreaming body all my life long, I have wasted enough time already, God knows; not that I regret having gone to Oxford, how could I? for I should be a very poor helpless kind of thing without Ted and you. Didn't I tell you that I meant to ask Street of Oxford if he would take me?[3] I intended to tell you, if I didn't; if that could happen, it would be glorious, for then I need not leave Oxford at all. Ah well, may it be so!

TEXT: Mackail, I, 82-83. Published: Henderson, *Letters*, 14-15. Extract published: *Memorials*, I, 117.

[1] Morris may have given Price the impression that he intended to leave the university without taking his degree, for Price noted in his diary on September 28: "Wrote to Morris . . . abusing him roundly for thinking of leaving Oxford." (See Henderson, *Life*, p. 30). Morris in fact returned and passed his Final Schools in the autumn of 1855.

[2] In the event, Morris signed and took his B.A. in 1856. It was not until the University Tests Act of 1871 that compulsory subscription to the articles of the Church of England was abolished.

[3] George Edmund Street (1824-1881), the leading architect of the Gothic revival, whose office at this time was in Beaumont Street, Oxford. Morris carried out his intention, and on January 21, 1856, signed articles of apprenticeship and began work with Street. In August the architect moved his headquarters to London. Morris went with him, but by the end of the year had abandoned the idea of becoming an architect.

14 • TO EMMA SHELTON MORRIS   Ex: Coll: Oxon.
                                                          November 11, 1855

My dear Mother

I am almost afraid you thought me scarcely in earnest when I told you a month or two ago that I did not intend taking Holy Orders; if this is the case I am afraid also that my letter now may vex you; but if you have really made up your mind that I was in earnest I should hope you will be pleased with my resolution. You said then, you remember, and said very truly, that it was an evil thing to be an idle, objectless man; I am fully determined not to incur this reproach, I was so then though I did not tell you at the time all I thought of, ⟨that you⟩ partly because I had not thought about it enough myself, and partly because I wished to give you time to become reconciled to the idea of my continuing a lay person. I wish now to be an architect, an occupation I have often had hankering after, even during the time when I intended taking Holy Orders; the signs of wh: hankerings you yourself have doubtless often seen — I think I can imagine some of your objections, reasonable ones too, to this profession — I hope I shall be able to relieve them — First I ⟨know?⟩ suppose you think that you have as it were thrown away money on my kind of apprenticeship for the Ministry; let your mind be easy on this score; for, in the first place, an University Education fits a man about as much for being a Ship-Captain as a Pastor of Souls; besides your money has by no means been thrown away, if the love of friends faithful and true, friends first seen and loved here, if this love is something priceless, and not to be bought again anywhere and by any means: if moreover by living here and seeing evil and sin in its foulest and coarsest forms, as one does day by day, I have learned to hate any form of sin, and to wish to fight against it, is not this well too?

Think, I pray you Mother that all this is for the best, moreover if ⟨the burden of⟩ any fresh burden were to be laid upon you, it would be different, but as I am able to provide myself for my new course of life, the new money to be paid matters nothing —

If I were not to follow this occupation I in truth know not what I should follow with any chance of success, or hope of happiness in my work, in this I am pretty confident I shall succeed, and make I hope a decent architect sooner or later; and you know too that in any work that one delights in, even the merest drudgery connected with it is delightful too — I shall be master too of a useful trade, one by wh: I should hope to earn money, not altogether precariously, if other things fail. I myself have had to overcome many things in making up my mind to this; it will be rather grievous to my pride and self-will to have to do just as I am told for three long years, but good for it too I think; rather grievous to any love of idleness and leisure to have to go through all the drudgery of learning a new trade, but for that also, good — Perhaps you think that people will laugh at me, and call me purposeless and changeable; I have no doubt they will, but I in my turn will try to shame them, God being my helper, by steadiness and hard work. Will you tell Henrietta that I can quite sympathise with her disappointment, that I think I understand it, but I hope it will change to something else before long, if she sees me making myself useful; for that I will by no means give up things I have thought of for the bettering of the World in so far as lies in me — Stanley and Rendal,[1] and Arthur, and Edgar shall keep up the family honour in the World, and perhaps even I myself shall not utterly disgrace it, so may Christ help the family of the Morriss.

You see I do not hope to be great at all in anything, but perhaps I may reasonably hope to be happy in my work, and sometimes when I am idle and doing nothing, pleasant visions go past me of the things that may be.

You may perhaps think this a long, silly letter about a simple matter, but it seemed to me to be kindest to tell you what I was thinking of, somewhat at length, and to try, if ever so unsuccessfully, to make you understand my feelings a little; moreover I remember speaking somewhat roughly to you when we had conversation last on this matter, speaking indeed far off from my heart because of my awkwardness, and I thought I would try to mend this a little now, have I done so at all?

To come to details on this matter, I purpose asking Mr. Street of Oxford to take me as his pupil: he is a good architect, as things go now, and has a great deal of business, and ⟨is⟩ always goes for an honourable man; I should learn what I want of him if of anybody: but if I fail there (as I may for I don't know at all if he would take a pupil) I should apply to some London architect, in wh: case I should have the advantage of living with you if you continue to live near London, and the sooner the better I think, for I am already old for this kind of work. Of course I should pay myself the premium and all that —

My best love to yourself, and Henrietta, and Aunt and all of them,

Your most affectionate Son
William

P.S. May I ask you to show this letter to no one else but Henrietta

MS: Walthamstow. Published: Mackail, I, 83-86; Henderson, *Letters*, 15-17.

[1] Morris, who frequently misspelled names, apparently misspelled that of his brother. In a letter to the William Morris Gallery dated November 7, 1958, Effie Morris, daughter of Thomas Rendall Morris, distinctly gave her father's middle name as Rendall. Her letter is a carefully written biographical sketch of the entire Morris family, composed with the knowledge that it would be consulted for research purposes, and is more likely than Morris's to be accurate in matters of spelling.

15 • FROM A LETTER TO CORMELL PRICE   [January 11, 1856]

I am to have a grind about Amiens Cathedral[1] this time, it is very poor and inadequate, I cannot help it; it has cost me more trouble than anything I have written yet; I ground at it the other night from nine o'clock till half past four a.m., when the lamp went out, and I had to creep upstairs to bed through the great dark house like a thief.

TEXT: Mackail, I, 96.

[1] The article Morris wrote appeared in the *Oxford and Cambridge Magazine*, February 1856.

16 • FROM A LETTER TO EDWARD BURNE-JONES   Oxford
May 17, 1856

Will you do me a great favour, viz. go and nobble that picture called 'April Love,'[1] as soon as possible lest anybody else should buy it.

TEXT: *Memorials*, I, 132.

¹ By Arthur Hughes (1832-1915), one of the Pre-Raphaelite painters. Morris had seen the painting at the 1856 Royal Academy Exhibition, which he had visited with Burne-Jones and Price. Georgiana Burne-Jones wrote: "Morris had been greatly delighted by the picture of 'April Love' and . . . made up his mind to possess it . . . but as by that time he had gone back to his work at Oxford, he wrote up to Edward, asking him to see about its purchase. . . . This reached Edward on a Saturday evening [apparently the same day], and by half-past nine on Monday morning he was off to the Academy, fortunately in time to 'nobble' the picture, and make Morris happy with the news." *Memorials*, I, 131-32.

Edward Burne-Jones drawn by Simeon Solomon, 1859.

17 · To Cormell Price   Oxford
                                                                July 1856

I have seen Rossetti[1] twice since I saw the last of you; spent almost a whole day with him the last time, last Monday, that was. Hunt[2] came in while we were there, a tallish, slim man with a beautiful red beard, somewhat of a turn-up nose, and deep-set dark eyes: a beautiful man. . . . Rossetti says I ought to paint, he says I shall be able; now as he is a very great man, and speaks with authority and not as the scribes, I *must* try. I don't hope much, I must say, yet will try my best — he gave me practical advice on the subject. . . . So I am going to try, not giving up the architecture, but trying if it is possible to get six hours a day for drawing besides office work. One won't get much enjoyment out of life at this rate, I know well, but that don't matter: I have no right to ask for it at all events — love and work, these two things only. . . . I can't enter into politico-social subjects with any interest, for on the whole I see that things are in a muddle, and I have no power or vocation to set them right in ever so little a degree. My work is the embodiment of dreams in one form or another. . . .

Yet I shall have enough to do, if I actually master this art of painting: I dare scarcely think failure possible at times, and yet I know in my mind that my chances are slender; I am glad that I am compelled to try anyhow; I was slipping off into a kind of small (very small) Palace of Art.[3] . . . Ned and I are going to live together. I go to London early in August.

TEXT: Mackail I, 106–107. Published: Henderson, *Letters*, 17–18.

[1] Dante Gabriel Rossetti (1828–1882), painter, poet, and one of the founders of the Pre-Raphaelite Brotherhood (see n. 2, below). Since Easter of 1856, Burne-Jones had been painting in London under Rossetti's guidance. Morris, still at Oxford, visited Burne-Jones nearly every week, and during these visits, met Rossetti. By the summer he had changed from young admirer to friend and disciple, especially enamored of Rossetti's doctrine that everybody should be a painter. Even before they had met, however, Rossetti had become a hero to Morris; and Rossetti, in turn, had expressed interest in Morris's poetry.

[2] William Holman Hunt (1827–1910), another founding member of the Pre-Raphaelite Brotherhood. The group was formed in 1848 by Rossetti, Hunt, and Millais, who were joined by James Collinson (1825?–1881), the painter; Thomas Woolner (1825–1892), the sculptor; F. G. Stephens (1828–1907); and Rossetti's brother, William Michael Rossetti (see next letter, n. 1). The "P.R.B." lasted until 1853, when the Brotherhood ceased to exist and Pre-Raphaelitism, as a movement, can be said to have begun. For the Brotherhood and the movement, see William E. Fredeman, *Pre-Raphaelitism: A Bibliocritical Study* (Cambridge, Mass.: Harvard Univ. Press, 1965); John Dixon Hunt, *The Pre-Raphaelite Imagination, 1848–1900* (London: Routledge and Kegan Paul, 1968); James Sambrook, ed., *Pre-Raphaelitism: A Collection of Critical Essays* (Chicago: University of Chicago Press,

1974); and Lionel Stevenson, *The Pre-Raphaelite Poets* (Chapel Hill: Univ. of North Carolina Press, 1972).

[3] Tennyson's "The Palace of Art," first published in *Poems* (1832), provided Morris and Burne-Jones with a shared image of the life of art.

18 • TO WILLIAM MICHAEL ROSSETTI

Red Lion Sq:
February 18, 1857

My dear Rossetti[1]

I beg to be forgiven for having left your letter so long unanswered —

I enclose a cheque for 10£; Jone's subscription and my own; I will try what I can do to forward the subscription elsewhere[2] —

Yrs truly
W. Morris

MS: UBC, Angeli-Dennis Papers.

[1] William Michael Rossetti (1829-1919), brother of Christina and D. G. Rossetti, and member of the original Pre-Raphaelite Brotherhood. A civil servant in the Inland Revenue Board from 1845 to 1894, he had ample time for his real enthusiasm, literature. He edited *The Germ*, the periodical which began on January 1, 1850 and terminated in May, only four issues appearing, and wrote its cover-sonnet. He contributed art criticism to the *Critic* and, later, to *The Spectator*. His first published book was *Swinburne's Poems and Ballads: A Criticism* (1866), a defense of Swinburne against hostile reviewers. He also edited the first English edition of Walt Whitman's poetry (1860) and wrote a life of Keats (1887). As manager of his brother's reputation and literary estate, he brought out D. G. Rossetti's *Collected Works* (1886), *Family Letters, with a Memoir* (1895), and *Rossetti Papers, 1862-1870* (1903). Although he was often a bottomless well into which family secrets dropped never to give back a sound, he has also been a source of essential materials for contemporary scholarship. Characteristically, his *Reminiscences* (1906) are notable both for what is omitted about D. G. Rossetti and for the information that is recorded.

[2] For Thomas Seddon (1821-1856), a painter who had died a few months earlier. The subscription mentioned here was probably got up by the Pre-Raphaelite Brotherhood, who, Grylls notes, "had a whip-round among themselves and other friends to try to help [Seddon's] family" (Rosalie Glynn Grylls, *Portrait of Rossetti*, London: Macdonald, 1964, p. 51). It may, however, refer to the matter which Doughty and Wahl note (I, 58, n. 5) namely, that after Seddon's death, D. G. Rossetti "helped to organize a public subscription to purchase his *Jerusalem and the Valley of Jehosophat from the Hill of Evil Counsel* for the nation." Thomas Seddon, brother of the architect John Seddon (1827-1906) and son of a cabinetmaker, had been a furniture designer as well as a painter and had also taken part in establishing a school of drawing in Camden Town in 1850. Doughty notes (p. 88) that in 1849 Thomas and his brother had become sympathetic associates of the original seven members of the Pre-Raphaelite Brotherhood, welcomed particularly at meetings and discussions because help would be needed with the new project, publishing *The Germ* (see n. 1, above).

19 • THREE LETTERS TO ALEXANDER MACMILLAN[1]

a. 13 George St: Oxford
October 25, 1857

Dear Sir

Having a volume of poems[2] which I intend bringing out, I wish to know if you would undertake to publish them, and on what terms?

I am
Dear Sir
Yours faithfully
William Morris

Alexander
Macmillan Esq;

[1] The publisher (1815-1896); younger brother of Daniel Macmillan (1813-1857), a Scottish bookseller who founded Macmillan and Company in Cambridge in 1844. In 1857, Alexander succeeded his brother as head of the firm, and in 1863 he transferred the business to London, at the same time opening a branch in New York.

[2] Morris had collected some of his poems into a volume, and given it the title *The Defence of Guenevere and Other Poems*.

b. 13 George St: Oxford
November 7, 1857

Dear Sir

Your letter to me was somehow mislaid so I have only just seen it.

I send you some of the poems on the chance of their being of any good, though I should tell you that I scarcely thought it likely you would undertake to publish them at your own risk: I suppose in case of no other arrangement being possible, you would not object to publishing them at my own expense.[1]

I am dear Sir
Yrs: truly
William Morris

Alexander Macmillan Esquire
Cambridge.

[1] In the event it was Bell and Daldy who published *The Defence of Guenevere and Other Poems*, in 1858, at Morris's expense. Generally regarded as the first volume of Pre-Raphaelite poetry, the dedication reads: "To my friend, Dante Gabriel Rossetti, Painter, I Dedicate These Poems."

Morris, age 23, at Oxford, 1857.

c.   13 George St:
                                                              Oxford
                                                              November 21 [1857]

My dear Sir

Three of the four manuscripts I sent you reached me today, the other (called 'Arthurs Tomb') is missing, would you be good enough to see if you have it, and if so send it to me —

Thanking you for the trouble you have taken —

                                        I am
                                        My dear Sir
                                        Yrs. faithfully
                                        W. Morris.

(A. Macmillan Esq.
Cambridge)

MSS: Berg.

20 • FROM A LETTER, RECIPIENT UNKNOWN   [France
                                                              October 1858]

      . . . to buy old manuscripts and armour and ironwork and enamel.[1]

TEXT: Mackail, I, 137.

   [1] This phrase occurs in a passage in Mackail (I, 136-37) in which the information seems to come from letters. Mackail's full sentence reads: "In October he was in France again, 'to buy old manuscripts and armour and ironwork and enamel.' "

21 • TO MARY NICHOLSON   41 Gt Ormond St.
                                                              February 6 [1860]

My dear Mary[1]

I wish you would be good enough to find me the big brass that used to hang up between the windows and bring it to me at Ormond St.[2] tomorrow (Tuesday) if possible; about 5 oclock will be the best time as I want to see you about your work.

                                        Yrs. faithfully
                                        W. Morris.

MS: Fitzwilliam.

   [1] Mary Nicholson ("Red Lion Mary") was the housekeeper at 17 Red Lion Square, where Morris and Burne-Jones took rooms in 1856. See Mackail, I, 112.
   [2] After their marriage on April 26, 1859 (see letter no. 22, n. 4), the Morrises went on

a six-week tour of Paris, Belgium, and the Rhine and then returned to London to live in furnished rooms at 41 Great Ormond Street while Red House (see letter no. 24, n. 3) was being built. See Mackail, I, 139.

22 • TO FORD MADOX BROWN

[Red House
Upton, Kent]
January 18, 1861

My dear Brown,[1]

Kid[2] having appeared, Mrs. Brown[3] kindly says she will stay till Monday, when you are to come to fetch her, please. I send a list of trains in evening to Abbey Wood met by bus, viz., from London Bridge, 2.20 p.m., 4.20 p.m., 6.0 p.m., and 7.15 p.m. Janey[4] and kid (girl) are both very well.

TEXT: Mackail, I, 160-61. Published: Henderson, *Letters*, 21.

[1] Ford Madox Brown (1821-1893), painter, was closely associated with the Pre-Raphaelite Brotherhood, sharing their preference for clear definition in drawing and accuracy of detail. In 1857, he had been invited by Rossetti to execute one of the paintings on the walls of the Oxford Union (see n. 4, below) but had declined. Brown's friendship with Morris grew, however, and Mackail indicates (I, 145) that Brown, along with Rossetti, was first to suggest the formation of the firm that started in April 1861 under the name of Morris, Marshall, Faulkner and Company (see letter no. 24).

[2] Morris's elder daughter, Jane Alice ("Jenny"), born January 17, 1861.

[3] Brown's second wife, Emma Hill (1833-1888) whom he married in 1848. She was the daughter of a Herefordshire farmer. "For two or three years Madox Brown kept his marriage a secret from all but his most intimate friends. This was as much owing to the want of female society amongst his friends as to his desire to educate his wife . . . her early days spent in a farm-house atmosphere had endowed her with few accomplishments and very little savoir faire." Ford Madox Hueffer, *Ford Madox Brown: A Record of His Life and Work* (London: Longmans, 1896), p. 60.

[4] Morris's wife, Jane Burden (1839-1914), whom he married in Oxford on April 26, 1859, R. W. Dixon officiating. The daughter of a groom, she met Morris during the summer of 1857, when he, Rossetti, Burne-Jones, Arthur Hughes, J. R. Spencer Stanhope, John Hungerford Pollen and Valentine Prinsep had gone to Oxford to paint frescoes, depicting scenes from the *Morte d'Arthur*, on the walls of the new debating hall of the Union Society (see letter no. 97, n. 2). Rossetti first noticed Jane Burden and asked her to sit for him and his friends. His pencil study of her, dated October, 1857, was the first of many drawings and paintings of her he was to execute in the following years. Morris, between 1857 and 1858, also made a pencil study of her; drew her as *Iseult on the Ship* (his painting for the walls of the Union was *How Sir Palomydes loved La Belle Iseult with exceeding great love out of measure, and how she loved not him again but rather Sir Tristram*); and made her the subject of his one surviving oil painting, *Queen Guenevere*, finished in 1858. On the back of this painting, Morris wrote, "I cannot paint you but I love you." Morris did not leave Oxford when, in November 1857, the painting in the Union was completed, and for the next year or so lived chiefly there, presumably, among other reasons, to be near Jane Burden. They became engaged in 1858. See Mackail (I, 117-38);

Jane Burden, age 19, drawn by Morris, 1858.

Jane Morris, c. 1860.

and Henderson, *Life*, pp. 43-45. However, in view of what we know now of Jane Morris's intimacies with other men during her marriage, intimacies which began early and lasted into the 1890's, we should take seriously Margaret Fleming's suggestion that Jane may never have loved Morris, even when she consented to become his wife, and that she was urged into the marriage by members of her family who hoped to profit from the connection. See "Where Janey Used to Live," *Journal of the William Morris Society*, IV, 3, Winter 1981, pp. 2-17.

---

23 • To George Price Boyce
Red House
Upton S.E.
[March 1861?]

My dear Boyce[1]

These are the Sunday trains wh: an omnibus meets to my crib, from London Bge.

$$\left.\begin{array}{l} 10 \text{ A.M.} \\ 6.30 \text{ P.M.} \\ 8.30 \text{ P.M.} \end{array}\right\} \begin{array}{l} \text{obviously} \\ \text{no use} \end{array}$$

That's a pity as I know you are not a good walker,[2] perhaps you might manage the 10 oclock train.

These are the weekday busses for Barjsos'[?] information please tell him viz (from London Bridge)

10 A.M.
11.20 —
3.20 P.M.

I hope you will manage to come on Sunday.

Yrs very truly
W. Morris

MS: Fredeman Coll.

[1] George Price Boyce (1826-1897), painter. Like Morris, he had intended to become an architect, but around 1849 gave up this plan to concentrate on painting, and at about the same time met D. G. Rossetti. He was a founding member of the original Hogarth Club, 1858, and owner of a house designed by Philip Webb, built in 1870.

[2] In 1849 Boyce had injured his hip in a skating accident, and he remained slightly lame for life.

---

24 • To Frederick Barlow Guy
8, Red Lion Square,
April 19, 1861

My dear Guy,[1]

By reading the enclosed[2] you will see that I have started as a decorator which I have long meant to do when I could get men of reputation to join me, and to this end mainly I have built my fine house.[3] You see we are, or consider ourselves to be, the only really artistic firm of the kind, the others being only glass painters in point of fact, (like Clayton & Bell)[4] or else that curious nondescript mixture of clerical tailor and decorator that flourishes in Southampton Street, Strand; whereas we shall do — most things. However, what we are most anxious to get at present is wall-decoration, and I want to know if you could be so kind as to send me (without troubling yourself) a list of clergymen and others, to whom it *might* be any use to send a circular. In about a month we shall have some things to show in these rooms, painted cabinets, embroidery and all the rest of it, and perhaps you could look us up then: I suppose till the holidays you couldn't come down to Red House: I was very much disappointed that you called when I was out before.

With kind regards to Mrs. Guy,

> Believe me
> Yours very truly
> William Morris.

TEXT: Mackail, I, 149-50. Published: Henderson, *Letters*, 21-22.

[1] Frederick Barlow Guy (b. 1826), the tutor who coached Morris for matriculation to Oxford after he left Marlborough College. At the time of this letter, Guy was headmaster of Bradfield College, for whose chapel Burne-Jones had designed three windows in 1857. See Mackail, I, 149.

[2] The prospectus announcing the establishment of Morris, Marshall, Faulkner and Co., "Fine Art Workmen in Painting, Carving, Furniture and the Metals." The original members of the firm were Ford Madox Brown, Edward Burne-Jones, C. J. Faulkner, Arthur Hughes, P. P. Marshall, Morris, D. G. Rossetti, and Philip Webb.

[3] Red House, Bexley Heath, Upton, designed by Philip Webb (see letter no. 34, n. 2). Georgiana Burne-Jones writes (*Memorials*, I, 213) that it was the necessity of furnishing this house that gave rise to the firm.

[4] Stained glass makers. John Clayton (1827-1913) had been Rossetti's fellow student at the Royal Academy Schools. In 1862 he adjudicated the International Exhibition in London, calling the work of Morris, Marshall, Faulkner, and Co. the finest of its kind exhibited. See Vallance, p. 60. Clayton's partner was Alfred Bell (b. 1832).

25 · TO DANTE GABRIEL ROSSETTI   8, Red Lion Square,
                                            London, W.C.
                                            [January 18, 1863?]

My dear Gabriel

I am sorry I can't come on Thursday as my brother is coming down to Upton it must be some day next week.

> Yrs ever
> W Morris

MS: UIowa.

Dante Gabriel Rossetti, self-portrait, 1855.

26 · To Edward Burne-Jones   In bed, Red House
                                                  [November 1864]

As to our palace of Art,[1] I confess your letter was a blow to me at
first, though hardly an unexpected one — in short I cried; but I have
got over it now. As to our being a miserable lot, old chap, speaking for
myself I don't know, I refuse to make myself really unhappy for any-

thing short of the loss of friends one can't do without. Suppose in all these troubles you had given us the slip what the devil should I have done? I am sure I couldn't have had the heart to have gone on with the firm: all our jolly subjects would have gone to pot — it frightens me to think of, Ned. But now I am only 30 years old, I shan't always have the rheumatism, and we shall have a lot of jolly years of invention and lustre plates together I hope. I need hardly tell you how I suffered for you in the worst of your troubles; on the Saturday I had begun a letter to you but it read so dismal (as indeed I felt little hope) that I burnt it.

I have been resting and thinking of what you are to do: I really think you must take some sort of house in London — unless indeed you might think of living a little way out and having a studio in town: Stanhope[2] and I might join you in this you know. I don't see how you can do with chambers, and it would be too like the old way of living — but all this you have probably thought of yourself. There is only one other thing I can think of, which is when you come back from Hastings come and stay with me for a month or two, there is plenty of room for everybody and everything: you can do your work quietly and uninterruptedly; I shall have a good horse by then and Georgie[3] and J. will be able to drive about with the kids jollily, meantime you need not be hurried in taking your new crib. Janey is exceedingly anxious that you should come and it is in her opinion the best thing you could do. I would give £5 to see you, old chap; wouldn't it be safe for you to come down here one day before you go?

TEXT: *Memorials*, I, 284. Published: Mackail, I, 164-65; Henderson, *Letters*, 22.

[1] A reference to the plan to add an additional wing to Red House for the Burne-Jones family, and to move the workshop of Morris, Marshall, Faulkner and Co. to Upton. (See also letter no. 17, n. 3.) The letter also refers to the death of the Burne-Joneses' son, Christopher Alvin, at the age of three weeks, and to Georgiana's illness. See *Memorials*, I, 283-85.

[2] John Roddam Spencer Stanhope (1829-1908) had been a pupil of G. F. Watts. One of the group who joined Rossetti in painting the walls of the Oxford Union, he became a member of the circle around Morris and participated in the decoration of St. Martin's-on-the-Hill, Scarborough (designed by G. F. Bodley), an early commission received by Morris, Marshall, Faulkner and Company (see letter no. 32, n. 2).

[3] Georgiana Macdonald (1840-1920) married Edward Burne-Jones in 1860. She was one of five sisters, four of whom became wives or mothers of men who left their mark on English life. Rudyard Kipling and Stanley Baldwin were her nephews and a brother-in-law was Edward Poynter, the painter. See A. W. Baldwin, *The Macdonald Sisters* (London: P. Davies, 1960). She was to become Morris's closest friend among women.

Red House.

27 • TO ALLAN PARK PATON

8, Red Lion Square,
London, W.C.
February 10, 1865

Dear Sir[1]

I am glad you like our sketch for the windows;[2] I enclose what I *think* is a correct diagram of the position of the figures but I can't be sure without the sketch; I think you had better let us have the small eyes[3] you mention, however small they may be, as we shall be sure in that case not to forget them.

I am Dear Sir
Yrs obediently
A. P. Paton Esq.   W Morris

MS: NLS.

¹ Allan Park Paton, Librarian of Greenock, Scotland, at this time.

² For the Old West Kirk in Greenock (demolished in 1926). Paton, who was secretary to a committee responsible for the restoration of the church carried out in 1864, had asked Rossetti's advice about where to go for the stained glass windows. Rossetti recommended the firm. See Sewter, II, 85-86, and also Doughty and Wahl, II, 531.

³ Possibly the "bulls' eyes"—the small, circular pieces of plain glass left at the end of a blower's pipe.

28 • To George Campfield
8, Red Lion Square,
London, W.C.
July 6, 1865

My dear Campfield[1]

It appears I am wrong about the way the patterns should go in the mouldings where they die off into each other it ought to be thus, ie

not two sets of patterns where the mouldings meet.

I shall send you another design next week and meantime please send a *rough* tracing ⟨of the⟩ of one of the archangels —

Write if you want anything — I hope you get on all right —
Yrs truly
W Morris

MS: Yates Coll.

[1] George Campfield, foreman of Morris, Marshall, Faulkner and Co. Campfield was a glass-painter who came to Morris's notice as a pupil of Ruskin in the evening classes at the Working-Men's College in Great Ormond Street. See Mackail, I, 148-49.

29 • To Frederic Madden
8 Red Lion Square
London
August 5, 1865

Sir[1]

My friend Mr. Warrington Taylor[2] of 3 Harwood Terrace Fulham who is already a reader is desirous of admission to the Manuscript Room as an artist.

I can recommend him as a gentleman and a person proper to enjoy this privilege.

I am
Sir
Your obedient servant
William Morris

Sir Frederick Madden KH &c &c

MS: BL, Eggerton Papers 2848.

[1] Frederic Madden (1801-1873) was head of the British Museum Manuscript Department, from 1837 to 1866. He was an original member of the Athenaeum Club, 1830.

[2] George Warington Taylor (1835-1870) was manager of Morris, Marshall, Faulkner and Co. from 1865 until his death.

30 · To James Arnold Heathcote   26, Queen Square,
Bloomsbury, London
February 19, 1866

Dear Sir[1]

I would be willing to let you my house at Upton for the time you mention for £100 a year, but couldnt afford to do anything to it for that sum — as ⟨the⟩ to the final purchase of it, I should be glad to know what you offer me for it on these conditions — I don't expect any difficulty about the title, and would not wish to put any obstacles in the way if you really wished to purchase.[2]

Your last note though dated the 16th did not reach me till Saturday evening, or I should have answered you before. I should be glad to see you here about the subject if you happened to be in London —

I am
Dear Sir
Yrs obediently
W. Morris

Capt. Heathcote

MS: Heathcote Papers.

[1] James Arnold Heathcote (1827-1877), the second owner of Red House. He was a retired commander in the Indian Navy and had established a maritime salvage firm in Kent. Why Morris addressed him as "Captain" is unknown. He may have received a promotion for retirement purposes or Morris may have used the title simply because he was writing to a naval officer. For information about Commander Heathcote, I am grateful to Col. James A. Heathcote, U.S.A.F.

[2] Although neither surviving letter to Commander Heathcote specifies when Red House was sold to him, an agent's advertisement (see next page) indicates that the house was still to let in June 1866. This amplifies Mackail's account, which tells us (I, 165) only that the Morrises moved from Upton to Queen Square, Bloomsbury, in November 1865, and that Red House was later sold.

31 · To James Arnold Heathcote   26, Queen Square,
Bloomsbury, London
March 7, 1866

Dear Sir

Excuse my long delay in answering your letter, I have been ill lately: as to the house, I would let it for the two years at the rate of £95 a year, but the lowest price for the freehold if you had the option of purchasing at the expiration of that term would be £1800; if you are willing to treat on this basis we could soon settle other matters and I should be happy to see you or write to you about it; ⟨otherwise⟩ but I cannot entertain

UPTON, NEAR BEXLEY, KENT.

To be ~~Sold or~~ Let,

A CAPITAL FREEHOLD RESIDENCE,

DISTINGUISHED AS " RED HOUSE."

Erected in 1859, on an elevated Position, commanding Extensive Views of the surrounding much-admired scenery ; it has exceedingly Dry Concrete Foundations, supporting very solidly-built Walls, faced with best Picked Kentish Red Bricks, stands in its own Grounds, approached by a Carriage Sweep, and affords the following accommodation :—

On the First Floor,—Three principal Bed Rooms and Dressing Room, a Large and Elegant Room, built as an Artist's Studio, capable of being converted into a Bed Room and Dressing Room ; a Noble Corridor, lighted with Stained Glass, of high artistic excellence, with a beautiful Southern View over the Kentish Hills ; fine Oak Landing and Staircase, Passage, Watercloset, and Two Servants' Bed Rooms (one for Three Beds) ; Drawing Room, 24 ft. by 18 ft., well lighted, and most elegantly and artistically decorated with the commencement of a series of Wall Pictures, by an Eminent Artist of the Old Water Colour Society. On the West end is a charming old English Oriel Window, looking North, South, and West.

There is access from this Floor to the High-pitched Roof above the Joists, forming a capital Store Room for Fruit, or could be made into an excellent Lumber Room.

On the Ground Floor,—A Fine Hall, entered through a Porch with a Lofty Gothic Arch, leading into a Lower Corridor, lighted with Stained Glass of the best character ; Garden Porch, leading out on to the charming Greensward, with Well, canopied in the Old English Style ; Dining Room, 24 ft. by 18 ft., handsome Dado Panelling, commodious Cupboard and Cellaret ; Library and Morning Room ; Kitchen, fitted with capital Range ; Buttery Hatch, Large and Light Pantry, ample Closet Room for China and Glass, Large Store Room, Scullery, Larder, Housemaid's Closet, Watercloset, Beer and Wine Cellars, Commodious Outbuildings, excellent COACH-HOUSE, and TWO-STALLED STABLE, WITH LOFT.

The Grounds are tastefully disposed, the Flower Garden with Plaisances in character with the House, Bowling Green, Orchard, and Productive Kitchen Garden, the whole containing more than an Acre.

There is an abundant supply of Spring Water, which has never failed in the hottest Summer.

Immediate Possession may be had.

The Fixtures and Fittings will be included in the purchase.

Water and Gas can be laid on if desired.

For Terms and Cards to View apply to

MR. MARSH,

Auctioneer, Surveyor, and Land Agent,

2, CHARLOTTE ROW, MANSION HOUSE.

June 1866

Agent's bill for Red House.

any lower offer than this — I should be obliged by your letting me know as soon as convenient what you intend to do about the matter.

Yrs faithfully
W. Morris

Capt: Heathcote

MS: Heathcote Papers.

---

32 • TO FREDERICK R. LEACH

26, Queen Square,
Bloomsbury, London
[late June 1866]

Sir[1]

I am informed by Mr. Bodley[2] for whom you have done some work that you would probably undertake the execution of certain decorations we are about to commence in Jesus Chapel. The work is to be in distemper to be done in the best & most workmanlike manner to be finished to the approval both as to colour and execution.

We shall begin on the ceiling of the tower. I shall be coming down to Cambridge with Mr Bodley on Thursday 5 July & should wish you by that time to have whitened sufficiently the tower ceiling for a ground. The white should have no blueblack mixed with it. If you could also manage it I should wish you to paint in at least one of the enclosed pattern on the smaller panels. This pattern must be placed so that the J H C can be read from the ground by one looking East.

I send with this patterns of colour for the flowers & leaves which I should wish to be closely followed. I shall be obliged by an answer by return as to whether you can do this & will then tell you by what train Mr. Bodley & I will come next Thursday.

Yours very truly
W. Morris

MS: Walthamstow.

[1] Frederick R. Leach of Cambridge was Morris's favorite decorator and carried out two or three jobs for the firm between 1866 and 1870. See P. Thompson, p. 30; and letter no. 39 and letter no. 48.

[2] George Frederick Bodley (1827-1907), architect. From 1840 to 1850 he studied with George Gilbert Scott (1811-1878). A designer of private houses and churches, he was a later nineteenth-century counterpart of the architects of the Oxford Movement (Pugin, Scott, and Street). The commissions he gave the new firm of Morris, Marshall, Faulkner and Co., in 1861-1862, were among their first. These were the decorations and windows for three of his own earliest churches: St. Michael's, Brighton; St. Martin's-on-the-Hill,

Scarborough; and All Saints, Selsey, Gloucestershire. The work done for Bodley quickly established the firm's reputation.

33 • To Charles Augustus Howell

26, Queen Square,
Bloomsbury, London.
July 3, 1866

My dear Howell[1]

Webb[2] and I are so very much ashamed of ourselves for not having done anything in the matter of Cruikshank[3] that we send a cheque for 2 guineas each as our subscription — it is to be hoped that this vast piece of generosity will wipe from your mind all remembrance of our disgraceful laziness.

Webb desires to join with me in praying you still to consider us worthy of your friendship

Yours ever
William Morris

C:A: Howell: Esq.

MS: Princeton T.

[1] Charles Augustus Howell (1840-1890) was born in Portugal, of a Portuguese mother and English father, and came to England when he was sixteen. From 1865-1870, he was secretary to Ruskin, and later became D. G. Rossetti's secretary and confidant. He allegedly took advantage of Rossetti's periods of depression and inattention to steal drawings and other objects of value from his employer. Doughty describes him (p. 372) as "renowned for wit, knavery, and brazenness" and writes (p. 396) that "[t]hings were always being 'lost' when Howell was about." Howell, at one time, affected a broad red ribbon across his shirt front, and said that it was a Portuguese decoration hereditary in the family, thus inventing a noble birth for his mother (his father was an impecunious drawing-master in Lisbon). Doughty notes (p. 454) that "Morris, who well knew [Howell], on being asked on one . . . occasion what the ribbon was, replied that he did not know, but as he knew Howell he was sure he had stolen it." Howell participated, in 1869, in the exhumation of the poems buried in the coffin of Elizabeth Siddal (1834-1862) and subsequently published as *Poems* by D. G. Rossetti in 1870. See Doughty, p. 416.

[2] Philip Speakman Webb (1831-1915), architect, and Morris's lifelong friend. Leaving the office of G. E. Street at Oxford, where he had met Morris, he opened a practice in London in 1859. Webb was the designer of Red House, and the architect for one church (Brampton, Cumberland) and about sixty houses, including 1 Palace Green, Kensington; Rounton Grange, Yorkshire; and Clouds, Wiltshire. He produced many decorative designs for the firm, of which he was a member, and was a co-founder with Morris of the Society for the Protection of Ancient Buildings.

[3] A testimonial fund on behalf of George Cruikshank to defray expenses of an exhibition of his works. Howell was the secretary of the fund. See J. Hillis Miller and David Borowitz, *Charles Dickens and George Cruikshank* (Los Angeles: W. A. Clark Memorial Library, 1971), pp. 92-95.

34 • To Henry Young Darracott Scott   26, Queen Square,
Bloomsbury, London
September 13, 1866

Sir,[1]

We beg to inform you that our Estimate for glazing the three windows in Refreshment room South Kensington[2] amounts to — £272.0.0. exclusive of fixing, packing, etc.

The character to be explained by our Mr. Morris in private interview with you.

We are, etc.
Morris & Co.[3]

MS: PRO.

[1] Henry Young Darracott Scott (1822-1883), served as a major-general in the Royal Engineers. In December 1865, he was employed by the Commission of the Great Exhibition at South Kensington, and on the retirement of Sir Henry Cole, was appointed secretary to the Commission. His chief responsibility was the Royal Albert Hall, design and construction of which were entrusted to him in 1866. After his retirement from the Army, he continued in his civil appointment at South Kensington, preparing plans for the completion of the South Kensington Museum.

[2] In 1867 the firm obtained its first really important commission in non-ecclesiastical decorative work: the decoration of the Green Dining Room at the South Kensington Museum. See Mackail, I, 176.

[3] Morris apparently did not write this letter. Correspondence of the firm has been included in this edition when apparently dictated by Morris, or written under his direction. The firm did not officially adopt the name "Morris & Co." until after its reorganization in 1875 (see letter no. 222b, n. 1) but seems to have used the title informally before that date.

35 • To Edmund Henry Morgan   26 Queen Square
Bloomsbury, London W.C.
November 27, 1866

Dear Sir[1]

The flat part of the ceiling I should fancy would be finished in about three weeks,[2] but I am sorry to say that it will be quite impossible to finish the figures round the coved part[3] by the time you mention; I am vexed that this should be the case, and would do anything that was possible that the College might not be inconvenienced, but work of this sort cannot be hurried, as the men who are able to do it are very few; if it was merely a case of flat painting we could make a push to get the work done quicker than usual by putting on more men, but for this artistic work they are not to be had. In short, we have only two men at the outside whom we could trust to do the work and they, with such help as I myself could give them, would take three months to finish it if they were to begin tomorrow; nay, with these short days they would probably be longer, neither would it be possible for us at present, at any rate for a fortnight, to spare one man from our atélier; add that cold weather may come which would prevent our working at all in a place like the Chapel. On the other hand since the more mechanical part of the Ceiling will certainly be finished in time, would it not be better to strike the scaffolding and look upon the work as put aside till Spring, at any rate, and in the meanwhile we could go on with the transept roofs, where we could work by candlelight, and if a frost came, wrapt up. At any rate at the risk of being troublesome I must deprecate any hurry with works of this kind; the opportunity (as you probably know) seldom happens to us to paint figures in churches on such a scale, and I am extremely interested in the work and want it to be done in the best possible way; at the same time if it were possible to finish the work in the time you mention I would strain every nerve to do so. I must mention that your letter on Saturday was the first we had heard about any definite time for the completion of the ceiling and we thought as there had been no hitch in the work since we began, and as we did not intend (in spite of all drawbacks) that there should be any, that the progress was satisfactory.

I hope to come to Cambridge on Thursday or Friday this week, I don't like to settle which day till I see whether Mr Bodley, (who is out of town today), can come with me on either of those days — perhaps I might be able to see you then, and in talk might explain better what our difficulties are.

I am
Dear Sir
Yours obediently
William Morris[4]

E. H. Morgan Esq.

MS: Jesus College.

¹ Edmund Henry Morgan (1838-1895), Dean of Jesus College, Cambridge, from 1866 to 1895, and Senior Tutor for the same period. He was popularly known as "Red Morgan" in order to distinguish him from the Master (H. A. Morgan) known as "Black Morgan." See *Alumni Cantabrigienses*, compiled by J. A. Venn (Cambridge: Cambridge Univ. Press, 1951), Part 2, Vol. 4, p. 461.

² See letter no. 39.

³ Lindsay notes (p. 131) that "about this time Morris and Webb designed Bodley's new ceilings at Jesus College Chapel, Morris doing a frieze of angels." The execution of the series of flat decorated panels for this new roof was left to F. R. Leach. On November 6, 1866, Morgan wrote to Bodley that "some astonishment was felt at the employment of a Cambridge workman in the execution of a work which was intrusted to *Mr Morris*, on the very favourable recommendation given by you." Bodley assured Morgan that Leach had been carefully instructed by Morris, and that "the figures of angels, in the panels over

the wall-cornice, will be executed by Morris' own men. The cartoons are prepared & matters put in hand. I wd. say that Morris finds Leach a very capable & able executant. The design & the exact shades of the colours are all done according to the directions given to him. Nothing of that kind is left to him. He is doing it quite well as Morris' own men wd." (Letter to Morgan, November 8, 1866, in Jesus College Library, Cambridge.)

⁴ This letter and the following one appear to have been written out by someone else and signed by Morris.

36 • To Edmund Henry Morgan
26, Queen Square,
Bloomsbury, London
December 3, 1866

Dear Sir

I was at Cambridge on Friday and saw the work which is going on satisfactorily, we shall be able to finish the ceiling by the first of April as you have arranged[1]

I remain
Dear Sir
Your obedt svt
W Morris

The Revd E. H Morgan.

MS: Jesus College.

[1] A letter from Warington Taylor to Webb, dated 13 November 1866 reads: ". . . Do see that Morris starts those angels for Cambridge roof now; he will never have them in time, and at the last moment will want others to do the work." (Victoria and Albert Museum, Reserve Case JJ35. Quoted by Henderson, *Life*, p. 80.) In *Morris & Company in Cambridge*, Robinson and Wildman note (p. 37): "Morris's own hand is to be seen in the row of stately angels in red, yellow and green around the cove of the ceiling. . . . The design . . . of the pairs of trees, with twisted trunks and laden boughs, which are interspersed with the angels, may be ascribed to Webb. . . ."

37 • To Allan Park Paton
26, Queen Square,
Bloomsbury, London
January 3, 1867

Dear Sir

The windows 60″ × 30″ we suggest should be filled with one figure each on quarry ground Nehemiah & Ezra. The cost would be for Nehemiah £41.5.0 for Ezra £48.5.0 As regards the window 9.10 × 4.6 in memory of Prof. Scott[1] from its large size we scarcely know what to suggest. We think a crucifixion treated historically would be a fitting subject but this would involve great expense for the cartoon the whole expense would probably be between £270 & £300

>We are
>Your obed servant
>Morris & Company

Vestry windows
Greenock
A. P. Paton Esq

MS: NLS.

[1] Alexander John Scott (1805-1860). Born in Greenock, he was minister, at one time, of the Old West Kirk in Greenock.

38 • To Charles Augustus Howell

26, Queen Square,
Bloomsbury, London
February 1, 1867

My dear Howell

I am ashamed that you should have had the trouble to write about the money to Mr. Mins, but I thought McShane[1] had paid him & told him to book the money against me. The poor old chap you see muddles one both in life & death however I have sent today the due sum.

I am very sorry you are seedy, hope you will be well enough to see me soon.

>Yrs Ever
>W Morris

MS: Princeton T.

[1] MacShane, elderly and ill, was the clerk who kept the books in "splendid order" for Morris, Marshall, Faulkner and Co., according to Warington Taylor (see Lethaby, p. 51).

39 • To George Campfield

26, Queen Square,
Bloomsbury, London
March 22, 186[7][1]

My dear Campfield

We send money £5. I think I shall be coming on Monday, but if any of the fellows ask when, say you don't know; you must manage to finish next week, Leach[2] and all of us. The escapades of our men have enraged the dons and they want to get rid of you.[3] I send the two last cartoons and with them a cartoon of an angel piping for the triangular space below the crossing arch. You must draw the wings (gold) yourself as I don't quite know what would show, they must be something like this [drawing][4] make the figure white on a vermilion ground quite bright and don't put in all the lines the cartoon shows. — It will be Monday pretty certainly only don't say anything about it to dons: and burn this letter.

Yours very truly
W. Morris

TEXT: Henderson, *Letters*, 22-23.

[1] Henderson, who is the only source for this letter, misdated it by exactly one year.

[2] See letter no. 32.

[3] It is not clear whether Morris means by "escapades of our men" the delays complained about by the college authorities (see letter no. 35) or activities unconnected with the work.

[4] Henderson does not reproduce the drawing but merely indicates its location in the manner done here.

40 • TO EDMUND HENRY MORGAN
26, Queen Square,
Bloomsbury, London.
March 26, 1867

Dear Sir

I went down to Cambridge yesterday taking two men with me to push the work in your chapel: Unfortunately I found that you had gone down for the day, or I proposed calling on you.

Everything seems satisfactory there but owing to very unusual weather of the last month the work has been much hindered, and I shall not be able to give it up to you this week; it will however be finished by the week after, (week ending April 7th). I hope by the Thursday or Friday —

Mr. Bodley has asked me to prepare a drawing for the decoration of the *wall* of the nave; in case you would like to have it begun before the scaffolding is struck: this I am doing, & could set Mr Leach at work on it when I come to Cambridge early next week if you think it advisable. I should add that under the circumstances our charges will be small apart from those of Mr. Leach —

I am
Dear Sir
Yrs obediently
W Morris

Revd. EH Morgan
Jesus Coll
Cambridge

MS: Jesus College.

41 • To Henry Young Darracott Scott
26, Queen Square,
Bloomsbury, London.
June 3, 1867

Sir[1]

With reference to the letter from the Department, 13 April: 67 bearing signature G. F. Duncome, we beg to inform you that our estimates are as follows:

No. 1. £53.9.0.
for the work already done by us in Refreshment room S[outh] K[ensington] museum
No. 2. To scaffolding, preparing colouring gilding & decorating ceiling of plaster work & designing patterns for the same.
To preparing & painting, etc —

Morris & Co.

MS: PRO.

[1] See letter no. 34 and notes 1 and 3. This letter (no. 41) is also not in Morris's hand.

42 • From a Letter to Edward Burne-Jones
[June 20, 1867]

Naturally I am in good spirits after the puffs,[1] but I reserve any huge delight till I see what the 'Pall Mall' and 'Saturday' say, one of which is pretty sure to act Advocatus Diaboli. However I fancy I shall do pretty well now; last week I had made up my mind that I shouldn't be able to publish 'The Earthly Paradise'[2] and was very low: I am as anxious as you are to get on with that work, and am going to set to work hard now.[3] I hope you won't let any rubbish pass without collaring it. I am too old now for that kind of game.

TEXT: Mackail, I, 185.

[1] Morris was referring to reviews of *The Life and Death of Jason*. The book was initially published (1867) by Bell and Daldy at Morris's own expense but when it was reprinted later in the year Morris received a substantial sum. In June, reviews were beginning to appear. A favorable (unsigned) review by Joseph Knight (see letter no. 43, n. 1) was printed in the *Sunday Times* for June 9, 1867. See Peter Faulkner, ed., *William Morris: The Critical Heritage* (London: Routledge and Kegan Paul, 1973), pp. 50-55.

[2] *The Earthly Paradise*, was published in three volumes, containing four parts, between 1868 and 1870. During the same period, a large paper edition in six volumes was also issued.

[3] This is presumably a reference to an illustrated edition of *The Earthly Paradise* that Morris and Burne-Jones planned but never carried out. However, Burne-Jones completed illustrations for "Cupid and Psyche," one of the stories for the month of May, and wood blocks were cut. These were discovered only recently, and an edition of "Cupid and

Psyche," illustrated by these blocks, was published in 1974, edited and with an introduction by A. R. Dufty (Clover Hill Edition, London). A detailed account of the making of the illustrations for *The Earthly Paradise* is given by S. C. Cockerell in "A Short History of the Kelmscott Press" (Sparling, p. 139) and by Joseph R. Dunlap, *The Book That Never Was* (New York: Oriole Editions, 1971).

---

43 • To Charles Augustus Howell
26, Queen Square,
Bloomsbury, London
June 20, 1867

My dear Howell

Many thanks for the trouble of book &c. — Knights[1] letter was mighty polite or more, and I should be very glad to see him; will you tell me what day you could come over to see me (grub) next week & I will write & ask him to meet you — his notice is a very handsome one, and so is his friend's in the Athenaeum, and there was another in The Spectator also flowing — so I am getting on pretty well —

Camon[2] to hand and very fine — many thanks. I reinclose Knight's letter — please write at once

Yrs affec:
W Morris

MS: Princeton T. Extract published: *CW*, 2, xv.

[1] Joseph Knight (1829-1907), drama critic of *The Athenaeum* from 1867 until his death.
[2] Possibly *The Lusiads*, an epic poem by the Portuguese poet Luís de Camoëns (1524-1580).

---

44 • To George James Howard
26, Queen Square,
Bloomsbury, London
July 25, 1867

My dear Howard[1]

Please excuse my rudeness in not answering your note before — it reached me however while I was away with Webb. I should have [been] very happy to have gone to see you but our time altogether was very short, and I didn't get farther north than York; many thanks all the same. I know something of Naworth Castle by Parker's book,[2] and it must be a very beautiful and interesting house —

Yrs very truly
W. Morris.

MS: Howard Papers.

[1] George James Howard, Ninth earl of Carlisle (1843-1911). An amateur artist, educated at Eton and Trinity College, Cambridge, he was Liberal M.P. for East Cumberland,

1879-1880 and 1881-1885, and succeeded to the earldom in 1889. During the 1870's, Morris took a sympathetic and active interest in Howard's political campaigns, and the Howard, Morris, and Burne-Jones families became close friends. George Howard gave the firm several commissions, including a number of stained glass windows and the decorations for the Howards' London residence at 1 Palace Green, built by Philip Webb.

² John Henry Parker, *Some Account of Domestic Architecture in England* (Oxford: J. H. Parker, 1853), pp. 211-12.

45 • To Morgan George Watkins   26 Queen Square
                                                          Bloomsbury, W.C.
                                                          August 21, 1867

My dear Watkins[1]

Thanks for your letter, with praise of my work[2] and news of old friends: I know Ottery well as I lived at a little place called Alphington with a person who was coaching me for 6 weeks[3] in the year before I came up to Oxford: I remember going to see the then Vicar (whose place I hope & suppose you hold), and going to the queer ante-dated old church, which is certainly one of the most remarkable & beautiful ones in England.[4] I hope now you have my address that you will see me, by dint of finding your way here, I am a married man too, & have 2 of the ποιηματα[5] you mention — Did I ever abuse Wordsworth? — I recant — though his cold unhuman, & somewhat prolix poetry has not much attraction for me, even now I'm grown old — As for my archaeology I'm afraid you will find little of it in Jason, and that my towns belong rather to the Cinque-Cento or Jacobaean period than the Homeric or rather pre-Homeric, and that there is more of Lincoln or Rouen than of Athens in them, let alone Tiryns or Mycenae, and that my wine is Bon Bourgogne not Chian, which latter assertion I hope to have the pleasure of proving practically & literally to you — I am going to Oxford for a holiday on Saturday with Jones, and Faulkner[6] (if you remember him), who is now a don of University, though not much like one I must confess.

                                        I am
                                        Yrs very truly
                                        William Morris

MS: Swales Coll.

¹ Morgan George Watkins (1835-1910), who was at Exeter College when Morris was there. He had been second master of the Grammar School and Canon of St. Mary, Ottery St. Mary, Devonshire, from 1858 to 1861. At the time of this letter, he was the rector of Barnoldby-le-Beck in Lincolnshire (he held the position from 1864 to 1885), and later became diocesan inspector of schools, 1872-1884, and then vicar of Kentchurch, 1888. He was also an antiquarian and naturalist.

² *The Life and Death of Jason.*

³ See letter no. 24, n. 1.

⁴ Probably St. Mary's, consecrated in 1260, which dominates the town of Ottery St. Mary. The aisles of the chapel have lancet windows which are pre-1260, and the church has a fourteenth-century wooden lectern, "one of the oldest eagle lecterns in the British Isles." (See Edwin Smith and Olive Cook, *British Churches* [London: Studio Vista, 1964], pp. 120-21 for description and photograph.) St. Mary's was "restored" by William Butterfield in 1850.

⁵ Offspring.

⁶ Charles James Faulkner (1834-1892) had been a member of the Morris–Burne-Jones circle at Oxford and was a founding member of the firm (he kept the books). By 1869 he had returned to Oxford, as a Fellow of University College, to teach mathematics. He later joined Morris in his socialist activities, founding the Oxford branch of the Socialist League. They remained lifelong friends.

46 • To Philip Burne-Jones
26, Queen Square,
Bloomsbury, London
October 18, 186[7?]¹

My dear Phil,²

I suppose you would like to know something about Jenny and May³ as you havn't seen them for some time: they are very well, and have been riding on donkeys over Hampstead Heath; the sum of 5 shillings have they dissipated in that amusement, 5 shillings each I mean: the house at Hampstead is like a rabbit warren because of the kids therein; only kids make more noise than rabbits; I was so incautious the other day as to wish, aloud, that one of their young friends was in the water butt with the lid shut down on her; and Jenny and May said they would tell her; so I have gained an enemy if a small one; her name is Isabella, and she can just make a noise!

Well I suppose you are coming home soon; I shall be very glad to see you — Shake hands with Margaret⁴ for me.
I am
Your affectionate Unc.

MS: BL, Add. MSS. 52708, typescript. Published: Compton-Rickett, 57-58.

¹ Morris had letterhead stationery in which a blank line was left for the date, with 186 already printed for filling in the year. When Morris omitted to write the digit for the year, I have given the date in the form shown here.

² Philip Burne-Jones (1861-1926), son of Georgiana and Edward Burne-Jones.

³ May Morris (1862-1938), the Morrises' second daughter, born March 25, 1862.

⁴ Margaret Burne-Jones (1866-1954), daughter of the Burne-Joneses. She became the wife of J. W. Mackail (1859-1945), classicist, professor of poetry at Oxford, and author of the standard biography of Morris.

47 • To George James Howard
26, Queen Square,
Bloomsbury, London
November 11, 1867

My dear Howard

I have only just got your note. I shall be very happy to come tomorrow I hope the fearful animal you mention is settled by this time.

Yrs very truly
W. Morris.

MS: Howard Papers.

48 • To Frederick R. Leach
26, Queen Square,
Bloomsbury, London
November 14, 1867

Sir,

There is a proposal to decorate a church in London[1] — Roof & wall decoration — Would you undertake to do work for us as at Cambridge?[2]

The Roof would be similar to Transepts. What would your charge be for the work in London and again the pattern on wall would be something like the one proposed at Cambridge. What would your charge be for that in London — Don't put your prices too low — and you must not be frightened if patterns are in some cases quite more elaborate. These patterns would sometimes crop the mouldings of archer.

We are
Yours Sincerely
Morris & Company

Mr. Leach.

MS: Walthamstow.

[1] Possibly St. Dunstan's, Stepney. See Sewter, II, 180.

[2] This refers to the work done by Leach in the decoration of the Chapel of Jesus College, Cambridge, and the installation of stained glass windows there. (See letter no. 32.)

49 • To Frederick Barlow Guy
26, Queen Square,
November 25, 1867

My dear Guy,

The plan[1] I think perfectly applicable to mosaic, but of course the designs want making out — avoid anything *spiky* in mosaic, it is too

[55]

May Morris in the 1860's.

easy, and looks so. I don't think it is worth while using the material unless the work is very elaborate; and there ought to be a great deal of gold in it; the part between the bands ought also to be at least of marble or alabaster. I don't want to discourage any reasonable plan, but I should think panelling the proper thing for your east end, picked out with colour and gold if you please; the next best I should think would be hangings. I scarcely fancy mosaics on such a small scale, and they are the proper decorations of curved surfaces, domes, and are the concomitants of a round-arched style and great magnificence of decoration in general. But on the whole panelling is the thing; couldn't your friend paint some figures and things on the panels? Anyhow, I will help if you wish it, with the designs, whatever you settle on.

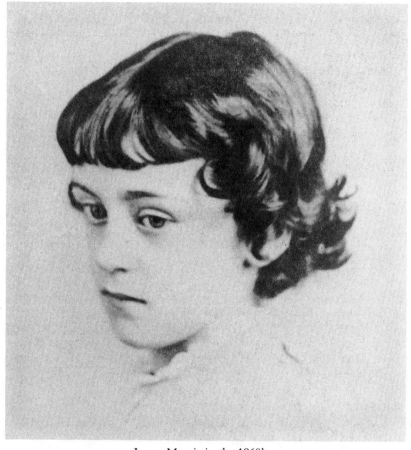

Jenny Morris in the 1860's.

I have to thank you very much for your friendliness with reference to Jason — it makes me laugh to be in the position of nuisance to schoolboys.[2]

Yours very truly,
W. Morris.

TEXT: Mackail, I, 191-92. Published: Henderson, *Letters*, 23.

[1] The ensuing discussion pertains to the decoration by the firm of the chapel in the Forest School, Walthamstow.

[2] Apparently, Guy had introduced Morris's *The Life and Death of Jason* into the school curriculum.

50 • To ALLAN PARK PATON
26, Queen Square,
Bloomsbury, London
December 19, 1867

Dear Sir,

The Hamilton window[1] will not be ready on *this* side of Christmas. You may expect it in January

If your exhibition[2] is yet closed we should be glad would you return the few drawings we lent you.[3] We took some of them out of our own frame where they usually hang as specimens.

We are Dear Sir
Your obedient Servants
Morris & Company

Allan Park Paton, Esquire

MS: NLS.

[1] A window depicting "Charity." It was installed in 1868 in memory of Menzies Sinclair Hamilton (1788-1861). See Sewter, II, 85.

[2] Presumably an exhibition held in connection with the restoration of the Old West Kirk.

[3] This may be a reference to Burne-Jones's cartoon for "Charity," which was begun in 1855 and later reworked in water-color as an independent work, dated 1867. Morris may also be referring to two small pencil studies and two drapery studies for the cartoon. See Sewter, II, 86.

51 • FROM A LETTER TO EDWARD BURNE-JONES   February 3, 1868

To-day I took first piece of copy[1] to printer. Yesterday I wrote 33 stanzas of Pygmalion.[2] If you want my company (usually considered of no use to anybody but the owner) please say so. I believe I shall get on so fast with my work that I shall be able to idle.

TEXT: Mackail, I, 193. Published: *CW*, 3, xxii.

[1] The first installment of *The Earthly Paradise*. The first volume of this work was published in April 1868. On its fifth printing, issued in November 1869, it was divided into Parts I and II (bound separately). The two subsequent and new volumes were therefore called by Morris Part III (published in November 1869 but dated 1870) and Part IV (published in December 1870). See Buxton Forman, pp. 53, 54, and 65.

[2] "Pygmalion and the Image," one of the stories for August. *The Earthly Paradise* consists of a prologue and two poetic narratives for each month, beginning with those for March.

Edward Burne-Jones in the garden of The Grange, c. 1872.

52 • To George Price Boyce
26, Queen Square,
Bloomsbury, London
April 14, 1868

My dear Boyce
Many thanks, I will come tomorrow about 12 noon if that will suit you; if you are out it dont matter as I am taking holiday, my book being done,[1] so don't trouble to answer; indeed I suppose there won't be time.

Yrs very truly
W Morris

MS: Princeton T.

[1] The first volume of *The Earthly Paradise*. See previous letter, n. 1.

53 • To Wilfred Heeley
10 Cheyne Walk
Chelsea
April 19 [1868?]

My dear Heeley[1]
We are coming to an end you see; there wont be many more sheets now, expect to be out by May 1.[2] I couldn't find the review of me in the Ecclectic.[3] Could you give me any help as to number &c — or perhaps it *wasn't* the Ecclectic after all. Hope you are pretty well and enjoying yourself, I have been sometime at Rossettis and shall be there the next week I fancy, ⟨so if⟩ but you may as well write to Queen Sq. — My kind regards to Mrs. Heeley[4] —

Yrs affect:
W Morris

MS: Princeton T.

[1] See letter no. 7, n. 8. In 1867 Heeley and his second wife were back in England for a year, living at The Grange with the Burne-Joneses, who took the house in November 1867. See *Memorials*, I, 306-307.

[2] The first volume of *The Earthly Paradise*.

[3] If the dating of this letter is accurate, it is likely that Morris refers to *Jason*. There was no review of *Jason* in *The Eclectic*, an American magazine. *The Eclectic* did review *The Earthly Paradise*, Part I, in its December 1868 issue.

[4] Josephine Heeley. During the year in England, she gave birth to a son. See *Memorials*, II, 7.

54 • To the Editor of *The Athenaeum*   26 Queen Square
                                                            April 20, 1868

In a notice of forthcoming works by me contained in your "Weekly Gossip" of last Saturday, there are some inaccuracies which I should be much obliged if you would correct. It is not my intention to republish 'Jason' in any other form than that in which it has already appeared; and the woodcuts mentioned in your paragraph, which have been designed as far as they go by my friend Mr. E. Burne Jones, illustrate, not the third part of the 'Earthly Paradise' (for there will only be two parts of that work),[1] but the whole. The time of publication, however, of this illustrated edition must, from the magnitude of the work, be very remote.[2]

WILLIAM MORRIS.

TEXT: *The Athenaeum*, April 25, 1868. MS: Draft of letter, Princeton T.

[1] In the event, *The Earthly Paradise* was published in four parts. Part IV appeared at the end of 1870.

[2] See letter no. 42, n. 3.

55 • Two Letters to Frederick Startridge Ellis

a.   26, Queen Square,
                                                            Bloomsbury, London
                                                            Wednesday [May 1868]

My dear Ellis[1]

Forgot to say, send Brighton what's his name to me at Leyton House[2]

Leyton
N.E.

as I shan't be in town till Saturday; & then I will send[?] you a note to your friend.

Yrs very truly
W Morris

MS: Princeton T.

[1] F. S. Ellis (1830-1901), bookseller, and publisher of Swinburne and D. G. Rossetti, among others. Introduced to Morris by Swinburne in 1864, Ellis became Morris's good friend, and in 1868, Morris's publisher (until retirement from the publishing business in 1885). After Rossetti's departure from Kelmscott Manor, Ellis took over the joint-tenancy and kept it until 1884. His bookshop at 29 New Bond Street, which he acquired in 1872, became, Doughty writes (p. xiv), "a kind of informal resort of the *literati* of the later Victorian period," with frequent visits by Ruskin, Tennyson, and others. Ellis acquired items for the British Museum between 1863 and 1877, including prints, drawings, and

manuscripts. Ellis also compiled monographs on *The Pembroke Book of Hours*, 1880, and *The Hours of Albert of Brandenburg*, 1883. Incipient tuberculosis forced him to retire from bookselling and publishing in 1885, and he took up residence in Devonshire, where he lived for the rest of his life. From 1890 to 1896 he edited a number of Kelmscott Press publications, including *The Works of Geoffrey Chaucer* (1896). After Morris's death, Ellis, along with S. C. Cockerell, became a trustee of the Morris Estate (Sparling, p. 90). For a useful account of Ellis's career, see Oswald Doughty, ed., *The Letters of Dante Gabriel Rossetti to His Publisher, F. S. Ellis* (London: Scholartis Press, 1928), pp. xiii-xvi, on which I have drawn here.

² Home of Morris's mother.

b.   26 Queen Sq:
                                                                          May 23 [1868]

My dear Ellis

Many thanks for the Brighton Herald with the notice of the Earthly Paradise, please thank Mr [Flat?] for me for his kind & sympathetic review, I am delighted to have been able to give him so much pleasure.¹

Yrs truly
William Morris

MS: Swales Coll.

¹ The *Brighton Herald*, May 16, 1868, published an unsigned review of the first volume of *The Earthly Paradise*. The reviewer had presumably identified himself to Ellis. Comparing the form with that of *The Canterbury Tales* he went on to equate Morris's achievement with Chaucer's. He wrote that there is the "same full, clear, unhurried and yet not lagging flow of imagery, drawn from Nature—the same knowledge of the human heart—the same mastery over the language in which old tales are told anew." He concluded: "We rejoice and are proud that such poems as these are written in our day. They are evidence that we are still strong and fresh in the power of song, as our forefathers were; that, morbid and prurient as our desires sometimes are, and overstrained as our own language sometimes is, yet the old vein that was opened hundreds of years ago is not worked out."

56 • TO WILLIAM ALLINGHAM   26, Queen Square,
                                                      Bloomsbury, London
                                                      May 23, 186[8]

My dear Allingham¹

I have just seen your card here; sorry to miss you. Can you come to grub next Wednesday (27th) Some other chaps are coming² — time 7 P.M. I shall be sorry if I don't see you before you go back again.³

Yrs very truly
W Morris

MS: Illinois.

¹ William Allingham (1824-1889), poet, and editor of *Fraser's Magazine* (1874-1879).

[2] In his diary for May 27, 1868, Allingham wrote that he went to dine with the Morrises and found himself at "a full dress party." Present were the Burne-Joneses, D. G. Rossetti, G. P. Boyce, the Madox Browns, Philip Webb, the C. A. Howells, Wilfred Heeley, the F. S. Ellises, Lucy Brown, Kate Faulkner, and Miss Heeley. See William Allingham, *A Diary*, ed. H. Allingham and D. Radford (London: Macmillan, 1907; rpt., Fontwell, Sussex: Centaur Press, 1967), p. 181.

[3] Allingham returned on June 8 to Lymington, Hampshire, where he had been staying. See his *Diary*, p. 182.

57 • RECIPIENT UNKNOWN
                                                    26, Queen Square,
                                                    Bloomsbury, London.
                                                    June 9, 1868

Dear Sir

Many thanks for your letter which needs no excuse at all; I have attended to the passages you mentioned, and corrected my blunders; amongst printers' blunders please notice this one in your Copy; on p 75 ⟨for⟩ in 'Where are my friends' for my read Thy; there are a few others some rather serious, some only absurd which annoy me very much, but which will be corrected in a second edition.[1]

I am delighted to have given you pleasure by what has given me a great deal of pleasure too, and it is kind of you to tell me so —

                                    I am
                                    Dear Sir
                                    Yours truly
                                    William Morris

MS: McMinn Papers.

[1] A second edition of the first part of *The Earthly Paradise* (which sold out quickly) was issued in midsummer. It was actually a reprint of the first volume with the words "Second Edition" inserted over the name of the publisher (F. S. Ellis); no corrections were made. See Buxton Forman, p. 53.

58 • TO PHILIP SPEAKMAN WEBB
                                                    26, Queen Square,
                                                    Bloomsbury, London
                                                    July 7, 1868

My dear Webb

I have spoken to Janey, & she would have no objection to seeing Mrs. T.[1] if it would do any good — I would have come it but it would have destroyed my mornings work — I shall see you this evening —
                                    Yrs ever
                                    William

MS: V&A, Warington Taylor Papers.

¹ Wife of George Warington Taylor. See letter no. 29, n. 2. Taylor was dying of tuberculosis.

59 • RECIPIENT UNKNOWN   26, Queen Square,
                                              Bloomsbury, London
                                              July 8, 1868

My dear Sir

I thank you very much for your kind letter — I am delighted to have given so much pleasure to one who has given me pleasure also, & I echo your wish that we may meet: though I think I have already seen you for a few minutes at our old place of business at Red Lion Sq:

I am
Dear Sir
Yrs truly
William Morris

MS: Doheny.

60 • TO BAYARD TAYLOR   Southwold, Suffolk
                                              August 18, 1868

Dear Sir¹

I am sorry to say that I shall be deprived of the pleasure of meeting you this time, as I am away from home, and unable to return for some days. I much regret missing a man with whom I don't doubt I should have so much sympathy. I return to town next Monday and my address then will be

26 Queens Sq
Bloomsbury.

I mention this in case by any chance your stay in London should be prolonged: in any case I hope we shall meet at some future time.

I am
Dear Sir
Yrs faithfully
William Morris

MS: PML.

¹ Bayard Taylor (1825-1878), American writer and professor at Cornell, known mainly for his translation of Goethe's *Faust*.

61 • To Charles Augustus Howell
26, Queen Square,
Bloomsbury, London
September 11, 1868

My dear Howell

The furniture came all right and looks very well though as you say scratched a good piece — many thanks for the plates they are very acceptable

as to the £20 don't think me a curmudgeon if I ask for it within a month or so as I am pretty hard up having been paying bills and muddling money away in that manner — I shall be glad to see you any day.

Yrs
W Morris

MS: Princeton T.

62 • To Charles Cowden-Clarke
26, Queen Square,
Bloomsbury, London
September 17, 1868

Dear Sir[1]

Your letter followed me about from place to place and reached me at last in London.

I thank you very much for it and the sympathy you express for my works; and am delighted to have been able to give pleasure to one so much interested in literature, and the friend of Keats, for whom I have such boundless admiration, and whom I venture to call one of my masters.

I am, Dear Sir,
Yours very truly
William Morris

MS: BL, Add. MSS. 45345.

[1] Charles Cowden-Clarke (1787-1877), Shakespearean scholar and schoolmaster. At one time he was Keats's teacher.

63 • To Charles Eliot Norton
26, Queen Square,
Bloomsbury, London.
September 21, 1868

My dear Norton[1]

Saga and poem came safely: many thanks therefore — I have been spending so much time in pleasuring lately, that I couldn't possibly go out for a whole day this week; and scarcely I'm afraid next week — but I will see how my work goes — Many thanks for the invitation whether or no.

Yrs very truly
William Morris

P.S. Shall I see you this week on any day but Tuesday or Thursday

MS: Harvard.

[1] Charles Eliot Norton (1827-1908), American scholar and man of letters, professor of history of art at Harvard from 1875-1898. He was an editor of the *North American Review* and helped found the *Nation* (1865). The Nortons regularly visited England, and spent the winter of 1868-1869 in London. Norton writes in a letter to Ruskin, September 19, 1868, of visiting Burne-Jones and seeing ". . . a good deal of Morris, who combines in a wonderful measure the solid earthly qualities of the man of practical affairs, with the fine perceptions and quick fancy of the poet. It was pleasant to see a famous author so simple, and so little of a prig. . . ." See Charles Eliot Norton, *Letters*, 2 vols. (London: Constable, 1913), I, 309-40.

64 • TO CORMELL PRICE   26, Queen Square,
                                             Bloomsbury, London.
                                             October 12, 1868

My dear Crom
There is a friend of mine called Magnússon,[1] an Icelander, with whom I am doing some translations and who is teaching me the tongue — not to split straws he is hard up, and would be glad of work: teaching of course would come handiest to him, Icelandic, Danish, Swedish, German, French or the dead tongues — he is a good philologist and scholar — I suppose there would be no chance of getting a place for him as librarian or secretary anywhere? I thought you knowing a many folks might help me to find him some work.

Yrs.
W. Morris

MS: Price Papers. Extract published: *CW*, 7, xvi.

[1] Eiríkr Magnússon (1833-1913), an Icelandic scholar who lived and lectured in Cambridge. He was introduced to Morris by Warington Taylor and taught Morris Icelandic, and then collaborated with him in translating Icelandic literature, beginning with the sagas. The first of these, "Gunnlaug Worm-tongue," was published in the *Fortnightly Review*, January 1869. Magnússon accompanied Morris on his first journey to Iceland in 1871.

26, Queen Square.

Bloomsbury, London.

Sept 21st 1868

My dear Norton

Saga and poem
came safely; many thanks
therefore — I have been spending
so much time in pleasuring
lately, that I couldn't possibly
go out for a whole day this
week; and scarcely I'm afraid
next week — but I will see
how my work goes — Many
thanks for the invitation
whether or no.

Yrs very truly

William Morris

P.S. Shall I see
you this
any day but
Tuesday
& Thursday

4883

Morris's letter to Charles Eliot Norton, September 21, 1868.

Cormell Price in the 1860's.

65 · To Charles Eliot Norton
26, Queen Square,
Bloomsbury, London.
October 15, 1868

My dear Norton

Many thanks; I can't manage to come on the Saturday, but I see that there is a train at 8.5 on Sunday morning which I will come by if I am right about it; it gets to Bromley[1] at 9.17. If I *dont* hear from you I shall conclude I'm right & come.

Yrs very truly
William Morris

MS: Harvard.

[1] The Nortons at this time lived at Keston Rectory, Bromley, Kent.

66 · To Cormell Price
26, Queen Square,
Bloomsbury, London
October 20, 1868

My dear Crom

All right I think there is no fear about Magnússon's accent; his address is 9 South Crescent
Bedford Sq. W.C.
I hope I shall see you soon in town —

Yours with love
W. Morris

Many thanks for taking the trouble. Eiríkr Magnússon is the Icelandic bloke's name by the way.

MS: Price Papers.

67 · To Edward Williams Byron Nicholson
26, Queen Square,
Bloomsbury, London.
November 7, 1868

Dear Sir[1]

It is true I am busy enough, but I can find time to look over your poem on the conditions that I shall take you at your word and say what I think of it, and that you musn't hurry me in looking over it[2] — Do you come to London this vacation? I shall be glad to see you here if you do.

Yrs. truly
W Morris

E. B. Nicholson, Esq.

MS: McMinn Papers.

¹ Edward Williams Byron Nicholson (1849-1912), classical scholar. Librarian of the London Institution from 1873 to 1882 and of the Bodleian Library, Oxford, from 1882 to 1912, Nicholson's interests included biblical criticism, comparative philology, folklore, music, palaeography, numismatics, and athletics. He wrote on many of these subjects, but there is no evidence that any of his poetry was ever published. At this time he was an undergraduate in Trinity College, Oxford.

² See letter no. 71.

68 • To Dante Gabriel Rossetti   The Grange¹
Sunday [late 1868?]

My dear Gabriel

Ned says he is very sorry but can't come because the Browns are coming to dine with him; he would have liked to have come very much. I answer for him as he is very busy with his picture² — I am coming not clean shaved, but with a contrite heart and great expectations of pleasure

Ever yrs affect
W. Morris

MS: Pennsylvania.

¹ Morris regularly had Sunday breakfast with the Burne-Joneses at The Grange, Fulham, where they began to live in November 1867. See *Memorials*, I, 306-307.

² Possibly "Phyllis and Demophoön," exhibited in 1870 but begun, Fitzgerald suggests (p. 119) in 1868. A study for the painting, possibly done in 1868, is in the William Morris Gallery, Walthamstow.

69 • To Thomas Rupert Jones   26, Queen Square,
Bloomsbury, London
November 16, 1868

Dear Sir¹

Many thanks for your letter; but I am afraid I have not studied deep enough to make any ideas of mine on the subject you mention of any value — the only source for the passage you have quoted, besides vague ideas about primitive people, ⟨was⟩ is the ⟨remembering⟩ same memory

of the practice of the early Scandinavians of scoring their weapons with
runes; of which practice I would think you would find examples in
many of the Sagas — a passage is quoted in the preface to Dasents[2]
'Gisli' from the Sturlunga Saga about a spear which had been made from
the fragments of the sword of that hero, 'Gisli,' which was marked with
runes (mála spiot) I cannot give you the passage now because I have not
by me Dasents book on the Sturlunga Saga; but I repeat that such things
can be read of frequently and as the Norsemen were early enough as
regards their position, and as some people have supposed the name at
least of *rune* to come from the Fins, and they themselves certainly con-
nected that people with magic rites, this might be of some interest to
you — only you probably know all about this much better than I do,
so excuse my useless letter & Believe me

Yrs faithfully
William Morris

T. R. Jones Eqre.

MS: Dunlap Coll.

[1] Thomas Rupert Jones (1819-1911), geologist and palaentologist. He became professor
of geology at the Royal Military College, Sandhurst, in 1862, and was president of the
Geologists' Association, 1879-1881.

[2] George Webb Dasent (1817-1896). A Scandinavian scholar whose translations were
widely read in nineteenth-century England. Morris read with pleasure all his translations
of Icelandic sagas, which included *Popular Tales from the Norse* (1859), the *Story of Burnt
Njal* (1861), and *The Story of Gisli the Outlaw* (1866). Elements in the style of the trans-
lations made by Morris suggest Dasent's influence: the kind that results when one writer
reads with absorption the work of another.

70 • TO CHARLES ELIOT NORTON
26, Queen Square,
Bloomsbury, London.
November 25, 1868

My dear Norton

I was extremely sorry to hear of your illness, though I was afraid that
day it looked something like it —

I am afraid I havn't got the MS. of the poem in question, but I shall
be very happy to copy it out again for you if that will have any interest
— I shall hope to see you often this winter. With kind regards to those
of your family who are with you

Believe me
Yrs very truly
W Morris

MS: Harvard.

71 • To Edward Williams Byron Nicholson   16 Cheyne Walk[1]
Chelsea
December 3 [1868]

My dear Sir

I have read your poem several times and this is what I think about it[2]
— To begin with disagreables it seems to me to lack the strong individ-
uality and devotion to the subject which one looks for in works that are
to last; and though I can't accuse you of plagiarism I see a reflection of
the poets of the day in it; on this however I don't dwell, because it
could hardly be otherwise in a man so young as you — but in fact it
doesn't leave impression enough upon one, either in style or ideas: of
minor faults (connected with this I think) I notice too much of the
machinery of the Classic works, and too great length of metaphor: but
let this pass till I can talk to you by word of mouth — on the other side
the verse is good, and there are indications of feeling throughout, and
of pleasure in the subject, (which is a very fine one). There is a great
deal of care and thoughtfulness in it, and it is both pleasant and easy to
read: this perhaps seems to you scant praise and liberal blame, but re-
member that I am criticising the poem entirely on its own merits; and
that you have the inestimable advantage of being very young, and that
you have (as I judge from your letters and position) a very ⟨good⟩ close
acquaintance with the classics which may be rather over powering in its
influence at least on your *style* — I repeat that I want to see more *weight*
in your work both of style and matter — but you must remember too
that I was to say all I thought of this work — and I assure you that I
think it quite good enough considering the circumstances (which must
be considered in such cases) for me to have said nothing but praise of
it; and I should very much regret if your experiment with me resulted
in your being discouraged by having the opinion of one man who for
aught you know may be a very bad critic; for I have no doubt you will
do better things, (though this is good, I repeat) if you look at matters
steadily and seriously, and do nothing but what you like very much
yourself.   finally you are yourself the best judge of what you are likely
to turn out and your letters to me were full of so much good sense and
modesty that I have no doubt that you will give your insight of yourself
full play —

I am anxious to see more of your work and should rather it were
rhymed, I think blank verse a snare to young poets —

When you come to see me at Queen Sq: please let me know ⟨when⟩
the day & time when you purpose a visit a day or two before hand, so
that we may not clash.

Again I must excuse myself for lecturing you, but as you have made me your school-master I can't help it; but I am afraid it isn't at all in my line.

I thank you very much for your expressions of sympathy with me, and wish you the utmost success and remain

Yours truly

William Morris

P.S. My old address in Queen Square will always find me: I keep your copy of the poem till I see you —

MS: McMinn Papers. Published: MM, I, 639-41; Henderson, *Letters*, 24-25.

¹ This letter was written from Rossetti's house.
² See letter no. 67.

72 • To Frederick R. Leach   26, Queen Square,
                                                                    Bloomsbury, London
                                                                    December 14, 1868

Sir

We send you the drawings & specification of the two screens¹ — The drawings are traced from the first designs & are not quite accurate — you had better go to Rattee's² & see the screens — they will tell you too whether it will be necessary to go to Beddington to paint the organ screen.   we suppose it will.

You will provide for painting the *doors* of the chancel screen *first* so as to be able [to] send them to us *here* as soon as may be — We shall paint all the panels — but no more — Can you lay or get laid a proper painting ground on the panels of the chancel screen? It would be desirable to have this done before the mouldings are painted —

Rattee would probably lend you fullsized correct profile of the mouldings — we should like to have these to make our patterns for you upon —

Tell us if you find any great differences between the drawings & the finished work —

In making your estimate you may consider that the pattern work will be simple & not very profuse but you had better err in excess than defect

We shall be glad to have your estimate as soon as you can make it —

Please return the drawings

We are your obt

Servants

Morris & Company

F. Leach Esq

MS: Walthamstow.

  [1] Organ screens for St. Mary's Church, Beddington, Surrey.
  [2] The building firm of Rattee and Kett of Cambridge, who had worked with Morris, Marshall, Faulkner and Co. on restoration and new work on the Church of St. Edward the Confessor at Cheddleton, Staffordshire. See *Building News*, 13 (April 1866), 245.

73 • TO EDWARD WILLIAMS BYRON NICHOLSON   26, Queen Square,
                                                Bloomsbury, London
                                                December 19, 1868

My dear Sir
    Tuesday at the same time about 3 pm would suit me better, as I have an engagement on Monday afternoon.
                                        Yrs truly
                                        W Morris

MS: McMinn Papers.

74 • TO FORD MADOX BROWN   26, Queen Square,
                                   Bloomsbury, London
                                   [February 15-17, 1869]

¼ to five
Your letter has only just come —
My dear Brown[1]
    Here be the florins — I am at Gabriel's but I suppose I can come on Friday. Gabriel I think is going on that night to honour his sister's[2] Cantata with his very unusual presence (at a concert!) but I should like very much to come; in fact I *will* come but I shan't be able to be with you before 9 I suppose
                                        Yrs ever
                                        W. Morris

MS: Huntington.

  [1] See letter no. 22, n. 1.
  [2] Christina Georgina Rossetti (1830-1894), poet, and sister of Gabriel and William. Devoted to Gabriel, she tended him during the frequent illnesses of his last years. On February 18, 1869 (a Thursday) a concert at St. James's Hall featured her *Songs in a Cornfield* set to a cantata by C. A. MacFarren. See L. P. Packer, *Christina Rossetti* (Berkeley: Univ. of California Press, 1963), p. 252.

75 • TO HENRY BUXTON FORMAN 26, Queen Square,
Bloomsbury, London
March 9, 1869

Dear Mr. Forman[1]

The window you saw here was for a little church at Dalton on Thirsk in Yorkshire, it is a new church.[2] I am glad you liked the windows at Brighton,[3] the little window at St Michaels is one of ours, the drawings are by Burne Jones, we always thought it a successful little window.[4]

Yrs very truly
William Morris

MS: Berger Coll.

[1] Henry Buxton Forman (1842-1917). He entered the Post Office in 1860 as a third class clerk and became Principal Clerk in 1885, Controller of the Packet Services in 1893, and Second Secretary of the Post Office in 1905. Despite his taking seriously his post office work (as Second Secretary he rose to a higher civil service rank than that obtained by any other literary man in his time in search of a sinecure), he was able to devote himself primarily and effectively to literature. His edition of Shelley's *Collected Poems* (1876) stood as the standard edition for fifty years. His publications included also Keats's *Letters to Fanny Brawne* (1878), Shelley's *Prose Works* (1880), and *Poetical Works and Other Writings of John Keats* (1883), as well as *The Books of William Morris* (1897). He has been praised for helping to set new standards of editorial practice and for adding a new dimension to descriptive bibliography. Unfortunately, his bibliophilia also got out of control on occasion. He has been implicated in T. J. Wise's literary forgeries, and *The Books of William Morris* contains (p. 85) one spurious work, "a privately printed pamphlet" dated 1876, "not for sale." Without Morris's knowledge or consent, Forman reprinted three of Morris's poems, "The Two Sides of the River," "Hopeless Love," and "The First Foray of Aristomes." See John Carter and Graham Pollard, *An Enquiry Into the Nature of Certain Nineteenth Century Pamphlets* (London: Constable and Co., 1934) and Fannie E. Ratchford, *Between the Lines: Letters and Memoranda Interchanged by H. Buxton Forman and Thomas J. Wise* (Austin: University of Texas Press, 1945). According to Forman, he first met Morris in 1869 and read proofs of the third part of *The Earthly Paradise* and, later, of *The Aeneids*. See Buxton Forman, p. 83.

[2] St. John's Church, built in 1868. In 1869, Morris, Marshall, Faulkner and Co. made the west window and nine windows for the nave. See Sewter, II, 59.

[3] In 1866, the firm made the east window for the Church of the Annunciation. See Sewter, II, 32.

[4] The Church of St. Michael and All Angels, Brighton, has windows made by the firm in 1862. Burne-Jones prepared the cartoon for the window in the baptistry and for the rose window, a depiction of the "Virgin and Child." Morris is probably referring to this rose window. See Sewter, I, Plate 60, and II, 32.

76 • TO CHARLES ELIOT NORTON May 13, 1869

My dear Norton

The Strong Man herewith;[1] I hope you will like him; there is no doubt a great deal that will strike you as coarse and rude in it, and a life very different from the ideal one of the future you were talking of yesterday; nevertheless I can't doubt that you will be interested in what is real; and to my mind also there underlies all the rudeness a sentiment and a moral sense that somehow made the hopeless looking life of our hero endurable; at any rate he did endure it in a kind of way that is a lesson I think to us effete folk of the old World.

I needn't ask you to excuse my own shortcomings in the translation as I know you will be only too ready to do so.

With kind remembrances to Mrs. Norton[2] and the rest of your party

Believe me
Yr most affectionate
William Morris

MS: Harvard.

[1] The Grettis Saga: The Story of Grettir the Strong, of which Morris, in collaboration with Magnússon, had made a prose translation. It was published in the spring of 1869.

[2] Norton married Susan Ridley Sedgwick in May 1862. She died in Dresden in 1872.

---

77 • TO EDWARD BURNE-JONES   26, Queen Square,
                                                    Bloomsbury, London
                                                    May 25 [1869]

My dearest Ned

I am afraid I was crabby last night, but I didn't mean to be, so pray forgive me — we seem to quarrel in speech now sometimes, and sometimes I think you find it hard to stand me, and no great wonder for I am like a hedgehog with nastiness — but again forgive me for I can't on any terms do without you.

Yours
W Morris

MS: Texas.

---

78 • TO CHARLES FAIRFAX MURRAY   [ca. May 25, 1869]

My dear Murray[1]

I was rude to you last night & drove you away from the Grange: please believe I didn't mean to be unkind, and forgive me.

I could explain all to you in a word or two if an explanation were necessary to you, which I doubt.

Yours affectionately
William Morris.

I am coming to you tomorrow morning: if you will be in.

MS: Texas.

[1] Charles Fairfax Murray (1849-1919), artist, collector, connoisseur, and close friend of Rossetti and the Morris circle. Murray was introduced to Morris by Murray Marks (see letter no. 265, n. 7) and "through Marks's interest, Murray received a commission to paint the portrait of Mrs. Morris in 1868 for Ellis, which led to more important commissions." See G. C. Williamson, *Murray Marks and His Friends: A Tribute of Regard* (London: John Lane, The Bodley Head, 1915). For a time Murray transferred Burne-Jones's cartoons to glass and did other work for Morris, Marshall, Faulkner and Co. He eventually became one of several artists whom Ruskin employed and sent to Italy to make drawings, in order to obtain records of "beautiful pictures, buildings, and scenes in danger of restoration or destruction." See E. T. Cook, *The Life of John Ruskin* (London: George Allen, 1911), II, 76. In 1873, Murray established a permanent residence in Florence, though he frequently revisited England. He became Italian secretary for the Society for the Protection of Ancient Buildings in 1877. He also sometimes functioned as a dealer, and in this capacity he secured Ruskin's most important purchase, a Verrocchio *Madonna and Child.* His relations with Ruskin appear to have broken off in 1883 when "Murray became pressing about money." See R. Hewison, *Ruskin and Venice* (London: Thames and Hudson, 1978), p. 106.

79 • To William Allingham

26, Queen Square,
Bloomsbury, London
July 14 [1869]

My dear Allingham

I am going out of town, to the 'outlands' with my wife who is very much out of sorts I am sorry to say, on Saturday I believe — I am glad you get on with Grettir.[1] as to your question veðrafjorð is ⟨weathe whethe⟩ *wether*-firth I should say; but hrutafjorð is so called once in Grettir Saga, the song on the slaying of Thorbiorn Oxmain viz — I havn't yet seen the Fraser with your article[2] in it, I shall get a look at it before I go —

I hope to see you when I come back in the autumn. Ned is pretty well and very hard at work —

Ever yours
W Morris

MS: Illinois.

[1] See letter no. 76, n. 1.

[2] Allingham's article, "On the Names of Places in Iceland," was published in the June 1869 issue of *Fraser's Magazine*, of which he was later the editor. The questions directed to Morris about Icelandic place names may have been mere politeness, since Allingham, who wanted the Norse word from which "Waterford" may have been derived, had apparently already queried Magnússon on the subject while writing the article, and had cited Magnússon as his authority. See *Fraser's Magazine*, 72 (June 1869), 792.

80 • TO PHILIP SPEAKMAN WEBB
Ghent[1]
Thursday
July 22, 1869

My dearest Friend

I just send a line in Janeys letter to you; if you went, (as I hope you did) to North-End on Tuesday you will have heard some news of us — Janey seems better than I feared she might be — Yesterday I took her for a drive on the quays & to see the Van Eyk.[2] She slept well and says she feels much better this morning. I called at North End on Saturday morning as you will have heard; they were both very very kind to me, though Ned seemed more moved at my going than I should have liked to have seen him — Will you be so kind as to write me a letter now and then, and tell me how things go on there — and other things as well. I have not seen a paper since I left — So far all goes pretty well, I can't look on far ahead, or try to forecaste how Janey may get on at Ems; it will be bad indeed to have to bring her back no better; I don't know how to face the fear of that.

I have done a little work already and hope to have the little tale[3] done (in rough) by then we are settled at Ems, and to get it together there — we go on to Mechlin today, Liege Friday, Aix Saturday, Cologne Sunday; so a letter reaching Cologne (Poste Restante) by Monday I should get.

My dear chap its not the least part of my troubles to think of all the trouble and worry I have given you, who no doubt had enough of your own already — but you have forgiven me, so I can do nothing but wish that you had a worthier, as you cannot have a more loving friend than

Yrs ever
WM

MS: BL, Add. MSS. 45342. Extract published: *CW*, 5, xii.

[1] The Morrises were en route to Bad Ems in hopes of improving Jane Morris's health. On July 16, 1869, Rossetti wrote to Alicia Margaret Losh (1801-1872) an elderly cousin of Alice Boyd (see letter no. 104, n. 4): "You will be grieved to hear that poor Janey Morris is very ill. She and her husband are going to Bad Ems on the Rhine, where she

has been told to go to drink the waters and take baths" (Doughty and Wahl, II, 708). Mackail notes (I, 201) that the Morrises spent nearly two months at Bad Ems.

² Probably Van Eyck's painting, *Adoration of the Lamb.*

³ "Acontius and Cydippe," one of the tales for October in Volume III of *The Earthly Paradise.* See also letter no. 82. In this sentence "then" may be a slip, Morris having intended "when."

81 • TO PHILIP SPEAKMAN WEBB   Fortuna Bad-Ems
                                     Saturday July 31 [1869]
Dearest Friend

That is really my address though it looks like chaff, and I am not like to move now during the time of our captivity; I am so jolly glad to have got over the journey on no worse terms, once or twice I felt quite enclined to give in, but here we are and Janey is certainly no worse than when we started; I even hope a little better; when you see Georgie next she will tell you about our rather evil arrival here, so I wont go over that joke again; suffice it to say that we are now pretty comfortably lodged, though by no means in a palace, the principal comfort being that the sun goes off our windows at 8 AM, and don't come on again all day; the weather has certainly been very hot, but so it seems to have been everywhere; I think we found Cologne hotter than this; there are good draughts blowing up and down the valley, and lots of shade everywhere, and that was all that we could possibly expect: J has seen the Dr. twice and has had 4 baths and a corresponding amount of luke-warm Spa-water which she drinks in the morning before breakfast; I took her a drive of about 5 miles and back on Thursday; she seemed better for it the next day; 2 other days I paddled her about the river in a machine like a butter-boat with a knife and fork for oars; this they call a gondola here; it is all very well for a mile or two while the river, artificially deepened and widened is without stream (there is a weir and lock about a mile below our lodgings, but none above as far as Nassau at any rate which is six miles above us) all very well without stream but presently the unlocked river runs like a mill-race; I tried it the first day, and made about 20 yds in half an-hour and then began to get back way; so I gave it up with hands blistered: however there is a nice green bank in shadow after 5 P.M. just this side of the rapids, and I suppose I shall paddle Janey there pretty often; till she gets better it is like to be her principal enjoyment as the carriage business shakes her too much; if ('when' I hope) she gets better there are splendid mokes and mules here, whereon she may climb the hills — bating the company, wh: is not to my taste, though I've no doubt better than I am, the place is well enough, and ½ a mile out of Ems is quite unsofisticate, except for the woods which look suspiciously like preserves; it is in fact a very lovely valley, though I think not the kind of place I should like to live in, one is so boxed in; it is rather like some of the lake-country but without the sour grow-nothing air of that soaking land — the valley is *very* narrow; first the river a rugged affair, with ⟨sand⟩ gravel-banks and all perhaps as wide as the Thames at Clifton-Hamden, then narrow green 'eres' sometimes on this side, sometimes on that, then the road on a sort of terrace, and then the hills, sometimes wall sided cliffs, sometimes roundish well cultivated downs wooded at the top; the roads have jolly fruit-trees each side of them and every good exposure has a vine-yard, looking very neat and ship shape, for they are just pruning them: everything seems to grow beautifully here, the apricots are stunning; but alas poor J. musnt eat em.

At the top of the gorge-side you come upon the bold uplands of the Rhine country, all covered with grain and oilseed crops; but its a strong pull to the top and till J is better I am not like to be able to get fairly up; I had a try yesterday morning and was a sight for a tallow boiler, but could scarcely get a glimpse & then was not fairly up: however as I say the country is a fine one in spite of my teeth; on our drive on Thursday we went through a funny-ragged walled village; so German! and so precious precious ragged! not dirty hardly, and scarcely squallid, but good lord, how ragged! I couldn't help thinking on our drive, though, how you and I and Charley[1] would have enjoyed a tramp up, or pull down this Lahn valley 11 years or so ago — As you may imagine the folks here are sharks, and I am so little used to watering places of any sort that I was rather frightened at prices at first; but thought it absolutely necessary to get decent rooms for J at once; these too wh: is a great point are quite close to the best (the government) Baths.   withal wine is good and cheap, and grub not over dear; dinner about 2/6 each per diem and very good.

There are a few oldish houses here, our windows look right on to the principal one, a rum old 17th century house, the old Kurhaus I believe — They keep early hours here; the band woke us this morning at 7 with Luther's Hymn played in thundering style — Well its a fortnight now since we set off; I have a kind of hope that J will get better but as I said before I dursn't look on far ahead — Wardle[2] has sent me on a packet of letters; the postage is heavy, and the most important of them was a bill for £1.12 to Quaritch[3] the bookseller; which perhaps he might pay: will it give you too much to do to open any letters for me;

if there were any secrets between us (as there are not) you would hardly come across them; one of Wardle's packets is on firm business and must be sent back — item there are sure not to be many of them. We have had a thunderstorm and about 2 hours rain here this afternoon but it is still very close as I have often noticed is the case just after summer storms — I keep this letter open till tomorrow.

Sunday. No letters this morning so I make an end; it rained heavily in the night and the river is pea-soup this morning; there is a little stream running even here: it has cleared off and is very bright — This morning I managed to scramble through Accontius & Cydippe; I have now got to knock it into shape, I am not sanguine about it — please give us a turn of your pen when you can: Janey sends her best love & I rest

Your most loving friend
W.M.

P.S. I forgot — will you ask Wardle to send round and ask Lucy Brown[4] if the soup-plates and delft cruets came safe to hand — the soup-plates are for you if you care about them — the cruet bottles have had tops to them — I think: Could you get Barkentyne to fashion these again; if you think it a fitting end to them — if not silver mounted corks would do I suppose though not so well — I bought them and the plates in Ghent on Georgie's birthday and meant them them [sic] the funny cruets for her — will you give them to her with my love when what is necessary is done; if it is done before I come home. perhaps they are broken though —

MS: BL, Add. MSS. 45342. Extract published: *CW*, 5, xiii-xiv; Henderson, *Letters*, 26-27.

[1] Charles James Faulkner. See letter no. 45, n. 6.

[2] After the death of Warington Taylor in 1870, George Y. Wardle became manager of Morris, Marshall, Faulkner and Co. "He had been employed by the firm as a bookkeeper and draughtsman since about 1866, and before that had been supplying drawings of paintings and patternwork from old East Anglian church roofs and screens. He remained manager until 1890." P. Thompson, p. 30.

[3] Bernard Quaritch (1819-1898), bookseller. Born in Saxony, at one time an employee of Henry Bohn in London, he opened his own business in 1847. Quaritch was to become a familiar figure to Morris, at first as a dealer from whom he purchased books and manuscripts, and later as the publisher of some of the books printed by the Kelmscott Press as well as of the Saga Library.

[4] Lucy Madox Brown (1843-1894), Ford Madox Brown's daughter by his first wife, Elizabeth Bromley (d.1846). She was half-sister to Oliver Madox ("Nollie") (1855-1874) and Catherine (1850-1927), children of Brown's second wife. Emma Hill. Lucy Madox Brown married William Michael Rossetti in 1874.

[81]

82 • To Charles Eliot Norton
Fortuna, Bad-Ems
Prussia
[August 5, 1869]

My dear Norton

Many thanks for your kind letter; you may guess that Ems is not exactly the place I should have chosen for a pleasure-trip, and that the day I leave it will have a white mark in my calendar, but the doctors said 'go,' and really they must have thought it so remote from suiting me, that I must needs hope they really thought it would do my wife good; we have been here for more than a week; but I cannot yet judge what effect it will have on her: I shall be very much out of sorts if it does nothing, as on all other grounds I can't but consider my stay here as so many weeks of my life thrown away; and I wish with all my heart we had been sent somewhere where we could have seen you and yours — As for my work I have finished the story from Laxdaela,[1] wh: I had begun when I saw you last: it has turned out very long, so much so that I am going to risk splitting the 2nd part of the E.P. into 2 vols and bring out one before Christmas, 'if all bowls row aright'.[2] The story in question I think on the whole the most important thing I have written; the deeper I got into the old tale the more interested I found myself, and now it is finished, I feel somewhat used up, and rather cold to subjects with less of life and nature in them; however I have another tale or two to turn out of hand, and must somehow string myself up to the task — On the way here, and here I have managed to scramble through a slight tale, Accontius & Cydippe, but I feel too torn up by the roots to be able to judge of it at present. If I write any song or sonnet here I will send you a copy with great pleasure, but I have nothing else by me either good or portable enough to send at present — Thank you very much though for asking for it.

The Lahn valley here is beautiful enough when one is clear of Ems but with a can't-get-out look about it that bothers me with my turn for stretches of chalk down and the like however I am grateful for its beauty as far as it goes, but of course can't leave my wife for long together, or I should feel disposed to stretch my legs a bit along some of the country roads. The place itself is as noisy and uninteresting as you would expect, with as fine a collection of fine feathers and foul birds as I have looked on for a long time — I for my part have come to Germany rather before my German was dead-ripe, but tis an ill wind &c, and the maids here find my performances on that intricate high-dutch instrument as good as a play, as was to be looked for.

I havn't seen a newspaper for a fortnight, or more but Ive a general idea that the English nation has been exercising its talent for compromise,[3] and that black and white are to be called grey in future — being at Ems and wanting to get back, I don't much care.

I heard good news of Ned by the last post;[4] I saw very good work of his before I left that would be new to you[5] — The address at the top of my letter though looking like a joke will reach me, if you have nothing better to do some idle half hour than to write to me again —

With best remembrances from my wife and myself to you all

I remain

Yrs affectionately

W. Morris

MS: Harvard.

[1] "The Lovers of Gudrun," Morris's retelling of the Laxdaela Saga and the concluding tale in Part III of *The Earthly Paradise*. Morris came to feel that this was "the best thing I have done" (letter no. 95).

[2] It was published in November 1869. This second installment was called Part III, however, since the fifth edition of the first volume (also issued in November 1869) was divided into two parts (becoming Parts I and II).

[3] Morris may be referring to the conflict between France and Prussia which was to result in the war that broke out August 1870. If so, the following note in Cormell Price's diaries for August 7, 1870 is apposite: "W.M. at dinner—long talk on French and Prussians—sympathy all with the latter, but not affection—W.M. says a confedern. of states is necessary or civilzn. will collapse."

[4] From 1867 on, Burne-Jones had been intimate with Mary Zambaco (b.1843), daughter of "Hadji" and Euphrosyne Cassavetti, cousins of the Ionides. In 1861 Mary married Demetrius Zambaco, doctor to the Greek community in Paris. She left Paris for London in 1866 with her two children, but without her husband. Mary Zambaco was a sculptress and medalist who also posed for Rossetti and Burne-Jones. The relationship with Burne-Jones, marked by attempts on his part to break with her, devastated his health. In January 1869, a seeming final crisis came when she insisted on a suicide pact in Holland Walk, Kensington, and then tried to drown herself in the Paddington Canal outside Browning's house, "bobbies collaring Ned who was rolling with her on the stones to prevent it, and God knows what else," Rossetti wrote to Brown on January 23, 1869 (Doughty and Wahl, II, 685). As a result, Rossetti continued, Morris and Burne-Jones started for Rome, "leaving the Greek damsel beating up the quarters of all [Burne-Jones's] friends for him and howling like Cassandra. . . . I heard today however that Top and Ned got no further than Dover, Ned being so dreadfully ill that they will probably have to return to London." The relationship, with all its strain, did not end with this crisis. In 1870, Burne-Jones "continued to draw Mary Zambaco and to bear her reproaches" (Fitzgerald, p. 126). Lindsay notes (p. 153) that "the affair dragged on at least until 1872." For an account of the entire episode, see Fitzgerald, pp. 117-31.

[5] This may be a reference to the Pygmalion series, 1868-1870. See M. Harrison and B. Waters, *Burne-Jones* (London: Barrie and Jenkins, 1973), pp. 96-99.

Fortuna Bad-Ems
August 9 [1869]

My dearest Friend

Both letters you mention in your last came safe; a many thanks for them; We would have answered your last before but Janey was not in sorts at all when it came; it seemed as though the long journey and the excitement of change & the rest of it had at last taken revenge on her; this naturally made me low, & so I refrained from writing till now when I can give you better news, for these last two days she has been much better, & I hope will get on again now — By the by Janey says with her love to you, that something is the matter with me & that she is afraid that you will have to call in *Kingsgate St*: (handy to you you know) for a nurse for me — is that broad-wheeled enough to cap your jokes — in fact I got a sort of cold in my limbs one night & fairly thought I should be laid up, but luckily (for J.) I sweated it off in the night — The last few days while Janey has been queer & bilious we have found it rather hard to get such grub as she could comfortably eat, however I have arranged that now; she gets on pretty well with the drink, and we both like the beer here; it is easier to digest I think than English beer, and doesn't make one sleepy —

Janey hasn't bathed for a few days, but hopes to begin again about Wednesday I shall see the Dr. at the same time I think and then get some definite idea as to when we shall be likely to get home; at present if things go well Sunday 12 Sept: seems like to be the day — I have something like hope about the water doing her good, and as to her late falling back I suppose it was to be expected; she hasn't taken her tonics since she came here, and the waters, the doctor says, are not at all tonic: yet I don't think today she is worse than before we left home in any way, and some of her symptoms are improved.

By the way the Dr. has just been and from what he says there seems to be hopes of our getting back sooner than we expected; but I musn't count on this; I shall be able to tell you more about this toward the end of the week — The weather has quite broken down today is a regular wet day and O lord can't it rain at Ems — I went a two hours walk yesterday up a hill-road; I think the country very jolly I must say; it all runs towards the big gorge in little gorges, the centres of which are all grass and hold the moisture like a cup and are as green as green can be, one little valley I came to was so jolly; a flat green space with alders round two sides of it, the great hills in the distance at one end and round the other the hills rising steep with great lanky beech woods — as dry as a bone —There is nothing of the common-place about the ordinary nature here, it is a wonderful country and fit for the breeding of German sentiment — I have been reading Carlyle's Wilhelm Meister and have got through a great deal of it; what a queer book it is, and how knowing and deep sometimes amidst what a sea of muddle and platitude I think Goethe must have been asleep when he wrote it: but 'tis a great work somehow. I have had a letter from Norton, I take it kind in him to write to me — Ellis also has written: have you seen him lately? I shall write to him by this post. Write again soon as I will. Janey excuses herself for not writing to you, saying that it makes her back ache to sit up to it — I have been reading Esmond to her lately; it is a pretty book, but weakish and Thackeray's *style* I think so precious bad — What news of Taylor[1] again?

> We rest
> Your loving friends
> J & W Morris

MS: BL, Add. MSS. 45342. Extract published: *CW*, 5, xiv-xv; and Henderson, *Life*, 103.

[1] George Warington Taylor, who was ill and who died early the next year.

84 • TO FREDERICK STARTRIDGE ELLIS [August 11, 1869]

Many thanks for you kind letter which was very welcome. If you are not joking I hope indeed you will come to Ems; I think you might even fish there; at any rate I have seen with my own eyes Germans catching small bream in the Lahn, and as they never strike when they have a bite, it is probable that the fish are very hungry. We have had pike and perch to eat withal, so I suppose those monsters inhabit the rather muddy waters of the Lahn: just at Ems it is all widened out into a kind of pond with nearly no stream, but from Ems to Nassau, about six miles (English), there is no lock, and the water runs in rapids. I am sorry for your disappointment at Lechlade, but at all events it is a jolly place. The country about here is very beautiful, there is no doubt of that, and the place itself I shall consider bearable if it does my wife any good, as I hope it will. I have been pretty hard at work, have finished one tale, and begun another since I left, so the book goes on.[1]

TEXT: Mackail, I, 201-202.

[1] Part III of *The Earthly Paradise*.

85 • To Edward Williams Byron Nicholson

Bad-Ems
North Germany
August 12, 1869

Dear Sir

I don't think I need hesitate much about subscribing to your review,[1] and shall be very glad to do so, wishing you all possible success: for your own sakes rather than mine I rather wish you had left the Oxford & Cambridge Mag: alone; for you know it was a failure, and on the whole deserved to be, though I am not ashamed of the part I took in it, though sometimes rather inclined to laugh thereat, nor should I have thought any body would have looked upon it from any other point of view than as a warning: however don't let what I say discourage you; for I am very much interested in your experiment, which no doubt ought to succeed, especially as your way of setting to work seems prudent and well considered; I do assure you, if you need that assurance that ours was *not* Your kind talk about my poems gratifies me very much, it is indeed a pleasure to be able to please thinking people — yet — don't think it ungracious if I take you to task for falling upon Tennyson, who after all is a *great* poet, and to my mind has well won his honours: no doubt you are right in the faults you find in your letter; no doubt Tennyson ought to have avoided them; but it is always unfair to judge a man by any but his best works, and (especially if he be a lyrical poet as T. emphatically is) the amount of these don't necessarily add to his claim to be considered a great poet; nor do I think it much matters that a man has written rubbish at some time other of his life if he ever does anything good; peoples minds grow in different ways, one man never writes anything bad, another flashes out and fades away as though the available part of his life was meant to be very short; again I say this is much more like to be the case with a lyrical poet than any other; I allow as a matter of course that Tennyson has little or no dramatic capacity, not enough for him to write even narrative poetry with success But if you think of the finish of In Memoriam, the pathos and feeling of the May Queen the delicate sentiment of Mariana, you must surely allow that he is a great poet — or what do you think of those few lines "tears idle tears"? Well I shouldn't have said so much only one sees a sort of reflex against Tennyson after a great deal of puffry of him; it is natural, it is a good deal his own fault, but it is a pity I think[2] — For my own works time will try them; but I am afraid that there is a good deal of ground for ⟨the⟩ what the critic of Temple Bar says, though very likely he don't say it in the right way, and though I can't really accuse myself of want of feeling;[3] I think these faults will not be so obvious in the next vol: for I have certainly felt them myself and tried to correct them — I havn't seen Temple Bar by the way. I have been obliged to split the remainder of the Earthly Paradise into two parts, of which I hope to publish one before this Xmas, and the other in May next — I am much interested in what you are doing with the Gesta Romanorum; do you know the old English translation edited by Sir F. Madden?[4] you ought to see it before you finish yours I think the ⟨book⟩ translation I know best is the French Violier des Histoires Romances published in the Libraire Elzivirienne, a pretty little book.[5] I have not been anything like so interesting as to fall ill, but have been very hard at work and am so still, though on account of my wifes ill health I have been obliged to spend a few weeks in this (to me) dreary place; I hope to be back in about a month. I have never mustered courage enough to get my photograph taken; I suppose I shall soon; Mrs Cameron[6] threatened me with the operation, but it has not come off yet, though I don't suppose I shall escape long.

I wish you good luck and thank you again very much for your letter and am

Yrs very truly
W Morris

MS: McMinn Papers.

[1] At this time, Nicholson was an undergraduate in Trinity College, Oxford, and apparently contemplated editing an undergraduate magazine. The plan was never carried out.

[2] In 1869, *Temple Bar* published a series of articles, "Poetry of the Period," by Alfred Austin (1835-1913), who became poet laureate in 1896. The first article, which appeared in May, condemned Tennyson as a bad poet. (In the articles for June and July, Austin took an equally dim view of Browning and Swinburne.)

[3] Austin's article for August discussed the poetry of Matthew Arnold and of Morris, finding Morris's the better of the two. Here Morris was responding only to Austin's reservations. The entire series of articles was republished as a book entitled *Poetry of the Period* (London, 1870).

[4] "The Man Born to be King," the second tale in the first volume of *The Earthly Paradise* partly follows the tale in the *Gesta Romanorum*. May Morris writes (*CW*, 3, xix,n.) that the English translation of the *Gesta Romanorum* in Morris's library "was a Roxburghe Club publication, edited by Sir F. Madden, 1838."

[5] Published in Paris in 1867.

[6] Julia Margaret Pattle Cameron (1815-1879), one of the great Victorian photographers (and a great-aunt of Virginia Woolf), known especially for her portrait studies of Carlyle, Darwin, Tennyson, and Ellen Terry. The composed thematic pictures, such as "Rosebud Garden of Girls," are Pre-Raphaelite in composition and treatment of details; they require consideration as a part of the Pre-Raphaelite pictorial achievement. A selection of Cameron's photographs was published as *Victorian Photographs of Famous Men and Fair Women* by the Hogarth Press in 1926 (reprinted in 1973), with introductions by Virginia Woolf and Roger Fry. There is no photograph of Morris in the book.

86 · To Philip Speakman Webb

Fortuna
Bad-Ems
August 15 [1869]

My dearest Friend

The root of all evil, is, if not *the* root yet one of the roots of this letter, lets get done with that first. I want to make myself safe from being kept in pawn, and set to hard labour at Ems (say sweeping up horse-dung, an office religiously observed here), I want £60 somehow; I suppose Wardle will be able to let you have it; if not would it strain your resources to be so kind as lend it me — failing this I don't doubt Ellis would let me have it; then will you be so kind as to pay it in to Praeds, and ask them what will be the best way of sending it; a letter of credit I suppose, either on some one here or Coblenz or Cologne. I havn't spent all I brought with me, but this week will see the end of it I fancy, and I want to speak rather before I'm hurt: I hope not to spend all that, but now we are here, it would be nothing short of madness not to stay here long enough to give the place a fair chance.

A month yesterday we left London, and 3 weeks tomorrow we came here: I have some hopes that we shall be at home again in 3 weeks from today, but don't like to think too much about it; though I catch myself now and then looking at the time-tables and considering which train we shall go to Cologne by: I get out for a walk every morning now, and if the weather looks well stretch my legs a bit, but always take my pocketbook with me and do a little work. This morning I walked to Nassau and back, 12 miles in all; it is a pretty quiet little town higher up the Lahn; Stein[1] the great Prussian statesman who did for the high tory party in Prussia was born there, was the swell of the place in fact. I also brought Paris' Death[2] to an end roughly; again I'm not very sanguine about the merit of it; but I shall get through the work I set myself to do here in some way, and have a month to turn over the first of the tales before I go to press when I come home — Ah hah! the letter you sent me wasn't sent on for nothing.[3] Janey got a pain in her back from laughing at it; I hope you read it right through. I felt so sheepish; I had to write back again a long letter to him thanking him but explaining to him that Tennyson wasn't quite a fool — however, if I havn't destroyed the poor young man's reason I should think he would make a decent editor; a better one than a poet, for unless his butter has blinded me, I should think he was a clever young chap — squints though. I have walked a little through the woods (beech mostly) but they are lonely and dismal except in the brightest weather and so precious full of ants as big as that; item on wet days the slugs there are bigger and uglier than any I have ever seen 4″ long, most of them a brilliant red-lead colour, but some like bad veal with a shell on their backs; the adders are lively too in this wet warm valley: yesterday morning I heard a rustle in the dry leaves behind me and out crept one as long as my umbrella of a yellowish olive colour and wriggled across the path as though he were expected; I kept feeling the legs of my trousers all the way home after that, and feel a little shy of sitting down on green banks now; however they are always wet. Item I never saw anywhere so many jays all round the edges of the woods they are at it all day long. Magnússons saga[4] has turned up and I have begun it; it is rather of the monstrous order but I shall go through with it partly to see what there is good in it partly to fill up the time — Sleeping does a good deal of that: I turn in at ½ past 10 which is about the time Janey composes herself to sleep; in revenge we get (I get) up early; this morning I was a long way on my road before 9 o clock. Janey says I am not to tell you how she is, because as soon as she has written to any one to say she is better, she gets worse; however I hope and rather think that, taking one day with another she *is* rather better: she is fast asleep now 4.10 P.M. and will write a line or two when she wakes up at the tail of this note.

My[5] finger-tips are sound as you see by this — and fit for much more hard labour — I feel that I have not much else about me that is good for anything, but I have a sort of presentiment (though of course you don't believe in such things) that I may make a rapid turn — and feel myself well all of a sudden — and then I have another presentiment that should this change come — all those I now call my Friends would also change — and would not be able to stand me.

Your most affectionate
W. & J. Morris

MS: BL, Add. MSS. 45342. Extract published: *CW*, 5, xvi; Henderson, *Letters*, 27; Henderson, *Life*, 103-104.

[1] Baron Heinrich Karl von Stein (1757-1831), Prussian minister of foreign affairs, forced to resign by Napoleon in 1808. After the Congress of Vienna, he spent his remaining years in the encouragement of German art and science.

[2] "The Death of Paris," one of the stories in Part III of *The Earthly Paradise*.

[3] Letter from E.W.B. Nicholson, to which Morris had replied August 12 (no. 85).

[4] The *Volsunga Saga*. See letter no. 95. Magnússon had translated it "in the course of the summer of 1869 and sent it out to Ems. . . . Morris now read the 'monstrous' tale of Sigmund, Signy, and Sinfjotli for the first time" (*CW*, 7, xx).

[5] Jane Morris wrote this concluding paragraph.

87 • TO FREDERICK STARTRIDGE ELLIS [Bad Ems
August 18, 1869]

Many thanks for your letter again, and the Temple Bar, which did not excoriate my thin hide in spite of a tender contempt with which Mr. Austin[1] seemed to regard me. Commercially I suppose I ought to be grateful to him and am so; from the critical point of view I think there is so much truth as this in his article, as that we poets of to-day have been a good deal made by those of the Byron and Shelley time — however, in another sixty years or so, when it won't matter three skips of a louse to us (as it don't matter much more now), I suppose we shall quietly fall into our places. I get about three hours' walk (with pocketbook, Mr. Publisher) every morning, and am in roaring and offensive health, keeping country hours, woke by the band (with a hymn-tune) at seven every morning and going to bed at ten every night. I shall want about a fortnight after I come home before I begin to feed the free burgher of Berwick-upon-Tweed with my immortal MS., and after that I hope there will be no hitch. Believe me, the longest and heaviest of sticks is buzzing about my ears, as you would find out if you had passed a week at this skin-'em-alive place; I'm not quite sure now if I shan't have to be sold to the Prussian government to sweep up horse-dung in Ems streets (they are very particular about it) — my God, what a bad bargain I should be!

I have not got any good wine at Ems, and perhaps they don't charge for such as they sell you! but the Grunhauser at Cologne and Coblentz was jolly that hot weather. Did you ever speculate as to what they fed German sheep on? deep thought at breakfast time has led me to suppose india-rubber to be their pabulum — this is not very encouraging to your journey to Ems,[2] but you see my wife is not strong enough to get to the restaurants here; I daresay we could get a tolerable dinner there.

Fishing I have not tried yet; I am too lazy to look up proper baits. The inside of a roll would be about as far as I should care to go. They don't seem to understand gentles[3] at Ems; nor have I seen anybody trying either worms or minnow, though there must be perch here somewhere; I have seen some big chubs about.

TEXT: Mackail, I, 202-203. Published: Henderson, *Letters*, 28-29.

[1] See letter no. 85, notes 2 and 3.
[2] Ellis visited the Morrises during their stay at Bad Ems. See letter no. 89.
[3] Maggots used as bait by anglers.

88 · To Philip Speakman Webb   Fortuna
                                                    Bad-Ems
                                                    August 20 [1869]

My dearest Friend

The notes came safe to hand yesterday morning; I thought I would see that all was right by dealing with the banker before I answered you — My dear chap I should be very willing to take the money as a gift with all the thanks you can imagine and all the gratitude (not much) I am capable of — I should be pleased to take a gift from you either greater or smaller, but I really don't think I want it, & I am sure you must; I think the money will be much more equally divided by your keeping it, than by your casting it on the dry and thirsty ground of a nee'r-do-well — the best of thanks all the same for the offer, and for the trouble of getting & sending the money — you must think I mean more by that than clumsy words will say; I am something of an Englishman and the words wont flow, 'tis one of the curses entailed on our blood & climate.

What a glutton at reading you must be to get through C.H in such a short time; I have done but little more than half of it, though certainly I never found it a tiresome or dull book nor, if one takes it on its own grounds, even prolix.

Of news from here there is little or none really, we are dull enough and sleep a great deal, and have a good deal of trouble in getting our dinner, as J. finds she can't eat the regular German feed; which certainly is rather greasy; you would never believe it if I had kept a diary of the amount of beefsteaks we had eaten, (the mutton can hardly be cut with a knife at all). Janey too has taken to beer; and I find it very jolly too, and sits much easier than our English beer: good wine seems dear at Ems though it was cheap enough at Coblenz & Cologne; but they make a fair rough red wine in the valley here, strong, but tastes *green*; the German *red* wine as far as I have tasted it, must from a critical point of view be considered a failure — but the beer I assure you is good and is only 6^d a bottle — at Coblenz we found the Mosel-wine very good; it was awfully hot weather, and all hands of us got through a deal of Grünhauser; but here I think the best wine I have drunk is the red wine of the valley as above, and they charge us ⁵1.6 a bottle for that — obviously too much — in spite of the cold weather the grapes are all turning now, and one can buy the black ones pretty cheap, but they are not sweet enough yet, though they are come to their full size pretty much; the biggest berries being about as big as an average sloe — the weather has picked up the last day or two, and today is lovely warm windy and fresh; and no sulks can quite prejudice me against the country here which is lovely; I went a walk in the uplands this morning about queer winding cart roads through grain fields dotted all over with apple-trees, everything of course being on the slope, and big hills everywhere in the distance, and thought what a delightful country it was if I had any business there.

I can't yet say at all any thing about our coming back; last time the Dr. called he said J ought to have about 12 more baths, that with a 3 days rest ⟨without⟩ before starting would let us start from here about Wednesday Sept: 1st. Janey does certainly seem better as to her specific grievance; but she is very weak; I suppose a warm bath every day would be like to make her so; the Dr. however don't seem at astonished about her, and we must be in his hands I suppose.   next week I hope to know some thing definite as to our getting back, meantime between walking, working & sleeping the time slips away somehow — I haven't taken to fishing yet, and don't think I shall, *pace Ellis.* I fancy I can dawdle about nearly as well without a rod as with one — I wish you had read Nicholson's letter through; however I will show it you when I come back —

Taylor is better then, I hope? I hope he don't think I am seriously vexed at any thing he has said, or otherwise than very much obliged by his friendliness; I think I understand the whole matter perfectly well; and know there is a great deal of reason in what he says,[1] though he is not at present quite master of the details — I hope your rheumatism is better: I know you are not the sort of chap to take care of yourself in spite of your preaching to others — as to me — I am disgustingly well, and quite ashamed of myself: only it is more convenient for the present that I shouldn't be ill, I mean to other people — good-bye write again when you can find time, and excuse Janey doing more than setting her hand to this as it tires her to sit up & write —

Your most affectionate friends
W Morris

P.S. I have picked you up two tunes — one called the 'The Last Rose of Summer' and the other the 'Mabel Walzes.' Seriously I have heard but one fine piece all this time.

Your affectionate
Janey

MS: BL, Add. MSS. 45342. Extract published: *CW*, 5, xvii–xviii.

[1] At this time there was some discussion of money owed the firm. Warington Taylor insisted that the debt collection be pressed, but the members apparently did not want to bother. In July 1869 Taylor had written to Webb: "Is everybody allowed to do as he likes? Ned, W.M. and Gabriel egg one another on to every kind of useless expense. . . . Our

balance sheets are strained to the last penny to please W.M. . . . I have written to the firm, to W.M. and to Gabriel. Everybody is doing his best to ruin us." In August he wrote again: "I do not care to push legal extremes, I only want the dignity of the firm maintained, and to let it be understood that we in no way sanction . . . the slightest irregularity of life. . . . Without some sort of tone is kept up the firm must sin, for no society ever lasted yet which ignored the fundamental principles of morality." See Lethaby, pp. 57-58.

89 • TO PHILIP SPEAKMAN WEBB

Fortuna
Bad-Ems
August 27 [1869]

My dearest Friend,

Many thanks again for your letter — Janey is better again today, in fact looks quite set up, after having had a doubtful and bad day or two; in case the North-End folk havn't heard from me before Tuesday please tell them this, as I wrote rather dismally to Ned yesterday morning. We hope to start from here on Tuesday week or thereabouts, but can say nothing clearer than that. Gabriel writing the other day to Janey proposed our going to Switzerland after we had done with Ems — tin apart wh: I suppose could be got up if necessary, I think there is too much to be said against going to make me think it is only my own wishes that make me decide against it — Janey objects strenuously, her digestion wants attending to more than can be done in a place where one doesn't know the manners and customs; item not being strong enough to go out there is nothing to interest her in a foreign country, and she misses a great many little occupations that wear the day away at home; item there are the kids; item there would be an extra journey of 10 days coming and going, and all journeys are to be dreaded now I think for her — Summa, she refuses to think of anything but going straight home when we have done here.

I am at work still, I find the Palace East &c,[1] wanted rewriting rather than tinkering, I want to finish it before we get back, so as to have some time for correcting it before going to press. As you will hear from the Neds, or perhaps from himself Ellis came here on Tuesday and stayed till Wednesday evening, he had been buying books at Hanover, and took me on the way back; he was as placid and jovial as usual, and on Wednesday morning we went a journey on the outside of mules, with some trepidation on his part — I went for the first time, into the Kürsaal,[2] and saw him stake a mild florin, which he doubled several times to his satisfaction, and then we departed — his luck has not tempted me to go in there again, it looked too dull — his coming rather put a spoke in the cart wheel of my muse; otherwise I was very glad to see him, and thought it very kind of him to come —

The weather has taken a turn here, and the wind is blowing from the east somewhere, and the sun is very bright and hot — the first day of it (the wind was west till then) reminded me of the 2nd or 3rd September/58 and Caudebec;[3] the grapes have got very good to eat at all events, but perhaps these are wall-grapes. Hum-drum is the style of our life here, varied only by a fit of dumps at Janey getting worse now and then: if I could I should like to go on working till the last minute, but I rather doubt my capacity to smother up my impatience to that extent —

Ned was so kind as to send me an illustrated copy of the review in Temple Bar, it was very pretty; did you see it before it went off? There is really nothing at all to tell you, at least when such a clumsy letter-writer as myself holds the pen; I will write at least once again before we leave here   This is the end of the letter unless Janey can write a word or two.

I[4] am sorry to hear you have not yet got rid of those rheumatic pains. I laughed at your joke about them if I did not understand it, but I won't say I did not.

> With both our love
> Yours most affectionately
> WM. Janey

MS: BL, Add. MSS. 45342. Extract published: *CW*, 5, xviii-xix.

[1] "The Land East of the Sun and West of the Moon," one of the tales for September in Part III of *The Earthly Paradise*.

[2] The room in which the spa waters were taken. It was customary to set up card tables in the Kursaal.

[3] See letter no. 20, n. 1.

[4] This paragraph was written by Jane Morris.

---

90 · TO PHILIP SPEAKMAN WEBB   Bad-Ems
                                                    August 29 [1869]

My dearest Friend

I write again to give you a bit of trouble: the Dr. here says that Janey can have an apparatus for the douche rigged up in the simplest way which will be quite satisfactory — as how, a tin box or cistern somewhat conical at its lower end, and flat against the wall, capacity 2 gallons; this cistern to be hung as high as it can conveniently be filled by jugs: a pipe from it, the first part of which may be of tin, with a tap at the end thereof, and a flexible tube (common india-rubber) of half an inch diameter to finish with — this is all; a fall of 8 ft; the Dr. says will give all the force necessary — Can you get this rigged up for me at once in the dressing-room adjoining our bedroom, and also get Stennett to make a scooped-out wooden stool like those one sits on at the Turkish Bath — If you don't fully understand it all a sketch by return would draw an answer from me in good time; but the whole thing is perfectly simple, and I should think our 2nd floor rooms must be 10 ft high so as easily to give height enough. The Dr. furnishes withal a prescription wh: gives the component[?] parts of the Ems waters, principally carbonate of soda, & common salt; and so all the essentials for going on with the course here are to be had at home: which is a great consolation to me, as these douches have certainly done J good, and yet I have no doubt she will be better at home — now — Janey seems getting stronger at last and I suppose there is little doubt that we shall leave about the 7th. She is in good spirits, but has nothing to do here, and is anxious enough to get home.

I am at work still but have got the fidgetts; I went a long walk in the heat of the day yesterday, to get rid of them; walked over the uplands till I came to a wood through wh: I had a lovely walk of an hour, taking a forest road at hazard: I thought I had fairly lost my way but it befel that I took the right turning, for at last I came upon a green-painted seat which showed I was near Ems; I drank a small lake of Seltzer water & white wine afterwards and got rid of my thirst, but not my fidgetts — however today much against the grain I wrote 120 lines — but have still got the fidgetts — I will write once at least again from here before we start and then from Cologne or Ghent or both —

Your most affectionate
W M.

MS: BL, Add. MSS. 45342. Extract published: Henderson, *Letters*, 29.

91 • TO PHILIP SPEAKMAN WEBB Bad-Ems
September 3 [1869]

My dearest Friend

Many thanks for your letter and the trouble you have taken about the douche affair, as also the architectural drawing a la Violet le Duc.[1] it seems all very handy, and I and Janey only note two things. 1st. let the tap not be more than 4 ft above the floor; 2nd don't forget the capacity of basin above 2 gallons; it had better be rather more than less I should think — I consider Janey really better now; she is stronger and the local trouble seems so much better, as to be nearly knocked on the head — Summa we intend to turn our backs upon Ems on Monday evening about 7 p.m. wh: will bring us to Cologne by 10: we think of staying a day to recruit at Cologne, so as to sleep on Wednesday at Liege, Thursday at Ghent, stop there Friday, get to Calais at midday on Saturday & cross at midnight in wh: case we shall get home about 7 Am on Sunday 12th   all this depends of course a great deal on how she stands the travelling at first; I will write you a line probably from Cologne, certainly from Ghent; and if you wish to write again, address Hotel Royal Ghent, so as to get to us no later than Friday morning (the 10th) —

I have little else to say except to thank you for bothering yourself about the little delft cruets;[2] I am glad they turned out well — I am pretty considerably fidgetty about getting over the time I can tell you but shall find enough to do what with one thing and another to pass the time till Monday — the idea of the journey makes me rather nervous too; there are two or three troublesome shiftings at custom houses and the like, but I hope all will go pretty well.

Yrs most affect:
WM.

Love from Janey

MS: BL, Add. MSS. 45342.

[1] Eugène Emmanuel Viollet-le-Duc (1814–1879), French architect and authority on Gothic art. He was a leader of the Gothic revival in France and designed the restoration of many medieval buildings, including the cathedrals of Amiens, Laon, and Notre-Dame de Paris.

[2] See postscript to letter no. 81.

92 • TO EMMA SHELTON MORRIS   26, Queen Square,
Bloomsbury, London.
Friday
[September 17, 1869]

My dearest Mother

We crossed on Sunday morning and got home safely, but after a very rough passage, which took us quite by surprise as there had not been ⟨a⟩ very much wind at Calais the day before, and it seemed quite calm at starting — owing to this no doubt Janey is not as well as I hoped she would be, as she seemed to bear the journey well up to this last point — however I still hope to send a better account to you in a few days; it was hardly to be hoped that she would not feel such a tossing about —

still I am naturally rather anxious — The children seem very well — We all send our love — When are you coming up to town?

> Yr most affect: Son
> W Morris

MS: Walthamstow.

93 • FROM A LETTER TO GEORGIANA BURNE-JONES[1] October [1869]

. . . about him which nearly drives me mad when I am in an irritable humour; but I behaved very well, though I felt rather crushed among so many clever people, and didn't say much. Brown I thought a trifle too genteel for a batchelor party. I prefer his company when the Westland Marston[2] element is absent — I am in short a narrow and monotonous bore — and being so, will not bore you any longer. Good-bye, and stand as long as you can

> Your most loving friend
> W.M.

Over page for 'October.' Show it to Ned if he is with you.[3]

MS: WPL. Published: Henderson, *Letters*, 30.

[1] See letter no. 26, n. 3.

[2] John Westland Marston (1819-1890), poet, playwright, and literary critic for *The Athenaeum*.

[3] The beginning of this letter is apparently lost. This passage is on a single leaf fragment on the reverse of which is "October," the introductory poem that precedes "Acontius and Cydippe" and "The Man Who Never Laughed Again" in Part III of *The Earthly Paradise*. See *CW*, 5, 122-23.

94 • TO CHARLES FAIRFAX MURRAY

> 26, Queen Square,
> Bloomsbury, London
> [November 15, 1869?]

My dear Murray

Herewith the space for the picture for the lay of Gudrun[1] —

> Yrs ever
> W Morris

MS: Texas.

[1] Presumably this referred to the unfinished illuminated manuscript, "The Story of the Volsungs and Niblungs," on which Morris worked until sometime in 1870. It contains miniatures painted by C. F. Murray. See letter no. 78, n. 1 and Fairbank, p. 66.

Georgiana Burne-Jones, c. 1860, drawn by Dante Gabriel Rossetti.

95 · To Charles Eliot Norton

26 Queen Squ:
Bloomsbury
December 21 [1869]

My dear Norton

I suppose I had better waste neither invention nor materials in excuses for not writing, so I will only say how very glad I shall be to hear from you again despite my 'lachesse'. I don't know if you have my book by this time, or have begun to deal with its somewhat elephantine bulk, wh: I should feel penitent about, only it is principally caused by the length of Gudrun which I feel sure is the best thing I have done — however no more of that. I have begun a translation of the Nibelungen[1] which I find very amusing; I have also another Icelandic translation in hand, the Völsunga Saga[2] viz, which is the Ice: version of the Nibelungen, older I suppose, and, to my mind, without measure nobler and grander: I daresay you have read abstracts of the story, but however fine it seemed to you thus, it would give you little idea of the depth and intensity of the complete work here and there indeed it is somewhat disjointed, I suppose from its having been put together from varying versions of the same song; it seems as though the author–collector felt the subject too much to trouble himself about the niceties of art, and the result is something which is above all art; the scene of the last interview between Sigurd and the despairing and terrible Brynhild touches me more than any thing I have ever met with in literature there is nothing wanting in it, nothing forgotten, nothing repeated, nothing overstrained; all tenderness is shown without the use of a tender word, all misery and despair without a word of raving, complete beauty without an ornament, and all this in 2 pages of moderate print. In short it is to the full meaning of the word inspired; touching too though hardly wonderful to think of the probable author; some 12 century Icelander, living the hardest and rudest of lives, seeing few people and pretty much the same day after day, with his old religion taken from him and his new one hardly gained — It doesn't look promising for the future of art I fear — Perhaps you think my praise of the work somewhat stilted; but it has moved us one and all in the same way, and for my part I should be sorry to attempt reading aloud the scene I have told you of before strangers. I am not getting on well with my work, for in fact I believe the Völsunga has rather swallowed me up for some time past, I mean thinking about it, for it hasn't taken me long to do — I had it in my head to write an epic of it, but though I still hanker after it, I see clearly it would be foolish, for no verse could render the best parts of it, and it would only be a flatter and tamer version of a thing already existing.[3]

My wife is better I think on the whole for the Ems sojourn, though still far from well: Ned, from whom I suppose you have heard lately, is pretty well, and working hard: Georgie gave us a little fright last week by falling decidedly ill, but she is much better now, and I hope will be none the worse for it. Webb is as usual working hard and looking thin (apropos I believe that Im grown thinner) Rossetti is hard at work on his poems[4] and I believe will publish in the spring: I hope so — thank you very much by the way for your extracts from The French Omar[5] — Ned has the book now.

Please give my kindest rembrances to Mrs. Norton and all your fellowship: my wife I believe intends writing to Mrs. Norton directly so I will send no message from her —

Yrs affectionately
W Morris

MS: Harvard. Extract published: Mackail, I, 73; MM, I, 471-73; Henderson, *Letters*, 31-32.

¹ According to May Morris (*CW*, 7, xxxiii), Morris abandoned the translation after completing 216 stanzas.

² *The Völsunga Saga: The Story of the Volsungs and Niblungs*, translated in collaboration with Magnússon, was published by F. S. Ellis in 1870.

³ Morris did in fact write an epic based on the *Völsunga Saga*, titled *Sigurd the Volsung*. It was published in 1876. See letter no. 311, n. 2.

⁴ Rossetti's *Poems* was published in April 1870. This volume contained the poems that had been buried with Elizabeth Siddal in 1862 and disinterred in 1869.

⁵ Possibly *Les Quatrains tr. du Persan* by J. B. Nicolas (Paris, 1807).

96 • To Algernon Charles Swinburne   26, Queen Square,
                                                Bloomsbury, London,
                                                December 21, 1869

My dear Swinburne¹

Many thanks for your kind letter and the criticism therein; I am delighted to have pleased you with the Gudrun;² for the rest I am rather painfully conscious myself that the book would have done me more credit if there had been nothing in it but the Gudrun, though I don't think the others quite the worst things I have done — yet they are all too long and flabby — damn it! —

I am glad you see anything to like in the Rhodope;³ I thought myself I had tried to make her too much of a character for the importance of the tale wh: is such a very slight one — Acontius I know is a spoony, nothing less, and the worst of it is that if I did him over a dozen times, I know I should make him just the same: I am hard at work now, but am making blunder on blunder, and if I could find anything else that really amused me except writing verses I would give up that art for the present, for I am doing no good.

Thorgerd plays a fine part in a beautiful episode of the Egils Saga where Egil loses his favourite son, and is minded to starve himself to death because of it; I could tell you more about it when I saw you. The whole story is very remarkable, admirably written and full of incident, but the most distinctly northern of all the Sagas, and Egil himself a strange savage character, though his poetry seems to me to have been really fine, but quite untranslateable.⁴

I am about an Icelandic translation now which quite throws all the other stories into the shade (for the story of Gudrun is told very disjointedly in the original, and generally in bald way very different from Njdla.) This is the Völsunga, the story of the Nibelungen in fact: I daresay you have read an abstract of it somewhere, but it would give you very little idea of the complete work. I should like very much to show you the translation which is nearly finished now; you couldn't fail to be moved by it Im sure —

I am proudly conscious of my position as *the* Christian poet of the age:[5] though I must risk that position first by communicating with you, and next by impugning the statement of holy writ, 'Blessed are those that seek, for they shall find', at least in my case —

Yrs affectionately

W Morris

MS: BL, Ashley Add. MSS. 3871. Published: MM, I, 642-43; Henderson, *Letters*, 30-31.

[1] Algernon Charles Swinburne (1837-1909). In 1859, while an undergraduate at Balliol College, Oxford, Swinburne became an enthusiastic admirer and follower of Rossetti and Morris. By 1869, however, he had established his own standing with *Atalanta in Calydon* (1865) and *Poems and Ballads* (1866), and though still an affectionate well-wisher, he clearly regarded Morris as a peer rather than a leader. In 1867 he had favorably reviewed *The Life and Death of Jason.*

[2] "The Lovers of Gudrun," based on the Laxdaela Saga, is the second story for November and completes Part III of *The Earthly Paradise.*

[3] "The Story of Rhodope" is the first tale for November in Part III of *The Earthly Paradise.*

[4] Morris may have been at work on the illuminated manuscript, which was never finished, of "The Story of Egil." See *CW*, 9, xxi, xxiii and Fairbank, p. 67.

[5] In *The Athenaeum*, December 25, 1869, the reviewer of the third part of *The Earthly Paradise* had praised Morris for "his Christian viewpoint."

97 · TO JAMES RICHARD THURSFIELD

[26 Queen Square
Bloomsbury, London
1869]

Dear Sir[1]

I am sorry you are in trouble about the works at the Union,[2] and hope I shan't increase it by my letter: I can speak distinctly about two of the pictures in question, Mr. Hughes', the one at the North end, and Mr. Burne-Jones' (Nimue and Merlin). Of these I think the design of Mr. Hughes to be quite among the best works of that painter, and a very beautiful and remarkable one: I think I have been told it is in a bad state; but I suppose something might be done to it. Mr. Burne-Jones' is a beautiful work, and admirably suits its space as to decoration; it would be quite absurd to cover it up. Mr. Pollen's,[3] opposite Mr. Hughes',[4] was never finished; two others, one by Mr. Prinsep,[5] another by Mr. Stanhope,[6] though not very complete in some ways, yet looked very well in their places I think. As for my own, I believe it *has* some merits as to colour, but I must confess I should feel much more com-

26, Queen Square, Bloomsbury,

London,

Dec. 21st 1869

My dear Swinburne

Many thanks for
your kind letter and the criticisms
therein; I am delighted to have
pleased you with the Gudrun;
for the rest I am rather painfully
conscious myself that the book
would have done me more credit
if there had been nothing in it but
the Gudrun, though I don't think
the others quite the worst things
I have done — yet they are all too
long and flabby — damn it! —
I am glad you see anything to like
in the Rhodope; I thought myself
I had tried to make her too much
of a character for the importance
of the tale wh: is such a very slight
one — Aclountine I know is a
spoony, nothing less, and the worst
of it is that if I did him over a
dozen times, I know I should

Morris's letter to Algernon Charles Swinburne, December 21, 1869.

[102]

make him just the same: I am
hard at work now, but am making
blunder on blunder, and if I
could find anything else that really
amused me except writing verses
I would give up that art for the
present, for I am doing no good.

Thorgerd plays a fine part in
a beautiful episode of the Egils
Saga where Egil loses his favourite
son, and is minded to starve him-
self to death because of it; I could
tell you more about it when I
saw you. the whole story is very
remarkable, admirably written
and full of incident, but the most
distinctly northern of all the Sagas,
and Egil himself a strange savage
character, though his poetry see ms
to me to have been really fine, but
quite untranslateable. I am
about an Icelandic translation now
which quite throws all the other stories
into the shade (for the story of Gudrun
is told very disjointedly in the original,
and generally in a old way very
different from Njala) this is the

Völsunga, the story of the Nibelungen in fact; I daresay you have read an abstract of it somewhere, but it would give you very little idea of the complete work. I should like very much to show you the translation which is nearly finished now; you couldn't fail to be moved by it I'm sure —

I am proudly conscious of my position as the Christian poet of the age: though I must risk that position first by communicating with you, and next by impugning the statement of holy writ; Blessed are those that seek for they shall find. at least in my case —

Yrs affectionately
W Morris

fortable if it had disappeared from the wall, as I'm conscious of its being extremely ludicrous in many ways.[7] In confidence to you I should say the whole affair was begun and carried out in too piecemeal and unorganized a manner to be a real success — nevertheless it would surely be a pity to destroy some of the pictures, which are really remarkable, and at the worst can do no harm there. I am sorry if this is 'cold comfort'; but I thought you would really like to know what I thought, and so here it is. I must thank you heartily however for the enthusiasm you have shown in the matter; and I wish I could be of more use to you.

Yours faithfully,
William Morris

TEXT: Mackail, I, 124-25. Published: Henderson, *Letters*, 29-30.

[1] James Richard Thursfield (1840-1923), naval historian and journalist. A fellow of Jesus College, 1864-1881, he was chairman of a committee appointed to inquire into the matter of the deteriorating paintings on the walls of the Oxford Union, done by Rossetti, Morris, and others in 1857. See n. 2 below.

[2] The Building Committee of the Oxford Union had commissioned D. G. Rossetti in 1857 to superintend the covering and painting of ten bays and the whole ceiling of the Oxford Union. He got together, for the work, Burne-Jones, Morris, Arthur Hughes, Spencer Stanhope, Valentine Prinsep, and John Hungerford Pollen. Morris finished the first picture and decorated the roof. But none of the group really knew anything of the technique of fresco painting, and the project was never finished. In the paintings that were completed, fading and running of colors began almost immediately. For a discussion of the Oxford Union murals, see Mackail, I, 117-26 and *Memorials*, I, 158-68. For an account of the redecoration of the ceiling by Morris in 1875, see K. L. Goodwin, "William Morris' 'New and Lighter Design,' " *Journal of the William Morris Society* (Winter 1968), pp. 24-31.

[3] John Hungerford Pollen (1820-1902). A friend of Ruskin, Turner, and Millais, he designed the ceiling of Merton College Chapel in 1850 and decorated many private houses. In December 1863 he was appointed to the office of Assistant Keeper of the South Kensington Museum and was also named Official Editor of its Science and Art Department. (See Anne Pollen, *John Hungerford Pollen, 1820-1902* [London: John Murray, 1919].) Pollen's picture was *How King Arthur Received His Sword Excalibur from the Lady of the Lake.*

[4] *The Death of Arthur.*

[5] Valentine Cameron Prinsep (1838-1904) had studied painting in Paris, and through his family, moved quickly into artistic-intellectual circles on his return to London. His picture was *Sir Pelleas and the Lady Ettarde.*

[6] *Sir Gawaine and the Three Damsels at the Fountain in the Forest of Arroy.*

[7] Mackail notes (I, 119) that Morris felt a morbid attraction to the subject of his painting: a man who was a failure and a rejected lover. The picture was entitled *How Sir Palomydes Loved La Belle Iseult with Exceeding Great Love Out of Measure, and How She Loved Not Him Again but Rather Sir Tristram.*

98 • To Kate Faulkner   Queen Sq:
                                                      Friday [December 1869]

My dear Kate[1]

Janey has been very poorly since you saw her, & though she is better
now, she is far from well and it would be very imprudent for her to go
out so she must put off coming; and I for my part must stay at home
with her this week at all events. I am sorry.

                                          Yrs very truly
                                          W Morris

MS: Princeton T.

  [1] Kate Faulkner (d.1898), sister of Charles Faulkner, was an embroiderer, gesso deco-
rator, wallpaper designer, and china painter. She worked for Morris and Co. from 1861
on, painting tiles as well as designing and embroidering. During the early years the firm
produced all its own tiles, the blanks being imported from Holland and then painted by
the Faulkners (Charles, Kate, and Lucy) and fired in a kiln in the basement of 8 Red Lion
Square. Kate Faulkner also did free-lance work in china painting outside the Morris firm
and designed wallpaper for Jeffrey and Company in 1883. See Callen, pp. 70, 223.

99 • To Mr. Delpierre   [1870?]

to Mr. Delpierre—[1]

Please give bearer my passport visée.

                                          William Morris

MS: Texas.

  [1] Unidentified, but possibly the French Consul in London. The fact that Morris re-
quired a passport suggests the date 1870 or later.

100 • To Charles Fairfax Murray   Queen Sq:
                                                      Saturday [1870]

I shall expect you if
I *dont* get an answer

Dear Murray

  I don't know what your [sic] are about, but if your sabbath-breaking
propensities are not too strong for you, you might come and dine here
tomorrow with me, & spend the afternoon, and look at my 'blooming
letters'[1] over wh: I have been working hard like a baby as I am.[2]   dinner
at one oclock, and I am going to ask Webb; do you mind him — have
you seen Nettleship[3] without his hat?

                                          Yrs affec:
                                          W Morris

MS: Texas.

¹ Large, floriated initials.

² In 1870, Morris began working on letters for illuminated manuscripts. His handwriting in this letter also suggests that it was written in 1870.

³ John Trivett Nettleship (1841-1902), painter, usually of animal subjects, and writer. His daughter Ida married Augustus John in 1900.

101 • THREE LETTERS TO EIRÍKR MAGNÚSSON

a.   [1870?]

My dear Magnússon¹

Can you come on Saturday for our reading instead of Friday: you can call anytime you please to see Mr. Wardle.

Yrs very truly
W. Morris

MSS: Iceland.

¹ See letter no. 64, n. 1.

b.   Queen Sq:
Sunday [1870]

My dear Magnússon

Please come a little later tomorrow (Monday) say 4 o'clock as I shan't be able to be at home at the usual time.

Yrs very truly
W. Morris

c.   26, Queen Square,
Bloomsbury, London
Thursday [1870]

My dear Magnusson

Can you come on Saturday instead of tomorrow? Excuse —

Yrs truly
W Morris

Eiríkr Magnússon, 1867.

102 · To John Watkins
26 Queen Sq:
February 10, 1870

Sir[1]

I should have been very happy to have sat to you for the portrait you mention, but I have already given a photographer one sitting for my portrait, and when it is completed, I will send it to the Editor of the Graphic.[2]

Thanking you for your note,

I remain
Yrs obediently
William Morris

J. Watkins, Esqr.

MS: Pforzheimer, Misc. 825.

[1] John and Charles Watkins of 34 Parliament Square, London. They were photographers to the Queen, Prince of Wales, and ex-Royal Family of France, and had photographed Charles Dickens, Eliza Cook, John Everett Millais, and George Cruikshank.

[2] This may be a reference to a photograph by Parsons which Morris was scheduled to sit for in June. See letter no. 118a.

103 · To William Bell Scott
26, Queen Square,
Bloomsbury, London
Monday
February 15, 1870

My dear Scott[1]

I am delighted that you are so pleased with 'Gudrun' and thank you very much for telling me so: I began a translation of that part of Laxdaela wh: bears reference to my story, which however I soon discontinued, finding that it was not necessary for my work: it happens to be the part most close to my poem, Gudrun's dream viz. I will lend it you along with my Laxdaela wh: has a Latin Translation, for the rest you will find a tolerably accurate account of the story in the notes affixed to Mallets Northern Antiquities published by Bohn, written (I think) by a man named Black.[2] The saga itself is full of interesting incident, but has no pretensions to artistic unity, being indeed what it calls itself, a chronicle of the dwellers in Laxdale: it is disjointed even for that withal, and in some important places very bald, much more so than in any of the good translated sagas: with that too were coarsenesses both of manners and character that seemed alien to other parts of the characters therein, and wh: I thought I had a right to soften or disregard: All these things, to my mind, joining with the magnificent story made it the better subject for a poem as one could fairly say that that story had never been properly told — Gudrun I should say is much more the stock 'stirring woman' of the north than I thought fit to make her, and bears a certain resemblance to Itallgerd Longcoat the wife of Gunnar of Lithend, who by the way was Kiartan's half-aunt of course she lacks the thievish qualities of the latter, as not even Laxdaela puts down the stealing of the Coif to her I fancy. Olaf Peacock is a noble character in the saga and his sentiments after the slaying of Kiartan are just as I have represented them — I think I have warranty for Ingibiorg too as I certainly have for Hrefna (she was Grettir's cousin by the way) and Kiartan & Bolli I am sure are pretty much the men that were in the old story-tellers mind. The last line of my poem is nearly the last word of the saga "þeim var ek verst er ek unni mest"[3] and seemed to ⟨give⟩ throw a light on Gudruns character from the beginning: on the whole I sleep in peace as to the bogy of Ari the Learned (the great grandson of Gudrun by Thorgils her last husband) or of Thurid, Snorri the Godi's daughter and his aunt who probably told him this story as she did many others according to Snorri Sturluson. Excuse this jaw of mine about my own work —

The Völsunga Saga is in the press; I insert in the text some of the songs out of Edda; the prose writer of Völsunga had already stuck in some; but had left out the best of all, the 1st lay of Gudrun (her lamentation over Sigurd dead): it is a wonderful poem, entirely free from any affectation or quaintness, as simple and direct as the finest classical poems — I don't doubt you will be very pleased with the whole book. I will send the book and MS. by P.D.C. tomorrow; you needn't hurry to send them back.

Please give my kindest remembrances to Mrs. Scott[4] and Miss Boyd,[5] and

> Believe me
> Yours very truly
> W Morris.

MS: Princeton T.

[1] William Bell Scott (1811-1890), Pre-Raphaelite poet and painter, friend of Rossetti, and occasional designer for the firm (he designed the "Indian" pattern). He was also associated with the South Kensington Museum as a decorator. See his *Autobiographical Notes* edited by W. Minto (listed in Abbreviations under Scott).

[2] Paul Henri Mallet's *Northern Antiquities*, translated into English by Thomas Percy in 1770. A new edition was published by Bohn in 1847, revised throughout and considerably enlarged. The additions included a translation of *The Prose Edda* and notes by I. A. Blackwell and an abstract of the *Eyrbyggja Saga* by Sir Walter Scott.

[3] "I did the worst to him I loved the most," the last line of "The Lovers of Gudrun" (*CW*, 5, 395). It is the aged Gudrun's reply when her son asks her whom among the men she had known she had loved the best.

[4] Scott married Letitia Margery Norquoy in 1852. She died in London in 1898.

[5] Alice Boyd (1823-1897), a painter and an intimate friend of Scott. In mid-career he and his wife retired to Alice Boyd's ancestral home, Penkill Castle, Ayrshire, Scotland, and he spent the rest of his life there.

104 • RECIPIENT UNKNOWN

London
February 25, 1870

Dear Sir

With many thanks for the interest you take in my works I have much pleasure in signing myself

Yours faithfully
William Morris

MS: Yale B.

105 • TO DANTE GABRIEL ROSSETTI

26, Queen Square,
Bloomsbury, London,
Friday [March? 1870]

My dear Gabriel

In spite of J's note I shall be in tonight; so if you are coming out you might come our way, as I rather wanted to ask you about the best form of answering the Editor of the Academy who has written to ⟨you⟩ me.[1]

Yrs Ever
W Morris

There will be cold meat about if you want a snack.

MS: Texas.

[1] Apparently with a request that Morris review Rossetti's *Poems*. This had probably been arranged by Rossetti, who, in his anxiety over the reception of the book, had contrived to have as many reviews as possible placed in the hands of friends. Morris's appeared in *The Academy*, May 14, 1870. See letter no. 113, notes 2 and 3. (*The Academy* had been founded in 1869 as a monthly. In 1871 it was converted into a fortnightly, and in 1874, into a weekly review.)

106 • TO ROBERTS BROTHERS

Queen Sq:
Bloomsbury, London
March 5, 1870

Dear Sirs[1]

I beg to acknowledge with thanks for moneys remitted on account of my royalty on The Earthly Paradise: I have to thank you (as I thought

I had done before) for the little pamphlet of reviews and for a copy of your edition: by some mistake you sent Mr. Ellis another copy of Pt: 1 instead of the new book: thanks all the same —

I shall have much pleasure in sending you my portrait this spring: but hitherto I have avoided the nuisance of sitting, but shall have to undergo the operation as soon as the sun will think fit to shine upon London, wh: I suppose will be in a week or two.[2]

Again thanks for your letter, and Believe me

Yrs truly

William Morris

MS: Texas.

[1] Roberts Brothers of Boston, Massachusetts, who published Morris's works in the United States. They were supplied with advance sheets of *The Earthly Paradise*, and while issuing Part III, printed *The Lovers of Gudrun* as a small separate volume. At the end of it is a collection of "Tributes to William Morris," originally a pamphlet that Roberts Brothers had compiled from notices appearing in English and American periodicals soon after the publication of the first volume of *The Earthly Paradise*. See Buxton Forman, pp. 58-60.

[2] See letter no. 118a.

107 • TO JANE MORRIS
26, Queen Square,
Bloomsbury, London
Monday [March 14, 1870]

Dearest Janey

I am glad to hear from Bessy[1] that you are better, I hope (rather against hope) that you are not deadly dull.[2] I have been hard at work, but have not done much except the translations as they are rather pressing now, and I want to get all my Volsung work done this week: then I shall set to work about Gabriels review, wh: I must say rather terrifies me. I dined at Leyton on Saturday   Rendal[3] came to fetch me: he is gotten awfully fat: has taken a house at Acton (close to London) and is thinking of setting up a poultry farm there: wh: I think rather a good idea if he will stick to it, and is pretty lucky.

Henrietta has been eating eggs all the week (apropos of poultry)   she didn't seem to like them on Saturday, but made out with a nice big mince-pie — Ned was to have come to see me on Sunday at 6 oclock; I waited till ¼ to 10 and then went to North End to see him, and he came in presently having come to me about 5 minutes after I went out; he is not in condition, poor sad dog! I read him my stanzas for the Volsunga and he thought them good.

As for other news: our lamp is now fairly broken, and I must look about for a new one; I don't know what to get — I did hope to be able to give you the news of my hair being cut this morning, but I had to stay in fair copying for Strangeways.[4] I send you a Spectator with a review[5] not bad as things go — It's awfully cold here, but sunny, to my comfort, as I suppose it must be tolerably pleasant in the sun on the parade down there — I shall write to the littles in a day or two and try to find something pretty to send them: Why havn't the little rascals written to me? I hope you find the lodgings pretty comfortable — Bessy seems rather disposed to go down to you, I suppose you would find room for her there.

Please write soon and tell us how you are and if you want books or anything.

Your loving
WM.

MS: BL, Add. MSS. 45338. Published: Henderson, *Letters*, 33. Extract published: *CW*, 6, ix.

[1] Elizabeth Burden (b.1842), Jane Morris's youngest sister and a skilled professional needlewoman. For an account of her work for Morris and Co., see letter no. 617.

[2] In March 1870, Jane and the children went to Hastings in order to benefit from the sea air.

[3] One of Morris's brothers.

[4] Strangeways and Walden were printers to F. S. Ellis, publisher of *The Earthly Paradise*.

[5] *The Spectator* for March 1870, xliii (pp. 332-34) contained an unsigned favorable review of Part III of *The Earthly Paradise*. The review is reprinted in Faulkner, pp. 112-18.

108 • TO FORD MADOX BROWN

26, Queen Square,
Bloomsbury, London,
Friday [April 1 or 8, 1870?]

My dear Brown

I don't know *when* you asked me to dine as you forgot to put in the day. On the whole however I had rather come on some day when Swinburne ain't there if you don't mind; my cowardice urges me to this, as I tremble before him; also he is much more likely to behave prettily when I am not there therefore my absence would be a double blessing to the rest of the company.

Withal I am hard at work which however wouldn't make me deprive myself of the pleasure of coming to your house on other occasions.   excuse my poltroonery, I am bourgeois you know & therefore without the point of honour.

Yrs. affec:
W Morris

MS: Huntington.

Ford Madox Brown, 1852, drawn by Dante Gabriel Rossetti.

109 • To Francis Xaver Hueffer   Queen Square
                                                     Saturday [April 1870]
My dear Hüffer[1]
Will you dine with me next Friday at 7 to meet Scott[2] & Brown &
Jones[3] —

                         Yrs truly
                         W Morris

MS: Berg.

[1] Francis Xaver Hueffer (1845-1889). Born in Germany, he settled in 1869 in England, where he worked as a journalist and editor, becoming music critic for *The Times* in 1879 and editor of *Musical World* in 1886. At the dinner which Morris gave, Hueffer met Ford Madox Brown, whose daughter Catherine he eventually married. The novelist and critic, Ford Madox Ford (1873-1939), was their son.
[2] See letter no. 103, n. 1.
[3] Edward Burne-Jones.

110 • To Jane Morris   26, Queen Square,
                                                   Bloomsbury, London,
                                                   Good Friday
                                                   [April 15, 1870]

                                                   (at least Bessy seems to
                                                   have gone to Church)

Dearest Janey
    Many thanks for note: I was glad to hear from you;[1] I thought the
wine would be useful: I went to Holland Park[2] on Wednesday; and it
seems they had heard lately of Stillmans[3] affairs, and were rather full of
them; I went by invitation to see Aglaia's[4] house yesterday afternoon,
& saw both the ladies, who were still on the subject. I am going to sit
to Watts[5] this afternoon, though I have got a devil of a cold-in-the-
head, which don't make it very suitable. It will be so precious dull here
till after Monday: how I do hate Easter, second only to Christmas:
however I'm going to Leyton on Monday: I make no doubt I shall come
down to you Wednesday afternoon but will write again meantime. My
cold makes me stupid today so I will shut up —
                         Your loving
                         W Morris

MS: BL, Add. MSS. 45338. Published: Henderson, *Letters*, 34.

[1] In early April, Jane Morris went to stay at Scalands, the home of Barbara Leigh Smith Bodichon (1827-1891), near Robertsbridge, Sussex. Barbara Bodichon was one of the founders of Girton College, Cambridge, and was a prominent advocate of women's rights. In political and artistic circles, she was known for her hospitality both in London and at

Scalands. Rossetti was also at Scalands in April, and Jane Morris remained until his departure in early May. See *CW*, 6, ix and Doughty, pp. 426-38.

2 Presumably to see Alexander Ionides. On Ionides and Stillman, see W. H. Stillman, *The Autobiography of a Journalist*, 2 vols. (London: Grant Richards, 1901), II, 464, 484. See also next letter, n. 1.

3 William James Stillman (1828-1901), an American landscape-painter, diplomat, and journalist. He was American Consul in Rome (1862-1865) and Crete (1865-1868), and *The Times* (London) correspondent in the Balkans and Italy from 1875 to 1898. In 1869, he met Marie Spartali (1844-1927) who had studied painting under F. M. Brown, posed for Rossetti, and was, May Morris wrote (MM, I, 74), Jane Morris's "nearest friend." Stillman's first wife, Laura Mack, had committed suicide in 1869, while they were in Crete. In 1871, Stillman and Marie Spartali were married. See Stillman, II.

4 See letter no. 111, n. 1.

5 George Frederic Watts (1817-1904), whose portraits of his contemporaries often became the standard ones. His painting of Morris, completed in 1871, is in the National Portrait Gallery, London.

111 · TO AGLAIA IONIDES CORONIO 26, Queen Square,
Bloomsbury, London,
Monday, [April 25, 1870]

My dear Mrs. Coronio[1]

If you will be at home I will call on Tuesday, and bring you your worsted.

Ned says you want to know how to read Chaucer; I will bring a vol: in my pocket, and with your leave will induct you into the mystery, wh: is not very deep after all: many thanks for your kind note — I have done my review,[2] just this moment — ugh! —

Yrs very truly
W.M.

MS: Berger Coll. Published: Henderson, *Letters*, 34.

1 Aglaia Ionides Coronio (1834-1906) was born into a family of wealthy Greek merchants from Constantinople who had gone into business in London in the 1830's. The children of Alexander Constantine and Euterpe Sguta Ionides included Aglaia, Luke, Alexander, Chariclea, and Constantine, with all of whom Morris was acquainted through their patronage of Pre-Raphaelite art and their artistic connections. Constantine Ionides (1833-1900) amassed a notable collection of paintings, prints, and drawings (including several Ionides family portraits by George Frederic Watts), which he left to the South Kensington (later Victoria and Albert) Museum. Of Aglaia Coronio and her place in Morris's life, Mackail says merely that "the friendship between her and Morris was affectionate and unbroken through life" (I, 290), a statement that Morris's surviving letters to her more than bear out. She married Theodore Coronio (d.1903) in 1855 and they had two children, Calliope (b.1856) and John (b.1857), according to an Ionides family tree compiled by Lady Butterworth in the 1930's, now in the possession of the British Library (bound typescript).

2 His review of Rossetti's *Poems* for *The Academy*. See letters no. 105, n. 1, and no. 113, n. 2.

Aglaia Ionides Coronio, c. 1870, drawn by Dante Gabriel Rossetti.

112 · To Jane Morris   Tuesday [April 26, 1870]

Dearest Janey

Many thanks again for note;[1] I am so rejoiced that you keep well; I scarcely dared hope you would get so much better. On Sunday I did a good days work at the Venusberg[2] and sat up till 3½ last night writing it all out; I think I may finish this last part this week, but then I have to rewrite a good deal of the earlier part. I had a pleasant evening on Friday with Brown and Hüffer: Ellis came in later and quite distin-

guished himself in the way of talk. I have just parted from Gabriel (&
oysters) at Rules: he is pleased with his binding and so am I[3]   the book
seems selling well   250 copies. I should think Stillman's remarks showed
his genuine taste; I don't suppose him to be a delicate or discriminative
judge of female beauty. I have sent in my review; I read it to Brown
on Friday and he thought it good: the Editor has asked me to write a
notice on the Academy pictures this year, but I have refused, as there
wouldn't be ½ a dozen pictures that I speak of without using more
forcible words than people expect to see in print. I dont suppose the
Volsungs will be out till the end of next week. The block[4] is promised
me by Tuesday; I have pretty much outworn my impatience about it
by now; I am going to receive Aglaia's bland flatteries on my way to
Neds this afternoon. I do rather wish she wouldn't butter me so, if that
isn't ingrateful so you needn't chaff me as one who cant see the fun of
it; I shall certainly come down for day or two next week and fetch you
up when you are ready to be fetched — do you want any more wine?

I am with love
Your loving
WM.

MS: BL, Add. MSS. 45338. Published: Henderson, *Letters*, 35. Extract published: *CW*, 6,
x.

¹ Jane Morris was at Scalands. See letter no. 110, n. 1.

² "The Hill of Venus" is the concluding tale of Part IV of *The Earthly Paradise*, pub-
lished at the end of 1870.

³ G. A. Simcox, reviewing examples of the art of bookbinding at the International
Exhibition of 1874, wrote: " 'Exquisite' is just the word for the well-known binding of
Mr. Rossetti's Poems, which imitates brass fretwork with the most lovely sobriety. The
cover of 'The Volsungs and Niblungs' is lovely too, but decidedly florid and even effem-
inate." *The Portfolio*, 5 (1875), 74.

⁴ Probably a reference to the metal block used to make the cover design for *The Völ-
sunga Saga*. The block was designed by Philip Webb.

113 · TO WILLIAM MICHAEL ROSSETTI
London
May 9 [1870]

My dear Rossetti¹

I send the Volsung story with this; I think you must be interested in
it. I couldn't you see get it ready against this months Academy: perhaps
thats as well as it might [be] comic to see a review on Morris by Ros-
setti, and another on Rossetti by Morris² in one number. The reception
of Gabriels book is satisfactory so far isn't it: I suppose we shall have to
wait till we see what the enemies say of what the friends say.³

Yrs very truly
W Morris

MS: UBC, Angeli-Dennis Papers.

[1] See letter no. 18, n. 1.

[2] *Poems* by D. G. Rossetti, published by Ellis, appeared in the last days of April 1870. Morris's review was published in the May 14 issue of *The Academy*, pp. 199-200. Morris proclaimed the volume "complete and satisfactory from end to end." He praised "the magnificent collection of sonnets . . . which, though there are some among upwards of eighty that are not free from obscurity, the besetting vice of sonnets, are nevertheless unexampled in the English language since Shakespeare's for depth of thought, and skill and felicity of execution." To Ellis, D. G. Rossetti wrote (Doughty and Wahl, II, 874-75) on May 14, 1870, that "Morris's article is direct and complete—an honour and a profit to the book." Apparently William Rossetti never wrote a review (of *The Völsungs*). A review by G. A. Simcox appeared in the August 13, 1870 issue of *The Academy*, pp. 278-79, reprinted in Faulkner, pp. 152-56.

[3] Dante Gabriel Rossetti had attempted to arrange for friends to review his volume. (Doughty lists, p. 442, those whom he successfully solicited for the purpose.) But Rossetti was upset by other reviewers, and by critics of the favorable reviews by his friends. In a letter to Ellis, April 28, 1870, he wrote (Doughty and Wahl, II, 857) "I expect *Spectator* and *Saturday* to be nasty. . . . An old foe of mine will I know have his fling somewhere, and I think it will be in one of the two."

114 • TO SIDNEY COLVIN

London
May 9 [1870]

My dear Colvin[1]

Herewith is a copy of the Volsung Story, great part of wh: I'm sure you can't fail to find sympathetic. If you can do anything for it in the press I think it would be worth while;[2] for the public are shy of Icelandic books & can't tell what the book may be by the title merely; and I am sure you would think it a pity that so important a work as this really is, should ⟨be⟩ drop quite unnoticed by the press.

I congratulate you on your article on Rossetti,[3] and am glad to think his book has had something like a worthy reception.

I suppose an article on Austin's book was yours too;[4] I thought it very satisfactory and am glad to think he got a rap on the knuckles.

Yrs very truly
William Morris

MS: Bodleian.

[1] Sidney Colvin (1845-1927), art and literary critic. He was Slade Professor of Fine Art, Cambridge, 1873-1885; director of the Fitzwilliam Museum, 1876-1883; and Keeper, Department of Prints and Drawings, British Museum, 1883-1912.

[2] No evidence that Colvin did review *The Story of the Volsungs and Niblungs* has been found.

[3] Colvin reviewed D. G. Rossetti's *Poems* in the *Westminster Review* for July 1870. He had written about them previously in the *Pall Mall Gazette*, April 21, 1870.

[4] See letter no. 85, notes 2 and 3.

115 • THREE LETTERS TO CHARICLEA IONIDES

a.   Sunday [1870?]

My dear Miss Ionides[1]

I am sorry but I can't come as I am going out to dinner as it is: I am very busy but hope to see you soon; I thought of calling on your sister one afternoon this week. May I dine on Wednesday week?

                                    Yours very truly
                                    W Morris

P.S. O me! What fearful paper I've written on, but I cant help it for I have got none else: so pray forgive it.

MSS: Texas.

   [1] Aglaia Coronio's sister. See letter no. 111, n. 1; see also letter no. 122.

b.   26, Queen Square,
                                                         Bloomsbury, London
                                                         Tuesday [May 24, 1870?]

My dear Miss Ionides

I have put off my mother; though by the way I hope you don't think I have made a mere excuse — and expect great pleasure in coming to you tomorrow: with many thanks,

                              I am
                              Yours very truly
                              W Morris

c.   26, Queen Square,
                                                         Bloomsbury, London
                                                         May 25, 1870

My dear Miss Ionides

You did ask us to dine today, didn't you, or your sister? I hope I didn't dream it, because unless we hear from you to the contrary we (Janey & I) are coming

                              Yrs very truly
                              William Morris

116 • TO CHARICLEA IONIDES

26, Queen Square,
Bloomsbury, London,
Saturday Morning
[Spring 1870?]

My dear Miss Ionides

I am very sorry but I can't come today as my wife is not well (though better than she has been,) & it wouldnt be kind to leave her alone to-morrow: so I will come on Thursday, please; by the train that leaves Waterloo at 3.30.   again I am sorry I cant come today

Yours truly
W Morris

MS: McMinn Papers.

117 • TO JOHN WESTLAND MARSTON

26, Queen Square,
Bloomsbury, London,
May 25, 1870

Dear Dr. Marston[1]

I have promised to go and see a friend in the country on Saturday: my visit will reach into Sunday, but I hope to be able to get back in time to come to you in the evening; ⟨but⟩ though it must remain a little uncertain—

I am with many thanks
Yrs truly
William Morris

MS: Huntington.
[1] See letter no. 93, n. 2.

118 • TWO LETTERS TO CHARLES FAIRFAX MURRAY

a.

26, Queen Square,
Bloomsbury, London
Monday [June 13, 1870]

My dear Murray

I am going to sit to Parsons the photographer ⟨at⟩ on Tuesday (to-morrow)[1]   could you come with me, or meet me there   I should be there by 11 at the latest.

Yrs very truly
W Morris

[121]

MSS: Texas. Published: *CW*, 2, xxvi.

[1] May Morris included one of Parsons' photographs in Volume 2 of the *Collected Works*: "The portrait of my father in this volume is done from a rather battered print of a particularly happy photograph by Mr. Parsons, a curious being with 'views' which unfortunately moved him to destroy all negatives later. . . . Except for the early daguerreotype, taken at the age of twenty-three, it is the earliest photograph of him that I know." (*CW*, 2, xxiv-vi.)

b. [June 21, 1870]

My dear Murray

I will be with you tomorrow, ⟨W⟩ Tuesday about 11 A.M. to finish the sittings: will that do.[1]

Yrs ever
W Morris

[1] In 1870 Morris made for Georgiana Burne-Jones an illuminated manuscript collection of poems (all by Morris, except for two translations from the Icelandic) which he called *A Book of Verse*. On the title page is a portrait of Morris by Murray based on the Parsons photograph referred to above (*CW*, 2, xxiv-vi). On the last page of the book Morris gave an account of its making: it contains seventeen miniatures by Murray, a drawing by Burne-Jones, and ornaments by George Wardle; it was begun in February 1870, and completed August 26 the same year. See *CW*, 9, xxi-xxii and Fairbank, p. 64. Scolar Press has published a facsimile edition of this manuscript: *A Book of Verse* by William Morris, with introductory notes by Roy Strong and Joyce Irene Whalley (1980).

119 • To G. W. KIRBY 26, Queen Square,
Bloomsbury, London
June 21, 1870

Dear Sir[1]

I have forgotten the title of the book, wh: however was a little book of old French Carol music, edited by a Mr. Sedding[2] (now dead I think) and published by Novello where I should think you would get it.

Yrs faithfully
W Morris

Mr. GW Kirby Jr.

MS: PML.

[1] Possibly George Kirby (1845-1937). A lecturer on music and an arranger of concerts, he was also in 1879 to become Curator of the City Art Gallery and Museum, York.

[2] Edmund Sedding (1836-1868), architect and musician, composer of carols and other pieces. He and Morris met while they were both apprentices in G. E. Street's office. The book to which Morris refers, *Ancient Christmas Carols* (London, 1860) contains a translation by him of "Masters in the Hall." See Buxton Forman, p. 216, and also Lethaby, pp. 16, 17.

120 • THREE LETTERS TO CHARLES FAIRFAX MURRAY

a.

26, Queen Square,
Bloomsbury, London
Saturday [June 25, 1870]

My dear Murray

I should be so much obliged if you could get on with the little pictures,[1] for I have done *all* the ornament here, including that to a fresh 'hawthorne brake'.[2]

Yrs very truly
W Morris

PS If you bring anything for me & I am out leave it with Wardle[3] —

MSS: Texas.

[1] See letter no. 118b, n. 1.

[2] The decoration for "Love and Death," on pp. 119 and 120 of *A Book of Verse.*

[3] George Y. Wardle, who did the ornaments for the first ten pages of *A Book of Verse.* See letter no. 81, n. 2.

b.

26, Queen Square,
Bloomsbury, London
Tuesday [ca. June 1870]

My dear Murray

I have got the writing all ready for you, & have looked out the cartoons of seasons: but don't know anything about the Spring baring her breast; it must have been some other drawing, but would suit my verses very well, so Ill find it:[1] will you come over here soon & when, to talk about these other illuminations; I should be so glad to get them done this month if possible.

Yrs truly
W Morris

P.S. Please don't show the little pictures to anyone before they are done.

[1] The page of *A Book of Verse* containing "The Lapse of the Year" (p. 40), has paintings of the four seasons depicted as minstrels. The figures were drawn by Morris.

c.

[July-August, 1870]

My dear Murray

Obliged to go out, Please leave the Venus[1] with Wardle, and he will give you the photographs — do as you please about the title page —

Yrs
W Morris

[1] The miniature illustration for "Praise of Venus," the last poem in the illuminated *Book of Verse.*

121 • To Dante Gabriel Rossetti   [August 1870?][1]
                                        7 p. m.

My dear Gabriel

I have only first got your note & am expecting ⟨Mr⟩ Ned tonight so I can't come — also I have asked Webb to dine (early) on Sunday expecting Janey back — so its all unlucky — but I will come round to dinner on Saturday if ⟨you⟩ I may   & see Janey & settle anytime you will for the drawing —

                                        Yrs   W Morris

MS: Iowa State.

[1] During the summer of 1870, Rossetti was in London and completed five drawings of Jane Morris, four of which were in her possession when she died. (See Virginia Surtees, *The Paintings and Drawings of Dante Gabriel Rossetti (1828-1882): A Catologue Raisonné,* [Oxford: Clarendon Press, 1971], pp. 176-77.) Morris, in this letter may be offering to purchase one of the four with a view to presenting it to Jane, or referring to one of the drawings in pastel, pencil, or crayon that Rossetti made of Jane at intervals in 1868 and 1869. It seems likely that this letter was written after the intimacy between Jane Morris and Rossetti began, and before 1872, when Morris's feelings about Rossetti made it unlikely that he would have been invited to dinner by him or would have accepted if asked.

122 • To Chariclea Ionides   26, Queen Square,
                                        Bloomsbury, London
                                        Saturday [September 1870?]

Dear Chariclea

I have to meet my wife at Paddington at 9 oclock on Tuesday next: it seems quite rude to say I will come to dinner if I may run away in time for that, and I can only plead in excuse my wish to see you. Kindest remembrances to Danreuter[1]

                                        I am Yours very truly
                                        William Morris

MS: Texas.

[1] Chariclea Ionides married Edward Dannreuther (1844-1905) in 1871. Born in Germany and educated in the United States, he settled in London in 1863, becoming one of the most prominent musicians in England, as a pianist, conductor, and writer on music. A supporter of new music, he was especially known as a friend and champion of Wagner. His writings include *Wagner and the Reform of the Opera* (1872) and *Wagner: His Tendencies and Theories* (1873).

123 • TO CHARICLEA IONIDES   Queen Sq:
                                                   Wednesday Morning
                                                   [November 1870?]

Dear Miss Ionides

I have just picked up a fine specimen of a cold and sore-throat; and dursn't face the white frost this evening: will you please make excuses for me all round: I am very much vexed, but I really dursn't come, I get so much knocked up by my colds: my wife is bad too; in bed these three days with sciatica & lumbago so we ain't particularly cheerful down here!

                                        Yrs very truly
                                        W Morris

MS: Yates Coll. Published: Henderson, *Letters*, 36.

124 • TO FORD MADOX BROWN   Monday 14th
                                                   [November 14, 1870]

My dear Brown

This week I am awfully busy, (it is hardly too big a word) over trying to get my book out before Christmas.[1] By next week I shall be free; but, don't you think it might be better to wait for the Christmas balance-sheet & trade-account.[2] If not, any day next week will do for me —

                                        Yrs ever
                                        W Morris

MS: Huntington.

[1] *The Earthly Paradise*, Part IV. It was published in December 1870.
[2] Of Morris, Marshall, Faulkner and Co., in which Brown was a partner.

125 • TO HENRY BUXTON FORMAN   26 Queen Sq
                                                   Bloomsbury
                                                   [November-December 1870]

My dear Forman[1]

If you have nothing better to do, will you come on Monday evening to dinner: to meet Burne Jones, Brown, and the Publisher[2] — batchelor fashion, as my wife is out of town — so no togs — I shall then be able to thank you viva voce for the trouble, (and a precious troublesome job too) you have kindly taken over my book.[3]

[125]

By the way I have translated the Frithiof Saga[4] & think it lovely — Stephen's translation[5] is vile[?] and not always correct — I am reading another love-saga — very graceful & pretty too. Viglundar Saga.[6]

Yrs very truly

W Morris

MS: UMass.

[1] See letter no. 75, n. 1.

[2] Frederick S. Ellis.

[3] Forman annotated the manuscript of this letter on November 7, 1911: "This letter was written on my finishing the proof-reading of The Earthly Paradise. The dinner was a most interesting occasion. I sat next to Burne Jones & greatly enjoyed his conversation and [illegible] his personality."

[4] Translated in collaboration with Magnússon and published in *The Dark Blue Magazine* for March and April 1871.

[5] George Stephens (1813-1895) was Professor of North European Languages at the University of Copenhagen. His *Frithiof's Saga*, published in 1839, is a translation into English of Esaias Tegnér's Swedish version, the latter based on two Icelandic sagas: *Thorstein Vikingsson* and *Frithiof the Bold*.

[6] Morris translated this, with Magnússon, as "Viglund the Fair" and included it in *Three Northern Love Stories and Other Tales*.

126 • TO JANE MORRIS

Queen Sq:
Friday
[November 25, 1870]

Dearest Janey[1]

I am so glad to hear of your well-doing: many thanks for your note: my cold is nearly gone: I am still hard at work over the proofs; but 'twill soon all be done: I expect to get a copy or two by about the 3rd in wh: case you will have it down there; but I dont suppose the book will be published before the 10th[2] — the other vols: have been moving a bit these past days; and Colvin's article has appeared; which I send herewith:[3] I think it may be considered satisfactory.

The weather has got beautiful here when it don't rain; but it rains a good bit. I went yesterday to order myself some new clothes; but was so alarmed at the chance of turning up something between a gamekeeper and a methodist parson, that I brought away some patterns in my hand to show Webb; but havn't seen him yet. I heard the thunder on Tuesday night & was astonished by it — I feel rather lost at having done my book: I find now I liked working at it better than I thought — I must try and get something serious to do as soon as may be.

best love to all of them. tell Emmie I shall have a Christmas present

[126]

for her which I hope may tend in some degree toward counteracting a youth spent in — ah! — Have the kids written? Such a rumpus this morning May enjoying a good tease and Jenny expressing herself in boo hoo —

I am with best love
Your loving
William Morris

MS: BL, Add. MSS. 45338. Published: Henderson, *Letters*, 37; *CW*, 1, xi.

[1] Jane Morris was in Torquay with Morris's mother and sister Henrietta.

[2] *The Earthly Paradise*, Part IV.

[3] Sidney Colvin's review of Part IV of *The Earthly Paradise* appeared in *The Academy* for December 1870 and is reprinted in Faulkner, pp. 119-23. See also letter no. 114, n. 1.

127 • TO JANE MORRIS   Tuesday
                                                [November 29, 1870]

Dearest Janey

I am so glad to hear you are getting on; and have little to say to you except that. I don't suppose the book will be out much before you come home: I think by the way you had better stay as long as you can, if it is doing you good: for it may save you having to go away again shortly.

I confess I am dull now my book is done one doesn't know sometimes how much service a thing has done us till it is gone: however one has time yet; & perhaps something else of importance will turn up soon — Meantime, one great event has occured — the ordering of a suit of Clothes: Ellis took me to a place in the city: where I was gratified by the tailor complementing on my great works before he measured me.

I think, yes I think tomorrow I shall entrust the head wh: accomplished the E. P. to the scissors & comb of a hairdresser.

Tell me the day you are coming back on: I shall be so very glad to see you dear.

Best love: I am sorry I am so stupid & can say so little — love to the kins-women

Your loving
William Morris

MS: BL, Add. MSS. 45338. Published: Mackail, I, 210; *CW*, 6, xi.

128 · To Jane Morris
26, Queen Square,
Bloomsbury, London,
Saturday
[December 3? 1870][1]

Dearest Janey

It was a great relief to know that you are better; I daresay getting home to some thing more amusing than — well — I send a P.O.O. for £5 drawn by William Morris in favor of Jane do:[2] Will that do?

I shall be so glad of you dear, when you come home — Picture[3] is hung up again; perhaps it looks better, but I can't see much difference, one *can't* see it and never will be able in that room. meanwhile the room looks very little altered for the new papering. The paint looks queer and 'foxy.'

The book won't be out till Tuesday; so its no use sending one down to you — As to the coming back; if you will let me know in case they are not coming on Thursday next ⟨I will⟩ and you have made up your mind to come that day, I will come down on Tuesday night or Wednesday morning, and bring you up: for Im quite sure you oughn't to make the journey alone, poor little dear — As for living, dear, people like you speak about dont know either what life or death means, except for one or two supreme moments of their lives, when something pierces through the crust of dullness and ignorance, and they act for the time as if they were sensitive people —

For me I don't think people really want to die because of mental pain, that is if they are imaginative people; they want to live to see the play played out fairly — they have hopes that they are not conscious of —

Hillao! here's cheerful talk for you — I beg your pardon, dear, with all my heart.

I am going this afternoon to get a little sentiment out of Aglaia, in case she's in: she is making quite a fine thing of her bookbinding, by the way.

Its horribly cold here whatever it may be at Torquay: though it will seem that those sort of places are always hot when they ought to be cool, and cold when they ought to be warm —

Goodbye dear child, love to all Kinswomen —

Your most loving
William Morris

MS: BL, Add. MSS. 45338. Published: Henderson, *Letters*, 35-36. Extract published: *CW*, 6, xii.

[1] Henderson, *Letters* dates (p. 35) this letter 3 October 1870. However, Buxton Forman writes (p. 65) that the book was not "really ready much before December; but at all events it was out well before Christmas."

² Abbreviation for "ditto."

³ A portrait of Jane Morris, in oils, which Rossetti painted in 1868 and altered somewhat in 1870. The inscription at the top of the picture reads: "Jane Morris A.D. 1868. D.G. Rossetti pinxit. Conjuge clara poetâ, et praeclarissima vultu, Denique picturâ clara sit illa meâ." (Famous for her poet-husband, and famous for her face, may my picture add to her fame.) See *CW*, 6, xii, and also frontispiece, *CW*, 5.

129 • To Jane Morris
26, Queen Square,
Bloomsbury, London
Monday
December 5, 1870

Dearest Janey

I think you are wise to stay;¹ especially as the weather is very bad here: and, if my vanity doesn't decieve me, I think I might make it pleasanter for you by staying the week with you; I should rather enjoy it than not, & I have now nothing special to keep me in town. So I intend unless I hear from you to stop me to come down by the 11.45 train on Wednesday and then you wont be obliged to stay the whole week unless you like; we can go back together when you please —

Your offspring are highly indignant at your bold step of not coming back: specially Jenny — As to the picture I didn't say it wasn't improved it visibly is; but it is darker you know if anything, and the light on it of course is the same — in addition I don't think the frame suits it: it wants something more florid, a big dark-toned picture like that.

So, Wednesday it will be unless anything happens on either side — Goodbye my dear: how shall I like the bag-pipers over head?

Best love to all
Your loving
W Morris.

MS: BL, Add. MSS. 45338. Published: *CW*, 6, xii-xiii.

¹ In Torquay.

130 • To Louisa Macdonald Baldwin
26, Queen Square,
Bloomsbury, London
[1871?]

My dear Louie¹

I am so sorry that I can't, but I am going to dine at the Grange this evening: I will come of course on Saturday. My kindest regards to Baldwin

I am
Yours affectionately
William Morris

MS: Texas.

[1] Louisa Macdonald (1845-1925), a sister of Georgiana Burne-Jones, had married Alfred Baldwin (1841-1908), an ironmaster, in 1866. Their son Stanley became Prime Minister in 1923.

131 · FOUR LETTERS TO CHARLES FAIRFAX MURRAY

a.

26, Queen Square,
Bloomsbury, London
[1871]

My dear Murray
Please give bearer Frithiof [1] I am asked to read it tonight — You shall have it back tomorrow morning — Send it all —

Yrs   W Morris

MSS: Texas.

[1] Morris began his illuminated manuscript (on paper) of "The Story of Frithiof the Bold" in 1871. The text is complete, but not the decorations. Ornamental work was done by Murray and, after Morris's death, two other artists were entrusted by Murray with additions. They were Louise Lessore (1882-1956), known for her decorated pottery, in collaboration with her husband, Alfred Hoare Powell; and Graily Hewitt (1864-1952). Morris's translation of *Frithiof the Bold* was also published in *The Dark Blue Magazine* for March and April 1871.

b.

26, Queen Square,
Bloomsbury, London
Saturday [1871]

My dear Murray
All right: will you come a little before 10 (to breakfast between ½ past 8 & 9?) & settle the room.

Yrs ever
W Morris

c.

26, Queen Square,
Bloomsbury, London
[between Spring 1871
and October 1872?]

My dear Murray

All right that's jolly: I will come over to you tomorrow (Friday) morning and settle about the space & writing & so get to work on the vellum ready for you.[1]

Yrs. very truly
W. Morris

[1] The only work done on vellum with the participation of Murray during this period was *The Rubáiyát of Omar Khayyám* begun in the spring of 1871 and finished in October 1872.

d.

26, Queen Square,
Bloomsbury, London
Friday
[between Spring 1871
and October 1872?]

Dear Murray

I am back as you see: if you have nought better to do will you come over and dine at ½ past 1 and spend the afternoon with me. I have rewritten those 2 leaves so you could take them back with you. A post card would oblige

Yrs ever
W Morris

132 · TO EMMA FRANCES POYNTER

26, Queen Square,
Bloomsbury, London W.C.
January 18 [1871]

My dear Miss Pointer[1]

Hearing that you were so much interested in the northern stories, I thought you might like to read the sequel[2] of the little tale I read a part of at the Grange some months ago: the little poems in it are very beautiful in the original (though very hard to translate; and the whole tale I think very beautiful & full of delicate touches.

It is one of the most popular tales out there, and the tune (a sort of plaintive chant) to which the poems are sung has been traditionaly preserved. The story of course is mere fiction, and is late in Saga Literature; that is, it was probably written between 1360 & 1390.

My copy will be rather troublesome for you to read I'm afraid; also I blundered in writing it out and wrote on the backs of 2 or 3 ff. however they are all paged: the blunder comes just at the end. Will you let me know if you get it safe, please, as it is my only copy, and send it back to me when you have read it at your leisure.

I have another translation wh: I believe is to be printed in a periodical soon, the Frithiof's Saga;[3] also of the romantic class, & very complete & beautiful

> I am
> Yours faithfully
> W Morris

 MS: UBC, Colbeck Coll.

[1] Emma Frances ("Fanny") Poynter (1840-1929), a sister of the painter Edward J. Poynter (1843-1906). See letter no. 26, n. 3.

[2] Possibly "The Story of Viglund the Fair," which Morris included in *Three Northern Love Stories and Other Tales* (Ellis and White, 1875). See his description of "Viglund" in the Preface.

[3] See letter no. 131a, n. 1.

---

133 • TO EDITH MARION STORY
26, Queen Square,
Bloomsbury, London, W.C.
May 10, 1871

Dear Miss Story[1]

Very many thanks for the Vellum which I got safely about 3 days ago: it is just the same size as the other and quite as good in quality. I will take advantage of your kindness again and ask you to get me the other 50 if you can really do so without inconvenience to yourself.

I am going what to me is a long journey this year; you in the middle of all your works of art and the luxury of a beautiful climate will shudder at my choice I fancy: still one will always be ready to go to Italy while the possibility of driving oneself to *Iceland* may fail one: for I am really going there this summer:[2] there is no art there at all, and there is nothing to interest most people there but its strangeness and wildness; yet I have felt for long that I must go there and see the background of the stories for wh: I have so much sympathy & which must have had something to do with producing & fostering their strange imagination: also to such a cockney & stay-at-home as I am there is a certain amount of adventure about the journey itself which pleases me. We don't start till the beginning of July, but I have a good deal of preparation of one sort or another to do beforehand, which breaks up ones time: we shall be back about the end of August; I suppose by that time you will have got to England.

The little ones are better, thank you, but have not lost their cough yet: I think I shall have to find a little house out of London for them to live in mostly, as I am beginning to be nervous about London for them.

Please give my kindest remembrances to your father & Mother &

Believe me

Yours very truly

William Morris

MS: Berger Coll.

[1] Edith Marion Story (b. 1844), daughter of William Wetmore Story (1819-1895), the American sculptor and writer who lived most of his life in Rome. In 1876, Edith Story married the Marquis Simone Peruzzi di Medici and became the Marchessa Edith Peruzzi. Robert Browning, or Charles Eliot Norton—probably the latter—could have introduced Morris to Story and his family, and Morris was writing at this time, as the letter indicates, because he wanted help in obtaining vellum from Rome.

[2] This is the first reference in Morris's *Letters* to plans for the journey to Iceland, which took place in the summer of 1871, Morris leaving from Granton on July 8, and returning to England the second week of September. May Morris writes (*CW*, 8, xv) that there were four in the party: Morris, Magnússon, and Faulkner were joined by W. H. Evans (1836-1900), a recent acquaintance of Morris who had been planning a voyage to Iceland on his own account. Cormell Price, as his diaries indicate, was asked to join the trip when it was being planned, but was unable to go.

134 · FROM A LETTER TO CHARLES JAMES FAULKNER [May 17, 1871]

I have been looking about for a house for the wife and kids, and whither do you guess my eye is turned now? Kelmscott, a little village about two miles above Radcott Bridge — a heaven on earth; an old stone Elizabethan house like Water Eaton, and such a garden! close down on the river, a boat house and all things handy. I am going there again on Saturday with Rossetti and my wife: Rossetti because he thinks of sharing it with us if the thing looks likely.[1]

TEXT: Mackail, I, 225-26. Published: Henderson, *Letters*, 41.

[1] In the surviving letters, this is the first reference to Kelmscott Manor. Morris took the house in joint tenancy with Rossetti in June 1871. Rossetti gave up his share in July 1874; for Morris, Kelmscott was to be a country home and the place he loved best for the rest of his life. The house is near Lechlade, a Cotswold village on the upper Thames.

[133]

Jane Morris and one of her daughters, 1860's.

Kelmscott Manor.

135 • FROM A LETTER TO CHARLES JAMES FAULKNER   [May 1871]

Don't forget to practise riding. I began this morning. By Gum the
great we shall have plenty of it there according to our program.[1]

TEXT: Mackail, I, 241.

[1] The trip to Iceland in the summer of 1871. May Morris writes (*CW*, 8, xv) that
Faulkner "was not in good health and thought the careless open-air life would benefit
him; this partly, but he went chiefly out of sheer affection for my father, interested in,
though not sharing his absorbing passion for the things of the North. He suffered untold
miseries on . . . salt water, endured the long days in the saddle the best he might, and
. . . was several times on the verge of illness. . . . Yet with all this, and not living in the
magic dream that possessed his friend, he managed to keep going by sheer pluck and
enjoyed it. . . . He was store-keeper and paymaster to the expedition."

136 • To Eiríkr Magnússon   26, Queen Square,
Bloomsbury, London, W.C.
Tuesday [May-June, 1871]

My dear Magnússon

Please don't come on Wednesday as I must do a bit of work on that day which I hoped to do today & cant: also my work in the city may keep me a little later than usual on Friday so don't co[me till][1] 4 on that day [I shall] be sure to be home by then.

Please write & tell me any news that turns up about the ship.[2]

Yrs very truly
W Morris

MS: Iceland.

[1] The bracketed words are conjectured, as a corner of this manuscript is illegible.

[2] The *Diana*, on which Morris, Magnússon, Faulkner, and W. H. Evans traveled to Iceland.

137 • To Louisa Macdonald Baldwin   26, Queen Square,
Bloomsbury, London, W.C.
June 1, 1871

Dear Louie

Will you kindly accept this book of me; it is heavy to carry West-a-way but will be very good reading when you get it there: it was one of my treasures in those times your memory serves you so well in;[1] and I think I know it pretty well by heart for these many days. I like to think that I remember past time well: I would not willingly forget anything that has happened to me in my life either good or bad. — and, apropos, don't forget my cribbage lessons — goodbye till I see you again.

Yours affectionately
William Morris

MS: Texas.

[1] This may be a reference to an early shared enthusiasm for medieval romance. Three volumes of Froissart given by Morris to Louisa Macdonald are in existence: a two-volume edition of his *Chronicles*, edited by Thomas Johnes (London: Bohn, 1852), which is inscribed, "William Morris / Exeter Coll: Oxon. / to Louisa Macdonald. / April 3rd 1857"; and H. N. Humphrey's *Illuminated Illustrations of Froissart* (London: William Smith, 1844), on a preliminary leaf of which there is a drawing of a dragon and an undated inscription, "Louisa Macdonald / from her friend / William Morris."

138 • To Charles James Faulkner   26, Queen Square,
                                                    Bloomsbury, London, W.C.
                                                    June 12 [1871]

My dear Charley

A bloke[1] has proposed to join our company whom I have seen, and who seems a quiet well conducted chap & not stupid, and having no objection to him but being a stranger: on the other hand he has the advantage of being used to wild travel, and will go where I choose to carry him & pay his due share of expenses, including Magnússon which will of course reduce our costs considerably — If you have any objection will you say so; otherwise I have none.

I have bought a cork bed for your use, but couldn't buy your waterproof coat without your trying it: if you get one yourself it should be that stout india-rubber stuff not the light-coloured M[agnússon] & I both have hoods to ours. Don't forget to get your thigh-boots — and order your breeches if you are going in them, as I shall. Magnússon advises us to take saddles with us after all: I have borrowed one from my mother What will you do? I have seen a second-hand one in very good condition & well made (in the shop we are getting our boxes made) for £4.4 including the bridle, wh: seems cheap to me — Shall I buy it for you? You could sell it no doubt if you brought it back in good condition. A gun I have borrowed I think I told you. I need not warn you perhaps to take an over plus of money out, especially as I must say I have my doubts about Mr. Zoga[2] being able to cash our crossed cheque out there.

I shall sign the agreement for Kelmscott this week I fancy, so would you be kind enough to see about a boat for me and let me know, what can be had for what: you know what I want.

Please answer any questions in this letter, as time is getting on now.

                                                    Yrs ever
                                                    W Morris

MS: Walthamstow.

[1] W. H. Evans. See letter no. 133, n. 2.

[2] Geir Zoega, a guide at Reykjavík. In his Icelandic Journal (1871), Morris wrote that Zoega "was to buy our horses amongst others; he is a big fellow, red-headed, blue-eyed and long-chinned, like a Scotch gardener; he talks English well . . ." (*CW*, 8, 23). Morris's Icelandic Journals were first published in *CW*; they have been reissued as *Icelandic Journals by William Morris* with an Introduction by James Morris (Fontwell: Centaur Press, 1969; New York: Praeger, 1970), comprising "A Journal of Travel to Iceland, 1871" and "A Diary of Travel to Iceland, 1873," and retaining the pagination of *CW*.

139 · To Philip Bourke Marston   Queen Sq:
                                                      June 12 [1871]

Dear Sir[1]

I have just come home to find your vol: of poems awaiting me:[2] please accept my thanks for it, and believe in my sympathy for your aims & good wishes for your success.

> I am
> Dear Sir
> Yrs very truly
> William Morris

MS: LC.

[1] Philip Bourke Marston (1850–1887), poet, was the blind son of J. W. Marston.

[2] Morris had probably received his *Song Tide and Other Poems*, published in 1871. Five additional volumes of his work were published: *All in All* (1875), *Wind Voices* (1883), and three posthumously: *Garden Secrets* (1887); *For A Song's Sake* (1891), a collection of short stories; and a final book of poems, *A Last Harvest* (1891).

140 · To Eiríkr Magnússon   26, Queen Square,
                                                 Bloomsbury, London, W.C.
                                                 July 1, 1871

My dear Magnússon

I have very great pleasure ⟨to⟩ in writing as to what I know about you, and certainly we have had enough intercourse both in friendship & in literature for me to be able to speak with certainty about your qualifications.

I am sure that no better man than you could be got to fill a librarians post,[1] both from your natural gifts for books; your conscientious accuracy and capacity of research, and your extraordinary power and appetite for hard work; your scholarly qualities and passion for philology, and intimate knowledge of it, joined to these other qualities must always make you one of the most useful of men in a place of learning.

I heartily hope both for your sake and the books that you may be connected in this way with the University.

> I am
> Yours very truly
> William Morris

to Eirikr Magnússon Esq

MS: Iceland.

[1] Morris wrote this letter in support of Magnússon's candidacy for the position of Un-

der Librarian in the University Library, Cambridge. Magnússon was the successful candidate and held the post until 1910, continuing, at the same time, to lecture on Icelandic language and literature in Cambridge.

141 • To Jane Morris   Queen Sq.
                                          Thursday [July 6, 1871]
Many thanks, dear Janey for your kind letter: I am so glad all is going well & that you are so cheerful: as also I am, though considerably journey-proud — I have spoken to Wardle about the papers, so you have only to tell him the number of pieces for each room:[1] only don't paper new plaster: Webb thinks a new flue might be made to that room into the other chimney: but that may ⟨take⟩ ⟨be made⟩ wait a while: let Lane do the garret if his estimate is reasonable — also let him clear the old window in the dining-room (room with cellar) —

I asked Philip[2] about cray fish; he says there are plenty and he seems to know about catching them: make him get a basket for them & begin the fishery as soon as they come on.

I have written a ballad about that story we were talking of on Sunday: I will send it you if I can get it copied in time. I am delighted that Victuals won't fail you: truth to say I was a little nervous on this point — How beautiful the place looked last Monday: I grudged going away so; but I am very happy to think of you all happy there, and the children & you getting well — Ned Webb & Faulkner dined here yesterday and we were all jolly enough.

Yesterday morning I saw Evans off by boat for Edinborough; such a packing as Charley and I had the days before; 12 blessed packages, however all is well there: I have made all my adieux & am off by the 9.15 P.M. train we go 3rd class but the train is good & comfortable.

Now I will say good bye dear for the present with all blessings on you — Kiss the littles and give them my best love. I shall write a line from Edinborough.

Live well & happy
                                          Your affectionate
                                          William Morris

MS: BL, Add. MSS. 45338.

[1] For Kelmscott Manor. Since Morris was busy preparing for his trip to Iceland, Jane Morris, the Morris children, and Rossetti were the first to live in the house. See also CW, 8, xxv-xxvi.

[2] Philip Comely, the cottager who looked after Kelmscott Manor.

142 · To Emma Shelton Morris   Granton by Edinborough
July 8 [1871]

Dearest Mother

We went down here on Thursday evening and took up our quarters at an inn overlooking the pier, and with a beautiful view down the firth: we sighted the boat at about ½ past 11 this morning, and after watching her for some time made out that it must be ours, as indeed it turned out.

Magnússon & I have just been on board and taken our berths — queer little dens enough, but the boat is trim and clean, & the cabins comfortable for so small a vessel: she has been a gunboat and carries the Danish mail-flag and looks a good sea-boat; we sail about 8 oclock tonight and are like to have a quiet time of it as long as we are under the lee of the land: but we shall be tossed about a bit afterwards I fancy.

I will write from Reykjavik where I shall be about next Friday: the boat has 5 passengers from Copenhagen and about 14 get on board here: the Captain looks a civil quiet man, and the steward also   they don't seem to talk much except Danish. The weather is somewhat showery here but is better today: all seems like to go well with us. We shall be off the Orkneys tomorrow morning. So goodbye for the present: I hope you will get into the new house comfortably: will you be living there when I come back?[1] let us know when you write; my address is simply

Poste Restante
Reykjavik
Iceland

with a 4d stamp, and you must post it on the 12 August.

My best love to yourself and Henrietta & Emma if she is with you: my haste must excuse a longer letter:

I am
Your most affectionate Son
William Morris

MS: Walthamstow.

[1] About this time, Morris's mother moved to a house called "The Lordship" in Much Hadham, Hertfordshire.

143 · To Philip Speakman Webb   Granton by Edinborough
July 8 [1871]

Dear Chap

We have been housed in an inn here overlooking the firth & the pier; and C.J.F.[1] and I watched the boat in about noon today, and ⟨Mr⟩ Magnússon & I boarded her and took our berths; and so behold a miracle is coming on; for we sail at 8 pm today.

She is visibly enough an ex gunboat rigged this fashion and looks trim enough but nowise great: the weather has been bright & showery these two days & the wind offshore: all seems like to go well: I would write longer but here is a Babel English Icelandic & German, yea and Scotch too.

With one remark I close, that when I really want to cut my throat I shall go to Edinborough to do so; it will be an easy matter so to do: Good[b]ye and be well and happy.

Your affectionate
W.M.

MS: V&A.
¹ C. J. Faulkner.

144 • To Jane Morris   Reykjavík, Iceland
                                            July 16, 1871

Well, my dear, here I am safe & quite well: I have written to the littles too, because I thought it would be fun for them: all goes well and we start up country tomorrow with 20 horses, such jolly little fellows the poneys are; they almost look as if they would talk: we had a very good and swift voyage out on the whole: the first day it was very calm, and so was the next morning (we didn't sail till Sunday ⟨on⟩ at 6 am) but after we passed the Orkneys we got a very heavy sea for some hours, and I was sick though not very ill, C.J.F being pretty much prostrate; that was on Monday; on Tuesday morning about 7 we reached Thorshaven in the Faroes, and went ashore for 12 hours: we went a long walk over the hills on the most beautiful of days and it was so calm that evening that the captain was able to thread the labyrinth of the islands, and a most wonderful sight it was: I have seen nothing out of a dream so strange as our coming out of the last narrow sound into the Atlantic, and leaving the huge wall of rocks astern in the shadowless midnight twilight; nothing I have ever seen has impressed me so much: we saw no land all Wednesday wh: was a very cold bleak day, though the wind was fair; but on Thursday morning about 3 Mag[nússon] called me up to see Iceland: I think I told you we were to go to Bernfirth in the East first of all; and we were just at the entrance to it now; it is no use trying to describe it, but it was quite up to my utmost expectations as to strangeness: it is just like nothing else in the world: it was a wild morning too, very black out to sea, and very bright sun under a sort of black canopy over Iceland. We coasted all that day and had fine weather at first, as we passed by the stupendous mass of glaciers they call Vat-najokull ⟨that⟩ where ice-rivers seem to run fairly into the sea: we sailed by Oræfa Jokull too with fair weather; it is the highest mountain in Iceland: after that the clouds settled on the land & it began to rain and blow & the sea soon ran very high: but the wind was fair & the ship went very fast: about 9 P.M. we were opposite Njals country and the ⟨sky⟩ clouds lifted a corner there to show a watery copper & green sunset very splendid: then about 2 am on Friday we made the Westman Islands, & stopped there to give & take letters: they were some time coming off and we had a good view of that wild collection of rocks, in which there showed great caves, with little beaches to them, a rare matter in the rocky coast we had seen: it was a doleful sight rather to see the poor chaps going back again in their walnut shell of a boat with 3 letters wh: was all their post.

next morning we had a good knocking about before we reached Reykjavik but I had got my sea-legs by then, and didn't mind it much: we got to Reykjavik about 3 in the afternoon this day (Friday) and went ashore soon, and were taken by Mag[nússon] to the house of one of his kinsfolk and are quite comfortable a-night on the floor a very small clean room, and are abundantly fed: the town itself might be in Canada, and is quite commonplace, but all the houses seem clean — inside —

We three worked hard at repacking all yesterday — and Oh my dear — do you remember the parcel from the Cooperative Store that they ought to have taken out of our case, and didn't send in time to do it? Well many a speculation we had as to what it would be; whether good to eat drink or wear; and I for my part said: perhaps it will be Floriline[1] and hair brushes — excitement there was when we got to it — and — may I never be forgiven if it did not contain these articles.

1st 2 doz bottles of scents.

Item 2 doz do of *Floriline*

Item 1 large box of violet-powder.

There! there! there! here is a laugh to end with: we howled so over it that we nearly killed the landlady with curiosity to know what it was all about.

Please dear Janey be happy & don't forget the date of letter to me. The boat starts back for England Sept 1st so I hope to be at home about the 8th (in London I mean)   if you are still at Kelmscott I will come at once to see you —

Be happy, I am with all love

Your most affectionate
William Morris

MS: BL, Add. MSS. 45338. Published: *CW*, 8, xvi-xviii; Henderson, *Letters*, 42-43.
¹ A commercial breath freshener.

145 • To Louisa Macdonald Baldwin Reykjavik Iceland
July 16, 1871

My dear Louie

Don't be too much astounded at the postmark: I only write to you to ask if you would write to me by the next boat out here, as letters will be enjoyable when I come back here: you put a letter into your post on August 11th with a 4d. stamp on it, and addressed,

William Morris
Poste Restante
Reykjavik
Iceland

and strange to say the miracle is accomplished, and I am made glad.

Strange you would think it if you had been sailing along the coast of Iceland, as I have been, and seen the end of the world rising out of the sea; shore and hills like nothing else in the world I should think: moreover, when you came to Reykjavik, that any body should send anything there by post, except a stockfish or a lump of fat, would astound you again: yet I have been here now since Friday afternoon, and am getting used to it, as one does to everything else in the world: but tomorrow is the exciting day as we begin our up-country journey with the help of 20 horses and 2 guides: as to horses, or poneys rather, my impression is, that 3 colts are born at the birth of every Icelander to help him in his journey through life: they, the poneys, are capital little fellows and look quite sympathetic — As for the men (and women) but specially the men, they seem to like anything better than hard work; in fact if I don't malign them they seem to be the laziest set of ragamuffins that ever sunned themselves (in the) on a door-step: how I sympathise with them: especially today wh: is a bright as may be, and would be very hot but for the N. wind that blows from Greenland on us here. I wish I could write longer but I have 8 letters to write and only a limited time of privacy to do it in: I hope to see you when I come back and talk it all over: please give my kindest regards to Mr. Baldwin, & believe me

Yours affectionately
William Morris

MS: Texas.

146 • To Emma Shelton Morris
Reykjavik
July 16 [1871]

Dearest Mother

Just a few lines to say that I am here safe and well after a prosperous voyage, and that we set out tomorrow on our riding with 20 horses: we have got a room to sleep in here in the smallest of cottages, wh: is however clean and neat: it is bright and hot here today though the wind is N. and blowing over the sea: I am eager for the journey as this little town is not in itself interesting: the poneys promise well; they are fine little chaps.

We did not go straight to Reykjavik but first to Bernfirth in the east; we came there about 3 on Thursday morning, and sailed all day along the coast: it was a most wonderful sight, as we passed by the two biggest mountains in Iceland; they are ice clad at the top, and the glaciers seem to run right down their sides into the sea: there were about 24 passengers in all; rather a tight fit in such a little boat; but they were all very good tempered 10 were English besides our Icelandic friends: and strangely enough 2 were known to me in one [way or?][1] other: the Captain & mate are very nice gentlemanly fellows, they are officers in the Danish Navy, and talk English well. The boat starts for the homeward voyage ⟨about⟩ on Sept: 1st so I shall be in London from the 7th to the 10th I should say: all depending on the weather. Magnússon has introduced me to several people here: some of them very interesting. My fellow travellers are as good tempered and helpful as may be, and we have had many a laugh already: we stopped a whole day (12 hours) at the Faroes, and went a long walk over the mountains to a ruined church[2] there; it is a strange & beautiful place & we enjoyed ourselves hugely.

The summer here has been hitherto one of the best on record; I don't know about the looks of the weather now, but we must hope for the best; and are at all events well prepared for everything.

I am sorry to have to send such a shabby note but I have a good deal to do, and have not a great deal of privacy either. You would laugh so if you saw this queer little town & the cottage we sleep in: we are well fed up to now, and I am quite well.

Best love to you and Henrietta, tell her I saw such beautiful hill flowers in the Faroes. I hope all goes on well with the moving.

I am
Your most affectionate son
William Morris

MS: Walthamstow.
  [1] Illegible.

² In his Icelandic Journal (1871) Morris described Kirkiuboe (Kirby) as a little white-washed church, the nearest building to the sea, while close by under a basalt cliff was the ruin of a stone medieval church. See *CW*, 8, 15.

147 • TO JENNY AND MAY MORRIS   Reykjavik, Iceland
                                                     July 16, 1871

Dear little daughters

Isn't it funny that I am writing to you from Iceland. I got here safe & sound about 4 oclock on Friday afternoon; we had a good voyage, and I was not very sick: one day we saw porpoises a long way off and when they saw the ship they swam after it as fast as they could, jumping out of the water so that you could see them all: they soon came up with the ship and played about her   it made one laugh so, because they looked like oiled pigs: we first saw Iceland about 3 oclock on Thursday morning; that was at a place called Bernfirth; it looked very wonderful; for there was a huge mountain like this ⛰ with clouds all round it: we saw several whales that ⛰ morning: afterwards we sailed along the coast & saw great ice mountains with rivers of ice looking as if they were running into the sea: this is a funny little town with more poneys than men in it, and we are lodging in such a queer little cottage, but very clean: we have bought 20 poneys for our journey, and we shall begin our journey tomorrow if all goes well: it is a very bright beautiful day today and very warm.

I hope you are very good and are kind to Mama and that you are happy at Kelmscott: it is not much like Iceland I can tell you. I send you some wild thyme I plucked this morning in the fields close by here: there are many pretty flowers about, but no trees at all; not even a bush about here, but the mountains are very beautiful.

I send kisses & love, my littles, and goodbye: I am writing to Mama too:

I am
Your most affectionate Father
William Morris

MS: BL, Add. MSS. 45339. Published: *CW*, 8, xix; Henderson, *Letters*, 41-42.

148 • TO JANE MORRIS   Stykkisholm on Broadfirth
                                                 Iceland
                                                 August 11 [1871]

Dearest Janey

This is a little sort of town by the sea-side, a trading station and there is come into the haven a Danish Schooner from Isafjolde (Icefirth) that will sail for Liverpool in a day or two: he has kindly offered to take letters for us and as there seems a chance of this reaching you before I do, I write. I have little time however as we go early tomorrow morning; I am tremendous in health and in very ⟨fair⟩ good spirits, and enjoy the riding very much; the poneys are delightful little beasts, and their amble is the pleasantest possible means of travelling: every body has behaved charmingly; even I have not lost my temper often: C.J.F. (from the other side of the table) begs to state that he would have been better tempered had it not been that riding has not been as enjoyable to him as to me, & even a black sheep skin has not made his saddle as soft as by rule of 3 it ought to be. We shan't get through above ½ our stores I fancy, people have been so hospitable; there has been but little roughing it, and I find sleeping in a tent very comfortable work even when the weather is very cold: the weather has been cold, and rather broken till the last few days: last Tuesday week we had a very bad day, riding over the wilderness in the teeth of a tremendous storm of snow rain and wind; it was an 8 hours job but I was not a penny the worse for it next morning. You've no idea what a good stew I can make, or how well I can fry bacon under difficulties. I have seen many marvels and some terrible pieces of country; I slept in the homefield of Njals house,[1] and Gunnar's,[2] and at Herdholt: I have seen Bjarj, and Bathstead[3] and the place where Bolli[4] was killed, and am now ½ hours ride from Holyfell where Gudrun[5] died: I was there yesterday and from its door you see a great sea of terribly inky mountains tossing about: there has been a most wonderful sunset this evening that turned them golden though: the firth we look on here is full of little islands that breed innumerable eider ducks, and a firth we crossed yesterday was full of swans: give dear love to the little ones and tell them I am going to try to bring them my pretty grey poney home; but if I don't they must not be dissappointed for there may be difficulties or he may not turn out well: his name is Falcon, and when he is in good condition he ambles beautifully; Fast and deliciously soft; he is about 13 hands high.[6] I wish you could see us to understand how jolly it is when we have got a good piece of road, and the whole train of 28 horses is going a good round trot, the tin cups tinkling and the boxes rattling (my word how the shine is taken off them!) I must 'premise' however that I am dirtier than you might like to see me: my breeches are a triumph of blackness, but not my boots, by Jove! I may mention in passing that an Icelandic bog is not good riding, and that the loose stones on the edge of a lava-field is like my idea of a half ⟨bro⟩ ruined Paris barricade: that there are no lice in Iceland and that itch is unknown: but Evans deposeth that there are fleas galore — however they dont bite — me.

Goodbye, my dear, I have so often thought of the sweet fresh garden at Kelmscott and you and the little ones in it, and wished you happy — Please write to mother with my best love: I would have written but time presses strongly — goodbye with all love.

Your loving
William Morris

MS: BL, Add. MSS. 45338. Published: *CW*, 8, xxiii; Henderson, *Letters*, 43-45. Extract published: Mackail, I, 261.

[1] For Morris's description of Njal's country, see *CW*, 8, 20-21, 55-57.

[2] A central figure in *Njal's Saga*.

[3] In the *Laxdaela Saga*, Herdholt is the home of Olaf Peacock. Bathstead is the place where Gudrun is born and brought up.

[4] A central figure in the *Laxdaela Saga*. He marries Gudrun after he deceives her into believing that Kjartan, whom she loves, has abandoned her.

[5] The heroine of the *Laxdaela Saga*. The theme is a triangle: Gudrun marries her lover's best friend. After the death of both men, she becomes Iceland's first nun and anchoress. She dies at Helgafell (Holywell) at an advanced age.

[6] Morris did bring back an Icelandic pony, named Mouse rather than Falcon.

---

149 • TO EIRÍKR MAGNÚSSON

Kelmscott
Near Lechlade
Monday
[September 11, 1871]

My dear Magnússon

I hope you are making yourselves comfortable in my house: I shall be home on Wednesday or Thursday when I hope to see you: meantime I take this opportunity for thanking you heartily for your kindness to me on our tour; and to tell you, what I am sure you will be glad to know, that I find it has done me a great deal of good both mentally & bodily and increased my debt of gratitude to Iceland. This is a very beautiful place here and I enjoy it very much, though I feel the climate rather, and miss the mountains somewhat. Give my thanks & kind regards to Mrs. Magnússon[1] and believe to be

Yours very truly
William Morris

MS: Iceland.

[1] Sigriður Einarsdóttir Magnússon (1831-1915) was the daughter of Einar Saemundson and Guðrún Ólafsdóttir. Her father was a hatmaker, but her family may have been well-connected, as Jón Sigurðsson, eventually president of the Icelandic Parliament (see letter no. 187, n. 1), was one of the witnesses at her marriage to Eiríkr Magnússon on August 13, 1857. She organized an exhibition of Icelandic handcrafts for the International Health Exhibition held in London in November 1884, and a similar display for the World Ex-

hibition in Chicago in 1898. She started a school for girls in Reykjavík which opened in 1891. I am grateful to Richard L. Harris for this information.

150 • To Emma Shelton Morris
Kelmscott
Monday
[September 18, 1871]

Dearest Mother

I am back here safe & sound after getting to London last Saturday: We had a very successful trip, all things considered, and I am as well as a man can be: all is well here & the place looking beautiful. I am coming back to London on Wednesday: when shall I come to see you & where? this last question stopped my telegraphing my safe arrival to you. I won't say anything more about my tour till I see you, except that it has done me a world of good both mind & body

Best love to Henrietta and all at home (I don't know who they will be.)

Your most affectionate Son
William Morris

ms: Walthamstow.

151 • To Emma Morris Oldham
26, Queen Square,
Bloomsbury, London, W.C.
[1871]

My dear Emma[1]

I don't see Warringtons[2] name in the directory, indeed I believe he is dead — from a public point of view that is no great loss as he was a regular old ignoramus and humbug — I don't know any thing about the Munich glass except that it is the worst that can be bought for money and, I believe the dearest: so I can't take much trouble in trying to spread the use of it — I should recommend Mrs. Turbot to go to Clayton & Bell in Regent St.[3] whom I have no doubt she will find businesslike and expeditious, and they do very fair glass now since we have taught them how to colour.

Thanks for kind enquiries we had a very pleasant time in Iceland, a time never to be forgotten: and I came back with the complexion of a trading skipper and much thinner.

Wardle is away, and I have lots to do which will excuse me for not writing longer.

Love to Joseph.

Your most affec: Brother
William Morris

MS: Walthamstow.

¹ See letter no. 1, n. 1.

² William Warrington (1786-1869), an artist who worked in stained glass and who attempted to imitate the appearance of medieval windows by brushing on large amounts of shoe polish. See Sewter, I, 9.

³ Clayton and Bell were able to make a convincing imitation of medieval glass. See P. Thompson, p. 117. See also letter no. 24, n. 4.

152 • TO LOUISA MACDONALD BALDWIN

Queen Sq
September 21 [1871]

My dear Louie

Many thanks for your letter, and more still for the lost one you were so kind as to write to me in Iceland: I was sure you would write to me if you could, and indeed I was so convinced that you had, that I went twice after the 1st time to rummage the post-office but found nought: I have got my Icelandic friends to write again to Reykjavik to see if anything is there, but my own impression is the same as yours, namely that Iceland is the country blessed by the presence of your letter.

I think I should have plenty to tell you of my travels if I saw you, but I am the worst of letter writers   besides I made a sort of a journal which I intend writing out, perhaps may manage to do so to part of it in time to send Georgie while she is staying with you, and then you can read it if you care to, any how you shall see it when it is done if you like, though I believe it will be but a poor specimen of its class. Moreover I confess to a dread of setting to work on it: it is true that the journey was alltogether successful, and that I think I have gained in many ways by it: but it seems such a long way off now, and there is a bit of one's life gone; and the world so much the narrower to me because of it: and when I look over it I am afraid of having to grin sourly at this bit of enthusiasm, and be puzzled at that bit of high spirits; and note here how I refused to acknowledge a dissappointment, and there how I pretended not to be weary — and in short — all the rest of it; something in its way like looking at a drawful of old letters — If anybody ever did venture on such a bold act, which I doubt.

I rather miss the mountains I must say, which is not what I expected, for I use to consider myself a hater of them: today I had to go out on business to a place near Wimbledon, and there was what people called a pretty view there, and I thought how dull it looked, and that after all people were right to build villas and plant red geraniums about it: my own little old house by Lechlade though is sweet and innocent enough, and though it has a sadness about it which is not gloom but the melancholy born of beauty I suppose it is very stimulating to the imagination.

I am going down there on Saturday, where I expect to enjoy making the acquaintance again of the little pony that carried me in my 6 weeks ride, the bravest & best tempered of little bea[s]ts: you should have seen him picking his way in one of those dismal bogs, where if you sneeze, the earth, or rather the roots of the grass, trembles violently: they say however that the Icelandic poneys get lazy among the fat pastures and soft air of England — small blame to them — I however am at work in spite of the luxuries, and in spite of what was worse   that my appearance, without any chain of cause and effect, was the signal for my friends flying away at a tangent.

My kindest regards to Mr. Baldwin, and goodbye.

I am Yours affectionately
William Morris

MS: Texas. Extract published: Mackail, I, 273-74; Henderson, *Letters*, 45-46.

---

153 • To Louisa Macdonald Baldwin   26 Queen Sq.
September 30 [1871]

My dear Louie

What a many excuses for a little matter: bless me! If you only knew what I expect of my friends that I can⟨t⟩ get hold of in such a matter! Such close attention, such anxiety on their parts such sincerity withal — O the cross-questioning of them after a reading! only ask Georgie — however I will say for myself that so long as their 'precious values'[?] don't 'break my head' I bear even sincere criticisms well.

Please send the M.S.S. and take my thanks for your putting it in my power to be of any use to you, which I scarcely hoped to be:[1] I will try to be sincere, but you know it is not very easy to say what one thinks if a friend's work is *not* to ones mind; you after all are the best person to say whether the book ought to be printed; I know you are clever and thoughtful, and are not likely to be wrong about it: forgive this piece of personality and be sure that I shall be really pleased to have the M.S.S. Withal Georgie told me you were writing a story, and praised it to me: and I think she is a better critic than I am — don't tell her I said so though.

As to the publishers; I can show the work to Ellis (mine) and if it is not in his way to publish it, no doubt he can set the thing on foot for you: I should think however he would publish it, on some terms or another, though its like enough you may have to risk the expences, publishers being naturally of a cautious turn: he is out of town now (Ellis) but I will speak to him as soon as he comes back, wh: will be in about a week; by that time I shall have read at least some of the MSS. I suppose —

I am
Yrs affectionately
William Morris

MS: Texas.

¹ In 1865, Louisa Macdonald had published "A Ghost Story" in *Victoria Magazine*. In the autumn of 1871, she was at work on a novel. "When the book was complete," according to A. W. Baldwin, "Morris wrote a long and patient appreciation of it, showing her its many faults, so that she had to recast it" (see *The Macdonald Sisters*, p. 193). This may refer to *Martyr to Mammon*, her first novel to be published. However, it did not appear until 1886.

154 • TO CHARLES ELIOT NORTON

26 Queen Sq:
Bloomsbury London
October 19, 1871

My dear Norton

How very kind it was of you to write to me at Reykjavik: I was delighted that you should form one of the packet I looked over, trembling lest anybody should be dead after having heard no news for nearly 8 weeks: as for you; you must have thought I was either dead or had forgotten how to write. I can make no excuse for not having done so, and can only say that I had by no means forgotten you — Georgie would say I fancy that that was the reason why I hadn't, in order viz. that the prick of conscience might keep you always in my mind.

Am I to defend myself for going to Iceland instead of Italy? I can only say in these matters one must follow ones instincts & mine drove me there: you see the change of life was complete: we were 6 weeks in the saddle: on 24 nights I slept in a tent: I got quite knowing about horses: I acquired a competent knowledge of the useful art of *cookery* — under difficulties too, I can tell you — for I was master-cook to the company. — don't you remember our argument about servants, at the Grange one night, & how I thought them immoral? (the use of them, I mean) — well here we were without them: for though our guides Gisti and Eyrvidr were engaged to serve us by the day yet they worked no harder than we, except where their knowledge was special, and they paid us no sort of defference except that of good-fellowship, for they were very good-tempered agreable men — now wasn't that delightful? — Then the people: lazy, dreamy, without enterprise or hope: awfully poor, and used to all kinds of privations — and with all that, gentle, kind, intensely curious, full of their old lore, living in their stirring past you would say, among dreams of the 'Furor Norsmanorum' and so contented and merry that one was quite ashamed of ones grumbling life — wasn't there something delightful & new about that also? Truly it would all have been nothing but for the memory of the old story-tellers; nay I think without them the people would have long ago sunk into stolidity and brutality — yet as it was all was enjoyment — or nearly all — almost every day's ride was a pleasure: I never got used to weariness of that starting in the morning, especially if the road was good and the day fair; the rattle and clatter as the horses (we had 30 of them) were got together and fairly set off: the anticipation of the unknown quarters we were coming to at night: then as to the look of the country, there is at least nothing commonplace about it; ⟨the⟩ its influence on the old story-tellers is obvious enough: often indeed the blank, barreness of some historical place, and the feebleness of the life that has taken the place of the old tragedies would depress one for a while, till one remembered the lapse of years, and the courage and hope that had been there.

Rewards I had at times too; as the sunny afternoon, when we mounted from a valley of black sand into a narrow shady pass, and presently as I looked up from my poney's head as we came to the brow of the pass, there lay before me the great valley of the Thing-meads bounded by great hills intensely blue in the clear sunny air: or the strangest ride we had up a dreadful valley close to Lithend, where the noble Gunnar of the Njal's Saga lived & died, on a bright hot day, when we rode through a great plain of stones that the outrageously strange-shaped cliffs rose from: and crossing 9 streams of the terrible-looking Markfleet came to a birch-wood in a little valley and lay there for an hour in a place that looked the very end of the world — it is an indescribable and miraculous looking country — the hills almost always rise from quite flat plains: they are grey with moss-grown lava; or black with scorial sand;[1] or burnt red: or striped green with the pastures on their sides. You always know when you are coming to a stead, for you see, a bright green patch about it, which is its túni or homefield. Sometimes though we would ride all day in the wastes; nothing with grey & black lava and sand, dotted over with tufts of sea-pink and Campion, and the grey roots of dwarf willow: the distant hills dark inky purple on a dull day; or blue from indigo to ultramarine on a sunny one.

Here is a sketch of where we went in the island in case you have a map by you.[2] We started from Reykjavik and rode east first into the country of the Njal's Saga, thence we turned north about the feet of Hecla to the Geysirs: then N. still into the great wastes, sleeping a night close by the big lake of Eyne-water (Grettir) & so into Vatusdal. (Waterdale) (In gimnud the Old). Then S.W. through Willowdale to Midfirth and Biarg there, where Grettir[3] was born & buried: thence west still through Ramfirth into Laxdale, and Herdholt there, the scene of my poem; we stayed 3 days there, making excursions to Soelingsdale the home of Gudrun, and went S.W. thence to Holy-fell, where she died, and where Snorri the Priest[4] lived before her: this is also head quarters of the Eyrbiggia Saga.[5] Thence we went right out to the end of the promontory dominated by the great mountain of Surfells-Jokul: then E. (having turned the corner) with the sea always on our right till we came to Hitdale (Grettir again). Thence to Burgfirth and Whiteriver-side, the scene of many stories but most notably of Gunnlaug the Worm-tongue's love and troubles. Thence S. to Reykholt where Snorri the historian[6] lived and was slain: then S. to the wonderful Thing meads — and so S. again to Reykjavik, having been away 6 weeks to the minute. Then on board ship in 3 days and home — and so glad to be there — in 9 weeks in all —

There — it was worth doing and has been of great service to me: I was getting nervous & depressed and very much wanted a rest, and I don't think anything would have given me so complete a one — I came back extremely well and tough, and set to work at once on a new poem[7] (which has nothing whatever to do with Iceland) You will see it someday I hope with illustrations by Ned thereto — we are both very much excited about it. I have to thank you for kindly sending me the photograph of the beautiful picture of Lippi's — what a lovely work it must be. I hope I shall one day see Italy — next year perhaps — I think I can sympathise with that as well as Iceland —

Please give my kindest remembrances to Mrs. Norton and the rest of your party. My wife is on the whole in much better health than she has been: we have taken a little house deep in the country where she and the children are to spend some months every year, as they did this — a beautiful and strangely naif house, Elizabethan in appearance though ⟨not⟩ much later in date, as in that out of the way corner people built gothic till the beginning or middle of last century: it is on the S.W. extremity of Oxfordshire within a stone's throw of the baby Thames: in the most beautiful grey little hamlet called Kelmscott.

I hope, but don't expect that you will enjoy Berlin[8]—

I am
Yours affectionately
William Morris

[153]

MS: Harvard. Extract published: *Memorials*, II, 24; Henderson, *Letters*, 45.

¹ Cinder-like lava.

² For a map of West Iceland illustrating the journey, see *CW*, 8, 252-53.

³ See letter no. 76, n. 1.

⁴ Snorri the Priest figures in the *Laxdaela Saga*. A chieftain of Helgafell, he was a kinsman of Osvif Helgason and a great friend of Gudrun. He fostered Gudrun's son, Thord Cat and helped Gudrun after the killing of Bolli Thorleiksson.

⁵ Mackail wrote (I, 262-63) that Morris translated the *Eyrbyggja Saga* in April 1870, that it was his first translation of an Icelandic Saga, and that Morris made an illuminated manuscript of it. Buxton Forman, however, seems to date (p. 83) Morris's translation and manuscript of the saga in early 1874. Finally, Alfred Fairbank lists (pp. 65, 67) two illuminated manuscripts by Morris of this work, the first prepared in 1865 and the second, seemingly the one to which Mackail refers, in 1870.

⁶ Snorri Sturluson (1178-1241).

⁷ *Love is Enough or The Freeing of Pharamond: A Morality* was published by Ellis and White in 1873.

⁸ The Nortons, in Italy at this time, were about to leave for Germany. In Dresden, Mrs. Norton died in childbirth, and Norton abandoned Berlin as a goal.

155 • RECIPIENT UNKNOWN

[Kelmscott
Soon after Christmas 1871]

Bossom told me that the hard winter had killed a huge number of the moor-hens. He said that when the frost was on they would come down to the open water by his barge and drink a drop or two and then die, poor things.

TEXT: Mackail, I, 235.

156 • TO CORMELL PRICE

26, Queen Square,
Bloomsbury, London
Friday [1872]

My dear Crom

I start from Paddington Station by ½ past 9 train tomorrow, and shall be very glad to meet you there.

Yrs. affect:
W Morris

MS: Price Papers.

157 • TO FORD MADOX BROWN

Queen Sq
Wednesday
[February 9-17, 1872]

My dear Brown

Would you find it too early to go down to Kelmscott by the *early* train on Friday next, which starts from Paddington at 10 AM. I think it would be pleasanter and it would be more convenient to me: we should get to the house by about ½ past 1. Please write by return as to whether it will suit you, ⟨and⟩ as I have to order the fly. if you agree to come, I can pick you up on Friday morning in my cab on the way to the station.

I am
Yrs ever
W Morris

MS: Watkinson Coll.

158 • TO LOUISA MACDONALD BALDWIN

Manor House
Kelmscott, Lechlade
February 13 [1872]

My dear Louie[1]

I have to ask your pardon for not saying something about your tale[2] before, and indeed not saying more about it now than that I have read up the last packet but one of those you have sent Georgie: In excuse I can say nothing but that I have been something more than busy; for I have been in trouble with my own work,[3] which I couldn't make to march for a long time; but I think I have now brought it out of the maze of rewriting and despondency, though it is not exactly finished, and I hope soon to finish reading your tale completely — I won't say anything about it till then, for fear that I should miss the real point of it.

I have come down here for a fortnight to see spring begin; a sight I have seen little of for years, and am writing among the grey gables & rook haunted trees, with a sense of the place being almost too beautiful to work in: Couldn't you & Baldwin come & meet me here as the spring gets on, & meet Georgie: She & Ned I expect next Saturday for a day's pleasure (to me) — I am sure you would enjoy the place — I don't know how many tulips there won't be when they come into blossom.

I am
Yours affectionately
William Morris

MS: Texas. Extract published: Mackail, I, 280-81.

[1] Mackail quoted from this letter but did not name the recipient. Henderson (*Letters*, p. 46), taking his text from Mackail, suggested that Morris was writing to Georgiana Burne-Jones. The entire letter, clearly addressed to Louisa Baldwin, has recently become available.

[2] See letter no. 153, n. 1.
[3] *Love is Enough*, published at the beginning of 1873.

Philip, Edward, and Margaret Burne-Jones in the garden of The Grange, c. 1872.

159 • TO GEORGE JAMES HOWARD   Horrington House
                                                   Turnham Green
                                                   Sunday evening
                                                   [February 1872?][1]

My dear Howard

You promised to come & dine here some day this week: I am not engaged any day except Thursday, but am like to be all alone as I find Ned is engaged all this week: so perhaps you would rather come someday early next week. I shall be very glad to see you in either case especially as I am like to have a dull week of it by myself as my literary work seems to have gone wrong, I can't think why.

Please let me have a line as soon as possible.

I am

Yrs affect:ly

William Morris

MS: Howard Papers.

¹ This letter has been erroneously dated. A better conjecture for the year is 1873, but this conclusion was reached too late to alter the sequence of the letters.

160 • TO FORD MADOX BROWN   26, Queen Square,
                                       Bloomsbury, London, W.C.
                                       Tuesday [May? 1872]

My dear Brown

Wont you and Mrs. Brown come and dine, say next Monday at 7. its a long time since you eat my salt.

In re cartoons, 'tis all a mistake: the only work given out has been the usual mechanical enlargement &c. done (& very badly) by Wiegand¹ and the touching up of other enlargements of Ned Jones' cartoons by Murray: the said Ned refusing utterly to look at them: Murray has also performed the same office for the lazy blackguard named *me*, and I think did them very well: but no original work at all has been done since the days when cartoons went a-begging I will see that you have the money for this one² — Please come on Monday.

Yrs ever

William Morris

MS: Huntington.

¹ Sewter notes (I, 19) that a "certain Weigand" joined the staff of Morris and Co. in 1861 and that he assisted Rossetti in the decoration of a cabinet made by the firm for the architect J. P. Seddon.

² Possibly for "St. Philip the Deacon," a window designed by Brown in May 1872 for the Church of St. Michael and All Angels, Waterford, Herts. See Sewter, II, 194-95.

161 • TO FORD MADOX BROWN   Kelmscott
                                       Tuesday [May 14, 1872?]

My dear Brown

I got your note & this one of Wardle's this morning, and Im afraid one answers the other: but I don't suppose it can be a matter of more than a week or so, as we have plenty of money owing us, and I will send you a cheque on the very first opportunity. I enclose a cheque (that I may not forget it once more as I have done so often to my shame) for

£1.7.6 which I borrowed of Mrs Brown on that troublous Sunday evening.

I will do everything I can to get the other money. I shall be in town tomorrow for 2 days.

> I am
> Yrs ever
> William Morris

MS: Huntington.

162 • To The Royal Literary Fund[1]
26 Queen Square
Bloomsbury
[ca. May 15, 1872]

My Lords and Gentlemen

It is well known to me that Miss Jones[2] is compelled to make her present application to the royal literary fund through pressure of circumstances and continued ill health, and that any additional details she may give are certain to be a correct representation of her case.

> I have the honour to be
> My Lords & Gentlemen
> Your obedient servant
> William Morris

MS: RLF.

[1] The Royal Literary Fund was founded in 1790 to assist writers and their families in need. The *Report* for 1978-1979 (p. 4) notes that "applicants must have published work of approved literary merit . . . and thus clearly establish their literary standing. . . . Some . . . cases assisted . . . include Samuel Taylor Coleridge, Chateaubriand, Thomas Love Peacock, Leigh Hunt, Richard Jeffries, Joseph Conrad, D. H. Lawrence and James Joyce." Although several members of the Pre-Raphaelite Brotherhood contributed to the Fund, and Ruskin served on its Council, Morris seems not to have made a contribution. I am grateful to Nigel Cross, archivist of the Fund, for the information given here.

[2] Martha Jones (b.1815), a writer of children's books. She had received three previous grants, in 1861, 1863, and 1865.

163 • To Eiríkr Magnússon
26, Queen Square,
Bloomsbury, London
May 23, 1872

My dear Magnússon

Im afraid I can't help you with the port and sherry, for I have not bought any for years, and the Hungarian don't deal ⟨with⟩ in those wines: on the other hand I have sent you ½ doz each of claret and German wine out of my cellar if you will accept them: the claret is sound but nothing grand, but 'tis the only claret I have at present. The white wine is very good Moselle wine: I would have sent you some Burgundy but I seemed to remember that you didn't like that wine —

I hope you will smash Burton[1] when you do fall on him: he is one of the curses of our humbugging society now-a-days.

I am wanting badly to get on with some of the translations Heimskringla[2] for example, and shall to ask your help therein: I hope to see you soon [the rest of this letter is missing].

MS: Iceland.

[1] Sir Richard Francis Burton (1821-1890), the traveler and travel-writer. He went to Iceland in the summer of 1872 and on his return published disparaging articles about the country in the *Morning Standard* and the *Mining Journal*. Morris and Burton were to meet later that year. Cormell Price noted in his diary, November 11, 1872, that Burton was present when Morris, at The Grange, read part of *Love Is Enough*.

[2] This translation was not finished for some time—until 1895, in fact, when the translation, done in collaboration with Magnússon, was published as Volumes III-VI of the Saga Library. See Mackail, II, 309. The *Heimskringla*, by Snorri Sturluson (1178-1241) is a chronicle of Norse kings from mythical times to 1177. The title comes from the first words, *Kringla heimsins* ("The circle of the world" or "The round world").

164 • TO FORD MADOX BROWN 26 Queen Sq:
Friday morning.
[June 1872]

My dear Brown

Come by all means and talk to Janey: She will be glad to hear anything you have to say about Gabriel.[1] For my part I am quite ready to do anything to help you in your work there: I mean to say for instance if staying there for a few days seemed desirable or in any place Gabriel goes to hereafter —

I am
Yours Ever
William Morris

MS: Huntington.

[1] Depressed by continuing attacks on his poetry and suffering from delusions of persecution, Rossetti attempted suicide on June 2, 1872, by taking an overdose of chloral. For two days he lay in a coma in the house of Dr. Gordon Hake. He then went to stay with Ford Madox Brown. Jane Morris was at Kelmscott; on hearing the news, she hurried back to London to be with Rossetti. On June 20, he was taken to Scotland by Hake and

Brown. In this letter, Morris's reference to "your work there" is possibly to Brown's care of Rossetti soon after the suicide attempt. If so, a plausible date for the letter is June 7 or 14. For a discussion of this period, see William E. Fredeman, "Prelude to the Last Decade: Dante Gabriel Rossetti in the Summer of 1872," *Bulletin of the John Rylands Library*, 53 (Autumn 1970), 75-121; (Spring 1971), 272-328.

165 • To Edmund Henry Morgan
26, Queen Square,
Bloomsbury, London
June 4, 1872

Dear Sir

Without the sketch at hand I find it difficult to say what could be done with reference to the colour of the ⟨sp w⟩ special window shown:[1] but there will be a good deal of red in the big transept window,[2] and therefore there must be some in the side windows thereof: on the whole I intend to get the *colour* of the windows principally by rich blues in the draperies: and my impression of the sketches you have is that there ⟨was⟩ is more white glass in the figures than I intended to use: as to the band below the foliage, I had some doubts as to whether there was not somewhat too much of it: we generally don't bring it lower than the shoulders, and I think it was higher in this case: but if we still thought it necessary to keep the same proportions between figures & foliage, we might introduce flowers & fruit in the latter. Where the drawing of the figures admitted of it I should use in some places considerable masses of red: you may be sure that I shall not depart from the plan of colour I spoke of to you, which implies the whole glass together being deep and rich in tone; but this cannot be done without a good deal of greyish colour to harmonize the fuller parts: finally I deprecate detailed criticism on a small sketch, and the College must surely see that it is necessary to give me some latitude in such matters. However I don't think they will find themselves objecting to what I mean to do; nor do I think I ⟨op⟩ am in any way opposed to what I suppose they want.

I am
Dear Sir
Yrs truly
William Morris

Revd. E. H. Morgan

MS: Jesus College.

[1] Possibly the window in the nave of Jesus College Chapel, south side, westernmost, consisting of four lights, done in 1872. The designs include "Moses," "Samuel," "David," and "Solomon" for the lights, and four small subjects in panels below: "Moses and the

Burning Bush," "Samuel and Eli," "David and Goliath," and "Solomon Building the Temple." The sketch design is dated 18 May 1872. See Sewter, II, 42, and Robinson and Wildman, pp. 38-39.

    [2] The south transept south window, which portrays the angelic hierarchy. See Sewter, II, 42, and Robinson and Wildman, p. 40 and Plates 28-37. See letter no. 213 for later improvements made to this window; it was completed in 1873.

166 • To Emma Shelton Morris   26 Queen Sq.
                                                      June 11 [1872?]
Dearest Mother

    The meeting last Thursday passed off quite quietly with no opposition, so the whole matter is settled: about which you can tell Arthur this: 1st that the mine will be reconstituted as a limited liability company.

2nd that every share ⟨will⟩ which now bears a liability of £9 will be multiplied by ten, ⟨so that⟩ with a liability of £5 each: so that each one of the ⟨new⟩ old shares will now be liable to a call of £50, or rather £48 because of the £1 paid up on the old shares.

3rd But there is no chance of all this money being called for, about £30 000 being the estimated cost of the new workings; and of course we hope to make good discoveries along before that is spent.

4th the object for raising this additional sum is the deepening of certain parts of the old mines that give indications of the probable discovery of good quantities of tin; and prosecuting other parts of the set for copper, which we have been obliged to lease alone hithertoo from want of funds & the low price of metal.

5 The Duke of Bedford[1] lowers our dues by one third in consideration of our undertaking these discoveries. You should tell him also that the price of copper is high and like to remain so.

    This last sampling we sampled somewhat more ore and of a better quality though still low. I will hope to come down soon but I am very busy, & in addition one of my friends is very ill,[2] indeed we thought him dying on Sunday, though there is good hope for him today, and this is a worry to me, & partly made me forget to write to you on Thursday.

                        Best love to all
                        I am
                        Your most affectionate Son
                        William Morris

MS: Walthamstow.

¹ Francis Charles Hastings Russell, Duke of Bedford (1819-1891), who owned the land on which the Devon Great Consols mines were situated.

² A reference to Rossetti's attempted suicide. See letter no. 164, n. 1.

167 • To Louisa Macdonald Baldwin
Queen Sq.
June 22, 1872

Dear Louie

Herewith I send by ⟨po⟩ book post my abortive novel:¹ it is just a specimen of how not to do it, and there is no more to be said thereof: 'tis nothing but landscape and sentiment: which thing won't do: Since you wish to read it I am sorry 'tis such a rough copy, which roughness sufficiently indicates my impatience at having to deal with prose.

The separate parcel paged 1 to 6 was a desperate dash at the middle of the story to try to give it life when I felt it failing: it begins with the letter of the elder brother to the younger on getting *his* letter telling how he was going to bid for the girl in marriage. I found it in the envelope in which I had sent it to Georgie to see if she could give me any hope: she gave me none, and I have never looked at it since — So there's an end of my novel writing I fancy, unless the world turns top-sides under some day.

Health and merry days to you, and believe me to be
Your affectionate friend
William Morris

MS: Texas. Published: Mackail, I, 287-88; Henderson, *Letters*, 46-47.

¹ Mackail notes (I, 287) that Morris, "feeling about for new methods of literary expression, had begun a novel of contemporary life" at about this time. The story, which survives as an unfinished fragment, concerns the love of two brothers for the same woman. (A love triangle involving two men and a woman is a recurrent theme in Morris's prose and poetic narrative writing.) The manuscript was sent to Louisa Baldwin at her request. The novel has been edited by Penelope Fitzgerald and published in the *Dickens Studies Annual: Essays on Victorian Fiction*, Vol. 10 (N.Y.: AMS Press) and by Journeyman Press, London, 1982.

168 • To William Allingham
Queen Sq:
July 1 [1872]

Dear Allingham

I expect you on Wednesday then — and there will be a bed for you tomorrow (Tuesday), only as we dine early here; please say if you are coming to dinner that evening too, If you can put up with a chop and a glass of wine at 7 p.m. as that can then be the Missis's supper — there is not the least trouble in this therefore; or if you find it convenient to come in later, let me know & I will expect you at the hour you name —

As for Ned I refrain from soiling my pages with the due term for his insolence.

Yrs.
W Morris

MS: Illinois.

169 • TO SOFFÍA EINARSDÓTTIR SAEMUNDSON

26 Queen Sq.
July 12, 1872

My dear Miss Saemundson[1]

I enclose a cheque for £10, which please tell me if you have safely. Also excuse my asking you to ask Eiríkr to let me have it back at his earliest convenience, as I find such things hard to come by, am in fact very poor this year.

I hope you are none the worse for your sojourn in Iceland and that you left our friends all well there.

With kindest regards to yourself & Mrs. Magnússon[2]

Believe me

Yours truly
William Morris

MS: Iceland.

[1] Soffía Emilía Einarsdóttir Saemundson (1841-1902) was one of Mrs. Magnússon's sisters and lived with the Magnússons in England for six or seven years. She had gone to Iceland with Morris and the Magnússons in July 1871 and seems to have stayed for the winter. On September 3, 1873, in Reykjavík, she married Síra Sigurður Gunnarsson (1848-1936), a priest, and Morris was at the wedding. Gunnarsson was also Morris's guide in 1871, earning extra money while studying for the priesthood. I am grateful to Richard L. Harris for this information.

[2] See letter no. 149, n. 1.

170 • TO EIRÍKR MAGNÚSSON

26, Queen Square,
Bloomsbury, London, W.C.
October 4 [1872]

My dear Magnússon

A letter this morning with yours (for which many thanks) from Porter[1] pressing the Tuesday dining, which I should like to accept if I may stay with you over Wednesday, and get our reading done that evening: otherwise I have offered to lunch with him on Wednesday. I needn't trouble you to write to me about the matter, but perhaps you would be so good as to tell Porter, as I have referred him to you. I shall come at any rate by the train you speak of, and will bring the books, Heimskringla[2] & all. Thanks for the correction of vísur,[3] I wrote the other rather thinking it was wrong, and hoping you would correct me.

Excuse this scrawl I am very busy this morning knocking off work in order to make this expedition —

Yours ever
William Morris

MS: Iceland.

[1] The Rev. James Porter (1827-1900), Master of Peterhouse, Cambridge, from 1876 to his death. As a Fellow, he took an active interest in the restoration of the College Hall and Combination Room, an undertaking that the firm began in 1868 and completed in 1874. See Sewter, II, 44-46.

[2] See letter no. 163, n. 2.

[3] Stanza.

171 • To Aglaia Ionides Coronio   Queen Sq:
                                                     October 8, 1872

My dear Aglaia[1]

I wrote you a letter some three weeks ago, and enclosed it to your mother: so I suppose you will get it some time or other: I am sorry you have been disappointed of it since you are so kind as to set any store by my letters. In case you don't get it however, I will repeat the chief news about myself; which is that I am bringing out my "Love is Enough." next month, without the woodcuts, as there seemed no immediate chance of Ned going on with them:[2] it has been all in the printers hands some time now, and we shall publish at the end of November: I should hope that you will be back earlier than would make it any use to send you a copy out there.

Other news is little of me: I am working hard at the Icelandic translations, and am also doing things for the firm: On Sunday last I spent the afternoon at the Grange and Ned and I went a walk about Hammersmith to see if we could find any house to let thereabout, but saw little or nothing: Yesterday I was up there again, and we went in great excitement to look at a house in that row of houses in the high road just before you come to ⟨the⟩ North End: but it turned out alltogether too small and wretched: Ned was very much dissappointed.[3]

I dined afterwards at your Aunt's,[4] and thought Mary[5] looking very well. I have been backwards and forwards to Kelmscott a good deal this summer and autumn; but shall not go there so often now as Gabriel is come there, and talks of staying there permanently: of course he won't do that, but I suppose he will stay some time: he is quite well and seems very happy.

I ought to be able to write you a long letter, and should very much like to, but I never felt so dry and stupid in my life as this morning. My work is absorbing me very much now, though it is not of the most serious: tonight I am going down to Cambridge to spend a day reading Icelandic with Magnússon.

The weather has been lovely here this autumn, but doesn't seem to have suited me very well, I have been queer several times, and am not very brilliant today — As to my mental health — I have had ups and downs as you may very easily imagine: But on the whole I suppose I am getting less restless and worried, if at the same time less hopefull Still there is life in me yet I hope. I am sorry you seem to find Athens a dissappointment; but I can imagine how revolting the contrast must be between the modern smartness and the ancient glory: I suppose too there are little or no remains of any mediaeval buildings or few even of the earlier Byzantine time that history has to take a jump from the Acropolis to the Stock exchange.

There the printer has just brought the last of the proofs for me to revise   it will be but a little book, under 140 p.p.

I am so stupid I must even leave off here and hope to write again before long: Write soon and let us know how you are getting on.

Goodbye —

> I am
> Your affectionate
> William Morris

ms: Yates Coll. Published: Henderson, *Letters*, 47-48.

¹ See letter no. 111, n. 1.

² According to Mackail (I, 285-86), Morris designed and made woodcuts of page borders of *Love Is Enough*, and some copies were to have been illuminated. Burne-Jones was to have drawn illustrations for some of the scenes. On October 7, 1872, Rossetti, who had returned to Kelmscott, wrote to W. B. Scott: "Morris has set to work with a will on a sort of masque called 'Love is Enough' which he means to print as a moderate quarto, with woodcuts by Ned Jones and borders by himself, some of which he has done very beautifully" (Mackail, I, 280). The significance of the abandoned plan is noted by Cockerell, "A Short History" in Sparling (p. 139); he writes persuasively that it anticipated the revival by Morris of the decorative features of earliest printed books when he started the Kelmscott Press. See also Dunlap, pp. 45-48.

³ At Queen Square the workshops of the firm were expanding, and encroaching on the

living quarters of Morris and his family. By the end of the year, the family had moved into Horrington House on Turnham Green Road, where they lived for six years. See letter no. 183.

⁴ Euphrosyne Cassavetti, mother of Mary Zambaco, was a "formidable 'Duchess', the terror of younger relations though not of her daughter." See Fitzgerald, p. 113.

⁵ Mary Zambaco (see letter no. 82, n. 4). From 1867 to 1872, she and Burne-Jones were lovers. His tender, intimate pencil drawings of her during this period are almost unique in his work. See Harrison and Waters, pp. 96-99, and Fitzgerald, pp. 112-15, 124.

172 • To Eiríkr Magnússon   26, Queen Square,
                                                  Bloomsbury, London, W.C.
                                                  Friday [October 18, 1872]

My dear Magnússon

After all I *am* going down to Kelmscott on Saturday: my wife press-ing me, & I not having seen her for 3 weeks. I will come some day next week down to Cambridge if you will have me. Come one morning & go away the next. *dont tell Porter.*[1]

I hope you are better by now —

                                        I am
                                        Yours most truly
                                        William Morris

MS: Iceland.

[1] See letter no. 170, n. 1.

173 • To Aglaia Ionides Coronio   Queen Sq:
                                                        October 24, 1872

My dear Aglaia

I am so grieved to hear of your troubles though I hope by the time you get this they may be bettered: I don't wonder that you crave for more comforts: for 'tis a different thing (since you compare Iceland & Athens in this) to sit over a sick child with nothing particular to do, and to get up every morning for a ride in the fresh air, not caring where you are to be at night, and in short with no sort of responsibility or anxiety about you: I am quite distressed that you should be so worried: I was hoping by the tone of your first letter that you would be having a not uncomfortable time of it with pleasant memories for time to come. When are you coming back again? you know how much I miss you so there is no need of talking of that anymore.

I should have answered your last letter before; but I have had a fit of low-spirits — for no particular reason that I could tell — which is over now for the present I hope. I am and have been hard at work on the Icelandic translations principally but my book will be published in about a months time: I suppose you see that Tennyson is publishing another little lot of Arthurian Legend.[1] We all know pretty well what it will be; and I confess I dont look forward to it.

I went down to Kelmscott on Saturday last till Tuesday, and spent most of my time on the river: it ought to cool you in dusty Athens there to hear of my Sunday on the Thames: a bitter north East wind and pouring rain almost all day long: however I enjoyed it on the whole; and Monday was fine & warm, so the *days* went well enough: but Lord how dull the evenings were! with William Rossetti[2] also to help us. Janey was looking and feeling much better.

It was such a beautiful morning when I came away, with a faint blue sky and thin far away white clouds about it: the robins hopping and singing all about the garden. The fieldfares, which are a winter bird and come from Norway are chattering all about the berry trees now, and the starlings, as they have done for two months past, collect in great flocks about sunset, and make such a noise before they go off to roost. The place looks as beautiful as ever though somewhat melancholy in its flowerless autumn garden. I shall not be there much now I suppose.

We are looking after a house in the west of London still; but a tolerable one after my wishes seems hard to find.

I am going to stay for a day or two with Ned next week I fancy. I have had a hardish time of it here all alone with Bessy;[3] with whom I seldom exchange any word that is not necessary. What a wearing business it is to live with a person with whom you have nothing whatever to do!

I am afraid my letters are stupid: one needs the flint and steel of question and answer to exchange ideas to any purpose — and after all one has so much to say that unless by some special luck one wanders about without fixing on any real subject at all.

Goodbye and I hope to hear better news of you soon.

> I am
> Your affectionate
> William Morris

MS: Yates Coll. Published: Henderson, *Letters*, 48-49.

[1] *Gareth and Lynette.*

[2] See letter no. 18, n. 1.

[3] Elizabeth Burden, Jane Morris's sister, who lived with the Morrises. Privy to the whole story of Morris, Rossetti, and Jane Morris, she may have felt that it was her sister, not Morris, who deserved sympathy.

174 • To Eiríkr Magnússon
26, Queen Square,
Bloomsbury, London, W.C.
Wednesday
[October 30, 1872?]

My dear Magnússon

I shall be very glad to have a Sunday with you if can come up on Saturday: would you send me a line on Friday if you can come: if I dont see you then I will ask you to be so kind as to deal with a list of visur which I will send up to you. I haven't seen Burtons Gothamite letter as yet;[1] when your answer is in type I should like to see both together.

The weather is dreadful here & I have a bad cold which is getting better I hope.

I have ordered 6 smoked legs[?] for you to begin with. You havn't sent the measurements for your paper yet by the way.

With kind regards to all

I am
Yours most truly
William Morris

MS: Iceland.
    [1] See letter no. 163, n. 1.

175 • To Eiríkr Magnússon
Queen Sq:
Monday
[November 4, 1872?]

My dear Magnússon

I am so sorry to hear that you are unwell. I hope by the time you get this it will be only a matter of history.   if I don't see you before I will come to Cambridge some day next week   meantime I enclose a list of visur that I have been unable to tackle: the Hákonar Mál[1] I have left for viva voce help. The whole end of the Hakonar Saga[2] seems exceedingly good & heroic in tone, and I have enjoyed it very much.

I am sorry to say that the Australian people have no mutton hams at present; so that must be put off.

The papers will go this afternoon; I hope you will like them when they are up.

I don't know how to get hold of the back numbers of the Standard, but am curious to see what that humbug Burton[3] has to say about Iceland: what was its date of publication?

I may be going to Kelmscott on Saturday next; but I think not: if I

do not go, which I would let you know about Thursday, may I hope
to see you on Saturday afternoon.

I have waded now all through the prose of the Grayfell Saga[4] but
couldn't make much of the visur: but I leave these till I see you.

I took the last sheets of my book to Strangeways[5] for press today, I
suppose it will all be out by the end of the month.[6]

Wishing you better than well, and with kindest regards to the family

I remain
Yours most truly
William Morris

MS: Iceland.

[1] A tenth-century poem by Eyvindr Finnsson on the death of the Norwegian king
Hakon the Good.

[2] "Hakon's Saga," one of the tales in Snorri Sturluson's *Heimskringla*.

[3] See letter no. 163, n. 1.

[4] Another story in the *Heimskringla*.

[5] See letter no. 107, n. 4.

[6] *Love is Enough*. See letter no. 171, n. 2.

176 · TO EMMA SHELTON MORRIS   Queen Sq:
                                    November 7 [1872?]

Dearest Mother

Just a line to let you know I got your note. I hope you are comfort-
able at Brighton in spite of the bad weather, which however is bettering
here a little.

I was at the meeting last Friday: there is nothing new, but I can't
think things look very bad in spite of the bad sales we have had lately.[1]
My new book[2] will be out about the 20 of this month. I suppose Brigh-
ton is very full just at present.

Best love to Henrietta & I hope you will both of you enjoy your-
selves.

I am
Your most affectionate Son
William Morris

MS: Walthamstow.

[1] Probably a reference to Devon Great Consols, the mines in which Morris had inher-
ited shares from his father. Morris held a directorship in the company at this time.

[2] *Love is Enough*.

177 · TO ROSALIND FRANCIS HOWARD   Queen Sq:
                                              November 14 [1872?]

My dear Mrs. Howard[1]

Thursday would suit me best; if ½ past 2 were not too early for you, it would give one plenty of light, if the day were tolerable as to sun.

I shall be very glad indeed to do anything I can, and consider it a day to be looked forward to.

> I am
> Yrs faithfully
> W Morris

MS: Howard Papers.

[1] Rosalind Francis Howard, Countess of Carlisle (1845-1921), wife of George Howard whom she married in 1864. She was active in the women's suffrage and in the temperance movements, and, like her husband, she directed her sympathy and energies to Liberal Party issues. She supported Home Rule, and from 1891 to 1901 was president of the Women's Liberal Federation.

178 · TO CHARLES JAMES FAULKNER   26, Queen Square,
                                              Bloomsbury, London, W.C.
                                              November 18 [1872]

My dear Charley

If you are not dead and buried I wish to ask you a question, which will involve you in the trouble of writing a letter: to wit; — Ned is thinking about Marlborough for a school for Phil and wants to know what reputation the school has at present; of course one means principally what sort of chaps they send up to the Universities and how show in the class-list — could you tell me anything about it?[1]

A chap (an Icelander) who went over in The Diana with us called on Saturday, & brought me a letter from Jon of Siðarendakob with a present of the Sturlunga Saga. Magnússon I expect to see to-day: I intend beginning to draw up a scheme for next summers travel straightaway:[2] and when you come up next we will begin making preparations for that delight?

How goes it with that tongue?

> I am
> Yours ever
> W Morris

MS: Walthamstow.

[1] Faulkner at this time was a Fellow of University College, Oxford, and could be expected to know something about the graduates of public schools.

² The letter was from Jón Jónsson (1828-1908) or Jon Soðlasmiðus ("saddle-smith") as he was called, whom Morris met on the 1871 Iceland journey and who served as his principal guide on the second trip in 1873, alluded to here. Faulkner was Morris's only traveling companion on the later trip, though this letter seems to suggest that Magnússon at first intended to be one of the party.

179 • EMMA SHELTON MORRIS

26, Queen Square,
Bloomsbury, London, W.C.
November 23 [1872]

My dearest Mother

Herewith I send a copy of my book: there is a review in today's Athenaeum, which you will like to see.¹

Janey comes home today: the little Jenny has been in town for more than a week and is very sturdy and well.

I am sorry to hear from Bessy that you have not been well.

Next Thursday is the General meeting again. last Friday we had the new contract for arsenic, & got a very good price for it.²

The weather is warm here; but rather apt to be wet, I hope you are having a good time of it down there again. Love to Henrietta.

I am
Your most affec: Son
William Morris

MS: Walthamstow.

¹ A favorable unsigned review of *Love is Enough* appeared in *The Athenaeum* for November 23, 1872.

² A reference to the activities of Devon Great Consols.

180 • TO AGLAIA IONIDES CORONIO

Queen Square
November 25 [1872]

Dear Aglaia

Many thanks for your letter: I am very glad to hear that you are getting on better; though indeed I heard from Webb some little time ago that so it was.

Janey has just come back from Kelmscott last Saturday, and is very well apparently, and in good spirits certainly.

I suppose you will have heard before this reaches you all about Mary's illness and how very ill she has been;¹ though I hope it will all come right now. I did not see Ned for a fortnight, and Georgie scarcely more:

it was a dismal time for all of us; but as aforesaid I hope it is well over. I dined at the Grange last Saturday, and found Ned in good spirits: he himself has not been well at all quite apart from other matters.

I am going with Janey tomorrow to look at a house in Hammersmith in 'Theresa Terrace': it is Mason the painter's house, who died about a month ago.[2] We must, it seems, turn out of this house next spring for Wardle wants it all for the business. I confess I won't look with pleasure at the prospect of moving; one gets a bit used to a house, even when as with me one feels as if living in a furnished lodging. However I shall keep my old study with the little bedroom still.

When I said there was no ⟨reas⟩ cause for my feeling low, I meant that my friends had not changed at all ⟨in dem⟩ towards me in any way and that there had been no quarrelling: and indeed I am afraid it comes from some cowardice or unmanliness in me.[3] One thing wanting ought not to go for so much: nor indeed does it spoil my enjoyment of life always, as I have often told you: to have real friends and some sort of an aim in life is so much, that I ought still to think myself lucky: and often in my better moods I wonder what it is in me that throws me into such rage and despair at other times: I suspect, do you know, that some such moods would have come upon me at times even without this failure of mine. However that may be though I must confess that this autumn has been a specially dismal time with me: I have been a good deal in the house here — not alone, that would have been pretty well, — but alone with poor Bessy: I must say it is a shame, she is quite harmless and even good, and one ought not to be irritated with her — but O my God what I have suffered from finding always there at meals & the like! poor soul 'tis only because she is an accidental person with whom I have ⟨had⟩ nothing whatever to do: I am so glad to have Janey back again: her company is always pleasant and she is very kind & good to me — furthermore my intercourse with G[4] has been a good deal interrupted not from any coldness of hers, or violence[?] of mine; but from so many untoward nothings: then you have been away so that I have had nobody to talk to about things that bothered me: which I repeat I have felt more than I, in my ingratitude, expected to: another quite selfish business is that Rossetti has set himself down at Kelmscott as if he never meant to go away; and not only does that keep me away from that harbour of refuge, (because it is really a farce our meeting when we can help it) but also he has all sorts of ways so unsympathetic with the sweet simple old place, that I feel his presence there as a kind of a slur on it: this [is] very unreasonable though when one thinks why one took the place, and how this year it has really answered that purpose: nor do I think I should feel this about it if he had not been so unromantically discontented with it & the whole thing which made me very angry and dissappointed — There, dear Aglaia see how I am show-ing you my pettinesses! *please* dont encourage me in them; but you have always been so kind to me that they will come out. O how I long to keep the world from narrowing on me, and to look at things bigly and kindly!

I am going to try to get to Iceland next year, hard as it will be to drag myself away from two or three people in England: but I know there will be a kind of rest in it, let alone the help it will bring me from physical reasons: I know clearer now perhaps than then what a blessing & help last years journey was to me; or what horrors it saved me from. But if I cant go, I shall have a fortnight or so on the river as a pis aller.

My poem is out now: you have not answered me as to whether I shall send it you or not; nor have you told me when you are coming home but your aunt told me incidentally the other day that you wouldn't be back till February; which seems a long time to me. Please write again soon to me: there was rather a long space between your last two letters.

Forgive my rambling and most egotistical letter and

Believe me
Your affectionate
William Morris

P.S. Many thanks about the pots: I will leave it all to you: you have a pretty taste in such matters.

MS: Yates Coll. Published: Henderson, *Letters*, 49-51. Extract published: Mackail, I, 288.

[1] Mary Zambaco. See letter no. 171, n. 5. See also Fitzgerald, p. 147.

[2] George Heming Mason (1818-1872). The house the Morrises eventually took was not Mason's, but another nearby, on Turnham Green Road. See letter no. 183.

[3] This is the first acknowledgment by Morris, in his surviving letters, that his accept-ance of the relationship between Jane Morris and Rossetti might have been the result of something other than stoical realism.

[4] Georgiana Burne-Jones.

181 • TO FREDERICK STARTRIDGE ELLIS　　　　26, Queen Square,
　　　　　　　　　　　　　　　　　　　　　Bloomsbury, London
　　　　　　　　　　　　　　　　　　　　　[December? 1872]

Dear Ellis

Vellum to be ready ⟨Fri⟩ in a week[1] — I find it no use to try for any thing but what we saw before, white, thick, the same on both sides, copiously dressed; they have no idea of any thing else; so I thought I had better order it; price stiffish 2ˢ/9ᵈ per sheet & Strangeways wants

60 sheets, so countermand it if you think it too dreadful £2.15 a copy: but you can get God Almighty's own price for them I know: only I thought I would tell you at once.

Yrs very truly
William Morris

MS: Texas.

¹ Presumably a reference to the vellum purchased for the four copies of *Love is Enough* printed on vellum. The dating of this letter is based on Buxton Forman's statement that the regular edition was through the press in November 1872. It seems reasonable to assume that the four vellum copies of the book, as well as the twenty-five on Whatman handmade paper, were printed soon after. See Buxton Forman, pp. 79-81.

182 · EIGHT LETTERS TO CHARLES FAIRFAX MURRAY

a.

26, Queen Square,
Bloomsbury, London, W.C.
Wednesday
[December 1872?]

Dear Murray

Will you come and dine on Sunday at 1 oclock — I have had a reinforcement of 50 more leaves of vellum from Rome and we might begin Ellis' book at once if you will.

Yrs. ever   W Morris

MSS: Texas.

b.

26, Queen Square,
Bloomsbury, London W.C.
Saturday [December 1872?]

Dear Murray

Come & dine tomorrow, 1 oclock

Yrs W Morris

c.

[1872?]

My dear Murray

All right 11 oclock tomorrow Wednesday

Yrs. ever
W Morris

d.   Thursday [1872?]

Dear Murray

Could you dine with me tonight at 7 & we would settle about the Oxford journey.

                              Yrs   W Morris

e.   Friday [1872?]

My dear Murray

I am going down to Kelmscott tomorrow, Saturday but shall take Oxford on the way as I want to buy a boat there; so I propose to drive over to Kelmscott thence: if you like that trip meet me at the G. Westerrn R.[1] at 10 A.M. and I will be there.   if not come any day you like next week not later than Wednesday, as I have to be in London again on Friday morning.

                              Yrs truly
                              W. Morris

[1] Great Western Railway.

f.   Saturday [1872?]

My dear Murray

How goes it? I havn't heard from you and the 2nd week of the fortnight is begun: I shall come up to you on Tuesday morning I think

                              Yrs ever
                              W Morris

g.   Sunday [1872?]

My dear Murray

I shall be in town again on Monday night, and if you don't come to see me on Tuesday about 1 oclock, I will come over on Wednesday morning.

                              Yrs very truly
                              William Morris

h.   [1872?]

My dear Murray

I've got my cold so bad that I can't come this morning   will come on Tuesday: perhaps you will have something to show by then.

Yrs —
W. Morris

183 • To Aglaia Ionides Coronio   Queen Sq:
January 23 [1873]

My dear Aglaia

I must ask your pardon for not answering your last kind letter before: but the fact is I have been waiting for a cheerful time to come to me; for I have been very dull and bad company but as the cheerful time wont come I must e'en write uncheerful for fear you should put down my silence to unfriendliness, which I hope may be far from me: also don't be alarmed for any domestic tragedy; nothing has happened to tell of and my dullness comes all out of my own heart: and — in short I am ashamed of it and don't like talking of it. I haven't sent you a copy of my book because 1st I heard from your mother[1] that you had had one sent from elsewhere, and 2nd because I have kept a big-paper copy in which I will write your name as soon as I see you.[2]

And now for news, such as I have got — and this time I really have a little: for we have cleared out of Queen Sq. as far as our domesticity is concerned: I keep my study and little bedroom here, and I daresay, as time goes on shall live here a good deal: for the rest we have taken a little house on the Turnham Green road,[3] about 20 minutes walk from the Hammersmith Station; and otherwise easy to get at because of the omnibusses: it is a *very* little house with a pretty garden; and I think will suit Janey & the children: it is some ½ hours walk from the Grange which makes it quite a little way for me; on the other hand I can always see anyone I want at Queen Sq: quite safe from interruption: so in all ways it seems an advantage — does it not? Withal I never have had any sentiment of affection for this house, though so much has happened to me while I have lived here. I have always felt myself like [illegible] lodger here. Nevertheless there is something profoundly dismal about the empty rooms here that strikes a chill on one. By the way I forgot one most decided advantage about the change — to wit, that Bessy will no longer live with us: rejoice with me over that.[4] Now I will break off for today and see if tomorrow will bring me anything pleasanter to say.

[176]

Jan: 24th. Well I *am* in better spirits strange to say; nay in good spirits for the time being howsoever that comes about — by little matters not worth talking of. I am going to have the little ones home to Turnham Green today: 'tis a month since I have seen them. Jenny is 12 years old now: bless us how old I'm getting. Except the work for the Firm, in which I am rather busy, I am doing nothing now but translations:[5] I should be glad to have some poem on hand, but it's no use trying to force the thing; and though the translating lacks the hope and fear that makes writing original things so absorbing, yet at any rate it is amusing and in places even exciting.

I fancy the Iceland voyage will be necessity to me this year: sometimes I like the idea of it, and sometimes it fills me with dismay: but I think 'tis pretty certain to do me good if I come back safe from it.

I hope to hear in your next letter to me that you are coming back soon.

Goodbye.

> I am
> Your affectionate
> William Morris

MS: Yates Coll. Published: Henderson, *Letters*, 51-53. Extract published: Mackail, I, 289-90.

[1] Euterpe Sguta Ionides. See letter no. 111, n. 1.

[2] *Love is Enough.*

[3] Horrington House, situated on the main road between Turnham Green and Hammersmith. Jane Morris described it as "a very good sort of house for one person to live in, or perhaps two." See Henderson, *Life*, p. 137. They lived in this house for six years.

[4] See letters no. 173 and no. 180.

[5] Possibly for the *Heimskringla*. See letter no. 163, n. 2.

184 • To Aglaia Ionides Coronio   26 Queen Sq:
                                                        February 11, 1873

My dear Aglaia

You see our letters crossed, and I'm glad I wrote to excuse myself before I got your letter⟨s⟩ taking me to task. I am in much better condition now than I was when I wrote last: I suppose the change has done me good: we are quite settled in our new house, and I find it very pleasant: my own room is particularly cheerful & pretty, and I can work in it with a much better heart than in the dingy room at Queen Sq: I go most days to the Sq: though, and come back when I feel inclined, or not at all if I feel inclined: all this involves a good deal of walking, which no doubt is good for me: it seems quite a ridiculously little way to the Grange now after the long way it used to be. Last Sunday Ned came to breakfast with me, and we had a pleasant hour or two.

I am very hard at work at one thing or another; Firms work for one thing: I should very much like to make the business quite a success, and it can't be unless I work at it myself. I must say, though I don't call myself money-greedy, a smash in that side would be a terrible nuisance; I have so many serious troubles, pleasures, hopes & fears that I have not time on my hands to be ruined and get really poor: above all things it would destroy my freedom of work which is a dear delight to me.

My translations go on apace, but I am doing nothing original: it cant be helped though sometimes I begin to fear I am losing my invention. You know I very much wish not to fall off in imagination and enthusiasm as I grow older: there have been men who once upon a time have done things good or noteworthy who have got worse with time and outlived their power: I don't like that at all. On the other hand all great men that have not died young have done some of their best work when they were getting quite old — however it won't do to force oneself about it, and I certainly enjoy some of the work I do very much, and one of these days my 'Heimskringla'[1] will be an important work.

Iceland gapes for me still this summer: I grudge very much being away from the two or three people I care for so long as I must be, but if I can only get away in some sort of hope and heart I know it will be the making of me. I am very much dissappointed that you are not coming back before: I quite looked for you this month.

Yes truly letters are very unsatisfactory; they would do very well if one could write them at our best times; but continually one has to sit down to them dull and cold and worried, with the thoughts all slipping away from us, till the sheet is filled up with trivialities — as this will be I fear — only there is something about the look of the writing of anyone one is fond of that is familiar & dear and saves one from utter dissappointment, and one feels that the stiff awkward sentences all about nothing or little have still something of a soul in them — Think what an excitement that day was for me when I got letters after 8 weeks in the Iceland journey: lord! how my heart did go thump thump as I gallopped up to the post office at Reykjavik!

Yes I think of you a great deal, my dear friend: as I looked out of my window on Sunday, I pictured you coming into the little garden till I could almost see you ⟨coming⟩ standing there.

I wonder how you will feel at the changes in the house here: Janeys room has already got the workmans benches in it: the big room is bare and painty; there is hammering and sawing & running up and down stairs going on; and all looks strange, and as yet somewhat wretched. it doesn't touch me very much I must say though: for this long time past I have as it were carried my house on my back: but the little Turnham Green house is really a pleasure to me: — may all that be a good omen! Yet you must come and see me here too when you come home, if you wont be too much terrified at my house-keeper who is like a troll-wife in an Icelandic story: with a deep base voice, big and O *So* ugly!

We have had cold weather enough lately; snow and a dreadful East wind, all of which I dont care a penny about to say the truth.

I am going to dine at the Grange this evening: I dined there yesterday week and we had the pleasantest evening together that has taken place for this long while.

On Saturday I am going down to Cambridge to Magnússon, to do Icelandic: as stupid over the language as you others who are such quick linguists would think me, I am really getting on with it now: when I am down there, which has been once or twice, we all talk nothing but Icelandic together.

Well I had best make an end now before I get too dull. Once again forgive me for not writing to you oftener: I have really had a hard time of it: but I hope things have taken a long turn now, and that I shall be something worth as a companion when I see you again, which I look forward to very much indeed   write soon again please and tell me how you are.

Goodbye then with love & best wishes:

I am Your affectionate
William Morris

MS: Yates, Coll. Published: Mackail, I, 290-92; Henderson, *Letters*, 53-55. Extracts published: *CW*, 9, xv; 10, ix.

[1] This translation was begun in 1872 but not completed until 1895. See letter no. 163, n. 2.

185 • TO GEORGE JAMES HOWARD Queen Sq:
February 18 [1873]

My dear Howard

I have a letter this morning from an old college friend[1] of mine and Ned's, which I send on to you bodily to save long-winded explanations. I don't think I need make any excuses for asking you to do what you can in the case, if the living is not promised, as Dixon is really an interesting man; the most single-hearted of human beings, with strong literary tastes, and of some originality and a good deal of learning: also (if that matters) of liberal opinions: he was a great chum of ours at Oxford, was a schoolfellow of Neds: though he has drifted out of sight pretty nearly I still look on him with a great deal of affection, as I have no doubt Ned does also.

I repeat that he is the best of men, and far from being stupid — also, as you may see, he is unlucky[2] and I don't think you could fail to like him if you got to know him —

I am
Yours affec:
William Morris

MS: Howard Papers.

[1] Richard Watson Dixon (see letter no. 7, n. 6). On February 17, 1873, Dixon, who was at the time minor canon and honorary librarian of Carlisle Cathedral, had written to Morris to say that the vicarage of Lanercost, in the gift of the Earl of Carlisle, had become vacant and to ask for Morris's help in trying to obtain it. "It has struck me," he wrote, "that possibly you may know enough of the Howard Family to ask this for me." Manuscript in Howard Papers.

[2] In his letter, Dixon had written, "I have been nearly sixteen years in Holy Orders and have never received more than £150 a year." Although his suit was unsuccessful at this time, Dixon in the following year did make George Howard's acquaintance, possibly as a result of Morris's efforts in his behalf, for in a letter to Cormell Price, August 18, 1874, he wrote that he had seen Morris and Burne-Jones at Naworth. Less than a year later he was able to write, in a postscript to a letter to Rossetti: "I have just been presented to a small living not far from Naworth and shall be moving thither in a few months." This was the vicarage of Hayton, in Cumberland, which Dixon held until 1883. Manuscripts in Howard Papers.

186 · TO EIRÍKR MAGNÚSSON

26, Queen Square,
Bloomsbury, London
March 18, 1873

My dear Magnússon

I will do my best to get the money £70 together in about a week's time: if this seems a cold answer, I must ask you to understand that though I seem comfortably off I am always rather lacking of *cash*: my only important resource being what I can get from the Firm here, which has so many irons in the fire that its banker's book often looks very thin. I don't mention this to make your request burdensome to you for I think myself bound to help you in any way I can, and that it is natural and right for you to ask for what you want of me, as I should of you in like haps, but only to excuse myself in case I should not be able to get the money speedily: however I hope for the best.

I am going away for a fortnight in about 3 weeks time, and should like to see you before then, so I must come up to Cambridge if you don't come to London.

I have at last done all those visur (28 of them such a job!) and should like to finish off the eleven left in the Olaf's Saga.[1] Also how about our little 3 story book Gunnlaug & Co.[2]

Once more my dear fellow please to believe it is a great pleasure to me to do any thing in my power to pleasure you

And believe
Yrs affectionately
William Morris

MS: Iceland.

[1] "The Saga of Olaf Tryggvason," one of the longer tales in the *Heimskringla*.

[2] A reference to *Three Northern Love Stories and Other Tales*. Buxton Forman writes (pp. 82-83) that Morris had mentioned (in a letter returning George Stephens's *Frithiof*, which Buxton Forman had borrowed for him) that "Viglund the Fair" would be added to "Gunnlaug" and "Frithiof," together with three other tales, to satisfy Ellis's request for a larger volume.

187 • To Jón Sigurðsson
26 Queen Sq:
Bloomsbury, London
March 18, 1873

Dear Mr. Sigurdson[1]

I have to thank you for the books of the Icelandic Literary Society[2] and to enclose a cheque for £7 which Magnússon tells me is my debt to the Society. I am very glad to belong to the society and wish it all prosperity. I hope this summer to renew one of the great pleasures of my life by going to Iceland again, and it would add very much to my pleasure if I should meet you out there.

May I speak on a subject in which I am very much interested, the publication of the Tristram's Saga:[3] all my literary life I have been deeply moved by that Cycle of Romance, as indeed I ought to be, being myself Welsh of kin, and I am very anxious to see the earlier version of that great story written in the noble language of the classical Icelandic time: I do hope it will not be long before we have the edition, which I hear is preparing in Copenhagen.

With best wishes for yourself your kindred & your countrymen,

I remain
My dear Mr. Sigurdson
Yours very truly
William Morris

MS: Iceland.

¹ Jón Sigurðsson (1811-1879), Icelandic statesman and man of letters. In 1833, he entered the University of Copenhagen and devoted himself to the study of Icelandic history and literature, an interest that continued throughout his life. As a political leader, he struggled for Icelandic Home Rule, which was achieved in 1874. In his Icelandic Journal of 1871, Morris wrote: "I went with Magnússon to see some of his friends; the most noteworthy of them was Jón Sigurðsson, the President of the Althing, a literary man whose editions of sagas I know very well: he seemed a shy, kind, scholar-like man, and I talked (Icelandic) all I might to him." *CW*, 8, 26.

² The Icelandic Literary Society published books of literary and historic interest. Among them were *Biskupa Sögur*, issued in six parts between 1856-1878, edited by Sigurðsson with others, and *Diplomatarium Islandicum*, started in 1857 and completed in 1919.

³ Possibly *Saga af Tristram ok Isönd samt Möttuls Saga*, edited and translated by Gisli Brynjulfsson and published in 1878.

188 · Two Letters to Eiríkr Magnússon

a.
26, Queen Square,
Bloomsbury, London
Monday [Spring 1873?]

My dear Magnússon

All right: the bed will be ready & I shall be glad to see you: when we can talk about matters: As to the book 'twas as much my fault as yours for being in an over hurry.

Yrs very truly
William Morris

MSS: Iceland.

b.
26, Queen Square,
Bloomsbury, London
March 22, 1873

My dear Magnússon

I enclose a cheque for £70. Please let me know if you get it safely. I think it would save time at our meeting if you were to send up your M.S. at once. I am in a great hurry as I am going out.

Yours ever
William Morris

189 · To Jane Morris   Florence[1]
                                           Sunday [April 6, 1873]

Dearest Janey

We ended our long journey yesterday: it had been very fine all the way: for my own part I was not over-tired, though the night journey from Paris was sufficiently wearisome. All is well here, and Ned in great spirits. We went out this morning to the Duomo and S. Maria Novella: but it has clouded over now and is raining.

You will hardly expect me to tell you of all the marvels in the limits of a letter; besides I am *such* a bad hand at it: I suppose in some respects we have come into Italy by the worst road: nevertheless it is all full of wonder and delight: one gets a bit tired of the eternal mulberry trees between Turin & Bologna but the passing of the Apennines thence to Florence is a wonderful journey; especially where you come out of a tunnel and see from the edge of the mountains the plain of Florence lying below you, with the beautiful old town of Pistoija within its square walls at the mountain's feet: it was something also to remember coming down into the plain of Piedmont out of the Alps; on the most beautiful of all evenings, and going (still between snow-capped mountains) through a country like a garden: green grass & feathery poplars, and abundance of pink blossomed leafless peach & almond trees.

The Duomo here is certainly the most beautiful church in the world outside; and inside I suppose would be if it had not been made as bare as the palm of my hand. The cloisters of S. Maria Novella though ⟨are the⟩ is what I have seen most to my mind here. We went through a market this morning and that was the greatest game: the lemons and oranges for sale with the leaves still on them: miraculous frying going on, and all sorts of queer vegetables & cheeses to be sold.

tis Palm Sunday today[2] and the people are going about with branches of olive boughs to serve for palms. The monks of S. Maria Novella make scents: I must bring you home a bottle.   also I must, if cash holds out, buy a toy for the littles from the jewellers shops on the Ponte Vecchio: the shops are a good deal shut today; so I couldn't see much there.

I suppose I shall stay here till next Friday, so don't write here again but write to The Hotel Lille & Albion
                         Rue St. Honoré,
                              Paris.

Best love to you & the littles: don't tell them I think of bringing them home a toy though. I hope you are much better.

                         I am
                         Your loving
                         William Morris

MS: BL, Add. MSS. 45338. Published: Henderson, *Letters*, 55-56; *CW*, 10, xi.

[1] In April 1873, Morris visited Italy for the first time. The trip lasted for two weeks, with one week in Florence, a few days in Siena, and a day's trip to Prato and Pistoja. Mackail writes (I, 293) that "with a mind still so full of his first journey to Iceland and so excited at the prospect of a second, it is not surprising that his first visit to Italy" was anticlimactic "and gave him little satisfaction." Burne-Jones, who was his traveling companion, stayed on when Morris left. See *CW*, 10, x-xi.

[2] This letter was misdated by May Morris and by Henderson, who dated it April 9, 1873. Palm Sunday, 1873, was on April 6.

190 • TO EMMA SHELTON MORRIS   Florence
                                                    April 9, 1873

Dearest Mother

We got here all safe last Saturday about 6 oclock and are lodged at The Lione Bianco via nuova vigna, a comfortable small inn, not very ⟨used⟩ much frequented by tourists. You may imagine we were pretty well tired with our journey as we hadnt slept since the Tuesday night except for some 4 hours at Turin: the weather has been somewhat broken & showery, and by no means hot — just like it would be in England in fact.

This is a bad week to be at Florence   the altar pieces are all covered & some of the galleries too: however it doesn't much matter as there is a great deal more to see as it is than I can ever get through in the time: on Monday afternoon we drove up to Fiesole, a queer wild showery afternoon but it looked very fine all the same   Yesterday we went to S. Miniato and enjoyed it in spite of the barbarous so-called restoration of the Church and destruction of the walls: Mr. Jones remembers it before its glory was departed.[1] We had a long morning in S. Marco which interested me as much as you can imagine: I shall value the very good book of it you gave me all the more for having seen it. This morning I have been buying scents of S Maria Novella for Janey —

We had very fine weather for our journey and a great deal of it I enjoyed very much especially the passage through the mountains from Bologna to Pistoja, where you suddenly come out above the plain of Florence — a most marvellous & beautiful sight. If the weather is pretty good, I shall try to get out to Prato & Pistoja tomorrow & come back in the evening. I suppose I shall turn my face homeward on Friday or Saturday next, but am not sure whether I shall have heart to make for Turin after being in Florence: also I shall be all alone.

I have just come in from seeing S. Croce; which indeed I had stumbled on for a minute before   Inside I think it is the finest church in

Florence: they were singing the Miserere there, and sang well though not so grandly as they used to, a friend says whom we have met here.

Give my best love to Henrietta. I will write you a line when I am safe back.

I am
Your most affectionate Son
William Morris

MS: Walthamstow.

[1] Mackail writes (I, 293) that "Burne-Jones . . . found [Morris] a rather exacting companion, and a little determined to make the worst of things. The interior of the Duomo at Florence depressed him with its chilly bareness: San Miniato was unfortunately in the death-agonies of a thorough restoration. . . ."

191 • TO PHILIP SPEAKMAN WEBB

At the sign of the White Lion
In the Street of the New Vine
Florence
April 10 [1873]

My dear Chap

April showers in Florence — that's the weather since we came here, and cold enough it has been too till yesterday evening when it began to get warmer: it is a lovely morning just now after a very heavy shower.

I have been merchandizing for the firm here, rather to Ned's disgust I am afraid; but can't be helped: I have bought a lot of queer pots they use for hand warmers (scaldini)[1] of lead glazed wast[?]; also I have ordered a lot of flasks wickered of all sorts of pretty shapes: I suppose they will be in England in about 6 weeks. I bought some things for the firm in Paris also: so I hope my journey wont be quite unfruitful even if I don't find anything in Thun. I shall start back from here on Sunday morning and hope, doing the Swiss detour & all, to be back in London on Thursday, next, this day week.

I ought to say a great deal about works of art here, but I had rather wait till I see you and we can talk over it: I am not at all dissappointed with Italy; but a good deal with myself; I am happy enough, but as a pig is, and cannot bring my mind up to the proper pitch and tune for taking in these marvels; I can only hope that I shall remember them hereafter. I daren't whisper this to Ned who is horribly jealous of the least signs of depression in me here, thinking that Florence ought to make a sick man well, or a stupid one bright. I venture to think though that there is another side to it, which may at least make one sad; change and ruin, and recklessness & folly, and forgetfulness of 'great men &

our fathers that begat us'[2] — it is only in such places as this that one can see the signs of them to the full.

Well you remember my ways at Troyes, dont you? and they are scarce likely to be better in Florence: Ned already complains of me that I seem to pay more attention to an olive-tree or a pot than I do to a picture — mind you though, an olive-tree is worthy of a great deal of attention, and I understand more of pots than of pictures; and he is a painter professed, so it isn't quite fair.

This is a dull letter to come from Florence: though by the way Florence seems to me, not dull certainly, but melancholy enough — but I thought you might like to know that I was alive and well, as is Ned also.

This is a nice little Inn that we are quartered in, and 'tis a great comfort ⟨to⟩ not to form part of the furniture of a gigantic Yankee-hutch. Herewith an end for the present. if you would kindly write me a line before I come home, write to

> Hotel Lisle & Albion
> Rue St Honoré.
> Paris

and post not later than next Monday.

> I am
> Your affectionate
> WM.

MS: V&A. Published: MM, I, 649; Henderson, *Letters,* 56-57.

[1] A small earthern brazier in which a charcoal fire was lit, the heated pot then being used to warm hands or feet.

[2] Ecclesiasticus, chapter 24.

192 • THREE LETTERS TO CHARLES ELIOT NORTON

a.   Saturday [April 26, 1873]

My dear Norton

I have been trying all this week past to get round to you,[1] but have been about so from pillar to post that I have really not been able: will you be in on Monday evening, and will it be convenient for me to come then?   if so don't take the trouble to write & I will come: if not, please send a line to 26 Queen Sq: to stop me.

> Yours affectionately
> William Morris

Philip Speakman Webb, 1873, painted by Charles Fairfax Murray.

MS: Harvard.

¹ The Nortons had been traveling in Europe. Mrs. Norton died in childbirth in Germany in February 1872; Norton returned to London and lived at 33 Cleveland Square.

b.   Saturday (also)
                                                                                    [April 26, 1873]

My dear Norton

My long-legged daughter,¹ whom I met as I took the other note to the post, has now some hour afterwards given me your message: many thanks then I will come on Tuesday.

Yours affectionately
William Morris

MS: Harvard.

¹ Probably Jenny.

c.   26, Queen Square,
                                                                               Bloomsbury, London, W.C.
                                                                               Tuesday [April 29, 1873]

My dear Norton

Many thanks: I shall be very happy to come on Thursday: I hope you are all well, and am

Yrs affectionately
William Morris

MS: McGill.

193 · To Eiríkr Magnússon   26, Queen Square,
                                                                           Bloomsbury, London
                                                                           May 3, 1873

My dear Magnússon

I hope you are well and flourishing: can you send me the address of the firm that sail the Queen; because I thought I had better find out if they are going to send her this year & when. I want to see you and have talk but have been rather driven from pillar to post since I came back from Italy: I had a very jolly time there while it lasted.

I shall be very glad to see you up here if you can get away: next week my wife will be away: so we could give you rather more roomy quarters than we were able last time —

Please give my kindest remembrances to the Good-wife and believe
me

Yours ever most truly
William Morris

I am in a hurry today

MS: Iceland.

194 • TO CHARLES JAMES FAULKNER   Queen Sq
                                                              May 26 [1873]
My dear Charley
   A note in a hurry to say: first that I have just been to a sadlers who
makes for the army and seen some pack sadles he has made for a man
who is going to Iceland:[1] they cost £4 apiece, or somewhat less if we
leave out, as I think we may, the breechings & breast straps: I forget
what the "Klyfsöðidlar"[2] we used last time cost: nothing like this of
course; but these are really good   Webb approved highly of them: they
are properly stuffed and all: shall I order say 5 of them?   we could no
doubt sell them either in Iceland, or better still over here next year. For
the rest Magnusson is *not* coming, and I cant help thinking we could do
with 5 loads, ie 8 boxes and a load of bundles.
   2nd the News from Iceland is that the spring has been fine; that Zoega[3]
has got the money, but — that horses are dear, but he will do the best
for us. Also Mr. Buist who sailed the Queen last year will write to me
to tell me when he will send this year.
   All this in great haste but please write by *return* about the pack sad-
dles. Are you coming up to town next Saturday?
                                             Yrs Ever
                                             W Morris

MS: Bodleian.
   [1] Faulkner was Morris's only traveling companion on the second trip to Iceland, during
the summer of 1873. On board the *Diana*, the ship that took them on both occasions,
they met John Henry Middleton (1846-1896) already known to Faulkner. This was the
beginning of a close and lasting friendship between Morris and Middleton, who was Slade
Professor at Cambridge, the director of the Fitzwilliam Museum, and then of the
Victoria and Albert. As an expert on Eastern art, he was able to give Morris help at the
time of his weaving and dyeing experiments. See *CW*, 8, xxx. Middleton married Bella
Stillman, daughter of William James Stillman.
   [2] Packsaddle.
   [3] See letter no. 138, n. 2.

195 • To Eiríkr Magnússon
26, Queen Square,
Bloomsbury, London
May 27, 1873

My dear Magnússon

If there is time and you think it worthwhile will you be so good as to write to Geir Zoega as to horse matter to wit that we shall be only 2 masters, and 2 fyljðarmen,[1] with 5 burden(s)-horse(s)-loads which makes but 18 horses for our full complement: also that I shall want no more than one 'klyfberi'[2] at most (if that) as I am going to order 5 pack-saddles here. I saw Maudsley's & thought them good: they were £4 apiece; but the smith will make them without some elaborate breech-straps & breaststraps (which latter you thought worse than useless) for £3–3– I think if I once had them I would not sell them: they have good cruppers so I dont see but that we might do without the breechings: Webb who is something of a hestmaðr[3] saw them & agreed with me about them Don't write if you think it needless.

I hope to see you on Saturday and am in meantime
Yours most truly
William Morris

MS: Iceland.
[1] Literally, "king's attendants."
[2] Packsaddle.
[3] Groom.

196 • To Frederick James Furnivall [June 1873]

Dear Furnival[1]

I sign my name with much pleasure and wishes for your success,[2] & am
Yours truly
William Morris

MS: Huntington.

[1] Frederick James Furnivall (1825-1910), one of the founders of the London Working-men's College in 1854, and an energetic figure in the world of letters. He contributed to *A New English Dictionary* (the original title of *The Oxford English Dictionary*), established many literary societies, edited Chaucer's works from manuscript, and supervised the issue of facsimiles of Shakespeare's quartos.

[2] In 1873 Furnivall was an unsuccessful candidate for the post of Secretary to the Royal Academy. Among those who testified to his qualifications were Tennyson, Morris, Charles Kingsley, John Robert Seeley (1834-1895), and Hippolyte Taine (1828-1893).

197 • TO EIRÍKR MAGNÚSSON   Queen Sq:
                                                       June 16 [1873]

My dear Magnússon

I can hear no news of Buist's Iceland farer: do you know anything about her? Because I suppose the Diana is to be looked for ⟨back⟩ at Granton back from Iceland towards the end of this week, and we ought to be taking our places by her then I suppose   Will you write me a line by return, and if you have heard nothing, I will write to Buist myself and get the matter settled; as this continued uncertainty is rather wearing to me I must come down and see you soon, probably next Saturday; but as you may imagine I am thrust to & fro by work a good deal.

                                              I am
                                              Yours most truly
                                              William Morris

MS: Iceland.

198 • TO EIRÍKR MAGNÚSSON   26, Queen Square,
                                                 Bloomsbury, London, W.C.
                                                 July 19, 1873[1]

My dear Magnússon

After all I cant come this Saturday, nor can Jones, but I will make a definite engagement to come on Saturday the 28th instant, and hope to bring Jones with me but wont be sure. I would have come next Saturday only I find staying in my only chance of seeing some friends whom I otherwise should miss on this side the Iceland journey: of course I am reckoning that we shall have to put up with going by the July Diana. In fact I am writing to Turnbull & Sabesen by this post.

Miss Saemundson's barrels have come at last: you shall tell me when I shall send them on to Granton

With kindest regards to Mrs. Magnússon & Miss Saemundson, and looking forward to the merry meeting of the 28th June.

                                              I am
                                              Yours most truly
                                              William Morris

MS: Iceland.

[1] Morris dated this letter "July" 19, a slip of the pen for June.

199 • TO AMELIA ANN BLANFORD EDWARDS   26, Queen Square,
Bloomsbury, London, W.C.
July 24, 1873

Dear Madam[1]

You may do as you please in the matter you speak of in your letter of the 18th June.[2]

I am
Dear Madam
Yours faithfully
William Morris

MS: Somerville.

[1] Amelia Ann Blanford Edwards (1831-1892), novelist and Egyptologist. Contributor to *Chambers' Journal, Household Words*, and *All the Year Round*, she also served on the staff of the *Saturday Review* and *Morning Post*.

[2] Possibly a request for permission to include Morris's work in *A Poetry Book of Modern Poets*, an anthology of English and American poetry edited by Amelia Edwards and published in 1878. It contained Morris's "A Christmas Carol" and four stanzas from "The Lady of the Land." However, a five-year hiatus between this letter and the book's publication is unlikely. Though the letter seems clearly dated "1873," possibly this is a slip or a misreading and the correct date is 1878.

200 • TO JOHN WESTLAND MARSTON   Queen Sq
June 24 [1873]

Dear Dr. Marston

My wife & I thank you very much for remembering us and asking us to your daughter's wedding:[1] we both hoped to have been able to come, but my wife is too poorly, I am sorry to say, to get out at all, and I myself am going in a few days to Iceland and don't yet quite know when which gives me such a heap of fidgetty work to do that I cannot get away from the office: so I must ask you to forgive my seeming churlishness in refusing.

Pray give your daughter and son in law my best wishes & congratulations

and believe me
My dear Dr. Marston
Yours very truly
William Morris

MS: Scripps.

[1] The older of Marston's two daughters, Eleanor, married the poet Arthur William Edgar O'Shaughnessy (1844-1881), author of *Epic of Women*, 1870, *Lays of France*, 1872, and *Music and Moonlight*, 1874. O'Shaughnessy was also a herpetologist and assistant in

the zoological department of the British Museum beginning in 1863. Morris, in earlier days, had probably become acquainted with him through Rossetti who was a friend of O'Shaughnessy.

201 • TO ROSALIND FRANCIS HOWARD
26 Queen Square
Bloomsbury, London
Tuesday [July 1, 1873]

My dear Mrs. Howard[1]

May I come in to see you on Saturday morning next? It will be good-bye then, as I go on this day week;[2] and what time please should I come? I shall be engaged from 3 onward.

Yours most truly
William Morris

MS: Howard Papers.

[1] See letter no. 177, n. 1.

[2] Morris planned to sail on Wednesday the 9th, or possibly the 10th, so left home Tuesday the 8th in order to get to Granton, the port. However, the boat was delayed and did not sail until the 11th. See letter no. 203.

202 • TO AGLAIA IONIDES CORONIO
26, Queen Square,
Bloomsbury, London
Monday [July 7, 1873]

My dear Aglaia

It will not be much out of my way to call on you tomorrow morning (Tuesday) on my way into town: I should be with you about 10 o clock if I can manage it:

I am
Yrs affectionately
William Morris

P.S. I don't go till Wednesday.

MS: Berger Coll.

203 • TO EMMA SHELTON MORRIS
Thursday, Granton
[July 10, 1873]

Dearest Mother

I am still here & shall be till tomorrow about 2 p.m. the ship being

[193]

late: I am rather wearied with waiting but it cant be helped. Today has been fine but rather windy and it is a beautiful evening now — I have just been to take our berths: there is nothing changed aboard the ship, but the Captain is a stranger to me.

If you write to me you must send off the letter on the 16th of August addressed

> Poste Restante
> Reykjavik
> Iceland
> via Granton.

I hope all things will go better than well with you while I am away. Give my best love to Hennie & tell her I *did* post that letter.

We had a very comfortable journey down here on Tuesday; and I am very well.

There are 4 or 5 big ironclads lying off here now: queer ugly-looking things.

Good bye dear Mother & take care of yourself.

> I am
> Your most affectionate son
> William Morris

MS: Walthamstow.

204 • TO EIRÍKR MAGNÚSSON
Granton
Friday Morning
[July 11, 1873]

My dear Magnússon

Just a line according to promise to say that we are all comfortably waiting till 2 today when Diana is off: late rather isn't it. C.J.F & I have taken the same berths that we had last time. It is bright & cold this morning & to say sooth seems to me to look like wind — but I won't cry out till Im hurt: all the more as an old dame of 80 I'm sure is going to make to voyage: of whom no doubt your wife has told you. God send she be no witch over whose head we shall have to draw a bag[?] before we knock it off! Many thanks for the letters   I shall not fail to use them.[1] Goodbye now and flourishing days to you.

> I am
> Yours most truly
> William Morris

MS: Iceland.
[1] Possibly letters of introduction.

205 • To Philip Speakman Webb   Granton
                                                 Friday Morning
                                                 [July 11, 1873]
Dear old chap

Here still you see, on a cloudy cold morning threatening rain we are to sail about 2 p.m. for everybody connected with the Diana seems to be leisurely enough. I feel as if I had been away several months already, but I suppose that will wear off by then I get to Iceland.

The Scotch people I have seen seem to me to keep well up to their character: 3 very drunken tradesmen we saw on Wednesday going along arm in arm obviously congratulating themselves on being the cream of the human race, were types to rejoice the heart of a Taylor.[1]

I found Edinburgh though to have a strong flavour of Scott & his novels this time. I went into the high Church (sadly bebuggered as it has been) rather a mean church always I fancy, but smelling strongly of Davie Deans[2] & the rest.

The Diana is not changed since '71 except for her Captain, unless it be that her flag is gone very nearly black in the interval. C.J.F & I have taken the same berths as last time: Lord how strange I felt to be in the little cabin again! I feel grave enough & not much as if this were a pleasant trip, but hope to get something out of it all; and (though you may think that unreasonable) to come back again at last. Meantime take care of yourself & remember that I am

                                    Your most affectionate
                                    WM.

MS: V&A.

[1] Possibly Tom Taylor (1817–1880), dramatist and editor of *Punch*, 1874–1880. He was educated, in part, in Glasgow. He wrote a play about Scottish people, *Arkwright's Wife: An Original Domestic Drama* (1873).

[2] Sir Walter Scott and Charles Dickens were Morris's favorite novelists, and this reference to a character in *Heart of Midlothian* anticipates the allusions to Scott and Dickens characters that seem to help Morris in his letters to express what he sees or feels.

206 • To Philip Speakman Webb   Reykjavik
                                                 July 18 [1873]
Dear old chap

We are off in a great hurry tomorrow morning; have got 15 horses & shall pick up 5 more in the Fleet-Lithe country. You can easily imagine that I am pressed for time, & am not alone & so you can ⟨eas⟩ forgive a few lines the easier.

I am so distracted that I really cant find anything rational to say even if I had time to say it. Nothing is changed here. We even sighted Iceland on much such a morning as last time, cold & bright as might be — a prodigious & glorious sight. The season is cold though and Hekla is covered with new fallen snow while in '71 there was no sign of it there.

Such a N W gale as we came in by this morning! last night we fairly had to turn tail before it at the last headland, and lie to under the lea of the land till the gale lulled for an hour or two about sunrise

More when I meet you again, which will be as soon as I come back that is not earlier than the 12th September.

Ever Your affect:
W.M.

ms: V&A. Published: Henderson, *Letters*, 58.

207 • To Jane Morris Reykjavik
July 18 [1873]

Dearest Janey

Here I am safe after having seen some part of the wonders that those see who are fools enough to 'exercise their business in the great deep'. In fact I have been very sick as was no wonder for we have had several rough days, especially last night when we fairly had to turn tail from the last headland and lie to under the lea of the land till the gale lulled a little: however no bones are broken & I am quite well now & so is C.J.F.

We are off tomorrow morning to my great satisfaction, except that it keeps me from writing a long letter to you my dear, as I should like to have done. Im afraid we shall have a coldish season, there is much more snow on the mountains than in '71. However all seems like to go well otherwise.

It is all like a kind of a dream to me, and my real life seems set aside till it is over Kiss my dear little ones for me & tell them I positively have no time to write to them, as you would easily ⟨see⟩ know if you saw me now amid the boxes with CJF & another man in the room:[1] I will send a letter to them from Akroyri (in the North) if I find a ship going to Iceland [*sic*].

My dear how I wish I was back, & how wild & strange everything here is. I am so anxious for you too it was a grievous parting for us the other day.

And this shabby letter! but how can I help it, not knowing whether I am on my head or my heels.

With all love to to you & the dear good little ones.

> I am
> Your loving
> WM.

P.S. We start back from here on Sept. 5th so dont expect me before the 12th.

MS: BL, Add. MSS. 45448. Published: *CW*, 8, xxxi; Henderson, *Letters*, 57.

¹ Possibly John Henry Middleton. See letter no. 194, n. 1.

---

208 • TO EMMA SHELTON MORRIS   Reykjavik
                                                                July 18 [1873]

Dearest Mother

We got in here safely this morning about ½ past 11 after a rather tedious voyage in which I was rather sick: it blew very hard the night before and we had to lay to under the lee of the land for 6 hours before we could get round the last headland   I am very well; and we shall start, well provided with tomorrow morning: meantime I am so hurried with many things that they must excuse me to you for not writing more copiously to you.

With dearest love to yourself & Henrietta

> Believe me
> dear mother
> Your most affectionate Son
> William Morris

P.S. I expect to be back in London about the 12th of September.

MS: Walthamstow.

---

209 • TO AGLAIA IONIDES CORONIO   Horrington House
                                                            Turnham Green
                                                            Sunday
                                                            [September 14, 1873]

Dear Aglaia

I am back safe you see and am very well, and happy: I landed at Granton on Friday morning, and got home about ½ past 10 in the evening. I called at your house on Saturday afternoon, & was very much

[197]

disappointed to find you out of town. I went to the Grange on Saturday morning, and had as joyous a meeting as you may imagine. The journey was very successful, & has deepened ⟨my⟩ the impression I had of Iceland, & increased my love for it, though I don't suppose I shall ever see it again: nevertheless I was very full of longing to be back, and to say the truth was more unhappy on the voyage out and before I got into the saddle than I like to confess in my letters from Reykjavik, but the glorious simplicity of the terrible & tragic, but beautiful land with its well remembered stories of brave men, killed all querulous feeling in me, and have made all the dear faces of wife & children, and love, & friends dearer than ever to me: I hope I shall not miss your face from among them for long. ⟨I hope⟩ please write and tell me when I shall see you.

You wrote a very kind letter to me at Reykjavik: you won't want to be thanked for it I know, but you will like to hear that it answered ⟨the⟩ its kind purpose & made me happier — What a terrible thing it is to bear that moment before one gets ones letters after those weeks of absence & longing!

Do you know I feel as if a definite space of my life had passed away now I have seen Iceland for the last time: as I looked up at Charles' Wain tonight all my travel there seemed to come back on me, made solemn and elevated, in one moment, till my heart swelled with the wonder of it: surely I have gained a great deal and it was no idle whim that drew me there, but a true instinct for what I needed. So goodbye for the present, & let us see a great deal of each other these coming days, and believe me ever to be

Your affectionate
William Morris

MS: Yates Coll. Published: Henderson, *Letters*, 58–59. Extract published: Mackail, I, 295; Noyes, 112.

210 • TO LOUISA MACDONALD BALDWIN

Horrington House
Turnham Green
September 14 [1873]

Dear Louie

I came back safe & well last Friday, and I am sorry to say *without* the poney for your little lad: this was not laziness on my part but was because I found the price of ponies gone up so much since I was last there that they are quite as dear there (for what they are) as in England: I mean that a poney of any character, & by no means *first* rate will cost from £8 to £10 there, and as it would cost £8 or so more to get it to Wilden the money say £17 seemed enough to buy a better beast than I could be ⟨sure⟩ reasonably sure of bringing you: add to this that they will probably be cheaper there next year, and that a letter from me to one or other of my friends there would be enough to get an average specimen at the current price their if you still wish it.

The old lady (age 77) turned out to be an ungrateful & stupid old creature as ever came out of Somersetshire (her native den) Yet one may be grateful to her for the following scene

on the Strand at Reykjavik a row of general shops fronting the sea, Mr. Tomsen's shop in the foreground:

Enter 1st the Lieutenant of the 'Diana' his hands in his waistcoat pockets, and he whistling 'see the conquering hero comes' to keep up his spirits — 2nd two sailors from the Diana carrying the old lady's bandbox & bundle —

3rd The Skipper of the Diana arm in arm with the OLD LADY. (costume of her: a drawn grey silk bonnet, a little white shawl, a purple chintz scanty gown beautifully flowered, white stockings & shoes with 'sandals')   captain: a fat red faced intensely good natured old naval officer:

4th The whole of the male population of Reykjavik who can spare time from doing nothing, looking anxious as to whether they will all be able to get into Mr. Tomsen's shop.

Old Lady to Lieutenant as they come on to Mr. Tomsens doorstep, who stands there (little polite red haired man) looking anxious as to how many of No 4 he can keep out of his shop —

Mr. Lieutenant (says she taking about 4ᵈ in small Danish money out of her pocket) will you take this.

Lieutenant — Thank you kindly. What am I to do with it?

O.L. Please to give it to the crew.

L. What shall they do with it?

O.L. I do not wish them to drink too much.

L. Shall they drink coffee with it?

O.L. O Yes Mr. Lieutenant, that would be very nice.

L: grins & pockets the 4ᵈ sterling & the whole of 1, 2, & 3 dissappear into Mr. Tomsen's shop, who manages to shut out no. 4 who takes its hands out of its pockets to take snuff & then settles itself to waiting till 1. 2. & 3 come out again—

This is literal truth: also that the old lady wanted to be Guy Faukesed about Iceland in a chair: also that she teazed Mrs. Magnusson to buy her a lamb that she might cook it herself in her own private room, & scolded her heartily because she couldnt get her one at once: also that

[199]

she slept on board ship with nothing over her but a sheet, though the thermometer was nearly at freezing point — also that she would hardly pay for anything, and (till the lamb came) was like to die of starvation (she told us she had £1000 a year) if someone hadn't given her some plovers.

I hear she went back by the return trip of the Diana, and, the weather being rough, was not much seen upon deck on the voyage: I still think she was the Flying Dutchwoman —

And now she is out of the story. We had a very successful journey did all we meant to do, and had fine weather on the whole: a great comfort, as wet weather makes daily riding little more than something to endure while it lasts, however amusing it may be to look back on, when it is well over. One day we rode through what we thought was a dust-storm mixed with drizzle, till a farmer told us that there must have been some irruption of the fire mountains as there was no sand thereabout, & that this was fine ashes. Skaþtar Jokul has been very un-quiet for years now, and the irruption in Jan: last was a much more tremendous affair than one would have judged by the slight notice of it in our papers: one priest told me that they saw it for about a fortnight, gushes of fire ⟨every⟩ ten times or so an hour, so that the long nights were quite light with it, and the short days all dark with the smoke — no one knows where ⟨it⟩ the crater was among the unreachable ice of the great Yokul: the big river of Skeiðará was nearly dried up by it for the time.

Our guides were very pleasant friendly fellows, as innocent of the great world as babies, and, apart from their daily labour, living almost entirely in the glorious past days of Iceland. One of them, Haldor by name, was born at Lithend where Gunnar lived and died. I suppose I shall never see them again — nor Iceland again, and the days of these two journeys there have grown inexpressibly solemn to me.

Please give my kindest remembrances to Baldwin & believe me

Yours affectionately
William Morris

MS: Texas. Published: Mackail, I, 296.

211 · To Aglaia Ionides Coronio

26, Queen Square,
Bloomsbury, London, W.C.
Friday [October 1873]

My dear Aglaia

I am very much dissapointed, and unfortunately I can't come on

Monday because I have made an appointment with a model on that day: for I am going to try to work hard once more, which I know you will be glad to hear.[1]

Could you come on Tuesday? I would keep that day for you. I hope you keep well yourself, and are in good spirits. Write me a word to say if Tuesday will do.

I am
Your affectionate
William Morris

MS: Yates Coll.

[1] Mackail offers the opinion (I, 301) that Morris's "practice in drawing now was not useless to him: and its effects may be seen, not indeed in any marked proficiency in drawing the human figure, but in a greater breadth and decisiveness of design in his decoration: a matter of no small importance when the designing of patterns for chintzes and woven tapestries became, as it did soon afterwards, one of his chief occupations."

---

212 • TO FREDERIC EVERY
26, Queen Square,
Bloomsbury, London, W.C.
October 6, 1873

Dear Sir[1]

I have been out of England for some months, & did not get your letter on my return, so no doubt it was mislaid here.

I need not say that I sympathise entirely with the objects you have in view, but I am afraid I should be no manner of use to you as a Vice-president but should be happy to subscribe as an 'Associate Member' if I may so express my sympathy for the Guild[2] —

Thanking you very much for the honour you have done me

I am
My dear Sir
Yours obediently
William Morris

Frederic Every Eqre.

MS: Berger Coll.

[1] In 1881, Every was a candidate for the secretaryship of the National Liberal Land Company and in a letter of support for his candidacy, Morris indicates that Every, in 1877, was also a member of the E.Q.A. See letter no. 665.

[2] The Trades Guild of Learning, before which Morris delivered his first public lecture, "The Decorative Arts," on December 4, 1877.

213 · To Edmund Henry Morgan
26, Queen Square,
Bloomsbury, London,
October 13, 1873

My dear Sir

I was sorry also for my part to miss you on ⟨Sat⟩ Friday: I have sent a telegram to have the whole of the lower part of the window back: for though I think that the alterations I had given orders for would have set the window right; yet I think I see my way to some alterations which would make the whole thing better.[1] I am not far from agreeing with you as to the colour of the lower part: but what I really think is wanted is to make all the two lower rows *darker* & greyer at once which will give the due value to the bright many coloured upper part: in which to say the truth the principal *pleasure* of the window must lie — Also now the big window is in I can see the Sybil window for the first time, and think the three single figures very successful:[2] but I want to have out the subjects and make them *very much* darker, and shall do the same with those of the nave windows: I think if you have a good look at the windows you will agree with me about this — Apart from this I think both the smaller windows very good colour; as to the big window I fully expected to have to make alterations after I had seen it in situ; and I am not daunted at having to do so on a biggish scale: to put so much colour into a window is a hazardous experiment: but I will promise you to get it right in the end.[3]

The alterations will not be long about. I will come & see the window when they are done & will give you notice of my coming.

I am
My dear Sir
Yours truly
William Morris

MS: Jesus College.

[1] For earlier correspondence about this stained glass window, see letter no. 165.

[2] A window in the south transept of Jesus College Chapel, east wall, southernmost, consisting of three lights. See Sewter, II, 43.

[3] After this window was completed, Morgan requested that one of the panels of the big window be altered so that it could be used as a ventilator. In a letter to Morgan, October 24, 1873, George Wardle wrote in an effort to dissuade the Dean from such a proposal: "Mr. Morris is horrified. He says it would be fatal to the window & you must really give it up. Could not a grating be laid in the floor to give air to the stove? Surely there are some means that the ingenuity of Cambridge could devise for feeding the stove without destroying the window. What a monster the stove must be to demand such a sacrifice. If it is to be done pray do not ask our connivance. That Mr. Morris will never give. Pray try something else. & if S. Gregory must be suspended in a ridiculous position to allow the necessary current of air to pass round his carcase — don't tell us you have done it. Please treat this protest as quite serious. Mr Morris would make no objection to your

proposal if he did not feel that his work would be endangered." (Letter in the possession of Jesus College.)

214 • To Louisa Macdonald Baldwin

26, Queen Square,
Bloomsbury, London
October 22, 1873

My dear Louie

Georgie says you would like to hear from me from time to time, which makes it a great pleasure for me to write: only I am one of the worst of letter-writers, & have little enough to talk about except that (to me) most interesting subject, *myself*. Georgie will tell you how inexhaustible I find that subject in talk with my friends, and so you must put up with your share of it if you want to hear from you [*sic*]. I am wanting to settle down now into a really industrious man: for I do not mean to go to Iceland again if I can help it, and it is strange what a hole in my life that determination has made. I have had a good deal to do of a trivial kind, & to say the truth have been busy enough over such things: but it seems I must needs try to make myself unhappy with doing what I find difficult — or impossible — so I am going to take to drawing from models again, for my soul's health chiefly, for little hope can I have ever to do anything serious in the thing. It must be six years now since I made a habit of drawing and I never, if you can understand that, had the *painters memory* which makes it easy to put down on paper what you think you see; nor indeed can I see any scene with a frame as it were round it, though in my own way I can realize things vividly enough to myself — also I am getting old, hard on 40 Louie, — so add all things together, and if I can tell you in six months time that I have been persevering in my drawing I give you leave therewith to praise my patience, though I can scarcely hope it will come to that.

It is wet & wild weather here now, but somehow I don't dislike it, and there is something touching about the real world bursting into London with these gales; and it makes me wish to travel in spite of my knowledge of how sick I should be at sea. It makes me feel lazy in the mornings though & I feel as if I should like to sit in my pretty room at Turnham Green reading some hitherto unprinted Dumas say about as good as the 3 Musketeers —

By the way did you ever steep yourself in that delightful series; did you ever read all the Vicomte de Bragelonne[1] & wish at the end that it was double as long: if not let me beseech you to do so now and be rewarded: did you ever read what I think Dumas' best book Olympe de Cleves?[2] I made Georgie read it once, and she enjoyed it very much, but we used to quarrel desperately about the character of the hero whether any woman could have stood him at all, I taking his part: I think I have rather altered my opinion now.

Excuse my saying abruptly good bye at this point, for I see it is ½[?] past 2 & I have an engagement to keep: I hope you will be able to read my writing.

Hoping to hear better news of you soon.

> I am
> Yours affectionately
> William Morris

MS: Texas. Published: *CW*, 22, xxxii-xxxiv; Henderson, *Letters*, 59-60; Mackail, I, 301.

[1] *Vicomte de Bragelonne* (1848-1850), the second sequel, in 26 parts, to *The Three Musketeers*.

[2] *Olympe de Clèves* (1852), the story of an actress and a Jesuit novice in the reign of Louis XV.

215 • TO CHARLES FAIRFAX MURRAY
Queen Sq
November 5, 1873

My dear Murray

Many thanks for both your letters: as to the pots, I think almost any of them would be good to get: those marked Ariursa seem very good: I fancy it must be the Venetian place but am not sure: the best way would be for you to order any of these you like best to the number of say 20 of each: and if you see anything else you like you need not send specimens, but send 20 of each again: they are sure to be salable here: so up to that number you have carte blanche: — so much for pots.

As to my Lancelot:[1] I think in any case I should like to make another MS of it again *myself*; also in any case you shall have the present MS. So if you think you could send it me *safely* I should be very glad to have it at once: otherwise it must wait till I see you.

I don't know about coming to Italy in the spring: if I go at all next year and the Master[2] goes I suppose I shall go with him. I came back from Iceland about the middle of September after a very lucky journey: I am thinner from it you will be glad to hear.

I am in a somewhat discontented mood at present: can get to no serious work, though I work many hours at trivialities: true I have made a step in getting models and have meant to take to drawing again: but I have so little hope about the whole affair that I can scarcely fix my attention on it so that it hardly seems worth the extreme worry and nuisance it gives me: however I shall keep it going a little longer & see what happens to me about it.

Can you talk Italian yet: you ought to be able to before I come out to see you: and I swear I *will* learn another sentence more than 'Si Cambia qui?' before I come out again.

> I am
> Yours very truly
> William Morris

MS: Texas. Extract published: *CW*, 10, xii, xvii.

¹ Among Morris's illuminated manuscripts May Morris lists (*CW*, 9, xx) "Lancelot du Lac (paper), portion of a manuscript in a very beautiful Italian script" and adds that Morris talked "of making another Lancelot manuscript."

² Edward Burne-Jones.

216 • FROM A LETTER TO HENRY BUXTON FORMAN   [26, Queen Square, Bloomsbury, London November 12, 1873]

Many thanks for your letter and the translation of Wagner:¹ I have not had time to read it yet: nor to say the truth am I much interested in anything Wagner does, as his theories on musical matters seem to me as an artist and non-musical man perfectly abhominable: besides, I look upon it as nothing short of desecration to bring such a tremendous and world-wide subject under the gaslights of an opera: the most rococo and degraded of all forms of art — the idea of a sandy-haired German tenor tweedledeeing over the unspeakable woes of Sigurd, which even the simplest words are not typical enough to express! Excuse my heat; but I wish to see Wagner uprooted, however clever he may be, and I don't doubt he is: but he is anti-artistic, don't doubt it.

TEXT: Mackail, I, 299. Published: Henderson, *Letters*, 60-61. Extract published: *CW*, 12, xiii.

¹ This was the libretto of *Die Walküre* by Alfred W. Forman (1840-1925), brother of H. B. Forman and the recognized English translator of Wagner's librettos. This one was done in alliterative verse and was later incorporated into Forman's translation of the entire *Der Ring des Nibelungen* (1877).

217 • FROM A LETTER TO HENRY BUXTON FORMAN   [December 8, 1873]

I would have answered your letter before (many thanks for it) but I had not quite made up my mind about the Stories in my translation book.[1] It stands thus now as I intended at first: the Story of Gunnlaug the Worm-tongue, printed in the Fortnightly some years back; the Story of Frithiof the Bold, printed before in the Dark Blue; the story of Viglund the Fair, never before printed: these 'three Northern Love Stories' will give the name to the book, but to thicken it out I add three more short tales; Hroi the Fool, Hogni and Hedin, and Thorstein Staff-smitten; the first of these three a pretty edition of a 'sharper' story and the same as a tale in the Arabian Nights.[2] The second a terrible story; a very well told, but late version of a dark and strange legend of remote times. The third simple, and not without generosity, smelling strong of the soil of Iceland, like the Gunnlaug.

TEXT: Mackail, I, 300. Published: Henderson, *Letters*, 61.

[1] *Three Northern Love Stories and Other Tales*, translated in collaboration with Magnússon and published by Ellis and White, 1875. Buxton Forman quotes (pp. 82-83) Morris as writing on another occasion about his plans "to make up a book big enough for Ellis's purposes."

[2] "The King, His Son, and The Seven Wezeers." See *CW*, 10, 4.

---

218 • TO EDWARD WILLIAMS BYRON NICHOLSON   26, Queen Square,
Bloomsbury, London
Thursday 1874

Dear Mr. Nicholson[1]

I am sorry to say that I was just going to write to you to tell you that one of my little girls was suddenly taken ill yesterday, and my wife is also unso[*sic*] unwell & very anxious so that I positively cannot come tomorrow or be away from home anywhere.

I hope you will understand that this is a positive necessity to me: I hope also that you will be able to put off your friends without seriously inconveniencing them.

When things seem going a little better I will write & ask you to name another day, I hope very shortly.

I am
Yours very truly
William Morris

MS: McMinn Papers.

[1] Nicholson (see letter no. 67, n. 1) was Librarian of the London Institution at this time.

219 • THREE LETTERS TO EIRÍKR MAGNÚSSON

a.

Horrington House
Turnham Green
Monday morning [1874]

My dear Magnússon

Imprimis will you be so kind as to let me have clearings up of the visur in Viglund from the one on p 82 (inclusive) to the end, & I will then turn out the whole matter strax:[1] to say the truth I am very much ashamed of not having done so before.

In secundis 'tis a long time since I have seen you, and I hope you will be up here soon: if not I must come up to Cambridge to see you, and make good the proverb.

Helgi works very steadily & seems getting on very well: I wish him luck & will do my best to push him.[2]

Please give my kindest regards to Mrs. Magnússon & believe me
Yours very truly
William Morris

MSS: Iceland.

[1] Icelandic word meaning "at once."

[2] Probably Eiríkr Magnússon's brother. He apparently did some drawing or copying for Morris for a short time, but the arrangement proved unsatisfactory and he soon returned to Iceland.

b.

26, Queen Square,
Bloomsbury, London
[1874]

My dear Magnússon

Enclosed are the letters for Haldor & Jón:[1] Helgi will explain Haldor's rash project which led to my perhaps rasher invitation. I am much bothered or I would write more at length
I am
Yours very truly
William Morris

[1] Haldor was Morris's guide in Iceland. For Jón Jónsson, see letter no. 178, n. 2.

c.

Queen Sq
March 25 [1872-1876]

My dear Magnússon

By all means I shall be delighted to see you: please let me know by what train you are coming on Saturday: we will if you don't mind sleep in Queen Sq on Saturday & go up to Turnham Green on Sunday morning.

Yrs most truly
W Morris

220 • Six Letters to George James Howard

a.

Queen Sq
Friday [1873–1875]

My dear Howard

10 AM at Paddington tomorrow (Saturday) only be a good 10 minutes early please, as there is always some confusion by these big GWR trains. Also bring a pipe with you: and if you don't like Latakia pure & simple a little baccy, as that is all I have down there. Don't mind the weather (wh: looks threatening now) as it will like enough clear up before we get there.

Yrs William Morris

MSS: Howard Papers.

b.

Queen Sq
Sunday [1873–1875]

My dear Howard

I will come on Monday with much pleasure: but as to Tuesday please excuse me, for I am getting quite low in spirits with doing so little work: make Colvin (whom I am sorry to miss) come on Monday.

Yrs affect:
W Morris

c.

Wednesday [1873–1875]

Dear Howard

Thanks, I shall be very happy to come: I hope Mrs. Howard is getting on all right, & that the little ones have not got the hooping-cough — mine make a fearful noise over it, but don't seem at all ill, so I am not anxious about them.

Yrs very truly
W Morris

Rosalind and George Howard, 1870's.

d.   June 19 [1873-1875]

My dear Howard

   Many thanks I will come: by the by if I am to put on togs will you let me know.

                                 I am
                                 Yours affec:
                                 W Morris

e.   November 24 [1873-1875]

My dear Howard
I think with excuses that I won't come *to dinner* tomorrow: but as I very much want to see you I will come in about 9 o clock PM if I may.
Yrs ever
William Morris

f.   Friday
Queen Sq:
[1873-1875]

Dear Howard
I am so sorry again that we must miss each other, but I am to meet Ned tonight by appointment, and so can't come.
Yrs affectionately
William Morris

221 • To Emma Shelton Morris   Saturday Morning
Horrington House
[1873?]

Dearest Mother
The book has just come to hand, many thanks for sending it: I was sorry to put you to the trouble. Janey thought the little (?) one looking much better.
Your most affectionate Son
William Morris

ms: Walthamstow.

222 • Two Letters to Walter Theodore Watts-Dunton

a.   [Jan-Feb 1874?]

My dear Watts[1]
I am sorry that I can't come tonight, or tomorrow night either, as I am going out both times: Will Thursday evening, say 7 o'clock do for me to call here? I rather expect to see Marshall[2] between whiles. Will you kindly write a line, best to Turnham Green I think
Yours very truly
William Morris

MSS: Bodleian.

[1] Walter Theodore Watts-Dunton (1832-1914), a solicitor who took up literary criticism in 1874. He wrote for *The Athenaeum*, was an intimate of Rossetti and his friends, and after 1879, shared "The Pines," the house at Putney, with Swinburne, where he became caretaker of Swinburne's life and affairs. In 1874, Watts (not yet Watts-Dunton) was acting for Rossetti and Ford Madox Brown during the controversy over the dissolution of Morris, Marshall, Faulkner and Company.

[2] Peter Paul Marshall (1830-1900), one of the original members of the firm, though the reason for his inclusion in the founding group is obscure. By training a surveyor and sanitary engineer, he was a friend of Madox Brown, and may have been invited to join the firm at Brown's suggestion. "He contributed several cartoons for glass, and a few designs for church decoration, but otherwise took little part in the work of the firm" (see Mackail, I, 147). Henderson, however, notes that Marshall did "some spirited designs for St. George and the Dragon stained glass" (*Life*, p. 69).

b.
26, Queen Square,
Bloomsbury, London
January 12, 1874

My dear Watts

I am sorry you called when I was out yesterday. They tell me that would write to make an appointment for ⟨our⟩ us to meet together:[1] so to save trouble I write to say that I shall not be free till Friday, as I am going to take my children to the Pantomime tonight & tomorrow I have got to go to Cambridge on business whence I shall probably not be back till Friday morning. So what & where will suit you, Friday, Saturday, Monday? Kindly write please.

I am
Yours very truly
William Morris

[1] The firm of Morris, Marshall, Faulkner and Co. was beginning to break up. Morris wanted it under his sole management; Ford Madox Brown felt that Morris was asking him to give up his share in the firm just when it was beginning to prosper. Rossetti and Marshall sided with Brown, who took legal advice and put the negotiations in Watts's hands. See letter no. 251, n. 2.

223 • TO EIRÍKR MAGNÚSSON
Turnham Green
Tuesday morning
[January 27, 1874]

My dear Magnusson

Thanks for proof: Old Strangeways I find makes so many ridiculous blunders that I don't think it worth while to send you the first proofs again, but the revises rather: there are one or two points I want to ask you about: those passages (glosses) about the Gunnars, and about the Things,[1] principally: also I dont quite agree with all your alterations: but we can leave all that for personal discussion when I see you which I think of doing (if may) next Saturday week, the 7th of Feb:

I have called Hrafn, Raven[2] you will see principally on account of the measure in my verses: but if you strongly object I dont press the point: I think by the way the visur in Gunnlaug are quite literal now: except perhaps the last; and of course I didnt feel myself bound closely by Jón þorkelson's[3] conjectural restoration of those two lines.

I sent Frithiof & a page or two of Viglund to press yesterday: I have not altered much in that, & think the visur read pleasantly, so I hope they are right. I will send you before the end of the week the music of Viglund[4] copied out by my wife & get you to write it out fair for the printer for me with the first quartrain both of Eigi má ek á aegi[5] & stoðum vit tweir túni[6] written along with the notes. The book seems like to come shorter than I should like; so I think of adding Norna-Gest[7] to the other tales: it is quite short, wont make more than thirty pages.

For the indexing I will sent you *two* revises: this will be near enough to being correct to answer the purpose and will save time, because I shan't send anything finally to press till I have seen you. I wish you good luck & send kindest remembrances to Mrs. Magnússon & Helgi: about the latter I enclose a question written fair on a slip of paper: as you see.[8]

I am
Yours most truly
William Morris

MS: Iceland.

[1] See *CW*, 10, 160.

[2] The husband of Helga, in "The Story of Gunnlaug the Worm-Tongue."

[3] Jon Thorkelsson (1822-1904), schoolmaster at the Latin School in Reykjavík and editor of a collection of Icelandic stories.

[4] See *CW*, 10, 98-99.

[5] "One cannot always on the sea . . ."

[6] "We two stood together in the homefield."

[7] This tale was not included.

[8] The slip of paper to which Morris refers has not survived.

224 • To Eiríkr Magnússon   26, Queen Square,
                                             Bloomsbury, London
                                             January 29, 1874
My dear Magnússon

I will bring down a MS book for Helgi to copy, and some more of my better MS with it, and then Helgi can do a few pages: I think his writing would do very fairly for what I want, though it isnt as pretty as mine: I needn't hurry him either, & if he got sick of it it wouldnt matter: about his future prospects we will talk when I see you and his work: I can't help thinking that if he can force himself to work hard & steadily he may do very well.

I don't suppose we shall quarrel much over the alterations: I am deeply impressed with the necessity of making translations literal: only they must be in English idiom and in un-degraded English at the same time: hence in short all the difficulty of translation. I told Strangeways to send you the revises: he has been extra stupid about everything this time, but I suppose all will come right in the end.

                                        Yours very truly
                                        William Morris.

 MS: Iceland.

225 • To Charles Fairfax Murray   Queen Sq:
                                             February 18, 1874
My dear Murray

I hear from Mr. Jones[1] that you have got to Rome, excuse me for saying 'at last': so I write to trouble you about a matter of my own: Vellum to wit:[2] I enclose a pattern of what I got thence before, & on the whole it is as you know very good: in the mediaeval books however the vellum is generally harder (on the smooth side) than this; so perhaps you might fall in with some more of that quality which I should prefer provided it is no thicker than mine and is 'pure' that is not surfaced with white lead: my patterns are certainly from the thinnest skins I had, & are whiter than some; I should prefer them with a little more colour if gettable: I see on looking at my patterns that they are from the best of mine, & if some of the skins were thicker I shouldn't mind because I could use those for bigger books. The size of my vellum is about 19 inches × 13 but so long as they are not much smaller that is not a matter of importance: will you be kind enough to see what you can do and let me know when you have found it out, & if you find anything different that you think will suit me send me patterns: and tell me what will be the cost of 100 skins of about that size, and I will send you the money straightway with many thanks for your trouble.

I have much improved by the way both in my ornament & my writing in that line since I saw you. Only I wish the devil I could do the pictures. A month or two ago I actually began having Colorossi[3] here to draw from, & did some very disheartening studies from him, & at last gave it up after making myself a laughing-stock by sending away about every other time. Have you done anything about the pottery[4] by the way?

I saw this morning the copy you have sent home of the Siennese picture & congratulate you on it, for it is very good.

Wardle asks me to enclose a slip to you in my letter which I do. We are commissioned now to do the next window to yours in Christ-Church at Oxford;[5] & I wish you could paint it, but I suppose you wouldnt care to even if you were in England. I hope you are well & will come home safe some time or other.

I am
Yours very truly
William Morris

P.S. You must ask for *writing* vellum because they also make famous bookbinder's vellum at Rome.

MS: Texas. Published: *CW*, 9, xxiv.

[1] Burne-Jones?

[2] According to Mackail (I, 303), Morris at this time was energetically undertaking and planning illuminated manuscripts on vellum. In March, he began a vellum manuscript of the *Odes* of Horace. At the same time, he planned to transcribe one of his own tales, "Cupid and Psyche," which was to include the pictures and designs made by Burne-Jones in 1869 for the original scheme of an illustrated *Earthly Paradise*. (See also letter no. 231, n. 5.) Toward the end of 1874, he began the *Aeneid* having at last "obtained a sufficient supply of vellum of the larger size required for a folio."

[3] Presumably the name of a model who had previously worked for Murray. Morris "was drawing for a time from [Murray's] models." See Crow, p. 71.

[4] See Morris's requests in a previous letter (no. 215) to Murray.

[5] Murray's window in Christ Church, Oxford, commemorated F. G. Vyner, who had been killed in Greece in April 1870. The window next to Murray's is the St. Cecilia window designed by Burne-Jones.

226 · TO EMMA SHELTON MORRIS
26, Queen Square,
Bloomsbury, London
Tuesday [February 1874]

Dearest Mother.

Yes I will go on with the money to Rendal,[1] at all events some of it, but Im afraid I am in arrears: suppose I say £10 now & then £2.10 per quarter for the rest of the year: I sent him £10 about Xmas time.

Janey comes back tomorrow with Jenny, but May stays behind — to be painted.[2] I hear good news of both of them.

I propose to come down next week one day: shall we say Tuesday? only I should be sorry to miss Henrietta again so if she wouldnt be at home that evening any other except Saturday would do.

I am hard at work though business is somewhat slack, as indeed it always is the first few weeks after Christmas: and the elections & all have made it worse this year.[3]

With best love to yourself & Henrietta.

I rest
Your most affectionate Son
William Morris

MS: Walthamstow.

[1] Morris's youngest brother. The money may have been due to him, as his share of the income from the Devon Great Consols. On the other hand, Morris seems to have agreed to send money he was not obliged to pay. The explanation may be that the income from the mining shares had dropped, but that Morris consented to keep up the old rate of payment as a way of helping Rendall, who, about this time, may have begun to fail in business.

[2] By Rossetti. In 1874, May Morris served as a model for figures in three of Rossetti's paintings. See Surtees, II, 341, 348, and 355.

[3] Parliament had been dissolved at Gladstone's request on January 26, 1874. The elections, the first to be held under the Ballot Act of 1872, providing for secret voting, concluded on February 17.

227 · TO AGLAIA IONIDES CORONIO
26, Queen Square,
Bloomsbury, London
Thursday
[March 5, 1874]

Dear Aglaia

Next Monday I suppose you mean the 9th of March that is: I shall be very glad to come at 4. I have missed you very much & never expected that it would be so long between the times of seeing you. I went down to my mother's yesterday & stayed there till noon today: I was very

[215]

dull when I went, & expected that it would make me duller; but some-how I found myself much better this morning, & am quite changed now; I can only hope it will last: I am ashamed of myself for these strange waves of unreasonable passion: it seems so unmanly: yet indeed I have a good deal to bear considering how hopeful my earlier youth was, & what overweening ideas I had of the joys of life.

The country touched me very much this time: so much so that I think some day soon before the spring has grown old I shall take my illumi-nating down to my mother's and stay there for three days — that seems a huge venture to me I assure you.

Write & tell me if it is not *next* Monday you mean, as I am sure I hope it is: otherwise expect me by 4 oclock. I am going this very minute to order my new clothes. Alas I am afraid they will not be ready in time.

Your affectionate
William Morris

MS: Yates Coll. Published: Henderson, *Letters*, 66-67.

228 • To George James Howard   March 6, 1874

My dear Howard
I should like very much to meet Dasent,[1] if it were only for the pleasure of talking of Icelandic matters once more: but I must say no this time because I have been out nearly every night this week, & Sat-urday & Sunday are my great work days. I must add too that I have no clothes but positive rags in which rags I should dread meeting a stran-ger. I shall have some more on Monday I hope after which I will come & see you.

Yrs affect:
W Morris

MS: Howard Papers.
[1] See letter no. 69, n. 2.

229 • To Charles Fairfax Murray   Queen Sq:
March 9, 1874

My dear Murray
Many thanks for your kindness in seeing to my vellum business at once: I am glad to find it is cheaper than I had expected: I think it would

be better for you to secure all that the woman has got, of both sizes; for I think the smaller size will be the same as the first little lot I had and as to the thickness: it might be a good deal thicker than what I sent you & yet not too thick even for smallish books: & for bigger ones thicker yet would be no harm: so please get all she has & order me 100 (one hundred) sheets of the May batch in addition: & then unless I live longer than I & the insurance offices think I fancy I shall have enough at all events till I go to Rome myself: which I hope wont be so very long after all.

By the way don't post the vellum till you hear from me that the first lot is here safe: and on what day did you post it? and did you *register* it? which would be the best thing to do in future. I have written today to the G P.O. here to inquire about it for I think it ought to be here by this time. I send you by registered letter ½ a £10 note out of which you can pay for the vellum sent & for that which the old woman has still got: about which by the way I couldnt quite make out by your letter if what was *left* of the larger size: the balance you can put to my credit in any future dealings — like the May batch — in such matters. By the way you must allow me without offense to pay for any vellum you want for yourself: since I shall consider myself the depot of that ware in England.

Well as to the babes: — Jenny is certainly big, has long coats now & looks like a quite grown up young lady: nevertheless she is not beyond a romp — to judge at any rate by the infernal row that she & Phil & Margery[1] made in our house last Saturday. May is at Kelmscott now being painted. I think of the two she is the more grown up, & writes quite like a young lady, Jenny rather appearing to dread the pen: nevertheless I think she too may be counted upon for any amount of row whenever that is asked for. I didn't forget to give your message to Jenny, & shall write it to May tomorrow.

I didnt understand your last paragraph about Webb: I told him however & perhaps he did. I dine with him at a tavern this evening to meet the master,[2] Stanhope[3] & Wallis,[4] & wish you were with us. Stanhope by the way dont care about Rome — What sort of impression has it made upon you? Thanks about the shirts: I told my wife about them.

I am with best wishes
Yours very truly
William Morris

MS: Texas. Published: *CW*, 9, xxviii.

[1] Philip and Margaret Burne-Jones.
[2] Edward Burne-Jones.
[3] See letter no. 26, n. 2.

⁴ Henry Wallis (1805-1890), a painter associated with the Pre-Raphaelites. He exhibited at the Royal Academy between 1854 and 1877 and later spent many years in the East, where he painted landscapes and became an authority on ceramic art. His best-known painting is "The Death of Chatterton," which was exhibited in the Academy of 1856, and for which George Meredith was the model. Wallis was at the time a friend of Meredith and his first wife, the former Mary Peacock Nicolls. In 1858, Wallis and Mary Meredith went off together to Capri. In 1861, they returned to England. Mary died of tuberculosis, and Wallis made his way back into artistic society, becoming something of a public figure and activist in behalf of cultural causes.

230 • To Louisa Macdonald Baldwin   26, Queen Square,
Bloomsbury, London
March 26, 1874

My dear Louie

Many thanks for your kind & friendly letter: it was very nice of you to remember my birthday which was solemnized yesterday by my staying at home all day & working very hard at illumination now my chief joy. Yesterday however was May's birthday, mine was on Tuesday on which sad occasion I was 40. Yet in spite of that round number I don't feel any older than I did in that ancient time of the sunflowers.

I very much long to have a spell of the country this spring, but I suppose I hardly shall I have so many things to do in London. Monday was a day here to set one longing to get away: as warm as June: yet the air heavy as often is in England: the town looks rather shocking on such days, & then instead of the sweet scents one gets an extra smell of dirt. Surely if people lived 500 hundred years instead of three score & ten they would find some better way of living than in such a sordid loathsome place: but now it seems to be nobody's business to try to better things — isnt mine you see in spite of all my grumbling — but look, suppose people lived in little communities among gardens & green fields, so that you could be in the country in 5 minutes walk, & had few wants; almost no furniture for instance, & no servants, & studied (the difficult) arts of enjoying life, & finding out what they really wanted: then I think one might hope civilization had really begun. But as it is the best thing one can wish for this country at least is, meseems some great & tragical circumstances, so that if they cannot have pleasant life, which is what one means by civilization, they may at least have a history & something to think of — all of which wont happen in our time.

— Sad grumbling — but do you know I have got to go to a wedding next Tuesday: to wit Lucy Brown & William Rossetti,¹ & it enrages me to think that I lack courage to say, 'I dont care for either of you & you

[218]

neither of you care for me, & I wont waste a day out of my precious life in grinning a company grin at you two old boobies (for they *are* old Louie, I mean for that sort of folly)[2] — No, I am going, woe worth the while! & hence these tears.

And so goodbye again with many thanks.

Yours affectionately
William Morris

MS: Texas. Published: Mackail, I, 302-303; Henderson, *Letters*, 61-62.

[1] They were married March 31, 1874.

[2] William Rossetti was forty-five and Lucy Madox Brown was thirty-one.

231 • To Charles Fairfax Murray

Queen Sq
March 26, 1874

My dear Murray

The vellum came to hand in good condition last Monday week: I would have written to tell you of it but was expecting every day an answer to my note with the ½ £10 note: please write by return & tell me if you have got this so that I may send you the other half. As to the vellum it is just the same as the last, & the smaller size is as I expected the same size as what I had the first time from Rome: this small thin vellum would be very useful if I were to do a tiny book as I have a mind to do:[1] so will you order me 50 sheets of it out of the May lot in addition to what I asked for before. Also to prevent mistake, as I know I am somewhat of a muddler in epistolary composition, I give my order again in full. 1st to buy all the woman has got in hand never minding whether it be thick ⟨and⟩ or thin: 2nd 100 sheets of the big (pretty much as it comes) out of the May lot: 3rd 50 sheets of the small as thin as may be out of the May lot. So much for that business & again many thanks to you for taking so much trouble.

As to what I am doing in my Scribe's capacity — I wrote a book (on paper confound it) of about 250 p.p. translations of unpublished Icelandic stories with pretty letters to each chapter, which looked well on the whole. I finished this early in February.[2] Now I am at work at an Odes of Horace[3] which will make about 100 pp of vellum octavo of the big sheets: the odes are short so there is nearly an ornamental letter to every page, which makes it a heavyish piece of work: however I have written about half & done 20 letters. To say the truth I have a mind to try and sell a book if I could find a customer: I work much neater now, & have got I think more style in the ornament, & have taken rather to the Italian work ⟨for⟩ of about 1450 for a type[4] — this kind of thing dont you know. I am very keen on the thing just now, & really enjoy my Sundays very much at it, and as you may imagine am very like to neglect my other work for it. However I believe I shall both have finished the Horace against you come home in the summer & shall also not be in the workhouse by then: & shall be very glad to see you after all this long time & have some of the pleasant times we used to have over again. I am rather thinking by the way of trying a Cupid & Psyche[5] for the market, painting in some of the master's pictures with it which he has given me leave to do: for belike the oddity of a poet illuminating his own poem might make it saleable: perhaps you would give me some help in the matter.

I was 40 years old last Monday & we kept that solemnity & May's birthday together yesterday: I staying at home & working hard at illuminating.

I have promised to take Jenny & May abroad this summer: but I don't suppose we shall get further than Belgium: money not being plenty at present: however even that will be amusing.

Goodbye, I hope to see you well & sturdy in the summer.   please dont forget to answer about the note.

> I am
> Yours affectionately
> William Morris

P.S. of course I shant want any more of the vellum till you bring it home in person

MS: Texas. Published: *CW*, 9, xxix.

[1] Of this book, Morris completed four trial pages, which are now in the William Morris Gallery, Walthamstow (MS J 578). The pages are approximately 2⅞ × 3¼ inches in size; the text is taken from the beginning of *The Story of the Volsungs and Niblungs*. See Joseph R. Dunlap, "The Road to Kelmscott: William Morris and the Book Arts Before the Founding of the Kelmscott Press," Ph.D. diss., Columbia University, 1972, pp. 190-91.

[2] The "Henthorir Saga," the "Banded Men," and "Howard the Halt," were done on paper, lightly decorated, and finished between 1873 and 1874, according to May Morris (*CW*, 9, xxi). This manuscript, prepared—like many of the others—as a present for Georgiana Burne-Jones, is now in the Fitzwilliam Museum, Cambridge.

[3] May Morris writes (*CW*, 9, xx) that the *Odes*, done on vellum, were "nearly finished" by 1874 but never completed.

[4] Morris possessed copies of four early manuals of handwriting: Vincentino Ludovico degli Arrighi, *La Operina Di Ludouico Vincentino, da imparare di scrivere littera cancellarescha* (1522) and *Il Modo de Temperare le Penne con le uarie sorti de littere ordinato per Ludouico Vincentino* (1523), Sigismondo Fanti's *Thesauro de Scrittori*, and Giovantonio Fagliente's *La Vera Arte de Scrivere*, published in the 1520's. He also owned two fifteenth-century Italian manuscripts which he may have bought at this time, and he is known to have studied similar work in the British Museum. See P. Thompson, pp. 135-36.

⁵ See Dunlap. *The Story of Cupid and Psyche*, illustrated with the wood engravings designed by Burne-Jones, was finally published in 1974 by Clover Hill Editions (London and Cambridge). It includes an introductory monograph concerning the illustrations, written by A. R. Dufty.

232 • TO AGLAIA IONIDES CORONIO
26, Queen Square,
Bloomsbury, London
Monday 3 oclock
[April 6, 1874]

My dear Aglaia

I was just setting off to come to you this afternoon when I remembered your ineradicable habit of writing to me at Queen Sq: instead of Horrington House, so I expected a note from you here & I came here instead where I hav'nt been since ⟨Tuesday⟩ Thursday, this being the Easter Holidays: it seems too late to call on you now as I could'nt get to you till after ½ past 3:

Unluckily tomorrow I have to go to my sister's at Weybridge in the afternoon:¹ so could I come on Wednesday or Thursday, or Friday — the sooner the better. It is a great dissappointment to me to have missed you: all the more from the selfish reason that I am not very well, & that an hour or two with you would have helped me to get along.

I intend to walk the greater part of my way home for I have not been out of the house since Friday morning when I went to the Grange: I have had my nose down on my vellum all the rest of the time & am somewhat weary of it though I cant help liking to see the page brighten while I am at it. I think I will try to do violence to my inclination & pound away at a poem good or bad before long. I wonder if I have gone stupid & cant though.

Well — please attend — if I am to come on *Wednesday*, write to me at *Queen Sq:* since I shall have to come back to the office on that morning after sleeping at Weybridge. But unless on special occasion 'tis always better to write to me at Horrington House: unless you write in the morning for me to get the letter in the afternoon. I hope all is pretty well with you

and rest
Your affectionate
William Morris

MS: Yates Coll. Published: Henderson, *Letters*, 70.

¹ Possibly Morris's youngest sister, Alice (Mrs. Reginald Gill).

233 • To Dante Gabriel Rossetti

26, Queen Square,
Bloomsbury, London
April 16, 1874

My dear Gabriel

I send herewith the £17.10 to you, not knowing where else to send it since Kinch[1] is dead. As to the future though I will ask you to look upon me as off my share, & not to look upon me as shabby for that, since you ⟨may⟩ have fairly taken to living at Kelmscott, which I suppose neither of us thought the other would do when we first began the joint possession of the house; for the rest I am both too poor &, by compulsion of poverty, too busy to be able to use it much in any case, and am very glad if you find it useful & pleasant to you.[2]

I am
Yrs affectly:
William Morris

MS: UBC, Angeli-Dennis Papers.

[1] Presumably the house agent for Kelmscott Manor.

[2] This letter was written after the dissolution of the firm had begun, and it was possibly the double estrangement from Rossetti—for business reasons and because of Jane Morris—that caused Morris to think about giving up his share in Kelmscott Manor. Rossetti at first was quite ready to take Morris at his word. On April 9, 1874, Rossetti wrote to the new house agent, sending the quarter's rent, and saying he would be glad to take a lease for seven or fourteen years. (See Doughty and Wahl, III, 1271.) However, no such lease was signed, and it was Rossetti who quit Kelmscott, leaving the house for the last time in July 1874.

234 • To Eiríkr Magnússon

26, Queen Square,
Bloomsbury, London
Wednesday [May 13, 1874]

My dear Magnússon

I cannot get away this week, but thought of coming down tomorrow week (Thursday in next week) for the afternoon & to look in with the order Porter promised me into the Fitz William on Friday morning.[1]

Also C.J.F & I have at last got all our presents ready for Iceland, & I am afraid I must trouble you to tell me *exactly* how to send them: I will have them all done up in parcels & will write notes to them which again I am afraid I must in some cases get you to translate for me: I have still been lazy over those visur, but will get them all done by next week.

With kindest regard to Mrs. Magnússon

I am
Yours very truly
William Morris

P.S. You must tell Porter I am coming I think

MS: Iceland.

[1] The reference to Porter may be in connection with a series of windows for the Combination Room and Hall in Peterhouse that Morris and Co. had begun in 1871 and were completing in 1874. See Sewter, II, 44-46.

235 • TO EIRÍKR MAGNÚSSON

26, Queen Square,
Bloomsbury, London
May 20 [1874]

My dear Magnússon

I am most unfortunately prevented from coming to Cambridge to-morrow by a very close friend of mine being very ill & in need of my presence continually.[1] Apart from the reason why I am very sorry not to be able to come. As to the presents I suppose all I have to do is to address them right & send them off to Salvesen's: I shall write with all of them & most of the letters must be in English: but I will still ask you kindly to translate one to Haldor & one to Jón which I will send you tomorrow.

Goodbye till I see you again which I hope will be next week if things go pretty well with me here.

Yours ever truly
William Morris

MS: Iceland.

[1] Possibly Edward Burne-Jones, who had recently gone through a period of severe depression. See Harrison and Waters, p. 110, and Fitzgerald, p. 155.

236 • TO EMMA SHELTON MORRIS

Horrington House
May 25 [1874?]

Dearest Mother

I write a line to wish you many happy returns of your birthday and all health & happiness: Janey says that you are coming up to town shortly: I hope you won't forget to come here in which case please let me have a line from you to warn me so that I may not be away by any chance.

I am expecting Arthur here this morning to talk about the D.G.C. I don't know what may happen at the meeting, but think that nothing will be done: things are looking a little better there, & the last sale was (comparatively) good as I daresay you have heard.

The children seem very well Janey on the whole better, but the hot weather is a bit knocking her up I doubt. What a sad time it has been for the gardens, but now I hope the summer is really coming: you will be looking very green & pretty down there.

Goodbye, dearest Mother with all love: best love to Henrietta.

I am
Your most aff: Son
William Morris

MS: Walthamstow.

---

237 · To Charles Fairfax Murray
26 Queen Sq
June 1 [1874?]

My dear Murray

I was going to write you a line to Pisa according to what you said in your note to my wife but it seemed so long out of date that I hesitated, & in meantime came your letter to the Master from which I made out that you would be still at Rome a while so take my chance of this finding you there but won't make it very long those chances considered.

First of course my wife told the bit of news about you that she got from your last letter but one concerning which I wish you all conceivable luck and happiness & expect to hear more from you when I see you —

Second I got the new vellum on Friday last: I counted 128 sheets of big & 50 of small all in good condition; I may have miscounted by a sheet or two: many thanks for sending it: it will set me up for a long time.

Let me hear from you as to when you are coming back.

I wont write more at present not knowing if you will get this.

Yours affectionately
William Morris

MS: Texas.

---

238 · To Rosalind Francis Howard
Hadham Nr. Ware
July 1874

My dear Mrs. Howard

I hear from Ned this morning that you will be gone North before I come back home on Thursday, so I shall have missed you, which I am very sorry for: I would have called before but George ⟨told⟩ was to tell me when it would be handy for me to do so, & I suppose he didn't reckon on my being away (as I practically am these days.

[224]

Janey & the children however are coming back home tomorrow. So I wish you goodbye without having said how do you do to you in person, & hope you will find the North-country pleasant to you.

I am
Yours very truly
William Morris

MS: Howard Papers.

239 • To Aglaia Ionides Coronio

Hotel du Commerce
Bruges
July 24 [1874]

Dear Aglaia

Many thanks for your kind letter & the jasmine blossoms from your window: I am very sorry to have dissappointed you about your letter, but I find it very difficult to get time to write, being always with the children and really having no time to ⟨itself⟩ myself to think at all: even now they are all here as I write while we are waiting to go out.

We have only had 2 railway journeys from Calais to Tournay last Saturday, & from Tournay to Ghent on ⟨Mo⟩ Sunday:[1] I must say I had no idea what heat was before, it was like being in a Turkish bath: after the 2nd one we by common consent determined to have no more of it than was positively necessary, & so gave up going to Antwerp & Mechlin, and hired a charabanc at Ghent to drive us to Bruges by road on the Tuesday: that was really a very pleasant drive, all among the pretty orchards the ripening wheat & oats, & the rye that they are already cutting, and so at last into Bruges by the ancient Gate of the Holy Cross: it took us all day, about 29 miles it is. We shall stay here till over Sunday, & then go to Ypres & then to Calais, & cross next Wednesday or Thursday night; I devoutly hope the first, for I most earnestly wish to be at home again: not that anything has gone wrong: on the contrary all is well & the children are very good: but travelling without time or space for musing is dreary work to me. We are all very much gnat-bitten, my right wrist is so stiff thereby that I really find it difficult to write so you must excuse a short letter   Bruges is a very beautiful place certainly, & I think I shall come over here one of these days when I have some litterary work to do, and stay here working for a few days by myself. Janey seems pretty well on the whole, and none the worse for the travelling for the present.

I had a letter from Ned yesterday not in high spirits I must say: he said he had seen you. I feel my imagination rather dull & torpid in spite

[225]

of all the change & beauty: I think 'tis the children being about, & the difference of age between us, & not knowing what they are thinking of. I am in the same room now as Janey & I were in when we came [to] Bruges on our wedding-trip: this morning we went to the Hospital of St John (where the Hemling pictures are)[2] and I looked in the book for my name & Murrays, & found them October 3rd 1870, & all the while I had been thinking it was only two years ago since I had been here.

I will write you another line before I come back to say exactly when we shall be in London. Goodbye meantime

I am
Your affectionate
William Morris

MS: Yates Coll. Published: Henderson, *Letters*, 62-63. Extract published: *CW*, 10, xv.

[1] In July, Morris and his family took a holiday trip to Belgium. It is worth noting that this trip, during which Morris and Jane Morris stayed in the room in Bruges they had occupied on their honeymoon, was taken the month in which Rossetti gave up his share in Kelmscott Manor.

[2] The *St. Ursula* and other religious paintings of Hans Memling (1430?-1495)—sometimes miscalled "Hemling" in the nineteenth century.

240 • To Emma Shelton Morris Hotel du Commerce
Bruges
July 24, 1874

Dearest Mother

A line to tell you how we all are which is very well, & also to say that before I left London I asked Mr. Wardle to pay £40 (forty pounds) into your account on the 28th of this month, which I suppose he will be able to do.

We have had but little railway travelling, only from Calais to Tournay & from Tournay to Gent: we found it so terribly hot on the railway that we quite gave up the idea of moving much, & so hired an omnibus at Ghent to take us here last Tuesday by road, & a very pleasant drive we had on a beautiful day with a shower or two to lay the dust through the ripe wheat & rye. It is very agreeable weather not much cooler & showery. I find Bruges scarcely changed at all: I saw my old signature in the book at St John's Hospital day four years old,[1] & this is the very same room which Janey & I occupied on our wedding-tour. This is really a beautiful place so clean & quiet too. I went into the Beguinage[2] yesterday — such a quiet pleasant spot among the canals — You can walk all round the ⟨walls⟩ town by the walls.

Janey seems very well considering the toil of travelling, and the children are very good & happy. We shall stay here till over Sunday & go on to Ypres on Monday evening, from Ypres to Calais on Tuesday and I think cross on Wednesday evening. Jenny & May were not a bit sick in coming over but enjoyed the sea vastly. I wonder if the weather has been as hot in England as here: one thing makes it worse here, that is the sandiness of the country, it is nothing but sand with a light loam over it: first rate for potatoes. all the grain looked well & they were already cutting the rye; but the country people I thought looked very poor

Goodbye Jenny & May are gone to lie down after dinner ⟨other⟩ & Janey too, otherwise no doubt they would send love: give my love to Henrietta & tell her we have not forgotten her commission: once more goodbye, dearest Mother.

I am Your most affec: Son
William Morris

MS: Walthamstow. Extract published: Mackail, I, 304.

¹ That is, four years to the day.

² Certain lay sisterhoods, established in the Netherlands and Germany, were known as béguines. Their communities, which were enclosed districts—little cities within cities—were called béguinages. The one at Bruges was founded in the thirteenth century.

---

241 · To ROSALIND FRANCIS HOWARD   Turnham Green
                                              Saturday [August 1874?]
My dear Mrs. Howard

I thank you much for your kind letter: you see I can't help it, but must keep away from my business even longer than on that morning: so I am coming by the night train on Monday which will land me at Naworth some early hour on Tuesday.¹ It is very kind of you to make so much of me, but I think 'tis you who are like to be disappointed with me, for I am getting an old man now and dull company.

Please give my love to George & also to Ned who will I daresay forgive my not writing to him in answer of his letter as I am to see him so soon. I hope he is better than when he left London, for he was looking poorly enough then.

I assure you it will be a great pleasure to me to see you again, & also not a light one to see the mountains once more and, as it were, sniff the wind from my beloved desert so much further north.

Believe me
Yours most truly
William Morris

MS: Howard Papers.

¹ In August 1874, Morris was a guest of the Howards at Naworth in Cumberland. Burne-Jones visited also, and a third guest was Richard W. Dixon. It was the first time since their Oxford days that Morris and Dixon were together for any length of time. Rosalind Howard wrote, "Morris arrived early this morning with such a diminutive carpet bag. He was rather shy — and so was I — I felt he was taking an experimental plunge amongst 'barbarians', and I was not sure what would be the resulting opinion in his mind. However, he has grown more urbane — and even three hours has worked off much of our mutual shyness. . . . He talks so clearly and seems to think so clearly that what seems paradox in Webb's mouth, in his seems convincing sense. He lacks sympathy and humanity though — and this is a fearful lack to me — only his character is so fine and massive that one must admire. He is agreeable also — and does not snub one. Not that I think he will like me — but he puts up with me. We shall jog along all right." See F. V. Lucas, *The Colvins and Their Friends* (London, 1928), p. 35. See also Mackail, I, 304, and letter no. 7, n. 6.

242 • TO AGLAIA IONIDES CORONIO

Naworth Castle
Cumberland
⟨Wed⟩ Thursday
[August 13, 1874]

Dear Aglaia

Though the weather is broken & stormy I have been passing a delightful life of doing nothing here: the place is so beautiful that one really does not want to do much, & doesnt feel it on ones conscience either. There are no visitors in the house but us & all is very pleasant: Ned & I pass our mornings in a most delightful room in one of the towers that has never been touched since William Howard of Queen Elizabeth's time lived there:¹ the whole place is certainly one of the most poetical in England: we had a long drive yesterday all along by the border, & I sniffed the smell of the moors & felt in Iceland again. The whole country side is most poetical & full of history & legend.

I think it has done Ned a great deal of good coming here: he is certainly better, & is quite cheerful & natural: the beauty of all this country moves him hugely.

I think we shall not come back till Sunday: I cant stay longer if I would, & I don't want to for many reasons.

I hope you are well & happy.

Your affectionate
William Morris

MS: Yates Coll. Published: Henderson, *Letters*, 63-64. Extract published: *CW*, 10, xvi.

¹ William Howard (1563-1640) is Sir Walter Scott's "Belted Will." Morris, an avid reader of Scott, knew this, as he also knew that Queen Elizabeth disliked the Howards, Lord William Howard having converted to Catholicism in 1584.

243 · To Frederick Startridge Ellis
Naworth Castle
Brampton, Cumberland
Thursday
[August 13, 1874]

My dear Ellis

Could you send me by *return* of *post* the Academy wh: contains my article on Gabriel[1]—

I am coming back on Monday, and will call round some time on Tuesday: this is a very jolly place; there are lots of becks & streams full of fish, but the water is very low and just as bright as glass, so tis hardly worthwhile for a bungler like me trying to throw a fly at their heads —

Yrs truly
W Morris

MS: Ray Coll.

[1] Morris's review of Rossetti's *Poems* had appeared in *The Academy*, May 14, 1870. (See letter no. 113, n. 2.) Like many notices of the book, it had resulted from Rossetti's efforts to have it reviewed by those loyal or sympathetic to him. What Morris had written that made it an urgent topic of conversation four years later at Naworth Castle is not clear.

244 · To William Allingham
26, Queen Square,
Bloomsbury, London
August 20, 1874

My dear Allingham

Thank you for your friendly announcement of your good fortune; of that side of it which is most important to you I had heard at the Grange a few days ago but the Fraser business is new to me:[1] I heartily wish you joy of both events and am ever

Yours very truly
William Morris

MS: Illinois.

[1] In June 1874, Allingham had become editor of *Fraser's Magazine* and on August 22 he married Helen Paterson (1848-1926), an illustrator.

245 · To Rosalind Francis Howard
26, Queen Square,
Bloomsbury, London
August 20, 1874

My dear Mrs. Howard

I was sorry to hear from Georgie this morning that you were no better but rather worse than when we were at Naworth. I would like you to understand, as well as my clumsy letter-writing will let you, how very happy I was those few days in the North, & how kind I thought you and George: I hope you will let me come again some time: and that then you will think me less arrogant on the — what shall I say — Wesleyan — tradesman — unsympathetic — with art subjects than you seemed to think me the other day: though indeed I don't accuse myself of it either: but I think to shut ones eyes to ugliness & vulgarity it wrong, even when they show themselves in people not unhuman: do you know when I see a poor devil drunk & brutal I always feel, quite apart from my æsthetical perceptions, a sort of shame as if I myself had some hand in it. Neither do I grudge the triumph that the modern mind finds in having made the world (or a small corner of it) quieter & less violent but I think that their blindness to beauty will draw down a kind of revenge one day: who knows, years ago mens minds were full of art & the dignified shows of life & they had but little time for justice & peace; and the vengeance on them was not ⟨the⟩ increase of the violence that they did not heed, but destruction of the art they heeded: so per-haps the Gods are preparing troubles and terrors for the world (or our small corner of it) again that it may once again become beautiful & dramatic withal: for I do not believe they will have it dull & ugly for ever: meantime what is good enough for them must content us: though sometimes I should like to know why the story of the Earth gets so unworthy. Now here I am preaching to you as Ned says men like to do: pray excuse it: please give my love & thanks to George & remind the children of me: especially Cecilia,[1] if I may say so.

I am
Yours affectionately
William Morris

MS: Howard Papers. Extract published: Mackail, I, 304; Henderson, *Letters*, 64; *Life*, 148.

[1] Cecilia Maude Howard, second daughter of the Howards, born April 23, 1868.

---

246 · TO WALTER THEODORE WATTS-DUNTON
26, Queen Square,
Bloomsbury, London
August 28, 1874

Dear Mr Watts

I find that two at least of our members wish to be out of the firm,[1] so could you tell me if their leaving us should be settled before we draw up our new articles of association: I suppose myself that it ought to be so but don't know: there will be no difficulties made on their side of the matter I should tell you as to valuation of their shares.

> I am
> Yours truly
> William Morris

MS: Princeton T. Published: Troxell, 71.

¹ Probably Ford Madox Brown and Peter Paul Marshall. See letter no. 251, n. 2.

247 • TWO LETTERS TO CHARLES FAIRFAX MURRAY

a.

> 26, Queen Square,
> Bloomsbury, London
> Wednesday
> [September 9, 1874]

My dear Murray

Will you come & dine tomorrow & have a bed: 7 oclock to dinner though I daresay the kids & J. would be glad to see you earlier though I shant be at home till then.

I will take care that you have a pudding

> Yours affect:
> William Morris

MSS: Texas.

b.

[September 1874]

My dear Murray

I am very sorry to miss you, but am summoned to a meeting in the City so must go: I have told the clerk to do up the vellum for you if you go to the office for it —

Let me know how you get on & where you are & I will write to you. — bon Voyage!¹

> Yrs ever
> W Morris

¹ Murray, who had been in England in September 1874, was apparently about to return to Italy.

248 • To Walter Theodore Watts-Dunton
26, Queen Square,
Bloomsbury, London
September 10, 1874

Dear Mr. Watts

Could you (if you are in town), come here next Monday or Tuesday to talk with me & one of the outgoers about our matter. Also we want the balance-sheet to refer to if you would kindly send it to us

With apologies for troubling you

I am
Yours very truly
William Morris

ms: Princeton T. Published: Troxell, 71.

249 • To Philip Burne-Jones
Horrington House
September 28, 1874
Sunday

My dear Phil

Many thanks for your letter. I am glad to hear that you are getting on well. I was in the upper 3rd when I first went to Marlborough though I only stayed in it a week: however I was a year older than you.

I havn't been well since you left: I have had rheumatism in my right foot and have been quite lame and pinned to my room where I have done many pretty letters:[1] Yesterday I was so much better that I thought it was all over, and so went to the Grange (in a cab) and slept in your bed so that I might have a merry morning today with your father: the merry morning we had sure enough, but alas! the rheumatism has crossed over and gone into the big-toe of my left foot so that I am nearly as lame as ever. I find all this a great nuisance.

If the frogs swarm in your hedge so do the spiders in our windows: so big and all mottled: when your father was here last Sunday he pulled down one big web but the spider had it up again by the next morning: I pulled it down again and the next morning there it was again.

I must write again when my toe has given over confusing my brain: Meantime Goodbye: Aunt Janey sends love and Jenny and May also: but I believe they will write soon.

The best of luck to you —

I am
Your most affectionate friend
William Morris.

Margaret and Philip Burne-Jones and Jenny and May Morris in the garden of The Grange, 1874.

MS: BL, Add. MSS. 52708 (typescript).

¹ Probably for the unfinished illuminated vellum manuscript of the *Aeneids* of Virgil, on which Morris and Burne-Jones were collaborating at this time. See *Memorials*, II, 56.

250 • TO WALTER THEODORE WATTS-DUNTON   26, Queen Square,
Bloomsbury, London
October 6, 1874

Dear Mr. Watts

I shall expect you then at *Horrington House Turnham Green* on Friday evening at 8 — to dinner of course, & shall be very glad to see you there apart from business. The house, by the way, is next door to the Roebuck and you can get there either by Kew & Richmond or Hounslow-Brentford bus, or by rail to Hammersmith Broadway either by the Gower Street line or the Temple Charing Cross line: there are also Hammersmith busses (more frequent than the Richmond) which will take you to the White-Hart, a bare 5 minutes walk from my house. Avoid the *Mortlake* — Richmond bus. It is 20 minutes walk from the Broadway to my house. but you can get a cab there. excuse my blundering directions but I don't know if you know our parts.

I rest
Yours very truly
William Morris

MS: BL, Add. MSS. 45345.

251 • TO DANTE GABRIEL ROSSETTI   26, Queen Square,
Bloomsbury, London
Wednesday
[October 21? 1874]

My dear Gabriel

Thanks for letter:¹ I have no objections to make, but we must settle how the thing can be done, as the money must be vested in trustees.²

For the rest your views of the meeting I think are not likely to be correct in any one point (except that Marshall will certainly be drunk) for I don't think *he* will venture to face the indignant members, I will tell you why tomorrow, which will be worth at least one grin to you, I flatter myself: Webb Ned & Faulkner have all promised to come; and though Brown refuses, I have asked Watts to attend (which he has promised to do) so as to report what we have to say to Brown. In short I consider it an important meeting, even if Brown don't come ⟨though⟩ & Watts said he would press him to do so. I expect to see Watts today, & he *may* bring me news of Browns being a little more reasonable though I confess I dont expect it.

We will talk the matter over tomorrow if you don't object.

Yours ever
William Morris

MS: BL, Ashley 3688. Published: Henderson, *Letters*, 24.

[1] Presumably a letter in reply to a request that he "attend a meeting of the Firm of Morris & Company at 26 Queen Square on Friday 23rd. inst. to consider what steps are to be taken in consequence of the announcement of withdrawal from the Firm of several members." This letter, signed "R.W.S. [Robert Smith?] pro Morris & Company" is dated October 13, 1874. Manuscript in UBC, Angeli-Dennis Papers.

[2] John Y. LeBourgeois, *Notes and Queries*, 216 (July 1971), 225, discussing negotiations that led to the dissolution of the firm, writes:

A meeting of the firm took place on Oct. 23, 1874. At the meeting the members attending—Morris, P. P. Marshall, Charles Faulkner, Edward Burne-Jones and Philip Webb; but not Rossetti or Ford Madox Brown—had decided that the firm should be dissolved and that three assessors should be appointed for the purpose of evaluating the company. At the meeting which followed on November 4, it was further agreed that a balance sheet should be drawn up as of Michaelmas 1874 in order to ascertain the firm's actual assets, and, although a protracted disagreement ensued over the value of the firm's 'goodwill,' the idea of assessors was never carried out.

For minutes of the October 23 meeting, and further comments on relations between Morris and Rossetti at this time, see next letter and its notes.

---

252 · To Dante Gabriel Rossetti

26, Queen Square,
Bloomsbury, London
October [24] 1874

My dear Gabriel

I enclose a copy of our last night's resolutions:[1] I do not see how Brown can object to them. ⟨as⟩

As to yourself I can't doubt that you will support this peaceful way of settling matters: in fact 'tis the only way left to get out of the dead-lock: so will you kindly *write* a word formally approving of the resolution.[2] As to the naming of the arbitrators, my own private ⟨way⟩ idea of the way of doing that is that Brown should name one and I another and that the third should be some stranger to us both; I am going to write him and tell him as much.

Marshall bore his execution with much indifference and good temper:

I suspect he smelt the advent of the golden shower and was preparing to hold his hat under the spout.

I am Yours ever
William Morris

MS: UBC, Angeli-Dennis Papers.

¹ The following is taken from the Minute Book of Morris, Marshall, Faulkner and Co., unpublished manuscript in the collection of S. L. and Helen Berger.

A meeting of the Firm was held at 26 Queen Sq Bloomsbury: Oct. 23, 1874. Present Messrs. Morris, Jones, Webb, Marshall, Faulkner.
1. Mr. Faulkner was asked to take the chair.
2. Resolved unanimously: —
    (i) that it is desirable that the firm be dissolved:
    (ii) that in order to ascertain the value of each share in the business 3 persons, not members of this firm, be appointed to act as assessors.
    (iii) that for the appointment of these assessors a unanimous agreement of the members of the firm be necessary.
    (iv) that a meeting of the firm be called at an early date to name the assessors & to consider the conditions under which they are to act.
3. Mr. Morris laid before the meeting two papers: -
    (i) a copy of a letter from Mr. Tupper, printer to the firm.
    (ii) a paper which had been ordered of Mr. Tupper by Mr. P. P. Marshall, with a printed heading as follows —

Morris, Marshall & Co.
9 Fenchurch Street
(and at 26 Queen Sq: Bloomsbury)
London. . . . 18. . . .

Resolved that this meeting disapproves of Mr. P. P. Marshall's proceedings in this matter and requests him to carry the business no further.

C. J. Faulkner
(Chairman)

Another meeting of the firm was held at 26 Queen Sq London W.C. on Nov. 4, 1874. Present Messrs. Morris, Webb, Marshall, Faulkner.
1. Mr. Faulkner was asked to take the chair.
2. Mr. Watts was present representing Mr. Brown, and Mr. White, Mr. Morris' solicitor was also present.
    The dissolution of the firm having been discussed, Mr. Watts on behalf of Mr. Brown said that as in the inception of the firm no member invested money, nor gave any time or labour without being paid at an agreed rate, the position of the several members ought to be considered as equal in respect to their claims on the assets of the firm — and further that he, Mr. Brown, considers that the goodwill ought to be taken at three years' purchase & ought to be included in the said assets. Mr. Marshall stated that in his opinion the goodwill was not worth 3 years' purchase, but that it might possibly be worth one year's purchase.
    Mr. Morris, Mr. Webb, and Mr. Faulkner gave it as their opinion that in the event of the dissolution of the firm there would be no goodwill.
3. It was agreed to have a balance sheet made out up to Michaelmas 1874 & to summon

[236]

a general meeting of the firm at the earliest possible period after its completion, to endeavor if possible to come to an amicable adjustment of the process of dissolution.

[2] Rossetti replied to Morris immediately (his reply is dated October 25): "I have received the minutes and notes from Q[ueen] S[quare] today. Of course I have no objection to the plan of appointing assessors. I don't see any object in my coming to the meeting on the 4th." The letter also contains a postscript, scrawled at the top: "I have been making a pattern for a new colouring of the marigold paper and will send it with remarks." John Y. LeBourgeois, who prints this letter as part of his discussion of the dissolution of the firm, believes that the postscript changes the accepted view that Rossetti took no part in the designing of wall papers by the firm. The postscript "also indicates," LeBourgeois says, "that Rossetti hoped to continue his relationship with the reorganized company, and, implicitly, his friendship with Morris." (See Notes and Queries, 216 [July 1971], 225.) Rossetti no doubt did want to remain associated with the firm; he was always anxious about money. As for a continuation of the friendship, the term is inadequate to describe the complexity of the relationship between Rossetti and Morris. Rossetti at this time was arranging to have his share of the settlement put in trust for Jane Morris, and he wrote to Watts that he would not attend a meeting on the 30th of October (apparently not held) because "You see my attitude to the world is that I give my share to Morris like the other members—still if this were publicly asserted by me in an emphatic manner and in open form it might give Morris the power of objecting to my modified course afterward if he chose. Thus I really think it seems necessary for me to stay away" (undated letter, typescript in Princeton T.). On the other hand, Rossetti and Morris had always been able to correspond about impersonal matters and continued to do so (see, for example, letter no. 391 concerning the S.P.A.B.). In a word, the dissolution of the firm probably made little difference to their difficult relationship, already profoundly affected by the attachment between Rossetti and Jane Morris.

253 • TO ROSALIND FRANCIS HOWARD

26, Queen Square,
Bloomsbury, London
October 24, 1874

Dear Mrs. Howard

I hope I shall not be troubling you if I write to tell you how grieved and distressed I was last night when Webb broke into a business-meeting here and told us this dismal news of George's illness:[1] I most fervently hope to hear better tidings of him soon.

It is most true that I scarcely knew how strong my friendship for you both was till my unhappiness at hearing of this misfortune proved it to me: though indeed you know I have, latterly especially, thought myself very much the friend of you & George. Excuse this blundering utterance of my sympathy for you and believe me always to be

Your affectionate friend
William Morris

MS: Howard Papers.

[1] Howard was ill with pneumonia. Shortly after, he left to spend the winter of 1874–1875 recuperating at San Remo.

254 • TO GEORGE CAMPFIELD

From Morris & Company,
26, Queen Square,
Bloomsbury, London, W.C.
October 30, 1874

My dear Campfield

Mr. Bowman[1] is out of work: if the Mile End Crucifixion is not given out[2] he had better have it if it is photographed: if not let him have a Calcutta figure:[3] he can at least do the flesh — Is the St. Thomas ready for him[4]

Yours
W.M.

MS: Dunlap Coll.

[1] Sewter lists (I, 101) Bowman as one of the chief glass-painters employed by Morris and Co. from 1877 to 1909, and notes (I, 46-47) that he also worked "as an occasional designer of foliage backgrounds, scrolls and other accessories for windows."

[2] Sewter lists (II, 134) a "Crucifixion" window by Burne-Jones, 1874, possibly for St. Benet's, Mile End, London. But the church no longer exists, and Sewter was unable to locate the window.

[3] Between 1873 and 1875, Morris and Co. did the west window for the Anglican Cathedral in Calcutta, India. Ten figures in all were designed by Burne-Jones for this window. See Sewter, II, 219.

[4] One of the figures in the lower tier of the window made for Calcutta Cathedral is titled "St. Thomas." See Sewter, II, 219.

255 • TO JAMES PORTER

26, Queen Square,
Bloomsbury, London, W.C.
[November 1874]

Dear Mr. Porter,[1]

Many thanks; my difficulty is that I dont want to lose the Icelandic lesson: so I am referring the matter to Magnússon and and if he can give me Wednesday evening I shall be very happy to dine with you on Tuesday: if not may I come to lunch with you on Wednesday: at all events I shall do myself the pleasure of seeing you, and the more doubtful pleasure of looking at our new windows in the hall.

I am
My dear Mr. Porter
Yours truly
William Morris

MS: Peterhouse.

[1] James Porter was Master of Peterhouse, Cambridge (see letter no. 170, n. 1). Between 1868 and 1874 the firm designed several windows and decorative wall tiles for the Com-

bination Room and Hall. For details see Sewter, II, 44-46; and Robinson and Wildman, p. 48.

256 • To Louisa Macdonald Baldwin
26, Queen Square,
Bloomsbury, London
November 15, 1874

My dear Louie

Many thanks for your kind and friendly letter, I would have written to you in answer to it before, but besides my usual 'don't know what to say', I have been dull as befits an Englishman in November. I am pleased that you remember my Mother under the Mold:[1] I have not seen Longfellows:[2] I should think he would make it literal at any rate. Mine is quite word for word; no very difficult task considering the likeness of the tongues.

Nothing happens to me here saving the usual run of work: I don't mean to say I complain of that though. I am going down to Cambridge in an hour to see a big window of ours in Jesus Coll: Chapel:[3] this means also a few hours reading of Icelandic with Magnússon, and two dinners one at Jesus & another at Peterhouse: My host at Peterhouse is a very good fellow, an Irishman nomine Porter, with so unappeasible an appetite for giving hospitality that 'tis said of him 'that he goeth about like a roaring lion seeking who may devour': his great friend is Fawcett[4] the polititian of whom of course you know: he is blind, owing to his father having shot him into his eye when he was a young man: I have a great respect for his courageous politics, and I believe he is really a good man: but — personally I don't find him a pleasure: a man must have a treasure of a soul to be agreable if he is blind: thats a fact: not that he is sulky or morose — quite the contrary.

I don't think I could read Jean Paul:[5] I can't help thinking that kind of thing is better talked than written.

I cant say that I get on with my drawing: but then I never expected I should: so I keep it up dreading the model day like I used to dread Sunday when I was a little chap.

Now I must say goodbye in order that I may put my clothes into my bag and sign the Saturday's check.

I am
Your affectionate
William Morris

MS: Texas.

[1] "The Mother Under the Mould," (*CW*, 24, 352). May Morris indicates (*CW*, 24,

xxxi) that it was one of a group of poems written at the time *The Earthly Paradise* was composed (1865-1870) and that they were all "part of the growth and development of *The Earthly Paradise* tales."

[2] Henry W. Longfellow, "The Musician's Tale: The Mother's Ghost," in his *Tales of a Wayside Inn*.

[3] Discussing the windows made in the 1870's for the Chapel of Jesus College, Vallance says (p. 74): "Of these the finest is undoubtedly the large window in the south wall of the south transept. The subject is the celestial hierarchy." See Sewter also, II, 42.

[4] Henry Fawcett (1833-1884) combined an academic career with active Liberal Party politics.

[5] Johann Paul Friedrich Richter (1763-1825), the German novelist and essayist who wrote under the name of Jean Paul and became known in England through Carlyle's praise of him. His novels include *Siebenkäs* (1796), *Titan* (1800-1803), *Flegeljahre* (1804-1805). His *Die Vorschule der Ästhetik* (1804) is one of the first studies of the novel as an art form.

257 • To Eiríkr Magnússon   Queen Sq:
                                              November 28 [1874]

My dear Magnússon

Many thanks for both your letters: I hope you will get settled comfortably soon down there. I think I told you that I was in trouble over my new poem; if that were once finished to my satisfaction I should be hot upon some more translation work, notably on Edda which I have quite made up my mind to publish some day or other: meantime I am going to publish a vol of poems consisting of the main part of my vol published first in 58, and such other things as I have about added to that:[1] about the same time I shall publish the Gunnlaug, the Frithiof & the Viglundr in one vol under the title of 'Three Icelandic Love Stories.' I don't know if you think that these require any alterations: I should rather like to rewrite the songs in Gunnlaug in alliterative instead of rymed verse, but I dont think it really matters. I am going to get my poem vol: together at once, & Ellis has promised to publish the saga on the day after the poems come out, as a reward of industry you see.[2] I shall go on with my reading very soon, & will avail myself of your kind offer to send you ⟨place⟩ chapter & verse of any difficulties by letter. I have not heard anything of Mrs. Magnússon: I hope she is better — I fancy I shall be in Cambridge on our stained-glass business in a short time & will look you up personally then.

                                I am
                                Yrs very truly
                                William Morris

ms: Iceland.

[1] A second edition of *The Defence of Guenevere* was published in 1875 by Ellis and White.

² *Three Northern Love Stories and Other Tales* was issued by Ellis and White in the summer of 1875.

258 · RECIPIENT UNKNOWN   26 Queen Sq
                                           Bloomsbury
                                           December 2 [1874]

Dear Sir

My friend Mr C. F. Murray writes to me from Italy that you were kind enough to undertake to bring home 2 vols: of M.SS. for me: in case you are come back I send round our boy with this to save you the trouble of posting or otherwise sending me the vols: and remain with many thanks

                              Yours obediently
                              William Morris

MS: Walthamstow.

259 · TO PHILIP BURNE-JONES   26, Queen Square,
                                           Bloomsbury, London
                                           Monday
                                           [December 7 or 14, 1874]

My dear Phil

What a shame not to have written to you before isn't it? But all my dearest friends will tell you if you ask them what a bad hand I am at letter writing: Even to your papa my letters have generally been of the briefest and woodenest.

Did you ever see my old room in A House — I thought it such a dismal place when I looked in there the other day[?]   a troublous life I led of it there for two years, after which I became a dignified person comparatively and was Captain of the room: are there still Captains of dormitorys?

Alas I did not fight enough in my time, from want of hope let us say, not want of courage, or else I should have been more respected in my earlier days: in the few fights I had I was rather successful, for a little, and thin (yes) boy as I was: for the rest I had a hardish time of it, as chaps who have brains and feelings generally do at school, or say in all the world even, whose griefs are not much shared in by the hard and stupid: nor its joys either, happily, so that we may be well content to be alive and eager, and to bear pain sometimes rather than to grow like rotting cabbages and not to mind it.

[241]

A hint to you on the mechanical part of battle: I was watching two little boys fighting in the street and it refreshed my memory of what used to go on at school: for each seemed afraid of the other and held his head down and hit round; and certainly the one who had stood up straight and hit out well from the shoulder would have got the best of it: and you may take it as a certain rule both in fisticuffs and all manner of fighting that if you are not afraid of being hit you can hit your enemy, and then the rest is a matter of endurance only.

Jenny and May are at my mother's this week: You may guess that they are eager for your return and the Christmas festivities. My word what a jolly time you will have of it! Nothing that has happened to me since I was [at?] school has given me quite as much pleasure as coming home for the holidays: make up your mind to that Phil; you will never be as happy again as you will be tomorrow week — though I hope with all my heart you will always be very happy and my good friend as I am

Your affectionate one
William Morris.

MS: BL, Add. MSS. 52708 (typescript). Extract published: Compton-Rickett, 127-28.

260 • TO EIRÍKR MAGNÚSSON   26, Queen Square,
                                                 Bloomsbury, London
                                                 December 29, 1874

My dear Magnússon

I am quite ashamed of having held my peace so long, & all the more as I must come before you with another apology; for in hunting up your corrected proofs of the book, no amount of search will bring to light sheets J & L, & one of these you have already sent me twice: I am really quite distressed at having to give you the trouble of going through them again: but it would be a great service to me if you could do so speedily, as I expect every day to have Strangeways threatening to break up the type. all owing to my abbominable sloth in the matter. As an excuse I must tell you that I have had very troublesome business on hand: one of those things that only happens to peaceable men like me once in a life-time.[1] I will tell you all about it when we meet. I am writing to Strangeways to send you J & L. also P & R which ends the text, as I already have your corrected M. N. O He shall also send you clean sheets of the finished text for index making As to preface I will set about a short one, & bring it with me when I come to see you, as I propose to do in about ten days   will you tell me of any day that will be agreable to you, next week, I was thinking of tomorrow week; Wednesday it is. Will you think of any necessary notes: I have Englished Högni & Heðinn from the Skalda[2] for that end. I will not leave the book now till it is done, but will carry it through hot-hand as far as my share goes. Ward[3] gave me some information about the orignes of the Hroi þáltr[?] curious enough. Lord, how I hate doing prefaces though! Give my kindest regards to all your party & accept my best wishes for you & yours.

> & Believe me
> Yours most truly
> William Morris

MS: Iceland.

¹ Probably a reference to the break-up of Morris, Marshall, Faulkner and Co.

² The story of "Hogni and Hedinn" is included in the *Skáldskaparmál* (Treatise on Poetic Diction). See *CW*, 10, 3. Morris's translation is one of the additional works in *Three Northern Love Stories*.

³ Harry Leigh Douglas Ward (1825-1906), medievalist and assistant in the department of manuscripts at the British Museum (1849-1893), where he catalogued Icelandic manuscripts. He also published a *Catalogue of Romances in the British Museum*, in three volumes, 1883-1910.

261 • TO AGLAIA IONIDES CORONIO   26, Queen Square,
                                                           Bloomsbury, London
                                                           January 1, 1875

My dear Aglaia

Shall I come round on Monday: I have been trying to come before & have not been able: I myself have been unwell, but am getting better — cold & — liver — if I may mention that organ to a lady: I beg to state that I have not the least idea where it lives

I was very sorry to miss you last Monday & that you had been unwell: I hope you will be much better on Monday.

> I am
> Your affectionate
> William Morris

MS: Yates Coll. Published: Henderson, *Letters*, 64-65.

262 • To Eiríkr Magnússon
26, Queen Square,
Bloomsbury, London
January 4, 1875

My dear Magnússon

Thanks for both your notes. as to Wednesday I am so full of indigestion that I think if it would be the same to you I will put it off till Wednesday *week* when I hope by eremitical fare, and quiet labour to have brought myself round again

You see 'tis so hard to deal with these things amidst boon companionship & enjoyment so I will say by your leave that I will come by the 12.5 train on Wednesday week the 13th January.

With kindest regards to Mrs. Magnússon & Lina

I am
Yours most truly
William Morris

MS: Iceland.

263 • To Jón Sigurðsson
26, Queen Square,
Bloomsbury, London
February 23, 1875

Dear Mr. Sigurðsson[1]

I send back herewith two parts of Flateyarbok[2] which Magnússon says were sent by mistake: I believe he will have written to you on the subject. I send also a cheque for £2.15s.9d. of which I owe you 1.15.9: ⟨&⟩ the other £1 being sent by Magnússon for Mr. þirrarðr[?] Kjerulf.

With best wishes & many thanks

I remain
Dear Mr. Sigurðsson
Yours very truly
William Morris

MS: Iceland.

[1] See letter no. 187, n. 1.

[2] The Flateyjarbók, the largest vellum manuscript written in Iceland, is a collection of songs, stories, sagas, and annals transcribed between 1387 and 1395. The manuscript is now in the Royal Library in Copenhagen. See also *CW*, 8, 238 (Magnússon's note concerning p. 97, line 32 of Morris's Icelandic Journal of 1871).

264 • TO EIRÍKR MAGNÚSSON
26, Queen Square,
Bloomsbury, London
February 23, 1875

My dear Magnússon
I am sending off the money to J.S. today. Thanks for Index & note: I must confess I have of late neglected Oddi for Mantua, Thingrskir for Rome, in short Ari hinn Froði for P Vergilius Maro:[1] but I am going home early this afternoon on purpose to mend my ways, & get to work on the final corrections which I hope wont take me many hours: and I shall instruct Strangeways to send you the revises straight to Cambridge. I am pretty well thank you, but weaker than I have been, & working harder at the same time. I did not get your letters till this morning as I was away from town, or I should have answered them before
With best wishes to you & yours
I am
Yours very truly
William Morris

P.S. By all means I will join the B.S.S.

MS: Iceland.
[1] Morris had begun to translate the *Aeneid* into English verse (see letter no. 265). The translation was published by Ellis and White in 1876. Ari Thorgilsson inn Frodi (1067-1148) was the author of the *Islendingabók*, a survey of the early political and church history of Iceland.

265 • TO CHARLES FAIRFAX MURRAY
26 Queen Sq:
March 11, 1875

My dear Murray
Enclosed you will find a ⟨pic⟩ tracing (full size) of one of six panels of our sideboard: ⟨on⟩ for which six we can afford £10 a piece if you care to undertake the commission: you can do any figure-work you please that you havn't used for C. & L. and paint it how you think best, understanding that the moulding & accessories will be probably gilded: the only conditions I impose on you are that the extremities should be well made out, & the surface pleasant & smooth — in short imagine me a medieval patron on that head: I enclose also a P.O.O for £5 for further disbursements on vellum: I would send more, but am scraping everything together to pay my thieves of partners, who have come to some kind of agreement ⟨to⟩ with me, if they don't cry off before the law-business is settled; which drags on confoundedly, & to say the truth bothers me more than I quite like to confess.

I got the vellum safe: though as by a miracle: for the box was quite smashed at one end: I daresay it was done in the last stages of the journey: but since it has happened it would be well another time to have the box a bit stronger: The vellum seems very good, though as you say rather over thin for my present needs: but I daresay I can pick out enough middling thick for my Virgil. By all means get me the 50 sheets of the bigger size sent, (or more if you can) which seems exceedingly good: by the way if it is any convenience in sending, or if it makes it any safer, the vellum might all be folded once (into folio). Many thanks for all the trouble you have taken in the matter.

As to my illumination work it don't get on just now, not because I shouldn't like to be at it, but because I am doing something else with Virgil, to wit, doing him into English verse: I have got toward the end of the 7th book, & shall finish the whole thing & have it out by the beginning of June[1] I hope: so you imagine I have not been quite idle: I shall keep you a big paper copy both of that & my new vol of Icelandic stories[2] & of the new edition of Guenevere.[3]

Gazing microscopically upon your letter I can perceive grumbling in it I think: as to the weather, console yourself by knowing what a devil of a time we have had of it here, & that the March E winds are only just beginning: and as to Italy console yourself by thinking how much the master would like to be there — yea & even myself. I don't agree with you & R,[4] but think on the contrary often enough that one can't know what rest is unless one lives among beautiful things or dignified nature. I suppose you have heard more or less about the storm in a teacup which went on here a few weeks back between Mr. R. & W.B. Scott & Tyrwhitt: it was all low and wretched, & Tyrwhitts book a most unutterable production.[5]

I have been in good spirits but not over well, the cold touched my liver up I think. I was going to see after your big book at last some 3 or 4 weeks ago, but found that Marks[6] had got it for some reason or other; can I do anything with DeCoverly[7] about it now?

As to the panels, if you care to do them, tell us when & where to send the doors (which are rather big by the way).

Also instead of that £5 P.O.O. I am sending ½ a £10 bank note by registered letter, & will send the other half on your answer acknowledging the receipt of it.

Jenny & May are very well, & I may say, devouring the sweets of knowledge. By the by those Roman pearls never came to hand at all.

Wishing you better weather & luck

I am
Yours affectionately
William Morris

MS: Texas. Published: *CW*, 11, xxii. Extract published: Henderson, *Letters*, 67.

[1] *The Aeneids of Virgil: Done Into English Verse by William Morris* was published by Ellis and White in 1876. Buxton Forman writes (p. 83) that he had a copy by the end of October 1875.

[2] Twenty-five copies of *Three Northern Love Stories and Other Tales* (1875) had been printed on Whatman's handmade paper. See Buxton Forman, p. 82.

[3] *The Defence of Guenevere and Other Poems* was reissued in April of 1875 by Ellis and White.

[4] John Ruskin.

[5] *Our Sketching Club: Letters and Studies of Landscape Art*, by Richard St. John Tyrwhitt (1827-1895), a painter, art critic, and admirer of Ruskin. In the *Examiner* for January 2, 1875, W. B. Scott published a harsh review, condemning the book generally and denouncing Tyrwhitt for appropriating the illustrations and text of Ruskin's *Elements of Drawing* (1856). Ruskin seized the occasion of a continuing debate in the columns of the *Pall Mall Gazette* on the subject of reviewing to defend Tyrwhitt and attack Scott. Ruskin's letter, published in the *Pall Mall Gazette*, January 11, 1875 (and reprinted in *Arrows of the Chace* [1880]), read in part:

> Mr. Scott is one of a rather numerous class of artists of whose works I have never taken any public notice. . . . My first acquaintance with Mr. Scott was at the house of a gentleman whose interior walls he was decorating with historic frescoes, and whose patronage I (rightly or wrongly) imagined at that time to be of importance to him. I was then more good-natured and less conscientious than I am now, and my host and hostess attached weight to my opinions. I said all the good I truly could of the frescoes, and no harm . . . and never since sought Mr. Scott's acquaintance further (though, to my regret, he was once photographed in the same plate with Mr. Rossetti and me). Mr. Scott is an honest man, and naturally thinks me a hypocrite and turncoat as well as a fool.

[6] Probably Murray Marks (1840-1918), the art dealer, who was a friend of Rossetti and often acted as his agent, buying blue china for him and also at times participating in the sale of his paintings.

[7] Roger De Coverley, a bookbinder from whom T. J. Cobden-Sanderson learned his trade. See Cobden-Sanderson, I, 94 and *passim*.

266 • To Louisa Macdonald Baldwin   26, Queen Square,
Bloomsbury, London
March 25, 1875

My dear Louie

It was very kind of you and I thank you very much for remembering me & my birthday: I have been a happy man with my friends; nor do I think as far as my constant affection & good wishes are concerned that I have done otherwise than to deserve the goodhap. I am in my second half of my life now, which is like to be a busy time with me,[1] I hope till the very end: a time not lacking content too I fancy: I must needs call myself a happy man on the whole: and I do verily think I have gone over every possible misfortune that may happen to me in my own mind, & concluded that I can bear it if it should come.

You would like to see my babies: they are such big girls — and so good; & even so handsome. Me! What a boy I feel still to have that responsibility on me for in spite of my 41 years I really don't feel a bit older than when Ned & I were living within sound of those tin-pot bells of St Pancras: well-remembered days when all adventure was ahead! Nay in some things I have run through a time when I was older — but by no means wiser — than I am now, between those days & these.

I shall be not very far from you next week: for I am going with Charley Faulkner, my inevitable travelling fellow, to look at my fatherland:[2] We are going to Shrewsbury, & thence to a College farm of his on the head-waters of Severn & Wye, where we are to have ponies and go 'over the hills & far away'; only for about a week in all though: 'tis a short journey, ⟨an⟩ but I think I shall love it: I think one sign of my increasing years is an increasing desire for travel that I may see the wonders of the world before it is all gone from me: but I suppose I shall get less & less of that pleasure for some time to come: for I am very busy both with my bread & cheese work, and also with my pleasure work of books. I am publishing a little set of Icelandic stories very soon:[3] also this summer a translation of the Æneids, which has been my great joy for months of late.

I was very sorry to hear of your trouble,[4] & wished & wish you all the solace of it that could be to people of feeling.

I dined at the Grange last night (my veritable birthday, by the way) and Aggy[5] was there also & seemed very well.

Perhaps you will let me come and see you one of the summer days, that faith of a very tenacious kind makes us still expect: my run west this time will be altogether too hurried to try it, or I was thinking of it.

Give my kindest regards to your husband & Edith[6] — and Believe me

Your very affectionate friend
William Morris

MS: Texas. Published: Mackail, I, 309-310; Henderson, Letters, 67-68. Extract published: CW, 11, xiii.

[1] Morris was about to assume sole proprietorship of the firm, reconstituted as Morris and Co. See next letter, n. 1.

[2] Morris's half-serious linking of himself to Wales is like the pleasure taken by George Meredith in the fancy that the Welsh origin of his name confirmed the existence of a poetic strain in his English character.

[3] *Three Northern Love Stories and Other Tales.*

[4] Hannah Macdonald, Louisa's mother, died on March 2, 1875.

[5] Agnes Macdonald, one of the five Macdonald sisters, had married Edward Poynter, the painter, in 1866.

[6] Edith Macdonald (1848-1937), the youngest sister, never married, and lived at Wilden with the Baldwins after her mother's death.

267 • TO EMMA SHELTON MORRIS   26, Queen Square,
                                                 Bloomsbury, London
                                                 March 25, 1875

Dearest Mother

Many thanks for your letter. I would have come to see you before now, but was obliged not to be out of the way while the trouble about the partnership was still about: I expect the deed now to be signed on Tuesday or Wednesday next;[1] after that I am going to fulfill an engagement I made last Christmas with Faulkner of going to Wales with him: We shall go on Tuesday or Wednesday night to Shrewsbury & then on the next day to the agent who lives near Llanidloes, & to whom Faulkner has written for ponies: we shall then have about a week's ride about the hills & so back: on my return I shall come down to you for a day.

I think it will do me good to go for this turn: I have been working very hard lately, & have been much bothered by this law business the past 6 weeks: my recalcitrant partners have behaved so badly that I felt half inclined more than once to throw the whole affair into Chancery: but law is too ticklish a matter for one to throw one's whole chances of livelihood into it: and I think I have done the best I could after all: though 'tis a deal of money to pay for shear nothing, and I doubt if their claims would have been recognized in the Court of Chancery — however 'tis all done now I hope —

Janey has been rather unwell of late   I suppose the bad weather has touched her up. The children are both very well, and are very good & dear.

The weather does seem to be changing at last: I hope you have been pretty well all through this cold & wretched spring.

Give my best love to Henrietta, I want very much to see her & You especially my dearest mother.

                                        I am
                                        Your loving Son
                                        William Morris

P.S. Love to Emmie also.

MS: Walthamstow. Extract published: CW, 11, xiii.

[1] Morris was referring to the dissolution of the firm (see letter no. 252). The final arrangements, not concluded until late March 1875, were these. Three of the partners, Burne-Jones, Faulkner, and Webb, waived their claims. Brown, Marshall, and Rossetti at

first stood firm on their legal rights, but in the end it was arranged that they should be compensated for the loss of interest at the rate of £1,000 each. The firm was reconstituted under Morris's sole management as Morris and Company, the name that had already been in use for some years in place of the longer one in which it had originally been registered. Burne-Jones and Webb continued to supply designs for stained glass and furniture. See Mackail, I, 305-308; and Henderson, *Life*, p. 150.

268 • To Jane Morris   Llanidloes
                                                             All fools day
                                                             [April 1] 1875

Dearest Janey

I am here safely this evening after a somewhat Gilpinian exit from Newtown The country is very beautiful & the weather fine: a great broad valley with the young Severn winding about it, fine hills all about not to say exactly mountains with passes here & there showing 'really' mountains in the distance: all the lower country beautifully wooded & not a few pretty black & white houses — tomorrow we go into much wilder country across the mountains to a town called Machhynlleth (don't try to pronounce it till I come home). This town is rather dirty & manufactory but has got a pretty town hall We had a good dinner with Charley's farmer — seemed a good fellow: I need not say that as he was not called Morris Roberts or Evans he was called Jones.

The best of loves to the littles: my next letter home I shall write to them & send love to you.

                                        Your
                                        William Morris

P.S. Picture to yourself the condition of poor Marshall by this time![1]

MS: BL, Add. MSS. 45338. Published: *CW*, 11, xiv.

[1] Possibly an allusion to P. P. Marshall's alcoholism and discomfiture over the terms of the settlement in the break-up of Morris, Marshall, Faulkner and Company.

269 • To Jenny and May Morris   Bull Hotel, Bala
                                                             April 5, 1875

Dearest Jenny & May

The Bull's head is the proper name though ⟨in spite of⟩ in accordance with the picture: 'tis a queer dull little grey town is Bala: but we are resting the horses here for a day: this morning I went out fishing in the rain up a very pretty river, the Welsh name of which will not stick in my head: I caught but two trouts which we had for dinner: the little town lies at the head of a Lake some 5 miles long which the Welsh call Llynn Teged: I don't know what that means: indeed I am but an ignorant person in Wales: the Country is pretty about the Lake but not so fine as some we have been through: we had a beautiful ride yesterday from Dinas Mowdwy up the Valley of the Dyfi (a river) till it came to an end, and then over the mountain necks into another valley, & so here. The Dyfi Valley was most beautiful, & I thought that it would be so nice to have a little house & a cow there, & a Welsh poney or two: the little houses are very rough outside but cleaner & trimmer inside than one might imagine: we had our lunch in one (a pot-house) yesterday, & they brought us the biggest loaf I ever saw: the Italian cake-bread was a mere joke to: it was very good to eat. Tomorrow we go to Dolgelly which is in a very mountainous country under Cader Idris; not more mountainous though than Dinas Mowddwy: the next day to Towyn, about a mile from the sea; and on Thursday to Dinas Mowdwy again by a road that runs on the other side of Cader Idris: and on Friday we set off to Oxford & London from that place so that I shall be back some time on Friday evening probably; & so glad as I shall be to see you & the Mammy!

We have seen something of Plinlimmon already: stopped at a farm of University Coll: under it or rather amidst it, (for 'tis a great spreading down-like thing not craggy,) on Thursday: the farm-house kitchen was such a nice place: there were some very pretty children there, but not a word could they talk of anything but Welsh, except one older girl.

Well goodbye my dear dears till Friday evening or so, & give my best love to Mammy.

I am
Your most loving father
William Morris

MS: BL, Add. MSS. 45339. Published: *CW*, 23, xv; Henderson, *Letters*, 68-69.

270 • TO AGLAIA IONIDES CORONIO   Towyn
                                                    April 7 [1875]

My dear Aglaia

I thought you might like to hear of my being still in the land of the living: I am in a little queer grey Welsh ⟨church⟩ town by the sea-shore on the flats under the mountains in the most Welsh part of Wales: we rode here through a rough mountain road this morning through rain and sunshine: it was very beautiful a great part of the way: desolate enough otherwhere, but always interesting to me. Tomorrow we ride down a long trench (as it were) on the other side of the mountains we passed ⟨yes⟩ today and that will be our last ride; for on Friday we shall take train home: I will try to call on you as I come home from business on Monday if I don't hear from you to stop me.

It is a great thing to have seen new country if it has any character, and a great deal of what I have seen is very impressive: about here the people talk very little English which I am glad to find; and in a queer way they are proud of their Welsh: they are mostly very polite & much better mannered than the same sort of people would be in England.

I will tell you more about it all when I ⟨saw⟩ see you: I have got a most villanous scratchy pen: so excuse the writing

I am
Yours affectionately
William Morris

 MS: Yates Coll. Published: Henderson, *Letters*, 69.

271 · To F. J. WEIDEMAN
26, Queen Square,
Bloomsbury, London
April 20 [1875]

Dear Sir[1]

Mr. Ruskin tells me you are studying decoration and wish for help from me. Both for his sake and for yours, since I hear that you are really interested in it, I shall be happy to do what I can, though I fear it may be but little, so will you call at 26 Queen Sq, Bloomsbury on Thursday or Friday next, if convenient to you between the hours of 11½ & 2, & you can see at all events what we are doing & explain to me more particularly what you want to do.

If Thursday or Friday are inconvenient to you, will you write & tell me when you like to call, and if I can meet you I will.

I am
Dear Sir
Yours faithfully
William Morris

MS: Yates Coll.
[1] Unidentified.

272 • To WILLIAM BELL SCOTT   Horrington House
                                                                  May 6, 1875

My dear Scott

I must ask you to forgive me for letting a week go by without taking any notice of the gift of your book;[1] but I do think you remember that I am a bad letter-writer, ⟨and⟩ even ⟨in an⟩ on ordinary matters, and often on extraordinary ones a helpless shamefacedness holds me back till I find I have committed an act of rudeness (as now) which I am very far from meaning: I trust to your good nature to understand that, and forgive me.

I was very glad to see your book with the poems that I first found so sympathetic when I came up to London years ago, when I was pretty much a boy; and also that there were other ones that seemed to me as good of which I have heard nothing meanwhile. Pray believe that I was touched & delighted by the affectionate inscription in the beginning, and though not more so (in some sense) by ⟨the⟩ my share of the dedication at the end, yet as much, amidst my surprise at the honour of it: for indeed I did not suppose you would have put me in the same place with A.C.S. & D.G.R.[2] both of whom I consider as for the more part unpassed masters over me in the art. I am sorry we have seen but little of each other for so long. I was thinking of coming in ⟨some⟩ one morning next week on my way to town to see if you would come over here some evening soon, & meet Ned Jones. I was very vexed that my Welsh engagement kept me from coming to you that evening you asked me.

With hearty thanks for your book & its dedication

                              I am
                              Yours affectionately
                              William Morris

 MS: Princeton T. Published: MM, I, 78; Henderson, *Letters*, 70-71; Vallance, 430; Scott, II, 212.

[1] *Poems*, subtitled "Ballads, Studies from Nature, Sonnets, etc.," illustrated by seventeen etchings by Scott and L. Alma-Tadema (London: Longmans, 1875).

[2] Swinburne and Rossetti. The *Dedicatio Postica* reads:

Now many years ago in life's midday,
I laid the pen aside and rested still,
Like one barefooted on a shingly hill:
Three poets then came past, each young as May,
Year after year upon their upward way,
And each one reached his hand out as he passed,
And over me his friendship's mantle cast,
And went on singing every one his lay.
Which was the earliest? Methinks 'twas he

Who from the Southern laurels fresh leaves brought,
Then he who from the North learned Scaldic power,
And last, the youngest, with the rainbow wrought
About his head, a symbol and a dower —
But I can't choose between these brethren three.

273 • To Charles Fairfax Murray   26 Queen Sq:
May 27 [1875]

My dear Murray

I was very glad to get your ⟨note⟩ letter & hear of your whereabouts and how you were. The vellum came all safe to hand: many thanks for it: I noticed that the smaller size seemed very good: but had not much time to attend to it much as I am very busy all sorts of ways. I have got my partnership business settled at last, and am sole lord & master here now, with never a Jawkins to refer unpleasant words to:[1] however 'tis a great blessing, & has set me working hard to make things go: I have somewhat slacked from the Virgil translation, as I found it not possible to get it out this summer, & easy enough to get it out by October: also I have begun one of the Master's pictures for the Virgil: I make but a sorry hand at it at first, but shall go on at it till (at the worst) I am wholly discomforted.

Meantime whether I succeed or not in the end 'twill be a long job: so I am asking you if you would do some of them, & what it would be worth your while to do them for:[2] I think I should have to see you before you could get to work on them; but if you dont come over here this summer, as I suppose you wont by your letter, I shall like enough be coming to Italy *next* year & we can talk about it then. I think the 4 seasons & Sun & Moon would do very well for the sideboard panels:[3] Wardle is enclosing a note in this about them: for the rest do just what you think good, in the matter.

Didn't you say something in your last letter about wanting some of our blue & green fine serge over there: if you will let me know what you want as to colour and the rest I will send you some as a gift if you will take it.

The Master is fairly well now, though lately he was but poorly, I think he had been overworking himself. I spent two days with him & Faulkner down at Oxford this Whitsuntide & we were very merry together: we saw Ruskin there: he was amusing, but refused to enter into our enthusiasm for the country & green meadows: said that there were too many butter cups & it was like poached eggs.

Last Easter I went with Faulkner for about a week's ride in Wales;

which was very amusing the look of the country was so exactly what I had expected, that I was quite surprised, to make a bit of a bull.

Mrs. Lock called about 6 weeks ago & brought Mrs. Morris the beads Many thanks for them. She & the babies send love: they are very big as usual, but I think Jenny will not grow much more up and down, as she is getting 'tall across'

I shall be publishing the Icelandic stories in a week or two I will send you an ordinary copy out there and keep a big one for you: I have also I believe a big paper Guenevere of the new issue for you.

After all I have no news for you, I am up to the neck in turning out designs for papers chintzes & carpets and trying to get the manufacturers to do them:[4] I think we are doing some good things in that way.

With best wishes for your welfare in your new estate

I am

Yours affectionately

William Morris

ms: Texas. Extract published: Mackail, I, 310; Henderson, *Letters*, 71.

[1] The character, in *David Copperfield*, to whom Mr. Spenlow always attributes a hard, unyielding attitude in business matters.

[2] Morris's illuminated manuscript of the *Aeneid* contains a number of half-page historiated miniatures by Murray after designs by Burne-Jones. See Fairbank, p. 68.

[3] Morris was referring to the offer of a commission to do six panels of a sideboard. See also letter no. 265.

[4] The listed wallpaper designs that Morris made in 1875 were the Marigold and Acanthus; the chintzes of this year were Tulip and Carnation; and the carpets, Lily, and Tulip and Lily. See Clark, pp. 14, 56.

274 · To Emma Shelton Morris 26, Queen Square,
Bloomsbury, London
May 27, 1875

Dearest Mother

I havn't forgotten your birthday & the date of it, & would have written earlier in the week, but I was not keeping count of the days of the month: I send you my best love & many happy returns of the day: item I send you a flower pot & saucer from some samples that they have just sent us from India, and which are still curiosities, as I suppose there are not 2 more in England at present out of the India House Museum.[1] I have just come from the DGC meeting &, I suppose, ended my business there, except for receiving my £100 which they were once again kind enough to vote us.[2] Stanley will tell you all about the meeting.

I am much better than I have been. I went down (or up) to Oxford for 2 days at Whitsuntide and I am going there about the middle of June again to take my M.A. degree; which is perhaps rather a 'fad' of mine; but I thought I might indulge it for once.   I hope you are keeping well, & enjoying this beautiful weather. Give my best love to Henrietta

I am Dearest Mother
Your most affectionate Son
William Morris

MS: Walthamstow. Extract published: Mackail, I, 324; CW, 11, xiv; Henderson, *Letters*, 73.

[1] On April 22, 1875, *The Times* had reported (p. 12) that the India Museum collection "would be opened at its temporary home at the South Kensington" Monday, May 25th.

[2] Probably a reference to Morris's resignation from a directorship in the Devon Great Consols Company. Mackail dates (I, 324) this letter 1876, though Morris clearly wrote 1875.

---

275 • To Eiríkr Magnússon
26, Queen Square,
Bloomsbury, London
May 27, 1875

My dear Magnússon

I called yesterday at the thrall Strangeways: so if you dont [get] the sheets at once all right please let me know:

Do you mind leaving out the note about the Flateyarbók in the preface?[1] You see my preface is written entirely to ignorant people; and your note I think would set people to hauling me over the coals for its' baldness & make them want to know how much I know of Syntipas & Sendibad & the Seven Wise Masters: exceeding small is that knowledge I do assure you. If you are anxious to have it in however, never mind: only I think 'twould be better to leave out the last sentence, in which you *name* Vigfússon & Myer:[2] they will know well enough what you mean without that.

I hope you are better now   I myself am getting round to my usual insulting health again

Yours very truly
William Morris

MS: Iceland.

[1] Apparently Magnússon did mind. The Preface to *Three Northern Love Stories* includes a note about the Flateyjarbók. The note begins by discussing the location of "Roi the Fool" in the Flateyjarbók and then elaborates upon the probable authorship and place of composition of the entire manuscript. See *CW*, 10, 4.

[2] Magnússon seems to have yielded on this point. There is no mention of Vígfússon (see letter no. 656, n. 2) and Myer in the note. See also letter no. 276.

276 • To Eiríkr Magnússon

26, Queen Square,
Bloomsbury, London
June 3, 1875

My dear Magnússon

Many thanks for last of the index which I have sent off to Strangeways at once. As to the note 'Flateyarbok': I will put it in except the last — 'kick on the arse' I must call it I'm afraid. Of course you mustnt suppose I don't see the value of the note: only as above my poor preface was not meant to be taken even by an ignoramus for a learned one. What a game Watts' book on Iceland will be when it comes out:[1] though I have somewhat spoilt the best part of it, to whit, that about the literature of the country, though I daresay not much: 'tis no use trying to explain what it was like except viva voce. Watts in his gratitude to me proposed to name me as having given him information on that head: fancy (if you can) my horror & adjurations!

I have been very much grieved & dismayed at what you told me about the poor Eastfirthers:[2] as to giving you names,[3] I am afraid any I could give you would be little use: rich men are most commonly damned stingy: of course I will do what I can in a money way myself: especially if I dont have to pay all at once, and I am pretty sure of getting something from my own immediate friends.

I am quite well now, thank you, and desperately hard at work, which after all is a great pleasure.

With kindest remembrances to Mrs. Magnússon & Lina

I am
Yours very truly
William Morris

I am very glad to hear that Thomas is coming out somehow
(P.S. of course I can give you names enough)

MS: Iceland.

[1] *Snioland; or, Iceland, its Jokulls and Fjalls*, by William Lord Watts, was published in 1875.

[2] In 1875, the volcano Askja erupted, devastating the northeast of Iceland and causing some emigration.

[3] Magnússon enlisted Morris's aid in founding a Mansion House Relief Committee to collect money for the distressed area. See Richard L. Harris, "William Morris, Eiríkur Magnússon, and the Icelandic Famine Relief Efforts of 1882," *Saga-Book* XX, pts. 1-2 (London: University College, 1978-1979), p. 32.

277 · TO FREDERICK WILLIAM FARRAR[?] 26, Queen Square,
Bloomsbury, London
July 6, 1875

Dear Sir[1]

I have seen a letter from you to my friend Burne-Jones in which you
mention your wish to have if possible a window from us: would you
be so good as to give us the measurements of the lights you wish to
fill, & if possible some indication of the subjects you want to have
represented, and I will give you at once something like an estimate of
the ⟨pr⟩ cost —

I need not say it will give me a great deal of pleasure to have anything
to do with the decoration of the Chapel.[2]

I am
Dear Sir
Yours faithfully
William Morris

MS: McMinn Papers.

[1] This letter was probably addressed to Frederick William Farrar (1831-1903), who was
headmaster of Marlborough College in 1875. He became Canon of Westminster in 1876
and Chaplain to the House of Commons in 1890. In 1895 he was made Dean of Canter-
bury.

[2] Of Marlborough College. The original chapel, for which Morris and Co. did the
window discussed in this letter, was replaced during 1883-1886 by a new building de-
signed by Bodley and Garner. See N. Pevsner, *Buildings of Britain: Wiltshire* (Penguin
Books, 1963), p. 304.

278 · TO EMMA SHELTON MORRIS July 17, 1875

Dearest Mother

I send you herewith a large paper copy of my new translation vol:[1] I
would have sent it before only the large paper copies were not ready: I
have told Ellis & White[2] to send you three weekly papers of today that
have very good reviews of the book:[3]

On Monday I am going down to Staffordshire on manufacturing
business & shall have to be at work there all the week.[4] The week after
I shall come and see you if I possibly can. Meanwhile I hope you are
keeping well in spite of this astounding weather.

Best love to Henrietta & yourself. My babies are very well: & work-
ing very hard

I am
Dearest Mother
Your most affectionate Son
William Morris

MS: Walthamstow. Extract published: *CW*, 11, xv.

¹ *Three Northern Love Stories and Other Tales.*

² David White was Frederick S. Ellis's partner at this time.

³ *The Athenaeum* for July 17, 1875 contained an unsigned review praising the book (reprinted in Faulkner, pp. 211-15). *The Saturday Review* of the same date also reviewed it favorably.

⁴ This is the first reference in the surviving letters to what had become a major new occupation for Morris: the study and practice of dyeing. Mackail writes (I, 311-16) that in the production of textiles by the firm, Morris had been frustrated by material that would not take color well and by inadequate dyes. To surmount these obstacles, Morris set himself, first, to learn the theory of dyeing, reading through French books of the sixteenth and seventeenth centuries, Gerard's *Herbal* (1597), and even Pliny. He then experimented in the little dye-house at Queen Square, dyeing with his own hands. However, these premises were too small for work on a scale that would meet the needs of the firm. He needed a regular dye-works, and for this, as well as further instruction, he went to Thomas Wardle (1831-1909), owner of a dyeing business at Leek, Staffordshire, and brother-in-law of George Wardle, Morris's manager at Queen Square. (The coincidence of names is explained by Thomas Wardle's marriage to Elizabeth, daughter of Hugh Wardle, a distant relative; George Wardle was her brother.) Thomas Wardle was already known as an authority on dyeing silk and cotton, and shared Morris's enthusiasm for reviving methods that had gone out of use. For about two years, from the summer of 1875, Morris made many visits to Leek, "where he and Wardle actually restored vegetable dyeing to the position of an important industry" (Mackail, I, 316).

279 • To Jane Morris

Care of Thomas Wardle Eqre.
Leek
Tuesday
July [20] 1875

Dearest Janey

Here I am all safe but with a woeful cold, which has upset my insides also a bit: twas an evil day yesterday, & is dull & sorrowful today: but the country is not half ugly about here, & not far off is very beautiful: the town also is not nearly as bad as I expected it to be: there is a raven here that says 'What' and looks upon most things as butchers meat, but especially tight legs.

Give my love to the dear babes: & tell them the weather will clear soon.

I am
Your loving
William Morris

MS: BL, Add. MSS. 45338.

280 • To Jane Morris
St. Edward St:
Leek
Friday [July 23, 1875]

Dearest Janey

It seems to be quite settled now that I cant get back till this day week: I really can't come away without having come here for nothing, not that I havn't got on fairly well, but I must see something more of results — The copper pots in the dye-houses full of bright colours where they are dyeing silks look rather exciting; but alas! they are mostly aniline. our own Establishment is very small but I daresay will for sometime to come turn out more goods by a great deal than we shall sell.[1] The country is certainly very pretty, a land of hillocks and little valleys, all curiously shaped. The last few days have been really beautiful except for a heavy shower just now.

On Sunday I am to have a days outing to Rowsly & Haddon. Perhaps I ought to have stayed at home & done my Virgil, but I have got so tired with being unwell these few last days that I shall be glad of a rest. I am much better now & getting all right.

The most of loves to the littles   I shall write to them next week.

I am
Your loving
William Morris

MS: BL, Add. MSS. 45338. Published: Mackail, I, 316.

[1] According to Mackail (I, 316) this soon proved untrue.

281 • To Emma Shelton Morris
Leek
Staffordshire
July 27, 1875

Dearest Mother

Many thanks for your note which Janey sent on: I find my business will keep me here till Saturday next so I shall not see you till some day *next* week: The country is very pretty hereabout though 'tis only 12 miles from the Pottery towns.[1] On Saturday & ⟨Sunday⟩ we went to Bakewell and slept there, & so back on Sunday to Leek: a very beautiful drive it is. I went into Haddon Hall[2] once more, and there I met an old acquaintance strange to say: Miss Katie Moxon that was to wit, with her husband & Miss Moxon.[3] I did not know her, but she did me & set her husband to ask: they sent their regards to you & Henrietta.

I shall be very glad to get back to my babies again: though I have not had an unpleasant time of it here on the whole, and hope I shall have advanced my work by the visit.

My best love to Henrietta.

The weather seems to have picked up here: the last 3 days have been dry & sunshiny though very cool at night.

Good bye with best love dearest Mother:

> I am
> Your most affectionate Son
> William Morris

MS: Walthamstow. Extract published: *CW*, 11, xvii.

[1] The "Five Towns"—Tunstall, Burslem, Hanley, Stoke-on-Trent, and Longton—which are the setting for Arnold Bennett's major novels.

[2] See letter no. 409, and n. 3.

[3] Catherine Moxon, the third daughter, and presumably Emma, the oldest daughter, of the publisher Edward Moxon (1801-1858), whose editions of nineteenth-century English poetry included Tennyson's *Poems* (1857), illustrated by D. G. Rossetti, J. E. Millais, and Holman Hunt.

282 • TO AGLAIA IONIDES CORONIO

Care of Thomas Wardle Esqe
St Edward Street
Leek, Staffordshire
Wednesday [July 28, 1875]

My dear Aglaia

This is a quiet morning for me, so I am writing to my friends, you amongst them.

I cannot get back before Saturday night I find, which I am sorry for, but it can't be helped: There are more difficulties in getting good colours & fast ones than you can easily imagine; but I hope to come to it soon.

Except for being away from friends I am comfortable enough here. Mrs. Wardle[1] went to the sea-side to her children at an early date; and the days pass very quietly.

Saturday & Sunday were holidays and we drove over into the Derbyshire dales & slept there on Saturday night.

The country is pretty all about and not at all smoky, though 'tis only 12 miles from Burslem, the worst of the pottery-towns. My work tries the patience but is tedious rather than hard: but it takes up pretty much all my time so that I have had little or no time for literary work —

For my comfort the last three days, or indeed four have been sunny & dry here: it was very dreary here at first in the sloppy weather.

My writing time is up so goodbye.

> I am
> Your affectionate
> William Morris

MS: Yates Coll.

¹ Elizabeth Wardle (1834-1902), an embroiderer. She married Thomas Wardle in 1857 and they had fourteen children. In 1879, she founded the Leek Embroidery Society, whose aim was to improve the general standard of embroidery. The work of the Society was done by its members, all female, in their own homes. It was emphasized that the work should be undertaken only by ladies "whose time was not money to them, and who did not expect to gain a livelihood by it." When Wardle opened a shop in New Bond Street, London, in 1883, which sold eastern silks and other materials, his advertising circular stated: "We shall have associated with us the Leek Embroidery Society which is now so widely known." The products of the Society were sought by churches especially, and during the 1880's and 1890's many church officials commissioned work from it. Around 1881, Elizabeth Wardle also founded the Leek School of Art Embroidery, which was closely allied to the Society. Sir Philip Cunliffe-Owen, then director of the South Kensington Museum, applauded the founding of the school in a letter to Wardle in 1881: "To found the Leek School of Art Embroidery—to provide a suitable home for it, to have a foundation for the maintenance of the same, including the payment of a mistress, would be a great and good work. It would enable classes of females to attend the schools of an evening; it would afford them the example of never having an idle moment, and further would help revive the great silk trade, and one branch of it, embroidery, which would respond to the growing taste for the same amongst all classes of society." See Callen, pp. 8, 226; Morris, *Victorian Embroidery*, p. 120; and D. G. Smart, ed., *The History of the Leek Embroidery Society*, Department of Adult Education, University of Keele, 1969, pp. 7-10.

283 • TO ROSALIND FRANCIS HOWARD

> Leek
> Staffordshire
> July 30, 1875

Dear Mrs. Howard

I am very vexed but not at all surprised, knowing, as I told you what a risky thing that transparent colour was: I dont believe it to be the paperhanger's fault. I am coming to town tomorrow, and will come round next Tuesday morning to breakfast if that will suit you; when I hope you will extend the clemency that you are enclined to show to somewhat dishonest tradesmen, to a somewhat honest one, as I boast myself.

I have been learning several very interesting things here, and love art and manufactures, & hate commerce and moneymaking more than ever:

I look forward very much to talking the whole matter over with you: though I daresay we shall differ on a point or two.

I am
Yours affectionately
William Morris

Please give my love to George.

MS: Howard Papers.

---

284 • TO THOMAS WARDLE   26, Queen Square,
Bloomsbury, London
August 3, 1875

My dear Mr. Wardle[1]

My bundle of fents[2] were very much admired by my artistic friends, and almost all of them seem good in colour when they come among our things here: the only draw-back to my satisfaction is the Prussian blue, which is a terrible dissappointment: all the more as one of the blues & one of the greens were among the best of the colours, and I had picked them out for orders at once: *but* they wash worse than Clarkson's[3] blues; in fact worse than any I have ever seen and it would be useless for us to sell them in their present state: this is wholly a surprise to me, as Hayworths washed pretty well, and we should have been contented with them in that condition: I enclose samples of Kay's & Hayworth's ⟨wash⟩ prussian's washed in *exactly the same way*: so you see it can be done: I beg to assure you that I am quite vexed for the trouble that this will give you, but you must not be too downhearted about it, for the madders ⟨were⟩ are really very good colours, and the yellows seem to wash pretty well. So we shall have some 12 & 15 fents to print from.

My explanation of the affair is this: Hayworth was a steam-colour printer & knew nothing about madder; Kay is a madder-printer & knows nothing about steam-colours. The last part of the sentence I will stick to till Kay produces a Prussian blue that will wash as well as 810, and you may tell him so. I blame myself for not making him soap some of the blue & green fents while I was there but you know I had troubles enough on hand.

What are we to do? First, can Kay be driven to make his blues as fast as Hayworth's? Second when can we have our indigo vats? We must give up blues & greens till one or both of these things is accomplished.

[263]

Meantime I need not say we must get on as fast as possible with the madders & yellows, additional orders for which I send down today.

I send you also a sample of the grey cloth we chose (6) and which the cloths you are now printing ought to match: will you [the rest of this letter is missing].

MS: Duke.

[1] See letter no. 278, n. 4.

[2] Samples of cloth, presumably the first experimentally dyed material produced by Morris under Wardle's guidance at Leek during July.

[3] In 1873, the firm made its first chintz design, Tulip and Willow. It was produced by Thomas Clarkson (of Bannister Hall, near Preston, Lancashire), the leading calico printer of the day. But Morris was not satisfied with the results, and the design was not put on sale until it was printed at the Merton Abbey works in 1889. See Henderson, *Life*, p. 155.

285 • To Eiríkr Magnússon Horrington House
August 3 [1875]

My dear Magnússon

I had just bought 1 doz silver tea-spoons as Faulkner & my remembrance-gift to Lina when I got your letter; an uninventive present I am afraid, but the heat has killed my imagination. I expect Einar to call tomorrow & he thinks of going to Cambridge so he can take the spoons to you: if he does not, I will send them. I wish you a most pleasant voyage, & hope you will find everybody well, and the country come in for a share of the hot weather that has fried my liver

Please give my best wishes to the bride, & to Mrs. Magnússon my kindest regards, & to Mrs. Gunnarson[1] as I suppose you will see her, & remember me in general to all I know that you come across: I am hurried & desperately hard at work, so excuse this short note —

I am
Yrs very truly
William Morris

MS: Iceland.

[1] See letter no. 169, n. 1.

286 • To Thomas Wardle 26, Queen Square,
Bloomsbury, London
August, 1875

My dear Mr. Wardle

Thanks for your letter. I am quite contented to wait a little about the indigo matter, and am meantime anxiously expecting the pieces of our order: the light shade in the sample received from Mr. Woodcroft is all right.

We send today some linen which pleases us, which we want you to print yard-fents of in any thing that is going; but no doubt madder would be the most important to do them in. We should like also yard fents of the wool serge and the thin chalis if you have enough of those materials; otherwise we will send you more.

I was very sorry to learn that your child was ill. I hope all is going on well with it now.

I have been looking about for a Gerard[1] for you, but have not met with a good one yet, but suppose I shall soon. Meantime I have sent you a copy of Philemon Hollands Pliny: a most curious book in itself & the translation a model of English:[2] altogether one of the most amusing books in the world to my mind.

I am going to Kelmscott on Monday for a week: and have faint hopes of picking up a perch though the weather is so queer I don't know what to make of it.

Pray give my kind remembrances to Mrs. Wardle, & to Mr. Woodcroft also: I shall on reflection send the message about the cloth straight to him in case you are away.

Thanks for the bit of chintz, which I thought a pretty design, though the loss of the green has injured it

> I am
> Yrs very truly
> William Morris

Thos: Wardle Eqre

MS: Duke. Copy in V&A.

[1] The *Herball or Generall Historie of Plantes* (1597) by John Gerard (1545-1612), issued in a revised edition by Thomas Johnson in 1633. One of its chief interests to Morris was its large number of beautiful woodcuts, which he enjoyed for their own sake and also used as an inspiration for designs. Mackail notes (I, 314) that the *Herbal*, "the old favorite of his boyhood," supplied Morris with "useful information about certain disused vegetable dyes."

[2] Pliny's *Historia Naturalis* was translated as *Natural Historie of the World* by Philemon Holland (1552-1637) in 1601. At his death, Morris owned a copy of the first edition of Holland's translation. It is interesting to note, too, that Morris gave a copy of the book to Buxton Forman, according to the latter. (See letter no. 291, n. 1.)

287 • To Emma Shelton Morris　　　　　　26, Queen Square,
　　　　　　　　　　　　　　　　　　　　Bloomsbury, London
　　　　　　　　　　　　　　　　　　　　September 1, 1875.

Dearest Mother

I propose coming down by the 5 oclock train on Monday next, and going to London again some time on Tuesday: I have not been able to get away before as Wardle is first going out of town and I am otherwise also very busy.

Best love to Henrietta

　　　　　　　　　　　　　　I am
　　　　　　　　　　　　　　Your most affectionate son
　　　　　　　　　　　　　　William Morris

MS: Walthamstow.

288 • To Thomas Wardle　　　　　　　　26, Queen Square,
　　　　　　　　　　　　　　　　　　　　Bloomsbury, London
　　　　　　　　　　　　　　　　　　　　September 3, 1875

My dear Mr. Wardle

The goods are not yet come to hand, but as I have a good deal to say I will begin my letter now. 1st. the yellow fent to hand this morning is very good. 2nd. I send herewith an order for green & blue pieces which I shall be very glad to have: only I must warn you that you will find them very much more difficult to get right (artistically) than the yellows or madders, assuming as think one must for the present that a dead match is impossible: in staining the blues so as to take away the coldness of the Prussian blue it is very difficult to avoid *dirtying* them too much; I should think that, if it can be used in steam colours, weld[1] would be better than the berry or bark for this purpose as the latter darken so much on soaping: the darker the blues are the more they will bear greening: any redness in the dark outline of the tulip destroys the sweetness of the colour — as to the colours ordered: the light colour in 987 would bear to be less green; it is also rather dirty 989 is good, but not so good as Hayworths 810 which leaves little to be desired, it is a once warmer and cleaner than 810; if 810 gets any dirtier or redder even but a little than it now is, it will be ruined.　in green 968 the lighter colour might be a little fresher: this fent washed very badly the darkening of the yellow in soap obviously ⟨helping⟩ making the evil worse,　967 leaves nothing to be desired if it were only faster: the colour is quite perfect.　the fent of marigold (unnumbered) might be a little lighter & brighter: it washed much better than the other greens. As to the fastness of blues & greens I shall be satisfied with such degree of it (in Prussians) as will allow them to be *cleaned* quite well; which cleaning I understood you to say you could undertake. Heyworth's blue I must observe was washed (I believe) when it first came to hand. If these blues & greens now ordered turn out satisfactory I will order a lot more at once, as they are much more important to me than the yellows; the remainder of which however please let us have as soon as possible. Indeed if it is convenient to you (as let me know at once) I will send you repition orders for the yellows to be executed while you are making experiments over the greens & blues.

And now for a battle about the 'Grey'. 1st Your quotation from Bancroft[2] as I read it without the context does not seem to me at all to the point: for he is aiming at getting the very thing that we are aiming at avoiding: the 'degradation' of the madder means that very brownish yellowish cast which in our eyes gives it all its character: the ordinary madder reds (except perhaps turkey red) being very poor colours not worth using: if we could not get this colour naturally we should have to imitate it by mixing other drugs with the madder, ⟨whic⟩ nor could we ever succeed in really imitating it: the other point he has at heart is the clearing of the grounds to a bright white, which would entirely destroy our cloths to our ideas.

While I am on that point I want to say this: might it not be good to clear the ground somewhat and then mordant[3] the cloths again, duely[?] all over and dye them up to the required shade, as then the cloths would wash perfectly, as they cannot be said to do now?

I break off the thread of my discourse to say that the goods are just to hand and to report upon them. 1017 Red Larkspur is certainly more even than any yet, in fact on that head there is not much to find fault with: nor is the ground a bad colour but on that head I refer you to what I have just written. It is not of course (and could not be) any match of 798. ⟨The fent primed on is better colour⟩ and not nearly as good, but though rather poor & faint is not bad colour I fancy soaping will improve it so we had better keep it for the present at all events: the fent primed on is much better colour but too brown (too much iron?) It seems to be the fent was stained and must at all events be called badly dyed: I suppose Kay is timid about the leaving in too long: I note here with reference to the twice dyed fent: will it help us to dye the grey at twice.

1018 yellow marigold — a bad match, being much too dark: otherwise satisfactory colour not bad & seems well printed.

1019 tolerable match but rather duller & darker than pattern otherwise satisfactory

[267]

The linens I see will want a separate set of experiments for them: the colours all come cold on them but you must remember that they are bleached: some look very fair as it is: but they all spoiled by the calendering;[4] they should be only just smoothed: if the fibre is crushed linen becomes quite valueless: in fact the calender is bad for all the cloths and I wish we could do away with it altogether.

A memo here: our clerk says that the pieces would be better preserved if they were rolled on wooden rollers: can you do this for us in future.

And now I must strongly impress on you the necessity of succeeding in *dyeing* the grey cloths (in printing them with steam colours we have succeeded) I am sure you understand that we want to get something *quite* different from the ordinary goods in the market: this is the very heart of our undertaking since we felt quite certain that the ordinary manufacturer throws away precious opportunities that the natural fibres & dyeing drugs give him, and we started this affair that we might watch for these, nor, as it seems to me have they quite escaped us: as to the difficulties ⟨of⟩ we have met with in dealing with materials in an unusual way, I must say that I am very much surprised that they are not more: and they are as aforesaid reduced to the evenness of the madder dyeing: on this head I feel obstinate in my opinion that Kay's manipulation is to blame and I am glad you are getting the new dyeing gear, & expect something from that: as to the sturmate of soda I am not quite convinced, and it certainly improves the quality of the colour: would it be of any use to pass the pieces through it *after* dyeing, as Kay did with the pinks? Of course we must give up preparing with it for the present however and do as well as we can as to the colours; I am anxious enough for more maddered cloths but leave you to arrange about all that: only let me know all you do, & send me any fents. This end of my letter is confused & hurried by people coming in: but if anything else occurs to me I will write again about it. Meantime don't be discouraged by anything I have said as I think we have done very well so far, & shall in time do great things I have no doubt.

I am
Yrs very truly
William Morris

MS: Duke. Copy in V&A.

[1] A yellow dye obtained from the plant of the same name.

[2] Edward Bancroft (1744-1821). Born in Massachusetts, he lived and practiced medicine for a while in Guiana and then went to England. He was acquainted with Benjamin Franklin and Joseph Priestley. In 1794, he published *Experimental Researches Concerning the Philosophy of Permanent Colours.*

[3] In dyeing, to treat or impregnate with a substance (mordant) that will fix color on cloth.

⁴ To pass cloth through a machine (calender) for the purpose of pressing and smoothing it.

289 · To Thomas Wardle
26, Queen Square,
Bloomsbury, London
September 8, 1875

My dear Mr. Wardle

The two pieces of carnation are to hand & look very well: only Martin should be more careful of his pins which very decidedly show at every repitition of the pattern. As to the red piece there would surely be some way of brightening the colour, which errs on the *dull* side: what does Kay do when he 'cuts' the pink tulip? Also in spite of theory, a rag of the piece having been soaped it shows a slight but decided improvement. The yellows that came up with the red washed very well.

The fents are not yet to hand: I will report on them as soon as I get them.

The linen 1023 looks very well by the way having had the marks of the beastly calender washed out of it.

I am
Yours very truly
William Morris

MS: Duke. Copy in V&A.

290 · To Thomas Wardle
26, Queen Square,
Bloomsbury, London
September 10, 1875

My dear Mr. Wardle

The woollen velvet is for the bold 2 ft: print: and we should like yard fents done of it in any colours that are possible and such as you think we should approve   A scrap done by Hayworth which we have in our book is labelled 'artificial alizarin': it is pleasant colour: but no doubt we had better do on this velvet whatever comes easiest at first.

The fents are just come.   in 1032 the greens are very well matched to 967: but the yellow mossing is too dark and especially too red: I hope this can be set right in the pieces, as otherwise it would be a very satisfactory print: especially if it will stand soaping pretty well: if the yellow is too far gone to alter never mind it is still very fair.

As to the others: 1029 is also good in colour, but not as good as 1032. 1033 is not a bad match for 964, but is a little too strong altogether:

however if you can print the pieces as well by all means do so. 1030 for 994 is too bright but not bad. 1034 is not much use, it looks dead & washed out: and 1031 for 964 is also no use being too bright & crude.

That is all I have to say about the fents: I hope to see the pieces soon — We have heard nothing as to price yet. We ought to be settling this soon.

I am
Yrs very truly
William Morris

MS: Duke.

291 • TO HENRY BUXTON FORMAN   September 14, 1875

My dear Forman[1]

Many thanks: I am at home (Horrington House Turnham Green) or at 26 Queen Sq: W.C till you hear from me to the contrary. I will consider about 'wrath' & 'forth' the only rhyme of that sort I have used,[2] I believe: I confess that personally I don't like it: though not having had the misfortune to be born in Aberdeen, I have no need to call happier people cocknies. at the same time I should defend the rhyme as quite allowable in another man's work *if he didn't use it too often*: because it is a fact that *no* South Englishman makes *any* diference in ordinary talk between dawn and morn for instance: & wrath & forth are less to be blamed than that, because the consonants at the end are so strong.

For the other things I will do my best, but things must be as they must thereabout: for I am too old to alter my mannerisms in a week: Please to believe that if I alter anything 'tis out of respect to my friends to Virgil & to myself, and not for the gaggling of critics: the more they gaggle the less I shall care. With which Welshism I end & am

Yours very truly
William Morris

MS: Wellesley.

[1] Buxton Forman had this letter tipped into his copy of Morris's translation of the *Aeneid*, annotating it as follows: "The letter inserted opposite relates to this translation of which I read proofs for Morris. (See 'The Books of William Morris', page 83.) The word 'gaggle' is from Philemon Holland's Pliny: Morris drew my attention to it in Ellis's shop when he gave me the copy of the work bearing his inscription on the 10th of August

1875—while the proof-reading was in progress. The Pliny was meant as a memento of a very pleasant episode in which each of us considered himself the debtor."

² In his translation of Virgil. This is a reference to Book II, lines 15-16.

292 • To Thomas Wardle   26, Queen Square,
Bloomsbury, London
September 21, 1875

Dear Mr. Wardle

The pieces are to hand 1028 is excellent colour & a very fair match: I wish ⟨you⟩ we had some more both of that and the carnation. 1032 is also fairly matched: the light green is a little duller than the pattern, and the yellow mossing is a good deal too dark the whole effect being gloomier than the pattern: however the yellow & green don't fight: and on the whole it looks very well: It stands soaping better than the the [*sic*] fents I brought up, but of course not well; I think a little better than Clarkson's 'willow pattern'.¹ I notice that the soap doesn't seem to affect the *dark* shade much. I hope now to hear some news of the blues: though I must tell you that the sight of such a fine colour that wont 'wash' has set me all agog again about the blue vat or the China-blue. we could make such glorious greens with them: how about the madders?

I am
Yrs very truly
William Morris

MS: Duke.

¹ "Willow pattern" may refer to the Tulip and Willow pattern of 1873, as printed by Clarkson, or to the Willow of 1874. See "Morris as Designer," MM, I, 34-62, and letter no. 284, n. 3.

293 • To Aglaia Ionides Coronio   26, Queen Square,
Bloomsbury, London
October 21, 1875

My dear Aglaia

Thank you for your note, & 'kind enquiries': I am exceedingly well and in good spirits, & shall be very glad to see you when you come back. We have got a few pieces of printed cloths here, and they are hung up in the big room, where they look so beautiful (really) that I feel inclined to sit and stare at them all day; which however I am far from doing as I am working hard: I don't suppose we shall get many people to buy them however; which will be a pity as ⟨they⟩ we shall be obliged in that case to give up the manufacture. Item, we have got a pattern of a woollen cloth that pleases me hugely, though I don't know if it would please you, for it looks quite like a medieval manufacture.

All this keeps me busy and amuses me very much, so that I may consider myself a lucky man, among so many people who seem to find it hard to be amused

I am
Your affectionate
William Morris

MS: Yates Coll. Published: Henderson, *Letters*, 72.

294 • To Thomas Wardle   26, Queen Square,
                                                      Bloomsbury, London
                                                      October 28, 1875

My dear Mr. Wardle

The two pieces of green for 967 are very bad indeed: they are not in the least to pattern, & I doubt if they will be of any use at all to us.

Meantime we are starving for the want of completion of really useful orders. What are we [to] do? the worst of the fents sent before for this colour was better than this: I confess I am quite discouraged: Kay does not seem to be able to do anything, even the simplest matching, and it is all a matter of luck how things go: I believe he thinks we can't do without him and that he can do anything he pleases: I don't suggest sacking him at once in the face of all the present orders, but we can't be forever under his hippopotamus thumb —

We want stock sadly: we have sold all the best of the little lot we had.

Would you like me to come down this side Christmas? I couldn't come next week but afterwards I might.

You must excuse my eagerness but I am sure we shall get to sell the cloths when we can get the stock.

I am
Yrs very truly
William Morris

MS: Duke. Copy in V&A.

295 • THOMAS WARDLE

26, Queen Square,
Bloomsbury, London
November 2, 1875

Dear Mr. Wardle

Thanks for your long letter: after what you say about the matching I will leave the matter in your hands, except for one thing, which has happened more than once and of which this morning gives us a strong example: to wit: Kay sends us a few days ago a fent of which No 1 is a strip as a pattern of how the finished good will be, when printed from the colour he has mixed for them: this morning the finished goods are to hand, and No 2 is a strip from them: now I can't believe that Kay has not altered the colour between the time that we said 'go on', and the printing of the pieces: mind I merely call your attention to this, for such a proceeding if he has done it, is so bewildering that one might as well be working in one's sleep. The fact is the man's mind is a perfect muddle: however no doubt we must put up with him at present, at least while we get cloths we can use. The strip you enclosed is not far from the two pieces, and if the other 3 come out so, they will be usable: the fault of them is that the blotch is too yellow, & the print too blue: the ground is good in them, & best in this last swatch.

As to the price per yard named by you the only thing *we* have to consider is the possibility of our selling the cloths at a profit (of some kind) ⟨now⟩ as I don't doubt you have no inclination to make the price burdensome to us. Now, we could do with those prices for all the goods we have had as yet, except the carnation, as the extra / 6ᵈ per yard falls heavily on a four colour print that doesn't *look* handsomer than the tulip:[1] and I have other patterns in hand with more blocks still to them, which I fear the / 6ᵈ a yard a block would prohibit from our customers: I suppose you doubt no more than I do, that when affairs are got more into shape the goods could be produced at a much cheaper rate: which makes me think that we had better go on paying expenses for a few months more: at the same time if your wishes go the other way I would be willing to agree to the prices named for 6 months ⟨but how should⟩ as I suppose you wouldn't object to considering the subject of particular prints:

Yet I doubt if it would not be fairer or all events pleasanter to us both for us to go on as before; having in my mind the possibility of badly-matched cloths coming up, which I should not think fit for us to offer for sale: though I should not be stiff in dealing with such matters: I do not know if your price would include the striking of fents, or to what extent it would do so: this brings me to reminding you that our cloths have as yet been very simple, and that we shall have some styles that may be more troublesome to get right; and there is the matter of the indigo*, which I think quite necessary for us, and which to my mind we ought to set to work about as soon as we have got any stock of our present styles, and have a little breathing-space: Please to consider all these matters, and I will do in the matter what on mature consideration you yourself prefer: meantime the quicker we can get through our orders the better.   these greens & blues seem a great sticker: however I must not meddle with the order in which the cloths are printed.

I am

Yrs very truly

William Morris

* how the indigo would help us in these greens! a certain depth of the vat, a certain strength of quercitron[2] or weld, & all would be done and sure

MS: Duke. Copy in V&A.

   [1] The first chintz that Wardle printed for Morris and Co. was the Tulip pattern, which had been put into production earlier in 1875.

   [2] A yellow dye made from the inner bark of the oak tree (*Quercus velutina*).

296 • TO CHARLES FAIRFAX MURRAY   26 Queen Sq:
                                                      November 4 [1875]

My dear Murray

   I write a line in a hurry (since I expect to see you soon) to say that I am very glad you are coming both on friendly grounds & also because I want you to undertake some of the Virgil pictures:[1] whereof more when we meet: all well here   the Virgil translation published today & big-paper awaiting you[2]

Ever Yours

William Morris

MS: Texas. Published: *CW*, 11, xxvi.

   [1] See also letter no. 273.

   [2] *The Aeneids of Virgil* of which, Buxton Forman notes, twenty-five large paper copies were printed on Whatman's handmade paper.

297 • TO EIRÍKR MAGNÚSSON   26, Queen Square,
                                                 Bloomsbury, London
                                                 [early November 1875?]

My dear Magnússon

   The bed is quite at your service on Thursday: on Friday I am sleeping in town: but I should think the female Judd could manage some sort of shake down for one.

As to your Slade Professor I suspect he knows that my general salutation to him would be 'kissi Rasa'! but he is not so far wrong in this instance: though I don't take it as a reproach but as a praise: in short I have translated [as] a poet and not as a pedant.[1]

Thanks for your kind appreciation of the book.

Yrs very truly
William Morris

MS: Iceland.

[1] Morris was probably defending himself against criticism of his translation of the *Aeneid*. If so, his salutation would have been aimed at Sidney Colvin, who was Slade Professor of Fine Art in Cambridge from 1873 to 1885.

298 • To Thomas Wardle

26, Queen Square,
Bloomsbury, London
November 5, 1875

My dear Mr. Wardle

Thanks for your letter. 1st as to prices, we must assume that matter settled for the 6 months; I must accept your offer about the 4 block carnation or I shan't be able to sell it at all.

I must say though, that I hope at the 6 months end ⟨I hope⟩ you will find it possible to reduce the prices considerably: if not I can't help seeing that the sale is likely to be very limited. The prices are more than double Clarkson's for block-printed cloths, and *his* prices are I am sure from the way we began business with him calculated above the usual scale. However it must all stand over till the 6 months are passed.

As to the fents that is pretty much what I expected, & seems fair. For the men, I am surprised that such creatures can exist — which I think I have said before: — but, seriously, you seem in your letter to admit all that I have ever charged them with, i.e. disregarding orders: if they had other qualities to make up for it this might be put up with, but as it is I believe they will beat you even in trying to carry out these first few orders of ours. One thing I must remind you of, that their obstinate refusal to make an ordinary match of *their own* patterns almost entirely nullifies whatever advantage may be derived from my artistic knowledge & taste, *on which the whole of my business depends*: however, the subject of these monsters of idiocy is a dismal one & I will say no more than to beg of you to impress on them the necessity of following out their instructions to the letter *whatever may be the results*. The new patterns I am about are not more difficult it seems to me than the old ones:

but I may be obliged to hold them back on the score of expense, which will be a pity, as the more patterns we have the more likely we are to get a general sale.

I send an order for re-executing the pieces of 967 for which you ⟨the⟩ have the colour mixed.

The pieces spoken of at the end of the week are not to hand yet.

I am

Yrs truly

William Morris

P.S. I enclose a 6 block pattern that they are selling to show what we have to contend with as to price: the buyers of this print would be a good deal our customers

ms: Duke.

299 • To Jane Morris

Kelmscott

Tuesday afternoon

[Postmark November 9, 1875]

Dearest Janey

It began to rain again before I got to Lechlade, at first to my infinite dissappointment: however when I got here and had had my lunch and, as it were, made myself free of the river by an insane attempt to fish, I began to feel very comfortable, and took out my work and looked at it. The floods are already very high, and as it is certainly going to rain for the nex[t] 24 hours I expect to see something curious. I don't think I shall come back before Saturday, as I really hope to do a pile of work here. I am rather short of victuals, as the booby Judd (female) only got me 1 lb of bacon instead of 3, as I ordered her: however there will be enough I daresay, till we can send into Lechlade: there is also 1 tin of Kangaroo meat.

My hands are still somewhat stiff with my work on the river — Lord! how cold it was — wind E. or thereabouts. I am obliged to write by candlelight though 'tis only 4 oclock.

Best love to my one daughter — wouldn't she have liked to have been out on the flooded river with me, the wind right in ones teeth and the eddies going like a Japanese tea-tray: I must say it was delightful: almost as good as Iceland on a small scale: please the pigs, I will have a sail on the floods tomorrow.

With best love goodbye[1]

I am

Your loving

W.M.

MS: BL, Add. MSS. 45338. Published: Mackail, I, 323; Henderson, *Letters*, 72-73. Extract published: *CW*, 11, xvii.

¹ Morris's reason for closing this letter with an uncharacteristic "goodbye" is uncertain. Possibly it was because Jane Morris was preparing to leave for a stay with Rossetti at Aldwick Lodge, near Bognor, Sussex. She did go later in November. In a letter to Theodore Watts-Dunton dated November 14, 1875, Rossetti wrote that by Monday or Tuesday he expected "Mrs. M and children if all goes well. Far from well she is, and will not, I judge, be able to sit at first, but I trust the air may really benefit her." (See Doughty and Wahl, III, 1370.) Grylls writes that Jane Morris was without her daughters at Aldwick Lodge and that she left in December in order to spend Christmas with them. Rosalie Glynn Grylls, *Portrait of Rossetti* (London: Macdonald, 1964), p. 167.

---

300 • TO JANE MORRIS

[Kelmscott]
[November 12, 1875]

Dearest Janey

I shall be home ⟨at⟩ tomorrow (Saturday) by about 3 p.m (afternoon) I have not fared ill on the whole, & today is very bright & lovely, though I wish there were a little more wind: the waters are higher than ever; I am just going out now to puddle about among them, though I scarce look for a sail.

I have made up with pigeons for the ⟨loss⟩ lack of bacon & fish, & so have done quite as well as my stomach will allow me. I hope you are better —

Love to the daughter.
I am
Your loving W M

MS: BL, Add. MSS. 45338.

---

301 • TO THOMAS WARDLE

26, Queen Square,
Bloomsbury, London
November 16, 1875

My dear Mr. Wardle

Thanks for your letter: I don't want to think I under estimate your difficulties, many of which no doubt I know nothing about: I want to point out to you however that our *essential* requirements as to colours are but few: the variety of the orders is a great deal due to the uncertainty of matching: If the matter were got to a matter of routine we should want these *standards* of colour and *no more* for the steam-colour styles —

⟨1 blue the⟩
⟨1 blotch⟩
1 blotch blue, which might be diluted into 2 more shades.
1 outline blue.
1 outline green which would be of an olive character.
1 blotch yellow-green to be diluted as above. ⟨(note⟩
1 blotch blue-green to be diluted. Note ⟨the⟩ here that the outline *blue* could be always used with these blue-green blotches so as to obviate the necessity of mixing a separate outline colour.
1 yellow greenish in character to be diluted for shades.
1 yellow, reddish in character as above for shades.
1 brown always dark & sometimes very dark.
To these one might add a black (if such a thing is to be got fast in steam-colours) and a shade or two of rust yellows or buffs, which would present no difficulty as they ⟨might⟩ would be such as are ordinarily used — With the above colours I can carry out any design I should care for that did not need the madder colours & setting indigo apart.

As to your oncoming troubles about the madder cloths, I have good hope that they will be less than you seem to look forward to: I don't think you *can* get a bad colour with the aluminious mordant on the *unbleached* cloth, so long as the ⟨y⟩ cloths are not starved of the madder: they can certainly always be lightened if they come too dark: the difficulty will be with those in which iron is used: in these I should say a light hand with the iron was the thing: also I note: in printing the tulip let the outline be always rather strong upon the blotch: otherwise the whole pattern looks dead & dull.

As to the indigo of course I quite agree to what you say about that: only when we once get it, Prussian blues & greens will be things of the past with us or nearly so. Apropos of that I send you a rag from the bed which heard my first squeak: my mother says it is about 6 years older than myself: I suppose it to be all indigo & madder except the yellow: the indigo is very nice and bright; whether it is dip-blue or china I don't know but it has certainly been blocked in some way: I have a yard or two in my museum, if you wish to see more of it.

Thanks for your kind remarks in conclusion & for sending me the Bœtian Ballad in question.

I suppose you will ⟨conclu⟩ consider it appropriate ⟨if I co⟩ to our own work if I conclude with wishing success to the old wooden plough.

Yrs very truly
William Morris

MS: Duke. Copy in V&A.

302 · To Thomas Wardle
26, Queen Square,
Bloomsbury, London
November 18, 1875

My dear Mr. Wardle

Your Yorkshire correspondent is too clever by half: Indigo seems scarcely to have been known in Europe (as a dye) till the end of the 16th century, and before that time nothing but woad[1] was used for blue as far as I can make out: of course in the way they use woad in the hot vat *now*, it has little or nothing to do with the colouring: but I think you will find O Neil[2] says that they still use woad for dyeing in some parts of France: I refer you to Bancroft[3] for all that.

I am scarcely sorry that you are compelled to prepare the pitch fork for Martin: if you could do at all with *two* men no doubt it would be a great help as you are then independent of their 'little ways'. I send you another bit of the old chintz: do you think it china or dip blue: and why do you think it French? I am anxious to see some madder-cloths.

Yrs truly
William Morris

MS: Duke. Copy in V&A.

[1] A plant (*Isatis tinctoria*), sometimes called dyer's or garden woad. The blue dye was prepared from its leaves.

[2] Charles O'Neill (b.1831), editor of *The Textile Colourist*, which he started. He was also the author of *Chemistry of Calico-Printing, Bleaching, Dyeing* (Manchester, 1860) and *Dictionary of Calico Printing and Dyeing* (London, 1862).

[3] See letter no. 288, n. 2.

303 · To Thomas Wardle
26, Queen Square,
Bloomsbury, London
November 23, 1875

My dear Mr. Wardle

I proceed to answer both your letters before I begin work this morning. 1st woad   Couldn't anything be learned in France about this subject, where they seem to have used it later than we at all events? The indigo on my natal print is *certainly* blocked in, as you would see if you had a bigger piece: I suspect Kay don't know as much on the subject as the present writer, who now sendeth you a piece of cloth pencilled on (nothing will do but the chewed willow twig) by his own hands:[1] it is very easy to lay on, but I fancy we shall not easily get it brighter than the enclosed specimen: I have a block, now in the cutter's hands very elaborate as to print, but very simple as to blotch on which we might at least try this blue: please however to refrain your natural grin of triumph when I mention that it is no use trying it on *un*bleached cloth.

Of course you would have children for the pencilling: our boys at 5/6 a week would be quite up to it.[2] I should have thought (with deference) that we scarcely wanted more printers: which observation brings me to saying a word or two on the subject of price since you mentioned it in your last: after this I will hold my peace about it till the six months are ended. I daresay you are right about the 6-colour prig[?] we sent you as to its being machine-printed: we know however that Clarkson's prints (for us) *are* blocked in. he charges us 1ˢ/5½ᵈ for a 2 print cloth, and for an elaborate 9-print cloth 3ˢ/9ᵈ. this is a *very* big block: I give you these as being the two ends of his scale. Of course we both hope & think that, when all goes smoother, you will be able to do the cloths as cheap as other people: meanwhile we have shown the cloths long enough to find that people start at the present prices we are obliged to charge. I must also remind you how much we suffer from imitators: these will be all agog as soon as they hear of our printed cloths being admired, and we must try not to give them the advantage of grossly underselling us; and also (to get away from the subject of price) we must be able to say (in the long run) that the goods are fast.

I don't think you should look forward to our *ever* using a machine. As to the mercantile branch, that is quite out of *our* way: but I see no reason why *you* should not try it, if you think it would pay; and I should be happy to help if you wanted any help in the designing way.[3] Of course we tried washing the /10¾ print before we sent it you — what can you expect from Prussia?

Re tussore:[4] You are quite welcome to send the prints to the India house:[5] as to the colours of them I don't like the green or the blue: if you print those colours make the blue deep, rich, & greenish & the green full and deep but with plenty of yellow in it: but I think that yellows browns & reds would be best for them: I suppose you can't use madder for them because it comes on too strong on the unmordanted parts: but I suppose Alizarine could be used: As to our using them the *only* drawback seems to be that they are made awkward widths for our present blocks. could this be got over? I like the look of them very much. By the way I think the Carnation would look well on the Tussore. I should say that I consider my pencil-blue as a good colour to go with the madders, and I am sure very good greens could be got with it: I should mention that I have used it unthickened, and that it is the glucose receipt that seems the best I have tried yet: I have not tried the receipt with the tin[?].

I have found a Gerard[6] for you at last; it ought to get to you tomorrow: it seemed a very good copy: but if it turns out imperfect please let me know.

I am Yours very truly
William Morris

MS: Duke. Copy in V&A.

¹ This piece of cloth is still with the original letter, now at Duke University.

² This is the first passage in the surviving letters indicating Morris's attitude to child labor. His position on the subject is still a matter in dispute.

³ Morris's readiness to supply designs for machine-printed fabric, while insisting that Morris and Co. would never use a machine for producing printed cloth, is a piece of evidence for sorting out his views concerning hand-craftsmanship versus machine work, and division-of-labor versus production by a single craftsman. His attitude toward machine work seems to embrace both his own personal rejection of it and a willingness to cooperate in "commercial" production utilizing machines. (For a discussion of this matter, see Peter Floud, "William Morris As an Artist: A New View," *The Listener*, 52 [October 7 and 14, 1954], 562-64, and 615-17.) Eventually, influenced by Marx, Morris was to qualify this notion, insisting that he was not opposed to machinery but to the enslavement of people to machines under capitalist methods of production. When the people became the masters of their machines, he was to contend, it would be proper to use machines for processes to which they were suited.

⁴ A coarse brown silk made in India.

⁵ Possibly the India Museum (India Office, Westminster), referred to by William Crookes (1832-1919) in *A Practical Handbook of Dyeing and Calico-Printing* (London, 1874), p. 356, as containing dyeing materials, including many not as yet used in Europe.

⁶ See letter no. 286, n. 1.

304 • TO THOMAS WARDLE

26, Queen Square,
Bloomsbury, London
November 26, 1875

My dear Mr. Wardle

I am sorry Nicholson should have done anything that seemed like throwing distrust on your work:¹ of course we knew nothing about it: as for myself I lead such a life of insults & sucking of my brains, that I have to put myself (mentally) in your position to sympathise fully in your annoyance: but of course I can fully understand that you would be much annoyed by it, as I have no doubt I should have been myself: and I must remark that you must rather put it down to want of delicacy than malice on Nicholson's part, otherwise he would scarcely have told you what he had done himself.

Finally I must beg you to consider our many difficulties in the way of getting anything good done, and not to leave us in the lurch and to receive the assurance again from me, if you need it, that I fully understand the value of working in open day with an honourable & sympa-

[281]

thetic person like yourself and am quite prepared to support you by any means in my power.

I am also as you must know most deeply impressed with the importance of our having all our dyes the soundest & best that can be, and am prepared to give up all that part of my business which depends on textiles if I fail in getting them so: however I don't in the least see why I should talk about failing which is after all impossible, as I have no doubt you ⟨fail⟩ feel yourself.

The silks by the Macclesfield dyer were not well matched, by the way, and to my inexperienced eyes seemed messed; what I have heard you call 'blind'. I don't understand why N. should have got them dyed; for we did not hurry him at all especially as I judged pretty well from what I had heard you say before that you were getting them done at Lyons.

I am
Yrs very truly
William Morris

MS: Duke. Copy in V&A. Published: Henderson, *Life*, 158. Extract published: Mackail, I, 312.

¹ Joshua Nicholson (1812-1885), silk manufacturer, a partner in J. and J. Brough, Nicholson and Co. On this occasion he had apparently bypassed Wardle and gotten someone else's firm to do the dyeing.

305 • To Thomas Wardle
26, Queen Square,
Bloomsbury, London
December 24, 1875

My dear Mr. Wardle

Thanks for your letter   I have been looking at the fents and will at once go into a detailed criticism of them.

1112 Indian diaper Deep red & faint purple: I like the colour very much and we are sending a small order for it, & would send a bigger, but the price makes it doubtful as a selling matter: it is very important that the red in it should be kept up to the present depth, & be no browner Martin might make the block register a little better I think.

1134 Purple & dark pink: we are going to order this too: keep the purple *quite* as dark.

1106. Flower de Luce madder red   The colour is poor, & seems to me to be starved; I have dyed it again in madder & soaped it, and I think either pattern would be good for this design: if you could get 2 fents to about this colour we could send you an order for them at once:

I may say generally that this design wants rich colour & a lightish ground, good contrast in fact, to be successful.

1121 Yellow larkspur is very good: only I note it is calendered heavily, please be careful of the finished pieces: we should like a fent of the ⟨Larkspur⟩ Flower de Luce in this colour, to order from.

1123 red lining will do if you can keep it as even in the pieces 1113 to 1137   the trials on bleached ground of no use for this pattern

⟨1104⟩ 1103–113⟨8⟩9 for 1036. The pattern marked passed is much the best: it however is not as good as our 1036 the blotch is bluer & duller: however it will be a good cloth so finished: the tinned pattern might be of use for some things but I prefer the soaped one as it is.

1104–1138 (for 1042) the passed pattern will make a pretty cloth, but it is considerably darker than our pattern: I don't like to suggest altering this pattern now as it is passed & is good in itself: but in repetitions of the order wouldn't more madder & more soaping be the remedy: I do think these light *soaped* pinks are pretty: and all your unsoaped patterns of them, in this last sent lot, seem to ⟨be⟩ me too dull: I think (as you seem to) that this might be cured by more madder: I think too that this must be the reason why the whites get cleared so much: it will [be] very important to remedy this in the 1-colour prints, that depend so much ⟨on⟩ in their richness of effect on having the ground full in colour.

1101–1127 (for 840) On the whole the one 1125 madder & Garrancine[1] soaped) seems to me the best: if the blotch were lighter (a little even) I should like it very much: at any rate this is the direction to work from only is the Garrancine quite fast? & if not would not more madder answer the purpose?   the 2nd trial 1119 & 1120 though not near the pattern are fine colours, & will be of use some day: We shall be quite ready to repeat the order for any madder pieces that come out well: all the more as my hatred against prussians grows with time: if we can once say 'yes' positively to the question 'will they wash'? we stand a much better chance of selling [getting?] the long price.

I think this is all there is to be said about the patterns in hand   I shall be writing again shortly.

Thanks for what you say about my wishes in this matter I echo back your compliments of the season even for the newcomer, who I hope is as yet undrowned.

> I am
> Yrs very truly
> William Morris[2]

ms: Duke. Copy in V&A.

[1] A dyeing substance obtained from the madder plant.

[2] A note following Morris's signature, but not in his handwriting, reads: "Kay   We had printed the outline on the bleached cloth for 981   May we go on with & if so how."

306 • To Thomas Wardle   Horrington House
                                                                              Turnham Green
                                                                              [January 8, 1876]

My dear Mr. Wardle   ·

I am at home today (as mostly I am on Saturdays) but G. W.[1] has sent
me up your letter and the fents, except the trial for 979, and as you
emphasize the return of post, I am doing my best to make up my mind
by candlelight. I think I had better say finish to 1153 (the twice soaped)
for the try at 1042, and ask you to try 1042 again: there is a pleasant
brightness about it which I dont want to forego. By the way has the
temperature of the dyebeck,[2] do you think, anything to do with our
failure in getting this desired brightness in the pinks: the books say
a *low* temperature is necessary for the successful production of
pinks.   there is a filminess about these fents for 1042 that bothers me.
I hope the 'bleeding' can be stopped: it makes this pattern look coarser
than it should, & if it went a little further it would quite spoil them.
1150 is a poor substitute for 840: it is so weak in colour and filmy also:
but I should have thought there would have been no great difficulty in
remedying this, either by strengthening the mordant or adding excess
of madder in the dyeing: of course I don't want this colour brown but
the original is rich and full: I must say I suspect garancine in the original
840: but do you think your 1150 has got as much madder as it will take.
The fent with the garancine in it I like very much, and I think I will
send an order ⟨if⟩ for it, though I feel quite sure that ordinarily garancine
does not stand so well as madder: I have soaped a bit of your fent, and
it stands it well enough however. I should have thought that pretty
much the same colour could have been got by the madder only, by dint
of getting the colour strong at first and soaping away at it afterwards:
though of course I know that the grounds of garancine cloths clear
much easier than the madder ones. Please dont forget that we want a
good strong colour for the one-colour prints of which we have now 3.
Our block cutter will be sending you the African Marigold next week[3]
I am anxious to see a fent of it though I suppose it will have to be done
with those accursed Prussians: shall you want any instruction about the
printing of this new block?

Finally I must say I am not happy at the way the madders are going:
we have not as yet got anything as good as the few pieces we had in
the autumn, let alone ⟨after⟩ fents that were got before; and that filmy
look bothers me very much. About Kay I have said all I need say I
suppose — but if you only could get an intelligent man, even if he were
only moderately experienced, it seems to me all would be gained.

As for me I am ready to spend any amount of time in pushing the

[284]

thing on: and I believe I could be of use now, since I know more about it than I did ⟨about the matter⟩ Only I must say that if I come down again for more than a day or two I should insist on not quartering myself on you.

There are a great many editions of Matthiolus:[4] some there are that have the cuts without the letter-press: pretty little books long in shape & very useful: I have the whole book a fine edition printed at Venice by Peter Valgrisius in about 1590; the cuts very big: certainly one of the best of the herbals: and the very beautiful herbal is Fuschias de Stirpibus (Dr Leonard Fuchs, — the Fuschia is named after him) a Basle book printed about 1530:[5] I have a poor copy of it[6] which I have found very useful: it is a rare book; but for refinement of drawing it is the best of all, as one would expect ⟨by⟩ from the date.

I am
Yours very truly
William Morris

MS: Duke. Copy in V&A.

[1] George Wardle, brother-in-law of Thomas Wardle and manager of Morris and Co. at Queen Square.

[2] The vessel containing the dyeing liquid; also the coloring matter contained in it.

[3] In describing this wallpaper pattern, Clark writes (p. 57): "Like *Pimpernel* wallpaper of the same year, this is an early, informal version of the vertical turnover structure, which Morris was to develop further as his knowledge of woven textiles increased." See also Clark, p. 65, for illustration.

[4] Pietro Andrea Mattioli (1500-1577). His *Commentarii in Sex libror Pedacci Dioscordis Anazarbei de Medica Materiá* (1544) represented the sum of botanical knowledge in Italy in the sixteenth century and was widely read. It was illustrated with small woodcuts. Another edition was printed in Prague in 1562 and was the first to be illustrated with large woodcuts. The first of the Balgrisi editions, which also contained large woodcuts, was printed in Venice in 1565. See Spencer Savage, "A Little Known Bohemian Herbal," *The Library*, 4th series, Vol. II, no. 2 (Sept. 1, 1921), 117-31.

[5] Leonhard Fuchs (1501-1566), German physician and botanist. The full title of his most important work is *De historia stirpium commentarii insignes* (Basel, 1542), which contains more than 500 outline illustrations, including one of digitalis, which was named by him.

[6] The copy listed in the Sotheby's Catalogue of the sale of Morris's books (1898) was printed in Basel, 1542.

307 · TO THOMAS WARDLE

26, Queen Square,
Bloomsbury, London
January 15, 1876

My dear Mr. Wardle —

I think there could be no harm in the Manchester visit: of course it must be an advantage to you to learn all you can; especially as their aims are so much more difficult of attainment than ours, even though we don't think them worth attaining to. Of course in getting new men you would have to let them know clearly the sort of thing we are trying to get, and you would know by now how to answer many of their objections.

The last six pieces of pink sent up vary very much from piece to piece; more than is convenient: one has bled sorely.

Many thanks for your hospitality and since you are so kind, I will certainly come to you when I come down. A few days notice will fetch me: but perhaps the longer days & better weather would be worth waiting for.

> I am
> Yours very truly
> William Morris

MS: Duke.

308 • TO EIRÍKR MAGNÚSSON
26, Queen Square,
Bloomsbury, London
January 24, 1876

My dear Magnússon

Since you put it in that way I can't say no: but you must put me up to all there is to do; as I was born *not* to be a chairman of anything: I suppose I shall see you on the morning of the day in question.

> Yrs ever
> William Morris

MS: Iceland.

309 • TO JANE MORRIS
Kelmscott
Wednesday afternoon
[Postmark January 26, 1876]

Dearest Janey

Here I am safely: The floods were facts enough, but the water has gone down a good deal since Sunday: I have been muddling about on the river and floods for excercise sake: It is a most beautiful afternoon: there are violets out, and ⟨the sn⟩ aconites, and the snowdrops are showing all about: Love to babies

> I am
> Your loving
> W.M.

Mr. Butcher sold me a piece of steak and 2 kidnies: I hope the first wont be tough.

MS: BL, Add. MSS. 45338. Published: *CW*, 11, xviii; Henderson, *Letters*, 73.

310 • To Frederick James Furnivall

26, Queen Square,
Bloomsbury, London
January 31, 1876

My dear Furnival

Thanks for your invitation, but ⟨it is⟩ you ask me to do a thing more remote from my inclination and powers at once than any thing else that I could imagine so I must say No.

I am
Yrs truly
William Morris

MS: Mayfield Coll. Published: *The Courier*, Syracuse University Library Associates, July 1962, 17.

311 • To Aglaia Ionides Coronio

26, Queen Square,
Bloomsbury, London
Monday [March 1876]

My dear Aglaia

I am very sorry to hear that you have the measles, am not at all inclined to laugh at you on that score: neither am I at all frightened & will come & see you whenever you wish me to — I was just writing this yesterday when everybody came ⟨&⟩ in and there was no more peace for me for the rest of the day. I hope you are better today: as to what I am doing, I am drawing patterns so fast that last night I dreamed I had to draw a sausage; somehow I had to eat it first, which made me anxious about my digestion: however I have just done quite a pretty pattern for printed work.[1] I am getting on with my poem, in quantity at any rate: I have (roughly) done the 3rd part: that is Sigurd & Brynhild are dead, & people are busy forgetting them after the fashion of our aimiable race: all that I have left to do now, if the last written parts turn out successful, is the revenge and death of Gudrun, which will be certainly short, and probably not difficult compared with what I have had to do.[2]

I am a little looking forward to having a rest someday soon: my rebellious inclinations turn toward Iceland, though I know it to be impossible, so I suppose it will be Kelmscott & the river someday soon. I was one day in the country on business last week: a dull place and a dull business: I am glad that arid weather has changed as I suppose everybody else is

Here is an end of a letter which if it amuses you you must be very hard up for amusement

I am
Your affectionate
William Morris

MS: Yates Coll. Published: *CW*, 12, vii; Henderson, *Letters*, 78-79.

¹ Possibly the Rose wallpaper. Other patterns which Morris designed in 1876 for printing, and the materials on which the printing was done, were the Mohair damask, Iris chintz, Bluebell chintz, and Snakeshead chintz. See Peter Floud, "Dating Morris' Patterns," *The Architectural Review*, 126 (July 1959), 14-20.

² *The Story of Sigurd the Volsung and the Fall of the Niblungs* was published by Ellis and White. Although dated 1877, it appeared in the winter of 1876. See Buxton Forman, p. 82.

312 • TO JANE MORRIS

26, Queen Square,
Bloomsbury, London
March 8, 1876

Dearest Janey

Thanks for your note: I was glad to hear that you were doing pretty well.¹ We came back from Marlborough on the Monday morning: we had a delightful drive to Silbury & Avebury on Saturday ⟨in⟩ through a wild stormy afternoon: Avebury is a beautiful place: the little village lies all within the earth-work of the old temple which, though not many of the huge stones are now left, is about 8 quarters complete, the church and a lovely old manor-house breaking the circuit in one place.

Sunday I must say was dullsome; for it rained hard all day: the others of them went to chapel in the morning which treat I refused: Jenny had a cold and so couldn't go with us to Dr. Farrars² to dinner in the evening: I don't think she suffered much from *that* loss however. Her cold is better now, and she has not stopped away from school. Phil by the way seemed very well, and played such a knife & fork as reminded me of my own better days: in short he ate like a Ghoul.

The Embroidery ladies gave me such a turn of it this morning I thought I should have been both walked & talked off my legs. I am withal in the thick of poetry blue-vats & business. I finished by the way, by buying *both* those pieces of embroidery for £160: I think I have as good as sold one of them: but of course I shall keep them till you come back.

I shall get one photographed. I don't think there is any more news: Give my best love to May — I am

Your loving
W.M.

MS: BL, Add. MSS. 45338. Published: *CW*, 11, xix; Henderson, *Letters*, 73-74.

[1] Henderson notes (*Life*, p. 163) that Jane returned to Aldwick Lodge, near Bognor, after Christmas (Doughty writes, p. 582, that she returned in March) where she was sitting for Rossetti's *Astarte Syriaca*. Jenny and May accompanied her, according to Henderson, but if this is true, Jenny must have returned home afterward.

[2] See letter no. 277, n. 1.

313 · To Lady Geary   26 Queen Sq.
                                      March 17 [1876?]

Mr. William Morris presents his compliments to Lady Geary[1] and has such pleasant recollections of her visit to him, that he regrets extremely that his work, which is especially heavy this year, will prevent him from accepting Lady Geary's kind invitation as he finds himself quite unable to go out anywhere because of it.

MS: SRO.

[1] Probably Fanny Isabella, née Prior (d.1901), second wife of Sir Francis Geary (1811-1895).

314 · To Jane Morris   Horrington House
                                      Saturday
                                      [Postmark March 18, 1876]
Dearest Janey

I won't press you to come back, then:[1] only let me know by return about when you intend coming: the point is that I have pretty well settled to go to Leek next Wednesday, & I intend when I go there to be about a fortnight away: Now if you were coming back say this day week, it would not stop my going, as I should ask Bessy[2] to keep Jenny company for those 2 or 3 days: but if you were going to stay much beyond that I should put off my Leek journey till after Easter as I should not like Jenny to be left parentless so long.

Of course when I made the arrangement for going I thought you would have come back today or Monday: I should like to go & get it over, and no doubt I am wanted there: but I don't know that my putting it off will much matter —

So let me recapitulate: write by return & say when you are coming back: if you will not be away for more than another week I shall go to Leek next Wednesday, & get Bessy to come here till you come home   if you are going to be away longer, I shall stay here till Easter over: Except by the way that I have promised to go with Webb to Kelmscott for 3 days at Easter-tide —

Give my love to May & thank her for her letter, & tell her that if I were not very busy over my poetry today I would write to her: I will try to do so on Monday.

It is fine & dry here today but very cold: I think the March dryness is going to set in.

I am with love
Your
W.M.

MS: BL, Add. MSS. 45338. Published: Henderson, *Letters*, 74–75.

¹ Jane Morris was still with Rossetti at Aldwick Lodge, Bognor.
² Elizabeth Burden, Jane Morris's sister.

315 • To May Morris

Horrington House
Tuesday Morning
[March 21, 1876]

Dearest May

Thank you for your letter: I should dearly like to have seen the storm. It is a hard frost this morning: this has been the coldest 'Blackthorn winter,' as they call it, that I ever remember. So I am off tomorrow to Leek and the dye-tubs. Mr. Tom Wardle has promised to get me a pair of sabots to work in: however even when I come back to Queen Sq I shall not be without the dye-tubs: for we have fitted up the old larder into a make-shift dye-house.

You shall come & see its wonders when you come home: also our Prussian Carpets of which we have bought many lately: it will all make you feel as if you were in the Arabian Nights — Even Mrs. Judd may help the illusion if you make up your mind that she is your regular old woman of that work 'a calamity of calamities, like the spotted green & yellow toad: or as we should say like a walnut shell spoiled.

Well, you may reckon how glad I shall be to see you & Mamma when I come back, which will be in about a fortnight

I hope you will be in a riotous state of health.

I am
My dear little May
Your loving father.
William Morris

MS: BL, Add. MSS. 45338. Published: MM, I, 652; Henderson, *Letters*, 75.

316 • FROM A LETTER, RECIPIENT UNKNOWN[1]   Leek
[March 22-April 6, 1876]

Wherein you are spiritless, I wish with all my heart that I could help you or amend it, for it is most true that it grieves me; but also, I must confess it, most true that I am living my own life in spite of it, or in spite of anything grievous that may happen in the world. Sometimes I wonder so much at all this, that I wish even that I were once more in some trouble of my own, and think of myself that I am really grown callous; but I am sure that though I have many hopes and pleasures, or at least strong ones, and that though my life is dear to me, so much as I seem to have to do, I would give them away, hopes and pleasures, one by one or all together, and my life at last, for you, for my friend-ship, for my honour, for the world. If it seems boasting I do not mean it: but rather that I claim, so to say it, not to be separated from those that are heavy-hearted only because I am well in health and full of pleas-ant work and eager about it, and not oppressed by desires so as not to be able to take interest in it all. I wish I could say something that would serve you, beyond what you know very well, that I love you and long to help you: and indeed I entreat you (however trite the words may be) to think that life is not empty nor made for nothing, and that the parts of it fit one into another in some way; and that the world goes on, beautiful and strange and dreadful and worshipful.

TEXT: Mackail, I, 327-28. Published: Henderson, *Letters*, 77-78.

[1] Henderson suggests that Edward or Georgiana Burne-Jones may have been the friend who received this letter. See *Life*, p. 165. It is equally possible that the recipient was Jane Morris. She told Wilfrid Blunt that her affair with Rossetti ended in 1875. Between No-vember and December 1875 she visited Rossetti at Bognor. She visited again in March, but only for a fortnight. It is possible that by March 1876 she had ended her intimacy with Rossetti and because of her conflicting feelings about this decision, became deeply depressed.

317 • FROM A LETTER TO GEORGIANA BURNE-JONES   Leek
Sunday
March 26, 1876

My days are crowded with work; not only telling unmoveable Lancashire what to do, but even working in sabots and blouse in the dyehouse myself — you know I like that. Your kind hope for my poem was vain I am sorry to say: T. Wardle rather insisted on my going out with him, so I yielded, not very loth, as I thought a country walk would not be amiss: so we took train to a station and then walked, first by a gim-crack palace of Pugin's,[1] Alton Towers[2] to wit, then to a village where your friend the novel-writer came from (called Ellaston, I rather think),[3] then to a village church, Norbury, with a strange very rich chancel to it, out of place in that queer way that things are in England, then up the valley of the Dove to Ashbourne, which I think Dr. Johnson had something to do with:[4] a dull walk that last, I scarcely know why, but Ashbourne church very fine and rich; and so home.

Some time this week I am going to Nottingham to see the hot vat in operation for flock wool-dyeing. When I was a very youngster, my father's mother,[5] then grown doting, used to promise me a journey to Nottingham, her home, if I were a *very* good boy.

Meantime I trust I am taking in dyeing at every pore (otherwise than by the skin of my hands, which is certain). I have found out and practised the art of weld-dyeing, the ancientest of yellow dyes, and the fastest. We have set a blue vat for cotton, which I hope will turn out all right to-morrow morning: it is nine feet deep, and holds 1,000 gallons: it would be a week's talk to tell you all the anxieties and possibilities connected with this indigo subject, but you must at least imagine that all this is going on on very nearly the same conditions as those of the shepherd boy that made a watch all by himself.

TEXT: Mackail, I, 324-25. Published: Henderson, *Letters*, 75-76.

[1] Augustus W.N. Pugin (1812-1853), the prominent architect of the early stage of the Gothic revival.

[2] Alton Towers was built by the fifteenth Earl of Shrewsbury between 1814 and 1827. Pugin's role was to make a number of alterations and additions for the sixteenth Earl, the most important of which were the building of the chapel in 1835 and of the Great Hall in 1836.

[3] Morris was referring to George Eliot, who was a friend of Georgiana Burne-Jones. The village was Ellastone, to the southeast of Leek near the Staffordshire-Derbyshire border. See also letter no. 320.

[4] Ashbourne was the birthplace of John Taylor, a cleric who was a schoolfellow and friend of Samuel Johnson. Johnson visited him many times.

[5] Elizabeth Stanley Morris, daughter of a naval surgeon. She died at eighty-five.

318 · To May Morris
St. Edward Street
Leek
March 26 [1876]

Dearest May

This is to wish you many happy returns of your birthday: I had too much to do to be able to write yesterday or the day before. I dye in the dye-house with sabots & a blouse on: you would laugh to see me. Yesterday we set the blue vat: it is much more than deep enough to drown you. I am going for a country walk today, & I believe have got to start soon so I can not write much more   I am sending a note to Mama at the same time: give my love to Jenny: I shall be very glad to come back:

I am
Your loving father
William Morris

MS: Swales Coll.

319 · To Emma Shelton Morris
at T. Wardle Esqre
St. Edward Street
Leek
March 26, 1876

Dearest Mother

Many thanks for your kind letter: You see I have got among the dyers again; ⟨so⟩ & I shall not be back till after Wednesday week (April 4th) so don't call in Queen Sq: till after that time: But when I am back I shall be delighted to see you there, and shall have many things to show you, nor will you interfere with my work in the least. I was obliged to come down here at rather short notice, or else I should have come down to Hadham first: I will come down when I come back to London.

Don't you remember how old Grandmother Morris use to promise me to go to Nottingham if I were a good boy: that reward I am now going to attain to, for I am going to Nottingham this week to learn something from a wool-dyer there: strange to say the manufacturer who is going to introduce me is named Shelton.

I am working very hard here & am learning what I hope will be useful & important to me: but I rather grudge being away from home. Jenny and I were all alone there for a fortnight: she was very good and companionable   Did she tell you how we went down to Marlborough together? it was very amusing.

Give my best love to Henrietta and with all love to you
Believe me
Dearest Mother
Your most affectionate Son
William Morris

MS: Walthamstow. Extract published: *CW*, 11, xx.

320 • TO AGLAIA IONIDES CORONIO   [St. Edward Street]
Leek
March 28 [1876]

My dear Aglaia
    I am at last able to write to you, and thank you for your letter: I have
a huge deal to do in a very limited time, for I am trying to learn all I
can about dyeing, even the handiwork of it, which is simple enough,
but, like many other simple things, contains matters in it that one would
not think of unless one were told. Besides my business of seeing to the
cotton-printing, I am working in Mr. Wardle's dye-house in sabots and
blouse pretty much all day long: I am dyeing yellows and reds: the
yellows are very easy to get, and so are a lot of shades of salmon and
flesh-colour and buff and orange; my chief difficulty is in getting a deep
blood red, but I hope to succeed before I come away: I have not got
the proper indigo vat for wool, but I can dye blues in the cotton vat
and get lovely greens with that and the bright yellow that weld gives.
    This morning I assisted at the dyeing of 20 lbs. of silk (for our dam-
ask) in the blue vat; it was very exciting, as the thing is quite unused
now, and we ran a good chance of spoiling the silk. There were four
dyers and Mr. Wardle at work, and myself as dyers' mate: the men
were encouraged with beer and to it they went, and pretty it was to see
the silk coming green out of the vat and gradually turning blue: we
succeeded very well as far as we can tell at present; the oldest of the
workmen, an old fellow of seventy, remembers silk being dyed so, long
ago. The vat, you must know, is a formidable-looking thing, 9 ft. deep
and about 6 ft. square: and is sunk into the earth right up to the top.
To-morrow I am going to Nottingham to see wool dyed blue in the
woad vat, as it is called; on Friday Mr. Wardle is going to dye 80 lbs.
more silk for us, and I am going to dye about 20 lbs. of wool in madder
for my deep red. With all this I shall be very glad indeed to be home
again, as you may well imagine.
    I am glad you liked my work at the show, though I don't think it

was much to make a row about; the silk piece I thought was the best. Mrs. Lewes came from this country-side, by the way: I went through the village where she lived, on Sunday: Ellaston, I think, it was called; a dull village; I seem to see a good few people about like the 'Aunts' in the 'Mill on the Floss.'[1]

I hope you are well.

I am your affectionate
William Morris

TEXT: Mackail, I, 325-27. Published: MM, I, 650; Henderson, *Letters*, 76-77.

[1] In the few references to George Eliot's works in his surviving letters, Morris is respectful rather than enthusiastic. May Morris notes (*CW*, 22, xxvi), "Of George Eliot he could only read with any great enjoyment the 'Scenes from Clerical Life' and 'Silas Marner.' "

---

321 • TO THOMAS WARDLE

26, Queen Square,
Bloomsbury, London
April 7, 1876

Dear Mr. Wardle

I got to Macclesfield half blind with a speck of coal in my eye, so that at last I had to go to a doctor to get it (the eye) turned up & down till it could be got cleaned: however I saw a good piece of the silk in the loom, and I am happy to say that it seemed quite satisfactory: the tram was not at all too light in colour, but perhaps it might have been better a trifle greener. the organzine[1] looked even enough as it lay in the warp, and was very good colour; the weaver said it was quite strong & wove very well, nor could I see any special dullness in the cloth: so you see we have been frightening ourselves for nothing: I need not say that I shall be glad to hear of the rest of the silk being dyed.

About the wool-dyeing: we think we could give you about 200 lb weight a week of the low quality wool you saw me dyeing: this is for our three-ply carpets made in Yorkshire:[2] if you had no more than this to do, could you undertake it, and if so at *about* what price? If this matter could be settled, we could try to make arrangements for the dyeing of our other woollen yarns to be done by you: they are of a finer quality & so would bear a higher price.

I find myself shortened for time so I must finish in a hurry merely saying that we shall be sending more orders for the prints in a day or two.

I am
Yrs very truly
William Morris

MS: Duke. Copy in V&A.

¹ A raw silk fabric made of threads of twisted strands.

² The first designs for carpets that Morris produced (in 1875) were for machine manufacture by the Royal Wilton Carpet Works and the Heckmondwike Manufacturing Company in Yorkshire. The latter firm, incorporated in 1873, carried out all the processes of carpet manufacture, from the treatment of the raw materials to the final touches on the finished article. See C.E.C. Tattersall, *A History of British Carpets* (Benfleet, Essex: F. Lewis, Ltd., 1934), p. 148.

322 • TO WALTER THEODORE WATTS-DUNTON

26, Queen Square,
Bloomsbury, London
April [12? 1876]

My dear Watts

Herewith I send the Aristomenes according to promise:¹ I still have my doubts however as to whether it will be possible to make a presentable extract from it: but I have dug out a sort of a ballad, which I fancy might do: if you think it not up to the mark, I can send you next week another one which I think as good of its kind as anything I have done: I am going out of town tomorrow (Thursday) but shall be back on Saturday; and at work here again on Wednesday next.

Do as you think good about the whole matter.

Yrs very truly
William Morris

MS: BL, Ashley MSS. 4902.

¹ "The First Foray of Aristomenes," published in *The Athenaeum* (May 13, 1876), pp. 663-64. It is an extract from the unfinished tale, "The Story of Aristomenes," which had been intended for *The Earthly Paradise* but grew too long for inclusion. The tale as Morris left it was first published in *CW*, 24, May Morris noting that it was printed "from the fair copy which my father gave later to Mr. Watts-Dunton" (*CW*, 24, xxx). In April 1876, Watts-Dunton was literary critic for *The Athenaeum*.

323 • TO THOMAS WARDLE

26, Queen Square,
Bloomsbury, London
April 13, 1876

Dear Mr. Wardle

Thanks for your note & for sending me the dyes & things. We have written to our Yorkshire manufacturers to see if they will give up the dyeing, & expect to hear from them shortly; ⟨it⟩ the matter must wait their answer now; so I can put off anything I have to say about the wool dyeing till then.

As to the Indigo coming off, I fancy *dark* colours of it always will a little: I tried the Nottingham dyed wool on white paper, and it left a trace: however I sympathize with your aspirations for perfection.

I send you 2 bits of Cretan embroidery for your museum: they are about 150 years old: and being borders of women's petticoats have been washed to death: the colour of the greener one pleases me very much: Mrs. Wardle will find some stitches in them worth looking at.

When you write next will you tell me what I owe you for Rossetti's dyeing book[1] that I may send you the £2 you lend me.

I find the book tough to translate,[2] and I suspect the receipts are very shady but it is amusing: I have made enquiries for that 1605 English book.

I am
Yrs very truly
William Morris

MS: Duke. Copy in V&A.

[1] The *Plictho* of Gioventura Rossetti, the first basic printed book on dyeing, was published in Venice in 1448. Sotheby's Sale Catalogue of Morris's library lists (p. 87, Lot 886) a copy of the book as follows: *Plictho de Larte de Tentori che insigna tenger Pañi telle Baubasi et sede si per larthe magiore come per la commune,* Venetia, 1540.

[2] It may have been difficult to translate because the text was written in Venetian dialect.

324 • To Thomas Wardle

26, Queen Square,
Bloomsbury, London
Wednesday
[April 19? 1876]

Dear Mr. Wardle

I have been away from business since Thursday last till this morning; or I would have answered you before about the Cheddleton Windows;[1] I am afraid it is too late now, and in any case I don't know how to describe a window, and also I have but a hazy memory about the Cheddleton work: I remember that the chancel was glazed with figures of Kings (including St Helena a queen) who had been helpers of the church. Charlemagne, Constantine, Alfred, St Edward Confessor, St. Louis, I remember.

Then there was the angel window, about which I have not so much to say about its reference to Mr. Boucher's late wife as even you had: they were beautiful figures, and fit adornments for a church, and that is all.

Then there was the baptism window with Naamon the Syrian for the type & the Baptism of Christ for antitype, and the four rivers of Paradise flowing above, in general symbolism of the whole subject: as for the two other windows I have been cudgelling my brain to remember the subjects, and I fairly can't I am afraid this is very poor help for you even if it reaches you in time

The embroidery was brought over [from] Crete by the English Consul: it was undoubtedly worked in the island: but there are strong marks of Italian influence in many of the designs I have seen.

I don't see why the German gentleman shouldn't try to sell our prints; I will write again about it.

I have been looking at the silk and can't quite make out what all the parcels are for: the organ[2] to match the other dyeing looks very well and so does the other as to colour I think I had better send it all on to Nicholson.

All right about Mr. Sleigh[3] & the Isaak Walton windows   I will do the best I can.

Cotton velvet fents satisfactory   I am glad to hear about the blue vat for wool: I left some wool with Gibson, perhaps it will be enough to go on with: I enclose bits of the Nottingham-dyed wool, 3 shades, for patterns, but should like a darker than the darkest and a shade between the 2 lightest: I should also like the same shades on wool very slightly yellowed with weld: or when I get your indigoes I will make green & greenish-blue patterns from them myself.

Many thanks about the black silk.

By the by if your indigo dyeing comes brighter than Nottingham so much the better.

Finally could you dye me 2 ½ pounds of floss-silk in the blue vat, 1 to match (or thereabouts) the organ for Nicholson, 2 to be about the colour of the 6 lbs sent to *us*.

Please tell Mrs. Wardle that I shall probably design a special rug for her wool-work. With kind regards to her.

> I am
> Yrs very truly
> William Morris

MS: Duke. Copy in V&A.

[1] Morris and Co. designed windows in 1864 for the Church of St. Edward at Cheddleton, Staffordshire. For details, see Sewter, II, 50. Wardle was preparing an article on this church, and had presumably asked Morris some questions about the windows.

[2] That is, organzine.

[3] John Sleigh (b.1826), author of *A History of the Ancient Parish of Leek, in Staffordshire* (London, 1883), quotes (pp. 166-69) from the paper written by Thomas Wardle in 1876 that describes Cheddleton Church (see n. 1 above).

325 • To Thomas Wardle   26, Queen Square,
                                          Bloomsbury, London
                                          April 25, 1876

Dear Mr. Wardle,

Re the wool dyeing: we want you to begin as soon as you can now, as our Yorkshire folks will be glad enough to drop it:[1] perhaps you and I will find out the reason for that before all is over. Meantime I want to give you an idea of the colours we shall want: as to matching, you know I am not likely to be very particular as to shade, though the kind of colour must be right: as to price, whatever costs me (taking an average over all) more than 6s. a lb. weight, will have to come out of my pocket: so I must cut my coat according to my cloth & use as little as I can help of the more expensive colours; but go on I *must* whatever it costs — so I will think no more on that subject.

I give you here a list of the colours we should be likely to want, you had better keep it as the names will serve you ⟨as⟩ to be used for nicknames when the affair is in working order: I append my idea as to how they would be dyed: I would send you patterns dyed by myself for each shade with an account of my way of dyeing it, & if that way were not practicable you would let me know I suppose — fastness and the right kind of colour being the only things I should deem essential: as to several matters of detail we must have instructions from the manufactures

We should begin by asking you to dye for 2 pieces (about 200 yds) of carpet: here then is the list:

1. Blue — *always* hot vat colour 3 or 4 shades
   2 Blue of green tint: blue vat as above, but very slightly yellowed with fast yellow weld I suppose. 3 or 4 shades.
2. Red
   a. scarlet: a full madder colour like I dyed at Leek.
   b. crimson: a full deep colour of cochineal with a little like I dyed at Leek,
   c. a brick red a poorer madder colour
   d. salmon, light madder colours 3 shades, the lightest very faint.
   e. pink; shades of cochineal & madder. 3 shades, the lightest very light.

[Note in margin] Will lac-dye help us in any of these colours — Will it be cheaper?

3. various shades of orange and buff to be got by weld mixed with the madder of above shades.
4. yellow:
   a. bright pure colour: weld: but these shades would be very light. 2 shades.

 b. deep ochre yellow: weld & madder: but these you would dye on the grey wool so as easily to get the colour darker 3 shades.

5. green

 a. yellow green blue vat & weld 4 shades.

 b. blue green do 3 shades.

 c. grey green do 4 shades.

[Note in margin] The darkest shade of any very dark all the duller shades on grey wool

6. black(?) what you would call a shocking bad rusty[?] black would be the nearest approach to it we should use: generally we should use a dark shade of blue vat either simple or slightly yellowed.

7. brown

 a. we should want 2 or 3 shades of cool brown like this.

 b. and 2 or 3 of red brown like this.[2] I have no idea as to how to dye these.

8. purple (very seldom) cochineal & blue vat 2 shades.

 This is a very copious list of the colours I should want. the thing that frightens me most as to price in it is the weld for the darker greens: because you once told me it was a costly dye: the deeper & richer madder & cochineal colours we should want very little of. We should no doubt use much more of greens & blues than anything else — I shall be sending you soon some worsted for embroidery to be dyed: but I am afraid it will be in rather small parcels. You will have to start me in patterns of blue by the by: as I am sure I cannot get on with my cold vat for them: it just amounts to sending me any amount of shades, & I will pick out the ones I like — will bark help us out with our greens? I mean is it to be considered a fast colour on wool?

 As soon as we can get this affair for the Yorkshire carpets on its legs, I shall try to arrange matters in like wise for other woollen goods that I hope will help us a bit. I hope it won't be long before you are ready to begin. We shall start with a new pattern, one of those I brought down to Leek.

 The black silk came to hand all right and was very much admired by the ladies, and also by me.

 Many thanks to you for getting it for me.

I am

Yours very truly

William Morris

per L.D.[3]

MS: Duke. Copy in V&A.

 [1] This is a reference to the machine-woven Morris Kidderminster carpets produced at Heckmondwike, Yorkshire. (See letter no. 321, n. 2.) Paul Thompson writes (pp. 98-99)

that after 1876, Wardle dyed the yarn, which previously had been dyed at Heckmond-wike.

[2] Morris drew two rectangles of color here.

[3] This letter, not in Morris's hand, was probably dictated by him to an employee of Morris and Company, possibly Lawrence Debney.

326 • To Thomas Wardle

From
Morris & Company
26, Queen Square,
Bloomsbury, London, W.C.
April 27, 1876

To Thomas Wardle Esqre.

Dear Sir/We have received the first piece of the blue damask from Nicholson and though it looks very well indeed the colour is so far unfast that it *rubs* off. For the curtains this will not matter very much but it makes the damask impossible for seats. This part of the order we have therefore countermanded and we wish your advice upon the next step.

1° Are you yet in position to dye this colour so that it will not rub off?
2° If you are, could you wash and redye the rejected silk without injury to its appearance and its working qualities?
3° If you cannot redye it blue for the present business could you dye it green in a solid way for some future business?
4° If it is necessary to dye fresh silk for this order, how soon could you do it? The loom for it is of course waiting, having been prepared for the silk we have set aside.

Truly yours,
M & C[1]

Before replying to query No. 2 perhaps you had better get from Nicholson a hank or two of the blue silk for experiment

MS: Duke. Copy in V&A.

[1] This letter is not in Morris's handwriting, but he may have had a hand in drafting it. Much of the phrasing seems to reflect his tone and style.

327 • To Thomas Wardle

26, Queen Square,
Bloomsbury, London
May 4, 1876

Dear Mr. Wardle

Thanks for the note about the Mercury[1] I shall be glad to have the whole piece. How about the wool-dyeing   I am very anxious to have it set afoot as so much of my work depends upon it.

I am

Yrs very truly

William Morris

ms: Duke. Copy in V&A.

[1] In 1876, "an improved process for the manufacture of red sulphide of mercury" was patented (see *The Textile Colourist*, 1[1876], 85). Another possibility is that Morris was referring to "dog's mercury" (*Mercurialis perennis*), a plant which dyes blue. See Ethel M. Mairet, *A Book of Vegetable Dyes*, 1916, p. 39.

328 • To Thomas Wardle
    26, Queen Square,
Bloomsbury, London
May 9, 1876

Dear Mr. Wardle

The price is certainly a stumbling-block in the wool-dyeing matter, but not more than I foresaw; nor can I think 1s/0 per lb. unreasonable for well-dyed wool, as we should have to do it: on the other hand I can't at all see my way to such an increase of business as would give us 200 weight per diem, though I think we might make a considerable increase before very long: at the risk of being thought importunate I must ask if you think you could undertake to dye our piece-goods (serges and Utrecht velvets) when the hank-wool-dyeing is fairly on its legs. The business in them would be trifling at first, but we think we could increase the sale if we could get them fast-dyed. As to going on with the enterprise of the wool-dyeing, I am determined to do so in some way or other; because so much of my work depends on the solving of the difficulty, that no amount of money could compensate me for the dissappointment if I had to give it up: at the same time I don't suppose the dyeing of our wools will ever be a profitable business to anyone, and no doubt it will be a troublesome one: so I for my part wish you to consider if it is worth your while to undertake it: which you must necessarily do for the pleasure of the thing than for commercial reasons: I think it only fair to put this before you, as the calico-printing has been such a troublesome affair; but of course I shall be very glad if you can ⟨make⟩ manage to do the ⟨bus⟩ wool-dyeing for us, as my only other plan would be to try to get a couple of men & do it in London, out Hammersmith way, as well as I could; and I have no doubt I should flounder about finely in the blunder-sea: If you elect to do it, I shouldn't think the clear month you ask a very long time, and I will try to have everything ready for you in good time.

[302]

I am glad to hear your opinion about weld, as I have a great affection for that vegetable: I have set my heart upon getting Kermes[1] somehow: I suppose you have no idea as to whom to ask further about it: I think of trying Constantinople as a possible place to ask about.

As to the printing, I am rejoiced to hear that things are like to go smoother. it was vexatious that the piece of blue didn't turn out right in tint; but it was altogether in the wrong direction and wouldn't go with our things at all.

I will ask you not to lose sight of the dip-blue printing: you will have 2 new sets of blocks for it soon.

About the indigo silk we have been rash certainly, but it can't be helped now.

Thanks for the paper about Cheddleton:[2] it amused me at breakfast this morning: for I happened to be here.

Yours very truly
William Morris

MS: Duke. Copy in V&A.

[1] The dried bodies of the females of certain scale insects (genus *Kermes*), formerly thought to be a berry; used for making a purple-red dye. Rediscovering the technique of using kermes, hardly known since the Middle Ages, was Morris's and Wardle's greatest success.

[2] See letter no. 324, n. 1.

329 · To William Grenley

Hart Street
Bloomsbury
May 16 [1876]

Dear Sir[1]

The quotation I think you will find is Gower's "Vox Clamantis" — Let my verse not be turgid, let there be in it no word of untruth; may each word answer to the thing it speaks of pleasantly and fully; may I flatter in it no one, and seek in it no praise above the praise of God. Give me that there shall be less vice amd more virtue for my speaking."[2]

I am
Dear Sir
Yours faithfully
William Morris

MS: Doheny.

[1] The envelope containing this letter is addressed to Grenley at 73 Vincent Square, Westminster, but I have been unable to identify him or explain the inside address.

[2] John Gower (1330?-1408) wrote *Vox Clamantis* (c. 1382) in Latin elegiacs. The poem narrates the Peasants' Revolt of 1381 and denounces political corruption in fourteenth-century England.

330 • To Emma Shelton Morris   26, Queen Square,
                                            Bloomsbury, London
                                            May 23, 1876

Dearest Mother

I write a line to wish you many happy returns of your birthday, and the best of good wishes in all ways and to send you my best love: I send by passenger-train also a parcel, containing 1st a little packet which Janey will explain, and also 2nd 20 yards of black silk to make you a gown This is part of a piece that my dyeing friend got for me direct from Lyons, and they call it the best that can be got for money: in fact it really looks good, & I hope you will find it so.

I have not been quite so well lately; I had a *little* touch of gout the other day, and have got to be very careful about my eating & drinking: I am head over ears in work, but that you know is a pleasure to me.

I hope you will like the change in the weather: I went into Northamptonshire on business last Thursday, & could see that the grass was not grown at all: I shall soon be coming down to have a look at you.

Give my love to Henrietta, and again I send love to you dearest Mother and am

                                            Ever Your most loving Son
                                            William Morris

MS: Walthamstow.

331 • To Mr. Grey   Scotswood Rd
                                            Newcastle on Tyne
                                            June 7, 1876

Dear Mr Grey[1]

The sentiment is good but a mere languid complacency[?] seems to me more dangerous that almost any other mood could be. At any rate I pledge myself, though I am a *very* busy man, to hang back in no way if any one will answer your question and mine of 'What is to be done?[2]

                                            I am
                                            Dear Sir
                                            (with many thanks)
                                            Yours faithfully
                                            William Morris

MS: PML.

[1] Unidentified.

[2] A penciled note on the back of the original, not in Morris's hand, states that he was "referring to the Bulgarian atrocities." See letter no. 339, which is similar in content.

332 • To Thomas Wardle   26, Queen Square,
                                                          Bloomsbury, London
                                                          June 20, 1876

My dear Mr. Wardle

I thought the letter L would look better if it were more emphatic, and so I have done it in white on black. Moreover as you have already one blue drug on your paper I thought it would be fairer to give Madder a turn, as it is a calico-printers sheet anchor so to say: moreover I had no figure of indigo to draw from: but if you like your other idea best & will send me a figure of indigo I will do it again: the Glastum[1] is nicely drawn & tells its story well; I think it would be a great pity to leave it out.

We have just got in two trial pieces of our 3-ply carpet woven of my dyeing-attempts, they both look very well, but as one of them is vat-blue we must leave that for the present: but the red one we want got into the loom as soon as may be, so I want to know if you can undertake 400 weight of wool for it; all cochineal & madder, and how long it would be in dyeing from the day you got the wool to hand: I will send you patterns of everything with notes as to how I got the colours, and as to which variations from pattern would be harmful & which would be of little importance

I have tried the weld on wool again and it has been in the window a fortnight, and has *not* faded but has gone a shade darker & redder: I think this must be because I had too much soap in the bath, as I certainly had for the feel of the wool: I used twice the weight of weld to the wool & got a strong bright yellow, much stronger than I could even use *as yellow*.

I have tried the weld on cotton (unbleached) also: one lot mordanted with red liquor, which turned out quite nought, and one with alum & tartar mordant and the ⟨wo⟩ yarn steeped before soaping in sulphate of copper: this seems a little touched by the sun but not much; perhaps it would have borne more soaping: I have your note with the pieces this morning about the cotton yarn dyeing, and shall therefore ask you to dye me some patterns of red and blue at once: I shall also want some greens, but will if you please make some patterns for these by dyeing some of your blues with weld. I have been looking at the pieces, and like them both very much, but especially the green, which is one of the best lots we have had: of course I cannot expect the Bolton cloth[2] to match the square-woven cloth closely: we want standards of the Bolton to match too: this obviously applies most to the maddered cloths: but I do not at all dislike the change in colour for a change —

I am very wishful to see a good fent of the honeysuckle pattern: also

The Honeysuckle design (chintz, 1876).

the green & blue carnation is much wanted, and also this same green as the Bolton on the plain cloth —

I am
Yours very truly
William Morris

P.S It will be a great pity if we can't match the shades of wool for red carpet pretty closely as it is very successfull   I send patterns for cotton yarn in another envelope

MS: Duke. Copy in V&A.

[1] A plant of the mustard family (genus *Isatis*) yielding a blue dye.

[2] Bolton, Lancashire, was especially noted for calicoes and muslins in the nineteenth century.

333 • TO THOMAS WARDLE

26, Queen Square,
Bloomsbury, London
June 26, 1876

Dear Mr. Wardle

Three weeks we had better say then, as I find we have still some of the old red carpet to sell. I send my mem: about the dyeing of my patterns: I am afraid you will think me little better than the departed Kay as to my want of method.

I have got a copy of Hellot (Paris 1750)[1] who is only about wool dyeing: he is very minute about the management of the vats, and I think might be of some use in that quarter, as he wanted to ⟨dye⟩ do with his vats as we do, viz make all the shades of blue to be used: he has an interesting chap: on Kermes, which he praises as the best and fastest of colours, as fast as madder: but I am afraid our chances of meeting with that drug are but slight.

I was amused to hear how you had kept your counsel about Kays departure when you were up here: I hope all will go well with the new man: I am waiting anxiously for your plant getting advanced enough to give us the dip blue: as well as the wool & silk dyeing.

By the by, I looked last Thursday at the trials we had dyed in the hydrosulphite vat; ⟨and found⟩ (those that you saw) and found the lighter silk considerably faded; the darker not noticeably so: the cotton a very little touched, and the wool quite unchanged: I can't help thinking that there might have been some foundation for the old idea that pastel & woad were faster than indigo: Hellot says that a vat of pastel only is better for the *light* colours, as it is hard to get them evenly dyed in a healthy indigo vat, & if they are dyed in an old & weak vat they are apt to be dirty. I should be glad to have the samples of cotton ⟨hank⟩ yarns dyed as soon as may be.

I have already signed the petition:[2] my daughter Jenny brought it me; I have handed it over to G.Y.W.[3] and he and I will be able to get a name or two I daresay.

Yrs very truly
William Morris.

P.S. Today we have bad accounts of another set of silk curtains of our selling: green this time, dyed at Lyons: as far as dyers are concerned I wish the days of Colbert[4] back again: it was red last time and Tours. I send the wool patterns over again to be sure of the numbers.

MS: Duke. Copy in V&A.

[1] Jean Hellot (1685-1766), French chemist and inspector-general of the royal dye-works, and author of *Théorie chimique de la teinture des étoffes* and *L'Art de la teinture des laines*. The Sotheby Sale Catalogue of Morris's library lists (p. 45, lot 432) the second of these which is described as follows: *L'Art de la Teinture des Laines*, calf, Paris, 1750.

[2] Possibly that presented on July 14 to Lord Derby by John Bright: it was a memorial, signed by members of Parliament and public figures, calling for nonintervention in the conflict between Turkey and Russia. For Morris's first surviving letter on the Eastern Question, see letter no. 351.

[3] George Y. Wardle.

[4] Jean Baptiste Colbert (1619-1683), minister of finance in the reign of Louis XIV noted for fiscal reform and the encouragement of new industries. In 1672, he sought to improve and control the operations of dyeing by promulgating a code of instructions for French woolen dyers and manufacturers.

---

334 • TO JANE MORRIS

Kelmscott
Friday
[Postmark July 9, 1876]

Dearest Janey

Here I am then all safe: I have passed the morning on the river: the fishing is bad; water low & bright: but I am not absolutely fishless, even as you foretold: for I am to dine off fish today, and am sousing (or Mrs. Comely is)[1] two small Jack for tomorrow or Sunday. The morning was not unpleasant, but this afternoon has turned out diabollically so: a strong East wind & a yellow blight are depressing even at Kelmscott — Ah, it is raining fast now, which I am glad of, as we may have a change tomorrow. The garden has suffered here much from the cold & wet, I mean to say as to vegetable, for it looks beautiful: the strawberry bed is a mass of blossoms; there no roses out except the yellow ones on the gable wall of the barn: but a fortnight hence, it will be a wonder for the roses: I must try to get down if only for a day at that time.

Would you please send me by return of post the baccy which is in my room at home You can easily make it into a parcel that will go by post & I shall get it on Monday: I am short of that article.

I shall not come back till ⟨Monday⟩ Wednesday if all bowls row aright: I enjoyed my morning on the river very much, though I lost the only really good perch I hooked, by my own stupidity, also by the same course of action a big chub.

Kiss those dear babies for me.

I am

With love

Your

WM

MS: BL, Add. MSS. 45338. Published: Henderson, *Letters*, 79.

¹ Mrs. Comely was housekeeper at Kelmscott Manor.

335 • TO JANE MORRIS

26, Queen Square,
Bloomsbury, London
Thursday 1876
[Postmark July 13, 1876]

Dearest Janey

I enclose herewith a P.O.O. for £10 drawn b[y] William Morris on the Deal office¹ in favour of Jane Morris: I hope you are pretty well contented with your palace; you will at all events have a spell of fine weather there: I only hope you wont be *quite* roasted before I see you again: I hear that Georgie & Madge² are off in a hurry to join you this afternoon: Georgie was out this morning when I called. Give my love to the dear babies & bid them write to me.

Your loving
WM.

MS: BL, Add. MSS. 45338.

¹ Jane Morris was at Deal, Kent, with Jenny and May for the summer.
² Margaret Burne-Jones.

336 • TO JANE MORRIS

26, Queen Square,
Bloomsbury, London
Tuesday
[Postmark July 18, 1876]

Dearest Janey

Thanks for your letter, I am so glad to hear that things go well so far: though of course I cannot help being anxious:¹ Yes, I got the dear things letters, and answered them on Sunday, (else I should have written to you) and very pretty letters they were. The news from here is little or none; e g. that I broke the strings of the venetian blind in my room last night; that no water came in to the cistern on Sunday, & very little yesterday; & so on. Item I was *not* the man that threw the medicine bottles at the dog last Saturday, and was fined a shilling for that righteous indignation.

I can't help thinking that you have not been so hot as we have been these last days; though last night and today it has been cooler: so much so, that, calling on Kate[2] yesterday evening, I found her refusing to go out with her mother because the wind was so cold: nay she durst not go near the window, for she said that the bitter north wind cut her in half. As for me, that the grumbling circle may be complete, I am longing for that tail of the glacier in Thorsmark,[3] or our camp in the wilderness at Eyrindarkofarver under the snow mountains: In fact though I don't feel unwell (and therefore ought to hold my noise, as you very truly say.) I am depressed and languid (say lazy) and don't care for my work, at any rate not ⟨my⟩ the bread & cheese part of it: though for want of finding any amusement in books on Saturday & Sunday I did manage to screw out my tale of verses,[4] to the tune of some 250 I think. By the way the Athenaeum has been very civil to me about that scrap of poem I published in it the other day,[5] though it was not worth publishing either, and sent me £20: it seems, such is the world's injustice & stupidity that it was a success — never mind, I shall pay for it when my new poem comes out.

I cannot tell you how pleased I am to hear that you think so well of Jenny: you don't say much about May: I suppose it can't fail to do her good: I think it would be a great pity to hurry them away if the place really seems to suit them, and if you can hold out there: I will give you as much of my company as work will let me: today week or tomorrow-week I hope to come down, and shall stay 3 days or so at any rate: I am looking forward to it very much. Take care of yourself my dear and tell me of anything you want: I think we had better spend that £20 in carriages at Deal? Well — give my dear love to the babes, and goodbye.

Your loving W.M.

MS: BL, Add. MSS. 45338. Extract published: *CW*, 12, xi; Mackail, I, 330.

[1] In the summer of 1876, Jenny Morris became subject to epileptic fits, and the anxiety acknowledged here was never to leave him. The worst sorrow of Morris's life, Bernard Shaw wrote, was his belief that Jenny's illness was an inheritance from himself. (Shaw presumably meant that Morris feared a connection between his own uncontrollable rages and Jenny's epileptic fits.) See Mackail, I, 328; and George Bernard Shaw, "More About Morris," *Observer* (November 6, 1949), p. 7.

² Kate Faulkner, sister of Charles Faulkner. She lived with her mother near the Morrises at Queen Square. See *CW*, 3, xxv.

³ Thorsmark is "a wood up in that terrible valley east of the Lithe." (*Icelandic Journals*, 1871, p. 48.)

⁴ He was writing *Sigurd the Volsung*.

⁵ "The First Foray of Aristomenes," published in *The Athenaeum*, May 13, 1876. See letter 322, n. 1.

337 • To J. H. Cooke
Horrington House
Turnham Green
July 24, 1876

Dear Sir

I send herewith a copy of my 'Earthly Paradise', of which I beg your acceptance, with some apologies for the weight of that specimen of literature, (in the scales at least)

I enjoyed my visit to Berkeley exceedingly; I think the castle can scarcely be matched among all the famous houses of England for romantic interest, using that much abused word in its best sense.¹

With many thanks for your kindness, which made my visit so very pleasant to me

I am
Dear Sir
Yours truly
William Morris

J. H. Cooke Eqre

MS: NYU.

¹ Morris was probably referring to Berkeley Castle in Gloucestershire, where Edward II (1284-1327) was imprisoned and murdered. It contains a large Gobelin tapestry (c. 1720), and many rugs, mostly oriental. See *The Connoisseur*, 137 (1932), 240-48.

338 • To Thomas Wardle
26, Queen Square,
Bloomsbury, London
August 1, 1876

Dear Mr. Wardle

I have been looking at the red wools, and thus report on them: the trial for 593 will not serve us for this job; as it is a good colour it had better be set aside for another carpet, since I understand you have dyed 40 lb of it: my pattern was dyed with what was left of the bath after dyeing the full colours 648 & 636: I find it stands well in the window   anyhow it would be very easy to get it by increasing the tartar in the mordaunt, & using the madder sparingly.

First trial of 614 is very good: 'tis a pity that the 200 sent to Yorkshire were not up to it; we don't want more than the 200 ff for this job so had better keep the 50 ff I understand you have dyed, for next carpet.

648 & 636 are not quite up to pattern: they seem to me to want more madder: also they are somewhat more orange than mine: query have they been soaped? and how about the dose of tartar? most of the receipts give too great a proportion of tartar for the colour I want, because they are aiming at scarlet: $1/4$ of alum & $1/12$ or tartar was what I used at Leek: I dyed some wool here the other day using $1/20$ of tartar, & a corresponding increase of alum: the colour came out a dead match of what I dyed at Leek.

605 is a very good match: please go on with it.

There are still 2 colours you have not sent us: the deep crimson warp & the light flesh shoot: we shall be glad to see patterns of them as soon as may be.

As to the cotton ⟨warps⟩ yarns: the blue are just what I wanted: but there has been some mistake about the reds, because we wanted them dyed with madder: it is not much use sending patterns to be woven in fugitive colours because when we come to the pieces the trouble of getting the colours comes all over again: I should be much obliged if you could give us patterns of these in madder, or as *near as you can*.

By the by I dont understand why the bit of welded cloth you sent us should have yielded to soap   the skein I dyed was only developed by soaping: I am going to green some of the blues you have sent me, & shall see what happens. I am anxious about the blue-dyeing   we can do but little till you are ready for that. I see with great pleasure that you have overcome the indigo printing, & what else I have to say today has principally to do with that: but I will begin with the steam-colour honeysuckle No 1.[1]

Please try a yard fent of this with the *print* not so red: I enclose a bit of water-colour on paper of the colour I want: the other colours will then be happy I think.

Pattern No. 4. Indigo & madder on Bolton: we must give up the madder for the print, it makes the ground so ugly: make the print the same as No. 1 corrected say No. 5. the blues and yellows are very good but the reds are wrong: make the light poppy blotch like enclosed pattern,[2] and the honeysuckle the very lightest shade possible madder of red.

Pattern No 3 half bleached. Again the blues and yellows are good, but the reds are wrong   they must be ⟨as for next above (No 4) the light

[312]

poppy as enclosed, the honeysuckle as light as madder red can be got: do one fent with steam print (as paper pattern) another with madder black.

Also do a fent with print as paper pattern, indigo blotch for ⟨big leaves⟩ blue as light as you can; yellow light as in No. 4. honeysuckle as ditto in No. 1. poppy two shades of salmon as to paper-pattern. Also: Please do 3 yds of fent with the print indigo as dark as you conveniently can: blue blotch indigo as light as you can, and send this up to us that we may give further instructions about it when we see what it looks like.

Please ⟨print⟩ do a fent of African Marigold³ with the ⟨blotch⟩ blue in indigo.

I have forgotten to note above that the print has bled in the places where madder comes over madder in these fents; can this not be remedied, as it spoils the effect terribly.

Also another fent: or two: as the corrected No. 3 and 4 but leave out madder blotch of poppy and ⟨print⟩ do ground in deep madder red as pattern. I shall be very glad to have these fents as soon as you possibly can, as this honeysuckle pattern has costs us a lot in blocks, & is one of the most important we have or are likely to have —

I note again that the pattern I send you for the poppy blotch seems to have been tinned[?]; I think ⟨it⟩ tinning[?] would improve all the madder colours in these fents; and would bring the colours nearest to the pattern I send, which I can't expect to be got *very* close on the bleached ⟨groun⟩ cloths.

I am
Yrs very truly
William Morris

Pattern of 653 cochineal carpet yarn arrived after the above was written. Dye the bulk same col.

Note. To prevent mistake we return samples of all the carpet yarns mentioned in this letter with numbers attached. The numbers on the patterns as received from you did not correspond with ours.⁴

MS: Duke. Copy in V&A.

¹ This 1876 Honeysuckle pattern for chintz is among Morris's best known designs. See Clark, pp. 56 and 64, for a discussion of its significance in Morris's development as a textile designer.

² Although Clark gives 1881 as the year of the Poppy design for wallpaper, it would seem that Morris had designed the pattern and attempted to use it for chintz, perhaps unsuccessfully, in 1876. See Clark, pp. 15, 35.

³ See letter no. 306, n. 3

⁴ This postscript "Note" is not in Morris's handwriting.

339 • TO MR. GYE[?]

9 The Cresent
Buxton
August 7 [1876?]

It seems to me a very dangerous mood you are in. At any rate I pledge myself though I am a very busy man, to hang back in no way if any one will answer your question and mine of 'What is to be done?'[1]

I am
Dear Sir
(with many thanks)
Yours faithfully
William Morris

To Mr. Gye[?] Aug 7

MS: Columbia.

[1] See also letter no. 331, with similar wording.

340 • TO THOMAS WARDLE

26, Queen Square,
Bloomsbury, London
August 19, 1876

Dear Mr. Wardle

I have the fents, and think some of them very successful, and so I can set the others aside for the present.

Fent marked 'execution of No 9 order': we are ordering 6 pieces of this: I hope you will be able to keep close to the fent, for in these many-coloured patterns so much depends on niceties: the main points to be careful about are 1st to keep the light yellow very light, and the dark yellow of its present greenish tint: the brown outline too is very important in these prints, and you have got it very good in both the two fents I shall be speaking of: the blue is quite as light as it ought to be, but is quite satisfactory as it stands: the pinks must be carefully kept from getting redder, & the lighter shades from getting darker: I assume that the prints here are not madders: couldnt they be got with madder another time?

Fent numbered 2 E & B blacks omitted. This is very pretty, and I am ordering 6 pieces of it: but couldn't the greens be got near enough to this in Indigo by printing over the blue-green once with yellow, & the yellow-green twice with yellow? You had better perhaps carry out the order as it is, and try a fent as I have spoken of it: I will send an order for this fent and also for the No 9 with the pinks in madder.

No. 10, 2 shades of Indigo, I am very much pleased with, and am ordering 6 pieces (or more if you like, & can insure them as good as pattern). I also send an order for a fent of it to be made with yellow and orange printed over it (if feasible): you see I want to make as much of this pattern as possible, as I consider it our best in effect.

This No 10 reminds me that I want a fent of the African marigold done with the blue in two shades of Indigo, and the yellow as before these two shades might be just as no 10.

The fent of the columbine[1] is still unlucky: this design has somehow turned out a failure — The cutting from the weld pieces, they are very faint, but *soaping* will yellow them though it wont make the pattern stronger: but I think thus they will do very well: I enclose a rag torn from your fent and soaped to show you what a difference it makes: but it would be better next time to get the mordaunt stronger. I am making some seasonible[?] experiments with walnut-peels on wool: they give very pleasant light browns at all events, and would be very useful for saddening[2] the colour is so clear.

By the by, why don't you try a little soap in the dyebeck[3] in the weld-dyeing? mightn't that do it.

I shall be delighted to meet you in Paris; only give me about 3 days notice.

I am shocked about the Roebuck:[4] It only shows that people now do not care about art and history — Can't you do anything? if words could avail I would be glad to help: you should buy the old house and live there: you would like it very much: and you should have the papers for nothing.

> I am
> Yours very truly
> William Morris

MS: Duke. Copy in V&A.

[1] This is probably a reference to the Bluebell pattern designed by Morris in 1876 for printed cotton. The name is derived from the figure of the bluebell in the pattern, rather than from the columbine which also forms part of the design. However, the pattern is sometimes called Columbine.

[2] In dyeing, the process of toning down colors by the application of certain chemicals.

[3] The shallow vessel that holds the dyeing liquid.

[4] The Roebuck was an inn, built in the seventeenth century, and moved—in pieces—to Leek from Shropshire. It belonged to the Loundes family. See John Sleigh, *A History of the Ancient Parish of Leek* (London, 1883), p. 235.

341 · To Thomas Wardle

26, Queen Square,
Bloomsbury, London
August 24, 1876

My dear Mr. Wardle

I have the four patterns of red cotton; the dark one is rather feeble as to colour, but the whole 4 would serve our present purpose (for the cotton damask) if they will stand light & air & soaping fairly, and if you can do our quantities for us, which would be small just at present: I tried soaping them this morning ½ hour's boiling in a strong solution of soap; I send you the results, to see if you think they ought to have stood it out better: I think myself they would serve our present purpose, but I imagine you will be able to get them better after a bit.

The madder wool for the carpet: when shall we have the balance? I shall be very glad to. Yesterday I tried dyeing the wool at twice, ⟨using the same qua⟩ halfing the madder ⟨at⟩ in each bath, and not raising the temperature over 160°F   the result was much *rosier* than the once-dyed, and would be useful for some things: though it don't matter for this, as you have got your strong colour (in the patterns sent) so good.

I have made some good green patterns from your blue-vat cotton yarns, and they have stood out 3 weeks of this torrid zone well; but the blue gave a little, *as the cold vat seems always to do*. Would you be ready to dye the greens (yarn) now. We are sorely in need of greens (indigo & weld) for linings by the way: can't you do anything for us?

I am very anxious about the blue-dyeing: we shall get into trouble about that silk, if we can't do something very shortly: and many things are standing still for want of fast blues in wool.

The indigo-*printing* seems quite a success now; I am very pleased & congratulate you upon it.

I am
Yrs very truly
William Morris

P.S. The cottons are not quite dry   the clerk will send them.

ms: Duke. Copy in V&A.

342 · To Thomas Wardle

26, Queen Square,
Bloomsbury, London
August 30 [1876]

Dear Mr. Wardle

We have up here 5 pieces of African Marigold on Bolton cloth, which are puzzling to me as they are 3 distinct colours: A (one piece) is quite satisfactory, B (two pieces) are greyer and not so good & C (two pieces) are quite bad: the blotch being almost purple: I am afraid we can do nothing with these 2 last (C).

What is to be done? Could you try the six pieces again to A? If it were a little bluer it would be no harm but the blotch going red is fatal.

The weld-dyed cloth is very pleasant colour: do the six pieces first as you suggest and we will make up the order to 12.

I note by the way that the pattern we sent you down to match the African Marigold seems to have faded.

Yrs very truly
William Morris

T. Wardle, Eqre.

P.S. Could nothing be done to raise the colour of the 2 bad pieces?[1]

MS: Duke. Copy in V&A.

[1] Some swatches of material are still with the original of this letter.

---

343 • TO JENNY MORRIS
Bull Hotel
Burford, Oxon.
[September 1876?]

Dearest Jenny

We got here very comfortably yesterday, and found the Windrush valley very beautiful: we are going this morning to Fairford & Kelmscott by way of Northleach & Foss Bridge: I could write you a long letter my dearest child, but my pen my pen! a needle: and of ink a mere dearth: so it gives me the fidgetts; so excuse me for this shabby little note.

& I am
Your loving father
William Morris

Burford is very nice & the Inn no worse than before, but why call it an Hotel?

MS: BL, Add. MSS. 45339. Published: Henderson, *Letters*, 139.

344 · To Aglaia Ionides Coronio Broadway Tower
Tuesday
[September 4, 1876]

My dear Aglaia

Here is the note then: I have been nearly a fortnight at Kelmscott off and on, and am going back there tomorrow till Friday when I am coming to town, but only for a day or two, after which I shall be going to Kelmscott again for a few days & then home. I believe I shall be at Horrington House next Sunday afternoon and if you are coming out that way I should be happy to see you: I am today at Crom Price's Tower[1] among the winds & the clouds: Ned & the children are here, and all are much amused: I am glad you have come back safe: & hope you have benefitted by Herr Wagner's instructive great work.[2]

I am
Yours affectionately
William Morris

MS: Yates Coll. Published: Henderson, *Letters*, 79-80.

[1] The tower at Broadway, Worcestershire, in the Cotswolds. May Morris described it as "a squat thing with turrets that Cormell Price rented . . . which overlooked a glorious view of many counties" (*CW*, 12, xii).

[2] The Bayreuth Festival was inaugurated in August 1876, with three performances of *Der Ring des Nibelungen*, and Aglaia Coronio had attended the series. Morris's dislike of Wagner was longstanding (see letter no. 216) but may have been sharpened at this time because he was at work on *Sigurd the Volsung*, derived from the same sources as *The Ring*. In the spring of 1877, when Wagner was in London conducting concerts at the Albert Hall, Luke Ionides tried to arrange a meeting between Morris and Richard Wagner, but the composer was detained by rehearsals and Morris met only Cosima. The entry in Cosima Wagner's diary (June 1) merely records: "Made the acquaintance of the writer Mr. Morris." *Cosima Wagner's Diaries, Volume I, 1869-1877* (New York: Harcourt Brace Jovanovich, 1978), p. 966. For discussions of Morris and Wagner, see Robert Gutman's Introduction to the *Volsunga Saga* (New York: Collier Books, 1962) and Henderson, *Life*, pp. 168-70.

345 · To Thomas Wardle 26, Queen Square,
Bloomsbury, London
September 16, 1876

Dear Mr. Wardle

Thanks for your note: I am glad we are getting on: but I am disappointed in not receiving the fent of the honeysuckle you promised me: I am very anxious to see it. Nicholson is ready for his cotton warps, I should be much obliged if you let him have the small quantities for trials speedily.

I am
Yrs very truly
William Morris

MS: Duke.

346 • To CORMELL PRICE
26, Queen Square,
Bloomsbury, London
September 26, 1876

My dear Crom
Many thanks: I send a bundle of proofs:[1] I am in a duce of a hurry And am

Yr affectionate
William Morris

MS: Price Papers.
[1] Presumably for *Sigurd the Volsung*.

347 • To THOMAS WARDLE
26 Queen Sq
October 9, 1876

Dear Mr. Wardle
I will come over by the night mail tomorrow (Tuesday) which will come to much the same thing as getting in on Tuesday night, as I shall be in Paris on Wednesday morning about ½ past 6:[1] I always sleep or doze on the journey: so I shall be ready for anything on Wednesday morning
I could not manage to [illegible] by the day train. I see the clerk of the weather has laid on a fine Sou-wester for me by the way, but it will do me good.

Yrs very truly
William Morris

MS: Duke.
[1] One reason Morris went to Paris to meet Wardle was to search bookshops for old books on dyeing. When Wardle returned to England, Morris remained and searched thirteen shops for such books. See letter no. 348.

348 • To Thomas Wardle
26, Queen Square,
Bloomsbury, London
October 18, 1876

Dear Mr. Wardle

Thanks for your letter, I am very glad [you like] the window, and you are most heartily welcome to it.[1] We had another thunder storm on Friday in Paris between 4 & 5 p.m. with huge hail; and it came on again just as I was leaving Paris, and lasted for 2 hours as we went along: it was very magnificent; I had a very smooth passage over.

As to the dyeing-books, I asked for them in 13 shops, and was treated with civil contempt in all except one, where I got Macquer,[2] and a useful looking book rather later in date by one Homassel[3] on dyeing wool silk & cotton, & printing: there is an article about weld-dyeing in this latter part   I send you an extract from this book about silk dyeing in indigo which (as far as the manipulation goes) [may] be useful to you: I notice by the way that he tells you to *gall*[4] cotton skein-goods, both for weld & madder: would you try this especially on the madder with a head or two of cotton: the galling is done before mordanting.

I have got to get these books bound they are so ragged: meantime I will send you an extract from Maquer: I also got another dye-book, Teinturier Parfait, that looks rule of thumb. Also a book with detailed description (with good plates) of the carpet-making we saw: this is part of the same series as Maquer and Macquer has also plates — also in the same series a book on cotton-velvet, because it had receipts for printing the velvet. The old chap will send me a Hellot as soon as he can get one; also I told him I would buy any old dyeing-books: so I expect to hear from him again.

We can only get down here 5 bushels of English Walnut-cods, but I shall get some more foreign ones: don't you think it would be worth while for you to try to collect some up there: I am sure they would help us very much in getting shades of colours: I find the London *leather-dyers* use them, but only the English nuts. I need not say I shall be very glad to hear of the blue dyeing getting into order.

With kind regards to Mrs. Wardle

I am
Yours very truly
William Morris

ms: Duke. Copy in V&A.

[1] Possibly at Wardle's request Morris had sent him a sketch made for one of the windows in Cheddleton Church. It is equally likely, however, that Morris refers to a window supplied for Wardle's own home. Morris did make windows for Wardle's house sometime in the 1870's. See Sewter, II, 203.

[2] Pierre-Joseph Macquer (1718-1784), French chemist. His *Art de la Teinture en soie* was published in 1763. Sotheby's Sale Catalogue of Morris's library, 1898, lists (p. 77, Lot 178) a copy of the 1763 Paris edition of this work.

[3] Hommassel's *Cours de l'Art de la Teinture* (Paris, 1809).

[4] Galls formed on oak trees have a high tannic acid content and can be used in dyeing.

349 · To Thomas Wardle

26, Queen Square,
Bloomsbury, London
October 24, 1876

Dear Mr. Wardle

Thanks for your letter, I hope we shall go on smoother for the future: you see our great difficulty with some of the patterns consists in the effect of them depending on very nice balance of colour: I cannot set these wholly aside, but in future I shall principally send you patterns which will less depend on nicety of shade; the new one is a case in point, and I shall be doing some even more broken than that. The African Marigold that went wrong it was a mistake to order, as its blue was a mere imitation of indigo: we will give you an order for it in two shades of indigo at once if you please, and according as it comes out leave it blue, or block yellow over it. By the way it might be worth while to pass a yard or two of the failure through the vat and see if it would turn out anything: we must try some experiments with the red 2-blue honeysuckle to see how best to block yellow over it: that was why I sent it back: these red indigos make very good greens, so we have that other string to our bow if we are at any time beat in the blues; only I should very much like to have a quite good 2 blue honeysuckle — we are sending you the order as you asked. Also order for the new pattern, dip-blue as originally intended, and as a single print in madder, & in indigo: if you like I can have the blue part of the ⟨part of the⟩ pattern cut for printing instead of dipping. The green cottons will do very well for trial pieces for Nicholson since they are bright and pretty.

Many thanks for your hospitable invitation; I shall certainly avail myself of it whenever I can, on all grounds.

As to the carpets, Mrs. Wardle shall have patterns from me whenever she wants them; And I will send down the book about the Gobelins carpets as soon as the binder has straightened it: you will find the plates so good that I have no doubt you will be able to set up a frame, a small one: for the big loom 30 ft long is a formidable-looking affair: by the way all the carpet-weaving at Aubusson used to be done by women. I will send Maquer also as soon as it comes from the binders. The tapestries are not to hand yet: I will let you know about them when they

[321]

are. A pattern of the carpet woven with your yarns is to hand: good, but considerably different to my pattern. The madders are none of them blue enough: the carpet is very scarlet in consequence. I dont suppose you will ever make a fortune out of our work, but if we can hold on a bit, and get something of a market as I hope this year or two coming to do, I can't help thinking it may make a fair little business, such as no doubt a Lancashire man would despise however: though I must tell you Mr. Clarkson[1] is exceedingly savage at losing any little bit of work he would have had from us.

> I am
> Yours very truly
> William Morris

MS: Duke. Copy in V&A.
  [1] See letter no. 284, n. 3.

350 • To Emma Shelton Morris
26, Queen Square,
Bloomsbury, London
October 24, 1876

Dearest Mother

I was very glad to get your letter, and hear that you were safe at home: I hope the Devonshire journey will take away your neuralgia. I was thinking of coming over next week, but must it off till your return: perhaps you will be able to look in here on your way to the west. Though we are going to make changes, of all which I will tell you when we meet, we have a fine show here: business is looking promising in spite of the bad times. My new book will be out in about a month.[1] Janey is bothered with the weather, and I am somewhat dyspeptic, but it don't go for much. Jenny is now regularly at her boarding house, and calls herself a 'poor exile': though to say the truth she likes it very much: she had a tumble last ⟨Saturday⟩ Friday, a *very* slight one, that was the first for 3 weeks. She looks so well that I can't help thinking she must soon get over it all.[2] May is rather poorly, she is not very strong, & looks much more of an invalid than Jenny. They have both been exceedingly good & dear girls of late.

  With best love to Henrietta

> I am
> Dearest Mother
> Your loving Son
> William Morris

MS: Walthamstow.

[1] *Sigurd the Volsung*.

[2] This is the second reference in the surviving letters to Jenny's epilepsy, which began in the summer of 1876 (see letter no. 336, n. 1). She was, intermittently, to be an invalid for the rest of her life.

351 • TO THE EDITOR OF THE *Daily News* 26 Queen Square
Bloomsbury
October 24, 1876

Sir

I cannot help noting that a rumour is about in the air that England is going to war;[1] and from the depths of my astonishment I ask, On behalf of whom? Against whom? And for what end? Some three weeks ago, if such a rumour had arisen, my questions would, I imagine, have been answered in this way:—"The English nation has been roused to a sense of justice (for at heart they are a generous people) by a story of horrors that no man has been able to gainsay; so they are going to war against the Turkish Government on behalf of certain subject peoples, whom the Turks conquered long ago but have never assimilated, and whom now, in their decrepitude, insolvency, and terror, they have been torturing and oppressing in the vilest manner, while they claim to be considered and treated as a civilized Government and a part of the comity of Europe. The end and aim of the war is to force the Turkish Government (who, to speak the downright truth, are a gang of thieves and murderers) to give these subject peoples, who are quite orderly and industrious, some chance for existence; to force the Turkish Government to agree to give these peoples some security for life, limb, and property, and to take order that they shall carry out their agreement (by occupying their territory or otherwise)—this is the end and aim of the war; and we and all Europe think it is a just and honourable aim, and that we are the right people to see it carried through; for we, a peaceful people, not liars (except in trade), we have nothing to gain by helping these luckless folks to live; and, though we are only their neighbours, in the sense that the Samaritan was to him who fell among thieves, yet we are in a kind of way responsible for their usage, for we have before this waged a great war to keep the Turks, their jailors, alive, thinking that we could make them a respectable and even a progressive people— so sanguine, and, to say the truth, such fools we were! However, except that we are still paying for it out of pocket, all that is past; we meant no harm then, and now we mean good and will do it."

[323]

If I had fallen asleep three weeks ago, and woke up yesterday, I should have expected some such answer to my questions of—For whom? Against Whom? and Why?[2] And I, a mere sentimentalist, should have rejoiced in such a war, and thought it wholly good: the people to be helped worthy of helping, the enemy thieves and murderers, all Europe our friends, no mouth to gainsay us but the mouths of thieves and murderers. Yes, I should have thought I had lived for something at last: to have seen all England just, and in earnest, the Tories converted or silenced, and our country honoured throughout all the world. In very truth, all this seemed on the point of happening three weeks ago, though without the terrible expense of a war; but alas, though I have not slept, I have awakened, and find the shoe quite on the other foot. The Tories are not converted; England is pretty much mocked throughout all the world. I must sorrowfully say, justly mocked, if, as I fear, we were not in earnest when we held all those meetings, and passed all those resolutions full of just anger, as it seemed. I say, not in earnest, because, to put all conventionalities aside, we know well that, in matters of peace or war, no Government durst go against the expressed will of the English people, when it has a will and can find time to express it; and, on the other hand, again setting aside conventionalities of "deliberation," "calm," "statesmanship," and the like, we know well that our Tory Government has determined to disregard, as utterly as if it had not happened, the seeming enthusiasm of repentance which the dreadful facts stated by your Correspondent[3] and Mr. Schuyler,[4] and confirmed by Mr. Baring,[5] seemed to awake, and which Mr. Gladstone's noble and generous rhetoric,[6] and Mr. Freeman's manly and closely-reasoned letters,[7] fanned into a seeming fire. We know, to speak plainly, that the new-made "brave" earl,[8] to whom "nothing is difficult," has at all events found it easy to see through a ladder, and is determined to drag us into a shameful and unjust war—how shameful and unjust no words can say. I say it would be impossible for even that clever trickster to do this, not only if united England were in earnest to gainsay him, but even if a large minority were but half in earnest and spoke, and said "No." And now, not even the wretched packed Parliament we have got is sitting. The cry for that was not believed; the members are too busy shooting in the country, and the nation is dumb, if it were not for the 2,000 working men who met last Sunday at Clerkenwell,[9] and who took it for granted, as everybody else I come across does, that the crossing of the Turkish boundaries by Russian troops would be followed at a greater or less time by England's declaration of war against Russia. And do you suppose the Turks do not take the same thing for granted?

I appeal to the Liberal party, and ask if it is not worthwhile their making some effort to avoid this shame. I appeal to the working men, and pray them to look to it that if this shame falls upon them they will certainly remember it and be burdened by it when their day clears for them, and they attain all, and more than all, they now are striving for: to the organizers of both these bodies I specially appeal, to set their hands to the work before it is too late, to drop all other watch-words that this at least may be heard—No war on behalf of Turkey; no war on behalf of the thieves and murderers! I appeal to all men of sense and feeling of all parties, and bid them think what war means, and to think if only perhaps this were an unjust war! What, then, could come of it but shame in defeat and shame in victory, and in the end ignominious undoing of all that the war should seem to do. I who am writing this am one of a large class of men—quiet men, who usually go about their own business, heeding public matters less than they ought, and afraid to speak in such a huge concourse as the English nation, however much they may feel, but who are now stung into bitterness by thinking how helpless they are in a public matter that touches them so closely. To these also I appeal to break silence at last, if they in any wise can, and to be as little hopeless as may be, for that all may perhaps help, and perhaps they as much as people more busy in such things; for the old proverb is true now as ever—"Like people, like priest." If this monstrous shame and disaster—if this curse—has to fall upon us, we cannot make Lord Beaconsfield or Lord Derby,[10] the Tory party or the House of Commons, our scapegoats; we must, our very selves, bear the curse, and make the best of it, for we put these men where they sit over us, and do their own will, such as it is; and we can put them down again if we choose. And, meanwhile till that happy day comes round, I say again that I firmly believe that a large minority, or even not so very large a minority of the English people, expressing their earnest will, would be enough to prevent any war; for, surely, even the Earl of Beaconsfield must hesitate before signing the death-warrant of so many men, if he has an excuse given him for it; since they say he is human, though, indeed, I scarce believe it. Any war could be stayed, much more, surely, such a cynically unjust and shameful one as this would be—nay, such a monstrously laughable one, if the world could laugh for shame and grief. This is the last word. I call on all those who attended those many-thronged and enthusiastic meetings throughout the country the other day to meet again. Let their organizers see to it. For I assure them that not the less because they have forgotten it were those babies murdered in Bulgaria—there were more, I believe, slain in Scio a while ago, but that is more utterly forgotten than these last—not the less were the poor souls robbed to their very shirts, it seems; not the less because they no longer heed it are people dying hundreds a day of cold and hunger out there; let those who attended those meetings, now they have rested, once more bring their imaginations to bear upon it all, and to take note that we have refused to help these poor people, that we have refused to take order that the like desolation shall not happen again, and have forced the Russians to do our share and their own of the business—for which we propose to go to war with them, after all we have said in our thronged and enthusiastic meetings! Can history show a greater absurdity than this, or greater fools than the English people will be if they do not make it clear to the Ministry and the Porte[11] that they will wage no war on behalf of the Turks, no war on behalf of thieves and murderers?

I beg with humility to be allowed to inscribe myself, in the company of Mr. Gladstone and Mr. Freeman, and all men that I esteem, as an hysterical sentimentalist; and I am, Sir, your obedient servant,

William Morris
Author of "The Earthly
Paradise"

TEXT: *Daily News* (London), October 26, 1876. Published: MM, II, 483-87; Henderson, *Letters*, 80-83.

[1] Morris became concerned about the Eastern Question during the summer of 1876. The broad issue was the old rivalry among Russia and the other great powers for control of the unstable Ottoman Empire. Events in Bosnia and Hercegovina eventually led to a Russo-Turkish war in 1877-1878; the Treaty of San Stefano which settled that conflict left Britain so dissatisfied that the Government approached the brink of war in order to compel a revision. The level of political activity in England ran high during this period, with frequent confrontations between opposing groups both on paper and in demonstrations. Among groups active in the cause of peace and the maintenance of British neutrality was the Eastern Question Association (E.Q.A.) formed in late 1876 for the stated purposes of watching events, spreading correct information, and giving expression to public opinion. Morris became treasurer of the organization, thus beginning his first period of political activism. Two detailed accounts of developments during these years are Richard Millman, *Britain and the Eastern Question, 1875-1878* (Oxford: Clarendon Press, 1979), and R. W. Seton-Watson, *Disraeli, Gladstone and the Eastern Question* (London: Macmillan, 1935).

The immediate crisis which precipitated this letter from Morris was the collapse of the Turkish government and an ensuing massacre of Christians. When Russia then threatened to invade Turkey, English popular reaction was divided between fear of Russian expansion and anger at the Turks. The Conservative Government under Disraeli warned that England would go to war if Russian troops crossed the border. Morris continued throughout the 1870's to oppose the policies of the Government that kept alive the possibility of British intervention.

[2] It is interesting that in his first important public comment on a political matter, Morris uses the "dream" as a rhetorical device. The dream recurs as a motif throughout his imaginative writing. It is apposite here to note that the dream is central to his two political prose romances, *A Dream of John Ball* (1888) and *News from Nowhere* (1890).

[3] The foreign correspondents of the *Daily News* were Edward Pears and J. A. MacGahon.

[4] Eugene Schuyler (1840-1890), an American diplomat, who was at this time secretary of the American legation at St. Petersburg and also consul general at Constantinople. He investigated alleged Turkish atrocities in Bulgaria, and before submitting his report to the State Department, permitted it to be included and published in J. A. MacGahon's *The Turkish Atrocities in Bulgaria* (London, 1876), a book that was widely circulated. It was said that his report did more to influence England than any other document of the Russo-Turkish war.

[5] Walter Baring (1844-1915), sent by the British Foreign Office to investigate reports of Turkish atrocities in Bulgaria. He described what he saw as "the most heinous crime of the century." See Seton-Watson, *Disraeli*, p. 60.

[6] Gladstone, supposedly in retirement at Hawarden, on September 6, 1876, published *The Bulgarian Horrors and the Question of the East*; on September 9 he addressed a huge open-air meeting of his constituents at Blackheath.

[7] Edward Augustus Freeman (1823-1892), English historian. Passionately anti-Turk, he had visited Dalmatia in 1875, when the revolt against the Turks broke out in Hercegovina, and had recently written a series of letters, published in the *Daily News*, in which he denounced the massacres in Bulgaria and also accused the British Government of inciting them by sending the Fleet to Besika Bay. See also letter no. 416, n. 4.

[8] On August 12, 1876, Disraeli had accepted a peerage, becoming Earl of Beaconsfield.

[9] The Patriotic Club had called a meeting for October 22, on Clerkenwell Green, to protest against the threatened war with Turkey. (See Andrew Rothstein, *A House on Clerkenwell Green* [London: Lawrence and Wishart, 1966], p. 50. Rothstein quotes *Reynold's Newspaper* for October 29, 1876 as his source.)

[10] Edward Henry Stanley, fifteenth Earl of Derby (1826-1893). Foreign Secretary (1874-1878) in Disraeli's second ministry. In 1876, he initiated the Constantinople Conference on the Turkish situation. He eventually opposed Disraeli's pro-Turkish policy and resigned twice, in 1878, in protest against the Government's apparent preparation for war. His career is well covered in Millman (see note 1 above).

[11] The government of the Turkish Empire, officially called the Sublime Porte. Justice, in former times, was administered from the gate of the Sultan's palace; hence the name.

352 • To Thomas Wardle

26, Queen Square,
Bloomsbury, London
October 31, 1876

Dear Mr. Wardle

I am very glad to hear of the 2 blue honeysuckle & look forward to seeing it: the matching in the ordinary prints seems going on much better now: I have sent instructions about the 3 blue (indigo) Af: Mar:[1] I think it promises well: the swatches you have sent up to mend the dirty indigo honeysuckle were too timid in the yellow: I have made out full instructions on that point, and, if you dont mind, I should like to get that matter settled, as we should then have a standard for mending any false shots in blue, besides adding usefully to our stock. As to snakehead please send us up strikings of the blocks on *paper* and I will get the blue cut at once: a word as [to] the fast blue-dyeing: you don't give me any distinct news of the vat, and there is that order pressing on us sorely: on the other hand I don't want to worry you about it, though I am so anxious to get my wools &c dyed: also on comparing that beautiful pattern of redyed silk that we have, with a scrap of it in the window, I find to my dissappointment that it has given a good deal in six weeks: all these things considered, I should be afraid to order the dyeing of any quantity of silk ⟨till⟩ in indigo (wool is different; the hot-vat wools have not yielded in the least) till the whole affair went on wheels: on the other hand it seems more than a pity to lose our order as we shall do if we put it off much longer: so I propose to get this silk dyed by you in the fastest modern way ⟨done⟩ possible; and should be glad to know what you could do for us: I am not wedded to any particular shade: any tint that was neither ugly nor dark would do: of course it would be a great advantage if it showed well by night: would Prussian blue do it? You remember what you were telling me about the silk in M. Marnas[2] drawing-room the other day. Meantime of course I think the hot-vat most important to my business, and am ready to get a lot of wool dyed at once in it as soon as it is ready — both skein & piece.

I send you Chaptal on Turkey Red to look at: I am afraid we shall not get the red skein cottons up to much unless they have *partly* gone through the Turkey red process:[3] please look at his observations on rouge brulé, which is in fact about the colour we want.

I hope to be able to send you Macquer & the carpet book fresh from the binder's next week. Nicholson has sent us a scrap of cotton stuff with the bright green cotton woven in: it *does* look too yellow; but so long as you can get the skeins less yellow I can give you a wide margin ⟨on that side⟩ in this matter. please get his cottons done as soon as you can, as we anxious to set him to work. Walnuts — I have been able to get very few of them, don't you think you might get some up there as you will be later than us: remembering all you have said to me about the difficulty of saddening silk, I cannot help thinking they would be very useful to us. I shall make you laugh when I tell you that on Saturday I tried another new dyeing material poplar-twigs to wit: I was promised a yellow out of them, but managed nothing nearer to it than a pleasant brown shading off to Nankin or buff colour. I am going to try them with [part of letter missing]

Af: Mar: looks very fine, but you must not forget to print the *heads* with a light shade of it: you remember there is a separate block for that purpose. I confess I feel rather low about the indigo-*printing*, but I must hope it will come all right. G. Y. Wardle is writing about the Prussian Af. M: and is sending more orders: I wish we could get the pieces more of a sort, I mean more evenly printed; if we could, it would suit us to order much bigger lots, say 20 or even 50 pieces instead of 6 at a time: we would risk the selling of them, if we could be sure of their being moreven.

I could come down between the 8 of Dec: & Xmas if convenient to you, for 2 or 3 days, if it were only about the colouring of these prints: I believe I am bound for Eaton about that time.[4] By the way shall we dispense with the ceremony of 'Mistering' one another, ⟨if y⟩ in future if you don't think it rude.

I am
Yours very truly
William Morris

MS: Duke. Copy in V&A.

[1] African Marigold.

[2] A member of a Lyon textile firm (Guinon, Marnas, and Bonnet), he developed a method for manufacturing aniline blue. The firm also obtained from lichens a product known as *pourpre française*. See William Crookes, *A Practical Handbook of Dyeing and Calico-Printing* (London, 1874), pp. 196ff.

[3] Jean Antoine Chaptal (1756-1832), French chemist. *The Textile Colourist*, 1876, no. 4, published an article (pp. 229ff.) entitled "Chaptal's Process" as part of a series on the production of Adrianople or "Turkey red." Morris refers to a work by Chaptal published in Paris in 1807 on "the art of dyeing cotton red."

[4] See letter no. 370, n. 2.

353 • TO THOMAS WARDLE   26, Queen Square,
                                                     Bloomsbury, London
                                                     November 5, 1876

Dear Mr. Wardle,

I am rather dissappointed with the 'honeysuckle': it is not up to the pattern: the blotch is too light, which takes the colour out of it, especially as the print is dark, which is not a drawback in itself.

Dyeing the other 'spoilt' honeysuckle does not do it much good: we had better wait to see if we can set it right by printing the yellow over it according to my instructions, as I think we can.

I confess I am quite in the dark about the requisites for the dye-shed you have just got roofed in: but I should like to come down when you have your vats going right so that we might set the wool dyeing going.

I am ordering some pieces of blue cotton, and according as they come out we can either leave them blue, or green them.

By the way I wanted you to try a fent of the spoilt African Marigold dipped in the blue-vat, since it is our only chance of using it.

Yours very truly
William Morris

MS: Duke. Copy in V&A.

354 • TO WILLIAM ALLINGHAM   Horrington House
November 14 [1876]

My dear Allingham

I am afraid that my wife will not be able to come on Friday, because our Jenny comes home from her (weekly) school on that day, & she would not stand her mother's absence: it was my stupidity forgetting this: the best way out of the difficulty, I think, would be for me to come by myself on Friday, and for you and Mrs. Allingham to come over here to dinner some day next week: would tomorrow week (Thursday) suit you? Please answer to 26 Queen Sq: or don't answer and I will come to you on Friday at 7 oclock and you can tell me about next week then.

I think your name well worth having and am very glad to have it:[1] I will tell you as much as I know about the affair ⟨on⟩ when I see you.

Yours very truly
William Morris

MS: Illinois.
[1] His signature on a memorial against war with Turkey.

355 • TO CHARLES JAMES FAULKNER   November 15 [1876][1]

I am very willing to receive you as a convert if you must needs ticket yourself so,[2] though I don't see the need, as both your views and mine being interpreted meant declaring ourselves enemies of that den of thieves the Turkish Government. As to the Russians, all I say is this: we *might* have acted so that they could have had no pretext for interfering with Turkey except in accordance with the unanimous wish of Europe: we *have* so acted as to drive them into separate interference whatever may come: and to go to war with them for this would be a piece of outrageous injustice. Furthermore if we came victorious out of such a war, what should we do with Turkey, if we didn't wish to be damned? 'Take it ourselves,' says the bold man, 'and rule it as we rule India.' But the bold man don't live in England at present I think; and I know what the Tory trading stock-jobbing scoundrel that one calls an Englishman to-day would do with it: he would shut his eyes hard over it, get his widows and orphans to lend it money, and sell it vast quantities of bad cotton. For the rest, I know that the Russians have committed many crimes, but I cannot accuse them of behaving ill in this Turkish business at present, and I must say I think it very unfair of us, who freed our black men, to give them no credit for freeing their serfs: both deeds seem to me to be great landmarks in history. However, I repeat, to finish, that my cry and that of all that I consider *really* on our side is 'The Turkish Government to the Devil, and something rational and progressive in its place.' If people say that latter part is difficult, I can only say that it is difficult to make a pair of shoes, or even a poem; and yet both deeds are sometimes done; — more or less ill 'tis true. . . .[3]

I do not feel very sanguine about it all . . . but since it is started and is the only thing that offers at present, and I do not wish to be anarchical, I must do the best I can with it.

TEXT: Mackail, I, 347-48. Extract published: Henderson, *Letters*, 99-100.

[1] Although dated 1877 by Mackail and Henderson, Mackail's transcript in his notebooks at the William Morris Gallery, Walthamstow, indicates that the date is 1876. This is confirmed by internal evidence.

[2] A reference to the preparations for the conference on December 9 at which the Eastern Question Association was formed. The immediate purpose of the conference was to promote resistance to Disraeli's alliance with the Turks. See letter no. 351, n. 1; see also E. P. Thompson, pp. 239-49.

[3] Mackail says (I, 348) that at this point in the letter Morris gives "details as to the action which it was proposed to take."

356 • TO ANTHONY JOHN MUNDELLA   26, Queen Square,
Bloomsbury, London
November 15, 1876

Dear Mr. Mundella[1]

I have a few names which you will find below: I can answer for all of them as feeling strongly and rightly about the matter; and they are mostly well-known men, and all will, I am sure, be useful in their own circles: their letters to me all express the desire that something should be done, and done as speedily as possible.[2] One or two of them ask for more papers, & I myself want a few more: will you kindly send me a few. Here are the names

William Allingham (Literary man) (Editor of Fraser)	12 Trafalgar Sq: Chelsea.
William De Morgan[3] (Artist, son of the Mathmetician)	8 Cheyne Row Chelsea.
F. S. Ellis (My publisher)	29 New Bond St:
C. J. Faulkner (not a parson) (Fellow and tutor of the Coll:)	University Coll: Oxford
W. B. Scott (artist, writer on art)	Bellevue Chelsea
Henry Wallis (Artist)	24 Brecknock Cresent NW.
Philip Webb (Architect, built Howards house)	1 Raymonds Buildings Grays Inn

I have added some private notes to show you who the men are: I hope for one or two more tomorrow or next day: a Cambridge Don and a well-known surgeon chiefly — here is another:

W. S. Stead[4]

Darlington

he is editor of the Northern Echo, but says expressly that he must *not* be put down so.

It seems very few; I wish I could do more.

I am
Yours very truly
William Morris

P.S. My Oxford friend reminds me of what has also occurred to me also; to wit, that money will be wanted some day soon: we are both of us ready as soon as it *is* wanted.

W.M.

MS: USheffield.

[1] Anthony John Mundella (1825-1897), the Radical M.P. for Sheffield. When Gladstone on September 6 published *The Bulgarian Horrors* and demanded that the Turks evacuate Bulgaria, the Radical wing of the Liberal Party supported him. Early in October, Mundella and his Sheffield friend, Robert Leader, discussed the calling of a national conference

on the Eastern Question. It was to be a popular movement, the politicians keeping in the background. In London, on October 20, the Labour Representation League held a rally of workers and presented the issue as a question of independence for oppressed Bulgarian Christians.

² As his October 24 letter to the *Daily News* (no. 351) indicates, Morris at this time also saw the issue as the need to aid an oppressed nationality. He therefore responded enthusiastically to Mundella's plan for a national conference.

³ William Frend De Morgan (1839-1917), artist, inventor, and author, best known today for the tiles and other ceramic ware he designed and manufactured. Early acquainted with the Pre-Raphaelite circle, he met Morris in the 1860's, and he worked for Morris and Co. designing stained glass and tiles in the 1870's. In 1871, he established a pottery works in Chelsea and rediscovered the process of making colored lustres. From 1882 to 1888, he was associated with Morris, but in 1888 built his own factory. In the later years of his life, he turned seriously to writing fiction.

⁴ Not W. S. as Morris wrote, but William Thomas Stead (1849-1912), at this time editor of the *Northern Echo*, a Darlington Liberal newspaper. In 1883 he succeeded John Morley as editor of the *Pall Mall Gazette* (see letter no. 422, n. 8) and remained in the post until 1890. He was known for his journalistic war against the traffic in child prostitutes in London and was instrumental in founding the Law and Liberty League. Stead was drowned when the Titanic sank, April 14, 1912.

357 • TO THOMAS WARDLE

26, Queen Square,
Bloomsbury, London
November 17, 1876

Dear Mr. Wardle

I send you down herewith Macquer & the carpet-book, wishing Mrs. Wardle all success in finding out how to do the carpets: I shall be ready with designs as soon as she can.¹

How about the blue-dyeing? I am expecting to hear of your vat being set every day   I read an account of the hydrosulphate-vat in the Textile Colourist of last month that interested me much;² it seems very simple: my only question is, is it as fast as the woad-vat? We have been trying the cuve-d'inde here after Hellot, but cannot make much of it: it has been greenish now and again, but we have never got any flurry upon it: never the less it will dye, but not a bright or a dark blue, though the wool will stand soaping.

I was at Kelmscott the other day in that beautiful cold weather and betwixt the fishing, I cut a handful of poplar twigs & boiled them, and dyed a lock of wool a very good yellow: this would be useful if fast, for the wool was *un*mordanted: the fishing by the way was so, so; no perch but one (2 lb 2oz he) but the pike rather good: I got one of ⟨£⟩5 lb on the pater noster.³

The yellow A. Mari: is up: very good: the last carnation needed the background-green to be brighter but the blues were very good: I thought the 2 indigo tulip very good: I hope we shall have some soon.

The fent of Snake-head is more scarlet than I meant: something more like the enclosed would be better; but anything between the one sent, and this, would do.

I am sorry to bother you about it but I should be *so* glad if you could get the blue & green cottons for Nicholson done soon: his moans are shortening my life: let alone that I want to see our cloth from him.

Yours very truly
William Morris

MS: Duke.

¹ See letter no. 321, n. 2. The designs mentioned here, however, are apparently for carpets to be woven on a hand loom.

² Although Morris refers to *The Textile Colourist* of "last month," he seems to have meant the November issue (Vol. 2, no. 11, pp. 233-61). This issue includes an article based on a talk given by George Jarmain at the Society of Arts in March and April 1875. There is a detailed discussion of blue-dyeing, although the vat described by Jarmain is the hydrosulphite vat.

³ A fishing line that has a row of hooks and bead-shaped sinkers.

358 · To Thomas Wardle
26, Queen Square,
Bloomsbury, London
[November 17-30, 1876]

Dear Mr. Wardle

I am in receipt of both your letters, and am obliged to you for being quite open on the subject of our troubles, and beg you to believe my communication to be wholly a friendly one, though I may have to say 'no' where you say 'yes.' The difficulties of your carrying on a private ⟨business⟩ manufactory for us, a business which *must* in the nature of things be rather what is called today an art than a manufacture, I feel, as I always have felt, to be immense: I can only wonder how you ventured to face them with your own difficult business to attend to, and I don't think you need take any shame to yourself if you conclude to give it up; neither do I think that the nature of the business will change, though time and use may wear it smoother in some places: I mean that I can never be contented with getting anything short of the best, and that I should always go on trying to improve our goods in all ways, and should consider anything that was only tolerable as a ladder to mount up to the next stage — that is, in fact, my life. To come to more detail — we have never expected in the printing to get a close match, but if the pieces are to be of any use to us they must differ from the pattern on the right side if at all: I must say also that I have always strained my artistic conscience to the utmost in dealing with doubtful cases ⟨to the very utmost⟩ and have kept many pieces ⟨with⟩ which, if I were dealing merely in a business way, I should have refused, and as a result we have a good deal of stock which is only half useful to us: You must allow that it [is] putting us in an awkward position if we have to be the only persons responsible for the pieces, when we have no control over the process of them: still I think we may venture so far as this: to accept the responsibility for all pieces, after having first seen and approved the fents printed from the stock of colour mixed ⟨from⟩ for the order: and it would help, I think, at any rate in difficult cases, if you would send us *all* the trial fents as you go on. I am aware that this would not save us from misfortunes, but I wish to meet you in the matter, as I can't help thinking you would not like to give up the affair: on the other hand, if you do wish to give it up, please understand I do not press you on the matter in the least: in that case I would take the whole business off your hands at such sum as you thought fair, only giving me some time to make payment (due interest paid meantime): also, I should ask you to keep the thing going at Leek for 3 or 6 months printing easy things, in order to get us a little stock, while we were looking about to start afresh during which time we would, if you pleased, pay all expenses: It is quite true that you are not likely to get your money back for some time for what you have spent on the dyeing operations, and what I have just said about the printing applies to this just as much or more: for me giving up the dyeing schemes means giving up my business altogether, and to give up the printing would be a serious blow to it, especially as last midsummer our balance showed a loss on that account of £1023.

To sum up the whole matter — the hitch over the printing seems to be the lack of constant artistic supervision on the spot; but since we can't have it, we must do the best we can by sending the fents about: as to the change in the business arrangement, ⟨I am⟩ (about taking the printed things) I am not much afraid of it for my part; for I have not sent much back, and I know you will do your best in the matter.

Yes, I do selfishly intend keeping the books, but the old fellow has promised to get more for me: Maquer may dissappoint you, it doesn't seem to me such an important book in its way as Hellot: I will send you ⟨round⟩ down the Volsunga Saga as soon as I get to my publishers. You will at any rate like the binding (Webb's design).[1]

Yrs very truly
William Morris

MS: Duke. Copy in V&A.

[1] Philip Webb had designed the cloth cover for the *Volsunga Saga* in 1870.

359 • To Francis Xaver Hueffer
26, Queen Square,
Bloomsbury, London
November 22, 1876

My dear Hueffer

Thanks for Your letter: I am more than very pleased that I am to fall into such good hands. I will tell them to send you a copy at once,[1] and also a copy of the Volsunga Saga, as I forget whether you have a copy. I shall be very happy to meet you again: if you are anywhere near Queen Sq pray come in: only at present I must ask you to take your chance of finding me in, as I have business on hand which makes my time not my own, and calls me away unexpectedly. On the other hand you will always for the present find me at home on Sunday afternoons & evenings, and we have a kind of a meal about 8 p.m. Or else (which I should like as well) will you come some evening to dinner: only in that case I am afraid I would only give you very short notice because of the above mentioned business: since Disraeli & the rest are as yet unhung. In any case I shall be delighted to see you again.

I am
Yours very truly
William Morris

P.S. I forgot: my address at home is Horrington House
Turnham Green
It is next door to the 'Roebuck' where the Hammersmith omnibusses stop, and within 5 minutes walk of the Turnham Green Station.

MS: NYPL.

[1] Hueffer wrote an article titled, "The Story of Sigurd and its Sources," which was published in the *Gentlemen's Magazine*, n.s. 19, pp. 46-56. In his review, Hueffer contrasted Morris's and Wagner's use of saga material.

360 • Recipient Unknown
26 Queen Sq:
Bloomsbury W.C.
November 24, 1876

Sir

I have the honour to inform you that I have been appointed Treasurer to the National Conference Committee[1] as its objects include, in addition to the holding of a Conference, the diffusing sound information on the Eastern Question throughout the Country, considerable expense will be necessarily incurred; I am instructed therefore to solicit your subscription

Cheques may be crossed 'Praeds & Co'
                                        I am
                                        Sir
                                        Your obedient Servant
                                        William Morris
                                        Treasurer

MS: Pennsylvania.

¹ See letter no. 356, notes 1 and 2.

361 • TO THOMAS WARDLE   26, Queen Square,
                                              Bloomsbury, London
                                              November 29, 1876

Dear Mr. Wardle

Thanks for letter: as to Nicholson, I dont see very well how we can mend it at present; please bear him as well as you can, as we all must bear disagreables: I wish I had my own looms, which would mend it all. — Red Cottons: may I ask was the mordaunt *thickened* at all? one book reccomends *half-thickening* for yarns: it can only be a matter of getting *enough* of the mordaunt on to the cotton.

Wool-dyeing &c: I must possess my soul in patience yet a while, which I will try to do.

Poplar-twigs: The pattern dyed among the perch showing no sign of yielding to 12 days window I tried the alum mordaunt, as you suggested and dyed about 3 lb of wool in 4 lbs of twigs: I enclose the darkest shade of the product, which I think very good: it took on the colour very quickly, say 10 minutes: soap made very little difference to it: as the colour is quite different to weld I think this would be a useful dye (if fast) for our wools: the lighter shades are more beautiful than this: I have only tried the cotton un-mordanted: it took nearly the same colour as the unmordanted wool, a bright buff I should call it: but I think the mordanted wools robbed the unmordanted.

Six pieces of indigo tulip are to hand: I am sorry to say I can't give a good account of them as blues they are *no* use to us, and they are so very uneven that I am afraid we shant make much use of them as greens: we must leave it a bit: only I must here make the remark that the unevenness is not by any means confined to the indigos: when I come down ⟨you⟩ we must talk about what is the best kind of *design* for these *printed* indigos: the fent of the overprinting of the spoilt honeysuckle is not right yet, but it is hopeful: wouldnt it be best to wait till I am down there before we do much more in printing yellow over indigo: when we once see the right kind of yellow, it will be much easier: the fent of ⟨blue⟩ indigo [the rest of this letter is missing].

MS: Duke.

362 • To Thomas Wardle   26, Queen Square,
                                          Bloomsbury, London
                                          December 11, 1876
My dear Wardle
   I am very sorry to be obliged to say, especially after your kind & friendly note, that I shall not be able to come down this side of Christmas: my political work, which I have taken up in such a way, that it is a matter of honour not to shirk it would prevent me getting away this week; and in addition I have picked up lumbago somewhere so that I can scarcely write, and so should be little use: as aforesaid I am very sorry for this: but perhaps as to the business it does not so much matter, as you have plenty of orders to go on with, & the fents can stand over: perhaps also the blue–dyeing will come on by then I can be housed with you; which I suppose will not be until the 'ruffians' (to whom I offer my congratulations on their youth, their holidays & their capacity for noise) have been swallowed by black Monday again.[1] I will make a point of coming then unless I am ill.
   You sent us a very fine clear pattern of Madder the other day: I hope the pieces will come as well: the indigo A[frican] M[arigold] was not up to the fine piece; I have put that latter out of stock for the present till we get more certain.
   Our meeting was a very great success, and to me a very solemn & impressive affair: I could not have imagined people would have been so enthusiastic[2]
   I will try what I can do about the photographs: they are rather hard to get at I fancy; but I think some may be had. Meantime I look forward very much to the pleasure of my visit when I do come, and am
                                          Yours very truly
                                          William Morris

MS: Duke.
   [1] Wardle had a large family.
   [2] On December 8 the National Conference on the Eastern Question was held at St. James's Hall. Among the conveners were Lord Acton, the Marquis of Bath, Robert Browning, Charles Darwin, J. A. Froude, William Lecky, C. E. Maurice, G. O. Trevelyan, Anthony Trollope, John Ruskin, W. T. Stead, Henry Broadhurst, and Auberon

Herbert (see the *Daily News*, December 5, 1876), and both sessions of the meeting were addressed by Gladstone. Admission was by ticket only: of the 89 M.P.'s who attended, 88 were Liberals; of the 23 peers only 3 were Conservatives. About 700 people came in all. At the end of the Conference the Eastern Question Association was formed to continue the work. Morris was elected Treasurer; the other officers were the Duke of Westminster, President; the Earl of Shaftesbury, Vice President; F. S. Pryce and George Howard, Secretaries; and F. W. Chesson and J. W. Probin, Honorary Secretaries. See also letter no. 351, n. 1.

363 • TO FREDERIC EVERY   Horrington House
                                              December 13 [1876]

Dear Mr. Every[1]

I am sorry that I shall not be able to come tonight, but my rheumatizm that was coming on last Sunday has fixed on me, and I cannot leave the house at present. After all except for my pleasure in the meeting it is of no great matter; as I feel that you will do better by yourselves.

The only thing I have to say about the whole matter now is that I think it important, that your meeting if you hold it should be *purely* of working-men; in which I don't doubt you will all agree with me.

                                              Yours truly
                                              William Morris

MS: Berger Coll.

[1] See previous letter to Every, no. 212.

364 • TO GEORGE JAMES HOWARD   26, Queen Square,
                                              Bloomsbury, London
                                              December 21, 1876

My dear Howard

Thanks, the cheque is to hand,[1] I am far from right again, but am going to act in all respects as if I were. Thanks for the 'Orient' card, though I am afraid I shan't be able to get round to him.

                                              Yrs affectionately
                                              William Morris

MS: Howard Papers.

[1] Apparently a contribution to the Eastern Question Association.

365 • To Emma Shelton Morris   Horrington House
                                                    December 26 [1876]

Dearest Mother

Thanks for your Christmas letter, and the best of good wishes to you. I suppose I shall be able to get away to you for a day about the beginning of next week: but Janey will write to you about it: our office is shut till Wednesday: so I have as it were four Sundays in a row: but I have abundance of work to do at home: We were all at the Grange on Christmas Eve & were very merry.

Give my love to all of them — & Believe me

                                                    Dearest Mother
                                                    Your most affectionate Son
                                                    William Morris

MS: Walthamstow.

366 • To Henry Holiday   26 Queen Sq.
                                                    Monday [1877?]

Dear Mr. Holiday[1]

You are welcome to the cartoons, though I don't think you will find any that will be of much use to you: I mean because they are not coloured, or got up to look like stained-glass at all: they are only drawings, and the men in the shop have to glassify them ⟨aft⟩ under my directions. This being the case I think the best way would be for you to come round here tomorrow & pick out what would suit you   I shall be in all day and would help you if it were only a matter of ½ an hour to do so.

                                                    I am
                                                    Yrs truly
                                                    W Morris

MS: UKansas.

[1] Henry George Alexander Holiday (1839-1927), painter and designer; husband of Catherine Holiday (see letter no. 385, n. 1). He joined Powell and Sons of Whitefriars, the glass manufacturers, as a stained glass cartoonist. In his *Reminiscences* he speaks (p. 94) of becoming associated with Morris and Burne-Jones in December 1862 when the foreman of Powell and Sons asked him to do cartoons for the firm. It is interesting that for several windows subsequently designed there is presently a question as to whether they are the work of Burne-Jones or Holiday (see Sewter, II, 105, 204). See also H. Holiday, *Reminiscences of My Life* (London: Heinemann, 1914).

367 • To Thomas Wardle
26, Queen Square,
Bloomsbury, London
January 4, 1877

My dear Wardle

Many thanks for your note, & kind wishes, which I return heartily.

I am still rheumatic, or whatever else the deuce is the matter with me; but I think a journey to Leek with all its pleasures would be likely to do me more good than harm: so I shall be happy to go down whenever you please after the beginning of next week.

I will send you a list of one or two fents that might be forwarded up to a certain point in readiness for finishing. I hope we shall be able to do something with the dyeing soon: we are waiting hard here for it. I thought by the way that you had been very lucky with the last snakehead print.

Yours very truly
William Morris

MS: Duke. Copy in V&A.

368 • To Aglaia Ionides Coronio
26, Queen Square,
Bloomsbury, London
Wednesday [1877]

My dear Aglaia

I was thinking of coming to see you tomorrow afternoon. I go to Kelmscott again on Friday, & don't quite know if I shall be back next week: will you write yes & no here.

Yours affect:
William Morris

MS: Berger Coll.

369 • To George Lillie Craik
26, Queen Square,
Bloomsbury, London
January 11, 1877

Dear Mr. Craik[1]

I have been out of town these 3 days past, or I would have answered you before: I am sorry I must say no to your kind invitation, I am not over well, & it takes me some trouble to keep on the safe side of gout and rheumatism, so that I really dare not go out.

                    I am
                    Yours very truly
                    William Morris

 MS: Yale B.

¹ George Lillie Craik (1837-1905), son of a Scottish minister, and an accountant by profession. In 1865 he married Dinah Maria Mulock (1826-1887), the author, and later became a junior partner in the publishing firm of Macmillan. The Craiks were acquainted with many members of the Pre-Raphaelite circle, and Mrs. Craik was godmother to Philip Bourke Marston.

---

370 • To Emma Shelton Morris   26, Queen Square,
                                                     Bloomsbury, London
                                                     January 13, 1877

Dearest Mother

Many thanks for your letter: I am sorry to hear you get well so slowly: also that Henrietta is so troubled: for myself, I have not quite lost my aches, but they are much better, & I feel quite myself otherwise.

I went down to Chester last ⟨Tuesda⟩ Monday to see the Duke of Westminster¹ on some business about the Chapel in his new house:² 'tis a huge place, but not at all a success I think: I was there on the Tuesday morning, and afterwards spent some 3 hours at Chester on a really beautiful day, which I enjoyed very much: the town is very little changed since I was there some 20 years ago: Yesterday I took the babes to the theatre (Macbeth) I think we all thought it ill done: they seem all well:

Today and yesterday are foggy in London, but not wet which is something.

Love to Isy³ & Henrietta, I am with much love

                    Your most affect: Son
                    William Morris

MS: Walthamstow.

¹ Hugh Lupus Grosvenor, first Duke of Westminster (1825-1890), who had been elected president of the E.Q.A. at the meeting of the national convention, December 8, 1876. See letter no. 362, n. 2.

² Eaton Hall, Cheshire. Alfred Waterhouse (1830-1905) had been commissioned to reconstruct the chapel and the library. The work took twelve years.

³ Morris's sister Isabella.

371 · To Philip Burne-Jones
26, Queen Square,
Bloomsbury, London
January 18, 1877

My dear Phil

I have found these two little blocks lying about: and so I send them at once, I will send a bigger one tomorrow: give my love to your Mother, and say I will write a line tomorrow or next day, but I don't quite know what day, next week I shall be going to Staffordshire.

I am
Yours affectionately
William Morris

MS: BL, Add. MSS. 52708 (typescript).

372 · Two Letters to Thomas Wardle

a.
26, Queen Square,
Bloomsbury, London
January 18, 1877

My dear Wardle

I have been expecting to hear from you or see you any day this week: I shall be ready to go down with you or to come to you if you are at Leek any day after next Monday: this week I have one or two designs to finish that keep me in town.

Yours very truly
William Morris

MSS: Duke. Copies in V&A.

b.
26, Queen Square,
Bloomsbury, London
January 20, 1877

My dear Wardle

Thanks for letter: Thursday will suit me very well: so I shall arrange for that day.

Yours very truly
William Morris

373 · FROM A LETTER TO GEORGIANA BURNE-JONES   Leek

January [27] 1877

My ill temper about the public was only a London mood and is quite passed now: and I think I have even forgotten what I myself have written about that most glorious of stories,[1] and think about it all (and very often) as I did before I began my poem.[2]

I had been reading the Njala in the original before I came here: it is better even than I remembered; the style most solemn (Dasent[3] now and then uses a word too homely I think, which brings it down a little): all men's children in it, as always in the best of the northern stories, so venerable to each other, and so venerated: and the exceeding good temper of Gunnar amidst his heroism, and the calm of Njal: and I don't know anything more consoling or grander in all literature (to use a beastly French word) than Gunnar's singing in his house under the moon and the drifting clouds: or do you remember the portents at Bergthorsknoll before the burning, and how Skarphedinn takes them? or Skarphedinn's death; or how Flosi pays the penalty for the Burning, never appealing against the due and equal justice, but defending himself and his folk stoutly against it at every step. What a glorious outcome of the worship of Courage these stories are.

TEXT: Mackail, I, 335. Published: Henderson, *Letters*, 84.

[1] *The Volsunga Saga.*
[2] *Sigurd the Volsung.*
[3] See letter no. 69, n. 2.

374 · TO AGLAIA IONIDES CORONIO   Litchfield

February 4 [1877]

My dear Aglaia

I have come over here with my dyeing friend to spend Sunday & am writing a letter or two while he is at church: I have been very busy last week & shall be busier still this, and shall not come back till the Saturday if even I can get away then.

This little town ought to have the prize for dullness over every other place in the world: but tomorrow will come, & I shall be back in the dye-house at Leek, to my great comfort. I shall be very glad to get back home again, I feel very much cut off from the trunk here, I mean away from London —

This is a short note, but I have nothing to tell you except about dyeing processes, so it must pass for the present.

I am

Yours affectionately

William Morris

MS: Yates Coll. Published: Henderson, *Letters*, 65.

375 • FROM A LETTER TO GEORGIANA BURNE-JONES   [Lichfield
February 4, 1877]

We have come over here to spend Sunday. Such a dull town is Lichfield, in a dull landscape: the church elaborate and complete, but so small as to be even petty: the old houses here seem to have been pulled down gradually by prosperous dulness, there are scarcely any much older than Johnson's time left; I daresay it was a sweet place enough while ago, when the old wood houses were standing. They have had some history even of late too; there is a stone in a house looking up into the Cathedral-close to mark where Lord Brooke[1] fell, shot through the head from the big tower of the church just as he was beginning the siege of it (he was a Parliamentarian) in 1642 — what a little time ago!

I shall be glad enough to get back to the dye-house at Leek tomorrow. I daresay you will notice how bad my writing is; my hand is so shaky with doing journeyman's work the last few days: delightful work, hard for the body and easy for the mind. For a great heap of skein-wool has come for me and more is coming: and yesterday evening we set our blue-vat the last thing before coming here. I should have liked you to see the charm work on it: we dyed a lock of wool bright blue in it, and left the liquor a clear primrose colour, so all will be ready for dyeing tomorrow in it: though, by the way, if you are a dyer, you must call it her.

Leek, Monday. I was interrupted there, and had no time for more at Lichfield: we drove from there this morning about eighteen miles to a station on the Dove, not a bad drive, through the last remains of Needwood Forest. I have been dyeing in her all the afternoon, and my hands are a woeful spectacle in consequence: she appears to be all that could be wished, but I must say I should like not to look such a beast, and not to feel as if I wanted pegs to keep my fingers one from the other. I lost my temper in the dyehouse for the first time this afternoon: they had been very trying: but I wish I hadn't been such a fool; perhaps they will turn me out tomorrow morning, or put me in the blue-vat.

TEXT: Mackail, I, 317-18. Published: Henderson, *Letters*, 65-66.

¹ Robert Greville, second Baron Brooke (1608-1643), parliamentarian general.

376 • To Jane Morris   Leek
                                                   Tuesday [February 7, 1877]
Dearest Janey

I have got your letter & the baccy-pouch   many thanks: the pouch is very pretty   I cannot get back till next Saturday, which will make 2 days more than the fortnight, but even then I shall have left a great deal unsettled: I shall leave Leek by the 4 p.m. train which will bring me back to you about ½ past 9. Please I shall want a bath when I come home: you may imagine that I shall not be very presentable   as to colour: I have been dyeing in the blue-vat today; we had to work it at 130° and a hot work it was, as you must keep the goods clean under the surface of the bath. It will be a difficult matter to arrange dyeing the shades: our vat is too strong at present for quite light shades: I have been red-dyeing also, but have not tackled the greens & yellows yet: I must try to do something in them before I go: I set myself too much work to do: that is a fact.

I am so sorry to hear you have been bad in the teeth: I hope May is better & that Jenny behaves well, dear child; give them both my best love.

I shall be heartily glad to come home again: I wish we were doing our own dyeing: these excursions are rather wearing.

We spent Sunday at Litchfield: a very dull town, with of course something to see it.

I am very tired this evening my dear so excuse longer writing.

                                                   I am
                                                   Your loving
                                                   W.M.

MS: BL, Add. MSS. 45338. Published: *CW*, 11, xx.

377 · JAMES RICHARD THURSFIELD
26, Queen Square,
Bloomsbury, London
February 16, 1877

Dear Mr. Thursfield[1]

I am afraid you must think I have been a long while answering your letter; I beg you to excuse my apparent neglect on the grounds that I found it hard to make up my mind what was right to do.[2] In the first place I thank you personally very much for moving in the matter, and I must say that nothing hardly would please me so much as such a recognition from my University, apart from considerations of fitness on my side: nor would laziness, or the various & heavy business on my hands ⟨have⟩ prevent⟨ed⟩ me from coming forward if I thought I could be of any real use: neither would a contested election frighten me, ⟨if⟩ though I don't like such things: It is therefore with the greatest regret that I find I must needs say 'no'; and this simply because I feel that I am not the man to fill the post: I suppose the lectures a Poetry Proffessor should give ought to be ⟨t⟩ either the result of deep & wide scholarship in the matter; or else pieces of beautiful & ingenious rhetoric, such, for example, as our Slade Professor could give;[3] and in both these things I should fail & do no credit either to the University or myself. It seems to me that the *practice* of any art rather narrows the artist in regard to the *theory* of it; and I think I come more than most men under this condemnation, so that though I have read a good deal & have a good memory my knowledge is so limited & so ill-arranged that I can scarce call myself a man of letters: and moreover I have a peculiar inaptitude for expressing myself except in the one way that my gift lies. Also may I say without offence that I have a lurking doubt as to whether the Chair of Poetry is more than an ornamental one, and whether the Professor of a wholly incommunicable art is not rather in a false position: nevertheless I would like to see a good man filling it, and, if the ⟨the⟩ critics will forgive me, somebody who is not only a critic.

I ask your pardon for writing so much about myself but your kindness has brought it on your head: with many thanks
I am
Yours very truly
William Morris

MS: Exeter College. Published: Mackail, I, 336-37; Henderson, *Letters*, 84-85.

[1] See letter no. 97, n. 1.

[2] Morris's friends had suggested that his name be put forward for the chair of poetry at Oxford, which had been vacated by F.H.C. Doyle (1810-1888) and not, as Mackail

thought, by Matthew Arnold. (See Mackail, I, 336.) In the event, the professorship went to John Campbell Shairp (1819-1885).

[3] John Ruskin.

378 • TO THOMAS WARDLE
26, Queen Square,
Bloomsbury, London
February [11-16] 1877

My dear Wardle

I have been expecting to hear some dyeing news from you this day or two past, and, not hearing, just write a line to make an extra note or two on our wants. 1st the trials for the Prussiate blues: has Nicholson sent you the silk? I assure you we are in sore disgrace about this matter at our end; and I am afraid our troubles over this matter will stand in the way of our market when we have got the dyeing into better order.

2nd Silk in the hot (hydrosulphate) vat: I got a goodish order for indigo curtains last week, which makes me more anxious still about this matter: will you do all you can in experiments as to the *evening* of the skeins: as regards *fastness* they cannot be very bad: excuse my pressing on you once more the wisdom of our forefathers in the de-greening & drying, Maquer & his 'banloire' to wit: by the way I think all silks and all *fine* wool goods & cottons should be soaped somewhat after the vat: or else there will be *some* loose indigo on them — and this would get us into trouble.

3rd all skein cotton goods should be dyed in the hot vat; and should be well bleached first: they will be dull else.

4th Piece dyeing: We shall be very glad as soon as you can do something in this, both in blue and other colours: I am sure we could have a trade in velvets & serges if we could get the colours good and fast: as it is whatever little beginnings we made two years ago have now come to nothing, because we durst not push them: it would be a pity to lose our chance now offered us by our new shop.[1]

5th The linings: I need only mention them: we need them sorely.

6th The skein wool-dyeing. How did Welsh get on with the 3 orders for red & pink I left behind? we shall be sending you lots of wool to dye as soon as I can get my patterns. I note about the blues that we have already dyed that, though they are average as to brightness, they are not as bright as some patterns we dyed here in our experimental hydrosulphate vat last summer: I send you samples to compare. However they are good enough to begin with.

7th. I want to be at my pattern making, and if I had my materials could go on at once on a very small scale.

8th Cotton prints. I think *all* pieces printed in Indigo or mostly in Indigo should be bleached.

9th Linen prints: I will give you orders for pieces as soon as you can get the goods to print on the right size & quality: as to the latter the ⟨piece⟩ pattern we had would do well enough.

10 the piece (blue) you greened is disappointingly uneven: there are obvious marks of the pressure of the rollers on it in stripes vertical or diagonal: I can't help thinking that this is not the right way to dye such *heavy* cotton goods: the colour otherwise was very good.

In a parcel just come Welsh sends a pattern of the scarlet warp: it is rather duller & flatter than my pattern: I still think he is wrong about the ageing; also that it would be better next time to enter the goods at 110° instead of 120°: the ageing I will try myself at once: when I say my pattern I don't mean the one I left behind which this matches exactly: but my old standard: as there are no more curtain blues sent up with this parcel I am afraid the vat has been empty; I shall be very glad to hear of her being full again.

Please give my kind regards to Mrs Wardle: I owe her many thanks (and you also) for making me so comfortable. I enjoyed myself hugely all the time.

I am
Yours very truly
William Morris

MS: Duke. Copy in V&A.

¹ In the summer of 1877 Morris and Company opened a showroom and shop at the corner of Oxford and North Audley Streets. The firm's letterhead gives the address as 264 Oxford Street.

---

379 • To ROSALIND FRANCIS HOWARD　　　　　26 Queen Sq:
February 28 [1877?]

Dear Mrs. Howard

I shall be very happy to come ⟨tomorrow⟩ Thursday; and the children shall come ⟨this day⟩ tomorrow week: many thanks for both invitations.

Yrs very truly
William Morris

MS: Howard Papers.

380 · To Chariclea Ionides Dannreuther   26, Queen Square,
                                                 Bloomsbury, London
                                                 Thursday. [March 1877?]¹

Dear Chariclea

I will come on Tuesday with pleasure: and am much obliged to you
for asking me — 'ok munda ek þegit hafa, þó at þú hefðir fyrr boðit.'²
I beg your pardon for that and am
                                        Yours very truly
                                        W Morris

MS: Berger Coll.

¹ The date of this letter is uncertain. Possibly it should be March 1871, around the time
the Dannreuthers were married. See letter no. 122, n. 1.

² "I would have accepted it, even if you had asked me earlier." Richard L. Harris has
called my attention to a passage in *The Laxdaela Saga*, XII, in which King Hákon
Aðalsteinfóstri gently chides Höskuldr Kollsson when greeting him: "Takit mundu vér
hafa kveðju þinni, Höskuldr, þóttú hefðir nökkuru fyrr oss fagnat, ok svá skal enn vera."
("We would have accepted your greetings Höskuldr, even if you had greeted us somewhat
earlier, but it shall be thus.") Morris may have adapted the line to his own purpose here.

381 · To Jane Morris   Horrington House
                                                   Friday [March 2, 1877]

Dearest Janey

I came back yesterday evening; I am to dine at Neds this evening &
shall send for Jenny tomorrow first thing.

Our Kelmscott journey would have been very successful in all points
except for a cold that I took down with me much as Ellis took baits: it
was a lovely night that brought us to Kelmscott, and we found the river
within its banks & in good condition next day: we fished all day, the
coldest & wildest in the year: fierce N. wind drifting snow. Showers &
frost, mixed with bright sun enough: I should have enjoyed it very
much indeed, but that my cold made me feel ill & cross now & then.
We got a few small perch & 3 pike, Ellis a big one 9½ lbs. at Goblin
Reach — he was so happy — Ellis, not the pike: we got back at 5 p.m.
I just about fit for bed; but I managed to stop up till 10. Wednesday it
froze very hard, but was sunny & beautiful so I wrapped up till I was a mere
bundle & went out: we fished all day & got no perch, but again 3 pike: I
the biggest, just as I was going to leave off: weight 6¼ lbs I was
much better on Wednesday evening: & we went home comfortably on
Thursday again bright & frosty: I gave my pikes to Wardle & Camp-
field.¹ I am still rather queer with the cold; but Monday or Tuesday
will break the neck of it. I saw Philip:² he looked dreadfully wasted I

am afraid the old idiot starves him: &, just fancy, they have chosen to bring him back to the cottage in the thick of this weather; I scolded them till they promised to bring him back till the warm weather set in.

I am glad you are going to stop a bit, as I don't suppose that 4 days could do anybody any good: I am afraid you have felt the cold badly. I shall stay at home all tomorrow with the babies.

Your loving
W.M.

 MS: BL, Add. MSS. 45338.

¹ See letter no. 28, n. 1.

² The Philip to whom Morris referred was probably Philip Comely, the cottager who looked after Kelmscott Manor (see letter no. 409). If so, the "old idiot" would presumably be Mrs. Comely.

382 • TO THE EDITOR OF *The Athenaeum*¹   26, Queen Square,
                                                  March 5, 1877

My eye just now caught the word "restoration" in the morning paper, and, on looking closer, I saw that this time it is nothing less than the Minster of Tewkesbury that is to be destroyed by Sir Gilbert Scott. Is it altogether too late to do something to save it — it and whatever else of beautiful or historical is still left us on the sites of the ancient buildings we were once so famous for? Would it not be of some use once for all, and with the least delay possible, to set on foot an association for the purpose of watching over and protecting these relics, which, scanty as they are now become, are still wonderful treasures, all the more priceless in this age of the world, when the newly-invented study of living history is the chief joy of so many of our lives?

Your paper has so steadily and courageously opposed itself to those acts of barbarism which the modern architect, parson, and squire call "restoration,"² that it would be waste of words to enlarge here on the ruin that has been wrought by their hands; but, for the saving of what is left, I think I may write a word of encouragement, and say that you by no means stand alone in the matter, and that there are many thoughtful people who would be glad to sacrifice time, money, and comfort in defence of those ancient monuments: besides, though I admit that the architects are, with very few exceptions, hopeless, because interest, habit, and ignorance bind them, and that the clergy are hopeless, because their order, habit, and an ignorance yet grosser, bind them; still there must be many people whose ignorance is accidental rather than inveterate, whose good sense could surely be touched if it were clearly put to them

[351]

that they were destroying what they, or, more surely still, their sons and sons' sons, would one day fervently long for, and which no wealth or energy could ever buy again for them.

What I wish for, therefore, is that an association should be set on foot to keep a watch on old monuments, to protest against all "restoration" that means more than keeping out wind and weather, and, by all means, literary and other, to awaken a feeling that our ancient buildings are not mere ecclesiastical toys, but sacred monuments of the nation's growth and hope.

William Morris

TEXT: *The Athenaeum*, March 10, 1877, 326. Published: Henderson, *Letters*, 85–86.

¹ This is the first surviving letter concerning the Society for the Protection of Ancient Buildings (S.P.A.B.), which Morris originated only months after he began his work for the E.Q.A. The decision to act seems to have been connected with two particular instances of restoration, Lichfield Cathedral and the parish church at Burford. After seeing the changes at Burford in September 1876, Morris "drafted a letter [which has not survived] urging the formation of a Society which might deal with such cases, and, if the destruction done by restorers could not be stopped, might at all events make it clear that it was destruction and not preservation." (See Mackail, I, 340ff.) Nothing came of this for several months. But at the beginning of March 1877, the proposed restoration of the Abbey Church at Tewkesbury apparently inspired him to take practical steps. The Society for the Protection of Ancient Buildings (familiarly known as "Anti-Scrape") was formally constituted at a meeting on March 22. Morris was appointed secretary. See also Henderson, *Life*, pp. 195ff.

² Faulkner notes that Morris chose *The Athenaeum* for his letter protesting Sir Gilbert Scott's plans for the restoration of Tewkesbury Cathedral "because in it, F. G. Stephens had been criticizing Scott's restorations for a number of years." Stephens was art critic for *The Athenaeum*. See Peter Faulkner, *Against the Age* (London: George Allen and Unwin, 1980), p. 91; see also letter no. 388.

383 • TO JANE MORRIS

26, Queen Square,
Bloomsbury, London
Tuesday [March 6, 1877]

Dearest Janey

I have come to the conclusion that it would be better not to come down with the babes: it would have to be an awful scurry: I should have to get back by the first train on Friday, & they will by no means hear of cutting into Monday: Georgie undertakes the entertainment of them on Friday which I know will please them very well: & they will be safe & comfortable there: so you need not be anxious. Don't come back in a hurry if it is doing you good: I will look after the babes on Saturday & Sunday. I am so driven today that I can't write more.

With love
Your W.M.

MS: BL, Add. MSS. 45338.

384 · TO THOMAS WARDLE

26, Queen Square,
Bloomsbury, London
March 7, 1877

My dear Wardle

The dip-blue patterns are some of them very good (in a way: but I think we had better stick to our own patterns for selling, and one of those at least on the roll is already in the market   the others soon would be if we began to take them up.

Wool-dyeing — I am sending today patterns for the warp & shoot[1] of a blue carpet and the wools are ordered for it (2 pieces, 200 yds i e) The thing to set you going fairly will be the greens; I am hard at work on the patterns for them, but have only got a big Bourges pot for my vat and find the wool-dyeing troublesome in it because the sediment kicks up so: in about a fortnight however I hope to be well through the green patterns, & will send them on as fast as I can: by the way a bit of yellow dyed with bark-liquor has already yielded to the light in our window; so we must stick to weld for the present, I think: we are sending you patterns for a *little* bit of indigo silk-dyeing, which I hope as well the green cotton skeins you will be able to do straight out: we musn't mind the stripiness of the blue too much just at first.

Item, I hope you will be able to get on with the red cotton skein dyeing, we want it much. Business is very flat with us, I am sorry to say, we ought to have begun the brisk time last week, and we have not this: but, to be thankful for small mercies, the chintz seems getting on steadily if slowly with the public.

Kelmscott: Well, we got but few perch certainly, & those small; the water was good though, but the weather awfully cold: with the pike we did better, and Ellis took one 9½ lb on a gut paternoster: my biggest was 6½ lb. I shall be very glad to get to the fly-fishing & shall thankfully take your guidance as to a rod when you are next in town.

I wrote to the Athenaeum yesterday: next week I shall have parson

& architect down on me, and may expect to finish in the work-house after all.

Yours very truly
William Morris

MS: Duke. Copy in V&A.

¹ In weaving, the shoot is the length of thread placed in one throw of the shuttle between the threads of the warp.

385 • To Catherine Holiday

Horrington House
Turnham Green
March 9 [1877?]

Dear Mrs. Holiday[1]

I have had all my time taken up for the past month with 'politics' so-called, till this week, when I found time for a little gout: if it had not been for these two pleasures I should have had some more to say to you about the embroidery before now.

I was quite delighted with the success of the door-hanging: I think it so good in colour and way of working that I am quite sure we can do nothing better: so as this first one is an order and is to be sent away I should be much obliged if you would put another *just like it* in hand: I know you dont like doing repetitions: but this is such a beautiful thing that I should think it a great pity if there were not more than one of it in the world.   as soon as I can I intend getting a small piece of work ready that might amuse you more. As to those beautifully coloured cushion-pieces you sent; I thought the sort of work rather too frail for the purpose, & proposed the quilting of the long stitches down with hair-lines of silk; even at the expense of losing some of the beauty. I think also I might find some better designs for cushions for you: in fact I have one, which I will send you if you please to do as you will with as to colour & style of work: with the caution however that durability is necessary for such things; especially when the work is as beautiful as you make it.[2]

I am
Yours very truly
William Morris[3]

MS: Berger Coll. Published: Henderson, *Letters*, 86-87.

¹ Catherine Holiday (1839-1924), married Henry Holiday (see letter no. 366, n. 1) in 1864. She was an invalid for many years and, doubting her strength, declined to take up tapestry designing and weaving, though Morris urged her to do so. Morris and Burne-

[354]

Jones were both enthusiastic about her embroidery, regarding it as skillful, bold, and original in color. Others who admired her work were G. F. Watts, William De Morgan, Cobden-Sanderson, and Holman Hunt. She was also a pianist and a strong advocate of Wagner's music. (See *The Times*, January 8, 1925, p. 14.) Paul Thompson writes (p. 111) that "by far the finest of Morris's embroideries are those which were specially designed for execution by Mrs. Catherine Holiday. . . . Morris left the colouring to her, dyeing silks himself to patterns which she sent him." A. B. Holiday, her great-nephew, corroborates this information in a letter to the present editor, saying that Morris would prepare designs for embroideries in pencil line, leaving Catherine Holiday to choose the colors and carry out the embroidery unaided.

² In *Reminiscences*, Henry Holiday wrote (p. 226): "My wife had for some time been practising embroidery, and had developed a technique of her own. William Morris, whom I had known for many years, saw some of this work, and admired it so much that he asked her to execute large designs of his, leaving the colour to her. One day he had been lunching with us, and, while walking up and down my studio, in the way he had of working off some of his superabundant energy, said to me in emphatic tones, 'You know, Holiday, I'd back your wife for heavy sums against all Europe in embroidery.' " Passage quoted by Henderson in *Letters*, p. 87.

³ Too late to make a change, I discovered that I was in error in dating this letter 1877 and that, moreover, it had been included in proper sequence among letters of 1878. See letter no. 502.

---

386 • TO EMMA SHELTON MORRIS
26, Queen Square,
Bloomsbury, London
March 9, 1877

Dearest Mother

Thanks for your letter; I shall be rejoiced to see you if you come up: please give me notice so that I may be sure to be in: we shall be partially flitting in about a fortnight I fancy: but there will be plenty of things here for you to see.

I knew more about that affair than you might fancy; for, first imagine, that outrageous blackguard had the coolness to write to me asking me to bail him: of course I did not answer his letter; and, as you say, I know nothing about him: I think myself 'tis the *madness* cropping up again; I don't think anything else can account for such monstrosities.

I have had a bad cold, which I have not quite got rid of: otherwise I am flourishing, and very hard at work, though we also share in the general depression of trade. I was down at Kelmscott for two days fishing with Ellis those cold days at the end of February.

With best love to Henrietta & yourself I am dearest Mother
Your most affectionate Son
William Morris

MS: Walthamstow.

387 · To Thomas Wardle   26, Queen Square,
Bloomsbury, London
March 13, 1877

My dear Wardle

The 'pattern-cards' of yellow over blue sent by Welch are not what I hoped as to colour; I mean to say for greening the blues: only those ⟨darkest⟩ on dark blue are of use for that end in a general way: I want quite a *bright clear* yellow like the enclosed water colour pattern for greening the lighter blues: how is it to be got fairly fast? are we to be driven to berries for it, or can't something nearer be got out of bark, especially if the blue is first washed off & finished?

I hope you read the Athenaeum of last week: I am going to keep the ball a-going now.[1]

Yours very truly
William Morris

MS: Duke. Copy in V&A.

[1] See letter no. 382.

388 · To Frederic George Stephens   26, Queen Square,
Bloomsbury, London
March 13, 1877

My dear Stephens[1]

Thanks in turn for your note; I knew of course that you were the author of the 'resistance' in the Athenaeum; I think hopelessness rather than anything else kept me from writing before, and I am ashamed of myself for it. But now what can be done?

The names I could be sure of for a society are but few: but I think we should begin as soon as may be, if the thing is in any way feasible: meantime I am unskilled in organizing this sort of thing; is it too much to ask you to do something to help; and when could I see you about it?

Thursday & Friday evening this week I shall be disengaged and at home at Horrington House: would you come over to dinner (7½) either of those days, and we might think of people to write to.[2]

Yrs truly
William Morris

MS: Bodleian.

[1] Frederic George Stephens (1828-1907), one of the original members of the Pre-Raphaelite Brotherhood. From 1861 to 1901, he was art critic of *The Athenaeum*. See letter no. 382.

[2] To enlist support for the establishment of the Society for the Protection of Ancient Buildings. Stephens was an original member of the S.P.A.B. and served on the committee that drew up a statement of views and aims for the new Society. See letter no. 391.

389 • TO JAMES BRYCE
26, Queen Square,
Bloomsbury, London
March 20, 1877

My dear Bryce[1]

Many thanks, but I am sorry to say that I cannot come on Friday as I have asked some men to dine with me; otherwise I should have liked very much to come.

It certainly does seem unbelievable that Russia really means to back out of everything now, but I must say it looks as if we shall be driven to believe it. I am disgusted with everybody's conduct in the affair.[2]

Yours truly
William Morris

MS: Bodleian.

[1] James Bryce, Viscount Bryce (1839-1922). Jurist, historian, statesman, Regius Professor of Civil Law at Oxford, 1870-1893; visited Russia in 1876 and published *Trans Caucasus and Ararat*, 1877; after visits to America in the 1880's, he wrote *The American Commonwealth* (1888). He was a member of Gladstone's last cabinet, and in 1877, was active in the Eastern Question Association. Bryce also became an early member of the S.P.A.B., and the exchange of letters between Morris and Bryce at this time may have been prompted by Morris's asking him to join.

[2] By this time it was apparent that efforts to promote peace, including the Conference of Constantinople, January 20, 1877, were failing, and that war between Russia and Turkey was imminent (Russia declared war on April 24). For a discussion of the events of February through April 1877, see Seton-Watson, *Disraeli*, pp. 168ff.

390 • TO THOMAS WARDLE
Horrington House
Turnham Green
March 25 [1877]

My dear Wardle

We held the first meeting of the Society for the Protection of Ancient Buildings at Queen Sq: on Thursday last, at which I was appointed Honorary Secretary; and I with Webb & George[1] are to draw up a program setting forth our views and aims, to submit to ⟨the⟩ a meeting on Thursday next; the said program having been agreed upon we shall ask the world in general to join: I think we shall make the program explicit enough to keep out pretenders; but it really is a difficult job, since everyone is ready to declare that he wants to protect ancient buildings, and even sometimes will take money for doing it. I really do hope we may do something, if only ⟨to⟩ we may make the architects a little more careful: my word, but they will be in a rage, if I have my way about the program!

I am much obliged to you about your determination to say no to Watts & Company; I think it would be awkward for their things to be dyed along with ours; besides those gentlemen are rather too ready to 'enter into our labours' without a word if they can get the chance.[2]

I have been thinking much since I saw you about beginning manufacturing in the small way as soon as I can: my trouble is that for the thing to be done satisfactorily it must be done in London (since I live there).[3]

I have asked my Kidderminster friend to see about a carpet weaver for me there; and besides I want very much to set up a loom for *brocade-weaving*: would it be possible to get a Frenchman over from Lyons under the present circumstances of the trade there? I would give a year's engagement certain to a real clever fellow who would do what I wanted him to do: I am dazzled at the prospect of the splendid work we might turn out in that time.[4]

The single piece of Snake-head that came up last week was very good: I don't know that I don't like it best of all that we have done.

I am studying birds now to see if I can't get some of them into my next design.[5]

We shall open our shop just after Easter I imagine, if that matters.[6]

> I am
> Yours very truly
> William Morris

MS: Duke. Copy in V&A.

[1] George Y. Wardle.

[2] A rival firm may have been copying Morris's designs. Watkinson discusses (p. 36) the jealousy and suspicion often found among decorating firms at this time.

[3] Morris was about to begin weaving in silk and wool in his own workshops.

[4] Morris eventually did hire such a person, Louis Bazin of Lyons (see *CW*, 12, xxii). According to the diary of F. G. Guy, son of Morris's old tutor, which Mackail quotes (I, 355-56), Bazin arrived on June 25, 1877, and by July 12 had set up his loom, a Jacquard, in Ormond Yard near Queen Square.

[5] The Bird pattern, in woven wool, was produced in 1878. See Clark, p. 58.

[6] The firm's new showrooms on Oxford Street. See letter no. 378, n. 1.

391 · To Dante Gabriel Rossetti   Horrington House
                                             April 3 [1877]

My dear Gabriel

Excuse my bothering you, but I want you to give us your name for the Committee of a Society that we are getting together now; don't be afraid, 'tis not political this time, but an attempt to put a spoke in the wheel of the 'restorers' of ancient buildings who have so grieved my soul: I think there is some chance of its being of use at last: Ned, Webb, Wallis, Boyce, Poynter, F. G. Stephens, Colvin are among the committee, & we expect to get many others big and little. I send with this a copy of the paper we intend putting forward to express our views & aims in the matter.[1] There are a few verbal alterations to be made in it, but it is substantially the ⟨one⟩ document agreed upon.

Please answer.[2]

Yours affectionately
William Morris

MS: UBC, Angeli-Dennis Papers.

[1] The Society's Manifesto. Written by Morris (and reprinted in every annual report without alteration ever since) it reads as follows:

A Society coming before the public with such a name as that above written must needs explain how, and why, it proposes to protect those ancient buildings which, to most people doubtless, seems to have so many and such excellent protectors. This, then, is the explanation we offer.

No doubt within the last fifty years a new interest, almost like another sense, has arisen in these ancient monuments of art; and they have become the subject of one of the most interesting of studies, and of an enthusiasm, religious, historical, artistic, which is one of the undoubted gains of our time; yet we think that if the present treatment of them be continued, our descendants will find them useless for study and chilling to enthusiasm. We think that those last fifty years of knowledge and attention have done more for their destruction than all the foregoing centuries of revolution, violence, and contempt.

For Architecture, long decaying, died out, as a popular art at least, just as the knowledge of mediaeval art was born. So that the civilized world of the nineteenth century has no style of its own amidst its wide knowledge of the styles of other centuries. From this lack and this gain arose in men's minds the strange idea of the Restoration of ancient buildings; and a strange and most fatal idea, which by its very name implies that it is possible to strip from a building this, that, and the other part of its history — of its life that is — and then to stay the hand at some arbitrary point, and leave it still historical, living, and even as it once was.

In early times this kind of forgery was impossible, because knowledge failed the builders, or perhaps because instinct held them back. If repairs were needed, if ambition or piety pricked on to change, that change was of necessity wrought in the unmistakable fashion of the time; a church of the eleventh century might be added to or altered in the twelfth, thirteenth, fourteenth, fifteenth, sixteenth, or even the seventeenth or eighteenth centuries; but every change, whatever history it destroyed, left history in the gap, and was alive with the spirit of the deeds done midst its fashioning. The result of all this was often a building in which the many changes, though harsh and visible enough, were, by their very contrast, interesting and instructive and could by no possibility mislead. But those who make the changes wrought in our day under the name of Restoration, while professing to bring back a building to the best time of its history, have no guide but each his own individual whim to point out to them what is admirable and what contemptible; while the very nature of their task compels them to destroy something and to supply the gap by imagining what the earlier builders should or might have done. Moreover, in the course of this double process of destruction and addition the whole surface of the building is necessarily tampered with; so that the appearance of antiquity is taken away from such old parts of the fabric as are left, and there is no laying to rest in the spectator the suspicion of what may have been lost; and in short, a feeble and lifeless forgery is the final result of all the wasted labour.

It is sad to say, that in this manner most of the bigger Minsters, and a vast number of more humble buildings, both in England and on the Continent, have been dealt with by men of talent often, and worthy of better employment, but deaf to the claims of poetry and history in the highest sense of the words.

For what is left we plead before our architects themselves, before the official guardians of buildings, and before the public generally, and we pray them to remember how much is gone of the religion, thought and manners of time past, never by almost universal consent, to be Restored; and to consider whether it be possible to Restore those buildings, the living spirit of which, it cannot be too often repeated, was an inseparable part of that religion and thought, and those past manners. For our part we assure them fearlessly, that of all the Restorations yet undertaken the worst have meant the reckless stripping a building of some of its most interesting material features; while the best have their exact analogy in the Restoration of an old picture, where the partly-perished work of the ancient craftsmaster has been made neat and smooth by the tricky hand of some unoriginal and thoughtless hack of today. If, for the rest, it be asked us to specify what kind of amount of art, style, or other interest in a building, makes it worth protecting, we answer, anything which can be looked on as artistic, picturesque, historical, antique, or substantial: any work in short, over which educated, artistic people would think it worthwhile to argue at all.

It is for all these buildings, therefore, of all times and styles, that we plead, and call upon those who have to deal with them to put Protection in the place of Restoration, to stave off decay by daily care, to prop a perilous wall or mend a leaky roof by such means as are obviously meant for support or covering, and show no pretence of other art, and otherwise to resist all tampering with either the fabric or ornament of the building as it stands; if it has become inconvenient for its present use, to raise another building rather than alter or enlarge the old one; in fine to treat our ancient buildings as monuments of a bygone art, created by bygone manners, that modern art cannot meddle with without destroying.

Thus, and thus only, shall we escape the reproach of our learning being turned into a snare to us; thus, and thus only can we protect our ancient buildings, and hand them down instructive and venerable to those that come after us.

² A note by William Michael Rossetti with this letter reads: "I am not now sure whether my Brother did or did not join The "Society for the Protection of Ancient Buildings" as a member: very likely he did, for he certainly sympathized in the object proposed. He did not however take any *active* part in the proceedings of the Society; & . . . he did not enter the Committee."

392 • To WILLIAM FREND DE MORGAN Horrington House
April 3, 1877

My dear De Morgan

I should be sorry indeed to force Mr. Carlyle's[1] inclinations on the matter in question, but if you are seeing him I think you might point out to him that it is not only artists or students of art that we are appealing to, but thoughtful people in general. For the rest it seems to me not so much a question whether we are to have old buildings or not, as whether they are to be old or sham old: at the lowest I want to make people see that it would surely be better to wait while architecture and the arts in general are in their present experimental condition before doing what can never be undone, and *may* at least be ruinous to what it intends to preserve.

Yours very truly
William Morris

TEXT: Mackail, I, 345-46. Published: Stirling, 112; Henderson, *Letters*, 87.

[1] Morris had asked De Morgan to persuade Thomas Carlyle to join the S.P.A.B. Carlyle wavered, and De Morgan, hearing that a letter from Morris might make a difference, asked for and received this one. Carlyle then wrote accepting membership, making a special allusion to the value of Wren's churches, buildings that Morris particularly disliked. See Mackail, I, 344-46, and Stirling, pp. 111-113.

393 • To the EDITOR OF *The Athenaeum* 26, Queen Square,
April 4, 1877

I am not quite sure that I should wish to see Tewkesbury minster "replaced in its former state," or one of its many "former states"; but, as it is clearly impossible, when one comes to think of it, for ourselves or our buildings to live again either in the 15th century or the 12th, it is hardly worth while to say much on this merely hypothetical matter of taste. On the other hand, I am sure that I do not wish the minster to look like a modern building, and I think Sir Edmund Lechmere also would disclaim any such wish,[1] though doubtless many others would not; and I assert that the more money is spent in altering its "present state" in the year 1877 and onwards, the more modern it will look. In truth, I am afraid that it will look much more modern than Sir Edmund Lechmere hopes; for I am older in restorations than he seems to be and pretty well know the value of assurances of strict care and such-like in restorations. They are always made even in the worst cases, and never kept even in the best: as, indeed, they cannot possibly be. Everybody who has had to do with old buildings knows what a perilous process is that business of stripping, so naively alluded to by Sir Edmund Lechmere, and how comprehensive a phrase "comparatively recent" can be made, nay, must be made very often when alterations once begin in an old building.

After all, the issue is narrow between Sir Edmund Lechmere and the restorers, and myself and the anti-restorers. Neither side wants a building to lose its ancient character; only the restorers think it will look even more ancient if it be worked all over under the "care" of Sir Gilbert Scott to-day,—which opinion we cannot admit. The issue being thus narrow, and the consequence of error so serious to lovers of art, I think it is but reasonable for the minority, to which I belong, to appeal to the public to wait. This is all the more reasonable, since if we are wrong no harm will be done. The unrestored ancient buildings are wronging no one in Church or State, as they are now; and it is but waiting a few years, and they can be restored then. Whereas if the restorers are wrong and have their way, they will hopelessly destroy all that is left us of our ancient buildings.

Prudence, we submit, should enlist the public on our side, for architecture is at present in a wholly experimental condition, as I suppose I need scarcely call on London streets to witness; and yet, such is the headlong rashness of our architects, that they have for the last thirty years made the priceless relics of mediaeval art and history mere blocks for their experiments: experiments which some of them must regret heartily, and sorely wish to "restore."

In my belief there is no remedy for the spreading of this disease, but for the public to make up its mind to put up with "comparatively recent" incongruities in old churches and other public buildings, and to be content with keeping them weather-tight; and if they have any doubts about the stability of the fabric, to call in an engineer to see to it, and let iron ties, and the like, do what they can. For my part, I cannot help thinking that they will soon find it easy to bear the absence of stained glass, and shiny tiles, and varnished deal roofs, and all the various upholsteries with the help of which our architects and clergy have striven so hard to "replace" our ancient buildings in their "former state," or, at any rate, in some "former state" imagined by themselves to be super-excellent.

William Morris

TEXT: *The Athenaeum*, April 7, 1877, 455. Published: MM, I, 107; Henderson, *Letters*, 87-89.

¹ Sir Edmund A. H. Lechmere, third baronet (1826-1894), Conservative M.P. for West

Worcestershire in 1877. In *The Athenaeum* for March 27, Lechmere had defended Scott against Morris's attack (see letter no. 382).

394 • To Thomas Wardle
26, Queen Square,
Bloomsbury, London
April 10, 1877

My dear Wardle

I was very sorry to hear that you ⟨wer⟩ are still laid up; it must be a confounded nuisance for you. We have already got some good names on the Committee of our Protection Society, and I think we shall get many more: Huggins[1] the writer of the letter you enclosed is to be asked by the way. I shall be glad of any suggestions of names from you, & will propose them as soon as possible.

We have a meeting here tomorrow night, but I dont suppose it will be a very important one; but in the next fortnight or so we shall be getting organized I fancy.

I am really rather sanguine as to doing some good, where ever any is left for us to do.

A word or two on business: the little lot of spun silk sent you by Nicholson must positively be dyed in indigo, as it is for a washing stuff and the prussiate would be of no use to us: I thought the dyeing of this small parcel would be of use in getting us into the indigo silk-dyeing, the want of which is now pressing us very sorely: we have more orders coming in for silk, and have a chance of setting that business on its legs if we can only get the indigo dyeing done: I really must implore you to do something to get us started in this line: I have given orders for 2 carpets (2 pieces each) to the Heckmondwyke people,[2] & I believe you have the wool by this time: I have sent wools to them of my dyeing for yard long samples of 3 or 4 things which I shall order as soon as possible: my blue dyeing is stuck here, as I havn't got my big pot fixed, & have broken my little one: will you send me 2 heads each of all the blue wools of ours you have that I may green them; and also a couple of heads of the enclosed darker colour.

The Heck-people have sent a pattern of the carpet done with the red wools dyed when I was at Leek: nothing could be better both as to tone and relief of colour — so that is settled.

The yellow over blue patterns are not the thing yet: unless the yellow is quite faint it seems to swallow up the blue altogether, and when it (the yellow) is light, it is also un-yellow.

Thanks for writing about the brocader[3] for me: I am sanguine as to doing something good if I could get a clever man. Thanks also for good wishes about the shop: I think it will answer though I can't say I am much excited about it, as I should be if it were a shed with a half dozen looms in it.

Hoping to hear a better account of you soon

I rest
Yours very truly
William Morris

MS: Duke. Copy in V&A.

¹ Samuel Huggins (1811-1885) wrote about architecture. His articles opposing restorations of cathedrals expressed views that the S.P.A.B. made its own.

² See letter no. 321, n. 2.

³ See letter no. 390, n. 4.

395 · TO THOMAS WARDLE
26, Queen Square,
Bloomsbury, London
April 13, 1877

My dear Wardle

I have both your notes, and have to thank you first, for getting me news of the brocader: I will clear off what I have to say about that first: We are willing to agree to his terms of 3000 fr: for the year, and think it would be prudent not to guarantee for longer, but if he suits us, no doubt the situation will be a permanent one for him: we agree to the travelling expenses of course: but I think before we strike a bargain we should see his specimens of work: meantime we send a parcel of examples of cloth such as we are likely to want as far as the weaving is concerned: they are all valuable, and some are not our own; so they must be taken care of & returned whole & in good condition: as a fixed wage is stipulated, we suppose he will work by the day, about how much per diem can he turn out: will he give us any idea of this? We suppose we shall have to find him standing-room for the loom: what space & height is wanted for this? As to the loom we should *by all means* want it big enough to weave the widest cloth that can be done *well* without steam-power: and it ought to be such as could weave a design 27 inches wide (Nicholson can only do us a 9 inch design) this width is what we have hithertoo had from Lyons. We should certainly want to weave damask. Your correspondent shall be welcome to the douceur,¹ which we shall be willing to add to if the matter turns out well: I hope he understands that we want a really intelligent man: if he turns out such, his position with us will be good; as we should surely be wanting more looms, and he would be foreman over the others.

As soon as we are agreed he must let us know when he can come, & send us some proper paper for pointing, in order that we may get a design ready for him without delay — Which latter word makes me express a hope that you will be able to dye us some silk against his coming: do you know for certain where we can best get our cards cut by the way.

So much for the brocader, when I have thanked you again very much for getting me on so far, and confessed that I am prodigiously excited about him. Thanks about the swivel silk indigo: I really don't think the unevenness will matter much unless it is beyond measure: I have seen old silks, blue & green, which were evidently stripy from the vat, & they didn't look the worse for it.

The tapestry is a bright dream indeed; but it must wait till I get my carpets going: though I have had it my head lately, because there is a great sale now on in Paris of some of the finest ever turned out: much too splendid for anybody save the biggest pots to buy: I will send you the illustrated catalogue to look at in a day or two. Meantime much may be done in carpets: I saw yesterday a piece of *ancient* Persian time of Shah Abbas (our Elizabeth's time) that fairly threw me on my back: I had no idea that such wonders could be done in carpets.[2]

We met again last night and are getting on I think: are going to ex-postulate with Ormskirk, Halifax and Cherry Hinton.[3] (*young* Scott's this last)[4] at once. As for the old bird, all I can say is that he is convicted out of his own mouth of having made an enormous fortune by doing what he well knows to be wrong.[5] — he is a damned old thief in short. I send some more circulars by all means distribute them.

By the way by a mistake (of ours) the floss & sewings I left behind at Leek has come back undyed; I send it back, & should be glad to have it dyed, as I am rather torn in pieces by my embroideresses.

Yours very truly
William Morris

MS: Duke. Copy in V&A. Published: Mackail, I, 351-52; Henderson, *Letters*, 89-90.

[1] A bonus or inducement.

[2] Shah Abbas I, The Great, of Persia (1557-1628 or 1629), the first royal patron of the art of carpet manufacture. He built the Royal Mosque at Isfahan and had carpet factories near the royal palace. This passage in Morris's letter is quoted at the head of a chapter in Sidney Humphries's *Oriental Carpets, Runners, and Rugs and Some Jacquard Reproductions* (London: Adam and Charles Black, 1910).

[3] According to the S.P.A.B. minutes for April 12, 1877, George Wardle (seconded by William De Morgan) proposed a resolution that the Secretary write to the authorities

about the churches of Cherry Hinton, Ormskirk, and Halifax, all threatened with restoration.

4 Probably George Gilbert Scott, Jr., one of the two sons of Sir Gilbert Scott who became architects and carried out some of the works left unfinished at their father's death.

5 In his *Recollections*, published in 1877, Sir Gilbert Scott acknowledged that he had redrawn the plans for the new Foreign Office, originally Gothic in style, because Palmerston insisted that the building had to be classical in style. He justified the compromise with his principle by saying his family needed the money: "I had no right to deprive [them] of what had become their property as much as my own, for a mere individual preference on a question of taste."

---

396 • TO GEORGE JAMES HOWARD
26, Queen Square,
Bloomsbury, London
April 18, 1877

My dear Howard

I am getting them printed and will send you them today. I hope. Meantime I *am* an inefficient Secretary: I am looking about for a new one, & am thinking of proposing *you*[1] — so you had better come to the next meeting   I wont fail to come tomorrow   I think things look very ugly indeed.[2]

> Yours ever
> William Morris

MS: Howard Papers.

1 Since Morris was secretary of the S.P.A.B., it would seem that the first part of this letter concerns the S.P.A.B. and that what Morris is getting printed is its manifesto. Howard was also a member.

2 The concluding part of this letter, from "I wont fail to come tomorrow . . . ," is apparently an abrupt shift in subject and refers to E.Q.A. business.

---

397 • TO THOMAS WARDLE
26, Queen Square,
Bloomsbury, London
April 18, 1877

My dear Wardle

Thanks for note & address; I should think they would do very well. I am sorry for Welch: it is a great curse both for him & for us. As to the silk dyeing, I am afraid we shall go but a very little way without facing the indigo-dyeing   we *must* try it, coute qui coute: I have done some skeins of floss for my wife's embroidery[1] down here, both green & blue, and they were fairly even; & I believe if I had had the due skill of a dyer to *handle* them properly they would have been all right: in

Morris in the late 1870's.

short, I think if they can be de-greened & dried evenly they will come even: at any rate when we have our own loom we can minimize the inconvenience of stripiness: &, to come back, we can't do without the indigo, stripy or not: by the way how about madder on silk; it gives the only thoroughly good orangy fleshy colours.

I am sending you orders for dyeing wools for two pieces of a new carpet; a *very* pretty one, though I say it as shouldn't: also for two pieces of curtain stuff; we should glad of them as soon as may be.

I remember the passage you quote from Ruskin[2] & it is most true.

Wishing you well out of your troubles of Welsh & beer and Morris & indigo

> I am
> Yours very truly
> William Morris

MS: Duke. Copy in V&A.

[1] Jane Morris executed embroideries on cloth and silk for Morris and Co., having early been instructed in the craft by Morris himself. She also worked a series of wall hangings for the bedroom in Red House. See Callen, pp. 104, 106.

[2] A member of the S.P.A.B., Wardle may have quoted, as did the Society, from Ruskin's *Seven Lamps of Architecture*: "Take care of your monuments, and you will not need to restore them; watch an old building with anxious care; count its stones as you would the jewels of a crown; bind it together with iron where it loosens, stay it with timber where it declines. Do not care about the unsightliness of the aid; better a crutch than a lost limb; and do this tenderly, reverently, continually, and many a generation will still be born to pass away beneath its shadow."

---

398 • TO MAY MORRIS
26, Queen Square,
Bloomsbury, London
April 24, 1877

Dearest May

Thank you for your letter: I am afraid Mama was not much *less* tired than she expected to be. I shall come on Saturday; & will write & let you all know by what train. If you or Mama write to me again you had better write to me at Queen Sq:

The Lyons brocader I find is named Bazin: I hope he won't be such a humbug as Aramis' Bazin:[1] we shall have him over soon.

I am very busy, but I enclose a line to Mama. Love to all dear daughter.

> Your affectionate Father
> William Morris

MS: BL, Add. MSS. 45341.

[1] See letter no. 390, n. 4. Bazin was the servant of Aramis in *The Three Musketeers*. Along with Scott and Dickens, Dumas was one of the few nineteenth-century novelists for whom Morris had any real enthusiasm. See letter no. 214.

399 • To Thomas Wardle
26, Queen Square,
London, W.C.[1]
April 25, 1877

My dear Wardle

Patterns of blue silk for swivels to hand: the colour seems satisfactory, though as you say a little duller than some: only if the lot is not dyed I should like the lightest a little lighter; if it is dyed, all right send it off: I don't think for this job it matters about the loose dye: in some cases however it would matter, & then I suppose you would have to soap the goods.

Green cotton shoot: we shall tell N[icholson] to try a bit; I don't think the stripiness will matter in that cloth; but the colour is a little poorer than pattern: at the worst you can put it into dark blue for us: but I think it will do.

I am very glad to hear that the Prussian silk is turning out better than we expected, but my moral for the whole affair is *vat blue for silk*: I have an idea or two about the printing which I must put off for want of time today.

Yours very truly
William Morris

MS: Duke. Copy in V&A.

[1] This is the first surviving letter written on letterhead paper showing the address of Morris's new showrooms. At the top is printed "Replies and parcels to be sent to Morris & Company, 26, Queen Square, Bloomsbury," above a double line. Under this, in a small box at top left, are the words "Show-room, 264, Oxford Street, corner of North Audley Street," and at top right is the address as shown here with a dotted line underneath for the date.

400 • To Jane Morris
26, Queen Square,
Bloomsbury, London
May 2, 1877

Dearest Janey

I have got a lot of work to do just now of the Boots and Brewer kind; for we are going to have a great anti-Turk meeting next Monday at St. James' Hall:[1] would you very much mind if I were to come down on Friday morning instead of Thursday night: there is a committee meeting tomorrow at ½ past 3, and I might be able to be there and catch the 4.45 train, and would do so if I could: otherwise I would be with you on Friday to dinner 1 o clock: you had better telegraph if you particularly want me on Thursday evening, and I will come at any rate.

There is a great stew in political matters, and our side will be done for and war certain if we don't raise the very devil over it. Picture to yourself a 3 years war, and the shop in Oxford Street, and poor Smith[2] standing at the door with his hands in his pockets!

There is a small meeting tonight at the Cannon St Hotel: I am going there to swell the crowd.[3]

Dear love to the babies:

Your loving
W.M.

MS: BL, Add. MSS. 45338. Published: *CW*, 12, xxi; Henderson, *Letters*, 90. Extract published: Mackail, I, 353.

[1] Russia had declared war on Turkey on April 24. *The Times*, May 8, 1877, reported (p. 12) that a meeting held in St. James's Hall on May 7 had been called to protest against any action being taken by the Government that might involve England in the conflict.

[2] Robert or Frank Smith. One was employed as sub-manager at the Oxford Street showroom and one at Queen Square. See letter no. 421.

[3] E. P. Thompson writes (2nd ed., p. 213) that "Russia's declaration of war threw the E.Q.A. and the L.R.L. into joint action. Henry Broadhurst called a meeting of 'Workmen's Political Associations and Trade Societies of the Metropolis' to meet at the Cannon Street Hotel on May 2nd, 1877, to support five anti-Turkish resolutions which Gladstone had tabled in the house." See also letter no. 402, n. 3.

---

401 • FROM A LETTER TO GEORGIANA BURNE-JONES May 4, 1877

I was at the working-men's meeting at the Cannon Street Hotel on Wednesday,[1] it was quite a success; they seem to have advanced since last autumn. Some of them spoke very well, nor would the meeting so much as listen to George Potter on the other side.[2] Burt (M.P. for Morpeth and who is, or was, a working man)[3] was chairman, and spoke excellently though shortly, with a strong Northumbrian tongue; he seemed a capital fellow. Meantime the Liberal party is blown to pieces, and everything is in confusion.[4]

TEXT: Mackail, I, 350.

[1] See letter no. 400, n. 3.

[2] George Potter (1832-1899), a trade unionist. He was a member of the London School Board at this time.

[3] Thomas Burt (1837-1922), a trade unionist and Liberal politician, M.P. for Morpeth from 1874 to 1918.

[4] E. P. Thompson writes (2nd ed., p. 214) that "incessant manoeuvres were going on among the [Liberal] parliamentarians to tone down Gladstone's five anti-Turkish resolutions."

402 · TO GEORGE JAMES HOWARD
Horrington House
Saturday Morning
[May 15, 1877]

My dear Howard

Your note didn't say on what day the christening was, so I suppose it was yesterday; but, as I slept in town on Thursday night, I didn't get it till the evening. I am sorry I have missed the affair.[1]

I duly went to Beaumont hall on Thursday night, and thought the meeting a success: it was all but unanimous on the Eastern Question, but a little fraternal dispute did somewhat confuse it at one time; I do not understand what it was all about, but believe that the claimant and De Morgan were at the bottom of it:[2]

I have settled with Broadhurst[3] for the two meetings to the tune of £49 about, which is within the estimate. By the way how is the £25 for the services of Messrs. Howell[4] & Broadhurst to be divided? I hope our committee won't go to sleep after this; *and* I hope our supporters will support us — with money — What news in that direction? When are you off? I hope I shall see you before you go. With wishes of good luck to my Godson

I am
Yrs affectionately
William Morris

MS: Howard Papers.

[1] Geoffrey Howard was born February 12, 1877.

[2] Probably a reference to the Tichbourne Case (1871-1873) in which Arthur Orton was imprisoned for perjury after he lost a trial in which he claimed he was Sir Roger Tichbourne (presumably lost at sea in 1854), heir to the Tichbourne estates. In 1877, a John De Morgan revived the case, called for the release of "Sir Roger," and tried to organize a demonstration in Hyde Park and march on the House of Commons in support of the right to be heard at the bar of the House. The demonstration, held April 17, was small and ineffectual, but was reported with disproportionate alarm, with the result that other would-be demonstrators were intimidated. *The Times*, May 24, 1877, reported that De Morgan had started a new political movement, "The People's Political Union," to demand parliamentary and social reforms.

[3] Henry Broadhurst (1840-1911), labor leader, previously a stonemason (see his autobiography, *Henry Broadhurst, M.P., The Story of His Life*). In December 1875, as a leader of the Labour Representation League, which actively opposed Disraeli's pro-Turkish policy, he attended the national conference on the Eastern Question. On April 24, 1877, Russia declared war against Turkey, and just after this, when the chance of Britain's entering the conflict was greatest, the E.Q.A. and the L.R.L. engaged in vigorous joint action to oppose such a move. See E. P. Thompson, 2nd ed., pp. 213-14.

[4] George Howell (1833-1910), who was secretary to the parliamentary committee of the Trades Union Congress from 1871 to 1875, was another leader of the L.R.L. who had attended the national conference on December 8, 1875.

403 · RECIPIENT UNKNOWN

26, Queen Square,
Bloomsbury, London
May 17, 1877

Dear Sir[1]

We have been very busy here the past week as you know, and intend to do our best to keep the thing going:[2] but at present, and in view of the great dangers that threaten us we cannot do any more publishing:[3] we have never had much money and the last fortnight of *dietetics* has shown us how necessary it will be for us to have some balance in hand against the next shocks — and the next — and the next, of the war party; this is our drawback against publishing *anything* (Gladstone's speech excepted).[4]

As to the peace at any price party, we should not put our principles in our pockets for them: For we think their objections wire drawn: at the same time, I do hope they will see the necessity of cordially supporting the only party that can save the country from war at present.

I must add in conclusion that our need of money is urgent, if we are to do anything serious, and that for our side to suppose itself safe now would be a most fatal mistake; so if you know any rich men who are of good will towards the Cause, you would be helping that Cause by putting our necessities before them: and I must say again that I think we have done good service, and I know we shall do more.

I am, Dear Sir,
Yours faithfully William Morris

MS: Inst. Rus. Lit. Published: *Notes and Queries*, June 1969.

[1] Leonid M. Arinshtein conjectures that the person to whom Morris wrote was a Russian woman, Olga Alexeevna Novikova (1840-1925), a journalist living in London who publicized the Russian cause at this time. See *Notes and Queries*, 214 (June 1969), 219-20. It should be pointed out that Arinshtein bases his conclusion on the fact that her articles were signed with her initials only and that Morris may not have known that she was a woman. However, the present letter was presumably written in reply to one he had received, and unless that were also signed only with initials, it is difficult to reconcile Morris's addressing the recipient as "Dear Sir" with Arinshtein's theory.

[2] On May 7, the E.Q.A. had held a large conference in St. James's Hall to force parliamentary action on Gladstone's anti-Turkish resolutions. On May 11, Morris had issued a manifesto "To the Working-men of England," signing it "A Lover of Justice." E. P. Thompson characterizes it (2nd ed., p. 214) as revealing the enormous effect upon Morris of his recent participation in the agitation, "the great stride forward in understanding the class issues which he had taken since his original letter [October 24, 1876, no. 351]." For the text of the manifesto, see Henderson, *Letters*, pp. 388-89.

[3] The person to whom Morris was writing may have written asking if the E.Q.A. would act as a publisher. It is true that just before Christmas 1877 Novikova published a book, composed of articles in the form of letters, titled *Is Russia Wrong? By a Russian Lady*. J. A. Froude wrote a preface. See Arinshtein, *Notes and Queries*, pp. 219, 220. See also Seton-Watson, *Disraeli*, p. 116.

[4] Gladstone's speech of Five Resolutions, May 7, 1877. See letters no. 400, n. 3 and no. 401, n. 4.

404 • TO JOSEPH JOHN JENKINS

The Society for
the Protection
of Ancient Buildings.[2]
26 Queen Sq. W.C.
May 22, 1877

My dear Sir[1]

I receive your name with much pleasure: as to the questions you ask, I think our statement which I forward to you herewith answers them generally; but I may say ⟨in⟩ furthermore, that we are by no means losing sight of the 'Caroline' buildings your letter alludes to, and that there is no one of our society that I know anything of who would not resist heartily the ridiculous transmogrifations that have been proposed for St Pauls, & carried out in many of the Wrenian Churches.[3]

As to Canterbury we are preparing a letter of remonstrance to be sent to the Dean[4] & Chapter, it is in good hands, and I suppose will get into print.

I am Dear Sir
Yours Faithfully
William Morris

MS: ULondon.

[1] Joseph John Jenkins (1811-1885), engraver and water-color painter.

[2] Morris wrote on paper with this letterhead printed in black letter.

[3] This may refer to a plan to obliterate Thornhill's paintings in the dome of St. Paul's and substitute mosaics.

[4] Robert Payne Smith (1819-1895), Dean of Canterbury from 1870 to 1895.

405 • TO THOMAS WARDLE

26, Queen Square,
Bloomsbury, London
June 4, 1877

My dear Wardle

I am very vexed to be obliged to put off the Kelmscott expedition; but I think you will excuse me when I tell you that I think I *must* be at our meeting on Thursday:[1] you see the beast of a Times Editor never put in my letter, and we must do something at once in the matter:[2] I shall go down next week for two days: and then if you would tell me afterwards any time you can come, almost any two days afterwards at a week's notice: you could get there pretty easy by way of Bletchley & Oxford if you were in Staffordshire There is nothing keeps me from going next week but Thursday's meeting.

Yours very truly
William Morris

MS: Duke. Copy in V&A.

[1] The diary of F. Guy, quoted by Mackail (I, 355), indicates that there was a meeting of the S.P.A.B. at the Oxford Street showrooms of Morris and Company on the evening of June 7.

[2] See letter no. 406. It was, in fact, published on June 4. Since he wrote in reply to letters of May 22 and 24, Morris had probably expected publication sooner and had not yet seen *The Times* for June 4. Editorial duties at this time were being handled by William Stebbing, acting for J. T. Delane who was ill.

406 • To the Editor of *The Times*   26 Queen Square. W.C.
[June 4, 1877][1]

Sir

As Mr. Loftie's[2] letter, quoted in your columns, calls on our Society by name, and as the letters of the Dean of Canterbury[3] and Mr. Beresford Hope[4] touch our principles closely, I venture to hope that you will give me space for a word or two on the subject of the restoration of the choir of Canterbury Cathedral. As to the present woodwork at the west end, it seems superfluous to praise it, as it is agreed on all hands that it is good, though in some people's minds I suppose it would be condemned as inherently unholy, because it is a post-Reformation work. But, good as it is, I cannot conceive what purpose it can serve when it is taken away from the place it was made for, and in which it looks both dignified and serious, as well as elegant; furthermore, what is to be the fate of the present stone screen when Sir Gilbert Scott's conjectural restoration of Prior Eastry's work is carried out? It is true that its surface has been destroyed by restoration, but it has been at least a true work of a good date.

It may seem a little matter to make a stir about a piece of clever joinery and carving of Charles II's time, when the great work of the 12th century Frenchman[5] is about it and above it, but I must confess to sharing that fear which Mr. Beresford Hope thinks has made reason unhelpful to Mr. Loftie; for I suppose that the proposed imitation, restoration, or forgery of Prior Eastry's[6] rather commonplace tracery is only the beginning of the evil day at Canterbury, and that before long we shall see the noble building of the two Williams confused and falsified by the usual mass of ecclesiastical trumpery and coarse daubing that all true lovers of art and history dread so sorely; that, in short, the choir of Canterbury will go the way of Ely, St. Cross, and Salisbury.

Sir, I think that our ancient historical monuments are national property and ought no longer to be left to the mercy of the many and variable ideas of ecclesiastical propriety that may at any time be prevalent among us.

> I am, Sir, yours obediently,
> William Morris, Hon. Sec. of
> the Society for the Protection
> of Ancient Buildings.

TEXT: *The Times*, June 4, 1877. Published: Henderson, *Letters*, 90-91.

¹ The letter, as printed in *The Times*, does not indicate the date on which Morris wrote it. June 4 is the date of publication. In this and all letters to newspapers and periodicals, brackets signify that the date given is the one of publication, not composition. When both dates are known, the one given in the upper right is the date of composition and the other is provided in the textual note as part of the information concerning publication.

² William John Loftie (1839-1911). He had attacked plans for restoring Canterbury Cathedral and had cited the S.P.A.B. with approval.

³ For the letter of the Dean of Canterbury, in which he explained his stand in the controversy and gave reasons for supporting the proposed restorations, see *The Times*, May 24, 1877, p. 14.

⁴ Alexander James Beresford-Hope (1820-1887), an architect who had been a Conservative M.P. (1841-1852 and 1857-1859). In his letter printed in *The Times*, May 24, he rejected Loftie's contention that "there is very little left of the old structure of Canterbury Cathedral older than the present reign" and defended the Dean of Canterbury's proposal to remove the stalls in order to reinstate the stone screen.

⁵ William of Sens, who rebuilt the choir after a fire in the Cathedral.

⁶ Henry Eastry was prior of Canterbury Cathedral from 1285 to 1331.

407 • To the Editor of *The Times*   [June 7, 1877]

The Society for the Protection of Ancient Buildings.

Sir

I am sorry to trouble you again in the matter of the proposed restoration⟨s⟩ of Canterbury Cathedral, but the Dean's letter shows that he has misunderstood both Mr. Loftie and myself ⟨in⟩ somewhat seriously, I think. He is mistaken in reading my letter as an approval of the schemes of restoration now afoot: on the contrary, I implied that the removal of the stalls now proposed would practically destroy a worthy work of art, which I ⟨estimate at much the⟩ value pretty much as Mr. Loftie does, and I expressed a dread, which I still feel, that changes would not stop there, but would spread to the ancient fabric of the choir: I believe myself to be justified in that fear by the well-known fact that assurances of the kind the Dean is now giving are ⟨difficult⟩ impossible to be kept to when restoration once begins.

I am glad to hear from the Dean that he dreads paint in restorations, though it is by no means the only thing to fear; but I protest strongly against the charge that I consider the ancient painted work of our churches ⟨(little enough is left unluckily) as coarse daubing.⟩ coarse daubing. I look on it rather with the greatest interest, and know that the art in it is often great, however rude it may be: it is the unfeeling and dead imitation of it so ⟨fatally &⟩ rashly ⟨used⟩ practised in restorations that I condemn.

But the Dean's most serious misunderstanding both of ⟨my lett⟩ Mr. Loftie's letter, & mine and of the general aim of our Society is in supposing that we wish our ancient buildings reduced to the state of ruins, whereas we earnestly press on their guardians the duty of keeping them in sound and orderly repair, so that they may never want 'restoration': Where Canterbury Cathedral has been unrestored it is in as good a state as in the 13th century, and, man's work as it is, has hardly begun to perish yet, nor will it for many a hundred years, if only the roofs be well kept: where it is restored — well, let the ghost of the Norman tower tell that tale.

The Dean's argument about divine worship I do not understand, coming from him;[1] in the mouth of an ultramontane priest I should take it to mean, 'Yes, we know our doings are in bad taste, but we don't heed that, since they ⟨attract⟩ beguile the Vulgar — let them be beguiled'. For my part, remembering well the impression that Canterbury Cathedral made on me when I first stood in it as a little boy, I must needs think that a great building which is obviously venerable and weighty with history is fitter for worship than one turned into a scientific demonstration of what the original architects intended to do: I think that these learned restorations are good on paper to be kept in portfolios, but not good in new stone for the use of people who are busy & in earnest.

I am, Sir
Your obedient Servant

ms: Berg. Published: Henderson, *Letters*, 91-93; MM, I, 158 (misdated July 7, 1877).

[1] Dean Smith had written: "Mr. Morris's Society probably looks on our Cathedral as a place for antiquarian research or for budding architects to learn their arts in. We need it for the daily worship of God." See his letter in *The Times*, June 7, 1877, p. 14.

408 · To Emma Shelton Morris
26, Queen Square,
Bloomsbury, London
June 10, 1877

Dearest Mother

I paid the £25 /5ˢ/[?] dividend on 100 D.G.C. shares, into your account at Praeds yesterday: I am glad you have got the money small as it is.

I hope you are very well this beautiful day. Love to Henrietta.

I am
Dearest Mother
Your loving Son
William Morris

MS: Walthamstow.

409 · To Jenny Morris
Kelmscott
Wednesday
[June 13, 1877]

Dearest Jenny

Thank you for your nice long letter;[1] my two day's holiday is coming to an end, and I am not very sorry, though I have fished diligently both days with moderate luck: the weather has been very dissappointing I must say: grey & dull, & today quite cold. I am glad you have been to Hardwick;[2] it is in a very genuine state still I believe: I think it must be 20 years ago since I went there with Aunt Emma. Haddon is the most beautiful of the places about there; and since it is not lived in by the grandees that own it and has nevertheless the roof on is in as good a state as one can expect an ancient.[3]

I have not seen the papers these two days; so if any thing is going on I am in the dark about it —

Philip seems a good deal better than when I was here in February:[4] he has been told he should go to the sea-side: it seems there is a hospital at Margate: does Aunt Emma know anything about it.

Lichfield Cathedral has been restored out of all knowledge especially inside: the town is queer & dull; but the Cathedral stands prettily beside a g[r]eat sheet of water: it must have been fine when its defensible walls were all standing. There are not many flowers out in the garden here: the tulips are over & the roses not yet come except one or two of yellow roses, that smell heavenly.

I wont forget your Grimm as soon as I get back: I am glad your

[377]

German-pronunciation turns out to be human: — though Uncle Ned would deny its humanity if it were like German by the way.

Goodbye, deary

I am your loving father
William Morris

MS: BL, Add. MSS. 45339.

¹ Jenny was visiting Morris's mother and sister at Much Hadham.

² Hardwick Hall, Derbyshire, the ancestral home of Elizabeth Talbot, widow of Charles Talbot, sixth Earl of Shrewsbury. Separated from Talbot (her fourth husband) in 1583, the Countess began converting the house, inherited from her own family, into a large mansion, known at the time as Hardwick Old Hall (she had been born Elizabeth Hardwick), and made extensive changes and additions. For a description of the house as she completed it, see Nikolaus Pevsner, *Derbyshire*, 2nd ed., rev. Elizabeth Williamson (New York: Penguin Books, 1978), pp. 221-29.

³ Haddon Hall, Derbyshire, owned by Lord John Manners, seventh Duke of Rutland (1818-1906), leader of the Young England Party. For a detailed and chronological description of the building, see Nikolaus Pevsner, *Derbyshire*, pp. 229-36.

⁴ See letter no. 381, n. 2.

410 · TO THOMAS WARDLE
26, Queen Square,
London, W.C.
June 22, 1877

My dear Wardle

I am going tomorrow week (June 30th) to Kelmscott: with Faulkner & probably De Morgan: the plan is to go down to Oxford on the Saturday afternoon, and sleep there: then to ⟨pull⟩ drive to Bablockhithe early on the Sunday morning, where we shall find our boat, and thence to pull, tow, sail, or whatnot, up to Kelmscott, about 20 miles distance: stop the Monday at Kelmscott, and pull &c. back to Oxford on the Tuesday.

What do you think of it, will you join? if so please let me know at once, & I will send you times of trains, and the like.

Yours very truly
William Morris

MS: Duke. Copy in V&A.

411 • TO THE DEAN AND CHAPTER OF CANTERBURY CATHEDRAL

June 22, 1877

To The Very Reverend the Dean
& the Reverend the Chapter,
of Canterbury Cathedral.[1]

The Society for the Protection of Ancient Buildings has heard with regret that it is the intention of the Dean & Chapter of Canterbury Cathedral, to remove from the Choir the ancient stalls which form such an interesting feature of the building. The Society feels it its duty to protest against such a course of action, which it considers injurious to the history, & art of the country. The Society begs to point out that this woodwork is remarkable for its intrinsic beauty, and although of comparatively late date, is a noble example of the art of its period, & in no way interferes with but rather adds to the Architectural Effect of the building. It is stated that these stalls conceal portions of more ancient work, part of the fittings of Prior Eastry, but as the work of that eminent architect is left in a very fragmentary condition, & any restoration must be, on the whole, conjectural as to design, and modern, as to workmanship, the Society feels that it would be a loss rather than a gain, to remove for the purpose of such restoration, a beautiful & untouched work of a former age.

The Society takes this opportunity of deprecating any attempt at imitating the supposed condition of the choir at any past period⟨s⟩ of its history, being convinced that however lamentable former destruction of ancient fittings & decorations may have been, the restoration of them is impossible, & can only lead to a condition of things still more grievous to all lovers of art, & still more destructive of the history and dignity of the Cathedral.

By order of the Committee.
William Morris
Hon: Sec:

MS: Ray Coll. Published: *The Athenaeum*, July 7, 1877.

[1] This letter, originally published in *The Athenaeum*, was also published by *The Times*, July 8, but *The Times* printed it as a news item, not a letter.

412 • TO AGLAIA IONIDES CORONIO

26, Queen Square,
Bloomsbury, London
June 25, 1877

My dear Aglaia

I don't know if you are very busy (as I have been) or if you would like me to call in some afternoon this week. Say Wednesday, or Thursday — Wednesday by preference —

Yrs affectionately
William Morris

MS: Berger Coll.

413 • To Thomas Wardle　　　　　　　　　26, Queen Square,
Bloomsbury, London
June 26, 1877

My dear Wardle

De Morgan and I intend going down to Oxford on Saturday next (30th) by the ½ past 6 train from G.W.R. at Paddington. I dont know whether it will suit you to come to London, or to go to Oxford by Bletchley. If you don't go down with us please let me know, and also write to C. J. Faulkner Esqre University Coll: Oxford & tell him when you are coming: I have told him you will do so.

by all means bring the rod if you don't despise chub: though if we do any fishing on Monday at Kelmscott it will more likely be paternostering or trolling.

The fishing was but poor when I went down that time — small shavers all. I havn't read your letter, I didn't know it would have to be sent back so soon.

Yours very truly
William Morris

MS: Duke. Copy in V&A.

414 • To George James Howard　　　　　　26, Queen Square,
Bloomsbury, London
June 29, 1877

My dear Howard

Re: Antiscrape: You have got the manifestos by this time I hope: Is Ormsby's name & address sent?[1] of course we are not responsible for every word in Stevenson's paper,[2] and of course there are many differences of opinion as to style amongst us. One of the useful things Ferguson[3] could do now would be to send me any names of *un*restored churches or buildings, & mention what sort of places they are: we are going to write to the guardians of such begging them to leave them alone. I have (by order) sent off a memorial to Dean Payne Smith,[4] he sent it back to me with a rude letter: I sent it back again with another letter in which

I tried, I fear in vain, to combine insult & politeness: he has not sent it back the second time.

E.Q.A. £20 from one Ellis not F. S. & 10.10 from Falkner are all our gettings of late. I am afraid people think all danger is over & that the Tories are muzzled. I don't: but now the Russians are fairly across a few days even may make a great difference. I suppose by the way the Government are really going to ask for that money.

Many thanks about coming down: but so busy I am! I can say nothing about it just yet.

Our Froggy weaver is over here and many a time in the day have I cause to curse that basest of jargons so grossly misnamed the Frankish or French tongue.

Yours affectionately
William Morris

MS: Howard Papers.

¹ Rev. George Ornsby (1809-1886), vicar of Fishlake (1850), prebendary of York (1879), and author of *Sketches of Durham* (1846) and *Diocesan History of York* (1882). An antiquary, he is listed as a member of the S.P.A.B. in the Report of the First Annual Meeting, June 21, 1878.

² John James Stevenson (1831-1908), architect and pupil of George Gilbert Scott. By 1878, Stevenson had come to agree with the principles of the S.P.A.B. and was at odds with his former teacher. At a meeting of the Royal Institute of Builders and Architects, May 28, 1877, Stevenson read a paper at which Scott took offense. See R.I.B.A. *Transactions 1876/77*, May 28, 1877, pp. 219-35, and June 11, 1877, pp. 242-68.

³ Richard Saul Ferguson (1837-1900), a barrister who devoted himself to the study of antiquities at Carlisle and served as its mayor in 1881 and 1882. He was elected a Fellow of the Society of Antiquaries in 1877, and of the Society of Antiquaries, Scotland, in 1880, and is listed as a member of the S.P.A.B. in the Report of the First Annual Meeting.

⁴ See letters no. 404, n. 4, and no. 411.

415 • TO FREDERICK STARTRIDGE ELLIS Horrington House
June 30 [1877]

Dear Ellis

I am very sorry, but I can't possibly come: next Thursday is a grand meeting of the Anti-scrape, as you would have known had you dutifully attended former meetings. I am however really very sorry on all grounds.

This evening I am going to Oxford, & C.J.F. & I are going to Kelmscott by water tomorrow; I shan't be back till Wednesday. I wish you were to be with us, but I thought it was no use asking you.

Yours very truly
William Morris.

MS: Princeton T.

416 · To George James Howard Horrington House
July 6, 1877

My dear Howard

It isn't about that last cheque of Bell's,[1] which we certainly received
& acknowledged: 'tis about one which he thinks he sent just after the
old St: James' Hall meeting: I have an impression of his having sent
something; but can find no trace of the earlier cheque; which is odd, as
it is the only case of the kind that has happened.

Thanks for the news about the Fratry; I think we may put a spoke in
their wheel since they havn't got the money:[2] I am going to write to
Ferguson[3] about it.

Things seem to me going very badly in Eastern matters: I suppose
the 'Russian collapse' in Asia has given the scoundrels heart over here:
of course you have seen Northcote's answer about Besika Bay,[4] which
the D[aily] N[ews] thinks satisfactory: so do not I: 'ax me no questions
& I'll tell you no lies', would have been his real words had he dared:
meantime our Committee are beat: there was a very bad meeting last
⟨Friday⟩ Thursday: Mundella not present: the Committee concluded to
do nothing, in spite of the protests of Broadhurst, Chesson,[5] Richard[6]
(who is all agog again) and myself: the fact is we don't know what to
do, and had better make up our minds to war: the beggars have tired
us out and we are beat. Yet I should like to give one more kick before
the knife goes home.

Yours ever
William Morris

ms: Howard Papers.

[1] Sir Isaac Lowthian Bell (1816-1904), metallurgist and industrialist, Liberal M.P. for
Hartlepool (1875-1880), baronet (1885). Morris and Co. had decorated Rounton Grange,
Northallerton, designed and built by Philip Webb for Bell between 1872 and 1876. For a
description of the house and of Morris's work in it, see Lethaby, pp. 93-95; and Girouard,
p. 418.

[2] Morris was perhaps referring to the restoration of the fratry of Carlisle Cathedral,
which had been undertaken by G. E. Street. The Dean and Chapter of Canterbury were
appealing for funds.

[3] See letter no. 414, n. 3.

[4] Northcote at this time was Chancellor of the Exchequer. (See letter no. 482, n. 2.)
The English fleet had been ordered to Besika Bay, at the entrance to the Dardanelles.
Since the Cabinet had debated landing 20,000 men at the same time, the sending of the
fleet alone was called a compromise. Replying to questions put to him in the House, North-
cote had said that Besika Bay had been chosen because it was a convenient station, one
from which the admiral could communicate quickly with the ambassador at Constanti-
nople or with the British Government. See *The Times*, July 3, 1877, p. 5, and July 7, p.
8.

[5] Frederick William Chesson (1834?-1888), a journalist on the staff of the *Morning Star*.
He was active in the E.Q.A.

[6] Henry Richard (1812-1888), an advocate of arbitration for settling international disputes.

417 • To John Ruskin

The Society for
the Protection
of Ancient Buildings
26 Queen Square, W.C.
July 10, 1877

My dear Ruskin

We all think it might do good to distribute a leaflet with a reprint of your words on restoration in the Seven Lamps:[1] will you allow me to do so? They are so good, and so completely settle the whole matter, that I feel ashamed at having to say anything else about it, as if the idea was an original one of mine, or any body's else but yours: but I suppose it is of service, or may be, for different people to say the same thing.

I needn't say I don't feel in very high spirits as to the amount of good our Society is like to do; especially since so little is left to save: yet it might be of use for the future if we could make people ashamed of the damage they have done; and at the worst one must say that we are driven to speak at last.

With best wishes

I am
My dear Ruskin
Yours affectionately
William Morris

MS: Fondation Custodia (F. Lugt Coll.), Institut Néerlandais, Paris. Published: Henderson, *Letters*, 93.

[1] The passage quoted at letter no. 397, n. 2.

418 • To Thomas Wardle

26, Queen Square,
Bloomsbury, London
July 10, 1877

My dear Wardle

Matter of the blue silk-dyeing for Bazin: 1st When you get it, which I hope will be at once: I hope you will carry it through at once: else — what a mess we shall be in! As to the dyeing itself: I have been trying again shortening the vat of lime as much as seemed possible: the silk came much redder out of the vat, but after washing off scarcely rubbed off at all though it was a dark shade: item: I acided some goods (stockings if I must confess it) they also don't rub off, & are pretty much as red as cotton would be.

As to the evening: I am sure that is a matter of drying: a head[1] that I dried in the sun & *wind* was quite even: 'tis a matter I think of keeping the threads apart while they are thoroughly oxidizing. Lastly I utterly distrust the cold vat & all his ways & works.

Of course I don't think we have hit upon the right vat for silk yet however we work it: I shall have another shy at the cuve-d-Inde sometime next week. I wish we were going on the river instead.

Yours very truly
William Morris

MS: Duke. Copy in V&A.

[1] A bundle of flax or silk of varying dimensions.

419 • To Emma Shelton Morris   26, Queen Square,
                                                Bloomsbury, London
                                                July 13, 1877

Dearest Mother

I shall never be too busy to see you if you would give me a day or two's notice: but I am afraid that Mrs. Bells work will be gone in two or three days.[1]

I think Janey will be going out of town in ⟨two or 3 da⟩ about a week with May who is ailing: she is thinking of going first to the Broadway Beacon —

With love
Dearest Mother
Your loving son
William Morris

MS: Walthamstow.

[1] Margaret Bell (d.1886), wife of Isaac Lowthian Bell (see letter no. 416, n. 1). The work Morris mentions was probably the embroidered frieze, "Romaunt of the Rose." Henderson notes (*Life*, p. 156) that Burne-Jones and Morris designed a frieze for the dining room at Rounton Grange which was "worked in wool, silk and gold thread on linen" by Margaret Bell and her daughters Florence Johnson and Ada Phoebe Godman and took them eight years to complete. See also Morris, *Victorian Embroidery*, p. 98.

420 • TO GEORGE JAMES HOWARD
26, Queen Square,
Bloomsbury, London
July 16, 1877

My dear Howard

All of A's[1] subscription acknowledged all right. I have just returned from the meeting: the room was full conventionally speaking; a great many bonnets present: speeches if possible duller than usual, I suppose owing to the necessity of respecting the feelings of the Tories, whose tails had been salted for the occasion: ⟨ap⟩ meeting not *obviously* enthusiastic: applause mostly called out by anything approaching politics — naturally — I hope they will get a lot⟨s⟩ more of money, but don't think they will.[2]

I find (as I suppose you know by now) that people here think the Disraeli part of the cabinet is best,[3] & that we are pretty safe — but I don't know: anyhow we should make all arrangements for a row if the time calls.

I will try to get to Naworth for 1 day or 2 before the end of the month: but it really is difficult to get away: I don't think May can come; she has been so seedy of late, that her mother doesn't like letting her escape her, as the young lady is a trifle perverse. Many thanks for asking us both.

It is as soppy here now as it can be in Cumberland I fancy —

Yours affec:
William Morris

MS: Howard Papers.

[1] Possibly George Douglas Campbell, eighth Duke of Argyll (1833-1900), who in 1877 was actively opposed to Disraeli's policy toward Turkey and Russia.

[2] *The Times*, July 17, 1877 reported (p. 11) that on the previous day a large meeting in behalf of Bosnian and Hercegovinian refugees had been held in Willis's Rooms. The Earl of Shaftesbury was chairman and Gladstone spoke. It was basically a fund-raising affair.

[3] Morris refers to Cairns, Northcote, Hardy, and Salisbury.

421 • TO LUCY FAULKNER ORRINSMITH
26, Queen Square,
Bloomsbury, London
July 20, 1877

My dear Lucy[1]

You are very welcome to any information our Misters Smith can give you either he of Oxford St. or he of here:[2] the Persian Rugs are up here: the really good ones are very expensive articles, because they are old & are no longer made. The modern oriental carpets that are made for the European market are very much deteriorated; especially in colour.

I have passed the word to the Smiths that you are to have every assistance in the matter.

Yours very truly
William Morris

MS: Walthamstow.

¹ Lucy Faulkner, sister of Charles and Kate Faulkner, was an embroiderer, designer, wood engraver, china painter, and writer. She began working for Morris, Marshall, Faulkner and Co. in 1861 and about that time married Harvey Orrinsmith. In 1878, she published *The Drawing Room, its Decoration and Furniture*. See Callen, p. 223.

² See letter no. 400, n. 2.

422 • TO GEORGE JAMES HOWARD

26, Queen Square,
Bloomsbury, London
July 20, 1877

My dear Howard

May can't come: many thanks all the same. My wife is bound to the Broadway Beacon for her health's sake, & cannot do without someone to keep her company out there. If I come it will be about Monday or Tuesday week I fancy but I am not sure that I shall be able to. I am much obliged to Brooke¹ for his kind intentions as to the conveying of May down.

Committee meeting yesterday: little or nothing to be done: but the parliament men say that the anti-war party is decidedly in the majority in the cabinet, & that there is nothing to fear at present. Lord Bath² had a talk with Pryce³ yesterday morning, and told him straight out that such was the case, & that all was going well: also they say that there are signs of a revolt among the Tories against Disraeli: one difficulty about that piece of dirt★ dissappearing is that Lord Derby⁴ won't serve under Lord Salisbury,⁵ nor vice versa; so the Duke of Richmond⁶ is talked of for prime minister's cloak: I should like it, it would be a piece of revenge for Lord Hartington⁷ on t'other side. After all I am uneasy about matters: and we seem getting so damned moderate & unparty; and in short I fear the Danai though gift-bearing.

We are pretty well for Brass: Morley⁸ has to pay, & we have about £700 in hand: I hope we are loaded & cocked ready for time & place, if that turns up: I shall look up Pryce about lists: I dont think he has done much yet.

Yrs affec:
William Morris

★ dirt — matter in its wrong place definition somewhere

MS: Howard Papers.

[1] Stopford Augustus Brooke (1832-1916), unorthodox churchman, poet and essayist, an acquaintance who shared some of Morris's interests. Brooke was a close friend of the Howards; he had met them in 1868, and for many years from 1870 onward, he spent a part of his holidays at Naworth. See L. P. Jacks, *Life and Letters of Stopford Brooke* (London: John Murray, 1917), I, 249.

[2] John Alexander Thynne, fourth Marquis of Bath (1831-1896).

[3] Frederick George Pryce (1842-1909), Secretary of the E.Q.A.

[4] See letter no. 351, n. 10.

[5] Robert Cecil, Marquis of Salisbury (1830-1902). In 1877 he was Secretary for India.

[6] Charles Henry Gordon-Lennox, Duke of Richmond (1818-1903).

[7] Spencer Compton Cavendish, Marquis of Hartington and Duke of Devonshire (1833-1908).

[8] John Morley (1832-1923) was editor of the *Fortnightly Review* at this time. He assumed the post in 1867 and held it until 1882.

423 • TO CATHERINE HOLIDAY   26, Queen Square,
                                             Bloomsbury, London
                                             July 20, 1877

My dear Mrs. Holiday

Thanks for your note: it is a little awkward doing curtains on speculation, because the length may be wrong: also I think for a curtain, an inside pattern would be necessary: would you like to take in hand that big coverlet you saw me at work on the other day? You might have it at once, because though I have not quite finished colouring it, there is enough colour to serve as a hint for you. It was to be darned with filosel[1] on that loose Indian cotton. I will send you the cotton and pattern at once if you please — I have also got another pattern you could have in about a weeks time: this might be done (for a door hanging) either solid on the white cloth, or with darned work on the cotton.

                         Yours very truly
                         William Morris

MS: Berger Coll.

[1] Filoselle, a silk thread less glossy than floss silk.

424 • TO JANE MORRIS   26, Queen Square,
                                             Bloomsbury, London
                                             July 27, 1877

Dearest Janey

I was very glad to get your letter, and to hear that you had got there at all events. I hope you have had pretty good weather; today is a beast here: but yesterday and Thursday were very fine, if a trifle cool.

I got a cheque from Ellis the other day:[1] better than I expected — £144 — but what is that among so many? I am working at the ferment vat, and this time I think I shall succeed more or less: My dinner parties came off with less success than might otherwise have been the case, since I really have had a touch of gout, which however has gone off, but left me careful of my meat and drink.

I had a letter from dear Jenny rejoicing in the idea of Kelmscott: I find it will be no very difficult job to get from Clay Cross to Honeybourne, as the line goes direct thence to Birmingham, & from B. to H is also a straight line: I am here working overtime at my dyeing: chiefly because of my ferment vat, which I hope to see look well on Monday.

Mother, it seems, has gone to Lullworth: I had a letter from her this morning.

With love to dear May
Your loving
W.M.

MS: BL, Add. MSS. 45338.
  [1] Possibly for *Sigurd the Volsung*.

425 • To Thomas Wardle

26, Queen Square,
London, W.C.
July 28, 1877

My dear Wardle

I write in real tribulation about the silk warp Bazin is idle, now; though in very truth he has been ill & in St Thomas Hospital meanwhile: we really must manage to begin at something, or I swear I will bolt

It really is very serious, all chaff apart.

We shall be able to set the dyeing agoing for the next piece as soon as the first warp is done. The next will not be blue — for our comfort.

Yours very truly
William Morris

MS: Duke. Copy in V&A.

426 · To Thomas Wardle
26, Queen Square,
Bloomsbury, London
July 31, 1877

My dear Wardle

I am afraid we must call it failure still: I don't like the colour, which seems to me flat & dull: let alone that the fastness is as described. May I ask a question or two? 1st was it dyed at the cold? 2nd has it been soaped? In any case it won't do: what shall we do with the silk? Could it be soaped to the bare bones & would there be enough colour left on it then to dye it some sort of green?

For the rest we pitched upon blue, so please you, because no other colour would do for the walls of our room, and so the order must stand: *but* as we can't keep the loom empty, we are telegraphing to warp the roller with white undyed silk, and are thinking of shooting it with Tusseh[1] also undyed (what a come-down): so please send us a pattern or two of bright good Tusseh, as golden in colour as may be: we shall weave that, wh: will give us a little breathing space for the blue. Meantime may I make a remark or two about the dyeing: to wit: I don't seem to find any difficulty in getting a colour like A (enclosed) in the vat set as for wool-dyeing: it was dipped 6 times in not overstrong vats; I think with you that fewer dippings in stronger vats would be better: the fibre seems to get choked after 3 or 4 dips. A has been soaped, & the soaping pretty stiffly didn't seemed to hurt the colour, as I dont think it would these dark colours: A comes off but not so much as the lighter colours you have sent me today: I have a head which I shall devote to the demons of soap, & see at what point (if any) the coming off would stop — A. was dyed at about 115°. The whole subject seems beset with difficulties: but I hold that what has been done once can be done again, and since the older dyers dyed indigo silks ⟨in⟩ perfect both as to colour & fastness; we *must* be able to do it somehow.

The past week I have been trying the Cuve-d-Inde — potash, bran, & madder: I find no difficulty in getting the Indigo dissolved to a certain extent, but cannot be sure that I have got it *quite* right: last Saturday I dyed about lb5 of wool, & left the vat still about as good in dyeing powers as I began: on Monday it was not as good, the fermentation obviously getting into the putrid stage: however it will still dye this morning —

I will send you a history of it when I chuck the stuff away. I have tried silk in it: the first dipped were much the same colour as from our hydro: vat, & about as unfast: I suspected too much alkali; & the latter dips, when the alkali was somewhat exhausted, have come duller, but

[389]

are certainly faster on. I enclose B and C of this lot: B has been dipped twice & soaped; C once and not soaped.

I shall work at this vat all the autumn, & report from time to time: of course if the hydro : vat could be made to do it would be much better, as this is obviously a troublesome matter.

Now as to our next piece for the loom: it is many-coloured, and will have a certain amount of blue & green in the shoot, light colours both: I think, as the piece is broken in colour, we may risk these in the ordinary hot-vat, which we know will give us *bright* colours, which last will be a necessity for the blue. We shall speedily send you patterns for the warp of this & a new roller: and I think we had better go on with it before the all-blue piece, since the white-Tusseh piece will give us respite: please let us lose no time in getting this latter done.

My respects to Master Ten when he comes, he will certainly be like a young bear, with all his troubles ahead if he has to learn blue-dyeing — how if it be Miss Ten though?[2]

Yours very truly
William Morris

P.S. I am going out of town: Broadway & Kelmscott for about a week next Friday.

MS: Duke. Copy in V&A.

[1] Also tussah, tussore: a coarse silk made in India.
[2] Wardle's tenth child was about to be born.

---

427 • To John Lucas Tupper

The Society for
the Protection
of Ancient Buildings
26 Queen Square
Bloomsbury
August 1, 1877

Dear Sir,[1]

In accordance with a resolution that was passed at the last meeting of the Committee, I am directed to forward to you half a dozen prospectuses and provisional lists, with the request that you would do your utmost to obtain fresh members.

The Committee would also be glad if you would forward to Mr H W Brewer[2] 28 Portland Road, Notting Hill, (who has consented to receive them) the names of all unrestored churches that come under your notice.[3]

I am, Dear Sir,
Yours very truly
William Morris
Hon Sec.

J. L. Tupper Esq.

MS: Spilstead Coll.

[1] John Lucas Tupper (c.1826-1879), a minor Pre-Raphaelite poet and artist whose work had appeared in *The Germ*. A posthumous edition of his poems, selected and edited by W. M. Rossetti, was published in 1897. Bornand notes (p. 11, n. 1) that Tupper's father, who owned a printing firm in London, "undertook the printing of *The Germ* and even financed the last two numbers"; he also printed for Morris and Co.

[2] Henry William Brewer (d.1903), a painter. He attended the first meeting of the S.P.A.B. in 1877, and is listed as in attendance at all subsequent meetings.

[3] At the first meeting of the S.P.A.B. a letter by Coventry Patmore (1823-1896) was read which suggested that the Society publish a list of unrestored churches in England. It was resolved at the meeting that part of the aim of the Society would be to "find out what ancient buildings are still left unrestored, and to what extent those that have been restored have suffered alteration." Patmore, an assistant librarian in the printed book department of the British Museum, 1846-1865, was a friend of Tennyson and Ruskin, and a contributor, in 1854, to *The Germ*.

428 • TO JANE MORRIS

26, Queen Square,
London, W.C.
August 2, 1877

Dearest Janey

We shall be with you on Saturday, but I don't know when: you had better tell the Lygon Arms to send & meet the first possible train at Honeybourne, & wait there till I come. I am sorry to hear that Crom is not coming till Monday, as I fully intended leaving for Kelmscott on Tuesday, & now I suppose there will [be] an outcry if I try it on: you see there will [be] so little to do at the tower all day long: I should have put off going down till next week if I had known: however it all doesn't matter. I am pretty well only: stomach upset by those hot days: & we all very much lowered by this bad news of the war.[1] Other news good: vat successful business doing well, *if* we could only get our money in, which I am determined to do, or 'periss in the attempt'.

I am so glad to hear you are getting on so well: I thought it would do you good: I confess I sigh for Kelmscott. I think Georgy & the children will certainly come. Love to little May

Your loving

W.M.

I hear from Emma today no news of Jenny, which I suppose is good news.

MS: BL, Add. MSS. 45338. Extract published: *CW*, 12, xxii.

¹ At the end of July, the Turks had driven the Russians out of Plevna. In an editorial, August 2, *The Times* wrote (p. 9) that it had become imperative for the Russians to hold the Balkan passes and prevent the Turks from taking Tirvona.

429 • To CORMELL PRICE   26, Queen Square,
                                                          London, W.C.
                                                          August 3, 1877

My dear Crom

I am going there today:¹ am sorry that I shan't ⟨see⟩ find you there: ⟨as⟩ come as early as you possibly can: because I want to take them² to Kelmscott & stay a day at least there before I get back to London the end of next week.

Yours affec:

William Morris

MS: Price Papers.
¹ To Broadway, where Jane Morris and May were staying.
² Morris's family.

430 • To THOMAS WARDLE   26, Queen Square,
                                                          Bloomsbury, London
                                                          August 3, 1877

My dear Wardle

The pattern out of dyed warp is a little disappointing: but I think soaping will mend it; especially as it is 2 or 3 shades too dark; I enclose two skeins of my dyeing: you will see that the soaped one differs little in colour but little from the unsoaped, & is *much* faster.

I think it worthwhile trying this before we warp the undyed: please report as speedily as possible: or what would be better, if the soaping succeeds warp it at once.

I should note that ⟨the⟩ my 'soaped' skein has been soaped 3 times the 'unsoaped' twice.

I am just off: so excuse haste.

Yrs truly
William Morris

If the colour after soaping is not fast, get a white warp made at once & send the samples of tussah shoot[1]

MS: Duke. Copy in V&A.

[1] This postscript is not in Morris's hand.

---

431 • To George James Howard
26, Queen Square,
Bloomsbury, London
August 15, 1877

My dear Howard

I have been away taking Jenny from Clay Cross, & the lot of them from Broadway to Kelmscott: I am afraid there is little chance of my coming now as my wife has some little trouble with Jenny's health, besides being but poorly herself; so it wouldn't be fair to spend what time I can spend away from my work except with her. When do you come up to town? I might get down for a couple of days later in the autumn.

Thanks for the Carlisle paper, I was glad to see that you put it on with such laudable strength: we are doing pretty much nothing at present; & indeed I think it would be a pity to throw away our little money while things are quiet: Sooth to say Pryce[1] only got about £30 at Manchester; but I think altogether we have got about £800. The lectures have dropped through for the present: but everybody seems to think that the chance of our interfering grows less & less: you know I distrust all that, but cannot think of anything to do. Meantime you see here are the Russians in a mess like people will get into if they let themselves be led by 'Kings & Scoundrels'; & the most dismal doings out there. Perhaps our people will get up heart to kick the Russians if they are well down: such has of late become our style.

Your affectionate
William Morris

MS: Howard Papers.

[1] See letter no. 422, n. 3.

432 · To Jane Morris

26, Queen Square,
London, W.C.
August 16, 1877

Dearest Janey

I shall come tomorrow (Friday) by the train that gets to Lechlade at
½ past 5 (the one we came by) I shall bring a hamper with me; so I
suppose Mrs. Hiett's fly had better be requisitioned. I may just as well
be at Kelmscott as here since everybody is away, & in consequence I
have nothing to do: however I shall be able to bring a bit of work with
me.

Please tell May to have a many worms ready for me: proper brand-
lings I must have: they are striped & dont smell nice — that is their
sign.

I have got everything you want I think: I hope the bonnet will come
to hand in moderate preservation.   by the way Crom is coming with
the Neds on Monday. Margery is wild with joy at the idea of coming.

Love to the babes.

Your loving W M.

I didn't get your letter till last night, as I slept in town on Tuesday.

Don't forget *the worms*.

MS: BL, Add. MSS. 45338. Published: *CW*, 12, xv; Henderson, *Letters*, 93-94.

433 · To Rosalind Francis Howard

Manor House Kelmscott
Lechlade
August 21, 1877

My dear Mrs. Howard

Thank you very much for your letter and its proposal: I have been
talking the matter over with Janey (meaning my wife), and have been
advising her to go if she thinks it feasible: I think she is quite inclined
to to it, thinking it will do them all good; for May is but poorly now:
⟨she will⟩ my wife will write to you in a day or two and tell you if she
thinks she can manage it: meantime we both of us thank you very much
for your kindness; especially as it would really be difficult to get so far
away without some such sort of help.[1]

For my part I can't think of anything likely to do Jenny ⟨good⟩ so
much good as a complete change of life & scene: and I know that my
wife thinks a winter in Italy would be of great use to herself. Jenny
seems much better at present; she has got terribly fat which bothers me
however. I am staying here for about a week and am glad of that bit of

rest for I have had a great deal of troublesome little business and manufacturing matters on my hands lately.

I return Mr. Congreves[2] letter, & again with many thanks Am

Yours very faithfully

William Morris

MS: Howard Papers.

[1] Jane Morris and her daughters were invited to spend the winter at Oneglia on the Italian Riviera. They left on November 21. See letter no. 456.

[2] Congreve may have been a banker or financial agent of the Howards, and Morris may have employed his services for financial arrangements needed for Jane Morris's stay in Italy. See also letters no. 473 and 477.

---

434 • TO THOMAS WARDLE   Kelmscott Lechlade
                                             August 27, 1877

My dear Wardle

Thanks for your letter: I suppose you have had the order to get the white warp ready; in fact I hope to see Bazin at work on it when I get back next Thursday:[1] when the white piece is out we shall I suppose put in the 4 colour damask; you had better get on with the warp for this at once (if you havn't had the order yet). There is both blue & green in the shute of this, but as the colour is all broken it will not matter so much as in an all blue pattern; or we might even use Prussiate once more. As to the blue-dyeing, I think it would be certainly a very good think to get a woadster over; though you know the old books all say that the woad vat is not good for silk: I don't know why, unless perhaps that the lime is bad for it: still he might help us in setting a potash vat (Cuve-d-Inde). I don't doubt after my recent trial that I should soon get to be able to manage this latter vat, though of course 'tis much less convenient than the hydro-vat: the one I set seemed to work very well; I dyed a good lot of wool in it, but rather[?] funked the silk; however I dyed several skeins, and they seemed faster on than the hydro- but the light colours yielded to soap pretty much as the latter did: it seemed to be hard to get *dark* colours on the silk. The vat was kept more than a fortnight: it was let to go cold for several days, & when heated again still dyed, though it stunk pretty loud when I threw it away. I suppose your new vat is smaller; I should think about 200 gals: would be about the right size: I should be very glad to come down & have a weeks work with you if it would not be too fearfully inconvenient: would it suit you in about 3 weeks hence? As to the dark blue warp already dyed: can anything be done with it? Couldn't it be soaped right down to the bones? The colour is very good & still darker than we want: or would it spoil the silk? I have the skein of shute I am sorry to say that it comes off too much. has it been soaped? I have got nothing to try it against, so can say nothing about the colour, which seems to me a little red, & if it is for the damask some what too dark.

Turning over my wife's silk box the other day I came across a skein of floss I had dyed about the same depth as this, which was a very good colour, and didn't come off at all: but I can't in the least tell why it should have been better: some skeins ⟨after⟩ wh: came off very much I greened after 2 soaps; after the greening they seemed fast enough, though the soaping hadn't seemed to help them much.

Of course I am much vexed at all this bother, but can see nothing for it but continuous trials: I think we had better work at this Cuve-d-Inde, as this was the old silk vat, and it *may* turn out that the hydro vat is unfit for silk whatever we do with it.

I wish the new young lady[2] all good, and with kind regards to Mrs. Wardle.

am Yours very truly
William Morris

MS: Duke. Copy in V&A.

[1] According to a diary kept by F. G. Guy, son of Morris's former tutor, as quoted by Mackail (I, 357), Bazin did not begin to weave until September 20. Guy worked as Morris's secretary and general assistant for a time, leaving in October 1877 to go to Oxford.

[2] Wardle's tenth child.

435 • TO EDWARD WILLIAMS BYRON NICHOLSON

26, Queen Square,
Bloomsbury, London
August 30, 1877

Dear Mr. Nicholson

Many thanks for your book[1] which I shall read with much interest & pleasure, though I think from my first glance I have seen some of the poems before.

As to the lectures, I can't do it:[2] it's true that I have made a kind of promise to lecture the Trade Guild of Learning and have repented it; but if I ever do give the lectures in question I am sure it will quite exhaust my feeble knowledge on the subject.[3] I assure you it is not laziness that hinders me, but the certainty that I cannot do it usefully.

Yours truly
William Morris

MS: McMinn Papers.

¹ *The Christ-Child, and Other Poems* (London: H. S. King, 1877).

² Morris may have been asked to lecture at the London Institution, where Nicholson was Librarian.

³ On December 4, 1877, Morris gave his first lecture, "The Decorative Arts," before The Trades Guild of Learning. In this lecture, Morris articulated many of the ideas and beliefs that he was to affirm for the rest of his life. He rejected the distinction between the "lesser" or decorative arts and the "great arts," which he named as architecture, painting, and sculpture. Asserting that humans *need* to decorate, he said that the purpose of decoration is to give people pleasure in the things they must use and the things they must make. He asserted that labor should be a pleasure, not a curse, and that when in the future the arts had become popular, art would "beautify" labor, and people would begin to find labor pleasurable. Conversely, when men had become equal, he said, they would be happy in their work, "and that happiness will assuredly bring forth decorative, noble, *popular*, art." The key word is popular: "I do not want art for a few," Morris said, "any more than education for a few, or freedom for a few." He anticipated that the development would require political and social change, too. Finally, he took the occasion to protest the restoration of ancient buildings and to define those buildings as "wrought into" the English countryside and as "completely a part" of nature as the land itself.

436 • To Thomas Wardle

26, Queen Square,
Bloomsbury, London
September 14, 1877

My dear Wardle

I have the shute resoaped; I find it still comes off, very disappointingly so considering that it is several shades lighter: however I certainly think it would be better to try it on the end of this white warp, so please wind off enough for a yard; less than that won't show: I must say it *is* uneven.

I think the second week in October would suit me well; I have to go ⟨ver⟩ over to Ireland about that time¹ & could come to you from Holyhead I should be delighted to look at the Grayling; but by the way I have not got my fly-rod; you took it away with you to get it mended: I send you back your winch: I must excuse myself for having used it as it was tied on to my rod. I hope we shall get through the dyeing of the 4 colour piece comfortably: I thought it would be better however, in case there is any hitch over the card-cutting &c for you to see what can be done with the dark blue warp & get it ready as soon as possible; you could then dye the shute while Bazin was getting the warp ready

I expect by the way to bring over another order for dark blue silk from Ireland: so we must mind our eyes. Allright about Macquer.

Yours very truly
William Morris

P.S. Am glad to hear about 1592.²

MS: Duke. Copy in V&A.

¹ F. G. Guy, as quoted by Mackail (I, 357) notes in his diary that Morris left for Ireland on October 8 (probably his first trip there). Morris was to call on the Countess of Charleville, Tullamore, King's County, "to advise her as to the doing up of her house," taking with him "patterns of carpets, silks, chintzes, etc.," and on the way back planned to stop at Leek and "stay there some while, making Tom Wardle look to his dyeing etc., helping a good deal in it too." The Countess was Emily Frances Wood (d.1911) who married Alfred Francis Bury, Earl of Charleville, in 1854.

² Presumably a lot number for dyed cloth.

437 • TO EIRÍKR MAGNÚSSON
26, Queen Square,
London, W.C.
September 27, 1877

My dear Magnússon

I have long looked at the drawings trying to think that there was some hope in them for selling purposes; but at last I am bound to say that there is none: you see they are not done in any recognized manner, though their conscientiousness is obvious, and I am afraid that is fatal to them: I send the roll back by pass: train with much regret.

With best wishes I am

Yours ever truly
William Morris

MS: Iceland.

438 • TO EMMA SHELTON MORRIS
26, Queen Square,
Bloomsbury, London
September 28, 1877

Dearest Mother

Many thanks for your letter: I am glad to hear that you are going to have another outing: I am back (we I should say) in London: I have had a very long holiday this time, which I must say I decidedly enjoyed: I am very well, & so is Jenny. Janey pretty well, & May middling: I hope great things for them from this Italian journey.¹

I am only in London now for about a week, & then I have to go to Ireland on business, after which I must spend a week at Leek over the dyeing & printing works: I hope to see you when you come back from Devonshire.

All well here: the business is doing well considering what a bad year it is for all kinds of business. With best love to everybody.

> I am
> Dearest Mother
> Your most affect: Son
> William Morris

MS: Walthamstow.

¹ See letter no. 433.

439 • TO CATHERINE HOLIDAY   26, Queen Square,
                                               Bloomsbury, London
                                               October 1, 1877

Dear Mrs. Holiday

I will do my best with the plum-colour you send me a pattern of: I think I can match it: I shall send you the yellow for the body of the work in a day or two; I daresay it won't be a dead match, but will certainly be the same sort of colour: so I must ask you to make the best of it; a little variety of colour will be no harm. I hope to dye the 2 blues and the sea-green this week.

As to our exhibition, I shall certainly wait for the coverlit¹ & for some other pieces of work also: I want to make an impression on the one hand, & to have some small pieces about for people to buy on the other.

> Yours very truly
> William Morris

P.S. I forgot to say that I have no pattern by me of the light blue silk for the big leaves   Will you kindly send it at once.

MS: Berger Coll. Published: Henderson, *Letters*, 94.

¹ For a picture of this coverlet, see Morris, *Victorian Embroidery*, Plate 51, p. 176.

440 • TO THOMAS WARDLE   26, Queen Square,
                                               Bloomsbury, London
                                               October 3, 1877

My dear Wardle

Thanks for your note; I propose coming next week, but ⟨am⟩ shall not be able to get to you till the Wednesday in the week, as I am obliged to go to Ireland on business on Monday. In fact I may not be able to get to you till the Thursday: I will telegraph from Ireland. I am going to send you our notes of the ferment vat, in case you like to start one a day or two before I come, so as to show by then I am [rest of letter missing]

MS: Duke.

441 • TO JANE MORRIS

Tullamore
Tuesday evening
[October 10, 1877]

Dearest Janey

I am safe and unsick across: the passage was very calm. The coast looked much more beautiful than I expected to see it. I did not sleep except for an hour on board, being prevented in the train by the jaw-bone of a fool.

A long journey from Dublin here through a curious country: it seems a little queer to be in Ireland, & I feel somewhat touched by it.

I am writing just before dinner; the letter won't go off till tomorrow, but I know I shall want to roll into bed as soon as I get upstairs, — not from whisky-punch however. I am lodged in an octagonal room which reminds me of Crom's tower, because that was hexagonal — You see the Irish charm is beginning to work already.[1]

I have told Wardle to send you a cheque for £5 at once: if he doesn't please blow him up: also ask for more:

Love to the babies: I hope they are good.

Your loving
W.M.

MS: BL, Add. MSS. 45338. Published: *CW*, 12, xvi; Henderson, *Letters*, 94-95.

[1] Morris was visiting the Countess of Charleville on business. See letter no. 436, n. 1.

442 • TO GEORGIANA BURNE-JONES

Leek
[October 18, 1877]

I slept on board for about two hours, and then stirred myself to get up and look, and when I came on deck we were just well in sight of land. It was much more beautiful than I expected to see: a long rather low cliffy coast on the right with a rocky steep island in front of it; and on the left a long line of mountains rather than hills going on and turning the corner, and casting up points a long way inland: the said mountains very lovely in outline. The sky was grey and sulky, but not unfit for the scene, and a thickish mist hid all the feet of the mountains, while a cloud or two was lying on the tops of them: it looked very like Iceland and quite touched my hard heart.

Dublin is not altogether an ugly town; the Liffey runs through the chief street much like the Seine at Paris, which is good: yet a dirty and slatternly city is Dublin, and Guinness seems the only thing of importance there. I set off about midday for my aristocrats;[1] the train running through a very flat country with the aforesaid Dublin mountains on the left; you pass the Curragh, where our army of occupation sits, a fine moorland swelling up towards the Dublin mountains: then you see Kildare, with a great ruined mediaeval church and a tall round tower beside it. Then the Dublin mountains die away, and the Slievh Bloom hills rise up on the left of the great plain; which is to say the truth nothing but bog, reclaimed, half-reclaimed, or unreclaimed: in Elizabeth's time thick forest covered it, but the oaks and all are gone now. The villages we passed were very poor-looking, the cotters' houses in outside appearance the very poorest habitations of man I have yet seen, Iceland by no means excepted.

Tullamore, my town, lies a little without the old Pale: my employers told me that it used to be the very centre of ribbonism;[2] even last year a man was slain there for "agrarian" reasons. They told me that an old man had told them how he had seen in the rebellion 20 miles of country burning in a straight line, the cabins and villages fired by the Orange yeomanry: the grandfather of the present young lady who owns the estate commanded the troops of that district in the war,[3] and his banners hang up very little the worse for wear in the hall of the house now — and these unreasonable Irish still remember it all, so long-memoried they are![4]

TEXT: Mackail, I, 358-59. Published: Henderson, *Letters*, 95-96.

[1] The Countess of Charleville. See letter no. 436, n. 1.

[2] A reference to the Ribbon Society, a Roman Catholic secret society formed in the early nineteenth century in Northern Ireland to oppose the rule of the Protestant majority. The Society worked primarily for land reform.

[3] The grandfather, through marriage, of the Countess of Charleville was Charles William Bury (1764-1835), who took an active part in suppressing the Irish rebellion of 1798, to which Morris refers. In that year he was created Baron Tullamore of Charleville Forest, and in 1806 was made Earl of Charleville. See *The Complete Peerage*, 3 (London: The St. Catherine Press, 1913).

[4] For some later comments by Morris on Ireland, see letter to Jane Morris, April 15, 1886, written when he was deep in the affairs of the Socialist League and went to Dublin to lecture.

443 • To Catherine Holiday

26, Queen Square,
Bloomsbury, London
October 24, 1877

Dear Mrs. Holiday

I am glad to hear you are getting on so well: I hope to be able to send your silks in a day or two dyed as well as I can. I don't know if you ever test colours by putting them in the sun on a card; I should advise you to do so: some colours on silk are so very fugitive; and though it doesn't matter so much for embroidery as other matters, yet it is as well to know what one has got to trust to. Many thanks about the anemoné: I am going down to Kelmscott in about a month; if the plant could stay unharmed in the earth till then, I should like to take it with me & plant it there.

I am longing to see the big coverlit finished: I will set to work now about designing a portiere as my note to Mr. Holiday explains.[1]

Yours very truly
William Morris

MS: Berger Coll. Published: Henderson, *Letters*, 96-97.

[1] See letter no. 444.

444 • To Henry Holiday

26, Queen Square,
London, W.C.
October 24, 1877

My dear Holiday

I enclose a cheque for £50, the sum I agreed to pay for the table-cloth, pending the sale of it. if I can sell it for £100 I shall owe Mrs. Holiday £40 more: at the same time I shall ask her to let me consider if I get an offer ⟨for⟩ at a less price, as it would be a pity to be obliged to stop the work for want of a market: if Mrs. Holiday would like any further payment on account of the work now in hand, I can manage it I think.

As regards the future, I am bound to be careful, as it is doubtful what market there is for these costly articles; the coming year will enlighten us a little on that point. I dont fancy it would be easy to get orders for curtains in the way you suggest: I will however get in hand a design for a portiere, which I will ask Mrs. Holiday to carry out for me in one or two ways and will see what our clients say to it: I should make the design less minute than the coverlit, & therefore easier to carry out.

Yours very truly
William Morris

MS: Berger Coll. Published: Henderson, *Letters*, 96.

445 · To Thomas Wardle
26, Queen Square,
London, W.C.
October 24, 1877

My dear Wardle

Thanks for sending the things, but I am afraid I must trouble you further, for Maquer, & my sabots & apron carelessly left behind in my retreat from Leek. Please thank Mrs. Wardle for sending me the spectacles, & tell her I am glad my coppers have gone so good a road.

I got to town all right, but not till after 10 oclock; the 8½ was a mistake I had to wait over ½ an hour at Stoke, & ¾ at Stafford: all of this didn't matter a rush; I only tell it for your own warning: I will send your coat back tomorrow with many thanks: I sent you this morning the Welsh book, which I hope you will like, though I can't praise the illustrations.

about the silk, I think the best way will be to send us up *at once* a good average pattern of both organ[zine] & tram;[1] we can then settle if we shall use the tram for this work or dye fresh: & will send you the roller for warping the organ at once. The *Widow Guelph*[2] has been enticing our customers from us & has got an order for tapestry that ought to have been ours:[3] So much for Kings & Scoundrels: you will have to join me in the end in crying death to the aristocrats! — or at all events to their coats.

Yours very truly
William Morris

MS: Duke.

[1] A double, twisted silk thread.

[2] Queen Victoria.

[3] Under Victoria's patronage, The Windsor Tapestry Works had been established on royal land at Old Windsor with the purpose of reintroducing the art of tapestry weaving. See *The Times*, January 15, 1875, p. 4.

446 · To Thomas Wardle
26, Queen Square,
London, W.C.
October 26, 1877

My dear Wardle

Thanks for note: it was not of the slightest matter about the train: I had a very comfortable journey ⟨over⟩ up.

As to the Paris journey I couldn't now go as my wife & family are going over about the 20th Nov: 'tis *possible* I might manage to kill 2 birds with one stone, and go then. Meantime any advice I can give is much at your service. I am glad you are going into the matter so energetically: 'tis true that we ought to have started the tapestry before: but you know the difficulties of *small* manufacturers: I have no doubt we can beat the 'tothers, who in all seriousness are welcome, like other folk to do their darndest: Jones is very much delighted at the idea of the work.[1]

My wife wants, if it is obtainable, some of the stout tusseh cloth, but wants to know how much she can have *at once*: if you have piece you can spare would you send it.

The patterns of the indigo silks are to hand: I am a little dissapointed with the look of the organ, but I think we had better use it: orders as to it and the tram will be sent on. Buré has just been, & we have been talking to Bazin, who wants an assistant; Buré will tell you about it if he sees you before I do.

I saw a piece of Japanese *tapestry* yesterday, of silk, very delicate in manufacture, and fine in colour.

Yours very truly
William Morris

MS: Duke.

[1] Edward Burne-Jones.

447 • To Emma Shelton Morris Horrington House
October 28 [1877]

Dearest Mother

You may chance to see in the papers an exaggerated account of our mishap at Queen Sq:[1] so I write to say that the affair will not be very bad for us; it was the detached building at the back that has been burnt, the place where our glaziers work: one window (Jesus College Camb:) was destroyed and part of another, together with some smaller pieces, and a stock of unworked glass, but we are fully insured, and so our only real loss will be the stoppage of work & inconvenience. I happened to be sleeping in the house that night, so I had a dissagreable waking enough: the fire broke out a little before 6 A.M. & the place was in a bright flame in five minutes afterwards; it was a great happiness that the house itself did not catch, as it easily might have done by that long wooden gallery: they had 3 engines at work and soon got the fire under, though I thought at one time it was spreading to the hospital next door, as indeed it did a little: but the firemen, being on the spot, soon overcame it. It would have been a terrible business if the houses at the back had caught, as I almost wonder they did not. On the whole I may well be thankful we have got off so well.

I got your kind & long letter at Leek to my great satisfaction: I had a pleasant time enough there; & matters are going well. It will be a curious time when Janey & the children are gone: of course I shall miss them very much, but hope much from their journey. I am thinking of letting my house here & living in one of the sets of rooms (still unlet) at Oxford St: I don't fancy such a long journey to & fro with an empty house at the end of it.

Best love to Henrietta: Janey & babes send love.

I am

Dearest Mother

Your most affectionate Son

William Morris

MS: Walthamstow. Published: *CW*, 12, xvii.

¹ *The Times*, October 29, 1877, reported (p. 6) a fire in the back workshop of Morris and Co. that had burnt out the roof and a floor, damaged the contents of the basement, and spread to the National Hospital for the Paralyzed and Epileptic, next door in Queen Square.

448 • To Thomas Wardle   26, Queen Square,
London, W.C.
October 29, 1877

My dear Wardle

I didn't think your letter curt, but I don't see any cause for anger & disturbance: it can't be any news to you that on the big scale people can dye cheap, nor did I doubt that it is generally nasty: the only question is what price is prohibitory to the public, with whom we have to deal, & who can stop our business altogether if they please: if I thought your trifling profit ⟨satis⟩ encouraging it was because I am not discouraged by having *lost* £1000 over the same experiment. The blue cloth is all at home: I will sent a pattern as soon as I can: Vickerman was the seller & dyer of the cloth: he charged us /1ᵈ per yd: (1 yd. wide) more for the dyed cloth than for the scoured, &, on our expressing astonishment at the small difference, explained that the cloth in the grease had to have less trouble expended on it if it was to be dyed than if it was to [be] left white: I only make this explanation because you asked about it. The whole question (again) is not a matter of competition with unfast & easy dyes, but what we can knock up together so as to make a business of it with everything done as well as it can be: It is useful, I think, to know what people charge in the ordinary way, even if we are not likely to come near their prices: this last remark to deprecate your anger. We will talk over the whole matter when you come up.

Thanks about the Tussah; Mrs. Morris must choose for herself.

As to the fire, the damage is considerable, to the stained glass only, but we are well insured. By the way you shall by all means see Barber when you come if you please — he thinks us cracked already, like M. Chatel.

Please do what you can for me about Bazins help: I want to get on: we are going to weave the 4-colour piece —

Yrs very truly
W Morris

 MS: Duke.

---

449 • TO CATHERINE HOLIDAY
26, Queen Square,
Bloomsbury, London,
October 29, 1877

Dear Mrs. Holiday

Many thanks for your kind note: I am glad to be able to give you a fairly good account of our mishap: it is the glazier shop, the nice-looking building at the back that is burnt: there is a good deal of stained-glass destroyed and material for it, but *nothing* else; also we are fully insured: of course there will be a good deal of trouble & loss from the stoppage of business.

As to the money-matters, I am sure that no one need be uneasy about taking money duly earned, as no one ought to grudge paying it, and so your mind may be quite at rest about that matter.

I am just beginning the design for the portiere, which I mean shall be much bolder & less minute than what I have hitherto done for you.

Yours very truly
William Morris

MS: Berger Coll. Published: Henderson, *Letters*, 97.

---

450 • TO ALFRED JAMES HIPKINS
26, Queen Square,
November 1, 1877

Dear Sir[1]

Many thanks for your kind note: you will be glad to hear that our loss will not be great by the fire & that nothing is destroyed that cannot be made good.

> I am
> Dear Sir
> Yours faithfully
> William Morris

 MS: BL, Add. MSS. 41631.

[1] Alfred James Hipkins (1826-1903), musician and historian of musical instruments, and a member of the S.P.A.B.

451 • To Eiríkr Magnússon   Queen Sq:
                                                 November 1, 1877

My dear Magnússon

Many thanks for your kind letter: what might have been a very bad business has happily turned out but a little one. Of course we are en-sured, & nothing has been burned which cannot be done again: the stained-glass works, are only somewhat hindered. I happened to be sleeping in the little room that night: it was curious to be woke up to look at ones own property all of a light low.

With best wishes

> I am
> Yours very truly
> William Morris

MS: Iceland.

452 • To Catherine Holiday   [November? 1877]

Dear Mrs. Holiday

The new silk would not be fit for anything but the darning, or some analogous method: for regular embroidery nothing will do but floss: I mean this stitchery

if it is wanted more durable the thing is either to work it finer & closer, or to quilt over long stitches with hair-fine silk.

for chain-stitch the only thing is twist: only they usu-
ally twist our silks over-much: which makes the work
look hard: the best thing to do with the stock of filosel
will be to use it in coarse work done with long stitches
quilted down with ordinary floss: only it will want a
special design for this, more colour than form & very
bold: we will try a table-cover of it when I come back.

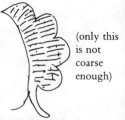

(only this
is not
coarse
enough)

Meantime I will order some silk of 2 or 3 quality nearly half as thick
again & with a little more twist: if too much twisted it will cover so
badly: I will get the colour for the ground of the portiere dyed at once
& have it sent to you.

Yours truly
W. Morris

ms: Berger Coll.

453 • To Catherine Holiday　　　　　　　　26, Queen Square,
Bloomsbury, London
November 8, 1877

Dear Mrs. Holiday

I send by bearer a hank of the pink & 1 of the blue-green: if the latter
be too raw it can easily be altered: the purple I have missed: 'tis a very
difficult colour.

I am almost ready to send you the new door-hanging: when it is quite
ready I will come & see you & talk about the colouring, which has to
be of a certain tone to go with a room we have done, as we are going
to offer it to a client who wants such an article: for the same reason I
think we had better content ourselves with using spun-silk in it as other
wise it might be too costly: but if we sell it you can do another in floss
which I agree with you would look very much better: and you shall
also colour it to your pleasure.

About the silks in general I will warn you again as to fugitive nature
of ordinary dyeing: no fancy (that is coloured) dyeing even pretends to
be fast: of course also the dealers in silks do not dye them themselves
& usually know nothing about the dyeing: I would not if I were you
use *any* silks except you know about their dyeing, unless it is for a little
piece, & when driven into a corner: I think I can get you the blood red
silk dyed fast, even if I cannot do it myself. Of course in all dyeing the
darker ⟨silks⟩ colours are the least dangerous, and the *very* delicate shades
however well they are dyed cannot be *positively* unchanging.

Could you let me have a piece of the many-coloured coverlit without very much hindrance to work: if so will you give it to the bearer: you shall have it back on Monday: I want to see it now I am shading the other (very roughly I fear)

Yours very truly
William Morris

MS: Berger Coll.

454 • To Thomas Wardle 26, Queen Square,
Bloomsbury, London
November 14, 1877

My dear Wardle

Like you I shall probably find one letter's space not enough for going into the whole matter of the tapestry, but I will begin: Let's clear off off what you say about the possibility of establishing a non-artistic manufactory: you could do it of course; 'tis only a matter of money and trouble: but, cui bono? it would not amuse you more than the Judson (unless I wholly misunderstand you) and would I am sure *not* pay commercially a *cheap* new article at once showy & ugly if advertised with humbug enough will sell of course: but an expensive article even with ugliness to recommend it: — I don't think anything under a Duke could sell it: however, as to the commercial element of this part of the scheme, 'tis not my affair, but on the art-side you must remember that, as nothing is so ⟨ugly⟩ beautiful as fine tapestry, nothing is so ugly & base as bad; eg. the Gobelins or the present Aubusson work: also tapestry is not fit for anything but figure-work (except now & then, I shall mention wherein presently) the shuttle & loom beat it on one side, the needle on the other, in pattern work: but for figure-work 'tis the only way of making a web into a picture: now there is only one man at present living, (as far as I know) who can give you pictures at once good enough & suitable for tapestry — to wit Burne-Jones — the exception I mentioned above would be the making of leaf & flower-pieces (greeneries, des Verdures) which would generally be used to eke out a set of figure-pieces: these would be within the compass of people, work-folk, who could not touch the figure-work: it would only be by doing these that you could cheapen the work at all.

The qualifications for a person who would do successful figure-work would be these:

1 General feeling for art, especially for its decorative side.
2 He must be a good colourist.

3 He must be able to draw well; ie he must be able to draw the human figure, especially hands & feet.
4 Of course he must know how to use the stich of the work.

Unless a man has these qualities, the first two of which are rare to meet with & cannot be taught, he will turn out nothing but bungles disgraceful to everyone concerned in the matter: I have no idea where to lay my hands on such a man, and therefore I feel that whatever I do I must do chiefly with my own hands. It seems to me that your weak point is that tapestry cannot be made a matter of what people now-a days call manufacturing, and that even so far as it can be made so, the only possible manufacturer must be an artist for the higher kind of work: otherwise all he has to do is to find house-room provide the frame & warp, and coloured worsteds exactly as the workman bids him. In speaking thus I am speaking of the picture-work: a cleverish woman could do the greeneries no doubt. When I was talking to you at Leek I did not fully understand what an entirely individual matter it must be: it is just like wood-engraving: it is a difficult art, but there is nothing to *teach* that a man cannot learn in half a day, though it would take a man long practice to do it well: There *are* manufacturers of wood-engraving e.g. the Dalziells,[1] as big humbugs as any within the narrow seas. I suspect you scarcely understand what a difficult matter it is to translate a painter's design into material: I have been at it 16 years now, & have never quite succeeded. In spite of all these difficulties if in anyway I can help you I will: only you must fully understand that I intend setting up a frame and working at it myself, and I should bargain for my being taught by you what is teachable: also I see no difficulty in your doing greeneries & what patterns turned out desirable, & I would make myself responsible for the design of such matters. With all this, I have no doubt that we shall both lose money over the work: you don't know how precious little people care for such things.

The carpets like the Savonnerie[2] ones is another matter quite: because you can get girls to do the work and it is really quite a mechanical matter: that seems to me quite feasible for you at once, & I should be glad to go into the matter with you: premising once more that I should like to have a frame of my own up here in this matter also.

This is so long a letter that in order not to recapitulate. Tapestry at its highest is the painting of pictures with coloured wools on a warp: nobody but an artist can paint pictures — but a sort of half-pictures, ie scroll-work or leafage could be done by most intelligent people (young girls would do) under direction.

The carpets can be done any day you like to set up frames & get

[410]

designs — which I will do for you. Finally I will help what I can: ie. if you choose to try one of Jones' designs I will do my best, distance and business considered, to overlook its progress: I assume however that you would have to begin with patterns & greeneries; & I think it would be interesting to see how much you could do such things for, by dint of employing girls or sharp boys. In this line I will make any designs you may want: and you in turn will teach me the teachable as aforesaid.

I am sorry if in anyway I appear also to have wet blanketted you: for I fully sympathize with your wishes to be busy in the matter: but I feel that it is such an important one that it is no use avoiding the facing of the truth in all ways, & I have accordingly given you my mind without concealment. As to business arrangements in case of our productions turning out marketable, I wait to hear what you have to say about the matter.

With best wishes
Yours very truly
William Morris

MS: Duke. Extract published: Mackail, I, 363-65; Henderson, *Letters*, 97-99.

¹ George (1815-1902), Edward (1817-1905), and Thomas (1823-1906) Dalziel, well-known engravers, draftsmen, and publishers. Their firm, Brothers Dalziel, was founded in 1839.

² A pile carpet of a velvety character.

455 • TO GEORGE CHARLES WINTER WARR

26, Queen Square,
Bloomsbury, London
November 14 [1877?]

Dear Mr. Warre¹

I enclose a paper in reference to the meeting we were talking of the other day: will you kindly answer; and also give me any names you think it would be useful to. I believe I could tell you more about the aims and organization proposed in the enclosed paper after to-night² if I could see you:

I am
Yours very truly
William Morris

MS: NYU.

¹ Although Morris spelled the name Warre, the letter was probably addressed to G.C.W. Warr (1845-1901), professor of classical literature and of Latin at King's College, University of London. Warr was a positivist who, with Morris's help, established the Trades Guild of Learning (before which Morris gave his first lecture) and who was also a member

of the Society for the Protection of Ancient Buildings. See E. P. Thompson, 2nd ed., p. 247.

² This may refer to a meeting of the S.P.A.B. held on November 14, 1877.

456 · To WILLIAM BELL SCOTT   26, Queen Square,
                                                Bloomsbury, London
                                                November 21, 1877

My dear Scott

Thanks for your note, & your invitations to come over: I will certainly do so in a day or two: though I am far from often in the neighbourhood of Chelsea: which, may I say it without being beaten, seems to me the most ingeniously out of the way place near London: I would have come to you before: only I have been getting my wife & daughters off to Italy, wh: has much increased my work: I have seen them off today, and shall be more able to get about.

                                    Yours very truly
                                    William Morris

MS: Princeton T.

457 · To CATHERINE HOLIDAY   26, Queen Square,
                                                Bloomsbury, London
                                                November 21, 1877

Dear Mrs. Holiday

I have now the drawing & tracing for the door-hanging all ready, and a tolerable stock of silks to begin with: I propose, if it is convenient to you, to come up on Monday next with it all so as to settle what has to be settled about it. Would about 3 in the afternoon do: or in view of the sort of weather we are having would it be better to come in the morning?

                                    Yours very truly
                                    William Morris

MS: Berger Coll.

458 · To JANE MORRIS   26, Queen Square,
                                                Bloomsbury, London
                                                November 23, 1877

Dearest Janey & dearest daughters

I have my dear May's note, and am glad to hear that you got to Paris otherwise than in small pieces in a hamper: I was certainly not rash like Palinurus,[1] & did not trust the sea overmuch: but 'twas no use saying too much about it before hand: nevertheless you have done pretty well in crossing when you did: for the wind rose to gale on Tuesday night with thunder; and yesterday was a most violent stormy day. Wouldn't it have been funny if I had got taken to Calais? in that case I would certainly have made the best of it, & gone on to Paris also.

I have no tidings to tell: I dined at the Grange in the evening: & I called in there this morning; and we talked of where you would be say at 10½ A.M. I thought about Culoz:[2] little Margery is prepared to miss you, my daughters very much: I dine at Webbs tonight, & shall have a quiet day on Saturday working at my lecture.[3]

There is a letter for you, Janey dear, from Alice[4] apparently; I will send it on next writing, wh: will be after I have heard from Cellar-Villa:[5] item: some lace has come without any note: I have put it a draw: it is bordering & rather pretty. I have found my Jenny's Motley[6] & will send that on too.

Last night was anti-scrape, a small & dullish meeting: I dined with Stevenson[7] before it. We have got some one to help froggy Bazin, but alas not the ideal '*personne*' that he spoke of, but a *person* of the ripe age of 58: a poor old ex-Spitalfield's weaver:

My dears you must tell me all about Cellar Villa & the glories of that most glorious of all ponds by whose shore you will get this: how glad I shall be to see you all again: it was tough work coming away from you I can tell you: A hundred thousand blessings on you all, my dears:

Your loving
William Morris

And after all — what larks!

MS: BL, Add. MSS. 45338.

[1] Aeneas's pilot, who fell asleep at the helm, tumbled into the sea off the coast of Lucania, and was murdered by the natives.

[2] A French town east of Lyons, on the route that Jane Morris and her daughters followed on their way to Oneglia.

[3] Morris's first public lecture, "The Decorative Arts," delivered before The Trades Guild of Learning, London, on December 4, 1877. See letter no. 435, n. 3.

[4] Possibly Alice Gill, Morris's youngest sister.

[5] Villa del Cava is the address on the envelope for this letter.

[6] Possibly John Lothrop Motley (1814-1877), an American historian. He is best known for *The Rise of the Dutch Republic* (1850), which Jenny may have been reading.

[7] Probably John James Stevenson, a member of the S.P.A.B. See letter no. 414, n. 2.

459 • To Jane Morris   26 Queen Sq:
                                                     November 29 [1877]

Dearest Janey

I was so glad to get Jenny's letter, & yours of today: Jenny said you were not well, but I could scarcely think you were like to be after such a demon ride as you have had: anyhow I was much consoled by your letter this morning: I will write the news in Jenny's note, all except this that the Homan[1] lot are off: I was firm about Sarah[2] & so they refused: not at all to my grief: I am now advertising the house at 3½ guineas including the cook's wages: I believe it will be just as easy to get 3 as 2 and really if I can't get a decent sum I may as well stop there considering the trouble and anxiety: I am ready to send you a cheque as soon as I know that my letters reach you. This I say because I wrote to you yesterday week, & neither you nor Jenny mention having got it. I say, *won't* the little wretches like it after all? I am so rejoiced that it is not disappointing to you, as indeed it could hardly be.

I have heard of a sort of a place for Edgar, from Miss Maud Stanley:[3] superintendant of a sort of boys home in Dean St: Soho: £60 per: an & good rooms: he is going to try for it on the principle of any port in a storm: but 'tis not fat.

I was indeed amused at the advent to Oneglia, though it must have been no joke to you at the time: now, my dear, don't let your celebrated thrift make you poison yourself with bad wine: but buy what you can drink: I expect a letter from May directly telling me all you are doing: I must say I should be glad to be out of Horrington House 'tis rather a doleful abode at present: I was thinking last Saturday of having Sarah up to read scraps of my lecture to her after the example of Molière; but refrained lest I should kill her with surprise. As I must write a line to Jenny and then get on with my lecture ⟨I shall not⟩ which is still heavy on my hands I must not write any more at present: but with all love am

Your loving
W.M.

P.S. I could surely send you out some compressed tea by post: Jenny's Motley I find was sent without the full address: it was addressed
                              Oneglia
                              North Italy.

 MS: BL, Add. MSS. 45338.

[1] Presumably prospective tenants. Morris planned to use rooms at Oxford Street and let Horrington House. See letter no. 447.

[2] Presumably the cook at Horrington House.

[3] Maude Alethea Stanley (1833-1915), a sister of Rosalind Howard. She started the first Club for Working Girls, and in 1877 was elected Guardian for St. Ann's, Soho. The school to which Morris referred was St. Andrews' Home for Working Boys. In her first book, *Work About the Five Deals* (London: Macmillan, 1878), Maude Stanley wrote that the object of St. Andrews was to provide a respectable home for boys 13 to 18 who had no parents. In addition, she indicated, it offered an evening school.

460 • To Jenny Morris   26 Queen Sq:
                                              November 29 [1877]
Dearest little Jenny

Thank you very much for your little notes, I am so glad you are safe at home and pleased, as I fancy you are.

Your Motley went yesterday. Let me see for news: First, Mr Irishman will not have Horrington House being alarmed at the aspect of the Ferocious Sarah — the more fool he! Next, & this is sad, poor Margery[1] has had a bereavement: her poor Persian Pussy: I had to help to dig it down into the cold earth last Sunday, for it had died suddenly in the night: and when I came in to breakfast there were the two elders not knowing how to break the news to Margery: however I think she has got over her grief by now: I was there yesterday evening, & Margery had with her, her little (?) friend Henrietta.

We shall soon be beginning our new piece of silk in colours; Bazin is troublesome about it; these weavers don't understand much about getting a pattern together; they can just weave & that's all. Apropos of frogs your fat friend is giving a series of lectures on French history:[2] Aunt Georgie attends them & says he is very funny: he is abusing Napoleon the Great chiefly; who indeed somewhat deserves it, if he cares about it: they are all Germans of the female sex at the said lectures which awful word reminds me of my own to come off next Tuesday: I went with Wardle to the place, & read Robinson Crusoe to him to see if I could make my voice heard; which I found easy to be done: yet I can't help feeling a little nervous at having to face my fellow beings in public 'a thatn's'.

I suppose you see or will see some sort of papers out there: there is nothing new at present: this afternoon I attend a meeting of the E.Q.A.

Dear little I must now get on with the aforesaid lecture, which hangs fire a little: love to the sister. I try to think of you all going about in the strange land, & miss you all very much, you may be sure my dears:

                              Your loving father
                              W.M.

MS: BL, Add. MSS. 45339. Extract published: *CW*, 16, xii; Henderson, *Letters*, 100.

[1] Margaret Burne-Jones.

[2] Probably the tutor with whom Jenny had studied either the French language or French history. See letter no. 470.

461 • To Jane Morris   26 Queen Sq:
                                                            December 3 [1877]

Dearest Janey

Just a line to say that I have your letter, I will send Daily News, Athenaeum & Spectator to you if you please. I finished my lecture yesterday after very hard work at it: I deliver tomorrow in a dismal hole near Oxford St: I am not sanguine as to its reception. I am expecting to see Mrs. Holidays coverlit tomorrow finished: I will tell you about it & the lecture & it when I write on Wednesday.

We have had a war-scare here, wh: I daresay George will hear of: My lord Beaconsfield was reported to have threatened Russia grossly in a conversation with an official personage. (Shouvaloff[1] no doubt): it was perfectly true that he did this, though of course 'tis denied: but his colleagues sat upon him, & Lord Derby shed a delightful stream of cold water on the heads of a set of rags who interviewed him in an almost providential way, begging him to do his best to get us into a row.[2] What a rage the Tory press were in!

Ned is going to take me to see Gilbert's 'Sorcerer' one day this week I believe: he says 'tis not so funny as Trial by Jury but very good. De Morgan called yesterday with that 2½ yds of boy called Eustace Balfour:[3] there is somebody else after the house: and De Morgan has somebody who might take it, & might if we liked perhaps take the lease off our hands: what do you say to this? Goodbye my dear with best love: also to the dear babes.

                                                    Your loving W M.

What larks!

MS: BL, Add. MSS. 45338. Extract published: *CW*, 16, xiii.

[1] Count Peter Andrevich Shuvalov (Shouvaloff) (1827-1889), ambassador to Great Britain, 1877-1879.

[2] On November 28, 1877, Lord Derby addressed himself to the fears and urgings of various groups demanding war to protect British overseas interests. He did not believe that British control of Afganistan was necessary to protect the British hold on India, nor that Constantinople was in imminent danger of falling to the Russians. He added that in any case, the fleet could not be sent there without the consent of the Porte, and concluded by reasserting the Government's policy of "conditional neutrality." See Seton-Watson, *Disraeli* p. 239.

[3] Eustace James Anthony Balfour (1854-1911), architect, and brother of A. J. Balfour (1848-1930). He was active in the S.P.A.B., holding the post of Honorable Secretary.

462 · TO CATHERINE HOLIDAY

26, Queen Square,
Bloomsbury, London
December 4, 1877

My dear Mrs. Holiday

I have the coverlit & am delighted with it: it is beautifully smooth: I shall put it in a flat box to keep it.

About money-matters: what am I to pay you for it: I am quite ashamed to appear to grudge paying for such a splendid & successful piece of work — but you know my difficulty which is with the stingy public: and if I could sell two or three grand pieces it would be encouraging both to you & to me: so I want to pay such a sum for it as would not make ⟨the⟩ my price prohibitive. I must say this looks mean when I must also add that I never saw a finer piece of work.

Yours very truly
William Morris

MS: Berger Coll. Published: Henderson, *Letters*, 100-101.

463 · TO CATHERINE HOLIDAY

26, Queen Square,
Bloomsbury, London
December 6, 1877

Dear Mrs. Holiday

I sent a cheque for £60 on account of the coverlit yesterday, and I suppose I must ask you to wait to see what I can sell it for as to the other money: I am afraid we are hardly likely to get £120 for it: you see this opens up the difficulty in a commercial way of the whole industry: meantime I am so glad that such a fine piece of work should be done that I am quite willing to forego any profit on it: but the question is what is to be done for the future? Can you suggest any smaller pieces of work that could be done? Cushions & the like say, or what else: by doing these you could be paid duly for your work, & the articles would be more saleable: I should like to know what sort of work you think would do for such articles, as the kind of work would influence my designs: I shall soon have your silks ready for the portiere or all but the darker one: only I find it very hard to get the very light colours in

[417]

'good' dye. I have not yet been able to get the cloth for filling up *the* table-cloth which is a great annoyance to me.

The coverlit is certainly most satisfactory.

> I am
> Yours very truly
> William Morris

MS: Berger Coll. Published: Henderson, *Letters*, 101.

464 • TO JENNY MORRIS   Queen Sq
                                                     December 7 [1877]

Dearest Jenny

Thank you kindly for your letter: I am glad to hear you are pitching into the Italian tongue: Yes I gave my lecture on Tuesday & I have only got your letter today — Friday: it went off very well, and I was not at all nervous, but made myself well heard: I send you the Architect which has got it all in: but I intend publishing it again myself.[1] I can send you some more books, my dear, if you like: have you a fancy for any? Why hasn't May written to me yet? is she too busy drawing.

You mustn't get dull you know out there, or back you will all have to come: I am going this evening with Uncle Ned & aunt Georgie to see the Sorcerer, which is a comic opera of Gilbert & Sullivan: I doubt if I shall care for it much though: On Tuesday I believe Mr. Webb & I are going down to Kelmscott for 2 or 3 days: the river has been much flooded Annie says but is going down a bit now: the weather has been entirely beastly for the past week. I am sorry you have had so much rain I didn't quite reckon on that: you must scold Mr. Howard for it, as I am sure he must *feel* responsible: I have been having an afternoon with Froggy, the Loom & our Coventry 'designer' so called: the loom was the wisest of the 4 of us & understood much more of what the others said than anybody else did — at least I think so. (Do you see anybody weaving or dyeing about there? I do so wonder what you all do with yourselves & what the place is like: in spite of photographs & things I really can't quite understand what sort of a place it is. Well, my dear daughter, since I have been dyeing this morning, I must go & try to get my hands cleaner least they shouldn't let me into the theatre after all

Best love, my dears, to you all   'tis getting on for three weeks since
I saw the last of you.

Your loving father
William Morris

What larks!

MS: BL, Add. MSS. 45339. Published: Henderson, *Letters*, 101-102. Extract published: *CW*,
16, xiii; Mackail, I, 360.

¹ The lecture, delivered before The Trades Guild of Learning, December 4, 1877, was
published as "The Decorative Arts" in *The Architect*, 18 (December 8, 1877), 308-12, and
as a pamphlet, *The Decorative Arts: Their Relation to Modern Life and Progress*, in 1878.

465 · To WILLIAM ALLINGHAM

26, Queen Square,
Bloomsbury, London
December 14, 1877

My dear Allingham
    Many thanks for your note: I was stupid enough to let a man from
the 'Architect' collar my lecture on the spot; so that the affair is at an
end: otherwise I should have been glad to let Fraser have it:¹ I am how-
ever going to publish it myself later on. I have seen nothing of you for
a long time, for which I am sorry.

Yours very truly
William Morris

MS: Iowa.
    ¹ Allingham was the editor of *Fraser's Magazine*.

466 · To JANE MORRIS

December 14, 1877

Dearest Janey
    I was very glad to get your letter: I thought what you say about
Jenny's tooth-cutting hopeful: I do hope you will soon get some good
from the change.
    I am just come back from Kelmscott where I was 2 days with Webb:
it was rather melancholy after our jolly times of last summer: we had 2
fine but very cold days: this morning brilliant but white-frosty. The
river had been much flooded, but was lower the first day, & I caught
two good pike: I should like to have sent you one in a letter.

[419]

Philip has been better, but he looks rather queer again now.[1] The blown-down tree *is* that one by the causeway gate: it makes a sad gap, for it was a fine branchy tree: a great mess it makes too: I shall write to Mrs. Turner[2] & ask her to bestir herself to get it moved, for it nearly blocks up the gangway altogether. Webb told Mitchell[3] what to do with the little window & he will get it done at once. The garden looked neat & nice.

I am going out to dine with Stopford Brooke tonight; but I fear I shall be irreverently reminded of a parson in the 'Sorcerers' by Gilbert which I saw the other night: he, the play-parson, was very funny, but all else I thought dreary stuff enough in spite of Ned.

I have a nice long letter from Jenny today; I will write first to May next to Jenny in a day or two: if I seem to write rather seldom & short you must remember, my dear, that I am one & you are 3: also that I am very busy with lots of really troublesome business that sometimes quite withers[?] me.

Miss Marshall writes bothering: says that she only got 13s/ for 8 days work at Bessys,[4] & so was obliged to give up working there: of course she lies; but she clearly didn't intend working there: am I to give her more than £2 for the table-cover (less the floss-silk) which she has just sent in? She says you gave her that for it & had done an eighth yourself:[5] I suppose Bessy will be able to give her the chair-back she asks for: she wants more silk too: why didn't she ask for all this before you went.

By the way, did you take a filter with you? if not, I must send you one, for it can't be good for you to drink water out there unfiltered. Shall I send you £50 at once?

Edgar has just been: it seems he has not got that place:[6] it was at best a miserable affair.

I am going to get to work at my 2nd lecture[7] at once: it bothers me not a little.

Heigh! here is an ill-tempered letter well it will remind you of me, my dear. So good-bye with best love to those dear babes.

I got Mays long & pretty letter all safe.

> I am
> Your loving
> W.M.

ms: BL, Add. mss. 45338. Extract published: Mackail, I, 360; Henderson, *Letters*, 102.

[1] See letter no. 381, n. 2.

[2] The Morrises' landlady at Kelmscott Manor. See *CW*, 8, xxx.

[3] Probably a local workman or builder.

[4] Apparently Elizabeth Burden in behalf of Morris and Company was employing others in needlework at this time. See also letter no. 617.

[5] It would appear from this letter that Jane Morris, too, acted in a managerial capacity with respect to women who executed piecework embroidery for Morris and Company.

[6] See letter no. 459.

[7] On December 19, Morris gave a talk at an antiwar meeting at Lambeth sponsored by the E.Q.A. See LeMire, p. 234.

467 • TO GEORGE JAMES HOWARD　　　　26 Queen Square
London
[December 18-19?] 1877

Things look bad. If you can come, you would help us much. Committee meets on Wednesday.[1]

W. Morris

G. Howard
Villa Bianchi
Italy

MS: Howard Papers (telegram).

[1] Presumably a committee of the Eastern Question Association; Morris, as Treasurer, would have been a member of their executive or steering committee.

468 • TO JANE MORRIS　　　　26 Queen Sq:
December 20 [1877]

Dearest Janey

I write just a line awaiting some letter from you or the babes: I am like to be very busy for the next 3 weeks: public matters pressing.　great things have happened since your letter to Georgie which she showed me this morning: the marshall[1] has given way; Plevna[2] has fallen; Servia is over the frontier[3] — and — things seem most like the Jew wretch and *that* old Vic forcing us into the war: you will see how the sprightly widow went to Hugenden & then said she would stay at Windsor Christmas over: & now Parliament is to meet for business on Jan: 17.[4] So we are all alive at the E.Q.A. & shall miss George very much in the matter.

I am so busy today that you must excuse a miserable scrap & I will write on Sunday to the babes more at large. Of course you will see all the public news as soon as you do this; but I am so bothered by it all that I can do little else. I even tried to flit a few words at a small meeting we had at Lambeth yesterday: I can't say I got on very well, but I did manage to get a few words out & get to the end.

I hope to hear from you tomorrow.

Your loving W M

Love to the babes, that goes without saying.

MS: BL, Add. MSS. 45338. Published: Henderson, *Letters*, 103.

¹ Maurice de MacMahon (1808-1893), French marshal and president of the Third French Republic. In an election held in October, the Republicans had won a large majority, and in December MacMahon was forced to accept a new Republican ministry under Armand Dufaure (1798-1881).

² Plevna, Bulgaria, defended by Turkish forces under Osman Pasha, fell to the Russians on December 10, 1877.

³ On December 14, Serbia declared war upon Turkey.

⁴ Disraeli and his Cabinet planned to summon Parliament early and ask for a "large increase of force." See Seton-Watson, *Disraeli*, p. 242.

---

469 • TO THOMAS WARDLE

Queen Sq:
December 20 [1877]

My dear Wardle

I send you today 2 vols of A Durer's copper cuts well reproduced somehow, which I hope you will accept & like. We are all in a flutter here about our inspired prime-ministers last stroke,¹ which I expect will keep me busy for 3 weeks or so: after which I hope to get to work with my tapestry design. Boyce² has lent me a very fine & interesting piece of the 16th cent: which I think you might like to study

Yours very truly
William Morris

MS: Duke.

¹ See letter no. 468, n. 4.
² George Price Boyce (1826-1895), the artist. See letter no. 23, n. 1.

---

470 • TO JENNY AND MAY MORRIS

Much Hadham
Christmas Day
December 25, 1877

Dearest Jenny & May

I have been so much about from pillar to post the last fortnight that I am hazy as to wh: of my babes I wrote to last so I will even write to both: and hereafter I shall solemnly write my letters in due order: 1st Mama 2nd Jenny 3rd May.

I have been much agitated for the past week by the goings on of an

August personage & my Lord Beaconsfield; but we hope to agitate others in our turn next week. I do not think it will really end in war: but the party of stupidity will do their best to bring it about: neither is there any doubt that the A.P. aforesaid is helping them and that this fact, strange as it may seem to us, makes many people, especially professional politicians, feeble in resistance. On the whole our side has got weaker, and many people are sluggish & hard to move, who thoroughly agree with us: on the other hand serious business-men & the like do shudder back from war, even those who are Turkophile: the EQA met in committee yesterday & agreed to do something, though not as dramatically as I could have wished: we are issuing a manifesto & asking people to stir:[1] however we meet again next Monday, & then I hope we shall arrange to have a big meeting before Parliament: meantime last Sunday we had a success, for a meeting[2] summoned of working men on Clerkenwell-Green to talk war turned all the other way by good management: item: the same rascal (which his name is Maltman Barry)[3] has summoned a meeting to Trafalgar Sq: next Saturday,[4] which I hope will go the same road.

So much for politics: I have seen several letters from your friends, so I know you have been busy in that matter. 'Tis a fine Christmas-day today though there has been a little snow. Edgar & his missis & baby are here, also Isabella and her naval officer,[5] & Ada: the latter is really much improved. We have just had a peppering little snow-shower, item: a cock-pheasant has been on the lawn just now: these are bits of Hadham news you know my dears: now they are coming in from Church, so I shall to give in.

I think it is rather funny of you my babies not to like Italian: let me tell you my Jenny that if you were taught it as the Professor taught you French, you would like it very much. Uncle Ned would tell you that a great deal of it is old Latin, older than Augustan or even Lucretian: theres for you, my dear.

Now I must leave off for everybody is chattering about me: give my best love to mama, & take my love to yourselves. I am whiles a bit dull without you: but still, Wot Larks!

Your loving father
William Morris

MS: BL, Add. MSS. 45339. Published: Mackail, I, 360-61; Henderson, *Letters*, 103-104.

[1] *The Spectator*, 50 (December 29, 1877) reported (p. 1632) that the E.Q.A. had issued a sensible circular. The *Daily News* published manifestoes of the Peace Society and the E.Q.A. See G. C. Thompson, II, 278, n. 1. *The Times*, December 31, 1877 reported (p. 6) that *Golos*, a Russian newspaper, had expressed satisfaction at an address recently issued by the Eastern Question Association in London.

² *The Times*, December 24, 1877, reported (p. 8) that on the previous day a meeting of about 2,000 workingmen had been held on Clekenwell Green "to consider [favorably] the Government policy toward the war in the East." One speaker said that a letter he had received from a group calling itself the "National Society for the Protection of British Interests in the East" had been sent to the wrong man. It was preposterous, he said, to think that the workingmen of Finsbury would demonstrate "to keep alive the moribund despotism of Eastern Europe."

³ Maltman Barry, author of *The Catechism of the Eastern Question* (London: E. Wilson, 1880). Sub-editor of H. H. Champion's *Labour Elector*, he was a mysterious figure in radical circles, said to have been a spy for Karl Marx and, later, for Lord Randolph Churchill (see Dan H. Laurence, ed., *Collected Letters of G. B. Shaw* [London: Reinhardt, 1965-], I, 358). Barry was a member of the First International, but by 1885 had become an agent of the Conservative Party. See Henry Pelling, *Origins of the Labour Party* (London: Macmillan, 1954; 2nd ed., Oxford: Clarendon Press, 1965), pp. 40, 146.

⁴ In concluding, the speaker who had scorned efforts to gain working-class support for government policy (see n. 2 above) said that the anti-Russian meeting convened for the following Saturday was a sham and that the means for the agitation "had been supplied by a certain noble lord, who had Russia on the brain." *The Times*, December 31, 1877, reported (p. 6) that in Trafalgar Square on the Saturday in question the "National Society for the Resistance of Russian Aggression and Protection of British Interest in the East" had called a pro-Turkish meeting. Maltman Barry was one of the organizers. Many of the working men present attacked the Society and its pretensions to represent them.

⁵ On the members of Morris's family, see letter no. 1, n. 1.

471 • To George James Howard

26, Queen Square,
Bloomsbury, London
December 27, 1877

Bloody end to the Turk

My dear Howard

I must really ask your pardon for wiring to you: but I thought you would scarcely like not to have warning if we thought of moving.

As to matters now I scarce know what to say: things may have changed so before you get this: the war-party is certainly exceedingly rampant; but on the other hand ordinary sensible people of all parties *do* shudder back from the leap of war: I don't fear that Parliament will do anything like an overt act of war, but I do fear that they may comit us to *the next move* unless they have unmistakeable proof that the country will not stand war with ⟨Turk⟩ Russia for Turkey's sake I believe we can give them this proof if we agitate now before Parliament meets:¹ though I allow that the silence of the ministers is horribly embarrassing to us, yet the whole country is without doubt putting the question of peace or war to itself; and I think it is highly necessary for us to seize upon any excuse (if you will) to get the country to commit itself to peace: if we do not no doubt we shall have one more chance, even supposing things come to the worst, of making the deuce of a row: but I would rather not be driven to our last ditch: and doubtless we have lost a lot of ground since the spring.

I note with thanks what you say about Froude[2] & Lord A. Russell[3] and will mention it.

At our Monday meeting we had a goodish Committee & agreed to publish a peace manifesto, wh: Mundella had got done by Harcourt:[4] Little else: a big public meeting hangs in the wind a bit;[5] we meet on Monday in Committee & I think if matters don't change for the better that we shall try it: *I* shall go for it, & so will Chesson. There is a meeting called by that beast Maltman Barry for next Saturday in Trafalgar Sq:[6] the faithful Broadhurst has arranged for the spoiling of it: what larks it will be! M[altman] B[arry] has been traced to Stafford House:[7] he has lots of money to spend, & has posters of his meeting all over the town: he tried on a preliminary one at Clerkenwell last Sunday, but our folk got there first, & held a peace meeting instead.[8] Of course the Peace Society are all agog: Lord! if Richard only knew how peaceable I feel[9] — The Russian is Madame Novikoff: her book is just coming out with a very good preface by Froude.[10]

As for my speaking at the Lambeth I made rather a mess of it: the audience was stupid & cold if friendly   it was a dull affair: but it looked well in the newspapers.[11] The sum of the whole seems to me that I don't think we shall go to war; but that if we do not stir now we may have to do so in a hurry & panic to stop war; wh: I think even then we could do. No one knows better than another what the ministry mean to do but of course the Widow Guelph is crazy for war in spite of all denials.

I have been feeling very anxious about my family & half regret that they have gone which is weak. When do you leave? I shall try to come out before you do, but I can only come out once. 'Tis right cold weather here

Yrs affectionately
William Morris

MS: Howard Papers.

[1] When Plevna fell on December 10, the main Turkish armies faced defeat. On December 19, it was announced that Parliament would be recalled three weeks early, on January 18, 1878, to consider the new crisis. See E. P. Thompson, 2nd ed., p. 215.

[2] James Anthony Froude (1818-1894), the historian.

[3] Lord Arthur John Edward Russell (1825-1892).

[4] Sir William George Granville Harcourt (1827-1904). The Peace Address of the E.Q.A. was published in *The Times*, December 28, 1877, p. 7. It was signed by the Duke of Westminster, President; Lord Shaftsbury, Vice-President; A. J. Mundella, Chairman of

the Committee; William Morris, Treasurer; George Howard, F. W. Chesson, Honorary Secretaries; and Edward S. Pryce, Secretary.

⁵ Perhaps a reference to a joint meeting of the E.Q.A. and the Labour Representation League—the "Workmen's Neutrality Demonstration" held in Exeter Hall, January 16, 1878. See E. P. Thompson, 2nd ed., p. 216.

⁶ See letter no. 470, notes 3 and 4.

⁷ The town house of George Granville Leveson-Gower, third Duke of Sutherland (1828-1892). He was an active supporter of the Turks and raised funds for relief of the Turkish wounded and for other pro-Turkish causes. See W. T. Stead, *The M.P. for Russia* (London: Melrose, 1909), I, 260; and G.E.W. Russell, *Portraits of the Seventies* (London: Unwin, 1916), p. 244.

⁸ See letter no. 470, n. 4.

⁹ A reference to Henry Richard, Secretary of the Peace Society (see letter no. 416, n. 6). An address, signed by Henry Pease, President, as well as by Richard, had also been issued by the Society. See *The Times*, December 27, 1877, p. 4.

¹⁰ *Is Russia Wrong? By a Russian Lady.* The author was Olga Novikova, a Russian journalist living in London who attempted to enlist British sympathy for the Russian cause. See letter no. 403, possibly written to her.

¹¹ See letter no. 466, n. 7.

472 • TWO LETTERS TO CATHERINE HOLIDAY

a.

26, Queen Square,
Bloomsbury, London
Thursday [December 1877?]

Dear Mrs Holiday

I was sorry not to see you: I will willingly pay the 40s. for the new cloth: of course I see that there is a great deal of work in it of a very careful kind: as to the colour it is lovely, nor do I think that anything could have looked better for the border than the light-blue: there is only one thing to be said further, wh: is that a *very little more* of the white and copper-coloured work in the body would improve it: would you mind doing this? it would be just a spot or two where the work looks a trifle unfinished for lack of it.

After all beautiful as this work is my mind is so perversely unarchitectural, and I am such a savage that I prefer the many-coloured work on the cotton.

One other thing before you begin the new piece of door-hanging: to wit: spun silk (filosel) is after all 'shoddy': would you find it harder to use net silk if it had a slight throw on it, that is what the Persian and Island Greek work is done with: say like floss only slightly twisted: the extra expense of material is not worth while considering when the *handiwork* is so costly.

Yours very truly
William Morris

MS: Berger Coll. Published: Henderson, *Letters*, 104-105.

b.
26, Queen Square,
Bloomsbury, London
December 27, 1877

Dear Mrs. Holiday

I send a hank of the pink wh: is right, & also 1 of blue wh: is near, & I think would do: I will see to the green at once. I am so sorry to hear that you have been ill: I am afraid that this cold weather, bright as it is will scarcely suit you.

Please thank Winny[1] for writing & excuse haste.

Yours very truly
William Morris

MS: Berger Coll.

[1] Winifred Holiday, daughter of Catherine and Henry Holiday. See letter no. 474.

473 • To Jane Morris
Queen Sq:
December 28, 1877

Dearest Janey

I have just sent the £60 to Mr. Congreve[1] & told him to keep the £28. I cannot help being depressed by what you say about Jenny: but it is too late to regret that you settled to go; & I do hope it will do you all good in the end: I am dull enough sometimes without you on the very few occasions when I have anything to think of except my work of some sort or other.

I was at mother's on Tuesday & Wednesday, the weather very bright & cold: company the Edgars & the Gilmores & poor Ada:[2] who by the by is really improved. Mother seemed very well indeed. We are still in a state of stew over the plot of 'the heart of a woman, (he might have said an old & ugly woman), & the head of an aged statesman', as Mr. J. Lemoine has it:[3] but I do hope that we shall get free from our fear this time.

However, the E.Q.A. is stirring a little, & perhaps next week we shall have a row.[4]

I am really sorry you find the weather so Icelandic at Oneglia: I tried to chaff Ned on that subject: but he was equal to the occasion & said he had always told me that the winter was colder in Italy than in England. I hope you wrap up well & have really warm things.

[427]

I am going to have a quiet evening over the proofs of my last lecture.[5] And then I must set to at the next,[6] wh: is much harder to do really. I enclose 3 notes for Jenny — Xmas cards I suspect: I am sick of that useless form of industry.

Annie Catherwood[7] I am told spent her Xmasday at the Grange, where she was very lively: Ned confides to me that he was not: I for my part decidedly enjoyed the country; it was so bright: only — let me confess & be hanged — I drank 2 glasses of port wine on Xmas day, & on the next morning there were signs of the toe-devil, & I had in my terror to fast more on the day after Xmas than Henrietta fasted on the day before: owing to which I am all right, and I had a very tolerable day after all, doing nothing but a very little walk to Mrs. Cornwalls farm. Also Isabella cut my hair in your absence with much success.

Mind and buy warm wraps against next month — Give my best love to those dear babes, & I am

Your loving

W.M.

MS: BL, Add. MSS. 45338. Published: Henderson, *Letters*, 105.

[1] See letters no. 433, n. 2 and no. 477.

[2] Ada Morris was one of the eight children of Thomas Rendall Morris. After his early death, the children were looked after by their aunt and uncle, Isabella and Archibald Gilmore. I am grateful to Miss Norah Gillow, Keeper of the William Morris Gallery, for this information.

[3] John Emile Lemoinne (1815-1892), a French journalist born in London. The references are to Queen Victoria and Disraeli.

[4] This may be a reference to a meeting held by the Chichester Association on January 7, 1878, at which Morris delivered a speech, "Address to English Liberals." (See letter no. 476; see also LeMire, p. 235.) However, there were meetings being held every day, all over the country, and Morris may be referring to a different one. A large meeting, for example, was held at Hawkstone-Hall, Westminster on January 7.

[5] See letter no. 464, n. 1.

[6] Possibly the "Address to English Liberals" (see n. 4, above) delivered before the Chichester Liberal Association, or a speech on the opening of the Dardanelles, delivered for the E.Q.A. at Willis's Rooms, London, on January 16, 1878. See LeMire, p. 235.

[7] Burne-Jones's aunt, his father's only sister, married James Catherwood in 1848. See *Memorials*, I, 31-33, 60.

474 · TO WINIFRED HOLIDAY 26, Queen Square,
London, W.C.
January 1, 1878

My dear Winny

Thank you for your letter: I see no objection to the outlining done in the clever way I have no doubt your Mama will do it in; and it certainly makes a very solid piece of work. I think a little variety in the colour of the veining, by using other yellows or the coppery pink, of which some has got into the trial and even perhaps white would be good in this piece.

I am very sorry to hear that your Mama is still so unwell: pray give her my kindest regards.

> I am
> Yours faithfully
> William Morris

MS: Berger Coll.

475 · To Thomas Wardle

26, Queen Square,
Bloomsbury, London
January 1, 1878

My dear Wardle

Many thanks for your note & kind invitation, which I shall be very glad to avail myself of in 2 or 3 weeks if it is still convenient to you: I am very anxious to see the tapestry in work & to try how I can manage it: I will bring down Boyce's specimen when I come: it is in all respects good & fit for talking over: also I want my Iceland wool tried on a rug: I will take the greatest pains in designing one when the frame is ready.

Bazin is beginning the coloured brocade today; I feel a little nervous about the result. He shot a little of that very uneven blue tram into the last warp: the result was encouraging; for I could not see that the unevenness mattered at all: this last fact may console you for the blue order we are giving you: G[eorge] W[ardle] is sending my memo: on it: *please* do it for us speedily: for our reputation depends on it.

I am still very nervous about this confounded war-fever: to hear people talk in London one would think it was a mere nothing for us to go into a big war: the course of which who can foresee?

I am getting my lecture No 1 printed,[1] I will send you a copy in a day or two: if you can supply me with the facts as to — how shall I put it? — the *improvement* of some other class of goods I will put an allusion to it in the place of 'heavy blacks' — this as showing my good-will to the good town of Leek.

As to yourself I send you all good wishes for you & yours and am

> Yours very truly
> William Morris

MS: Duke. Copy in V&A.
[1] See letter no. 464, n. 1.

476 · To Jenny Morris

26, Queen Square,
Bloomsbury, London
January 4, 1878

Dearest Jenny

As this is a sort of New Years Day letter I am writing to May as well: I have written what may be called the domestic news to her, & so here goes for politics to you: The last few days have been anxious, nobody knowing anything as to what was going on: today things look better; for Lord Carnarvon[1] has spoken to a deputation, who came to him about African matters, both sensibly and well, as you will see when you get the papers;[2] which will also tell you how the Russians have refused our mediation:[3] you may fancy how the wretches of the Telegraph tried to whip up public opinion about that: but the Globe & Standard are both moderate: nevertheless we are *all* of opinion that we must go on agitating: personally I don't like it; for I have found myself pledged to go to Chichester on Monday to speak at a Liberal Association:[4] I have spent the whole morning at Broadhursts & am to go there tomorrow also: for we are going to hold a great meeting on the 16th in conjunction with a working-man's committee:[5] you see we want to finish with them for good & all this time: 'tis as bad as the Russians over Kars:[6] are we always to be liking it?

The Trafalgar Sq: last Saturday was disgracefully reported by the Daily News: the Times was much better about it:[7] it was a glorious victory for us: though I believe some blood was shed (from noses): the enemy had spent huge time & trouble & plenty of money all to be spoilt in the end. I was not there, but Faulkner was, & one or two of our Committee went to look on. I am really beginning to hope that Disraeli will be kicked out this time; but am afraid that he will draw back, and say he meant nothing: you may be sure that the Empress Brown[8] has a great deal to do with it all: what a rage she will be in! For I really cannot think that the country will go to war when all is said: it would be too monstrous: the London working men have now got their backs well up on our side.

Lo here a long letter all about politics   there are other scraps of news in Mays letter. Goodbye my dear.

Your loving father
William Morris

ms: BL, Add. mss. 45339. Published: MM, II, 68; Henderson, *Letters*, 106.

[1] Henry Howard Molyneux Herbert, fourth Earl of Carnarvon (1831-1890), Colonial Secretary in Disraeli's second administration, 1874-1878. See Arthur Hardinge, *The Life of Henry Howard Molyneux Herbert*, ed. Elisabeth Countess of Carnarvon (Oxford: Oxford Univ. Press, 1925).

² *The Times*, January 3, 1878, reported (p. 10) that Lord Carnarvon had assured a deputation of merchants of support against "native uprisings." He also spoke of the Eastern Question and said that the Government's attitude was "neutral as regards the belligerents." Morris here passed over the subject of "African matters," and Carnarvon's assurance of support against native uprisings seems not to have offended him. This apparent lack of interest in imperialism in Africa was to change by the time of the Sudanese War. See letters to May Morris, February 20, 1885 and J. Mavor, March 27, 1885.

³ In December 1877, the Sultan had appealed, without success, for the intervention of the Powers. He then appealed to the British Government, and on December 27, Lord Derby instructed Lord Augustus, Ambassador to Russia, to offer Britain's good offices. However, the offer was refused by the Russian Government (see Seton-Watson, *Disraeli*, p. 247-48). In *The Times*, January 2, 1878, the correspondent in St. Petersburg wrote (p. 5) that the Russian Government was favorably disposed to peace proposals but insisted "that they should come directly from the Porte in the usual way."

⁴ On January 7, 1878, Morris gave his "Address to English Liberals." See LeMire, p. 235.

⁵ Henry Broadhurst had organized a workmen's committee to participate in the Eastern Question Association. He was in charge of organizing the large public meeting held in Exeter Hall on January 16, 1878. See Broadhurst, pp. 79-84.

⁶ A Turkish fort captured by the Russians during the Crimean War and exchanged for the Crimea in the negotiations in 1856 ending the war.

⁷ See letter no. 470, n. 4.

⁸ See letter no. 477.

477 • TO MAY MORRIS   26, Queen Square,
                                            Bloomsbury, London
                                            January 4, 1878

Dearest May

Why don't you go a donkey riding with the others then, & what do you do with yourself? As you see I did not have a bad Christmas-day on the whole though I miss you very much my dears   I am busy indeed with the E Q.A. I will refer you to Jenny's letter for political news so that I may not make both my letters alike as I am writing to her as well

Do you know that the Widow Guelph is setting up a stained-glass manufacture as well as a tapestry one?¹ Old Mrs. De Morgan² calls her the Empress Brown;³ which seems to me funny as I hope it will to Mama: about 3 weeks ago I spent a whole evening at the De Morgans, & found Mrs. De Morgan very nice & talkative: I like her very much.

I hope you lost the 9 francs again very soon, or gave it away or spent it? By the way *can* one spend money at Oneglia, except in (thrifty) victuals & drink? Tell Mama that I think I had better send her a filter & then I could send one for the Howards also in the same parcel: I have sent her the money & got an acknowledgement from Mr. Congreve.⁴

Aunt Georgie Phil & Margery went off on Tuesday to spend 10 days with Mrs. Wyndham at Wilbury:[5] fancy her being at a tory house at this crisis!

This is a short letter but I am so busy: Please give best love to Mama & tell her I scarcely know how to stay at home if it were not for the work.

Froggy Bazin began the new piece of brocade yesterday: it looks very well; but quite different as to the ground from what I expected.

I am
Your loving father
William Morris

MS: BL, Add. MSS. 45341. Published: *CW*, 13, xxii.

[1] See letter no. 445, n. 2.

[2] Sophia Elizabeth Frend De Morgan (1809-1892), William De Morgan's mother. She was an early advocate of women's suffrage and an active promoter of higher education for women. Her books include *Memoir of Augustus De Morgan by His Wife, with Selections from His Letters*; a book on spiritualism, *From Matter to Spirit*; and her own memoirs, *Threescore and Ten*, edited by her daughter Mary.

[3] John Brown (1826-1883), the Queen's Highland servant, had reputedly become Queen Victoria's lover. (See Tom Cullen, *The Empress Brown* [London: The Bodley Head], 1969). Cullen writes (p. 21) that "Morris and William De Morgan . . . disputed the credit for first having thought up the title." E. P. Thompson ascribes the epithet to William De Morgan (2nd ed., p. 216). It would appear from this letter, however, that Sophia De Morgan thought it up.

[4] See letter no. 433, n. 2.

[5] Wilbury House, near Salisbury, home of Percy Scawen Wyndham (1835-1911) and his wife Madeline Caroline Eden (d.1920), for whom Philip Webb built Clouds. Wyndham was Conservative M.P. for West Cumberland from 1860 to 1885, a protectionist, and outspoken on the Eastern Question. See *The Times*, March 14, 1911, p. 11. Wilbury House is described in Nikolaus Pevsner, *The Buildings of Britain: Wiltshire* (Penguin, 1963), pp. 510-11. Clouds was begun in 1877 but was not completed until 1886; three years later it was destroyed by fire.

478 • TO AUBERON EDWARD WILLIAM MOLYNEUX HERBERT

26 Queen Sq: W.C.
January 6, 1878

Dear Sir[1]

Thanks for your letter: in these days, when things shift with such strange quickness, advice soon becomes out of date, & I daresay mine is so already: anyhow who can say what will have happened before next Wednesday week.

Meantime since you have issued your tickets & advertized the meeting[2] I do not see how you can draw back now: I have asked all my friends to attend; but they are not many: I may be able to get rid of a few more tickets usefully: will you please send me ½ a dozen more. I hope you will get some good speakers; and again be careful to whom you give your tickets.

I don't suppose that the meeting will do any harm to ours in the evening,[3] wh: I hope everybody will attend who wishes well to the cause, as it will be I think an important one.

Yours truly
William Morris

MS: Schimmel Coll.

[1] Auberon E.W.M. Herbert (1838-1906), brother of the fourth Earl of Carnarvon. A political theorist, he was originally a Conservative but became a Liberal M.P. for Nottingham, 1870-1874. In 1872, he declared himself a republican and was later to champion Charles Bradlaugh, become a disciple of Herbert Spencer, and profess agnosticism. He also took a strong interest in the labor movement. In 1884, he published *A Politician in Trouble with His Soul*, and in 1890 launched a periodical called *Organ of Voluntary Taxation* as a continuing forum for his economic theories.

[2] A committee had been formed to promote free navigation through the Dardanelles, and a meeting had been called for January 16. Members of the committee were E. A. Freeman, the Rev. Cannon Liddon, Dr. Humphrey Sandwith, Auberon Herbert, and C. E. Maurice, who was the Honorary Secretary (see G. C. Thompson, II, 284). At the meeting, Morris delivered a speech on the "Opening of the Dardanelles." See LeMire, p. 235.

[3] A meeting of workingmen, held at Exeter Hall, "to protest against England being dragged into war." See *The Times*, January 17, 1878, p. 6. A. J. Mundella was president and among those on the platform were Morris, Lord Granville, Auberon Herbert, I. Lowthian Bell, Joseph Arch, and F. W. Chesson.

479 • TO JENNY MORRIS

26, Queen Square,
Bloomsbury, London
January 14, 1878

Dearest Jenny

I thank you & May for your dear little letters; & now I am writing a line to send you my very best love which I hope you will get on your birthday, my dear, and I wish you may always be as happy as a bird. I think I had better keep my present for you till I come out; for like enough we might covet something in Genoa or Florence mightn't we? I daresay you will not think it too shabby of me to write a hurried letter, because you may well imagine what a busy time I am having of it with the Dardenelles Meeting coming off on the afternoon of the same day that the big meeting does:[1] I am to speak at the Dardenelles one: it will be but a little meeting I fear: indeed we most of us thought it would be better to put it off a bit: but Mr. Howard will know what an obstinate man Mr. Auberon Herbert is — & so we have to do our best. Things still look very serious: on Saturday morning we had another scare, after they had looked quieter through the week. This morning there is nothing new. You will see the account of the lecture the Turks had at St James Hall on Thursday: and about the Duke of Sutherland's speech, wh: everybody is laughing at so:[2] also the Morning Post had an article saying that the Russians took the Shipka Pass by treachery.[3]

So much for the '*poor*' Turks as their friends call them now. I am just going in to the Faulkners Kate is better, I think. I am sorry I am obliged to hurry so: please give best love to Mama & May, & my dear once more I send you my very best love to yourself as you well know.

Your loving father
William Morris

MS: BL, Add. MSS. 45339. Published: MM, II, 569.

¹ See letter no. 478, notes 2 and 3.

² *The Times*, January 11, 1878, reported (p. 8) that on January 10, the Duke of Sutherland had presided at a meeting at which A. Bothwick had given a lecture entitled "The Eastern Question." In proposing a vote of thanks to the lecturer, *The Times* continued, the Duke of Sutherland spoke of "the wonderful way in which the Russians worked their agents. . . . [T]heir mode of procedure was like that of a snake which licked its victim all over before he swallowed it. Now the agents chosen in this country were Mr. Gladstone, and General Ignatieff, and when he mentioned Mr. Gladstone of course he included a couple of dukes, a marquis, an officer of the army, and a number of clergymen who travelled with their eyes in their pockets."

³ On January 9, 1878, the Russians took Shipka Pass and the Turks retreated in disorder. There was panic in Constantinople and the Sultan asked for an armistice. See Seton-Watson, *Disraeli*, p. 263.

480 • TO JANE MORRIS
26, Queen Square,
Bloomsbury, London
January 19, 1878

Dearest Janey

I am so glad of your news being good: I *will* write to you this time in spite of the babes: 'tis May's turn next, I think. Now I'll tell you all about things as well as a short letter may do.

The Agitation is over for the present I suppose: Parliament has met: the Queen's speech was the usual shilly shally, but hinted at asking for money ⟨&⟩ wh: everybody thought would be asked for; but Northcote[1] in answer to Hartington[2] said they would not ask for the money till, 'unexpected events' happened: Dizzy's speech was angry but perfectly empty: Argyle[3] made a very good & determined speech; so that I think the liberals will vote against the money if it *is* asked for: which I don't think it will be unless any really unexpected event should change the general views of the country: there lies the danger: what one fears is that Dizzy has bidden the Turks *not* to make peace, but to draw on the Russians to Constantinople: I confess I fear the effect of a Russian siege of that city on the *ignorant* public; and meantime we expect every day to hear of the Russians at Adrianople. There is no doubt that the last fortnight's agitation has stopped Dizzy from asking for money & proposing a Gallipoli Expedition: that is to say from proposing immediate war: this is encouraging: but the danger will not be over till peace is signed. As to the agitation: I must confess I have been agitated as well as agitating: you will have got the newspapers by this time with a sort of report of our proceedings including the speech of me, & its — may I call it amicable indiscretion:[4] of course I said more, & more connected words than that: the little meeting was very noisy, but I call it a success considering the slight care with which it was got up: at least it quite refused to cheer the Empress Brown: you see I had to speak at the end by wh: time the peace-party desired to fight for peace, & the war-party was blue with rage. The evening meeting was magnificent:[5] orderly and enthusiastic; though mind you, it took some very heavy work to keep the enemies roughs out; and the noise of them outside was like the sea roaring against a lighthouse; and though the overflow meeting at Trafalgar Sq: was in our favour on the whole, yet there was opposition there also:[6] you will have seen about our music: wasn't it a good idea? I think Chesson suggested it first, & then they set me to write the song, wh: I did on the Monday night.[7] It went down very well, & they sang it well together: they struck up while we were just ready to come on to the platform & you may imagine I felt rather excited when I heard them begin to tune up: they stopped at the end of each verse and cheered lustily: we came on to the platform just about the middle of it. Mundella made a first-rate chairman, & the speaking was much above the average: and the opposition *inside* was so small as to be quite insignificant, & even that soon got cowed into silence. I send you enclose 3 'London Lads':[8] I have a bundle here, & if you want more for the Howards I will send on again.

I am very tired with it and shall enjoy a week of dyeing & designing next week if Dizzy will let me have it. I am sorry to hear that Sarah is lonely: I bid her to go out every Sunday: & next Thursday I am going to give a dinner party. Webb Vinal[9] & Wardle.

I have had a nice little letter from May: give my best love to them both, & take it yourself.

Your loving
W.M.

Of course dear Jenny has got my letter.

MS: BL, Add. MSS. 45338. Published: MM, II, 570-72; Henderson, *Letters*, 106-108. Extract published: Mackail, I, 361.

¹ See letter no. 482, n. 2.

² See letter no. 422, n. 7.

³ George Douglas Campbell. He opposed the Conservative government's policy on the Eastern Question. See letter no. 420, n. 1.

⁴ On January 17, *The Times* report of the meeting held the previous day included (p. 6) the following paragraph: "Mr. W. Morris spoke in strong terms against the 'war-at-any-price-party'. . . . He praised Gladstone (Three cheers were heartily given, while in response to a similar call in the case of Lord Beaconsfield . . . cheers mingled with hisses). . . . He . . . also [said] . . . that the Court was using all [its] influence . . . (Cries of 'No, no,' and 'Three cheers for the Queen'). [Morris then being] reminded by the chairman that it was undesirable in a Constitutional country in which Ministers were responsible to the people to introduce the name of the Sovereign into political discussions, he concluded by expressing his regret that fortune had placed at the head of affairs in England a man without genius (Cries of 'Oh! Oh!'), but only a galvanic imitation of it, to whose shiftiness the nation . . . must oppose a steady resistance. (Renewed cries of 'Oh, oh')."

⁵ See letter no. 478, n. 3.

⁶ The account in *The Times*, January 17, said (p. 6) that an overflow meeting was arranged for later in the night, in Trafalgar Square, but that the meeting became a scene of conflict between the workingmen's "neutrality" party and "a numerous Turkophile contingent."

⁷ Broadhurst says (p. 81) that Morris wrote the song at his suggestion and that it was intended as a prelude to the chairman's address at the meeting.

⁸ The verses were as follows.

1. Wake, London Lads, wake, bold and free!
        Arise, and fall to work,
    Lest England's glory come to be
        Bond-servant to the Turk!
    Think of your Sires! how oft and oft
        On freedom's field they bled,
    When Cromwell's hand was raised aloft,
        And Kings and scoundrels fled.

2. From out the dusk, from out the dark,
        Of old our fathers came,
    Till lovely freedom's glimmering spark
        Broke forth a glorious flame:
    And shall we now praise freedom's dearth
        And rob the years to come,
    And quench upon a brother's hearth
        The fires we lit at home?

3. O, happy England, if thine hand
 Should forge anew the chain,
The fetters of a tortured land,
 How were thy glory vain!
Our starving men, our women's tears,
 The graves of those we love,
Should buy us curses for all years,
 A weight we might not move.

4. Yea, through the fog of unjust war
 What thief on us might steal,
To rob us of the gifts of yore,
 The hope of England's weal?
The toilsome years have built and earned,
 Great men in hope have died;
Shall all the lesson be unlearned,
 The treasure scattered wide?

5. What! shall we crouch beneath the load,
 And call the labour sweet,
And, dumb and blind, go down the road
 Where shame abides our feet?
Wake, London Lads! the hour draws nigh,
 The bright sun brings the day;
Cast off the shame, cast off the lie,
 And cast the Turk away!

⁹ Possibly C. G. Vinall, one of the three Honorary Secretaries of the S.P.A.B.

481 · To William Bell Scott   26, Queen Square,
                                                  Bloomsbury, London
                                                  January 19, 1878

My dear Scott

I enclose 6 London Lads:¹ the singing went off very well on Wednesday & the whole meeting was a great success: there is no doubt of the political working man being with us.

Many thanks for your kind word about my speech: at any rate I got it out, however *indiscreet* it was: Please to remember that the meeting did *not* cheer the Queen after all.² I do not feel easy about the present state of things; but I suppose we must wait till the enemy makes the next move before we can do anything else.

                                                  Yrs Ever
                                                  William Morris

MS: UBC, Penkill Papers.
 ¹ See letter no. 480 and its n. 8.
 ² See letter no. 480, n. 4.

482 • To Mary Katherine Stanley [January 26, 1878?]

Dear Lady Stanley[1]

Many thanks for your note & enclosure: I am afraid if 'tis true that the very Gods fight in vain against stupidity, we stand but small chance against Northcote:[2] otherwise I cannot believe that the nation can long put up with such blatant rubbish: I must needs hope for the best.

Yours very truly
William Morris

 MS: Howard Papers.

[1] Mary Katherine Stanley (1848-1929), daughter of Sir Isaac Lowthian Bell and wife of Edward Lyulph Stanley, Rosalind Howard's brother.

[2] Sir Stafford Henry Northcote (1818-1887), first Earl of Iddesleigh. Private secretary to Gladstone, 1842, and a Conservative M.P. from 1855-1885, he became an important speaker for the opposition and a close associate of Disraeli. He was commissioner for settlement of the Alabama Claims, 1871, Chancellor of the Exchequer, 1874-1880, and leader of the Conservative Party in the House of Commons, 1876-1885, after which he sat in the House of Lords.

483 • To May Morris

26, Queen Square,
Bloomsbury, London
January 26, 1878

Dearest May

Things have changed again since I wrote last: Yesterday morning *everybody* thought that the game was up and we were sure of war. Lords Carnarvon[1] & Derby had resigned: the fleet was ordered to Constantinople & Northcote announced that he was going to ask for money; while Dizzy made a disgraceful booming[?] speech:[2] today things seem more hopeful again: the Porte has accepted the terms of the armistice.[3] Lord Carnavon spoke very well in the House last night, & Dizzy prevaricated: the Tories meantime are trying to keep Lord Derby in; and he is a poor creature and will probably yield: the Liberals will certainly resist the vote of credit: (six millions). The Fleet has been ordered back to Besika Bay but I see this afternoon's newspaper posters have up that it has entered the Dardanelles: in that case there must have been some very foul play: but I can scarcely believe it. I have been all the morning at a committee meeting of the E.Q.A.[4] where we were passing resolutions to be published on Monday: what this means in a full committee Mr. Howard will very well know. & what a job ⟨that means⟩ it was Nobody can tell how it will all end: the government have behaved disgracefully: they are all liars except Lord Carnarvon: we are not planning any big meeting yet, though what Monday may bring no one can tell: we are anxious enough, but not dispirited. I havn't heard from any of you for some time past: I hope you are allright: the weather here, which has been very warm & muggy, has now turned bright and cold.

Love to you all, my dear: & don't work too hard at your play-acting, though it be Larx: I was reading Joe & Pip aloud at the Grange last night.

Your loving father
William Morris

MS: Bentham Coll.

¹ See letter no. 476, n. 1.

² *The Times*, January 26, reported (p. 6) Disraeli's denial that sending the fleet to the Dardanelles signified a violation of neutrality. In answering Lord Carnarvon, however, he said that the occupation of Constantinople by the Russians would not be viewed by the British with indifference.

³ See letter no. 479, n. 3. See also Seton-Watson, *Disraeli*, p. 264.

⁴ *The Times*, January 28, 1878, reported (p. 10) that a meeting of the E.Q.A. had been held on Saturday (January 26) with A. J. Mundella in the chair. The meeting, in essence, continued to protest against the Government's request for a six-million-pound military appropriation.

484 • RECIPIENT UNKNOWN

26 Queen Sq
Bloomsbury WC
January 30, 1878

Dear Sir¹

I thank you very much for the honour you offer me, and I ⟨am⟩ accept it with pleasure if it does not involve my giving my address within the next week or so, as I am very busy with all sorts of work, that will not be delayed.

Meantime pray believe that if I can be of any use to such an important & interesting community as yours I shall consider myself well rewarded for any trouble I may have to take in the matter.

I am
Dear Sir
Yours faithfully
William Morris

MS: Monterey.

¹ This letter may have been addressed to John Henry Chamberlain (1831-1883), chairman of the Birmingham Society of Arts, and is possibly a reply to an invitation to be its president. (See letter no. 498.) On February 2, 1879, Morris gave a lecture, "On the Art of the People," as the annual presidential address. See LeMire, p. 235.

485 • To SIDNEY COLVIN   26 Queen Sq:
                                             January 30, 1878

My dear Colvin[1]

I fear it is quite impossible at present: I am (alas!) on the stump po-
litical whether I like it better or worse; and I can't help thinking that
next week will be a stormy one: and if things go wrong I shall to speak
seriously be in no heart to do anything but the most hum-drum part of
my necessary business: in which to say the truth I am grievously behind
hand at present:

I am very sorry: for I should have liked to have been of any use (as
small as it might be) to your school & scholars.[2]

                                             Yours very truly
                                             William Morris

MS: Bodleian.

  [1] See letter no. 114, n. 1.

  [2] Colvin had asked Morris to speak at the distribution of prizes at the Cambridge School
of Art on February 21. Although Morris declined the invitation in this letter, two days
later he changed his mind (see next letter). For the text of Morris's address, see *The
Cambridge Chronicle and University Journal*, February 23, 1878, p. 4. See also LeMire, p.
235.

486 • To SIDNEY COLVIN   26 Queen Sq
                                             February 1 [1878]

My dear Colvin

Many thanks for your kind note: I should feel ashamed at having to
be pressed to do what will be but little service to you; only I am really
hard at work at anti–Dizzy, & cannot even insure myself against black
eyes: I attended a market for that commodity last night, but happily
came away without them. Any how I will come on the 20 or 21st by
which time if all is not over one way or other, there will at least be a
lull.

I am sadly afraid you rather underestimate the danger of war: the 2
parties are now distinctly face to face on the matter; and I must with
grief say, that I rather more than doubt that the counting of heads ⟨wou⟩
in the country would go for peace: this would not matter if a tolerably
peaceful cabinet were in power: but I am *sure* that the cabinet, or if you
will Dizzy & the Rump plus the 'Empress Brown' are fully determined
to have war if they can: however events move very quickly nowadays

and an hour or two may prove me wrong, as I devoutly hope it may.
Please tell me all I am to do at this affair.

Yours very truly
William Morris

MS: Trinity College.

---

487 • To George James Howard   Queen Sq:
                                            February 1 [1878]

My dear George

Many thanks for your letter. I have just been conning[?] the begin-
ning of the great debate: I need only note that the stock-exchange anti-
Russianism seems to have got into the blameless Cross:[1] people think
the division will come off on Tuesday, & Chesson tells me positively
that some few of the liberal M.P.s will still go on opposing in Com-
mittee; so that 'tis hoped it will be a fortnight before the whole thing is
over. I hope things will change before then: for at present they look
very black, and not only to me I must tell you. In the first place if ever
we indulged in the idea that the anti-war party were in the majority,
(as you know I never did) that idea is now fading away: if as I suppose
he will, the beast Dizzy makes up his mind to war, I am sorry to have
to say, that he may fairly ⟨say⟩ claim to have the majority of the English
people with him: I am sure we shall only be kept out of war (if at all)
by what happens out of England.

As to our agitation, on Tuesday night we took a bad beating at Shef-
field:[2] the Tories in the house were all cock-a-hoop over it: this is a *very*
serious affair, and I am afraid will stimulate war meetings widely: yes-
terday was a stormy day: the stock exchange blackguards plus some
imported roughs stopped (before it began) poor Mr. Merriman's[3] meet-
ing on our side, made a regular riot outside the Cannon St Hotel & then
went to the Guild-hall, where they had it all their own way.[4]

In the evening I went to a meeting at Stepney, a biggish meeting of
quite 1000: Tom Hughes in the chair: it was managed badly, & turned
out a bear-garden;[5] no human being could be heard; no pretence was
made to listen to either resolutions or amendment: the resolutions were
declared carried, and after some rather poor fisticuff work, our quiet
non-coms[?] having retired we were obliged to leave the hall (at 10
P.M.) in possession of the malcontents: all this however is small detail,

[441]

but I hear just now that the City business was serious, and was managed regardless of expenses.

We have a committee meeting for next Monday, & meantime have just held an informal meeting at Broadhurst's rooms (some of us) and to say the truth we are floundering rather: between ourselves Mundella is rather cowed by that Sheffield meeting: and is afraid of most things — Still I hope something will be done — if the Gov: make any overt act — I truly hope it wont be too late — The great shaft in our quiver is a *great* demonstration in Hyde Park:[6] Howell[7] & Broadhurst say they can make it sure if money does not lack, and that I think we are sure of.

I wont pay you the bad compliment of saying your absence don't matter, which is in fact far from true.

I hope I shall be able to come over while you are still there, & that all these troubles will be behind us then.

Yours affectionately
William Morris

MS: Howard Papers.

[1] Richard Assheton Cross (1823-1914), Home Secretary from 1874 to 1880. Previously considered a moderate, he had begun to criticize the parliamentary opponents of the Government's Russian policy. See Seton-Watson, *Disraeli* p. 306.

[2] *The Times*, January 30, 1878, reported (p. 10) that a meeting had been held in Paradise Square, Sheffield, the previous day to consider the Government's war vote and to pass a resolution on the Eastern Question. There was a large crowd, and the proceedings were disorderly. Eventually a resolution was passed requesting the House of Commons to reject the proposal that six million pounds be voted for military preparation.

[3] J. J. Merriman, a solicitor, and chairman of the executive committee of the City Conference in Favour of Peace and Neutrality.

[4] *The Times*, February 1, 1878, reported (p. 12) that on the previous afternoon a meeting in the neighborhood of Cannon Street had been called by the City Neutrality Committee "to protest against the vote of six millions for War purposes." In the Cannon Street Hotel, a meeting of the City Liberal Club was disrupted by " 'Conservative workingmen' and other Conservative organizations." Later, the demonstrators went to the Guildhall, where they formed themselves into a meeting of Conservatives, presided over by the Lord Mayor (who had joined them), to express confidence in the Government.

[5] *The Times*, February 1, 1878, reported (p. 12) that "a very turbulent meeting was held last night in the Stepney School-hall, Stepney-green. Mr. Thomas Hughes, Q.C. [1822-1896, author of *Tom Brown's Schooldays*] presided. A resolution in opposition to the vote of credit was carried amid great uproar."

[6] This may refer to a meeting planned for Hyde Park on Sunday, February 24, which was organized by Auberon Herbert and Charles Bradlaugh, Broadhurst having dissociated himself from a Sunday meeting.

[7] See letter no. 402, n. 4.

488 • To Jane Morris   Queen Sq:
                                                           February 1 [1878]

Dearest Janey

I write just a short line to say that I am all right; safe in wind and
limb, and not very likely to risk either at present; though I was at a
very noisy meeting last night down at Stepney, where we had a bare
majority: I have been writing to G. Howard today about the 'situation':
I must say I feel gloomy enough about it, though I cannot suppose it is
hopeless: meantime our people are much dispirited with the defeat at
Sheffield, and the row yesterday in the city, at which latter place there
were some 7000 people they behaved very disgracefully, as you will
see in the newspapers: they had 400 roughs down in waggons from
Woolich Dockyard, & generally played the gooseberry: people on our
side had to hide away in cellars & places & get out anyhow: all of this
is very enraging, & I am beginning to say, well if they will have war
let them fill their bellies with it then! However perhaps the Government
don't mean so much as they seem to mean: it may be bluster to satisfy
the rump in and out of parliament. I feel very low & muddled about it
all: but we have one shot in the locker yet, to whit, a big, *a real big*
demonstration in Hyde Park; which however is both expensive & dan-
gerous; especially in England, where it sometimes rains.[1]

I hope you are having better weather and also that you are all better
yourselves: I was very glad to hear good news of Jenny: did she get my
letter on her birthday? Would she like any book sent out to her there
do you think? She hasn't written to me for ever such a time:

All private matters going well

Best love to babies my dear

Goodbye.

                                        Your loving
                                        W.M.

MS: BL, Add. MSS. 45338. Published: Henderson, *Letters*, 108–109. Extract published: MM,
II, 573.

    [1] See notes to letter no. 487 for details of meetings mentioned by Morris here.

489 • To Jane Morris   Queen Sq:
                                                           February 4, 1878

Dearest Janey

I send the tea, 2 lb thereof by post; wh: is expensive but it don't
matter:

I am very well; but still anxious work it is: though the news this morning is that the armistice is signed at last:[1] the fact is that the liberal party are funking, owing to the Tory successes against our meetings: I was at a committee-meeting this morning where I must say our counsels were perplexed: I can only say one must be patient, and hope; but I for one feel very bitter & angry.

It must be said that the debate *ought* to be very damaging to their (the Tory) cause: they have not a word to say: scarcely even lies: the debate will end on Thursday;[2] but I fear our friends durst not *obstruct*, and of course the government will have a large majority.

And after all if the country will have war, let it, and try a little ruin for the purging of its folly.

I shall write to Jenny in a day or two: best love to them & you: I am very busy.

Your loving
W.M.

MS: BL, Add. MSS. 45338. Extract published: Henderson, *Letters*, p. 109.

[1] On January 31, 1878, Turkey and Russia signed an armistice at Adrianople.

[2] The parliamentary debate over the request by Disraeli for six million pounds for military preparations.

490 • FROM A LETTER TO CHARLES JAMES FAULKNER   February 5, 1878

I am full of shame and anger at the cowardice of the so-called Liberal party. A very few righteous men refuse to sit down at the bidding of these yelling scoundrels and pretend to agree with what they hate: these few are determined with the help of our working-men allies (who all along have been both staunch and sagacious) to get up a great demonstration in London as soon as may be, which will probably be Saturday week.[1] There will certainly be a fight, so of course you will come up if you can.

TEXT: Mackail, I, 361. Published: Henderson, *Letters*, 109.

[1] The demonstration was held in Hyde Park on February 24, a Sunday. It was planned by delegates of workmen's clubs, trade societies, and political societies who met on February 15 with Auberon Herbert as chairman. (See *The Times*, February 16, p. 5.) For a report of the demonstration, see the *Daily News*, February 25, 1878, p. 10. See also letter no. 498.

491 • To Aglaia Ionides Coronio
Monday
[February 11?, 1878]

My dear Aglaia

I heard something of what I was very sorry to hear from your letter, from Ned the other day; & I should have written at once, only I thought you would like to tell me yourself before I said anything about it. I am really very much grieved that you should be in trouble, though my ignorance of City business keeps me from knowing how serious the matter may be. I shall not be able to dine with Aleco[1] on Thursday next, as it is Anti-scrape again,[2] and I must not miss it this time as I did last: but I could call in on the afternoon towards the end of the week probably: say Friday?

I find no one seems confident, or other than anxious about matters, in spite of the armistice being signed — who can trust such a pack of liars as our government are?

Yours affectionately
William Morris

MS: Yates Coll.

[1] Alexander Ionides, Aglaia Coronio's younger brother.

[2] The S.P.A.B. met twice monthly, the first meeting usually being held in the middle of the month. This suggests that the date of the meeting to which Morris refers may have been February 14 and that this letter therefore may have been written on February 11.

492 • To Jenny Morris
Horrington House
February 11 [1878]

Dearest Jenny

I do not think you naughty for not having written before; in fact I am glad that you have plenty to do, & havn't so much time for letters: you see with us here, there are so many and such great events crammed into a short space, that the time seems long: the past week, as you will see by the papers, has been a very agitating one: on Monday (this day last week) there was a meeting of the E.Q.A.[1] & it was obvious that our party in Parliament were getting out of heart: so some of us conscious how dangerous things were getting, met at Mr. Broadhursts & talked about holding a great demonstration in Hyde Park to keep up their spirits: I set off with Mr. Auberon Herbert to beg money for it to S. Morley's[2] a big merchant in the city, & then we went to the house of Commons & beset members in the lobby, which we had to do on the Wednesday again: on that day the Tories had a meeting in Exeter Hall, wh: turned out a very poor affair, the room only 2 thirds full &

plenty of opposition:[3] on Thursday morning I went to Auberon Herberts, & we concocted an address for the meeting; but lo as we came into the Strand in the afternoon the newspapers had in them, 'The Russians in Constantinople & Gallipoli': here was a spoke in our wheel! no one talked of anything else that evening: I heard that the confusion in the H of Commons was beyond everything; that [it] was like a French revolutionary assembly: Mr. Foster, as you know withdrew his amendment, & only 96 liberals voted against the money vote: many people thought that war would be declared in a few hours.[4] But next day (Friday) things looked much better, & our people began to pluck up heart again: in the evening I was at a meeting of the ⟨Committee of the⟩ Workmans Neutrality Committee,[5] & the meeting, about 50 people, went as a deputation to the House to thank the 96: we were received in a room called the Conference-room, which has a sort of screen across it; and the scene (apart from the seriousness of the situation) was as good as one of your plays, my dear: for some of the Tory MPs had smelled us out, and came blustering into the other end of the room, and while some of our MPs were gravely & solemnly bowing & yes-ing to us ⟨there⟩ in the hither end, James[6] & Chamberlain[7] were having a pretty little quarrel with the intruders at the other end.   well things went much better that evening: Gladstone made a very good speech[8] & when the division came off again about 30 more voted for us than on Thursday: also the government made moderate speeches, and though ⟨Lord Derby⟩ the fleet has gone for Constantinople, Lord Derby has, so to say, wrapped it up in cotton wool: and this morning we all were thinking that things were looking better; nor indeed is it easy to see on what excuse we can go to war: but at noon is a new surprise got ready for us, & a curious one — *the Turk won't let our ships pass the Dardanelles.* The worst part of it all is that the war fever is raging in England, & people go about in a Rule Britannia style that turns one's stomach: they tried a big meeting at Cremorne[9] on Saturday; but I put a spoke in their wheel,[10] & it was not a great success for them: nevertheless though one foresaw that ⟨it⟩ all this would happen it is nasty when it comes: ask Mr. Howard how he likes being at the mercy of the veracity of Beaconsfield, the sagacity of Northcote, & the tenacity of Derby. With wh: 3 long-tailed words I will end politics, my dear; tell Mama that business is fairly good at 26 considering the state of trade: we have let our 2nd floor at Oxford St:

We have had a longish spell of cold & raw weather: best love to you to May & Mama. & goodbye   I have just got a letter from May.

Your loving father
William Morris

MS: BL, Add. MSS. 45339. Published: MM, II, 574; Henderson, *Letters*, 109-11. Extract published: *CW*, 16, xiii.

[1] *The Times*, January 28, 1878, reported (p. 10) that a meeting of the E.Q.A. had been held on Saturday (January 26) with A. J. Mundella in the chair. The meeting, in essence, continued to protest against the Government's request for a six-million-pound military appropriation.

[2] Samuel Morley (1809-1886), Liberal M.P. for Bristol.

[3] *The Times*, February 7, 1878, reported (p. 10) that a meeting had been held in Exeter Hall on Wednesday, February 6. The tickets bore the words, "Loyal and Patriotic Meeting."

[4] On January 31, W. E. Forster (1818-1886), Liberal M.P. for Bradford, had moved, as an amendment to the motion that the House go into a Committee of Supply, a statement that Britain was not threatened by the Russo-Turkish War and that there was no reason to vote "unnecessary supplies." With the news on February 7 that the Russians had entered Constantinople, Forster withdrew the amendment. The House then voted to go into a Committee of Supply. See *The Times*, February 1, pp. 6-8; and February 8, pp. 6-8. See also the *Annual Register*, 1880, Part I, 12-22.

[5] The Workmen's Neutrality Committee, of which Henry Broadhurst was secretary, worked with the E.Q.A. See letter no. 476, n. 5.

[6] Henry James, Baron James of Hereford (1828-1911), Liberal M.P. for Taunton.

[7] Joseph Chamberlain (1836-1914), Liberal M.P. for Birmingham at this time.

[8] Gladstone quoted a parody called "Tennyson to the Rescue": "Ring out your battle-cry,/ Vote this War Supply./ This must we have or die—/ Vote the Six Millions!/ Yours not to reason why/ Ours not to make reply,/ Ours but to say 'You lie'/ Vote the Six Millions!"

[9] *The Times*, February 11, 1878, reported (p. 9) that on Saturday there had been a political demonstration in Cremorne Gardens. Sir Coutts-Lindsay (1824-1913), the chairman, said that it was a meeting of all parties to assert that the Government's duty was to defend Britain's honor and interests in any conference held.

[10] Possibly a reference to an attempt to amend the resolution by Sir Coutts-Lindsay, made at the outdoor meeting, in support of the Government; see Coutts-Lindsay's letter to *The Times*, February 11, 1878, p. 9.

---

493 • TO EMMA SHELTON MORRIS

The Grange,
North End Road,
Fulham S.W.
February 17, 1878

Dearest Mother

Many thanks for your letter: it is nearly a week since I heard from the Italians:[1] all seemed to be going well then: they could scarcely, I think have more beautiful weather than we have had today: they seem now to have settled down and got more at home. I am very well, though I have of late been busy about work that I don't like at all, though my conscience wouldn't let me refrain from doing it.

However for good or for ill it must soon be over, & I shall be free again to get to my special work: I am afraid that there is still great danger of war: no one can tell from hour to hour what is going to happen: one can only hope that it will end well yet. Love to Henrietta.

I am

Your most affectionate Son

William Morris

MS: Walthamstow.

¹ His family, who were staying with the Howards in Italy.

494 • To James Bryce

26, Queen Square,
Bloomsbury, London
February 18, 1878

My dear Bryce

I write in a great hurry to say that the meeting at wh: Gladstone is to speak is on *Thursday* next, and that I hope you will manage to be there as I think it a very important affair:¹ I will send you some ½ doz tickets.

As to the Hyde Park Meeting I am enclined to agree with you: but some of the working men plus Herbert have taken it up,² & go on it will in rather a scatter brained way: and yet I think it will not be a failure; many of the men are very hot about it.

Many thanks for the cheque: am I to use it for the Gladstone meeting, for wh: we want money sorely, or is it simply for the E.Q.A. that body is not acting as yet in the matter of this meeting I must tell you; it is the affair of the working mens Committee. I will take care that you have all information about Thursdays Meeting.

I shall be very happy to meet your friend almost any day when there is a lull in all this troublous work

Yours very truly
William Morris

MS: Bodleian.

¹ This meeting was canceled. Another at which Gladstone was to speak was planned for the Agricultural Hall, Islington, on February 25. *The Times*, February 16, reported (p. 5) that the purpose of the meeting was to hold the Government to its policy of neutrality and "at the same time to secure the . . . independence of the provinces . . . freed from Turkish oppression." This meeting, too, was never held. See letter no. 497 and G. C. Thompson, II, 364–65.

² See letter no. 490, n. 1.

495 • TO JAMES BRYCE
26, Queen Square,
Bloomsbury, London
February 18, 1878

My dear Bryce

I will come home with you with pleasure if it turns out possible on Thursday: as to tomorrow's meeting:[1] pray come *if you possibly can*

Yours very truly
William Morris

P.S. You had better come to the Hall not later than ½ past 7

MS: Bodleian.

[1] This may have been the meeting of the E.Q.A. to which Morris referred in letter no. 497. It may have been held in conjunction with the Workmen's Neutrality Committee; the latter group did meet on February 19 and decided to postpone the meeting scheduled for the Agricultural Hall. See also letter no. 494, n. 1.

496 • TO JAMES BRYCE
26, Queen Square,
Bloomsbury, London
[February 20, 1878]

My dear Bryce

It was wrong of me to say I would come: I really am pledged to Colvin;[1] but I didn't know quite what I was saying just now: it is no use: now I am out of the noise & away from the sophistry of spoken words, I cannot help saying that I am overwhelmed with shame at our double failure:[2] and who knows what will happen? Whatever does, we are now at the mercy of the Tories: if they want war they will have it, nor shall we be able to say one word to stop them: it will be quite impossible to get the working-men to a meeting on the subject again. I can't think that a riot made by the war-party would have hurt either us or Gladstone a bit: and now I am sure they will hold meeting after meeting, and triumph, as they well deserve to do.

Yours very truly
William Morris

MS: Bodleian.

[1] To deliver an address at the distribution of prizes at the Cambridge School of Art. See letter no. 485, n. 2.

[2] Possibly the cancellation of the meeting scheduled for February 21, at which Gladstone was to speak, and the manner in which the Hyde Park demonstration for February 24 had been organized. See letters no. 490, 494, and 497.

497 • To Jane Morris
26, Queen Square,
Bloomsbury, London
February 20, 1878

Dearest Janey

I suppose I shall have a letter from one or other of you tomorrow, but I shall scarcely be able to answer it, as I am going to Cambridge to give an address at the School of Art (for Colvin). As to my political career, I think it is at an end for the present; & has ended sufficiently disgustingly, after beating about the bush & trying to organize some rags of resistance to the war-party for a fortnight, after spending all ones time in Committees, & the like; I went to Gladstone with some of the workmen & Chesson, to talk about getting him to a meeting at the Agricultural Hall:[1] he agreed & was quite hot about it, and as brisk as a bee: I went off strait to the Hall, & took it for tomorrow: to work we fell, & everything got into into train: but — on Monday our parliamentaries began to quake, and tease Gladstone, and they have ⟨now⟩ quaked the meeting out now:[2] the E.Q.A. was foremost in the flight, & really I must needs say they behaved ill in the matter: Gladstone was quite ready to come up to the scratch & has behaved well throughout: but I am that ashamed that I can scarcely look people in the face though I did my best to keep the thing up: the working-men are in a great rage about it, as they well may be: for I do verily believe we should have made it a success; though I don't doubt that there would have been a huge row: there was a stormy meeting of the E.Q.A. yesterday, full of wretched little personalities, but I held my tongue — I am out of it now; I mean as to bothering my head about it: I shall give up reading the Papers, and shall stick to my work. Of course after this fiasco it will be impossible to hold another meeting in London on the subject: we have been terrorized by the medical students[3] & the civil(?) servants, and are now slaves of the Tories for life. On the other hand it must be said that things look much less like war than they did: so we must even hope. I will write again soon: to May this time.

Best love to you & all: I am so sick of it and so vexed but I shall not let it bother me overmuch.

Your loving
W.M.

MS: BL, Add. MSS. 45338. Published: MM, II, 576; Henderson, *Letters*, 111-12. Extract published: Mackail, I, 362.

¹ See letter no. 494.

² The reason given for postponing the meeting in the Agricultural Hall was "the altered aspect of affairs, resulting from the departure of the fleet from the immediate neighborhood of Constantinople." The planning committee may also have been influenced by the

threat of violence and, should it occur, its consequences in so large a hall and in so great an assembly of people. The committee, in any case, agreed to the postponement of the meeting. In a circular signed by Henry Broadhurst, they announced their decision, saying that they were obliged to accept the advice of those insisting on this step but that they did not share the view that the meeting should be postponed. (See G. C. Thompson, II, 364-65; see also *The Times*, February 21, 1878, p. 10, quoted by Thompson.)

[3] There was a rumor that workmen employed at Woolwich Arsenal planned to break up the meeting and that they were being encouraged by the Government in this intention. A letter in the *Daily News*, February 21, from a medical student in University College Hospital, reported that a stranger at the Hospital had called attention to a notice requesting all medical students to "meet on Thursday in Trafalgar Square and march with bands and flying colours to Agricultural Hall, there to hoot down Mr. Gladstone." See G. C. Thompson, II, 364-65, n. 2.

498 • TO MAY MORRIS   26, Queen Square,
                                                               Bloomsbury, London
                                                               February 25, 1878

Dearest May

I have just got Mama's letter with news of you at last: I say at last, for it is the first I have heard of you for 10 days. I am tired out with my political business, &, as I told Mama in my last, it has pretty much come to an end; since the people are gone crazy, & are quite determined on war if the Government can find any excuse for picking a quarrel; about which there is still some doubt.

It was a very bad business putting a stopper on the Agricultural Hall meeting; I can't help suspecting some under-hand work was stirring in the matter. Yesterday came off the Hyde Park Meeting, (in wh: I had no hand) the Tory organization was too strong for us & broke it up in point of fact:[1] I am just going to a meeting of the E.Q.A. but I scarcely hope that they will try to do anything.

Well I am off this afternoon for a days holiday to Kelmscott: I shall be back on Wednesday evening. On Thursday I went to Cambridge & gave an address (on Art) to the School of Art ⟨at Cambridge⟩ there over which Colvin is President: it was quiet work & not unpleasant after all the London hubbub — did I tell you that they have made me President of the Birmingham Society of Arts for the current year: that means a speech early next year.[2]

Tell Mama I will send her the rent next time I write: also the book: did you get Old Deccan Days?[3]

And now just listen! You are not (the lot of you) to leave me without any letters for a fortnight again: or by George I'll go to Iceland: where after all perhaps we shall have to go if these English Swine persist in their folly.

Good bye my dear May, & best love to all of you, my dears & take care of yourselves.

Your loving father
William Morris

MS: BL, Add. MSS. 45341. Extract published: *CW*, 16, xiv.

[1] The *Daily News*, February 25, 1878, reported (p. 10) that a large crowd had assembled and that Auberon Herbert began the meeting, saying that its purpose was to protest against any action which might lead to war and to confirm the right of free speech. At this point, members of the "National and Patriotic League," under a Lieutenant Armit, rushed in and broke up the meeting.

[2] See letter no. 484.

[3] *Old Deccan Days: Or, Hindoo Fairy Legends, Current in Southern India*. Collected from Oral Tradition by Mary E. Frere, with an introduction and notes by Sir Bartle Frere and illustrated by C. F. Frere (London: Murray, 1868).

499 • TO JENNY MORRIS

Horrington House
March 6 [1878]

Dearest Jenny

Thank you for your nice letter. I am at home today & have been since Sunday, because I can't help it, being lame with gouty rheumatism, or rheumatic gout: I can't get down stairs, but I find the long room very comfortable: I don't suppose I shall be prisoner for more than one more day now, as I am not very bad. I duly went to Kelmscott with Ellis & uncle Edgar getting down there on Monday-week evening: the fishing was not very good: we got a good many little perch but only one big one; & Edgar got 3 smallish pikes: on the other hand Ellis captured a monster under the willow on the Berkshire side of the Old-Weir pool: he weighed 17 lbs: I thought we should never have got him into the net he was so big: but somehow I don't seem to care about fishing like I did: I suppose I am getting too old for it: this big pike bit a gold-fish, which Ellis had brought down with him. I am sorry to say that poor old Philip is worse again:[1] he comes down for an hour or two in the day & sits by the fire-side; but he seems very weak: I doubt he cannot last long.

The new window is made, & the little room looks much the better for it: but the stupid Mitchell has daubed the wall outside with nasty whitey-bluey cement about the joints: however I don't doubt we can scrape it off & set it right: the poor old tree is cut up, or all but, & ready to be carried away. Mouse[2] looks shaggy & well in his winter costume, & the 2 pussies are as clean as ever.

I have been so long now without doing any work, I mean my proper work, that I have very little news to tell you about that. We have got a fresh piece of work (darned) from Mrs. Holiday, which is prettier even than the coverlit; but perhaps I told you about that.

Margery is quite well now: only she has had another pet-trouble: a pretty little green parroquet wh: her papa bought her as a tooth-taking-out-reward has died after a short illness: I am glad my dears that you have not yet taken to pets: for they are a *nuisance*.

We have had such lovely weather for the last 3 or 4 days: but today is grey and blowing a gale from the S.W. it was baddish down at Kelmscott: but this has altogether been the finest & warmest February I remember & the warmest winter — so far.

Now for cold & eastwinds I suppose.

Little Mr. Leigh[3] who comes to see me for my gout has grown so fat: he had better take care, & be warned by me!

I enclose a scrap of a note for Mama.[4]

As to politics: we are very glad that the peace is signed;[5] and I don't know what the war-party will do for a pretext now: no doubt also they will have to get rid of Lord Derby first. Things at any rate look better.

Well, my deary, goodbye with best love to May & Mama.

Your loving father
William Morris

P.S. The Empress Brown is hard at work at her rival establishment: I am sure she expects to get the whole of the ornamental upholstery of the Kingdom into her hands: let her tremble! I will under-sell her in all branches. I will send Mama her money as soon as I can get to Queen Sq:

MS: BL, Add. MSS. 45339. Published: Henderson, *Letters*, 112.

[1] See letter no. 381, n. 2.
[2] The pony Morris brought back from Iceland in 1871.
[3] Richard Hodges Leigh, a London surgeon.
[4] It has not survived.
[5] Russia and Turkey signed a peace treaty on March 3, 1878 at San Stefano.

500 · TO AGLAIA IONIDES CORONIO
Horrington House
Thursday Evening
[March 7, 1878]

My dear Aglaia

I am much better today, and shall probably manage to get up to town tomorrow, where I have little odd business jobs to do that are pressing, and which I can do in spite of the limps. I have just got your note with the photograph, wh: *is* the one I was talking about:[1] but I feel most ashamed of getting it in this way. Many thanks for your being so kind as to come & see a gouty old fogy (wh: is what I must now set myself down for), and for your kind offers. I expect to be quite well by Sunday: I could come round some afternoon next week I think: which would suit you.

My Mother & Sister called this afternoon; so what with the bright weather & feeling better I had a goodish time of it.

The photograph is a great beauty: but I feel about up to the mark of Lord Beaconsfield for extracting it in that way.

Do you see by the way how very pro-Greek the Daily News is: it is trying hard to *shove* Lord Derby in that direction:[2] only you must remember that that the Greeks would never have been in that mess but for Lord Derby — no I havn't seen Fun.[3]

Yours affectionately
William Morris

MS: Yates Coll.

[1] A photograph of St. Sophia.

[2] Lord Derby supported the Greeks of Epirus and Thessaly, who, rebelling against Turkish rule, demanded reunion with Greece.

[3] A weekly periodical.

501 • TO THOMAS WARDLE
26, Queen Square,
Bloomsbury, London
March 8, 1878

My dear Wardle

I enclose a warp from a 16th cent: piece of tapestry, wh: as you see, is worsted: the pitch is 12 to the inch: nothing in tapestry need be finer than this: in setting up your work you must remember that as tapestry hangs on the wall the warps are horizontal though of course you weave with them vertical,   that is the way the warp goes I mean. If you please to send   me the space of your loom, I will make a design for   ⟨the⟩ it (the space).

Thanks for sending me Arnold's lecture,[1] with the main part of which of course I heartily agree: the only thing is that if he has any idea of a remedy, he dursn't mention it: I think myself that no rose-water will cure us: disaster & misfortune of all kinds, I think will be the only things that will breed a remedy: in short nothing can be done till all rich men are made poor by common consent: I suppose he dimly sees this, but is afraid to say it, being, though naturally a courageous man, somewhat infected with the great vice of that cultivated class he was praising so much — cowardice to wit.

A Greek friend got me the photographs of St Sophia: I will try to get them again.[2]

As to Jones' pictures: the difficulty is to get them, as he is always a good way ahead: I should recommend you to write to him, & ask ⟨yo⟩ him to let you have something at the price you can afford, when he has such a picture going: you would get something you would like I have no doubt for from £150 to 200.

Today I am in town, but I was lame till today, though not very bad.

Yours very truly
William Morris

MS: Duke. Extract published: Mackail, I, 365-66; Henderson, *Letters*, 113.

[1] Matthew Arnold's lecture, "Equality," delivered in February 1878 at the Royal Institute, published in the *Fortnightly* for March 1878, and afterward included in his *Mixed Essays* (1879). Arnold argued, in this essay, that social inequality in England was the result of medieval laws of bequest. He looked forward to equality, but he argued that the defect of socialism and communism was that they were content with a low, materialistic standard of well being. He continued that the impulse to cultivate manners promotes equality. Returning to economic causation, he said that the remedy in England must be a change in the law of bequests, but that this was not a matter of practical politics. He concluded his lecture by asking only that his audience think about the problem.

[2] Aglaia Coronio. See letter no. 500.

502 • TO CATHERINE HOLIDAY
Horrington House
Turnham Green
March 9 [1878?]

Dear Mrs. Holiday

I have had all my time taken up for the past month with 'politics' so-called, till this week, when I found time for a little gout: if it had not been for these two pleasures I should have had some more to say to you about the embroidery before now.

I was quite delighted with the success of the door-hanging: I think it so good in colour and way of working that I am quite sure we can do nothing better: so as this first one is an order and is to be sent away I should be much obliged if you would put another *just like it* in hand: I know you dont like doing repetitions: but this is such a beautiful thing that I should think it a great pity if there were not more than one of it in the world. As soon as I can I intend getting a small piece of work ready that might amuse you more. As to those beautifully coloured cushion-pieces you sent; I thought the sort of work rather too *frail* for the purpose, & proposed the quilting of the long stitches down with hair-lines of silk, even at the expense of losing some of the beauty. I think also I might find some better designs for cushions for you: in fact I have one, which I will send you if you please to do as you will with as to colour & style of work: with the caution however that durability is necessary for such things; especially when the work is as beautiful as you make it.

I am
Yours very truly
William Morris

MS: Berger Coll. Published: Henderson, *Letters*, 86-87.

503 · To JANE MORRIS   Queen Sq
March 12 [1878]

Dearest Janey

I am much distressed at the bad news: we must remember however what a trying time spring is for all that sort of thing. I went to Reynolds[1] yesterday & found he had gone & would not be back till the 1st week of April: they wouldn't give me his address: so all I could do was to write to him & beg him to write to you: I enclosed his prescription & gave him all the information I could: the letter will be sent on to him, as he has a brother Sawbones in London to open his letters: It also struck me that it might be good to try Radcliffe's[2] nostrum of bromides again: so I have orders to Morrison to send you a month's allowance of his last prescription: you know all about it and might use it safely I dont doubt. I see Reynolds's is hashish or bhang like Monte-Christo & the Arabian Nights.

I will certainly come out at the end of April whatever happens: will sell my books for journey-money if need be. I don't suppose you have read Galt's novels:[3] so I am sending you 2 vols, as they amused me last week as I lay up with gout: he wrote about Scott's time, and is certainly good — always as far as his real turn goes.

I want to talk to you about the Mcdonald's house (that was)[4] now I have been over it twice: if you could be content to live no nearer London than that, I cannot help thinking we should do very well there: you can get a cab to the house in a quarter of an hour: and certainly the open river and the garden at the back are a great advantage: the house itself is just about big enough for us, and the rooms are mostly pretty: the drawing room is (since Mc: knocked a bedroom into it) a great long

Kelmscott House.

room facing the river: the draw-back to the *house* is a dreary room at
the back: high darkish and ugly-windowed: but we should only want it
as a subsidiary 'larking room', so needn't mind it much when it is duly
whitewashed: besides we might keep hens in it; or a pig, or a cow; or
let it for a ranter's chapel. The Garden is very long & good: it also has
a draw-back — now, of being overlooked badly down one half of it,
because the wall lowers there: but we might stick up a great high trellis
(as the wall would be ours) wh: would effectually shut out the over-
lookers: on the other side there are other gardens & all is quite pretty.
If the matter lay with me only I should set about taking the house: for
already I have become conscious of the difficulty of getting anything
decent: as to such localities as Knightsbridge or Kensington Sq: they are
quite beyond our means: a fairish house in such places means £250 per
ann and they almost always want a premium; which last I *cannot* pay.

Best love to all of you, my dears: and I will certainly come out. My gout is nearly gone, but still hangs about a little.

Your loving

W.M.

MS: BL, Add. MSS. 45338. Published: MM, II, 577-78.

[1] John Russell Reynolds (1828-1896), a specialist in nervous disorders and, from 1893 to 1895, president of the Royal College of Physicians.

[2] Charles Bland Radcliffe (1822-1889), physician, one of the first to do research on the electrical physiology of muscle and nerve. He was also a friend of the Burne-Joneses. (See *Memorials*, passim.)

[3] John Galt (1779-1839), poet, novelist, dramatist, and essayist, best known for his biographies of Byron and Carlyle and for his studies of rural Scotland.

[4] George Macdonald (1824-1905), poet and writer of prose romances. The Morrises did take the house, which Macdonald had called The Retreat and which Morris renamed Kelmscott House after Kelmscott Manor. About the naming of the house, May Morris wrote (*CW*, 13, xvii) that Morris objected to "The Retreat": "[H]e declined, he said, to pass his days in a house with such a name; 'people would think something was amiss with me and that your poor Mama was trying to reclaim me.' The aggressively beshuttered appearance of the front to the river inevitably suggested the nick-name of 'The Shutters,' which lingered for a year or two in familiar talk."

504 • TO JANE MORRIS   March 18 [1878]

Dearest Janey

I *did* write after doing all I could of what you wanted: but no doubt by this time you will have my letter, so I needn't say anymore about that. This letter to you is about house-hunting; you must pardon me for troubling you about it; but I do not like the idea of leaving all to be done after you come home; lest we should have to hurry into some den of a place at the last moment: besides any house we take will want some doing up; and 6 months would be all too short to get the lease-wrangling over in time to be sure of our having leisure for the doing up.

1st about the Mcdonalds house (The Retreat) — I have been there again with Webb: and I have heard from the Miss Cobdens[1] who lodged with Mcdonald for some time. The latter give a very unfavourable account of the house, & I can't help thinking that your information comes by some road from them: their information is obviously exaggerated, and I should say that they hated the house, & probably the Mcs also: my 3rd visit established the fact that the house was quite dry, and also in very bad repair; there was no smell about: the house could easily be done up at a cost of money, & might be made very beautiful with a touch of my art: even the dreary room could be made habitable: you

[458]

could have a very nice room looking into the garden, and sufficiently to yourself to be comfortable and there would be nice rooms for each of our maidens. The long drawing-room could be made one of the prettiest in London: the garden is really most beautiful, & there is a private door at the end leading out into Hog Lane close to the high road. Cross examination of the woman who takes care, & has been about the house off and on all the time the Mcs were there, could only draw out *for certain* that the cellars had been flooded at abnormal high-tide that happened 3 years ago: Webb thought that this might be easily guarded against, as it does not come up through the drains (since the house drains into the main sewer not into the Thames): meantime they are quite dry at present. There is a real green-house down the garden, if you care for that, and capital stabling & coach house; so that we might perhaps manage to keep a pony & trap.

Summa: the objections are two: 1st can you do with living so far from London? This is really the important point; for the threat of un-healthiness that the Miss Cobdens threw out I don't believe in, except that doubtless the drains want seeing to; as they probably will in any house we take: there is no doubt that the house is exceptionally dry. The situation is certainly the prettiest in London: you may mock at this among the olives beside the Midland Sea but to us poor devils of Lon-doners 'tis something: now, my dear, you must settle whether I am to go further in this matter; as though 'tis certain that I am enclined to it I would not think of it again if you feel that you would not like it.

No. 2. I have seen a house at the corner of Earl's Terrace: the place I have no doubt you would like: looking into Holland Park on one side, and into Edward Sq: garden on the other: the house is big enough for us, and being not quite modern, is without gross vulgarity; on the other hand it is both scrimply and dull, and the chief rooms look pretty much North: the garden is just a yard, no more: nevertheless if you come to think of it you will find that you won't get a garden or a house with much character unless you go out about as far as the Upper Mall: so I think this doubtful paradise of Earls Terrace worth considering if you say no to the 'Retreat.' I don't think either you or I could stand a quite modern house in a street, say at Notting Hill: I don't fancy going back among the bugs of Bloomsbury: though tis a healthy part & we might do worse: we might as well live at York as at Hampstead for all we should ever see of our friends: I am told that about Fulham and Putney are pretty houses to let: that would be as far off as the Mall: but what do you think of it? Earls Terrace is certainly delightfully accessible: the rent is £140: ridiculous, you say, for what is after all a *lodging*, not a house: but that I shall have to pay either in rent or in repairs wherever

I go: rents have risen so: please let me hear from you at once about these matters, and say straightout what your views are; for it would not do for either of us to agree to go into a house, in wh: one or other would pray for an earthquake to knock it down.

I am writing to Jenny: I am dreadfully anxious about you.

Your loving

W.M.

MS: BL, Add. MSS. 45338. Published: Henderson, *Letters*, 113-15. Extract published: Mackail, I, 372.

[1] Richard Cobden (1804-1865), advocate of free trade, Member of Parliament, and a leader of the Anti-Corn Law League, was survived by five daughters. Three of them became well-known through their marriages: Jane, wife of Thomas Fisher Unwin (1848-1935), the publisher; Ellen, wife of Walter Richard Sickert (1860-1942), the painter; and Anne, wife of Thomas James Cobden-Sanderson, the bookbinder, who added her name to his own.

505 • TO JANE MORRIS   [before March 28, 1878]

Dearest Janey

Description of the Retreat on the upper Mall Hammersmith.

top floor 3 garrets: one very large, window looking west: one fairish but darkish (might make another window:) one quite small: too small for sleeping.

2nd floor 3 bedrooms: No 1 a very pretty room about 17 ft sq: looking S. & W. No 2 smaller but good, looking S. No 3 small, no fireplace: big enough for spare-room-between 2nd & 1st floor: more modern part of house; a very large room, about 21 ft × 17 ft looking N. (fine view into garden) and W. (call this A)

1st floor 1st a very long drawing-room say 35 ft × 17. 2 fire-places 5 windows facing S. (river). 2nd a queer little den of a bathroom with gas & water laid on: Ground floor. 3 rooms. ⟨2 on ea⟩ one on each side of street door: No 1 smallish, cheerful. No 2 about 18 ft × 15 ft. a good room — the 3rd is the dismallish *handsome* room: ('tis really very handsome) same size as big bedroom but very lofty: looks N into garden door between it and front room No 2: I believe by dint of cheerful papering, book cases & the like it might be made a very good dining-room.   the Mcs have done their best to make it look dismal.   there is a big pantry on this floor (& Oh I forgot (as Jenny says) a *beautiful* linen closet close to the big bedroom on the floor above. Kitchen-floor. No 1 a fairish kitchen facing S. No 2 a good back-kitchen with fire-place &

copper: No 3 what was the original kitchen turned by the Mcs into a diningroom faces N: a very big room: the cellars are lower than the kitchen & are very big

The stables are big & good   a big loft: harness room & 2 bedrooms both with fireplaces, *if* we kept a gardener-&-groom he would or could inhabit these. Otherwise the one room might have a bed in it for Crom to sleep in: or it would be a general sulky-room.

There is a good garden & root house, besides the large green house.   a tank in the former for watering purposes: there are 2 arbours: there are of big trees 1st a walnut by the stable: 2nd a very fine tulip-tree halfway down the lawn. 3rd. 2 horse chestnuts at the end of the lawn: beyond that is a sort of orchard (many good fruit trees in it) with rough grass (gravel walk all round garden): then comes the green-house & beyond that a kitchen: garden with lots of raspberries. This is the plan of garden [see drawing on next page]:

This is pretty accurate as to proportions: only the orchard is rather longer than I have drawn it & the kitchen garden not so long: the walls are covered with fruit-trees: Margery says the raspberries were very good & many there: the lawn is in good condition: sweet grass & not mossy —

I should suppose that you would occupy the big bedroom: the two dear maidens would occupy the 2nd floor rooms (*very* nice ones) & you might hand over to me the 2 ground-floor ones for bedroom & study since your drawing-room would be so big.

The house, as I said in my last, wants small repairs badly but the floors are very good: much better than they would be in a modern house: I should of course send Vinal[1] to report professionally on it: as to expense, if you are offered a house in good repair they make you pay premium, so it comes to the same thing.

I must tell you that I have gone over the Earls Terrace house again and find it won't do at all: there is no room in it for us: 4 bedrooms (including servants) a den, a bath-room and a dressing room: 2 draw-ing-rooms, 2 dining-rooms: the only way to make the drawing room livable in would be to knock them into one as they have been — the whole house mean & un-roomy beyond description: the rooms very *small*: the garden like a prison yard & very *tiny*: without a shrub in it: I don't think either you or I could live there. I find that a good house with a moderate garden nearer London than Hammersmith costs £300 a year: we had much better keep a pony and trap at Hammersmith than burden ourselves with a heavy rent. as it is, we need not expect to get *any* house for less than £120 or 140 — including the repairs: rents have risen prodigiously in the last 6 years   I must say I am more strongly

To Hammersmith High road

New road into the Mall

Stone b—y new house 3

Chapel

a nursery man

High Lane / down into the Lane

2 little houses (pretty)

Greenhouse — Kitchen Garden

orchard

arbour

a very high laurel

Tank   asparagus

tulip tree

Stable

Lawn (the Mall)

with rough grass (gravel walk) all round garden; then comes the green-house & beyond that a kitchen-garden with lots of raspberries.

This is the plan of garden

This is pretty accurate as to proportion: only the orchard is rather longer than I have drawn it & the kitchen garden not so long; the walls are covered with fruit trees; Margery says the raspberries were very fine; & many; the lawn is in good condition: evergreen & not-mowing?

than ever in favour of taking the Retreat (we might re-name it) and I ought to take some steps in the matter as soon as may be: it would not be too early for us to take any house from Midsummer and I would begin by offering £85 rent, as I am going to spend so much in doing it up.

So much for all that. I also shall be so glad to see you all again — I have had but a dreary time of it — Thank dear Jenny for her orange-flowers.

I will send on Osborne's Islam: there was an attack on it in the Athenaeum tother day: said it was inaccurate[2]

Your loving
W M.

ms: BL, Add. mss. 45338. Published: Henderson, *Letters*, 115-17.

[1] See letter no. 480, n. 9.
[2] R. D. Osborne, *Islam Under the Khalifs of Baghdad* (London: Seeley, 1877), was reviewed unfavorably in *The Athenaeum*, March 9, 1878.

506 • To Jenny Morris   26 Queen Sq:
                                                            March 18 [1878]

Dearest Jenny

Thank you for your little letter: both you and Mama must please to get quite well against I come over;[1] or else how the wonder are we to wander about Venice & the Lombard cities: won't it be nice to see those places?

My gout has practically gone now: I wrote last Tuesday to Mama: so I suppose our letters must have crossed: but I shall put this into the post with my own hands.

I have had some photographs of St Sophia at Constantinople got for me: it is a very beautiful place: I have been reading a lot about the Byzantine Empire in Finlays[2] book of late (in gout-time): it is very interesting though somewhat dreary: however if we go to Verona and Padua we shall see (what with Venice and all) quite the pick of the Italian mediaeval architecture   I have been engaged in studying architecture from the more practical side in London: to wit, I have been house-hunting; and don't feel very exhilarated with the results of the chase. For the rest, I am working hard to do a little business before I come out: the time is drawing near now.

As for politics, I am now out of it: I breakfasted with poor Mr. Herbert last Tuesday, and we were both chop-fallen enough: the scene in the Parks yesterday-week was most disgraceful:[3] so I am told for I didn't go there: both houses of parliament went to look on; and all the thieves in London went to labour at their vocation. Edgar told me that they caught (the philo-Turks, (ie the thieves)) a gentleman with a fez-cap & put him up to speak on their side: he was a rich man with rings and a watch and plenty of money in his pockets: but in 3 minutes his friends had all that from him and he went away with no more gold on him than the poorest man in the park.

Meantime the war party at home here are jubilant, and make up their minds that we are going to war: I can't help thinking that they will find themselves jockied in their turn.

Well, my dear, good-bye: I will write again to May before the week is out.

Your loving father
William Morris

MS: BL, Add. MSS. 45339.

¹ Morris joined his family in Italy toward the end of April. See letter no. 525.

² George Finlay (1799-1875), an historian who resided in Greece, where he saw much of Byron. His *History of Greece*, which had first appeared serially, was published in 1874.

³ *The Times*, March 11, 1878 reported (p. 9) that the attempt to hold a peace meeting the previous day had failed. Auberon Herbert and Charles Bradlaugh were pushed and hustled from their positions by a group of men "bearing colours, and singing 'Rule Brittania.' " A fight ensued. On both the "Peace" and "War" sides "persons were trampled under foot" and "heads were indiscriminately punched." See letter no. 498, n. 1.

507 · To May Morris

26, Queen Square,
Bloomsbury, London
March 21, 1878

Dearest May

I am writing to you a line to send my love to you on your birthday: I don't send anything else: for I daresay we shall find some bonny-die at Venice hereafter.

News I have but little   I have written a long memo to Mama about the house, wh: with my work is what I have chiefly to think of now. I went to a little meeting at Mr Bryce's the night before last, to talk to some Armenians about their chances in the Congress:¹ they were queer looking fellows of this type ⟍⟋ but one man from Tabreez in Persia was better looking. ⟋ I have seen a very pretty thing this week; that is an exhibition ⟨ of eastern things at the Carpet-man's Vincent Robinson's.² he has bought a room complete from Damascus walls, ceiling, window and all and 'tis put together properly with only the due amount of light in it — due in Syria I mean not in

London — it is all vermillion & gold & ultramarine very beautiful and is just like going into the Arabian Nights: he has also the most beautiful tiles, and brass & copper engraved bowls & vessels very fine: one little casket of the 13th century I thought the finest piece of metal-work I had ever seen on that scale.

There is a new piece of Mrs. Holiday's work come in of late, yellow on light yellow silk with a greenish bluish border: very lovely colour — but I must take care, or I shall rouse jealousy.

I have not much to tell you about politics: the war-party have by no means given over trying to get us involved: their chief occupation now is to abuse Lord Derby, who is become our chief support — so low we have fallen!

My dear, I hope you will have a nice birthday, & will get happier & happier as one year goes over another in birthdays to come.

Your loving father
William Morris

MS: BL, Add. MSS. 45341. Published: MM, II, 578-79.

[1] The Congress of Berlin, held from June 13 to July 13, 1878, was called at the insistence, initially, of Austria to see that the final drawing of boundaries and disposition of the question of the Straits following the war between Russia and Turkey were consistent with treaties existing among the European powers. Its aim, therefore, was to substitute new boundaries for those imposed by the Russians at the Treaty of San Stefano, signed on March 3. As a result of the settlement reached at the Congress, Armenia was to remain a province of Turkey.

[2] Vincent Joseph Robinson (1829-1910), a connoisseur of oriental art, author of *Eastern Carpets* (1882), and director of the India section of the Paris Exhibition in 1889.

508 • To George Macdonald

26, Queen Square,
Bloomsbury, London
March 22, 1878

Dear Mr. Macdonald[1]

I have been thinking of taking the house you used to live in on the Upper Mall, which in many respects would suit me very well; but I have heard some doubts thrown on the healthiness of the place, and have thought it best to ask you directly what the fact of the matter is: I should be very much obliged by your telling me about it: of course I am prepared if I take the house to do all things necessary to the drainage & the rest. I am by no means a fidgetty person about these matters, & of course I know by this time all that can be said about Hammersmith in general: I also know how very fidgetty many people are on (these matters⟩ this side and I discount largely unfavourable reports about the health of places.

Asking your pardon for troubling you

I am

Yours very truly

William Morris

G Macdonald, Eqre.

MS: Berger Coll.

¹ See letter no. 503, n. 4.

509 · TO JANE MORRIS

26, Queen Square,
Bloomsbury, London
March 26, 1878

Dearest Janey

House again! Of course I see nothing unreasonable in your objections to living so far out: nay I feel them myself & they make me very uncomfortable, because I don't think we shall manage to get what we want nearer: you see this is practically what we want in a house: servants rooms kitchen & the rest: then 1st 2 nice airy rooms (though they needn't be very big) for our dear maidens: 2nd a good & quiet room for you, my dear: 3rd either a biggish room for my study to hold a bed for me also, or some den for my bed, & a fairish room for my study: nor 5th can we quite do without a spare room: 6th 2 sitting-rooms and (especially if only 2) one of them to be decidedly a good room: this, I think, is the least we can do with, and from all I can see I fear we shall not meet with such a big house for less than £300 anywhere Kensington-or-west-away, nearer than Hammersmith, that you would like to go to: also, at the risk of being considered self seeking I must say that in the ordinary modern-Cromwell-Rd-sort-of-house I should be so hipped that I should be no good to anybody; nor do I think that either you or the girls would get on in such a place.

As to the Earls Terrace house I tried my utmost to think that it would do, as the place was obviously good: I dismissed all prejudice from my mind; but the net result was that there was not so much room as in Horrington House, besides its being unutterably mean & work-housy, & the garden (what there was of it) most dreary: it plainly wouldn't do. You have not said what you think of trying Bloomsbury again: the worst of that is that you & the children would be much cut off from the Neds: as for me I could get about no doubt: also I confess I fear the

[466]

dirt: no house can be kept clean in Bloomsbury: St John's Wood & the Regents Park I have always hated: besides I believe good houses are dear there: I do not know what the deuce to do.

Well — to change the subject: I have just had the babes letters: I will write a line to them tomorrow: meantime I have sent Mr. Congreve[1] £50 and asked him to send you the balance after paying the rent: item I send off today by post Islam under the Khalifs.[2] I didn't know Brook[3] was coming out so soon: else I would have sent the books & tea by him I will send a little tea tomorrow.

How about my coming out? Suppose I were to come just about when the Howards leave; stay a day or two at Oneglia just to see what sort of a life you have been living; & then go as straight to Venice: we needn't go with the Howards, as I should be there to take care & we should meet them at Venice: then stay about a week at Venice, & back by the Lombard cities to Milan: see Florence next time would that be feasible, as it certainly would be very nice?

Winter has reached us at last: bright & sunny with fierce snow & wind-storm between: and oh so cold!

I dined at Hadham[4] last night: H[enrietta] was better & mother very well. Rogers cut my hair this morning in the presence of my kins-women & the parrot: wh: last was delighted, & mewed & barked & swore & sang at the top of his vulgar voice.

Best love
Your loving
W.M.

P.S. Mind a poney & chaise at the retreat.

MS: BL, Add. MSS. 45338. Published: Henderson, *Letters*, 117-18.

[1] See letter no. 433, n. 2.

[2] See letter no. 505, n. 2.

[3] Possibly Stopford Brooke, who was a friend of both the Howards and the Morrises. See letter no. 422, n. 1.

[4] Much Hadham, Hertfordshire, where Morris's mother was living.

510 • TO JENNY AND MAY MORRIS   26, Queen Square,
                                            Bloomsbury, London
                                            March 27, 1878

Dearest daughters

Many thanks for your happy birthday notes: also May for your baccy pouch: the shape of which is very pretty & the colour: only I shall ask you to put silk strings to it as cotton on cotton sets my teeth on edge:

of course 'tis indigo. So you see, Jenny, I was at Grandmama's yester-
day: it looked very pretty, but how cold! if you still understand what
that word means. The March snow came on with a sudden & mighty
squall on Sunday about 3 p.m: ⟨and⟩ that capsized the Eurydice[1] as you
will read, drowning many poor fellows: I was at the Grange & noticed
it but had no idea it was so fierce: there has been an Icelander over here,
the secretary of the Land's Hofðingi (Governor) whom I have seen: he
says, what must your summer be since you call this winter: but he
thinks London a very nasty place and is shocked by the aspect of the
'residuum' in the streets: as he well may be — well I suppose the tories
& the said residuum will have their way, & to war we shall go: it
reminds me of the rascal Louis Napoleon and his residuum: I have been
and am reading Victor Hugo's Histoire du Crime[2] & am much inter-
ested with it. I will bring it out with me.   but a very few more letters
before I shall see my dears again & then WHAT LARX.

Goodbye, dear daughters

Your loving father
W.M.

MS: BL, Add. MSS. 45339.

[1] The *Eurydice*, a wooden sailing frigate, had capsized off the Isle of Wight. There were
only two or three survivors. The accident was reported in *The Times*, March 25, 1878,
p. 9.

[2] Victor Hugo's *Histoire d'un Crime: Déposition d'un Témoin* (Paris: Calmann Levy, 1878)
was reviewed in *The Times*, March 22, 1878, p. 4.

511 · To Thomas Wardle   26, Queen Square,
                                                    Bloomsbury, London
                                                    March 28, 1878

My dear Wardle

I find I cannot possibly get away next week: it is now but about 3
weeks before I go out to Italy: I think I could manage a day or two the
week after next: I shall have a narrow piece of pattern you might use
for your tapestry trial. I will write again if the week after next you could
have me.

Your very truly
William Morris

So Sir G[1] is gone: I don't suppose it will make much difference either
for or against: but I am glad we began before he went off.

MS: Duke.

[1] Sir Gilbert Scott died on March 27. *The Times*, March 28, printed an obituary and
also carried (p. 9) a leader on Scott's work which was far from enthusiastic.

512 • To HENRY BROADHURST
26, Queen Square,
Bloomsbury, London
March 29, 1878

Dear Mr. Broadhurst

I have much pleasure in sending the cheque;[1] I was going to write to you this morning: I send this by hand: I have not been very well & have been much driven owing to my business work having fallen into arrears of late.

The situation is queer enough now: isn't it?[2]

I am
Yours very truly
William Morris

H Broadhurst Eqre
Please send receipt.

MS: LSE.

[1] Possibly for the Hyde Park meeting held on February 24, 1878. See letter no. 490, n. 1.

[2] This probably is a reference to events that occurred during the previous week. On March 22, the terms of the Treaty of San Stefano were published in the London press. On March 27, Disraeli had proposed to the Cabinet that reserves be called up and that—with Indian troops brought through the Suez Canal—posts in the Middle East be occupied to gain command of the Persian Gulf and the country around Baghdad, thus to neutralize the new Russian influence in Armenia. In response, Lord Derby, who had for some time exercised a restraining influence within the Cabinet, resigned on March 28 as Foreign Minister. He was succeeded by Lord Salisbury. See Seton-Watson, *Disraeli*, p. 364; *The Times*, March 29, 1878, p. 7.

513 • To JANE MORRIS
26, Queen Square,
Bloomsbury, London
April 2, 1878

Dearest Janey

I have arranged to take the house: I had first a long & satisfactory letter from MacD[onald]. We can easily house the 3rd maid, & I think 'tis a good idea: the stable could also easily be turned into a gymnasium, & the maidens could have the 2 queer little rooms above for larking rooms: there is no doubt that if we had made up our minds to come nearer in we must have been prepared to sacrifice everything to position, and even then we should have had to pay at least £180 to £200 rent: Luke[1] gave me a very bad account of the Earls Terrace houses. I do think that people will come to see us at the Retreat (fy on the name!) if only for the sake of the garden & river: we will lay ourselves more for company than heretofore. You must remember also that 'tis much nearer to the Grange; & I have made Kate Faulkner promise to come & stay with us. So let us hope we shall all grow younger there, my dear.

As to my coming out; it shapes to be, that I shall get to you about the 21st April: Ned is going to take Philip to see the real frogs (of Paris) & it would be pleasant to go so far in company: he intends for the 18th or 19th but he is a queer one, & I think wants to go by the Channel Fleet or the Castalia or dry-shod or some such game; so that may delay me: I will of course tell you the day and hour of my leaving Paris for Turin, & in return you must give me such information that I may not be landed a dumb beast of an Englishman at Rome or Beneventum or — Constantinople.

Which last word brings me to the 'situation': Yesterday morning I suppose there were few people in England who didnt think war as good as declared:[2] but it is strange how a feeling of backing out on both sides seems growing this morning so that I should not wonder if the Jingoes were dissappointed after all. E.Q.A. as good as dead.

Goodbye my dear best love to dear babes.

Your loving
W.M.

ms: BL, Add. mss. 45338. Published: Henderson, *Letters*, 118-19.

[1] Luke Ionides.
[2] See letter no. 512, n. 2.

514 • To Catherine Holiday

26, Queen Square,
Bloomsbury, London
April 2, 1878

Dear Mrs. Holiday

Thanks for your notes, and your suggestion about the money: it would be prudent to nurse our buying powers till we begin to sell: I still think we had better not show the things *publicly* till we get up our exhibition.

The additional work on the yellow quilt seems wrong somehow (or some of it does) I think I can lay my finger on the how & why when I see you again: I will send you the twisted silks for the chain-stitch work: I will send a pattern of the new silk as soon as I get it.

Note please about the chain-stitch work, that all shading in it should be of this fashion I mean worked round & round in rows.

I am just off to a Committee meeting of the Association:[1] I doubt they will not do much: meantime there seems to be a better feeling about this morning; and until war actually comes I must needs hope for the best.

Yours very truly
William Morris

MS: Berger Coll.

[1] The Eastern Question Association.

515 • To Thomas Wardle

26, Queen Square,
Bloomsbury, London
April 4, 1878

My dear Wardle

I am really very vexed, but I cannot get down to Leek this side of my Italian journey: this week a spurt of politics in which I was bound to share, has destroyed all my work and left me only next week & a day or two in the week after for doing what I positively *must* do before I go: I am the more vexed as judging from your note I might have been of some use to you about the silk printing: however I send you some notes of combinations of colour which I think would succeed, & shall be happy to see the patterns & advise accordingly: nay, if you thought it positively necessary (since you are pressed for time) I would run down by night-train one day next week & come back by night-train the next day.

I should be very glad to have specimen of the embroidery silk with the slight throw before I get away; & then I could send you patterns & you could dye some for us while I am away.

I fancy you will like to sign the enclosed (name 'description' & address) I was at the deputation[1] yesterday: I saw that some of your townsmen were on the list of names: I don't know if they were really there: I thought the speeches ⟨were⟩ of the 2 lords were very discouraging ⟨an⟩ unleader-like &, to use a plain word, cowardly.

I hope you will let me come down in the summer: I am driven from pillar to post at present.

Yours very truly
William Morris

MS: Duke.

[1] *The Times*, April 4, reported (p. 8) that on the previous day Lord Granville and the Marquis of Hartington (the leaders of the Liberal Party in the Houses of Parliament) had received at the Westminster Hotel a national deputation wanting to know the Liberal Party's position in the current crisis.

516 • To ROBERT BROWNING
The Eastern Question Association
34 Great George Street,
Westminster S.W.
April 5, 1878

Dear Mr. Browning

I know you will excuse my sending you the enclosed paper for your signature whether you feel you can sign it or not: I know you have been with us hitherto, and I confess I should very much regret it if your name did not appear in this protest,[1] which may, and I should think, probably will be the last, whether war or peace jumps out of the bag.

Yours ever truly
William Morris

MS: NYU.

[1] A peace memorial was being circulated, asserting that there was no justification for war between Britain and Russia. See S. Hutchinson Harris, *Auberon Herbert, Crusader for Liberty* (London: Williams and Norgate, 1943), pp. 198-201.

517 • To AGLAIA IONIDES CORONIO
26, Queen Square,
Bloomsbury, London
April 5, 1878

My dear Aglaia

You had better come & look over our stock of dyed silks & you shall have any of them you please in such quantities as I can spare: or shall I make a selection?

As to the cheque — you must allow me to remark that though 'tis 5 days too late, I am not quite so easily taken in as that: so into the fire it has gone: why you would never be able to use up £3-worth of silks if you lived to be a hundred (as I hope you may).

Yours affectionately
William Morris

MS: Yates Coll. Published: Henderson, *Letters*, 119.

518 • RECIPIENT UNKNOWN
Horrington House
Turnham Green
April 6 [1878]

Dear Sir

Many thanks for the cheque for £3 which has duly come to hand: I send you what of the memorial forms I have with me:[1] if you want more, you will get them speedier by writing to E. S. Pryce Esqre[2] 34 Gt. George St. Westminster, to whom I will also ask you to send the signed papers: I am afraid also as a matter of form we must ask for your friends & your own signatures ⟨at the⟩ below the memorial form itself, as they have to be appended to the memorial before it goes in to the authorities (Mr. Cross I believe in this case).[3]

Unless my memory fails me you are in orders: if I am wrong pray accept my apologies.

Yours very truly
William Morris
Treasurer Eastern Question
Association

MS: Huntington.

[1] The peace memorial which was presented to Queen Victoria. See the *Daily News*, April 12, 1878, p. 5. See also letter no. 516, n. 1.

[2] Edward Stisted Mostyn Price (1851-1932), Secretary of the E.Q.A.

[3] Richard A. Cross, the Home Secretary. See Letter no. 487, n. 1.

519 • TO THOMAS HUMPHREY WARD   26, Queen Square,
                                           Bloomsbury, London
                                           April 7, 1878

Dear Sir[1]

Thanks for your letter about the book of selections of English Poetry and your kind remarks about myself in the matter.[2] But apart from ⟨the⟩ my having no available time to take the subject in hand, I am quite sure that I am not a fit person to do it: nor to speak quite plainly do I think the scheme a very promising one. It seems to me that selections of passages ⟨of⟩ from poets are only of value in peculiar cases, as for example when the ⟨art⟩ poet is lacking in constructive, though abundant in lyrical power; or if, as is so common among our Elizabethan poets, he is a man of some poetical gifts, but is not strong enough to break through the pedantry of the time in which he lives, except on rare occasions. A selection from Chaucer's poetry could not possibly mean anything except reprinting one or more of his poems complete; nor do I think that there is anything to be said about him or his works that has not been already very well said: and in any case I am quite sure, as above, that no one could say what was to be said worse than I should. I ask your pardon for putting in a word which seems to discourage

[473]

your plan, about which I have no right to speak; but I think it due to you to give some reasons for my refusal.

Yours faithfully
William Morris

MS: Texas.

¹ Thomas Humphrey Ward (1845-1926), author and journalist, whose wife, Mary Augusta Arnold, was the novelist Mrs. Humphrey Ward.

² This letter probably refers to *The English Poets*, selections with critical introductions by various writers, and a general introduction by Matthew Arnold, edited by Thomas Humphrey Ward, 4 vols. (London: Macmillan, 1880). Ward had apparently asked Morris to make selections from Chaucer and to write the introduction to them.

520 • To Catherine Holiday

26, Queen Square,
Bloomsbury, London
April 8, 1878

Dear Mrs. Holiday

I think the more we can afford to fill up the leaves, stems, and all, the better; but I must leave it finally with you: I am sending you rather a poor lot of silks (twist) except in pinks; but the boy can dye for¹ for you of ordinary colours, while I am away. I send patterns of the silk that is suggested as the substitute for the shoddy (filosel) of these 1 & 2 are very good silk 3 fair and 4 baddish: I mean as to quality: but the point is how are they as to amount of twist, size, & the like: will you please give me a report on them as speedily as you can; as I have no other patterns than these, please dont use them all up, and send me back the balance.

Our memorial is going on fairly well: I suppose you have seen last night's speeches: Lord Derby's is very remarkable, & ought to damage the government if anything can.²

Yours very truly
William Morris

MS: Berger Coll.

¹ Presumably "four." It appears that Morris wrote "fore," and crossed out the "e" but forgot to add the "u."

² Although Morris dated this letter April 8, he probably wrote it on April 9. *The Times*, April 9, reported (pp. 6-7) that on the previous day, Lord Derby, speaking in the House of Lords, had said that the calling out of the reserves was not his only reason for resigning from the Cabinet. He thought that there was no greater emergency than before and still hoped for a settlement through diplomacy. If there were war, who would be Britain's allies, he asked, and concluded by urging that the Government not rush into unwarranted declarations. The peace memorial Morris mentions was presented to Queen Victoria later in April.

521 • To May Morris
Queen Sq
April 8, 1878[1]

Dearest May

This is the last letter I shall write to *you* (to thee) before I come out:
Wot larx! I must write one more to Jenny, one more to Mama, and
then we shall meet: how nice it will be!

We will settle all about the travel back when I come out, tell Mama;
and meantime I am sure that Venice & gondolas will suit her back: &
whatever happens I will take you and Jenny to see Verona & Padua. I
hope you will like the new house: I past by there last Sunday when the
tide was high, & the sun was shining, & it looked all very cheerful —
for London. My poor children, how black & bare and ugly you will
find London when you come back! As for me I am much excited at the
idea of throwing a stone into the Midland Sea; let alone the famous
Venice and the Lombard cities.

Politics — Perhaps we had better forget them: last night however was
the first of the great debate: the most noteworthy speech was Lord
Derby's who (strange to say) alone of all men from the beginning of
the whole affair, has said what he really means — in blundering words
enough to judge by the report, but unmistakeable: no government but
Lord Beaconsfields could stand against such a speech: but Lord B is
really adored by four-fifths of the English Nation.

Now Mama must send me minute instructions as to how to get to
Oneglia. I intend starting from London either next Saturday-week or
next Monday week. I can't tell quite wh: ⟨I should go⟩ or perhaps on
the Sunday between: in any case I should go by the night mail; wh:
would mean starting for Turin from Paris by the evening train next
day. I have such a lot of work to do before I go, including doing what
I can in getting our memorial forward.

Your loving father
William Morris

Best love to Mama & Jenny

MS: BL, Add. MSS. 45341.

[1] Morris misdated this letter which, from internal evidence, seems to have been written
on April 9. See letter no. 520, n. 2.

522 · TO JANE MORRIS 26, Queen Square,
Bloomsbury, London
April 11, 1878

Dearest Janey

What is to be said? What would you like best yourself? Will not the babes be dreadfully dissappointed not to see Venice? My own feeling about the matter is, that though I should have been glad for work-reasons not to have gone yet now that all arrangements have been made I should indeed like to go.

Nevertheless prudence says that £100 though not nice in itself is useful: and you know my work cries out at me: still I should insist on coming out if the Howards are not to bring you home: & once out, why not Venice? and once at Venice, our only way back to Milan will be by the Lombard cities. Summa if the Howards don't come back out I go: if they do you settle it for me yes or no: only dont dissappoint my babes too much.

You may tell G. Howard from me, that though he would have been of great use earlier in the year he may now just as well come back for the boat-race[1] as the general election: (if there is one and I suppose he is better informed about it than I am) ⟨no man⟩ Except for Scotland, Birmingham, and a few boroughs in the NE and S.W. no man will have any chance of getting in, unless he is for supporting the Jew in the war policy: the peace-party are in a very small minority: pray insist on this earnestly to him: *there is no doubt of it.* Still tis like enough that our master & his Whig allies may give us peace, and on any terms I shall be glad of that: but still even in that case Mr. D will be the darling of this people — or in any case — in short for some years to come, ⟨we shall be⟩ until perhaps great disasters teach us better, we shall be a reactionary and Tory Nation. I believe myself that the best way would be for all worthy men to abstain from politics for a while; so that these fools might be the sooner filled with the fruit of their own devices.

There enough of that! Please take council with the babes about the coming out: I should be glad to come & glad to stay; so that I see you all soon. The weather today is triumphantly horrible: it has rained hard for 30 hours with chill & wind.

Love to babes,
Your WM.

MS: BL, Add. MSS. 45338. Published: Henderson, *Letters*, 119-20.

[1] The Oxford-Cambridge boat race took place on April 13, 1878.

523 · To the Editor of *The Times* 26 Queen Sq:
Bloomsbury
April 15, 1878

Sir,

The question asked by Lord Houghton[1] in the House of Lords on Thursday elicited from the Bishop of London[2] an acknowledgement that the scheme proposed some few years back for the wholesale removal of the City churches is continuing its destructive course unimpeded.[3] Four more churches are to be sacrificed to the Mammon-worship and want of taste of this great city. Last year witnessed the destruction of the fine church of St. Michael's, Queenhithe, and All Hallows, Bread-street, which bore upon its walls the inscription stating that Milton had been baptized there. St. Dion's Backchurch, a remarkable building by Wren, is now in course of destruction, while within the last ten years the beautiful church of St. Antholia, with its charming spire, and the skilfully designed little church of St. Mildred, in the Poultry, All Hallows, Staining (except its tower), St. James's, Duke-place, St. Bennet, Gracechurch, with its picturesque steeple, the tower and vestibule of All Hallows-the-Great, Thames-street, have all disappeared. Those for the removal of which a Commission has been now issued are as follows: — St. Margaret Pattens, Roodlane; St. George, Botolph-lane; St. Matthew, Friday-street; and St. Mildred, Bread-street, all works of Wren, and two of them—St. Mildred, Bread-street, and St. Margaret Pattens—possessing spires of singularly original and beautiful design. It must not be supposed that these are the only churches which are in danger, but their proposed destruction serves to show the fate which sooner or later is in store for the whole of Wren's churches in this city, unless Englishmen can be awakened, and by strong and earnest protest show the ecclesiastical authorities that they will not tamely submit to this outrageous and monstrous barbarity.

From an art point of view the loss of these buildings will be irreparable, for Wren's churches form a distinct link in the history of the ecclesiastical art of this country.

Many persons suppose that by preserving St. Paul's Cathedral, that architect's great masterpiece, enough will be left to illustrate his views upon ecclesiastical architecture, but this is far from being the case. For, grand as St. Paul's undoubtedly is, it is only one of a class of buildings common enough on the Continent — imitations of St. Peter's, Rome. In fact, St. Paul's can scarcely be looked upon as an English design, but, rather, as an English rendering of the great Italian original, whereas the City churches are examples of purely English renaissance architecture as applied to ecclesiastical purposes, and illustrate a style of architecture peculiar not only to this country but even to this city, and when they are destroyed the peculiar phase of architecture which they exhibit will have ceased to exist, and nothing will be left to record it. The Continent possesses nothing in the least resembling our City churches, and the fact that they are all found in such close proximity to one another only serves to make them the more valuable for purposes of study. One great merit which they possess is shown by the fact that, although they are diminutive in point of size, scarcely any one of them being above 80 ft. long, they possess a dignity of proportion, a masterly treatment as to scale, which renders them far more imposing than many buildings double and treble their dimensions; the relation which they bear to each other and to the great Cathedral which they surround, enhancing by their thin taper spires the importance of the majestic dome, and relieving the dulness and monotony of the general sky line of the City, all serve as unanswerable arguments for their preservation. Surely an opulent city, the capital of the commercial world, can afford some small sacrifice to spare these beautiful buildings the little plots of ground upon which they stand. Is it absolutely necessary that every scrap of space in the City should be devoted to money-making, and are religion, sacred memories, recollections of the great dead, memorials of the past, works of England's greatest architect, to be banished from this wealthy City? If so, alas for our pretended love of art; alas for the English feeling of reverence of which we hear so much; alas for those who are to come after us, whom we shall have robbed of works of art which it was our duty to hand down to them uninjured and unimpaired; alas for ourselves, who will be looked upon by foreign nations and by our own posterity as the only people who have ever lived, who, possessing no architecture of their own, have made themselves remarkable for the destruction of the buildings of their forefathers.

> I am, Sir
> Your obedient servant,
> William Morris,
> Hon. Sec., the Society for the
> Protection of Ancient Buildings.

TEXT: *The Times*, April 17, 1878. Published: Henderson, *Letters*, 120-22.

[1] Richard Monkton Milnes, first Baron Houghton (1809-1885). He was educated at Trinity College, Cambridge, where he was an "Apostle" and a friend of Tennyson, Hallam, and Thackeray. A writer and Member of Parliament, Milnes made his home a meeting place for writers and political figures.

[2] John Jackson (1811-1885), Bishop of Lincoln, 1853-1868, and of London, 1868-1885.

[3] *The Times*, April 12, 1878 reported (p. 6) that Lord Houghton had asked the Bishop of London whether any city churches of architectural or historic merit were to be de-

stroyed as a result of shrinking congregations and the combining of parishes in the City of London. The Bishop replied that five commissions had been established to report on the union of parishes. He went on to list the churches and to indicate which parishes had been combined.

524 • TO THE ECCLESIASTICAL COMMISSIONERS FOR ENGLAND AND WALES

The Society for
the Protection
of Ancient Buildings
26 Queen Square
Bloomsbury
April 17, 1878

My Lords and Gentlemen,

On behalf of the Society for the Protection of Ancient Buildings, a Society whose objects are explained by the circular enclosed herewith, I beg[1] most respectfully to address you with regard to the works proposed to be done to the Collegiate Church of Southwell Minster.

The Society recognises with satisfaction that since the building has been under the control of the Commissioners the security of the fabric has been considered and its condition as regards stability improved, but at the same time many alterations have been made which in the view of the Society have been destructive of its artistic and historical character.

The removal of the modern fittings of the choir, which were in themselves of no great value, but inasmuch as the removal also involved the destruction of the very interesting side screens, was a step which the Society greatly regrets should have been taken, and the rearrangement of the pewing of the choir appears to them to have been an entirely unnecessary alteration, as though the design of the pewing was modern and poor in quality it was quite adequate to the requirements of cathedral service.

It is understood that the Commissioners have sanctioned a scheme for removing the present low-pitched roofs and the flat ceilings and substituting high-pitched roofs, open internally, throughout the church.

Against this proposal the Society desires to enter its energetic protest, and respectfully asks the Commissioners to reconsider their decision for the following reasons, which the Society trusts that the Commissioners, as guardians of one of the most important public monuments in the kingdom, will not consider unworthy of their consideration.

The proposed alteration, if carried out, will necessarily involve the destruction of the present wooden ceilings of the nave and transepts.

[479]

These ceilings were laid shortly after the fire of 1711, and are in all probability rude but still not unsatisfactory copies of those which were destroyed by the fire. They have an excellent effect, are broad and simple in design, and are much more in accordance with the architecture of the church than an open roof.

The ceilings are of oak and are apparently perfectly sound, no flaw being perceptible from the floor of the church. The outer roofs do, it is true, admit water in places after heavy rains or continued snow, but as they are covered with slate this is no more than what would occur in the roof of any other building of a similar size.

The Norman nave was in all probability covered originally with a flat roof similar to Gloucester and St. Albans. This was replaced in the Middle Ages by a pitched roof; but we have no evidence to show that the alteration was an improvement, but, on the contrary, the subsequent removal of this roof and the substitution of a flat roof tends to show that its effect was not found satisfactory.

Although the present roof dates back no further than the beginning of the last century, it is indisputable that the lowering of the roofs took place at least a century earlier, as Hollar's[2] engraving of the cathedral (which was made in 1672) seems to show them in their present condition.

All trace has been lost of the design of the mediaeval roofs, so that any restoration must be entirely conjectural, and therefore unsatisfactory, when regarded from an antiquarian or architectural point of view.

A matter of even greater importance arising out of the contemplated raising of the roofs is the obliteration of the wooden lantern between the western towers, which would be swept away if any other roof is substituted for the present.

In all probability the destruction of this lantern was not present in the mind of the Commissioners when the question of the alteration of the roofs was under consideration, and the Society earnestly hopes that now that the entire effect of the proposed raising is brought to their notice that the Commissioners will hesitate before they give their sanction to a proposal which will inflict an irreparable injury upon the church, and deprive it of one of its most interesting and characteristic features.

The lantern is perhaps unique of its kind, and though exceedingly simple in design, it is so dignified in expression and adds so much to the charm of the church that its removal would be a source of the deepest regret to all who are truly interested in what is most native in one of our first and best preserved national monuments.

The Society trusts that the Commissioners will, for these reasons, refrain from carrying out an alteration which is perfectly unnecessary and uncalled for, which will in no sense add to the safety or beauty of the church, and that they will devote the funds at their disposal to the preservation in its present state of the interesting building committed to their charge.

It would be a lasting disgrace to the century if it should happen that through injudicious interference the Collegiate Church of Southwell, after having escaped the rapacity of Henry VIII and the followers of Edward VI, and has come down to us almost unimpaired in its essential features from very nearly the earliest historical times, should in these last days have its identity destroyed, and its value as a national record placed in jeopardy by a mistaken zeal for restoration.

I have the honour to remain, my lords and gentlemen, your very obedient servant, (Signed)

William Morris, Hon. Secretary.

TEXT: *The Architect* (London), August 30, 1878.

¹ Morris may not have written this letter though it does bear his signature. See letter no. 578.

² Wenceslaus Hollar (1606–1677), Bohemian etcher who worked mainly in England. His engraving of Southwell Cathedral is in the third volume of William Dugdale's *Monasticon Anglicanum*, published in 1673.

525 • TO EMMA SHELTON MORRIS   April 17, 1878

Dearest Mother

I am off on Saturday night. I shall get to Oneglia about 6 on Tuesday evening. It will interest, I daresay, to know that I am making arrangements to take the house I told you of on the river-side: I hope to get all settled so as to get the repairs begun as soon as my back is turned.

I drink my tea out of the blue cup every day now.

Your most affectionate Son
William Morris

P.S. Best love to Henrietta

MS: Walthamstow.

526 • TO JENNY MORRIS   26, Queen Square,
Bloomsbury, London
April 17, 1878

Dearest Jenny

I shall not trouble any of you with long yarns today as I shall see you so soon: I am going to leave London on Saturday (20th) by the night

[481]

mail, & Paris on Sunday night; so that I shall get to Oneglia by Tuesday evening. So 'Why row?'

It is April weather now thunder & lightening at this moment. but warm: I hear from ⟨you⟩ May that the hot weather makes you all very lazy; which will suit me to a turn.

Your loving father
William Morris

Mama on 'tother side.[1]

MS: BL, Add. MSS. 45339.

[1] The half of the letter paper containing the note to Jane has not survived.

527 • TO GEORGIANA BURNE-JONES Genoa
April 27, 1878

We entered this ancient city yesterday evening by no means triumphantly: we had a lovely drive on Thursday morning to a hill town with an ancient stone or two in its buildings, which are now nothing but tatters of disorder: yet it was agreeable and not very dirty. Diano Castello it is called: people used to run there when the Saracen Vikings burnt Diano Marina and the shore in general: unhappily, though the drive was pleasant, and the evening wandering among the olives was pleasant, I felt the seeds of gout in me all day, and woke yesterday morning with that plant flourishing vigorously; but I didn't like to keep them stuck at Oneglia, as all preparations had been made for departure: so about midday we got away, and I found myself in a carriage somehow along with my dear Jenny, and a very pleasant ride we had to Genoa with my gout seemingly decreasing: but when we all met at the station there was a long way to go to the omnibus, and the octroi[1] objected to the box of medicines (thinking them syrops), and I could not walk or even hop well, so I got stuck, till a chap took me up on his back: but even then I behaved so ill as this, that when he set me down against a wall (lacking nothing of Guy Fawkes but his matches and lanthorn) things began to dance before my eyes, my knees went limp, and down I went, thank you, and enjoyed a dream of some minute and a quarter I suppose, which seemed an afternoon of public meetings and the like: out of that I woke and found myself on the ground the centre of an admiring crowd, one of the members of which held a brandy bottle to my lips which I had the presence of mind to refuse and call for water. Poor May, who was with me, was very much frightened, but was very good: even then I had to be Guy Fawkesed upstairs at the

Hotel, chuckling with laughter, till they landed me in this present pala-
tial suite of rooms: so I'm not likely to be able to tell you much of
Genoa, I fear. Murray, who is still with us, has taken the two girls out
for a walk; I can't help thinking that they will enjoy the port and streets
of a big town after the quiet of Oneglia, though I, for my part, when I
wandered among the olives above the sea the other day, felt as if I
should be well contented to stay there always; it really was a most
lovely spot: and it was pleasant to have the high road close by it and to
hear the jingle of bells as the carts went by, though when you were
among the olives you could not guess of any road near: the trees went
on terrace after terrace right up to the top of the low hill: you could see
nothing else: nothing can be imagined more beautiful and soothing.

This confounded gout and Guy Fawkesing of mine has of course put
off our journey to-day, but I am much better now, and I hope we shall
get on to Venice to-morrow: we shan't attempt stopping at Verona,
where we can easily put up on our return: you see if we were once at
Venice, Janey and the girls could amuse themselves in any case; and as
for me 'tis clear that Venice must be the hobbler's Paradise. Can't you
imagine what a time it was for me when I looked out at the window at
Oneglia and saw those three all standing together?

TEXT: Mackail, I, 366-68. Published: Henderson, *Letters*, 122-23.

¹ Possibly Morris means the fare collector.

528 · TO CHARLES FAIRFAX MURRAY   Venice
                                                   Hotel de L'Univers
                                                   April 29, 1878

My dear Murray

We hadn't at all a bad journey yesterday, though my wife is very
tired today, and I am still lame, as, though my r[ight] foot is nearly
well the enemy has got into the left: I am glad that nobody told me of
Lake Guarda, it was a wonderful surprise for me, that moved me more
than anything I have seen: of course we *had* to change at Milan, & as
the train was very full we had to get into separate carriges. I went about
in a Gondola today past & up to the ducal Palace, but I couldn't manage
to crawl across the Piazetta: nevertheless I enjoyed myself hugely.

This is a queer ramshackle old house: very cheap, but attendance bad:
it has a nice platform of its own over the water: it is near the iron bridge
(damn the iron bridge!) & beside the Academia. The Ducal Palace looks
very different from what I imagined as to colour: I mean the diapred

[483]

part of it: people paint it white & red; but I see the red is the faintest pink: this looks better than I expected:

I hope to write again

Yours very truly
William Morris

MS: Texas.

529 • EXCERPTS FROM THREE LETTERS TO GEORGIANA BURNE-JONES[1]

a.   [April 29, 1878]

What a strange surprise it was when it suddenly broke upon me, with such beauty as I never expected to see: for a moment I really thought I had fallen asleep and was dreaming of some strange sea where everything had grown together in perfect accord with wild stories.[2]

b.   [early May 1878]

It is sad to think that our children's children will not be able to see a single genuine ancient building in Europe.

c.   [Torcello
May 12, 1878]

it was a great rest to be among the hedges and the green grass again, and to hear the birds singing; swifts are the only songsters in the city.

TEXT: Mackail, I, 368-69.

[1] These excerpts, almost certainly taken from letters to Georgiana Burne-Jones, form part of a narrative sequence arranged by Mackail (I, 368-69).

[2] According to Mackail, Morris was referring to his first sight of Lake Garda.

530 • To Aglaia Ionides Coronio
Hotel de L'Univers
Grande Canal
Venice
May 2 [1878]

My dear Aglaia

We have all got here & this is our 4th day at Venice: I think the girls but May more especially are the better for their sojourn: as to Janey I should have said the same for her till she got here, but now she seems to have broken down, which is a great dissappointment to me: the weather is very dull & close, which may have something to do with it. As for myself, I have made rather a mess of it, for my cold turned at the end of last week into gout or rheumatism or a mixture of both; which is very obstinate, and keeps me still quite lame; so that all I have seen of Venice as yet has been from 2 gondola rides: I got on pretty well in the long journey from Genoa here, & it was a beautiful day; so that after all if the worst come to the worst I have seen a good deal to remember even as it is; & I suppose I may reckon on getting about in the course of 2 or 3 days: we think of staying here about 10 days in all, & then going home by way of Milan stopping at Padua & Verona also at least. I should think Verona right under the mountains would suit us all better than the lagoon — wonderful as the place is in all other respects.

I found the place at Oneglia a most beautiful spot to live in: I don't think I should ever have tired of the olive-woods.

Yours affectionately
William Morris

MS: Yates Coll. Published: Henderson, *Letters*, 123-24.

531 • To Charles Fairfax Murray
Hotel de L'Univers
May 4 [1878]

My dear Murray

I enclose some pills which I hope will come safe & not *much* squashed: my gout has now at last turned the corner, & today I managed to hobble into S Marks: but I have wasted 5 days here, & am still lame enough. The weather is now beautiful here: bright clear & rather hot: I have got a comfortable room now: We leave about the end of next week for Padua. I am bein hollowed at to come out as we are going a drive, to Lido I believe.

Yours very truly
William Morris

MS: Texas.

532 · To Georgiana Burne-Jones [Padua, May 15, 1878]

What a beautiful and *pleasant* place it is with the huge hall dividing the market place, and the endless arcades everywhere: or the Arena Chapel in the midst of the beautiful garden of trellised vines, all as green as the greenest just now. Yesterday was a stormy day, and in the afternoon the girls and I were caught in a shower as we were wandering about; however, it was but wandering in an arcade till it was over, and as the pavement was clean and dry I sat down with great content with my back to the wall. A dyer's hand-cart took refuge by us with a load of blue work (cotton) just done: I was so sorry I could not talk with one of the men, who looked both good-tempered and intelligent. In the evening we went to a queer old botanic garden and heard the birds sing, and then we were driven along the road outside the walls. The rain had cleared off but left great threatening clouds that quite hid the Alps, but the small mountains to the west of Padua were quite clear and blue, and set me longing to be among them. It was a beautiful evening, but damp I doubt; but how sweet the hay smelt!

[Verona, May 16, 1878][1]

'Tis a piping hot day, not a cloud in the sky. I have just been into Sta. Anastasia, which is hard by: a very beautiful church, but appeals less to the heart than the head, and somehow don't satisfy that: also though 'tis meant to be exceedingly Gothic and pointed, it is thoroughly neo-classical in feeling. S. Zeno is not quite what I expected: 'tis a round-arched Gothic church, just as S. Anastasia is a pointed-arched Renaissance one. I am more alive again, and really much excited at all I have seen and am seeing, though sometimes it all tumbles into a dream, and I do not know where I am. Many times I think of the first time I ever went abroad, and to Rouen, and what a wonder of glory that was to me when I first came upon the front of the Cathedral rising above the flower-market. It scarcely happens to me like that now, at least not with man's work, though whiles it does with bits of the great world, like the Garda Lake the other day, or unexpected sudden sights of the mountains. Even the inside of St. Mark's gave one rather deep satisfaction, and rest for the eyes, than that strange exaltation of spirits, which I remember of old in France, and which the mountains give me yet.

I don't think this is wholly because I am grown older, but because I really have had more sympathy with the North from the first in spite of all the faults of its work. Let me confess and be hanged: with the later work of Southern Europe I am quite out of sympathy. In spite of its magnificent power and energy I feel it as an enemy; and this much more in Italy, where there is such a mass of it, than elsewhere. Yes, and even in these magnificent and wonderful towns I long rather for the heap of grey stones with a grey roof that we call a house north-away.

TEXT: Mackail, I, 369-70. Extract published: Henderson, *Letters*, 124-25.

¹ Mackail in his notebook summarizes a letter to Georgiana Burne-Jones dated May 16, 1878 as follows: "(Padua): finished next day at Verona. Remembrance of his first journey abroad and exaltation at Rouen."

532a • TO GEORGE JAMES HOWARD   Verona
                                                       May 18 [1878]

My dear George

Here we are & have been all yesterday: I am still not quite myself; & I am sorry to say that my wife is quite poorly; so that I doubt if we can get away from here tomorrow (Sunday) & we shall certainly have to miss Milan. I think she has picked up a touch of fever somehow, but she is better today than she was yesterday, so I am not so anxious as I should have been; nevertheless 'tis a great trouble for all parties: it is terribly hot here; not a cloud in the sky, Wind S.E. it would be quite unendurable but that there is always a wind on the water.

Padua we all thought a most delightful town, as full of character as could be: the precinct of the Arena Chapel is a paradise, and St. Antony & its cloisters is very fine & noble. As for Verona its general beauty & interest is beyond all praise, & I don't know when I have been so moved by any place as I was last night at the look-out from the Arena; a lovely and cloudless evening: but perhaps I am a little dissappointed with the architecture as architecture: St Zeno is very beautiful & *elegant* the porches at the Cathedral are splendid & all the porches round-arched or pointed are elegant: but to be critical, everything is elegant rather than solemn or poetical. St Marks, Torcello, Fiesole, St Mincarto, the Baptistry at Florence: these (but the first above all) are what I have seen in Italy that really move me: the rest that I have seen I must say seem to me very inferior to good French & English Gothic. Nevertheless Verona is a wonderful place, and on the whole most beautiful: ah, if only one could have some nice grey, cool, wholesome, weather to see it in! The Roman Gate & the Arena are what has pleased me most here.

We were all very loathe to leave Venice, Janey especially; she never ceases longing for the gondola and its easy travelling. I confess I dread the journey home for her very much. This Inn is not a very nice one, & it *is* dear doubtless: it swarms with the Anglo-Saxon going to or coming from the Tyrol: the Paduan Inn, the golden star (the Eagle is extinct) was comfortable & obliging. I have got 2 vols of G. Sand[1] which I am going to read to punish myself for being so gout-crusty at Venice: I expect this penance will expiate the more part of my sins. Of course I have seen no papers since Tuesday: Wishing you all luck, & with best remembrances to all

I am
Yours affectionately
William Morris

MS: Howard Papers. Extract published: Henderson, *Life*, 183.

[1] Possibly *Histoire de ma vie* (1854-1855).

---

533 • To Emma Shelton Morris   Paris
                                                                May 23 [1878]

Dearest Mother

We have all got safe so far as this, and are going by the mail tonight, so that we expect to be home tomorrow morning. We came all the way from Turin yesterday, starting on Tuesday evening: it was a beautiful bright day yesterday, and I enjoyed the journey through France; especially as I had always been that way by night before: Janey bore the journey wonderfully, & the children were not very tired. Unluckily we cannot get about much here, as it is a very wet bad day, and I am still rather lame in one foot.   the weather got very hot after we left Venice, and I think it was that wh: brought back my rheumatism a little: however it has not been bad since. We were all very sorry to leave Venice; but I think Janey the sorriest: you see she found the water-carriage so pleasant. I hear that it got very hot after we had left: we stayed 2 days at Padua, & 3 at Verona on our way home, and were very much delighted with them. I suppose Paris is very full of English; at any rate this Inn (St James', Rue St Honoré) is.

I have to wish you many happy returns of your birthday, and all blessings, my dearest mother: I will come and see you when I get right in the legs again.

Best love to Henrietta, I think Janey is writing to her.

I am
Dearest Mother
Your most affectionate Son
William Morris

MS: Walthamstow.

**534 • FROM A LETTER TO GEORGIANA
BURNE-JONES[?]**   [London, May 25, 1878]

I am still plaguy lame, a very limpet, but am not so devil-ridden as I was. I think that came of that infernal furnace-heat we were in, the last few days of Italy: it was such a relief when the cool mountain breezes woke me out of a doze as the train laboured up the last slopes before the great tunnel: and going through that merry Burgundy country with a fine windy sunny day I got quite merry myself.

TEXT: Mackail, I, 370.

535 • TO WILLIAM ALLINGHAM   Horrington House
                                                 June 6 [1878]
My dear Allingham

I have been out all the forepart of the week, so I could not come out now; else one certainly should go to St. Albans, and I should have been very pleased to have been there with you. Of course we are not going to let Scott quite alone: but I don't know about attacking him in detail: I mean to say, fighting as to whether he has done such & such, and not done it:[1] the human mind is shockingly given to lie when convenient (as witness Sir Stafford Northcote yesterday)[2] and about such small matters the public is none the wiser, and soon gets tired of controversy concerning 'You did' and 'I didn't.'

But I daresay you don't mean the thing to be taken up like that, and your visit to St. Albans is just the thing to help you to say that a re-stored building no longer looks like an ancient one, that the surface history is all gone, and with it the venerableness of the sense of lapse of time, and the pleasure of looking at a work of man that has withstood it, — and the like. I am very sorry I can't be with you, though I must say it would give me a great deal of pain to see St Albans now, as I have seen it once or twice while it was still in a genuine state: a strange and most poetical looking half mile of church.

                                                 Yours very truly
                                                 William Morris

P.S. On the whole, the Anti-Scrape Society is doing well.

MS: Illinois. Published: *Letters to William Allingham* (1911), 231-32; Henderson, *Letters*, 125.

[1] *The Times*, May 10, printed (p. 4) an article titled "St. Albans," in which the resto-ration of the abbey by Gilbert Scott was described, as was the work carried on after his death by his sons, G. Gilbert and J. Oldred Scott. The article discussed the method by which the south wall had been brought back to the perpendicular.

536 • To Frederick William Chesson
26, Queen Square,
Bloomsbury, London
June 28, 1878

My dear Chesson

I have both your notes, and as to the 1st question I shall be quite ready for my [part] to agree to spending the £5 from the balance of the Agricultural-Hall-Meeting fund,¹ of which there is in my hands £23 odd.

As to the rooms in Gt George St, we cannot do otherwise than agree, I think: will you write to Mr. Platt?²

The balance of the E.Q.A. account is £123

I am
Yours very truly
William Morris

MS: PML.

¹ See letter no. 494, n. 1.
² Possibly the landlord of the building in which the E.Q.A. meeting was held.

**537 • To the Ecclesiastical Commission
for England and Wales**
The Society for
the Protection
of Ancient Buildings
26 Queen Square
Bloomsbury,
July [29] 1878

Dear Sir

The Society for the Protection of Ancient Buildings has had under consideration your architect's observations in reply to the letter addressed you in April last.

The Society is glad to find that the building is in charge of an architect so careful and conservative as Mr. Christian,¹ though it disagrees with the opinions expressed in his letter. Bearing in mind the objects of the Society, this letter is neither satisfactory nor reassuring. Believing that your architect concurs in its estimation of the responsibility which attaches to the custodians of a national record such as Southwell Minster, and of their obligation to preserve it from change, the Society brings the following further remarks to the notice of your Board.

As regards the fittings of the choir the Society still remains of opinion that, poor though they were, they fulfilled the requirements of the service of the church by providing seats for clergy, singers, and people. If stalls and benches of oak, and tile floors, be requisites of cathedral service, the Society must acknowledge these were lacking.

As to the removal of the galleries, the Society thinks it was unnecessary. It is true that the galleries which existed in the choir aisles hid some of the architecture, but in a church like Southwell, which was never intended to be seen from base to apex in the naked way modern restorers seem to think becoming, they concealed nothing that is not sufficiently expressed elsewhere. The galleries, screens, tombs, and such like obstructions, impart a fitted look to a big building — they help to give a homely and inhabited appearance to the edifice, and it is their removal and destruction that has made so many of our large churches so cheerless.

The loss of the side screens is a more serious one, and the Society again expresses its regret at their removal. Your architect admits they were well modelled, he does not allege they were in bad repair, but says they were only removed after most careful consideration, and after Mr. Street's opinion had been taken by the Bishop, and that they were put together in a most flimsy manner. The Society urges that this is no justification for their demolition. It understands Mr. Street also advised the removal of the fourteenth century screen, and it regrets that the same influence was not used to save the side screens that prevailed against Mr. Street's opinion in the other case.[2]

As regards the roof of the nave, the Society does not dispute that the marks on the central tower, and the moulded arched openings below, of which it was aware when its letter was written, indicate the former existence of a high pitched roof, but the timbers of this were in all probability concealed internally by boarding. It *does* dispute the existence of an open roof, meaning thereby a roof the timbers of which were visible from the nave of the church.

No adequate reason is given in your architect's letter for the necessity for new roofs. He disagrees with the Society as to the value of the flat ceilings, which he considers dwarf the church; says that the roofs were made of the cheapest and rudest form consistent with strength, and that *his* view and that of most persons interested in the church is that the substitution of open roofs would be an enormous improvement to the interior. Here is no justification for the removal of the present roofs and flat ceilings, the latter of which, in the Society's view (the Society numbering many persons also interested in the church), have an excellent effect, are broad and simple in design, and, though in later style, agree with the architecture of the church. The Society hopes your Board will give further consideration to this matter, and not needlessly remove the existing roofs for the sake of what is a very problematic improvement.

The Society's opinion that the restoration of the mediaeval roofs must be entirely conjectural is not disputed by your architect, who, by means of the indication of the level of the collar beams, the lines showing the old pitch on the central tower, and examples of ancient framing, proposes to substitute open roofs for the existing ones, thus destroying a ceiling 167 years old, which is probably unique, to add one more to the many imitations of ancient roofs which have of late years been so freely produced.

Your architect cannot understand why the Society should advocate the retention both of the flat ceilings and of the "lantern"[3] at the western end, which he says it is no part of his design to remove. It does so because it wishes to save *both* the "lantern" *and* the flat ceilings. No doubt the roof was raised over the western bay for the reason your architect states. The builders took advantage of the peculiar conditions to do something striking and characteristic. A roof of higher pitch than the present one would cover over the "lantern" and enclose the great west window, thus doing away with the necessity that originated the "lantern" which without the flat ceiling would be both useless and meaningless.

May the Society suggest that if the present roof timbers and their covering be unsound, or if the pitch of the roof be insufficient for slates (though your architect in his reply does not say so) they might be repaired or renewed, or the exterior covered with lead, without the demolition of the flat ceilings. More urgent reasons than are given for the removal of the old roofs and ceilings are necessary to satisfy the Society that it is not possible to preserve them.

The Society thanks your Board for giving it the opportunity of explaining its views at greater length.

Believe me, yours faithfully,
William Morris, Hon. Sec.

The Secretary, Ecclesiastical Commission

TEXT: *The Architect* (London), August 30, 1878.

[1] Ewan Christian (1814–1895), a restorer and designer of buildings. His work included the restoration of Carlisle Cathedral and the design of the National Portrait Gallery. In 1850, he had been appointed consulting architect for the Ecclesiastical Commission.

[2] For correspondence on this subject, see *The Architect*, August 30, 1878; for a report of

the S.P.A.B. meeting on October 23 and a letter in reply to Street signed by Newman Marks, see *The Architect*, November 1, 1878. For further exchanges between Street and Christian, and for comment on their dispute, see *The Architect*, September 13, November 8, 15, and 22, 1879. See also letter no. 578.

³ A crown-like addition to the tower added for ornament or to admit light.

538 • To Emma Shelton Morris   26, Queen Square,
                                                                    Bloomsbury, London
                                                                    July 31 [1878?]

Dearest Mother

I am safe at home again; after a very successful trip. I write in a great hurry to say that they have made a mistake about that £40 supposing that it was to be instead of paying 40 on the 180 shares still in my name: if you have paid anything on them I will pay you back at once: if not I will pay the £40 to Mr. Allen.

I hope much you are well & Henrietta also: my best love to you & her.

Your most affec: Son
William Morris

MS: Walthamstow.

539 • To the Editor of *The Times*   26, Queen Square,
                                                                    Bloomsbury
                                                                    August 1, 1878

Sir,

As honorary secretary of the "Society for the Protection of Ancient Buildings," I cannot help expressing my satisfaction, which I have no doubt will be shared by all my colleagues, at the letter which appears in *The Times* of to-day from Lord Carnarvon, as chairman of the Society of Antiquaries of London, with reference to the contemplated alteration of the roof of St. Albans Abbey.¹

I have no doubt that the opinion expressed by Lord Carnarvon represents the feelings of antiquaries and men of taste throughout the country very generally.

Our society has already written to the "Restoration Committee" of St. Albans deprecating the contemplated alterations.

I am, Sir, your obedient
servant,
William Morris

TEXT: *The Times*, August 2, 1878.

¹ Lord Carnarvon wrote that the accidental building of flat roofs had made the central tower magnificent. He insisted that if it were left as it was it would continue to be interesting as the record of additions and alterations made by generations over centuries.

540 • TO FREDERICK STARTRIDGE ELLIS
26, Queen Square,
Bloomsbury, W.C.
August 6, 1878

Dear Sir

In a few days the speech delivered by Mr. Gladstone[1] on Tuesday last in support of Lord Hartington's resolution[2] will be published in pamphlet form. I am associated with Mr. Sellar, Hon. Secy. of the Liberal Central Association[3] and Mr. Chesson, Hon. Secy. of the Eastern Question Association in a private effort to raise a fund to promote the *gratuitous* circulation of this speech in the constituencies. I should feel much obliged if you could contribute to this special object. I may add that Mr. Gladstone has revised the speech.

Yours faithfully
William Morris[4]

F. S. Ellis Esq
39 New Bond Street

MS: Ohio.

¹ Gladstone's speech was fully reported in *The Times*, July 31, 1878, pp. 6-7.

² On July 30, the Marquis of Hartington had moved resolutions expressing the satisfaction of the House that the Treaty of Berlin had ended the Russo-Turkish War and that self-government had been extended to some populations in European Turkey. He had moved, in addition, an expression of regret that Greek claims had not been met, and an assertion that Britain's guarantee of Turkey's Asian frontiers had unnecessarily extended Britain's military liabilities and had, moreover, been given without the knowledge of Parliament.

³ Alexander Craig Sellar (1835-1890) was legal secretary to the Lord Advocate (1870-1874), and later served as Liberal M.P. for Haddington Burghs (1882-1884) and Lanarkshire, Patrick division (1885), and as Liberal whip (1885-1889).

⁴ The formal address and careful handwriting suggest that this was a form letter, sent to Ellis among others. It may not have been penned by Morris but was certainly signed by him.

541 • To Mr. Bowman
26, Queen Square,
Bloomsbury, London
August 8, 1878

Dear Mr. Bowman[1]

Sir R. Alcock's book[2] came yesterday, & I received it with much pleasure; it seems very interesting: pray thank Sir Rutherford very much for me: I shall be very glad to see him when occasion serves.

Yours very truly
William Morris

MS: Berger Coll.

[1] See letter no. 254, n. 1.
[2] Sir Rutherford Alcock (1809-1897), a diplomat who had held foreign service posts in Europe and Asia. Morris was referring to his *Art and Industries in Japan*, published in 1878.

542 • To the Editor of *The Times*
26 Queen Sq:
Bloomsbury
August 26, 1878

To the Editor of the Times[1]

Sir

Though the Committee for the restoration of St Alban's Cathedral have determined to alter that church by putting a high-pitched roof on the nave in the place of the present flat one, the Committee of our Society cannot ⟨yet⟩ give up all hope that the public in general may yet interest itself in the matter, and refuse to support a scheme regarded by so many archaeologists as rash and destructive: in this hope we beg the favour of space in your columns to enable us to protest once more against what at the least we must call a dangerous alteration of an ancient & famous building.

Into the artistic ⟨questions⟩ matters of the relative advantage of a high or a low roof in the abstract; and the respective merits of the earlier or later styles represented at St. Albans, we do not wish to enter, conceiving that both this ⟨and⟩ as well as the archaeological point of dispute as to whether the ⟨earlier⟩ church once had a high-pitched roof ⟨are⟩ is beside the question: the point that we wish to lay before the public is that the church is already covered with a roof which can be repaired so as to be thoroughly substantial without risking the stability of the walls, and without altering the architectural character of the building, or making it other than it has grown to be through a long period of interesting history: of that history the present roof is a genuine part; it conceals or injures nothing more artistic or splendid than itself; ⟨and, taken in conjunction⟩ the long unbroken line of parapet ⟨that results from such a roof being used⟩ of mixed materials fitted to this roof must be allowed by everyone to hold its place amongst strong & remarkable architectural effects, the loss of any one of which would be a loss to the variety and interest of art. To replace this roof with a high-pitched one is an undertaking involving so much expense that the Restoration Committee shrink from the task of raising money to carry out ⟨out⟩ the work with proper materials, and propose to use deal and slate instead of the present oak and lead; if this is done it will lay on the future guardians of St. Albans a heavy burden of expenses for the repair of such perishable ⟨materials⟩ substitutes: but ⟨in⟩ whatever material is used, the proposed new roof will involve possible danger to the fabric of the walls, and certain change in some of their architectural features, such as the parapets for instance: nor can we hide from ourselves that under cover of these necessary, (and in any case regretable) changes, the mistaken zeal of the restorers will probably lead to quite unnecessary changes most destructive to the artistic and historical interest of the ⟨this great monument⟩ the building: we fear, in short, that it ⟨will lead to⟩ will end in the entire modernization of this great monument; a result which we are sure the public in general, even that portion of it which is not specially interested in archaeology, will heartily regret.

With this fear in our minds we wish to appeal to the public to notice that the opinion of archaeologists and artists is at least divided on the matter; ⟨and⟩ we wish to point out to it that the risk of loss to the nation through possibly mistaken alteration is greater out of all proportion to its advantages than the risk incurred by possibly mistaken inaction: if the fabric of St Albans Abbey is watchfully constantly & reverently repaired, it will not be too late when the views of our Society are proved to be wrong beyond all question, to put a high-pitched roof on the nave; or indeed to pull down the whole Church and rebuild it: but if the proposed alterations take place, and it be found some few years hence that our views are reasonable, as we confidently think it will be, then indeed it will be all too late for reparation, & no regrets will wish back the inimitable work of our forefathers, which our rashness and egotism will have destroyed forever.

> I am,
> Sir,
> Yours obediently,
> William Morris
> Hon: Sec: on behalf of the
> Committee of the Society for
> the ⟨Preservation⟩ Protection
> of Ancient Buildings

MS: NYPL. Published: MM, I, 165: Henderson, *Letters*, 126-27.

[1] This letter was apparently never published in *The Times*.

543 • To Thomas Wardle   Kelmscott, Lechlade
                                                              September 9, 1878

My dear Wardle

Thanks for your letter: I am very glad to hear that Mrs. Wardle is better; it must have been very trying for one so active to be laid up like that. Thanks for asking me to come again: if it would suit you, I think I could get away in about a month's time: I am sorry to hear of Martins desertion: as to the dress-pieces printing, I can see no objection though it will take some study on my part to think of what will be really worth doing: we will talk it over when we meet. The public ⟨are⟩ is very hard to move, and I sometimes think I have a toughish job ahead of me in dealing with them before I finish. I shall have to tell you of a nice piece of rascality played on us by certain of our manufacturers: this sort of thing really sickens one.[1]

I saw lately such a beautiful old house some 20 miles from here: I really think the finest Jacobean house I have seen: lots of old furniture & embroidery in it, & 2 rooms hung with their original tapestry (English without doubt). Chastleton the name is: the S.P.A.B. had some dealings with the spinster owner of it.[2]

If it is fine I am going to take my daughters to Oxford tomorrow by water.

Yours very truly
William Morris

MS: Duke.

[1] Writing about the designs for Kidderminster Carpets, Vallance says (p. 107) that the designs were not registered, and that one of them, the "Lily," was pirated by a manufacturer who produced it on his own account after making a minor alteration. Confronted by Morris, the manufacturer admitted the truth of the charge. Parry, probably referring to the same incident, has noted (p. 78) that Morris learned that the Heckmondwike firm were selling the "Lily and Tulip" pattern to his competitor, Maples. He and G. Wardle visited Sir John Maples to complain, but Maples insisted that he was doing no wrong and was rather benefiting everyone involved.

[2] Chastleton House, Oxfordshire, built in the seventeenth century by Walter Jones, a wool merchant. The owner to whom Morris refers was Miss Whitmore Jones. See H. A. Evans, *Highways and Byways in Oxford and the Cotswolds* (London: Macmillan, 1905), pp. 140-45.

544 · To Henry James Jennings

Sigurd p: 375.

King Atlis' men are bidden to cut the heart from the living Hogni, the son of Giuki, as he lies bound after the battle in the hall, and to bring it to the King: Atli's councillors bid them wait lest they disgrace the King by slaying his prisoner by night, for, "night-slaying is murder-slaying' as the saw runs: the slayers are shaken in their purpose, all the more as they are awed by the majesty of the fallen Niblung; they say:

—— The King makes merry, as a well the white wine springs,
And the red wine runs as a river; and what are the hearts of kings
That men may know them naked from the hearts of bond & thrall?
Nor go we ⟨go⟩ empty-handed to King Atli in his hall."

Thus the sword-carles spake to each other; and they looked & a
                                                   man they saw,
Who should hew the wood if he lived, & for thralls the water
                                                   should draw,
A thrall-⟨bound⟩ born servant of servants, begetter of thralls on the
                                                       earth:
And they said: "If this one were away, scarce greater were waxen the
                                                   dearth,
That this morning hath wrought on the Eastland; for the years shall
                                               eke out his woe,
And no day his toil shall lessen, & worse and worse shall *he* grow."

They drew the steel new-whetted, on the thrall they laid the hand;
For they said, "All hearts be fashioned as the heart of a king of the
                                               land."
But the thrall was bewildered with anguish, and wept and bewailed
                                             him sore
For the loss of his life of labour, and the grief that long he bore.

But wroth was the son of Giuki, and he spake: "It is idle & vain,
And two men for one shall perish, and the knife shall be whetted
                                             again.
It is better to die than be sorry, and to hear the trembling cry,
And to see the shame of the poor: O fools, must the lowly die
Because kings strove with swords? I bid you to hasten the end,
For my soul is sick with confusion, and fain on the way would I
                                           wend.

Horrington House
Turnham Green
October 21, 1878

Dear Sir[1]

Above I have written out a few lines from my poem of Sigurd, &
have explained whereabouts in the poem they come.[2]

Yours faithfully
William Morris

Henry J. Jennings, Esqre

MS: Huntington.

[1] Henry James Jennings (born c.1840), writer and editor. In 1878 he was editor of the
Birmingham Daily Mail. (See his autobiography, *Chestnuts and Small Beer* [London: Chap-
man and Hall, 1920]).

[2] Since Morris wrote the lines out as part of his letter, they are included here. They
come from Book IV, "Gudrun," of *Sigurd the Volsung*, published in 1876.

545 • TO FREDERICK STARTRIDGE ELLIS

26, Queen Square,
Bloomsbury, London
Wednesday
October [23 or 30?,] 1878

My dear Ellis

Alas! no, I can't come even at all: I am glad you are having such a
good time: I can't imagine greater pleasure than Kelmscott under such
weather ⟨the⟩ as the last few days: though it looks wettish today. Which
however wont matter for you.

I hold you to your promise for November.

Yours very truly
William Morris

MS: Schimmel Coll.

546 • TO FREDERICK WILLIAM CHESSON

26, Queen Square,
Bloomsbury, London
October 28, 1878

My dear Chesson

Thanks for your letter: I enclose the cheques received to the amount
of £35.1 & a cheque for £10 from the Ag: Hall-balance   I have written
to Lord Bath[1] asking him to send the £10 he promised. I am glad to
hear so much has been done with the speech.[2]

[499]

Though I don't doubt it myself I suppose some members of the E.Q.A. might doubt whether we could have any dealings with the Affghan matter:[3] so I should think a new committee[4] would be better: anyhow something ought to be done; and perhaps might be done with some effect upon ⟨the⟩ public opinion now.

Yours very truly
William Morris

MS: PML.

[1] See letter no. 422, n. 2.

[2] Gladstone's speech in Parliament, July 30, 1878, reported in *The Times*, July 31. There were plans to publish it as a pamphlet. See letter no. 540.

[3] In the summer of 1878, a Russian mission was accepted by the ruler of Afghanistan. The British responded by launching a military campaign to gain control of Afghanistan's foreign relations and exclude the Russians, which led to the second Afghan War of 1878-1879.

[4] After the second invasion of Afghanistan, a new Afghan Committee was established. The officers were: Chairman, Lord John Laird Mair Lawrence, Vice-Chairman; Henry Fawcett; Treasurer, Francis W. Buxton; Hon. Secretary, Frederick William Chesson; and Secretary, John Noble.

---

547 • To William Bell Scott

Morris
Kelmscott House
Upper Mall, Hammersmith
[Autumn 1878?]

Take train at South Kensington for Shaftesbury Road (4 minutes walk) or to Hammersmith Broadway (10 minutes walk.)   ask for River Court Rd which leads on to the Mall.[1]

MS: Fredeman Coll.

[1] These directions for reaching Kelmscott House are included here on the assumption that they were mailed to William Bell Scott, for whom they were prepared. It is probable that the slip of paper on which they were written was enclosed with a letter which has not survived. Morris wrote out his address (cf. letter no. 552, n. 1).

---

548 • To Thomas Wardle

26, Queen Square,
Bloomsbury, London
November 11, 1878

My dear Wardle

Thanks for the patterns, & also for the kermes[1] wh: latter came to hand this morning: I thought the patterns very good: the darkest kermes colour especially so: I fancy that with less or no tatar we might get it more crimson: The question now is, where & how to get kermes in tolerable quantity, & at a price to make it usable ⟨for⟩ from a commercial point of view: it is a great pity it can't be got at for artists colours, as it makes the only satisfactory lake.[2]

Yours very truly
William Morris

MS: Duke.

[1] See letter no. 328, n. 1.
[2] A purplish-red pigment.

549 • To DANTE GABRIEL ROSSETTI   Westminster Palace Hotel,
                                        November 18, 1878

My dear Gabriel

Excuse my bothering you, but I want your name badly at once: it won't be any trouble to you to sign the paper,[1] if as I suppose you agree.   in haste

Yours Ever
William Morris[2]

Please don't chaff

MS: UBC, Angeli-Dennis Papers.

[1] Presumably a memorial protesting against the second British invasion of Afghanistan.
[2] This letter is written on paper headed "Afghan Committee" followed by the names of the officers. See letter no. 546, notes 3 and 4.

550 • To GEORGE JAMES HOWARD   26, Queen Square,
                                     Bloomsbury, London
                                     November 20, 1878

My dear George

As you will see by the papers we are keeping the memorial open for signature; so I suppose we now want numbers as well as names: as to the latter there seemed never to be any danger of our being swamped by EQA names: the great mass of them were new: I don't know if you feel enclined to sign so late, but if, as I suppose numbers are (is?) a desideratum you might get us some.

Though the war will of course (I suppose) be declared, I cannot help think that matters political look brighter — perhaps because matters commercial look so very much the reverse. We have not much to grumble at in that way yet: but I rather shudder at the thought of /79 when London will begin to feel the pinch.

Yours affectionately
William Morris

P.S. Brampton Windows: the guards are ordered since it cannot be helped.[1]

Of course in a way 'tis too late but I think it will do good too. I think it *would* be useful to put some sort of pressure upon Hartington — if liberals could agree on it; a great *if* I fear.

WM.

MS: Howard Papers.

[1] In 1878, Morris and Co. made two windows for St. Martin's Church, Brampton: the westernmost window on the north side and the north aisle middle window. See Sewter, II, 29.

---

551 • To Sidney Colvin

26, Queen Square,
Bloomsbury, London
December 8, 1878

My dear Colvin

M. Yriarte[1] well-known as a writer on Venice has been for the past month there making a detailed ⟨acco⟩ report of ⟨its⟩ the present condition of S. Marks; he was stirred up to this by Wallis:[2] the report is now ready & we think it would be a good thing to get it into some English paper: it will probably be over long for the Times; & the next best paper for publicity would be, I should think the XIX Century. Could you speak of it to any of their people & if you could (or if not) would you write a line to H. Wallis, Esqre

29 Brecknock Crescent
NW.

The paper would be longish, & not at all controversial, pretty much a statement of facts: M. Yriarte has been architect to the French Government in times past, I should mention.

Yours very truly
William Morris

MS: Fitzwilliam.

[1] Charles Yriarte (1832-1898), Inspector-General of Fine Arts in the French Government.

[2] See letter no. 229, n. 4.

552 • To John Simon

Kelmscott House,
Upper Mall, Hammersmith.[1]
December 14, 1878

My dear Simon[2]

Very many thanks, & I should have liked to see the nice people, & especially yourself; but unfortunately my work will make me too late for 7 oclock dinner on Monday & too tired I expect for anything but bed, so I cannot come.

I hope you will find your way over here some day soon: 'tis not such a very long way off.

Yours very truly
William Morris

MS: DeGruson Coll.

[1] This is the first surviving letter written on stationery imprinted with the Kelmscott House address.

[2] John Simon (1818–1897), Liberal M.P. for Dewsbury, Yorkshire, from 1868 to 1888. He was one of the first Jewish barristers to be admitted to the Middle Temple and was a founder of the Anglo-Jewish Association.

553 • To Charles Howard[?]

Kelmscott House
Upper Mall, Hammersmith
January 7 [1879]

Dear Mr Howard[1]

Unfortunately, I *am* engaged on Saturday; so would you kindly come on Monday. Any time will do, if you could let me know before hand.

I am so very sorry for the cause of your not coming today, & I hope you will not risk any recurrence of your cold by coming Monday, but will stay at home unless you are quite in form.

Yours very truly
William Morris

MS: Bodleian.

[1] Possibly written to Charles Howard, George Howard's father. See letter no. 604, n. 2.

554 • To George James Howard

26, Queen Square,
Bloomsbury, London,
January 17, 1879

My dear George

My confounded digestion is so bad that I really cannot venture to sit at a dinner-table with anybody: but I will come in tomorrow a little after 9 oclock P.M. if that will do. I am very sorry to hear of Mrs. Howards mishap   I hope to hear good news of her tomorrow.

Yrs affectionately
William Morris

MS: Howard Papers.

555 • To Georgiana Burne-Jones[?]   [March 1879]

I am writing in a whirlwind of dyeing and weaving, and even as to the latter rather excited by a new piece just out of the loom, which looks beautiful, like a flower garden.

TEXT: Mackail, I, 375.

556 • To Roberts Brothers

26, Queen Square,
Bloomsbury, London
March 4, 1879

Dear Sirs

Thanks for your note. I should be happy to write a preface if I thought it would improve the book, but on the contrary I think it would rather *flatten* the whole thing:[1] you have always Mr. Magnussons & my translation of the Icelandic originals to ⟨fall⟩ refer to; & the German Nibelungen Noth is well known & has been translated more than once. Of course I should be glad to correct any mistakes that could be pointed out to me: I do not *remember* any at present.

I am
Dear Sirs
Yours truly
William Morris

Messrs. Roberts Brothers

MS: Mayfield Coll. Published: Syracuse University Library Associates, *The Courier* (Winter 1965), 24.

[1] In early 1879, Roberts Brothers planned to issue a second American edition of *Sigurd the Volsung*, the first having been successful. It was possibly Thomas Niles, director of business, who thought that a preface or introduction by Morris would make the new

edition even more attractive, and who elicited this reply. See Syracuse University Library Associates, *The Courier* (Winter 1965), 23-25.

557 • TO CATHERINE HOLIDAY
26, Queen Square,
Bloomsbury, London
March 4, 1879

Dear Mrs. Holiday
You are quite welcome to make the transfer you speak off: I should be glad on the one hand that the Jones had the colouring they saw & liked: and as to the other I am quite sure I can trust you with the colour & am glad that you should have any pleasure in the carrying out of the work.
I am sorry to hear that you have been so unwell, & hope to hear better accounts of you:

Yours very truly
William Morris

MS: Berger Coll.

558 • TO HENRY OCTAVIUS COXE
26, Queen Square,
Bloomsbury, London
March 5, 1879

Dear Sir[1]
Though I cannot claim any further acquaintance (personally) with you, than that of having been once introduced to you at the Bodleian, (of which introduction however I have very pleasant recollections) yet I venture both as an artist and as a member of the University to trouble you with a letter laying before you the claims to consideration of my friend Mr. W. B. Richmond, who is a candidate for the Slade Professorship now vacant:[2] He is both a very scholarly artist, and in practice a most successful one: besides possessing a large share of the invention and imagination necessary to the making of an original artist he is a master of the knowledge of materials and processes which is unhappily rare among artists nowadays, and I know few men who equal him ⟨for⟩ in enthusiasm for [his?] art, and industry in its practice. I believe if he were appointed to the Chair, he would enter on ⟨his⟩ its duties with great spirit, & with full intention of making it of practical use to the

[505]

members of the University; and I should think it a piece of good fortune for us to have obtained his services:

My wish to see the vacant chair worthily filled must be my excuse for troubling you on this subject, hoping you will excuse me on these grounds.

I remain
Dear Sir
Yours faithfully
William Morris

The Revd. H. O. Cox

MS: Bodleian.

[1] Henry Octavius Coxe (1811-1881), Librarian of the Bodleian Library. In that office, he was automatically on the board of seven who elected the Slade Professor of Art.

[2] Sir William Blake Richmond (1842-1921). The son and grandson of portrait-painters—his father was George Richmond (1809-1896), a successful artist who was inspired, as a young man, by William Blake—W. B. Richmond continued the family tradition, succeeding as a portrait-painter, although he also painted subjects from classical mythology, and did the mosaic decorations for St. Paul's Cathedral. He supported the S.P.A.B. and shared Morris's zeal for fishing (he and Morris were neighbors in Hammersmith). His candidacy for the Slade Professorship was successful and he held the post from 1879 to 1883.

559 · To Henry Howard Molyneux Herbert   26, Queen Square,
Bloomsbury, London
March 12, 1879

My Lord[1]

I have received a letter from Lady Florence Herbert[2] kindly inviting me on your part to pay you a visit at High Clere[3] next Saturday; I am very sorry to lose the opportunity of making your acquaintance, but I find that my necessary work & necessary rest make it impossible for me to get away from London, or indeed go out anywhere; and this is particularly the case at present, as I am in the midst of rather harassing work: so with many thanks for your kind invitation, I feel obliged to decline it.

I am
My Lord
Yours faithfully
William Morris

MS: Berger Coll.

[1] See letter no. 476, n. 1.

[2] Lady Florence Herbert (d.1886), the Earl of Carnarvon's sister-in-law, married Auberon Herbert in 1871. She was the sister of Francis Thomas de Grey Cowper, seventh Earl Cowper (1834-1905), a Liberal politician.

[3] For a description and photograph of Highclere Castle, see Girouard, pp. 130-36.

560 · To WILLIAM EWART GLADSTONE

The Society for
the Protection
of Ancient Bldgs.
9 Buckingham St.
Strand, W.C.
March [17?] 1879

The Rt Hon: W. E. Gladstone M.P.

Sir,

The Committee of the "Society for the Protection of Ancient Buildings" has had its attention called to a letter from you published in the Guardian expressing your approval of a scheme for the restoration of the ruins of St Germain's Church in the Isle of Man: the Committee feels that this approval, coming from one so deeply & sincerely interested in the welfare of the arts as you are well known to be, will have great weight with the inhabitants of the island; yet it cannot but think also that the scheme, though set on foot with the best intentions, is likely to be injurious to the arts: it has ventured therefore to desire me to write to you and point out why it thinks the scheme for the (so called) restoration of St Germains Church should be abandoned. The Committee considers the islet on which the church is built with its group of curious buildings to be a monument of the deepest historical interest, connected as it is on one side with the Early Christianity and Civilization of Ireland, and on the other with the domination of the Norsemen, since the church itself has features borrowed from its once mother church of Drontheim: the Committee knows by experience that, however skilful the architect employed may be, a great part of the historical value of this strange islet will disappear if the ruins of the little Cruciform Church on it are to be restored, it appeals to the opinion now almost universal among those who have studied the subject deepest, that whatever may be said of more partial "restoration" the restoration of a ruin is impossible, & that the attempt to restore such a work can only result in substituting a frigid & dead academical study of an ancient building for the living through mutilated remains of it.

On the score of convenience the Committee do not think the Manxmen will be great gainers by the "restoration" of this little building: & it begs to remind you that Bishop Wilson[1] himself to whose memory it is proposed to restore the Church, got the consent of the Tynwald[2] to unroofing a portion of it so that the lead might be used for building a church in a more convenient place: the Committee also wishes to state its opinion that a new church fitted for the wants of the people of the district might be handsomely built for a less sum than would be necessary to the so-called restoration of St Germains Church. At the same time, the Committee is informed that the Crypt of the Church is in danger of falling in & thinks that some means of keeping it up ought to be tried, though whatever is done, it thinks should be mere obvious props & stays against its further ruin.

For the rest the Committee ventures to beg you to reconsider your approval of this scheme; believing that you recognise to the full, the value of these ancient national monuments and the historical associations connected with them as most important instruments towards the education and refinement of the people at large: the Committee believes also that you will excuse it for troubling you with this letter on a subject of such general public interest

I have the honour to be on behalf of the Committee Sir

> Your obedient servant
> William Morris
> Hon: Secretary
> "The Society for the Protection
> of Ancient Buildings".

MS: BL, Add. MSS. 44459, Gladstone Papers.

[1] Thomas Wilson (1663-1755) became Bishop of Sodor and Manx in 1697. In 1707, he published *Principles and Duties of Christianity, in English and Manx*.

[2] In the Isle of Man, an annual convention attended by the governor (representing the sovereign), a council acting as the upper house, and the House of Keys, at which the laws which have been enacted are proclaimed to the people.

561 • To Mr. Shipton

26, Queen Square,
Bloomsbury, London
April 7, 1879

Dear Mr. Shipton[1]

These are something like my 'heads':[2] difference between 'ancient' & 'modern' art: by modern I mean art that began at the fall of the Roman Empire — by ancient art till then: ancient art falls into 2 divisions, archaic, symbolic art (Egypt Assyria &c) and naturalistic, perfect art (Greece): Egyptian the earliest known art: at its best 1400 years B.C. Egyptians great colourists: very skillful in industrial arts: good dyers weavers cabinet-makers potters &c in earliest times: Eastern in feeling: Assyrian less orderly than Egyptian, derived from Chaldean, in which probably originated many of the mysterious types that were blindly followed in ornamental forms: Ancient Persian derived from Assyrian but showing marks of their Aryan blood in their columnar architecture. Greeks probably borrowed some forms from Assyria by means of the Phoenicians. in Greek architecture pattern-ornament very subordinate: perhaps unduly so, pride of intellect narrowing the Greek mind, & demanding perfection in all art, & therefore having no room for suggestive, striving, & imperfect art: progress more to be desired than immoveable perfection; which would indeed be impossible. Roman art partly derived from Greek, partly from unknown sources: their invention of the arch, & ⟨its⟩ the great stimulus of this invention to architecture: architecture thenceforward pliable & popular fit for all climates countries or manners: Roman ⟨art⟩ pattern-work stimulated by the art of mosaic: ancient art changing into modern: the 'barbarians' bring new blood into the ancient world & new life to the arts wh: were languishing: the Parthians conquer⟨ors of⟩ Persia, and are a nomade people without art: Romes contest with Parthia sets Persia free: the new Persian Kingdom (the Sassamians) their art developed from ⟨the⟩ Assyrian & Chaldean, the forms of it Zoroastrian symbols of good & evil & the creation of all things: the connection of Persia with Byzantium: the change of styles suddenly gaining new life in Byzantium & becoming modern art; the certainty of its admixture with Asiatic art: its becoming free and capable of giving expression to the thought of the whole people: the splendour & swiftness with which it spread ⟨of⟩ over the whole world; if popular art has become degraded, it can scarcely die & will one day certainly take a fresh start, and do all we require of it.

— I am writing this without my M.S. but I think this is the substance of it: I send herewith my Birmingham Address[3] which may interest you.

Yours very truly
William Morris

MS: St. Bride.

[1] Not identified. Morris kept a daily journal in certain years (1881, 1887, 1893, 1895, 1896), and there is a reference to a Mr. Shipton on February 13, 1881. For this journal, see BL, Add. MSS. 45407-45411.

[2] The following outline probably pertains to "The History of Pattern Design," a lecture delivered by Morris before the Trades Guild of Learning, April 8, 1879. See LeMire, p. 235.

[3] Probably his "The Art of the People," presidential address delivered at the Birmingham Society of Arts on February 19, 1879. See LeMire, p. 235.

562 • TO THE EDITOR OF *The Architect*

The Society for
the Protection
of Ancient Buildings
9 Buckingham Street
Strand, W.C.
April 8, 1879

Sir

As there seems to be an impression growing up in the mind of the public that the above Society is actuated by feelings of disregard for the structural preservation of ancient buildings, and as such an impression is likely to seriously interfere with the important objects which they have in view, I have been requested by the committee of the Society to ask you to insert their most emphatic denial of any such sentiment on their part. The urging on the public of the necessity of doing structural repairs to ancient buildings in time to prevent decay and keep out wind and weather is one of the primary objects of the Society; and they have on several occasions had to deplore, in the case of ancient buildings brought under their notice, that money which ought to have been expended on the structural repairs has been worse than wasted in utterly destroying the beauty and historical value of the interiors.

I am, Sir,
On behalf of the Committee,
Your obedient servant,
William Morris, Hon. Sec.

TEXT: *The Architect* (London), April 19, 1879, p. 239.

563 • TO THE METROPOLITAN BOARD OF WORKS

The Society for
the Protection
of Ancient Buildings
9 Buckingham St:
Strand
April [25-30,] 1879

To the Chairman & members of
the Metropolitan Board of Wks
Gentlemen

The "Society for the Protection of Ancient Buildings" observes with the deepest regret that it is proposed by your honorable Board to raise & open up the Water Gate of York House at the foot of Buckingham St: in order to form an entrance to the Embankment Garden

[510]

The Society desires to protest in the strongest manner against this proposal as being unnecessary mischievous & damaging to an interesting monument as well as involving considerable expenditure of public money for a purpose which in the opinion of this Society is worse than useless

In its present position the Gate serves to mark the ancient course of the Thames and gives emphasis to the Embankment constructed by your honourable Board. It also indicates the site of an ancient historical house, and recals some of the most interesting annals in the history of our country

The proposed raising cannot be effected without considerable danger to the fabric of the Gate and will necessarily entail considerable expense. In its present position a very small sum would suffice to protect it from the weather but if raised and opened out as proposed a foundation must of necessity be constructed and other works will, in all probability, be considered requisite to render the Gate worthy of its prominent position which will lead to an outlay the extent of which cannot be estimated and which will have the effect of entirely destroying the historical & artistic value of the Gate.

The Society desires to impress upon your honorable Board the importance of the Gate as a specimen of the art and an illustration of the domestic habits of a time long past and impossible to be renewed, and submit that as no public necessity exists for its removal that the Board should preserve the Gate as an interesting artistic & historical monument.

It would in the opinion of the Society be desirable if the Gate passed into the possession of your honorable Board to clear out the rubbish with which the Gate is encumbered, to build a retaining wall, to keep back the earth[,] repair the roof, as well as exposing the steps, but they deprecate in the strongest possible manner any attempt at raising it "restoring" the stone work, or in any way adding to the structure as it at present exists.

> I am, Gentlemen,
> On behalf of the Committee
> Your very obed Servant
> William Morris
> Hon: Sec

MS: Greater London Council, Inner London Educational Authority, Department of Civic Design and Architecture

564 • To William Ewart Gladstone
The Society for
the Protection
of Ancient Buildings.
9 Buckingham Street,
Strand, W.C.
May 5, 1879

Dear Sir,

The Committee of this Society desire me to thank you for your letter of the 21st ⟨ult:⟩ March. The Committee is quite prepared to take its stand on the principle that the "restoration," in the literal sense of the word, of an ancient monument is impossible; and that if its rebuilding should be for any reason necessary, that rebuilding would involve a loss to art of its genuine character, as complete as would the repainting of an ancient picture. For the rest the Committee is convinced that not only will reverend & constant care and attention to small repairs assuredly preserve any church which is still in use without the necessity of resorting to so called "restoration," but that even a ruin may be so dealt with in the same spirit that it may be kept standing for the study and instruction of the public through many generations without the substitution of modern imitative for the ancient genuine work.

I have the honour to be, on behalf of the Committee,

Your very obed Servant,
William Morris
Hon: Sec:

Rt. Hon: W. E. Gladstone. M.P.

MS: BL, Add. MSS. 44460, Gladstone Papers.

565 • To Eiríkr Magnússon
26, Queen Square,
Bloomsbury, London
May 8, 1879

My dear Magnússon

I enclose a draught of a letter to the Athenaeum which can go next week,[1] I being away till this morning.   if you would like to correct at all pray do so. I have not seen Vigfusson's Prolegomena, perhaps I had better do so, & then I could alter the first sentence to, 'I have noticed.'[2]

Yrs very truly
William Morris

MS: Iceland.
[1] See letter no. 567.

² Guðbrandr Vígfússon (1828-1889) was an Icelandic scholar who settled in Oxford; from 1884 until his death he was Reader in Scandinavian language and literature. At the end of 1878 he published an edited volume containing the *Sturlunga Saga* and other works in which he apparently failed to give any credit to Magnússon for the translations he and Morris had done together. Morris attempted to put this right by giving a detailed account of their collaboration (see letter no. 567).

566 • TO FREDERIC GEORGE STEPHENS   Kelmscott House,
Upper Mall, Hammersmith.
[May 12, 1879?]

My dear Stephens

Alter this as much as you please:¹ I hope it is not too long. I got my bag last night after a long hunt for the house-keeper. Sorry we couldn't go home together.

Yours ever
William Morris

MS: Syracuse.

¹ See letter no. 567.

567 • TO THE EDITOR OF *The Athenaeum*   26, Queen Square
Bloomsbury
May 12, 1879

ENGLISH TRANSLATIONS FROM THE ICELANDIC.

I have noticed that Mr. Vigfusson, in his recently published Prolegomena to the Sturlunga Saga, speaks of me as the sole translator of the English versions of the Grettis Saga and the Gunnlaugs Saga Ormstungu, omitting to mention the name of Mr. Eirikr Magnússon, my *collaborateur*.¹ As a matter of fact, when we set about these joint works, I had just begun the study of Icelandic under Mr. Magnússon's mastership, and my share in the translation was necessarily confined to helping in the search for the fittest English equivalents to the Icelandic words and phrases, to turning the translations of the "vísur" into some sort of English verse, and to general revision in what might be called matters of taste; the rest of the work, including notes, and all critical remarks, was entirely due to Mr. Magnússon's learning and industry.

I should explain that the Gunnlaugs Saga, which was first printed in the *Fortnightly Review*, when republished in our 'Three Northern Love Stories,' went through a very careful revision, in which we both shared.

Mr. Magnússon's responsibility and labour was, therefore, much greater than mine in these works, though if his pleasure in that labour was half as much as mine, it was great indeed. The recollection of the great services he rendered to me in the matter, and indeed, I think, to the public in general, makes me venture to trouble you with this letter.

William Morris

TEXT: *The Athenaeum*, May 17, 1879, 632-33. Published: Henderson, *Letters*, 127-28.

[1] See letter no. 565.

568 • TO JAMES BRYCE
26 Queen Square
Bloomsbury, London,
June 3, 1879

My dear Bryce

The meeting is arranged for half past 2 on the 28th & we shall ask you to move the first resolution.[1] I could give you any number of instances unluckily of restoration sweeping the history from old buildings: I saw them at Salisbury 'restoring' the traces of the 13th cent: painting by laboriously painting imitations of it, or rather of what they thought it had been, over the old work; the same thing is now being done at Norwich Cathedral: I daresay you have seen the dulness of the sham mediaeval ornament which has disfigured so many of our churches, the grotesqueness copied, but not the life of the incomplete, but growing art. Of course one of the commonest forms that restoration has taken among ourselves has been the clearing away of all later additions to a building; e.g. perpendicular windows from a Norman church (as at Southwell) & this has been done by many men who should know better. Perhaps the point of the whole matter is, that the workmen of the old buildings were intelligent members of the body artistic, & yet that the whole weight of history *forced* them as it were to work in a certain style; they could not help dating a building for us, giving us clear indications of the tendencies & aspirations of their own times: if you go to Westminster Abbey, & look at the western part of the nave, you will see how the 15th cent. men finished the 13th cent. church: their work carries on the earlier work worthily and handsomely, & is in no way discordant from the earlier work, but at a glance it is clearly of its own time: compare with this the work now going on in the porches of the N. transept: these had been tampered with I suppose about Wren's time with no light hand certainly, but London smoke had hidden the worst faults of it, & I have no doubt that the main outline

of it was that of the 13th cent. architecture: all the more as it was cer-
tainly French in tendency like the choir; & that outline was broad &
stately: then look at the 'conjectural restoration' of the porches tame &
lifeless, with thin reedy imitations of the beautiful growth of 13th cen-
tury carving, done by men, who if you bid them would as lief carve
the strip work of James' time as the cherubs' heads of Queen Anne:
why on earth was it necessary to tack on this bit of poorly designed
finery to the transept, to confuse future times by setting them to won-
der how the men who built the matchless choir & apse could have
carpentered this together. At St Albans there are in the west front bits
of work of Abbot Trumpington's unfinished work, of the very best
English work; they are now threatening to take the life out of these
most precious fragments by restoration. Do you remember how strange
& romantic the unfinished Cologne Cathedral once looked? how stupid
the present completion of it looks I myself can bear witness. St Cross
at Winchester: have you seen that simple & majestic piece of early work
since its bedizenment: Ely you must have seen: I never saw it before it
had been daubed over like a music hall; but what it must have looked,
the rich choir the amazing lantern & that finest of all Norman naves —
what they must have looked when they were all grey & venerable to-
gether I can partly imagine: I hear that they threaten the *Lady* Chapel
(so called) now: it is the richest piece of Edwardian architecture I know.
St Albans by the by, & the rash move of putting a new high roof on
the whole nave is a very strong case; because Sir Edmund Beckett's[2]
highhanded proceedings have been so widely objected to. I could tell
you however of dozens of bad cases enough & I have spun out this
letter unconscionably: I shall be very glad to have your resolution at
your convenience.

Yours very truly
William Morris[3]

MS: Walthamstow (copy). Published: Henderson, *Letters*, 128-29.

[1] At the annual meeting of the S.P.A.B. on June 28, Bryce moved the first resolution:
"That this meeting, recognizing the value of Ancient Buildings to the Student of History,
whether general or local, deprecates all alterations in and restorations of such buildings
which may obliterate their historical character and features."

[2] Sir Edmund Beckett, fifth Baronet and first Baron Grimthorpe (1816-1905), was chan-
cellor of the province of York from 1877 to 1900. He engaged in theological controversy
(opposing revision of the New Testament), was active as a church designer, and was
prominent in the restoration of St. Albans Cathedral.

[3] This letter exists only in a copy made by Mackail.

569 · THREE LETTERS TO JAMES BRYCE

a.
26, Queen Square,
Bloomsbury, London
July 4, 1879

My dear Bryce

I ⟨am⟩ have only just got your letter, as I have been away for the last 2 days, and I am sorry to say I can't come as I am engaged meanwhile, which seems to be my bad luck whenever you have asked me: otherwise not even the hope of getting up at 3½ AM would have kept me away.

Yours very truly
William Morris

MSS: Bodleian.

b.
26, Queen Square,
Bloomsbury, London
July 15, 1879

My dear Bryce

I have delayed answering your note about the Greek voyage because I have been trying to see if I could bring both ends together & be able to go; but I find no straining will do it & that to my vexation I must give up all thoughts of it; as indeed I must of any holiday longer than a fortnight at a time this year: you see I have some things to do that cannot possibly be done by deputy without serious damage to my work; & this year I have set on foot two or three things that will certainly stick fast if I am not on the spot to push them on, and sticking fast means in these cases giving up what I have bound myself to do.

Very many thanks all the same.

Yours very truly
William Morris

c.
26, Queen Square,
Bloomsbury, London
July 28, 1879

My dear Bryce

I really cannot: you see it would take me six weeks really in all: also besides my work I don't like to leave my family for so long, as my wife is unfortunately weak in health this year: many thanks all the same.

Yours truly
William Morris

570 • TO CHARLES FAIRFAX MURRAY — 26, Queen Square,
Bloomsbury, London
August 14, 1879

My dear Murray

That stretcher is ready for you if you have time to do anything before
you go:[1] those damned lawyers[2] kept me at Leeds for nearly a week, &
upset all my plans: I believe I am going out of town for a day or two
on Monday evening but I am not sure: I shall be at home at Hammer-
smith on Saturday and Sunday at all events. My wife & children went
N. on Monday.

Yours very truly
William Morris

MS: Texas.

[1] Possibly for the unfinished *Heimskringla* on vellum. See *CW*, 9, xxi.

[2] Morris may have met with lawyers in Leeds in connection with the pirating of the
"Lily" design for Kidderminster Carpets. See letter no. 543, n. 1.

571 • TO JANE MORRIS — The George Inn
Amesbury, Wilts,
Tuesday
August 19, 1879

Dearest Janey

. . . We got to Salisbury last night, and to-day drove here through
the lovely chalk valley by the water (Avon) side after having spent 2 or
3 hours at Salisbury and an hour at old Sarum, which is a wonderful
place: we have had as much rain as we could do with to-day, and just
at present 'tis raining cats and dogs: but up on the downs rain really
don't matter, for there are no nasty sloppy trees or things about: 'tis
nearly as good as Iceland (and much drier).

This is a village hard by Stonehenge which is its chief attraction,
though it is a beautiful place, with a very fine church: I was very much
impressed by Stonehenge, which is a very strange place indeed; and I
should like to live on Salisbury Plain, (since I can't live on Bláskogaheiði)
I should be so well, and the scent of the wastes is delightful. Tomorrow
we drive on to Marlborough, and shall get there about 3 p.m. we ex-
pect, so that we can drive at once thence to Avebury: Jenny perhaps
will remember that and Silbury Hill.

Not much news from home: the big rug came duly out of the loom,
and turned out very well: Campfield is to come and draw a bit more
on to my warp,[1] so that after this week I shall get on very well I hope. . . .

I believe this letter to be somewhat scatter-witted, but the room of this nice little Inn is small, and Webb is teaching a stranger small-boy cribbage, which makes a noise. Now I will write if I can to-morrow (Marlborough) to the girls, or the next day (Uffington probably). Meanwhile best love to them and luck in horse-manship.

Best love and good-bye
Your W.M.

TEXT: *CW*, 18, xxii.

¹ For the "Cabbage and Vine" tapestry.

572 • To Jenny Morris Kelmscott House,
Upper Mall, Hammersmith
August 23, 1879

Dearest Jenny

Though May wrote first to me, yet as I have your letter fresh in my memory I will write to you this time: the said letter by the way I did not get till I was leaving Kelmscott this morning early. We left Amesbury on Wednesday morning, a very unpromising one, Scotch mist with occasional dashes of thicker rain: however we got better weather as we went on: we went right up the Avon Valley and very beautiful it was; then as the river narrowed we turned off towards a little scrubby town called Pewsey that lies in the valley between the Salisbury & the Marlborough downs: it was all very fine & characteristic country especially where we had to climb the Marlborough downs at a place that I remembered coming on as a boy with wonder & pleasure: Oare Hill they call it. We got early in the afternoon to Marlborough & walked out to see the College & so strolled away to the Devil's Den, & back in the dusk. The next morning we set out early for Avebury in weather at first much like the day before; however it cleared before we reached Silbury & was quite fine while we were thereabout for 2 hours, after which we drove on towards Swindon intending Lechlade & Kelmscott that evening. The Downs end at a village called Wroughton & we could see a large piece of England from the slope of it, Faringdon clump not at all in the background: we got another trap at Swindon where they warned us that we should have to go through the waters to get to Lechlade: we went through Highworth a queer old village on a hill, & sure enough we could see waters out from thence, though they turned out to be only from the little river Cole: at Highworth we found that they were mending the bridge into Lechlade town, & that it would be closed; so at Inglesham we had to turn aside to strike the road that leads

[518]

over St. John's Bridge: sure enough in a few yds: we were in deep water enough, right over the axles of the wheels: the driver lost his presence of mind, not being used to floods you see, & pretty nearly spilt us in the ditch; but we just saved the carriage & after some trouble got into the high rd: by Buscot Parsonage; though even there for some time the said rd: was also a river: so over St. Johns Bridge & safe to Kelmscott. But opening the gate there, lo, the water all over the little front garden: in short I have never seen so high a flood there: there was a smart shower when we got in & then a bright clear evening: the next day was bright & clear between strong showers with a stiff S.W. gale: of course we could do nothing but sail & paddle about the floods. We got up very early this morning & up to London amidst heavy rain & clouds of lowering smoke; but it has cleared up this evening & is pretty clear though threatening for tomorrow: thus much about my holiday.

I shall send a note ⟨from⟩ to Mamma with this & will write to May next time. I am so glad you are enjoying yourselves, but Mamma gives a poor account of herself.   anyhow I expect you are having better weather than we are.

Love to Mamma & May & good bye my dear.

Your loving Father
William Morris

MS: BL, Add. MSS. 45339. Extract published: Mackail, II, 2-4; Henderson, *Letters*, 129-30.

573 • To May Morris   26, Queen Square,
Bloomsbury, London
September 4, 1879

Dearest May

I was very glad to get your letter, & hear that things are a bit better with Mama: as for me, I have little to say because I have been living very quietly since I came back: I went on Sunday afternoon to see Mr. Carr. at Bedford Park[1] those new houses you know on business, on the whole the place looked pretty, especially as they have kept the trees mostly: they have pulled down rather a nice little house in the high road & are building a square (Westcroft Sq:) in the garden thereof.

Those little beasts of girls have been helping themselves to the apples & pears &c; the servants were in a fine taking about it; they dropped down so heavily on Katey the goggle-eyed, who seems to have been the one caught, that when I went to blow her up in the morning, I found her so penitent & beblubbered that I nearly burst out laughing, and fortunately had no need to make a long harangue.

Since last Friday the weather has been perfectly heavenly here: all yesterday there was not a cloud in the sky; today is not so good, as the wind has shifted E and London smoke is on our heads: but, my dear May, I do think London is a nice place for ones holiday: in the autumn, mind you, when one cannot be 'amused.'

Nevertheless I am going to Naworth, but on *Sunday* night instead of ⟨Monday⟩ Saturday, so expect me on Monday morning next, grimy & with but few buttons on my clothes.

The drawing-room is done at last & looks very nice: the hangings much improved by the dusting.

Best love to Mama & Jenny.

Your affectionate Father
William Morris

MS: BL, Add. MSS. 45341.

¹ In *Richard Norman Shaw*, Reginald Blomfield writes that "about 1876-77 a Mr. Jonathan Carr undertook the construction of an artistic suburb which was called Bedford Park." One expression of the mark it made was the "Ballad of Bedford Park," a parody containing the following stanzas:

> Then each at t'other winked his eye
> and next they did prepare
> A noble Clubhouse to supply
> with decorations fair.
>
> With red and blue and sagest green
> were walls and dado dyed,
> Friezes of Morris there were seen
> and oaken wainscot wide.

In his notes to the ballad, Blomfield writes that it was not Shaw but E. J. May, his assistant, who designed "the noble Clubhouse," and that Shaw was on friendly terms with Morris. See Reginald Blomfield, *Richard Norman Shaw, R.A., Architect, 1831-1912* (London: Batsford, 1940), pp. 33-36.

574 • To Thomas Wardle

26, Queen Square,
Bloomsbury, London
⟨August⟩ September 5, 1879

My dear Wardle   (Truro Church)

We have had a row with the Bishop¹ on the subject: according to our information a clean sweep was to be made of everything; the Bishop denied this, but in an unsatisfactory manner: his letter to you seems queer: the only part of the old church I have seen figured is the remains of a 3-aisled church of a very rich and peculiar perpendicular style (Cornish in short) not as much 'debased' as Henry VIII's Chapel at Westminster, and as satisfactory a piece of architecture as any in England: as to its condition, of course I don't know: George says he will go to Truro & have a look at it. I may mention that Pearson, the architect of the new church is one of the very worst of the destructives, especially if he comes across latish work.[2]

I also am sorry we missed each other.

Yours very truly
William Morris

P.S. With your permission, I will keep the Bp's letter to show to the Committee.

MS: Duke.

[1] Edward White Benson (1829-1896), who became Archbishop of Canterbury in 1882. At this time, he was Bishop of Truro.

[2] John Loughborough Pearson (1817-1897), the architect for the new cathedral of Truro, had restored Lincoln Cathedral in 1870. Over the course of his career, he took part in the restoration of Westminster Hall, the north transept of Westminster Abbey, and the cathedrals at Peterborough, Canterbury, Bristol, Rochester, Chichester, and Exeter.

575 • To May Morris   Kelmscott House,
                                                Upper Mall, Hammersmith
                                                September 15 [1879]

Dearest May

All right then, so be it. But, my dear, I do not think you will come by the Great Western, as you write, but more probably by the ⟨Great Northern⟩ North Western: item, since the unwisdom of our ancestors (and I must say they were fools not to be able to say 24 oclock) has arranged that there shall be 2 10.35s in the 24 hours, do you mean AM or P.M. You must please tell me either by letter or telegraph which you mean. As to Willesden Station; don't try it: it is a mere trap for the unwary; everything is arranged so that you shall miss your trains there; there are scarcely any men about, & what there are refuse to answer questions: the first time I went there I got into the wrong train; the second time I was so exacerbated by the coolness ⟨that⟩ of the officials, that I had to offer to fight the only one I could find: fortunately for me he refused battle: but if you try the place, you may get back to Naworth, or you may get to Aberdeen, or Truro, or Northampton, or Norwich or Boulogne but to Hammersmith you will never get, unless you walk there — carrying your luggage, which would be wearying:

no, *put yourselves in a cab* at Euston & come straight to Hammersmith.

I did my business in the heavy woollen country, & got back home about 7 p.m.: on Saturday; a most miserable wet ⟨day⟩ evening it was to be sure: but yesterday was lovely, & this morning it is clearing up after a heavy fog.

I was also very sorry to miss Mother, but cool reflection of course assured me that there was no chance of doing more than catching my train: apropos of that, please remind mother to tip William (I think) he of the red-head, as I saw nothing of any body at the Castle, but one kitchen maid: such attraction had fat pigs for all the world except Jenny & me.

Best love to mother, my dear, who I hope is keeping well, or better, I should say. Also to Jenny.

> Your loving father
> William Morris

MS: BL, Add. MSS. 45341. Published: Henderson, *Letters*, 131.

576 • TO THOMAS WARDLE   Kelmscott House,
                                              Upper Mall, Hammersmith
                                              September 15 [1879]

My dear Wardle

Many thanks for your kind & genial invitation; but I am sorry to say I must say no to it as I am only just back from a week in Cumberland: (your letter came while I was away) & next week I am going to Kelmscott for about a fortnight. I am really very sorry I can't come all the more as I am so glad to learn that Mrs. Wardle is getting better. I send this to Leek, in case you don't call in at Queen Sq: today.

> Yours very truly
> William Morris

MS: Duke.

577 • TO CHARLES FAIRFAX MURRAY   26, Queen Square,
                                              Bloomsbury, London
                                              September 16, 1879

My dear Murray

Thank you for your letter; all the more as laziness had to be overcome in writing it; as heaven help us is much the case with this: Not having heard from you before you left I did *not* send for the cartoon, till after your letter reached me: & then I couldn't get it because Mr. Rutson is away, & there seems to be nobody to answer questions: could you please tell us what to do, as in a week or two, I shall be able to get to work on the cartoon. Meantime many thanks for doing it.

I was away last week at Naworth and found my babies very flourishing but my wife so, so,: I think she will take a turn at the sea-side presently before the winter comes on.

I wonder if there is any chance of our getting to Italy next year: I will let you know if there is, & then you can give me advice as to time & place.

Yours very truly
William Morris

MS: Texas.

578 • TO FREDERIC GEORGE STEPHENS

26, Queen Square,
Bloomsbury, London
September 25, 1879

My dear Stephens

As far as I can remember the Southwell correspondence was ordered by the Committee to be published in the *local* papers: if it wasn't sent to the Athenaeum it was because it was thought that it would [be] too bulky for that paper: I will send your note to the Secretary[1] as a reminder to him not to forget to let you have first pick of anything that is likely to be useful to you in future: by the way I wrote none of the letters in question, & they ought not to have been signed with my name, but with the Secretary's.[2]

As to the report of Annual Meeting, it is in type, I think, but has not been sent to Members yet: because the Committee is all out of town & the Secretary has been taking his holiday; rather a long one I should say.

Please come to the meetings whenever you can: I don't like the business falling into the hands of too few people.

With thanks for your letter

I am
Yours very truly
William Morris

MS: Bodleian.

[1] The Secretary of the S.P.A.B. at this time was Newman Marks.

² For correspondence on Southwell Minster signed with Morris's name, see letters no. 524 and 537.

579 · To Ellis and White

Kelmscott House
Upper Mall, Hammersmith
[September 27, 1879]

Dear Sirs
Please send to
Kelmscott Manor
Lechlade
Charles Kingsley's 'Hypatia' 1 Vol:

Yours faithfully
William Morris¹

MS: Princeton T.

¹ This postcard is not in Morris's handwriting.

580 · Excerpts from Four Letters to Georgiana Burne-Jones [?]

a.

[Kelmscott,
October 3, 1879]

Somehow I feel as if there must soon be an end for me of playing at living in the country: a town-bird I am, a master-artisan, if I may claim that latter dignity.

TEXT: Mackail, I, 375.

b.

[Kelmscott,
October 13, 1879]

As to poetry, I don't know, and I don't know. The verse would come easy enough if I had only a subject which would fill my heart and mind: but to write verse for the sake of writing is a crime in a man of my years and experience. . . .

I have seen a many wonders, and have a good memory for them; and in spite of all grumblings have a hope that civilized people will grow weary of their worst follies and try to live a less muddled and unreasonable life; not of course that we shall see much of that change in the remnant that is left of our days.

TEXT: Mackail, II, 1-2. Published: Henderson, *Letters*, 132.

c. [Autumn 1879]

Lord bless us how nice it will be when I can get back to my little patterns and dyeing, and the dear warp and weft at Hammersmith!

TEXT: Mackail, I, 375.

d. [Kelmscott,
late Autumn 1879]
I am sitting now, 10 p.m., in the tapestry-room, the moon rising red through the east-wind haze, and a cow lowing over the fields. I have been feeling chastened by many thoughts, and the beauty and quietness of the surroundings, which latter, as I hinted, I am, as it were, beginning to take leave of. That leave-taking will, I confess, though you may think it fantastic, seem a long step towards saying good-night to the world.

TEXT: Mackail, II, 2. Published: Henderson, *Letters*, 132.

581 • To George Price Boyce Kelmscott
Nr Lechlade
October 13, 1879

My dear Boyce

I have sent on your letter to Colvin, thinking he would be the readiest: if he can't do it, perhaps the best way would be for one of us to write it in our mother tongue & get it translated:[1] I am all right, thank you — considering my great age — I foresee that we shall all have to make great exertions & do a deal of disagreeable work, if we are to keep our Society together. This you will understand, I know, since you are so decidedly one of the few who really have the matter at heart.

Fogs seem to have settled down on us too now; though till yesterday they were clearing about noon into lovely afternoons.

Hoping to see you soon

I am
Yours very truly
William Morris

MS: Scripps.

¹ This letter probably refers to the start of the protest against the restoration of St. Mark's, Venice. Colvin, Slade Professor of Art at Cambridge, was active there in organizing opposition (see his letter to *The Times*, November 19, 1879). Morris, in the third Annual Report of the S.P.A.B., wrote that it was in October that he received news that the west front of the church was to be rebuilt.

582 • To William Bell Scott

Kelmscott
Nr Lechlade
October 13 [1879]

My dear Scott

We have been wandering to Oxford & elsewhere where letters were not sent on, which accounts for my not answering you before: many thanks for your note: we should be very glad to do the work in question, & thank you much for putting it in our way: I don't remember about Sir Kelk's glass¹ but I rather think we did *not* do it, that it slipped through our fingers.

I am going back next Wednesday: De Morgan & his sister² have been staying with us this past week: I don't think I have much news about other fellows: Ned Jones has been ill, as perhaps you may have heard, but is all right again now: Hunt (Holman) has called on me once or twice lately, not much changed in look from years ago. I am delighted to hear that you are so much better: when do you come up to town? & when will you come & see us? We make rugs now in the stables on the mall: also I have taught myself the art of tapestry-weaving, the signs of which might amuse you. If you are writing to me again please address to Queen Sq: as before, since I am fixed in London again from next Wednesday onward.

Yours ever
William Morris

P.S. Yes, I was at Naworth, & saw Bewcastle for the first time, & the rimed stone there on a lovely day: what a strange place it is: also I saw the mine nicks of Thirlwall for the first time; a wonderful piece of country: I had been away before from Salisbury over the downs to Marlborough & so by Avebury to Swindon & here: I saw Stonehenge for the first time, and was much impressed by it: though the earth & sky nearly met, & the rain poured continuously, nothing could spoil the great stretches of the Plain, & the mysterious monument that nobody knows anything about — except Fergusson, who knows less than nothing³ —

W.M.

MS: Fredeman Coll.

¹ Sir John Kelk (1816-1886), contractor for the buildings of the South Kensington Museum for the International Exhibition, 1862.

² Mary Augusta De Morgan (1850-1907), a writer of children's books, which were illustrated by her brother and by Walter Crane, and author of a novel, *A Choice of Chance* (1887), under the pseudonym "William Dobson." She nursed Morris in his final illness, and in 1905 went to Egypt where she was in charge of a reformatory for children. She was also credited with powers of clairvoyance. See Stirling, *passim*.

³ James Fergusson (1808-1886), author of *A History of Architecture in All Countries from the Earliest Time to the Present Day* (1865-1867), and *Rude Stone Monuments* (1872). He maintained that Stonehenge was of comparatively recent construction.

583 • To the Editor of the *Daily News*

26 Queen Square
Bloomsbury, London
October 17, 1879

Sir

I suppose most Liberals will heartily endorse the views expressed in the letter of an "English Liberal" published in your columns of October 14, and many, I hope, are only too anxious to translate the precepts of that letter into action if they only knew how. I fancy the first course many of these will take will be to look round to see if there are any existing organizations which may help them to that action. Under these circumstances, I trust you will not think it out of place for me to lay before them the claims of the National Liberal League¹ on their support, an organization which, though but in its infancy, has already begun its missionary labour, as your impression of October 8 testifies in its report of the League's proceedings of the evening before, when Mr. George Howell read an able paper on the Land Question. Its aims for the future are precisely and solely those indicated in your correspondent's vigorous letter, and are based on Liberal principles at once decided and broad. Its promoters understand well what our chief stumbling-block is — not the body of crystallized Tory opinion that writes so many of our journals and votes so patiently in the House of Commons, but rather the mass of no opinion which, having in itself no principles, is naturally led to the poll by the first plausible cry that can manage to excite it into a temporary vitality. I suppose we may take your correspondent's suggestion of a mission to us Southerners from the far North as a piece of banter, but I think both that we in London deserve it and that London must save its own political soul, and by its own efforts make itself a light instead of a dark spot on the political map. I have strong hopes that the National Liberal League may help towards this end, which means no less than London leading in Liberal principles, instead of being a drag on them; and, considering of how many elements London is made up, that in its turn will be a token of the whole nation waking to reasonable political life. Meantime it is, I submit, a hopeful sign of that awakening that a body like our league should be set on foot in London, and receive abundant encouragement both from London and the country at large.

I am, Sir,
Yours obediently
William Morris
Treasurer to the National
Liberal League

TEXT: *Daily News*, October 18, 1879.

[1] Morris at this time was Treasurer of the National Liberal League, which had been founded in the late summer of 1879. Mackail notes (II, 7) that the League was a working-class association formed largely by radicals who had earlier organized themselves in opposition to the Eastern policy of the Government. Other officers of the League were George Howell, Chairman, and Henry Broadhurst, Secretary.

584 • FROM A LETTER TO MAY MORRIS[?]　　　　[October 18, 1879]

My tapestry is standing idle till I have drawn out some more which I shall accomplish towards the end of next week I hope: meantime I rather feel the loss of it on the days I am at home. The big rug is out of the loom to-day and looks much better than I expected.

TEXT: *CW*, 13, xxvii.

585 • TO THE EDITOR OF THE *Daily News*　　　　October 31, 1879

I have just received information, on the accuracy of which I can rely, that the restoration of the west front of St. Mark's at Venice, which has long been vaguely threatened, is to be taken in hand at once.[1] A commission is called for next month, to examine its state and to determine whether it is to be pulled down immediately or to be allowed to stand till next year. The fate of such a building seems to me a subject important enough to warrant me in asking you to grant me space to make an appeal to your readers to consider what a disaster is threatened hereby to art and culture in general. Though this marvel of art and treasure of history has suffered some disgraces, chiefly in the base mosaics that have supplanted the earlier ones, it is in the main in a genuine and untouched state, and to the eye of anyone not an expert in building looks safe enough from anything but malice or ignorance. But anyhow, if it be in any way unstable, it is impossible to believe that a very moderate exercise of engineering skill would not make it as sound as any building of its age can be. Whatever pretexts may be put forward, therefore, the proposal to rebuild it can only come from those that suppose that they can renew and better (by imitation) the workmanship of its details, hitherto supposed to be unrivalled; by those that think that there is nothing distinctive between the thoughts, and expression of the thoughts, of the men of the twelfth and of the nineteenth century; by those that prefer gilding, glitter, and blankness, to the solemnity of tone, and the incident that hundreds of years of wind and weather have given to the marble, always beautiful, but from the first meant to grow more beautiful by the lapse of time; in short, those only can think the "restoration" of St. Mark's possible who neither know nor care that it has now become a work of art, a monument of history, and a piece of nature. Surely I need not enlarge on the pre-eminence of St. Mark's in all these characters, for no one who even pretends to care about art, history, or nature, would call it in question; but I will assert that, strongly as I may have seemed to express myself, my words but feebly represent the feelings of a large body of cultivated men who will feel real grief at the loss that seems imminent—a loss which may be slurred over, but which will not be forgotten, and which will be felt ever deeper as cultivation spreads. That the outward aspect of the world should grow uglier day by day in spite of the aspirations of civilisation, nay, partly because of its triumphs, is a grievous puzzle to some of us who are not lacking in sympathy for those aspirations and triumphs, artists and craftsmen as we are. So grievous it is that sometimes we are tempted to say, "Let them make a clean sweep of it all then: let us forget it all, and muddle on as best we may, unencumbered with either history or hope!" But such despair is, we well know, a treason to the cause of civilisation and the arts, and we do our best to overcome it, and to strengthen ourselves in the belief that even a small minority will at last be listened to, and its reasonable opinions be accepted. In this belief I have troubled you with this letter, and I call on all those who share it to join earnestly in any attempt that may be made to save us from an irreparable loss—a loss which only headlong rashness could make possible. Surely it can never be too late to pull down St. Mark's at Venice, the wonder of the civilised world?

TEXT: *Daily News*, November 1, 1879; *The Architect*, November 8, 1879.

¹ Mackail notes (II, 5) that by this time large-scale restoration of St. Mark's had been proposed and that Morris was the "soul" of the movement of protest. The campaign,

carried on both by an independent St. Mark's committee (of which Morris was an active member) and by the S.P.A.B., offended the Italian government. It had a strong influence, however, in preventing the demolition and rebuilding of the western façade. Morris spoke and wrote untiringly in this cause.

586 · To CORMELL PRICE

The Society
for the Protection
of Ancient Buildings
9, Buckingham Street,
Strand, W.C.
November 1 [1879]

My dear Crom
   We are hard at work doing that very thing:[1] we are rather cornered by want of lists; could you old chap get & send here, or tell me where to get lists of the Public School Masters who I know would sign: I will send you our memorial tomorrow   meantime in thundering haste
                              Your affec:
                              W.M.

MS: Price Papers.

   [1] Presumably addressing to the Italian government a memorial protesting the rebuilding of the west front of St. Mark's, Venice. See letters no. 581, n. 1, no. 585, and no. 587.

587 · To JOHN RUSKIN

26, Queen Square,
Bloomsbury, London
November 3, 1879

My dear Ruskin
   I am much grieved at having to disturb you with the news which you will find on the enclosed slip: but some of us think that it may be possible to put off [at] any rate the threatened destruction, and we purpose getting up some kind of memorial, which we believe our Ambassador would present to the Minister of Public Works:[1] both Ned Jones & myself believe that the way in which you could help the matter most, would be by writing a letter to the Times, which paper in spite of any ill-will would be obliged to give it a place:[2] and I am sure that both those who wanted rousing, & those who, though roused, want encouraging into definite action would be much helped by the sort of words ⟨you would⟩ that would come from you on the subject. Ned Jones was at Cambridge on Saturday & found people much excited & very indig-

[530]

26, Queen Square,

Bloomsbury, London,

Nov: 3rd 1879

My dear Ruskin

I am much grieved
at having to disturb you
with the news which you
will find on the enclosed slip;
but some of us think that
it may be possible to put off
any rate the threatened destruction,
and we purpose getting up
some kind of memorial, which

Morris's letter to John Ruskin, November 3, 1879.

we believe our Ambassador
would present to the Minister
of Public Works: both Ned
Jones & myself believe that
the way in which you could
help the matter most, would
be by writing a letter to the
Times, which paper in spite
of any ill-will would be
obliged to give it a place.
and I am sure that both
those who wanted rousing,
& those who, though roused,
want encouraging into

definite action would be much
helped by the sort of words
~~that I said~~ that would come
from you on the subject.
Ned Jones was at Cambridge
on Saturday & found people
much excited & very indignant
about it; so that I have
some hopes that we may
stop the ruin for the present.
Yours affectionately

William Morris

nant about it; so that I have *some* hope that we may stop the ruin for the present.

Yours affectionately
William Morris

MS: Berger Coll.

[1] The memorial was addressed to the Minister of Public Works, but it may have been received by the Minister of Public Instruction, under whose jurisdiction St. Mark's came. Sometime in November, Francisco de Sanctis (1817-1883) was appointed to this post (see *The Times*, November 22, 1879, p. 5). He was an historian and critic of Italian literature and had served as Minister of Public Instruction in previous governments.

[2] There is no letter from Ruskin in *The Times*, but in the issue for December 24, 1879, there is an announcement (p. 9) of an exhibition of photographs of St. Mark's with notes by Ruskin. He also sent a message to the Oxford meeting in the Sheldonian Theatre held on November 15 (see letter no. 588, n. 2).

588 · TO ROBERT BROWNING

26, Queen Square,
Bloomsbury, London
November 7, 1879

My dear Browning

I dont know if you have heard of the proposed rebuilding of the front of St Marks at Venice, which terrified us suddenly & not a little, since though we knew it would one day come, we thought would be put off year after year: it is now only a matter of doubt, whether it is to be taken in hand *at once* or next year. — that is unless some expression of opinion among cultivated men ⟨could⟩ should stop it. Some of us have been doing our best to do so, in various ways, & amongst others have moved the Dean of Ch: Ch:[1] to take the chair at a meeting to be held at Oxford on Saturday 15th Nov: 2 pm.[2] If you would consent to be present, & say something of what I cannot but think you must feel on such a misfortune, it would go far to make the meeting.[3]

You see I almost assume that you agree with me in the matter, but if any objections come across you, I should be very glad to answer them: to me such a thing happening would mean never going to Venice again, & trying to think that it had vanished, undegraded by such a luckless stroke of fortune: and almost everyone I know feels much the same about it I think —

I am
My dear Browning
Yours very truly
William Morris

MS: Princeton T.

My dear Browning

I dont know if
you have heard of the proposed
rebuilding of the front of St
Marks at Venice, which terrifies
us suddenly & not a little, since
though we knew it would one
day come, we thought would
be put off year after year:
it is now only a matter of

doubt, whether it is to be
taken in hand at once or next
year. — That is unless some

Expression of opinion among
cultivated men should stop it.
Some of us have been doing our
best to do so in various ways,
& amongst others have moved
the Dean of Ch: Ch: to take
the chair at a meeting to be
held at Oxford on Saturday
15th Nov: 2 pm. If you would
consent to be present, & say something
of what I cannot but think you
must feel on such a misfortune,
it would go far to make the
meeting. You see I almost
assume that you agree with
me in the matter; but if any
objections come across you,
I should be very glad to know

them: —— to me such a thing
happening would mean never
going to Venice again, &
trying to think that it had
vanished, undegraded by such
a luckless stroke of fortune:
and almost everyone I know
feels much the same about it
I think: ——

I am
My dear Browning.
Yours very truly
William Morris

Morris's letter to Robert Browning, November 7, 1879.

¹ Henry George Liddell (1811-1898), Dean of Christ Church, Oxford, from 1855 to 1891, and father of Lewis Carroll's Alice.

² The meeting, held in the Sheldonian Theatre, marked the first occasion on which Morris appeared in public at Oxford. *The Times*, November 17, reported (p. 9) that a resolution of protest directed to the Italian Government was passed and that a memorial would be circulated for signatures.

³ Browning did not attend. On November 10, 1879, he answered Morris's letter, sharing in general Morris's feelings about the proposed restoration and adding objections of his own to work already done at St. Mark's (see letter no. 592, n. 1). But he concluded by saying that he would not participate in the meeting at Oxford. "I never speak," he wrote.

589 • To William Ewart Gladstone
                                26, Queen Square,
                                Bloomsbury, London
                                November 7, 1879

Dear Sir

I believe you have heard from Mr. Burne Jones that we of the Society for the Protection of Ancient Buildings have been terrified by receiving information that it is proposed to *rebuild* the great façade of St. Marks at Venice, perhaps immediately, & certainly next year: there are a great many who do not belong to our Society, & who perhaps, do not go all lengths with us, are scarcely less terrified than ourselves, & some stir is being made in the matter, & we believe that we may get many & important signatures to a memorial which we are preparing for presentation to the Italian Minister of Works:¹ we believe it would go far to ensure the success of our plans if we could obtain your ⟨report⟩ support since we well know that no one outside Italy has so much influence there as yourself: I write therefore (at the instance of our Committee) to ask you if I may send you our memorial with any hope of your according your support to it, or otherwise helping ⟨it⟩ us.² Any information as to the matter that I can give I will lay before you fully; but it occurs to me that I may as well meet one objection at the outset: It may be said that the state of the building is dangerous, & that the only way of preserving any record of it is to rebuild it however deplorable the loss of its present lovely surface may be: I should say in answer ⟨1st⟩ first, that, I am morally certain that there is no danger to be feared for the structure, & that two well known & very learned architects³ have assured me that they do not believe it is any danger whatever: but secondly, even if be, it must be obvious to anyone who thinks of it that the engineering side of architecture could hit on some expedient which would make the building sound again without seriously disturbing its surface, which latter I cannot suppose any one who really understands art could endure to see altered.

[538]

I feel that I owe you some apology for disturbing you at a time when you have work on your hands of such importance to all of us, but the importance of the subject-matter of my letter will I know not be denied by you, and I hope will excuse me.

I am
Dear Sir
Yours obediently
William Morris

To the Rt: Hon: W. E. Gladstone.

MS: BL, Add. MSS. 44461.

¹ See letter no. 587.

² *The Times*, November 29, 1879 reported (p. 10) that Gladstone had signed the memorial.

³ One of the architects may have been G. E. Street, who, according to Morris's third Annual Report to the S.P.A.B., 1880, had made a special journey to Italy. This Report refers to a letter by Street in *The Times*, November 21, 1879. However, Street, in his own report to the S.P.A.B. of his Italian trip (dated March 19, 1880) said that he had not been in Venice in nearly three years (see *The Architect*, 23 [May 22, 1880], 353). The other architect may have been John James Stevenson or William Burges, who also reported on St. Mark's (see *The Athenaeum*, [November 22, 1879], 607). Along with Street, Burges attended the November 15 meeting in Oxford.

590 • TO HENRY HOWARD MOLYNEUX HERBERT　　26, Queen Square,
Bloomsbury, London
November 8, 1879

My Lord

I suppose you will have noticed something of what is going on in the matter of the 'Restoration' of St Marks at Venice, & that some of us are doing what we can to save that beautiful work from the last degradation: the Society for the Protection of Ancient Buildings will presently be writing to you as President of the Society of Antiquaries, to ask for the support of that body: meantime I venture on my own responsibility to ask a favour of you: the Dean of Ch: Ch: [Christ Church] has consented to call a meeting at Oxford on the subject, and to take the chair at it; and it would be a great help to the meeting if you would take a part in the proceedings: The subject is attracting so much attention, & so many are horrified at the rashness of the proposed 'restoration' that we really are hopeful of at least delaying the stroke, and it is in this hope that I trouble you thus, which I should otherwise have been very loth to do: but feeling sure of your good-will in the matter, I have thought myself bound to get your active help if I could. The meeting is fixed for Saturday 15th Nov: 2 PM   I need not say I shall be very happy to give you any information you may ask for as to present & past conditions of the building if you have not seen it lately.

I am
My Lord
Yours faithfully
William Morris

To the Rt: Hon The Earl of Carnarvon.

MS: Monell Coll.

591 · To Anthony John Mundella[?]

The Society for
the Protection
of Ancient Buildings
9, Buckingham Street,
Strand, W.C.
November 10, 1879

Sir

In the belief that you will agree with the opinions expressed in the enclosed memorial on the above named subject, which is being widely circulated amongst lovers of art, we earnestly hope that you will sign it, and use all your influence to further the object it has in view.

I am
Sir
Your obedient Servant
William Morris
Hon: Sec: of the Society
for Protection of Ancient
Buildings

MS: Sheffield.

592 · To Robert Browning

The Society for
the Protection
of Ancient Buildings
9, Buckingham Street,
Strand, W.C.
November 11, 1879

My dear Browning

Thanks for your letter:[1] as to the pavement, though I spent many days last year in the Church I can't say I mastered the whole pattern, so I couldn't say to what extent the big pieces had really replaced the patterned work or were parts of the original design: *some* of them I know were: as to the so-called restoration, nothing could have been worse, it could not even be called an imitation; though I cannot say that any imitation would have been much better: It seems to me that all that needed doing was to mend the far-gone places. As to the danger to the Church from the pavement being on the wave of course that is visionary: some of our archeologists think that it was orginally ⟨built⟩ laid so: however that may be tis certain that it has been wavy for hundreds of years. But at present it is an affair of putting the finishing stroke on the whole church by rebuilding or renewing the west front, which visibly to everybody's eyes is in a good condition. Whether they will actually *rebuild* it as our correspondent words it, or only renew the surface I know not, nor can I think it greatly matters except to a pure antiquary; they will most certainly in either case destroy its qualities as a work of art: I am afraid too, whether they rebuild or merely 'restore,' they will set to work at the mosaics in the vaulting of the portico, which in spite of their rudeness are most beautiful & imaginative; and *because* of those qualities combined quite impossible to be imitated.

As to making a noise about it at present, the point of that is, to speak frankly, that they have given us an opportunity of appealing to people who might not otherwise be easy to move, by this wholesale threat, & to miss that opportunity would mean, even at the best, allowing them to go on mauling the building piece-meal, till there was nothing left worth preserving: so to end my boring letter I enclose our memorial to which I do most particularly wish for your signature.

Yours very truly
William Morris

MS: Scripps.

¹ Browning's letter, dated November 10, reads in part: "I feel quite painfully enough, and perhaps to spare, on the subject of almost any 'restoration': but it is many years ago since I noticed that every trampler's foot was apt to send flying a lozenge of red or green marble,—and last year, after long absence, it struck me that great slabs of marble, looking already oldish, had replaced corresponding spaces of the fine patternwork I remember in the nave . . . [O]f the outrage on the Front—I could guess little so dreadful as that! If there is any 're-building' (your word) the rebuilders should be throttled between the two red pillars, which have done similar and worse service of old . . . how can the fresh and raw compete (or harmonize) with the old mellowness imbrowned by the sunny summers so long? Giotto's tower at Florence used to affect one painfully, in my time, with its splicings of bright white stone, in and out the rich colour about them. . . .

"Of another terrible project I heard—which seemingly has escaped you, but, I believe, will assuredly be carried into effect: a road from the railway to St. Mark's, for omnibuses. This may befall, since it is a money-procuring project . . ." (manuscript in Pforzheimer Library).

593 • To James Beal
26, Queen Square,
Bloomsbury, London
November 12, 1879

Dear Sir[1]

I shall be very happy to have my name on Mr. J. Morley's Committee;[2] as there are few men whom I [would] rather see representing an important constituency.

I am
Dear Sir
Yours faithfully
William Morris

J. Beal, Eqre.

MS: GLRO.

[1] James Beal (1829-1891) took an active part in establishing land and building societies and was a member of the City Guilds Reform Association.

[2] See letter no. 422, n. 8. The reference here is to John Morley's second (unsuccessful) attempt, in 1880, to enter Parliament. See also *The Times*, November 6, 1879, p. 10, and November 12, p. 10.

594 • To Richard Chamberlain
The Society for
the Protection
of Ancient Buildings
9, Buckingham Street,
Strand, W.C.
November 12, 1879

My dear Chamberlain[1]

I will come by that train then: as to the meeting,[2] it would be well to have some big photographs wouldn't it: also what chance would there be of a resolution in favour of our memorial (which I send).   at any rate it might lie in the room for signature.

Yours very truly
William Morris

MS: Birmingham.

[1] Richard Chamberlain (1840-1899), Mayor of Birmingham. He signed the St. Mark's memorial.

[2] For a report of this meeting, held in Birmingham, see *The Architect*, 22 (November 22, 1879), 298-99. See also LeMire, p. 236.

595 • To the Editor of *The Times*

The Society for
the Protection
of Ancient Buildings
9, Buckingham Street,
Strand, W.C.
November 22, 1879

Sir

I note with great pleasure the remarks your Italian Correspondent quotes as expressing the opinions of the Ministry of Public Instruction in Italy,[1] but the answer to their retort on our newly-acquired tenderness for their glorious monument is as simple as that retort is natural and reasonable. It is that 15 years ago we had but little tenderness for our own buildings, nor do I think in the long run they will feel aggrieved at our eagerness to save them from some of the same loss that we ourselves have suffered: perhaps they scarcely know with what pleasure some of us would hail their interference with our affairs of a like kind here. Meantime, Sir, I beg to appeal, through your columns, most earnestly to those Italian gentlemen, mentioned by your correspondent, and whose names will surely be always honoured by all lovers of art, to do their utmost to induce the authorities to forbid for the future all meddling with the matchless mosaics and inlaid works which are the crown of the glories of St. Mark's. The news that the so-called restoration of the lovely pavement, now unhappily once again progressing, had been stopped by the authorities would do more than anything else to allay our fears, and would make many of us who at present dread that we shall never dare to see Venice again look forward with redoubled pleasure to our next visit to the most romantic of cities.

I am, Sir,
Yours obediently,
William Morris

TEXT: *The Times*, November 24, 1879.

[1] *The Times*, November 22, 1879, printed (p. 5) a dispatch from its correspondent in Rome who reported the indignation of the Ministry of Public Instruction, whose officials were saying that there had been no protest when Austria had restored or rebuilt the whole of the northern side.

596 • From a Letter to Edward
         or Georgiana Burne-Jones

November 24, 1879

Yes, the Memorial has flourished and Dizzy did actually sign it on Saturday; I have many a worrit over it and even now I am not quite sure what to do with it; for this morning is news from Italy that the Minister has sent word to the Prefect of Venice to stop the restoration of the Mosaic. What this means I don't quite know, but I hope it is the stopping of the work on the pavement, because I feel sure that we have saved the west front already. I suppose in any case, even if the Memorial is a mere formality, it will have to go; we have to hand it to the Ambassador here[1]: I must say it seems to me extremely absurd that we can't send it by post as to an ordinary mortal. In truth what has really worried me in this matter has been all the ridiculous rigmarole and social hypocrisy one has to wade through.

TEXT: *Memorials*, II, 96; Published: Henderson, *Letters*, 132.

[1] General Luigi Menabrea. See letter no. 631, n. 1.

597 • TO THE EDITORS OF VARIOUS ITALIAN NEWSPAPERS

9 Buckingham St
Strand, London
November 27 [1879]

To the Editor of —— [1]

Sir

We have noticed with much pain that the Italian Press believes those English persons who have of late ventured to criticize the past and prospective restorations of St Marks at Venice, intend by that criticism to cast a slur on the Italians of being specially incompetent or careless in dealing with their ancient buildings: Our Society is most anxious to deny that there is any foundation for what they regard as a charge against them of injustice and prejudice; it begs to assure you that its utterances, whether of its members as individuals, or in its collective form do not fairly bear any such construction.

The Society is well aware that the Italians can be charged with no greater errors in this matter than any other nation which is the inheritor of an ancient civilization. Those errors, being errors of principle and not of accident only the Society was founded to combat, in England first, but thence, if possible throughout the world.

The Society has from the first, been fully alive to the difficulty and delicacy of addressing a foreign nation on its own affairs, the importance of the subject only could have driven it to take such a course; but it is firmly convinced that if it had done less, it would have betrayed the cause of art.

Perhaps our best defence against the charge of having attacked the Italian Nation specially, will be found in the enclosed paper, which is the original program of our Society published three years ago,[2] and which, as above-mentioned, was addressed primarily to our own countrymen, pointing out to them that support and constant care, and not restoration so-called, were ⟨the⟩ what ⟨the⟩ our ancient buildings demanded of us.

We believe that if you would be so good as to print this document in your valuable paper, your many readers would see that we have not been more indulgent to our own country than to yours; and perhaps it is not extravagant to hope that its publication in Italy may attract to us many who agree with ⟨us⟩ our principles, but who have hithertoo been more or less defenceless from isolation.[3]

We write to you, Sir, in full confidence that your love of justice will not permit you to refuse us the only means in our power of setting ourselves right with the Italian people and preventing that misunderstanding which is so lamentable between people who ought for all reasons to cultivate relations of mutual esteem.

> We have the honour to be
> Sir, Your obedient servants
> William Morris, Hon Sec of
> SPAB
> Newman Marks Sec:

MS: Huntington.

  [1] This letter was apparently written to be sent to a number of Italian newspapers.

  [2] The manifesto of the S.P.A.B., written by Morris in 1877.

  [3] During the June 1880 annual S.P.A.B. meeting, W. B. Richmond read a message to the members from an Italian antiquarian who had written to the Society regarding St. Mark's: "The article of Mr. Morris came at the right time. It was so full of fire and hit the mark exactly. I published it in the Rinnovamento."

---

598 • TO THE EDITOR OF *The Times*   9, Buckingham Street,
                                                     Strand
                                                     November 28, 1879

Sir,

The information of an official character given yesterday in your columns confirms remarkably that which we received a month ago from our correspondent at Venice.[1] The fact that the works had been taken out of the hands of the local authorities and that a Commission was to be called to consider in what way they were to be carried further, while it made us anxious lest those works should be of a yet more sweeping character than what had hitherto been done, yet seemed to afford an opportunity of urging the opinion that the exercise of the utmost conservatism was needed if St. Mark's was not to be practically destroyed by well-meant efforts to restore it.

That opinion we still think is worth the consideration of the Commission now sitting, especially since it has been supported by the large and influential body of cultivated people that has signed the memorial preparing for presentation to the Minister of Public Instruction in Italy, the signatures to which comprise, we believe, the names of the greater part of all those whose study of the subject and interest in it give them the best right to have an opinion thereon.[2]

> I am, Sir,
> your obedient servant,
> William Morris
> Hon. Sec. of the S.P.A.B.

TEXT: *The Times*, November 29, 1879.

[1] On November 28 *The Times* reported (p. 9) that "the whole destructive work against which the outcry was raised has been stopped. . . . The Ministry of Public Instruction has taken the matter into its own hand. Whatever may prove to be necessary in the way of restoration or of repair will be done, but with the utmost care and tenderness." The correspondent was probably John Bunney, Fondamenta San Biagio, Venice. Bunney was listed in the S.P.A.B. membership.

[2] On November 19, 1879, the memorial had been published in *The Times* (p. 8) with the names of some of those who had signed it.

599 • TO CATHERINE HOLIDAY

26, Queen Square,
Bloomsbury, London
December 5, 1879

Dear Mrs. Holiday

The difficulty of sending the embroideries to America[1] seems to me that the risk is too great: for if they do not chance to be sold they will undoubtedly be spoiled by exposure & turning over: this to say the truth would make me rather afraid to send our own: the other one (for I don't quite know if its ours or yours, only that it isnt paid for) is a little stouter and might come off better: but I confess I don't advise you to risk it — simply ⟨on those⟩ for that reason.[2]

> Yours truly
> William Morris

MS: Berger Coll.

[1] By 1878 Morris and Co. had a number of American agents, the chief of whom were Cowtan and Tout, Inc. of New York. See Parry, p. 136.

[2] Holiday undertook to sell her embroideries to America on her own.

600 • To Pietro Saccardo   26 Queen Square
                                                Bloomsbury, London
                                                December 13, 1879

Dear Sir[1]

I beg to acknowledge with many thanks the receipt of your courteous letters and the interesting enclosed plan of the foundations of the Basilica. In reply I can only say that it would be presumptuous for me to argue on a matter of technical detail with a person of your experience in the matter all the more as I am not a professional architect; at the same time, I still hold to my opinion that when the public in Italy comes to acknowledge that any rebuilding or any restoration of their glorious Church would be a disaster to art and to them, the renowned engineers of Italy will not find it impossible under any circumstances ⟨of nothing[?]⟩ to devise some scheme for keeping the Basilica standing for ages to come without any change in its external aspect.

Meantime, my dear Sir, will you allow me to trespass further on your courtesy by presenting to you my friend, Mr. J. J. Stevenson,[2] a distinguished English Architect, and a member of our Committee, who has been deputed by that Committee to report to us the present state of St. Mark's Basilica. We believe that your intimate knowledge of the building will be of great use to him in his survey of it, and that you will not grudge him that help, as we cannot doubt that you fully understand the good-will which our Society bears both to the Italian People and to Venice, and permit me to add, since you have made us acquainted with you by your letters, to yourself also.

                                I am, Dear Sir,
                                Yours Obediently,
                                William Morris

Signor P. Saccardo

MS: Mander Coll. Published: Henderson, *Letters*, 133.

[1] Pietro Saccardo fought against replacing the twelfth-century mosaics in St. Mark's with new ones by an Austrian artist. (See letter no. 592.) Saccardo later wrote a number of books on St. Mark's, including *The Mosaics of St. Mark's* (1896).

[2] John James Stevenson; see letter no. 414, n. 2.

601 • To Rosalind Francis Howard   26, Queen Square,
                                                Bloomsbury, W.C., London
                                                December 13 [1879]

Dear Mrs. Howard

Ned Jones & I went to look at the effect of the gold paper against the picture, & found to our grief that it would not do:[1] yesterday I went there to meet him that we might try something else, but the morning was so bad that he could not come out: this morning I find that you suggest leaving the matter till you come up to town: but meanwhile, I, knowing that it would be impossible to get the work done unless we began at once, have set Leach's[2] men at work to forward the job, so that the Drawing Room will be finished next week in the way you wished; & the boudoir has been prepared for final painting & hanging which would now take less than a week to do at any time: Ned and I are going to look at the room again on ⟨Mon⟩ Sunday, so that I shall be able to report again on Monday, so that if you agreed to our suggestions, there would still be time to finish the room before you get back. I hope I have not done wrong in setting Leach to work: if I have, I must plead the usual excuse of fools, that I have acted for the best.

— Dining Room.

I am bound to ask your pardon for having neglected this job; but I did not quite understand what was to be done except the writing (which by the way is a very difficult business):[3] I am now going to set to work to design ornaments for the mouldings round the pictures, the curved braces of ceiling, and the upper part of the panelling. I fear there is little chance of getting any of this done before your return (I mean executed on the wood-work) but I will do my best to get everything in train to start it on the first opportunity: meantime I have thought it best to tell Leach's man to varnish only the lower part of the panelling, doors & shutters, &c, where the ornament will not come.

Yours very truly
William Morris

MS: Howard Papers. Published: Mackail, II, 52-53.

[1] Morris and Company were decorating the Howards' London house, at No. 1 Palace Green. See also letter no. 604.

[2] See letter no. 32.

[3] The dining room was decorated with a series of panels painted by Burne-Jones and Walter Crane, which illustrated the story of Cupid and Psyche.

602 · To Thomas Wardle

26, Queen Square,
Bloomsbury, W.C., London
December 15, 1879

My dear Wardle

I have just read your memo: about the blue-printed velvet: I *have* seen it, and I am sorry to say that I consider it rather disastrous: in fact I cannot possibly offer it for sale in its present state; you know better than I do whether any thing can be done to better it. I should add that no sets of the prints are ever passed without my seeing them: By the way *is* the blue velvet an indigo print? I thought it was not. The way to guard against this mishap with this print in future; will be to print it *at least* as strong as the approved pattern: to make it ⟨stronge⟩ weaker is sure to *ruin it*.

Yours very truly
William Morris

MS: Duke.

603 • TO INGRAM BYWATER
26, Queen Square,
Bloomsbury, London
December 15, 1879

My dear Bywater[1]

I am rather sorry that the Oxford Memorial was not set on foot at once: however I don't know that it matters much since the meeting was of so public a character:[2] anyhow by this time all the good has been done which could have been done by any action in England, and I think it would be better to let the matter rest for the present, & hope for the best: I admit I am not very sanguine, though 'tis clear that we have had some effect on their views

I think the scheme of pulling down St Clements Danes has been abandoned, but we will make enquiries.

Yours very truly
William Morris

MS: Dunlap Coll.

[1] Ingram Bywater (1840-1914) was a Greek scholar and Fellow of Exeter College. From 1879 on, he was a delegate to the Oxford University Press.

[2] The meeting held in the Sheldonian Theatre, Oxford, on November 15, in connection with St. Mark's, Venice. See letters no. 588, n. 2 and no. 589, n. 1.

604 • TO ROSALIND FRANCIS HOWARD
26, Queen Square,
Bloomsbury, London
December 15, 1879

Dear Mrs. Howard

Thank you for your kind letter: Ned & I duly went to Palace Green yesterday & our joint conclusion was that the *best* hanging for the walls of the boudoir would be the enclosed madder-printed cotton: it brings out the greys of the picture better than anything else: also I think it would make a pretty room with the wood-work painted a light blue-green colour like a starling's egg & if you wanted drapery about it we have beautiful stuffs of shades of red that would brighten all up without fighting with the wall hangings: if you could like this & would let me know some day this week, I could get all finished against you come home, but if you still have doubts we would leave the room in a forward state for finishing To complete the business part of my letter I may as well give you the price of the red stuff: 2s/ per yd. yard-wide, which would come to less than the gold sunflower would have done.

Janey is but poorly, thank you: Any cold weather is bad for her you know: today indeed is not cold but is damp & miserable; I am getting more & more dissatisfied with living in London — but what am I to do?

I do not know enough of Wortley[1] to say if he is a muff, but doubtless his principles could be packed in a very small box: I suppose he is ambitious, a very bad vice — or — who is *she*?

Like everyone else who knew Mr Charles Howard[2] I have often thought of him and his kindness & straightforwardness: it moved me much to see his new made mound among the old tombs at Lanercost last summer.

My girls are well I think, & have been having rather a merry time of it: I cannot say I look with much favour on most of the young men who have been about here — and I hope they don't.

Please give my love to George & dont forget the babies.

Yours very truly
William Morris

MS: Howard Papers. Extract published: Henderson, *Letters*, 154-55.

[1] Charles Beilby Stuart-Wortley (1851-1926), elected Conservative M.P. for the borough of Sheffield in the general election of 1880 and in the same year married to Beatrice Trollope, a niece of Anthony Trollope. She died soon afterward; in 1886 Stuart-Wortley married Alice Millais, a daughter of John Everett Millais. See *The Times*, April 26, 1926, p. 9.

[2] Charles W.G. Howard, Mrs. Howard's father-in-law, who had died on April 11, 1879. A son of the sixth Earl of Carlisle, he was Liberal M.P. for East Cumberland at the time of his death.

605 • To William Ewart Gladstone
The National Liberal League
19 Buckingham Street
Strand, London, W.C.
December 22, 1879

Sir,

We, the members of the Executive Council of the National Liberal League, beg to be permitted to send our congratulations to you on your seventieth birthday. We would much rather have had the pleasure of meeting you at a banquet or some other great gathering of our fellow-countrymen in London; but since that is not possible, we take the only other means open to us of expressing to you our heartfelt pleasure and our unfeigned satisfaction that you are still spared to devote your great talents and unwearied energies to the services of our common country. We earnestly hope that these services will for very many years be placed at the disposal of that party to which you and we belong, and whether as its leader, which by your nature and our desires you ought to be, or in any other capacity, we shall ever gratefully remember your noble devotion and self-denying efforts for the welfare of all classes of the community and for the furtherance and establishment of liberty and justice thoughout the world.

We remain your faithful
servants,
George Howell, Chairman
William Morris, Treasurer
Henry Broadhurst, Secretary

By order of the Executive Council, December 22, 1879

TEXT: *Daily News*, December 23, 1879.

606 • Two Letters to Emma Shelton Morris

a.

26, Queen Square,
Bloomsbury, London
December 31, 1879

Dearest Mother

Just a line to wish you a happy new year: with all possible health; also please give the same wishes to Henrietta, who I hope is better.

Janey is only pretty well, the changeable weather has somewhat upset her. The children are very well: they have been rather gay this Christmas: Mr. Cormel Price is staying with us, this week.

[551]

I have sat down to write amid business going on; so I am very much muddled, & will finish with ⟨wishing⟩ giving you my best love.

Your most affectionate Son
William Morris

MSS: Walthamstow.

b.
26, Queen Square,
Bloomsbury, London
January 7, 1880

Dearest Mother

I have ordered Diosy to send 4 dozen of the claret, which please accept as a new year's gift, & if by accident he sends *you* the bill please send it on to me.

I have to thank you so very much dearest Mother for your splendid gift of the piano: I shall be calling at Broadwoods[1] tomorrow & shall hear about it

Janey is bad with neuralgia I am sorry to say: otherwise all well.

Your most affectionate Son
William Morris

[1] The piano manufacturing firm founded by John Broadwood (1732-1812).

607 · RECIPIENT UNKNOWN
26, Queen Square,
Bloomsbury, London
January 19, 1880

Dear Sir

I answer your questions with pleasure.

My poem[1] is founded on the Scandinavian version of the Niblung story, which I had previously translated with the help of my friend Mr. Eirikr Magnússon, a learned Icelander: The book is published by Messrs. Ellis & White under the title of The Story of the Völsungs & Niblungs, & includes translations of the part of the poetic Edda that relate to the Niblung story. You may rely on this book for being a word for word translation of the originals.

The subject of the relation between the German & the Scandinavian version of the great northern Epic is too intricate to be discussed in a hasty note: but one may say broadly, 1st that, the German poem is only a fragment of that Epic: 2nd that in its present condition it is of various

Emma Shelton Morris, 1879.

dates, & 3rd that the earliest part of it is later in form (much later) than the Eddaic poems.

By saying this I do not mean to say that it is derived from the Icelandic poem: and in any case it is a very noble work.

I am

Dear Sir

Yours truly

William Morris

MS: Present location unknown.

[1] *Sigurd the Volsung*. See letter no. 311, n. 2.

608 · THREE LETTERS TO AGLAIA IONIDES CORONIO

a.

26, Queen Square,
Bloomsbury, London
January 23, 1880

My dear Aglaia

Thank you kindly for the little packet of Levantine wool: owing to my own mistake it isn't quite what I was thinking of: I ought to have asked for woolen *yarns*; ie the wool spun into threads, however I daresay this will be useful also. Thank you also for writing about the Broussa Velvet:[1] I confess I thought it so cheap at the price, that, though I had no money I hankered after it so much that I could not make up my mind to say *no*, which however I now do.

As to the kermes, I am even now engaged in the last experiment: I fancy it is just the same as the sample.

I suppose I shall meet you at Lukes on Monday: if you are in town next week, I should like to call on you one afternoon: say Wednesday — or Friday.

Yrs affectionately
William Morris

MSS: Berger Coll.

[1] A silk velvet produced in Broussa, Turkey, which has a long history of textile manufacture and has also been a center for sericulture. Linda Parry of the Victoria and Albert Museum has suggested that Morris probably had in mind "the traditional Turkish patterns of pomegranate and artichoke more than any particular technique when he referred to this term, and it is likely that he was thinking of the typical cushion and divan covers made in the area. Usually rectangular in shape, these consist of tree of life or pomegranate or artichoke central motif with semi-geometric borders. The patterns on these pieces are woven in pile with flat, often metallic backgrounds."

Morris, 1880.

b.
26, Queen Square,
Bloomsbury, London
Wednesday
[January 28?] 1880

My dear Aglaia

I can come in on Friday afternoon if you please: thanks again for the bag of kermes, which I have given to Wardle to make into lake.[1]

Yrs affectionately
William Morris

[1] Lake is a reddish color, usually obtained from cochineal. Morris planned to substitute kermes for the cochineal.

c.
26, Queen Square,
Bloomsbury, London
January 30, 1880

My dear Aglaia

I enclose a cheque for the amount: it don't matter about the kermes: one expects to pay for one's whistle.

Thank you very kindly for all the trouble you have taken in the matter; I am really ashamed to give you so much trouble.

Yrs affectionately
William Morris

609 • To Thomas Wardle
26, Queen Square,
Bloomsbury, London
February 4, 1880

My dear Wardle

Thanks for note: I have been making enquiries in Greece about the Kermes; & at last have got full particulars on the subject through M. Tricoupi[1] the well-known politician out there: about 4 years ago there was a small demand for it (πρινοκόκκι is the Greek name) & a certain amount was gathered which is all which is in the market at present & of which (in Greece) about 4000 lb is left: the price of this on board ship at Patras is about 6d/. per lb: the place where it grows is in the Morea (about Tripolitza) & in Acarnania, but the latter is inferior: it is exported chiefly to Tunis for dyeing the fezzes. That now in the market is old & therefore doubtless not very good: I have had a sample of about 6 lb, which I have tried as a dye & am getting tried as a lake: the colour is much the same as I got from your sample, but perhaps not quite so full — ⟨So m[?]⟩ a Greek merchant has sent us another sample of ⟨6 lb⟩ eleven pounds, which will be here in about a month.

Now all this is old: *but* it is gathered in June & July & ought to cost no more than about 3/6 per lb. if fresh gathered: in which case it would also be stronger: so I have ordered 200 okes, ⟨that⟩ (an oke is nearly 3 lbs) of this gathering if I can get it at 12 drachmas per oke, which would bring it to about 3/6 per lb; at which rate it might be used for tapestry & embroidery worsteds, though scarcely for regular weaving or carpet work: perhaps you would like to share my order & make it a little more, which I fancy would make it easier to get at a moderate rate. I am supposing that the Algiers kermes comes from the Morea; but I am not sure: it used to be gathered in Granada: about Valencia — see Hellot.[2]

I think whereas the Moorish kermes seems to be doubtful as to quality, & but little below what I have given for the Greek I had better leave it alone.

Yours very truly
William Morris

MS: Duke.

[1] Charilaos Tricoupis or Tricoupi (1832-1896), who had been Prime Minister of Greece in 1875 and regained that position in 1880.

[2] Jean Hellot. See letter no. 333, n. 1.

610 • To John Henry Chamberlain   26, Queen Square,
Bloomsbury, London
February 6, 1880

My dear Chamberlain[1]

I will breakfast with you on the 20th with much pleasure[2] I dont care so long as I get back to Hammersmith early in the evening.

As to Burne Jones the news is bad, he will not accept: he wrote me a letter which I meant to have sent on to you, but I have somehow mislaid it: however I remember the gist of it, which was this — that the thing was so much out of his usual way that for any other town he would have said no at once, but felt Birmingham had a claim on him for something, but that for him unused [to speaking,] it would be so difficult to say what he really had in him to say as it ought to be said, that he was bound to refuse on the ground of its taking up too much of his time which he could use much more profitably for Birmingham as well as other places: in short he took the thing so seriously & would obviously have been so glad to accept it if he thought he could, that I could press him no further.[3]

What do you think of Holman Hunt, or Poynter,[4] or G. E. Street? I suppose you wouldn't poison the latter from professional jealousy. Excuse haste: if I find E.B.J.'s letter I will send it on.

Yours very truly
William Morris

MS: Fitzwilliam.

[1] John Henry Chamberlain (1831-1883), architect, Vice-President of the Royal Society of Artists, and Chairman of the Birmingham Society of Arts.

[2] Morris was to be in Birmingham to deliver his lecture, "Labour and Pleasure versus Labour and Sorrow," at the School of Design on February 19. See LeMire, p. 237.

[3] Burne-Jones had been invited to succeed Morris as president of the Birmingham Society of Arts. He declined, giving as his reason the difficulty of writing and delivering the presidential address. For the text of Burne-Jones's letter, written to Morris but intended for the Committee of the Royal Society of Artists, see *Memorials*, II, 98.

[4] Edward John Poynter (1836-1919), painter, president of the Royal Academy, and husband of Georgiana Burne-Jones's sister, Agnes Macdonald.

---

611 • TO ANTHONY JOHN MUNDELLA

Kelmscott House,
Upper Mall, Hammersmith
February 9, 1880

Mr. William Morris has much pleasure in accepting Mr. & Mrs. Mundella's[1] kind invitation for Saturday, the 21st instant

MS: USheffield.

[1] See letter no. 356, n. 1.

---

612 • TO JANE MORRIS

26, Queen Square,
Bloomsbury, London
February 13, 1880

Dearest Janey

All well here: I was very glad to get your note:[1] today is perfectly lovely here & the weather is looking settled. I don't see how you could be likely to be much better in a week's time; & I don't think a fortnight is long enough for you to get benefit from the turn. I go to Birm[ingham] on Wednesday & shall not be home again till the Friday evening — I have been asked to dine at Mundellas on the Saturday after, & couldn't very well say no: but I would beg off if you wanted me to come down on that day.

Any how if you stay over next week I could come to you whether

Jenny comes or not. I told her about Hadham, and she seemed to like the idea: so she will write to Mother

I have been working my head off over the Birmingham address:[2] I shall finish it tomorrow: but I doubt if it will be worth reading when its done.

I am writing this in a hurry at Queen Sq: so I can't tell what I am writing.

Oh! as Jenny used to say, here is £10 by registered letter.

Also my address at Birmingham will be care of W. Kenrick, Eqre[3] The Grove Harborne Birm

Both Jenny & I thought that May's account of the house shaken by the waves was delightful We have had wild weather enough till quite lately.

I do so hope you will get better this week, my dear; & let May give me a bit of news.

With love to you & May

Your loving
W.M.

MS: BL, Add. MSS. 45338.

 [1] Jane Morris was with the Burne-Joneses at Rottingdean.

 [2] See letter no. 610, n. 2.

 [3] William Kenrick (1831–1919) was Chairman of the Museum and School of Arts Committee, Birmingham City Council.

613 • To Jane Morris   26, Queen Square,
Bloomsbury, London
February 16, 1880

Dearest Janey

I am so sorry I was a false prophet about the weather: but surely when this gale has blown itself out we shall have it good.

Jenny is going to dine with the Miss Cobdens[1] this evening: She has been a very good girl & amused me; also I have not been a disobedient parent.

The chest is stuck in its place by means of the united efforts of Mathews[2] & myself, & Jenny and I put away the embroidery in it last night.

You will be amused to hear that Mr. Buller cast up yesterday *very* politeful: but I shall take care that he don't get on to the old footing again.

I have finished my lecture[3] such as it is, and am ready for a start on

[559]

⟨Thursday⟩ Wednesday: I suppose I shall hear before then what is to be arranged about Jenny, & also whether you are coming back or not.

If you want any more cash before I come back, please write to Wardle who will sign checks this week. It is rather clearing up here & I hope it is with you. Yesterday afternoon we had it not bad.

I suppose you have heard that Phil passed his matriculation exam:[4]

> Love to you & May
> Your loving
> W.M.

MS: BL, Add. MSS. 45338.

[1] See letter no. 504, n. 1.

[2] The gardener at Kelmscott House, employed by both the Morrises and the Richmonds.

[3] See letter no. 610, n. 2.

[4] Philip Burne-Jones matriculated at University College, Oxford, in 1880, but there is no evidence that he took his B.A. degree.

---

614 • TO AGLAIA IONIDES CORONIO

Kelmscott House,
Upper Mall, Hammersmith
Tuesday Evening
[February 17, 1880]

My dear Aglaia

I believe I said I would come if I could: since then a meeting has intervened, which I can't decently shirk, and also I have to go to Rotting-dean to my Kinswomen on Wednesday evening: I am really very sorry; but from pillar to post is a feeble metaphor to express the driving of me. Would next Monday suit you? it is my best day at present, & I would undertake to come that day — Pray how is Miss Vaughan?[1]

> Yours affectionately
> William Morris

I don't come for the books: but I really am ashamed you should so load me with presents & take such trouble for me.[2]

MS: Berger Coll.

[1] Possibly Kate Vaughan, the dancer, keenly admired by both Burne-Jones and Ruskin. See *Memorials*, II, 121.

[2] Written diagonally at upper left-hand corner of the letter.

615 • TO SIDNEY COLVIN
26, Queen Square,
Bloomsbury, London
February 20, 1880

My dear Colvin

I will submit the cloth to a piece-dyer to see what he thinks of it, & if he thinks the stripes will not show after-dyeing I will get it dyed: otherwise I will tell you. You see it seems to us that the stuff is the natural colour of the wool, in which case the present colour cannot be got rid of before redyeing.

Yrs truly
William Morris

MS: Bodleian.

616 • TO CONSTANTINE IONIDES
26, Queen Square,
Bloomsbury, London
February 22, 1880

My dear Ionides[1]

Mrs. Lyell, a client of ours, who is about building a house wishes to see the effect of your stained panelling in your dining room, would you kindly allow her to do so.

Yours truly
William Morris[2]

MS: Berger Coll. (copy).

[1] Constantine A. Ionides, wealthy Greek ship owner, patron of the arts, and brother of Aglaia Coronio. See letter no. 111, n. 1.

[2] This letter is taken from a handwritten copy of the original.

617 • TO GEORGE HECTOR CROAD
26, Queen Square,
Bloomsbury, London
February 28, 1880

Sir[1]

Miss Elizabeth Burden, who is a candidate for the post of superintendant of ⟨the⟩ needlework of the School Board for London, has been employed by me for some years as an embroideress, and an arranger of such-like work: She is a first-rate needle-woman, and in general matters well educated: while doing work for me, she had to keep troublesome & complicated accounts concerning designs, materials, & wages, which she carried through very competently & with great accuracy.

I have no doubt that her careful business habits combined with her complete mastery of the theory ⟨of⟩ & practice of all kinds of needle-work would fit her well for discharging the duties of the place she is applying for.

> I am
> Sir
> Yours faithfully
> William Morris
> (of Morris & Co)

to G. H. Croad Eqre
The Clerk of the London School Board

MS: Bodleian.

[1] Croad (1829-1902) was the first secretary to the newly established London School Board in 1870.

618 • To Emma Shelton Morris

> Kelmscott House,
> Upper Mall Hammersmith
> March 3 [1880]

Dearest Mother

I am so sorry I cannot come on Thursday, but I am engaged two deep that day; ⟨as⟩ indeed ⟨for⟩ I cannot get away at all till Monday, when I will come if convenient to you: we will then talk about Jenny.

We are having very wild weather here, but seasonable, being March.

Janey is better on the whole I think, but still weak & complains of head-ache.

Give my love to my Jenny, also to Arthur & Henrietta.

> With best love
> Your loving Son
> William Morris

MS: Walthamstow.

619 • To Edward Williams Byron Nicholson

> 26, Queen Square,
> Bloomsbury, London
> March 5, 1880

Dear Mr. Nicholson

Thank you: I shall be very happy to come on the 17th.[1]

> Yrs truly
> William Morris

MS: McMinn Papers.

¹ Probably to attend a lecture by John Ruskin. At this time, Nicholson was Librarian of the London Institution (see letter no. 67, n. 1). *The Times*, March 18, 1880, reported (p. 11) that on the previous evening Ruskin had lectured at the London Institution on "A Caution to Snakes," a subject, he said, appropriate to St. Patrick's Day. The theater had been filled to capacity, and because of the great demand for tickets the talk was scheduled to be repeated on March 23, 1880.

620 • RECIPIENT UNKNOWN

26, Queen Square,
Bloomsbury, London
March 16, 1880

Dear Madam

I am so very busy at present, that it will be quite impossible to pre-pare any lecture for the College. I am really ⟨fr⟩ very sorry, for it is a great pleasure to me to address such a sympathetic audience.

I am
Dear Madam
Yours truly
William Morris

MS: Berger Coll. (copy).

621 • TO CHARLES ELIOT NORTON

26, Queen Square,
Bloomsbury, London
March 30, 1880

My dear Norton

I am ashamed to write to you after this long silence, & all the more as I am writing now asking you to ⟨to⟩ do something for me: Mr. G. Y. Wardle my manager, is travelling in America with the purpose of trying to disentangle people's ideas as to our business, & to show them what kind of things we are really making, and what our aims are: he would be very glad therefore to be introduced to anyone who is interested in these matters, and I thought you might be able to help him herein, & I was sure that you would do so in that case: hence this *interested* letter.¹

I may add that I believe you will find Mr. Wardle sympathetic in matters social, political & literary, as well as in matters artistic.

I make this letter short because I am genuinely ashamed of myself for not writing to you before; but will write longer when I am not writing about my business.

I am
My dear Norton
Yours very truly
William Morris

MS: Harvard.

¹ George Wardle arrived in America the following month. Enclosing Morris's letter, he wrote to Norton:

Tremont House
April 22, 1880

Dear Sir

I beg leave to present in this way a note of introduction from Mr. William Morris, which I would have handed to you personally but I fear to intrude on you at an inconvenient time. It would give me great pleasure to call on you & to have the advantage of your advice in the business which has brought me to America if you would kindly indicate the hour which would be most agreeable to you.

Believe me Dear Sir
Very truly yours
George Wardle

Professor Charles E. Norton

Wardle made another trip to the United States a few yers later when he was sent to take charge of the Morris exhibit at the Foreign Fair, Boston, 1883. See Buxton Forman, p. 195.

622 • To WILLIAM DE MORGAN   [March 31-April 4, 1880]

Election Day, 1880¹
How sweet the never-failing Spring comes round,
Up comes the sun we thought the sea had drown'd
Rending the clouds that darkened England's heart,
Right tears the veil of stealthy Wrong apart,
And we, long-worn, long faithful, glad of face,
Hoist the torn banner to its ancient place . . .

That's the first part—Hurrah—I will do the rest if I can—Gladstone for Middlesex!²

TEXT: Stirling, 114.

¹ Morris never completed this acrostic, but during the general election of 1880, when Sir Charles Dilke and the historian Charles Harding Firth (1857-1936) were standing for the same constituency, Morris, Burne-Jones, and De Morgan bombarded each other with postcards containing electioneering propaganda, sometimes in the form of acrostics. See

Stirling, p. 114. The first day of polling was March 31, 1880, and different places voted on different days through about the first week of April.

² Herbert John Gladstone (1854–1930), W. E. Gladstone's youngest son, was defeated in the Middlesex election, April 3, 1880.

623 • To Henry Broadhurst   Kelmscott House,
                                                 Upper Mall, Hammersmith
                                                 April 4, 1880

Dear Mr. Broadhurst

I don't know if 'tis the fashion to congratulate new–made M.P.s,¹ but you know I am not a formality-hunter, so I will not hesitate to do myself the pleasure of telling you how glad I am that your success forms a part of the general victory: and a very important part it forms to my mind, since I know you are one of those who will work hard to make this no mere temporary & party triumph, but a new start ⟨of⟩ on the road of progress & freedom: How to broaden & deepen the stream of radical principles, keeping meanwhile the government both alive & steady, without harassing or frightening it,— that is the question I fancy; & to answer it, & practically carry out the answer, will be no light work, & will be worth our very best pains.

However the first step is gained, I must say to my great surprise, & surely now all will be well & better.

Wishing you all health & happiness in your new sphere of usefulness,

                                        I am
                                        Dear Mr. Broadhurst
                                        Yours very truly
                                        William Morris

Henry Broadhurst, Eqre M.P.

ms: LSE.

¹ Broadhurst (see letter no. 402, n. 3) was elected Liberal M.P. for Stoke-on-Trent. Morris writes here as a fellow officer of the National Liberal League. See letter no. 583, n. 1.

624 • To Jane Morris   Castle Mona Hotel
                                                 Douglas, Isle of Man
                                                 Tuesday Evening
                                                 April 7 [1880]¹

Dearest Janey

I shall not go to England till Thursday morning; this will mean getting to Liverpool by about 3 p.m. So I shall not be home till quite late.

I am not having a bad time of it here: the inn is pleasant with a beautiful garden; the weather beautiful: just a little thunder storm this afternoon

I have got to dine with the Governor[2] tonight & he is to take me to Peel tomorrow. The island seems really beautiful.

We hear that Gladstone is in for Mid-Lothian; but that H.G.[3] is out for Mid-sex — also that East Cumberland has gone awry;[4] which grieves me. Still on the whole all seems well. Mr. Wiggin[5] who has beat a Tory in Staffordshire I met at Birmingham.

So poor Mr. Bell[6] has lost his seat. Love to the girls.

Your loving
W.M.

MS: BL, Add. MSS. 45338.

[1] April 7 was a Wednesday. Morris probably made a slip of the pen in writing the day or the date. His visit to the Isle of Man may have been connected with plans on the part of the island administration to restore St. Germain's Cathedral. There is mention of it in the S.P.A.B. Annual Report, 1880.

[2] Henry Brougham Loch (1827-1900).

[3] Herbert Gladstone, W. E. Gladstone's son.

[4] George Howard was defeated in his bid to keep the seat he won when his father died in April 1879.

[5] Henry Wiggin, a manufacturer who was the successful Liberal candidate for Birmingham.

[6] Isaac Lowthian Bell, who had been Liberal M.P. for Hartlepools since 1875. See also letter no. 416, n. 1.

---

625 • TO FREDRICK WILLIAM CHESSON

26, Queen Square,
Bloomsbury, London
April 28, 1880

My dear Chesson

I understand by your note that you have paid *both* bills, & so send you a cheque: there is still a balance of about £80 in favour of the E.Q.A.

Yours truly
William Morris

MS: PML.

626 • To George James Howard
Kelmscott House,
Upper Mall, Hammersmith
Tuesday
[May 1880]

My dear Howard

I can't leave home this morning as I am expecting a man to come whom I shall have to direct. I can call tomorrow morning if that suits; if it does *not* please a card.

Meantime I told Wardle yesterday that you were wanting a scheme & estimate, & he will be setting to work on it: I am afraid I can say little from my side as to the cost till he has made out the arithmetic of the window[1]

Yrs affectionately
William Morris

MS: Howard Papers.

[1] In 1880-1881, Morris and Co. made the east window for St. Martin's Church, Brampton. In an entry in his account book dated May 1880, Burne-Jones, who did the designs, wrote: "To Brampton window — a colossal work of fifteen subjects — a masterpiece of style, a chef d'oeuvre of invention, a capo d'opera of conception — fifteen compartments — a Herculean labour — hastily estimated in a moment of generous friendship for £200, if the firm regards as binding a contract made from a noble impulse, and in a mercenary spirit declines to re-open the question, it must remain — but it will remain equally a monument of art and ingratitude — £200." See Sewter, II, 29-30; the manuscript volumes of Burne-Jones's accounts with Morris and Co., 1861-1896, are in the Fitzwilliam Museum, Cambridge.

627 • To Anthony John Mundella
26, Queen Square,
Bloomsbury, London
May 21, 1880

My dear Mundella

There is on hand something like an agitation (as you doubtless know) for abolishing the 'students days'[1] at the National Gallery, & letting the public in every day as is done at the Louvre and other continental galleries; In common with most artists I know I think the wish to have it so is reasonable, & I dont see any objection to it: somehow it has fallen into the hands of Mr. Coope[2] to take the bill in hand which means to give force to the wish above-mentioned.

Now I hope you won't think me a busy-body for asking if it would not be possible for Government to take the wind out of the sails of the Tory member for Middlesex (bad cess to him!) by doing the thing themselves; & I think if they could also manage to put an end to the annual cleaning-shutting-up epoch at the N.G. the public would be very pleased. I know some people feel strongly on these points & I don't think anybody scarcely would grudge the alterations if they could be made.[3]

This is a new character I address you in; I heartily congratulate you on the change.[4]

I wonder sometimes as I walk through the streets and look at the people if they are the same flesh & blood as made things so pleasant for us in the spring of /78; and I feel enclined to say, what the deuce then *was* it all about?

Pray don't take the trouble to answer this if you are too busy, but just give it your best consideration.

Yours very truly
William Morris

MS: USheffield.

[1] Days on which art students were permitted to make copies of paintings.

[2] Octavius Edward Coope, Conservative M.P. for Middlesex and a partner in the brewery of Ind Coope and Co.

[3] The bill to abolish "students' days" never came to the floor of the House, and Mundella took no part in the question.

[4] Mundella became a member of the Privy Council in 1880.

628 • To Emma Shelton Morris
Kelmscott House,
Upper Mall, Hammersmith
May 23, 1880

Dearest Mother

I write a line to wish you all imaginable health & happiness on your birthday.

I am afraid you won't think much of my gift which should come by post: the Birmingham people have paid ⟨the⟩ me the compliment of printing some copies of my last address on large paper, & have sent me 3 copies:[1] so as it will be something of a rarity, & as you have my other large paper books I thought that perhaps you might like to have this: when you have read it, if you will let me have it back I will get it nicely bound for you; which I would have done before sending it you, only they have but just come.

We are enjoying the weather here very much now though my garden wants rain sorely.

Wardle is still in America,[2] & by consequence I have still a good deal of extra work to do I think so far we are doing better than last year:

I begin my exhibition of my hand-made rugs this week — from which though I expect more honour than money.[3]

Once more, dearest Mother, I send my best love and most earnest good wishes,

and I rest
Your most loving Son
William Morris

MS: Walthamstow.

[1] "Labour and Pleasure, versus Labour and Sorrow." See letter no. 610, n. 2. See also Buxton Forman, pp. 97-98.

[2] See letter no. 621.

[3] According to May Morris, in May 1880 Morris and Co. had a special show of Hammersmith rugs at 449 Oxford St. for which Morris wrote a circular, quoted by Mackail (II, 4), in which he said his intention was "to make England independent of the East for the supply of hand-made Carpets which may claim to be considered works of art." May Morris wrote that a "hammer in black or in white, with a blue zig-zag (for the river) was the maker's mark worked into the edge of the rugs . . ." (CW, 13, xxiii). See also Buxton Forman, p. 194.

629 • To John Ruskin
26, Queen Square,
Bloomsbury, London
May 26, 1880

My dear Ruskin

I venture to trouble you by writing to ask you to do what would give a great deal of pleasure to many people, & do them a great deal of good, and would be as you well know a very great pleasure to me personally. Our Society For the Protection of Ancient Buildings holds its Annual Meeting on June 23rd at Society of Arts' Room, and it would be the making of the said meeting if you would kindly agree to take the chair at it, and say some words, which no one can say as well as you, for a cause which you yourself made a cause: if this would not be too great a burden on you, I think we deserve the encourgement your voice and presence would give us: we are again going to stir the St Marks' matter, and though I confess I am not very hopeful of success, I feel somehow as if we ought to try if anything can be done by iteration, however weary a job it be.

But even if we do nothing in this case, & in many others, yet I do think we may save here & there some fragment of art, and to my mind it would be worth the trouble, & years of our little Society's life, if we could but save one little grey building in England.

This is the spirit we have been working in, & therefore we are in a

⟨ll⟩ way pledged not to be discouraged by anything, as long as there is anything genuine, however humble, to save.

I know you will help us if you can, therefore I will not say anything further to press you, but hope for the best.

If by any chance you object to taking the chair could you be present & speak nevertheless?[1]

Will you kindly let me know, & once more excuse ⟨by⟩ my troubling you.

Yours affectionately
William Morris

MS: Yale O.

[1] Ruskin apparently refused (see S.P.A.B. Annual Report, 1880). The chair was taken by Stanley Leighton (1837-1901), Conservative M.P. for North Shropshire, 1876-1885, amateur artist, and author of *Shropshire Houses, Past and Present* (1901).

630 • To Aglaia Ionides Coronio

26, Queen Square,
Bloomsbury, London
June 7, 1880

My dear Aglaia

I only got your note this morning, or you should have had an answer before. Please tell Aleco, that I am sorry but that I am engaged 2 deep to meetings, & if I don't go to one I must go to the other, so I can't come to him.

Janey will be very glad to see you on Wednesday, & I will call on you with much pleasure on Friday.

Yrs affectionately
William Morris

MS: Berger Coll.

631 • To Luigi Federico Menabrea

[June 1880]

Your Excellency[1]

The Committee of the S.P.A.B. have been informed that it is intended to attempt to raise the Baptistry at Ravenna,[2] which has sunk into the marshy ground some 2½ metres, to its original hight ⟨preparator⟩ with a view to the restoration of the building: The Committee ⟨beg most respectfully to address your excellency on this subject⟩ of the S.P.A.B., though representing a body of students of art founded & supported in England, feel in common with all archaeologists, such an intense interest in this building, which, small as it is, is of the utmost importance to art and history, that they venture most respectfully to address your excellency on this subject.

They cannot help fearing that the operation proposed, though doubtless it will be carried out with great skill & care, will be dangerous to the interest of ⟨this most⟩ the monument: for ⟨in the first place⟩ they cannot see how it can be possible to effect the proposed change without shaking the mosaics of the walls and dome so seriously as to imperil their stability; and it will be admitted on all hands that these early & curiously historical mosaics are the chief treasure of the Baptistry, & that ⟨their loss, or⟩ their destruction, or any injury to their genuine condition would be an irreparable loss to all lovers of art. Even if the mosaics are not shaken out of their places by the engineering work contemplated, the Committee fear that they would be so disturbed by it that extensive repairs in them would ⟨become necessary⟩ be undertaken, which they think would be a serious evil.

The Committee of &c. therefore beg with all humility to ⟨suggest to your⟩ pray your Excellency ⟨that⟩ to reconsider any such intention of raising the building as may exist, and to substitute for this plan careful repairs of the fabric such as may be necessary for rendering it generally stable & excluding injuries ⟨and the prevention of such injuries as might result from exclusion of the weather⟩ to it likely to result from weather, and the preservation of the rare mosaics in a genuine condition: they believe that this care will be most gratefully acknowledged by the many visitors to the famous city of Ravenna.

With many apologies to your Excellency for troubling you with this letter, ⟨we beg to⟩

> We have the honour to be
> Your Excellency's
> Most obedient humble Servants[3]

MS: Huntington.

[1] Luigi Federico Menabrea (1809-1896), Italian ambassador to England (1876-1881).
[2] See *The Times*, November 27, 1879, p. 5; and Morris's letter to *The Times*, no. 632.
[3] There is no signature on the manuscript, but the letter is in Morris's handwriting.

632 • TO THE EDITOR OF *The Times*   [June 9, 1880]

To the Editor of The Times[1]

The Baptistery Ravenna

Sir

The Committee of the Society for the Protection of Ancient Buildings has noted with much interest and satisfaction the letter of your correspondent in your impression of the 19th ⟨ultimo⟩ May, & has directed me to write to you, begging you, since the ⟨nam⟩ Society was mentioned in the letter, to insert a few words ⟨explaining its⟩ explanatory of its views on this point.

The Committee are aware that the building needs repair badly enough; but it cannot help feeling that the plan of raising it bodily is fraught with danger to the fabric, however skilful may be the engineer who conducts the operation: ⟨moreover⟩ the risk to the precious mosaics at any rate is undeniable, whatever may happen to the main structure of the walls, and these mosaics are in fact the very thing about the building that it is worth spending money and pains to preserve: it need scarcely be said that if they be shattered to pieces by the proposed engineering operation no restoration of them will be possible on any terms.

But furthermore the Committee thinks it has reason to fear that ⟨even if the building⟩ a so-called restoration of the interior decoration ⟨may⟩ will be attempted whether the jacking-up of the Baptistery be successful or not: such restoration the Committee deprecates most earnestly, feeling that it is ⟨echoing the⟩ expressing the universal opinion of Archaeologists in asserting, that whatever may be said for or against the restoration of other buildings, even any suspicion of genuineness ⟨even⟩ cast on the decorations of this most historical monument would sorely damage its interest; and that if, as is too common in such cases, the restoration ⟨really meant⟩ turned out to be the discarding of the old work, & the substitution of a modern imitation, ⟨in its⟩ all interest would be taken from the Baptistery.

Your correspondent suggests that if the Society for the Protection of Ancient Buildings has any ⟨su⟩ practical suggestions to make on the subject, it would be well for it to send out some of its members to confer with those who are dealing with the matter; the Committee has only to say that if it were honoured with any such invitation, it would accept it with great pleasure, & with every wish to treat the question ⟨with⟩ in the most practical manner, & with all possible moderation; since it has no other desire than that the Baptistery of Ravenna should be preserved from ruin ⟨for the⟩ by any feasible means.[2]

> I am Sir (on behalf of the
> Committee of &c.)
> Yours obediently
> William Morris
> Honorary Sec:

My dear Mr Marks, please copy & send on signing my name & dating from Buckingham St.

MS: Huntington. Published: *The Times*, June 12, 1880.

[1] The text of this letter is taken from Morris's handwritten draft. Five lines at the beginning of the letter were entirely crossed out by Morris after numerous changes. They read as follows: "The Committee of the Society for the Protection of Ancient Buildings, has directed me to express ⟨its⟩ ⟨the⟩ ⟨the pleasure it⟩ its satisfaction in seeing ⟨this subje⟩ the subject of the proposed repair of this building made public in your columns."

[2] On April 20, 1880, *The Times* had published (p. 5) a letter from Henry Wallis in Ravenna commenting on the condition of the Baptistery and saying that he thought the mosaic decoration the only valuable part of the building which was in a state of great disrepair. On May 19, a dispatch sent by a correspondent in Rome and dated May 10 appeared in *The Times*, quoting Wallis's letter: "In any way to endanger such a monument . . . is a matter which concerns the whole of intelligent Christendom." In 1875, this dispatch continued, the Italian Commission for the Preservation of Ancient Monuments had been established (earlier than the S.P.A.B.) and reported that the Baptistery should be raised from the swamp into which it was sinking. The correspondent mentioned the problems of jacking up the Baptistery and concluded: "If the S.P.A.B. has any . . . suggestions they surely would be willingly received," proposing that the S.P.A.B. send a couple of competent persons to evaluate the situation and previous plans.

633 • To Henry Holiday   26, Queen Square,
                                              Bloomsbury, London
                                              July 6, 1880

My dear Holiday

I suppose combing the 'fleece' means they were carding wool: in fact a fleece, which is not skin & hair together, that is a fell, but the clip of the sheep: this is a wool comb wire & wood.

                    Yrs truly
                    William Morris

MS: Berger Coll.

634 • To Samuel Waddington   26, Queen Square,
                                              Bloomsbury, London,
                                              July 21, 1880

Dear Sir[1]

I am sorry that I cannot help your book: I believe I have written but one sonnett[2] in my life, and that one was not such as I should care to see reprinted in any Collection.

                         I am
                         Dear Sir
                         Yours faithfully
                         William Morris

S. Waddington Esqre.

MS: Berger Coll.

[1] Samuel Waddington (1844-1923), a poet and author. He published *English Sonnets by living writers, selected and arranged, with a note on the history of the "sonnet"* (London: Bell and Sons) in 1881. Presumably he had wanted to include something by Morris in this volume. Several editions of his own poetry were published, in addition to a monograph on Arthur Hugh Clough (1883) and an autobiography, *Chapters of My Life* (1909).

[2] It is not true that Morris wrote only one sonnet, and it is difficult to conjecture which he had in mind. Some possibilities are "Summer Dawn" from *The Defence of Guenevere* (1858), reprinted from the *Oxford and Cambridge Magazine* (1856) where it had appeared under the title "Pray But One Prayer for Me"; "Near But Far Away" which May Morris prints (I, 539) and dates as belonging to *The Earthly Paradise* period, presumably 1866 to 1870; and the sonnet facing the title page of the *Grettis Saga* (1869). This last was reprinted by Buxton Forman, pp. 56-57, n. 1.

635 • To Eiríkr Magnússon

26, Queen Square,
Bloomsbury, London
July 21, 1880

My dear Magnússon

Herewith the draft letter: I have made it as short as I could, so that it might be read; for the same reason I have not spoken perhaps as strongly as I feel, 'moderation' being much beloved by officials.[1] I hope my writing may be of service to you: as soon as I have your remarks on it I will send a clean copy to the great man.

O the Dean![2] What a crusty little beast he is! in defence of flunkyism he can rage like a bear robbed of her whelps.[3]

Yours very truly
William Morris

MS: Iceland.

[1] See letter no. 636.

[2] Arthur Penrhyn Stanley (1815-1881), Dean of Westminster from 1864 until his death.

[3] Presumably a comment on a letter from the Dean to *The Times*, July 20 (p. 8), in which he defended a plan, recently abandoned, to erect a monument in Westminster Abbey to Prince Louis Napoleon (the only son of Napoleon III), who had been killed while fighting with British troops in the war against the Zulus in 1879. See also letter no. 637.

636 • To the Consular Department, Foreign Office

26, Queen Square,
Bloomsbury, London
July 22, 1880

Sir

I am informed that a memorial has been forwarded to you praying you to consider the advisability of establishing a British Consulate at

Reikjavík the chief town of Iceland; I venture therefore to address you on the subject, as being especially interested in that country, and having some knowledge of its past history & present hopes. I sincerely think it would be of advantage both to Iceland & this country if England had an official representative at Reykjavík: that Iceland though poor has resources at present more or less neglected is clear to me both from the evidence of history & personal observation of the country: its trade with England has much increased since my first visit in 71; and I may add that the tendency of its trade in general is towards *direct* communication with the British isles, even apart from those goods (ponies chiefly & live sheep) for which they are the sole customers: in some cases this is inevitable, the wool for instance the most valuable export of Iceland which I believe is eventually nearly all worked up by British Manufacturers, and is always sure of a good market amongst them.

It is a lesser matter, though one perhaps worthy of consideration, that the number of English tourists to Iceland increases yearly; & it is obvious that it would be a great advantage to them to have a British representative to whom they could apply for help & advice.

In the case of its being thought good to establish a consulate at Reikjavík I make bold further to say a word or two in favour of the claims of my friend & collaborateur Mr. Eiríkr Magnússon to the office: apart from his great aquirements in philology & Archeology, he is a man of great general cultivation: he also understands English German & French, & talks those languages well: he is also a man of strong common sense, great industry & good business qualifications: I believe I may say in short that he is a good specimen of that type of a highly educated & wide-minded Icelander that has attracted so much attention throughout Europe. I may add that I believe that his appointment to such a post would be very acceptable to the public both in Iceland & in Denmark:

I beg to apologize to you for trespassing on your invaluable time, & must ask you to believe that I would not have thought of doing so if I had not been urged to it by the strong good-will to Iceland & its people nourished by many acts of kindness & hospitality (on their part) which is certainly shared by all who have had much to do with that interesting people.[1]

MS: Iceland.

[1] The manuscript of this letter has no signature, but the handwriting is Morris's.

637 · To John Simon
26, Queen Square,
Bloomsbury, London
July 22, 1880

My dear Simon[1]

Thanks for the P.O.O. As for the reserved trifle; let us hope that one day there will be a committee for trundling *out* of the Abbey some cartloads of monuments; say 20 thousand ton: send the trifle to that.

Item, if you want somebody to chaff: don't you think the Dean rather deserves it, for not giving way with fewer words and better temper?[2]

However perhaps he is happy now as well as we — so all's well.

Yours truly
William Morris

MS: McWilliams Coll.

[1] See letter no. 552, n. 2.

[2] See letter no. 635, n. 3. See also *The Times*, July 22, 1880, p. 12, for second letter by the Dean defending his position.

638 · To Henry Wallis
9 Buckingham St
August 4, 1880

St Marks Committee

My dear Wallis

I understood when I saw you last that we were to meet here at ½ past 4 today; so I came; but after waiting till ¼ past 5 concluded there must be some mistake; so I write. Ruskin written to by Jones has telegraphed to say that he joins: Burne-Jones joins also Walter Crane[1] (asked by me) the latter is to ask W. Spottis Woode (P.R S.)[2]

Civil note from the American Legation on Lowells[3] part, accepting. Also from Mark Pattison[4] Rector of Lincoln Coll: Oxford accepting. Also from Talbot[5] Warden of Keble Coll: accepting. So please put these names down, which will give us a tolerable list pro: tem:.

I suppose you had better notify their being on the Committee officially. Talbots letter being humble as well as civil I answered at once. I have also a letter from Max Müller[6] declining, but speaking sympathetically of the movement.

I sent my letter to Lowell to the American Legation.

Ruskins address is:

Brantwood
Coniston
Lancashire

[576]

on Tuesday next I go out of town for a week. I have no letter yet from the Dean of Ch[rist Church].[7]

Yours very truly
William Morris

MS: BL, Add. MSS. 38831 (St. Mark's, Venice, Committee Papers, 1879-1882).

[1] Walter Crane (1845-1915), the well-known illustrator, designer, and painter. Between 1863 and 1896, he was especially successful as an illustrator of children's books. He designed wallpapers for Jeffrey and Company from 1874 and had produced over fifty designs by 1912. He also designed fabrics for various manufacturers, including Wardle and Company, and one tapestry (the "Goose-girl," 1881) for Morris and Company. Other decorative work included designs for pottery and ceramics, ornamental plasterwork, mosaics, and designs for stained glass. He and Morris first met in 1870 and became closely associated in the Socialist League and in the founding, in 1888, of the Arts and Crafts Exhibition Society, of which Crane became president. He remained in this position, with the exception of the period 1893-1896 when Morris was president, until 1912. In 1893 he became Director of Design at Manchester Municipal College, and in 1898 was appointed Principal of the Royal College of Art at South Kensington. He wrote *The Bases of Design* (1898) and *Line and Form* (1900), based on his lectures. See Crane's *An Artist's Reminiscences* (Macmillan, 1907) and Anscombe and Gere, pp. 113-14.

[2] William Spottiswoode (1825-1883), mathematician and physicist, the son of a partner in the publishing firm of Eyre and Spottiswoode. He was president of the Royal Society from 1878 until 1883.

[3] James Russell Lowell (1819-1891), the American poet. He was minister to Great Britain from 1880 to 1885.

[4] Mark Pattison (1813-1884), a follower of Newman during the Oxford movement, and a contributor to *Essays and Reviews* (1860). Among his works are a life of Isaac Casaubon (1875) and a life of Milton (1879). In 1883, he dictated his *Memoirs* to the year 1860; these were published posthumously. Pattison may have been the model for George Eliot's Mr. Casaubon in *Middlemarch*.

[5] Edward Stuart Talbot (1844-1934) was Warden of Keble College from 1869 to 1888. From 1896 until his death, he was Bishop successively of Rochester, Southwark, and Winchester.

[6] Max Friedrich Müller (1823-1900), an orientalist and philologist, and one of the founders of the study of comparative mythology.

[7] Henry G. Liddell, who was active in St. Mark's Committee affairs at Oxford.

639 • TO EDWARD WILLIAMS BYRON NICHOLSON 26, Queen Square,
Bloomsbury, London
August 6, 1880

Dear Mr. Nicholson

It is I on the contrary that have to ask your pardon for not answering your note before: but the fact is I was trying to screw myself up to the sticking-point of saying *either* yes or no: at last with some misgivings I say yes, in the hopes that I shall have something to say: so please fill up the *last* day possible (March 10th) for me: My subject might be called '⟨on⟩ the Prospects of Architecture in Modern Civilisation'[1] if that be grammar. That name would embrace all I have to say on the arts; but I should not probably get much into detail. Among the R.A.'s would Poynter be gettable: or get Street to give a lecture on St Marks at Venice: he is sound on this point & it might do good.

I do not know much of the French Roman de la Rose, but cannot suppose it possible that it should be without metrical law, if one reads it right.

Yours very truly
William Morris

MS: McMinn Papers.

[1] The final title of the lecture, which was delivered at the London Institution, March 10, 1881, was "The Prospects of Architecture in Civilization."

---

640 • To Georgiana Burne-Jones   [Kelmscott House
                                                  Upper Mall, Hammersmith]
                                                  August 10, 1880

Little things please little minds; therefore my mind must be little, so pleased am I this morning. That is not logic, though I suspect the conclusion to be true; but again I doubt if the 'Ark,' which is veritably the name of our ship, can be considered a little thing, except relatively: item, it is scarcely a little thing that the sky is one sheet of pale warm blue, and that the earth is sucking up the sun rejoicing.

Jenny and I went out before breakfast to see the craft. She is odd but delightful: imagine a biggish company boat with a small omnibus on board, fitted up luxuriously inside with two shelves and a glass-rack, and a sort of boot behind this: room for two rowers in front, and I must say for not many more except in the cabin or omnibus. Still what a joy (to a little mind) to see the landscape out of a square pane of glass, and to sleep a-nights with the stream rushing two inches past one's ear. Then after all, there is the romance of the bank, and outside the boat the world is wide: item, we can always hire a skiff for some of the party to row in and stretch their muscles, and in that way I propose to start this afternoon about 2½ after dining here.[1]

Rathbone[2] can't come, being too hard at work after all: so our males will consist of Crom, Dick[3] and Meorgan [a child's mispronunciation of De Morgan's name][4] besides self. Yesterday morning, also a very beautiful one, I had qualms about leaving the garden here, which really, as De Morgan said on Sunday, is a very tolerable substitute for a garden: item, after doing a good deal of small necessary work at Queen Square I had qualms about leaving my business; but to-day I have none — I think I know now why I fatten so.

More and more I think people ought to live in one place — pilgrimages excepted. By the way, I give my third lecture to the Trade Guild of Learning in October;[5] that will be my autumn work, writing it, if I have any quiet time away from home. Also I have promised to lecture next March at the London Institute[6] — subject, the prospects of Architecture in modern civilization. I will be as serious as I can over them, and when I have these two last done, I think of making a book of the lot,[7] as it will be about what I have to say on the subject, which still seems to me the most serious one that a man can think of; for 'tis no less than the chances of a calm, dignified, and therefore happy life for the mass of mankind.

I shall find my long carpet out of the loom when I come back — but I am not a bit anxious about it now, the river will wash all that away.

TEXT: Mackail, II, 8-10. Published: Henderson, Letters, 133-34. Extract published: CW, 13, xxxiv-xxxv.

[1] The trip that Morris, his family, and friends were about to make was a voyage on the Thames from Kelmscott House in London to Kelmscott Manor, above Oxford. The itinerary, and much that Morris observed along the way, provided the outline and the descriptive detail for the river journey in News from Nowhere (Chapters XXII-XXVIII) written ten years later. Morris's diary for 1880 (manuscript in British Library) indicates the route taken and helps to date some of the letters written in August.

[2] Possibly Harold S. Rathbone, a pupil of Ford Madox Brown. Rathbone had helped Brown with cartoons for stained-glass window designs executed for the old firm and, in 1894, was one of the founders of the Della Robbia Pottery Company of Birkenhead.

[3] Richard Cecil Grosvenor (1848-1919), fifth son of Baron Ebury. He was a member of the S.P.A.B. and a close friend of William De Morgan.

[4] Information in brackets added by Mackail.

[5] Morris lectured on "Some Hints of House Decoration," on November 13, 1880. See LeMire, pp. 237, 295.

[6] See letter no. 639, n. 1.

[7] Morris's first collection of essays was published by Ellis and White in 1882 with the title Hopes and Fears for Art. The subtitle read, "Five Lectures Delivered In Birmingham, London, and Nottingham, 1878-1881." Included were the following: The Decorative Arts (reprinted as The Lesser Arts); The Art of the People (reprint of the 1879 Birmingham address); The Beauty of Life (reprint of Labour and Pleasure versus Labour and Sorrow); Making the Best of It (paper delivered to the Trades Guild of Learning and the Birmingham Society of Artists); and The Prospects of Architecture in Civilization (delivered at the London Institution). See Buxton Forman, p. 99-100.

Georgiana Burne-Jones, c. 1880.

641 • To Georgiana Burne-Jones   Kelmscott
                                                    [August 19, 1880]

We came to our first lodging (Sunbury, some six miles above Hampton Court) very late, about half-past ten, and queer it was the next morning to note how different the place was to our imaginations of it in the dark: item: the commonplace inn was a blow to the romance of the river, as you may imagine. Crom and I slept on board the Ark that night: perforce. A cloudy morning when we started, which at first much disappointed me after the splendid evening we had come in by: nevertheless I was in spirits at the idea of getting out of the Cockney waters, and we were scarcely through the lock we had to pass at starting before the sun was out and hot again: the river was nearly new to me really hereabouts and much better than I expected, especially from Chertsey to Staines; it is full of strange character in many places; Laleham, for instance, with its enormous willows and queer suggestions (at any rate) of old houses on the banks: we dined luxuriously on the bank a little below this, and had tea on the grass of Runneymead which, (as I remembered) is a most lovely place, on such an afternoon as one can scarcely hope to see again for brightness and clearness. When we had done tea, it became obvious that we should never get to Maidenhead (as we had intended) that night, so after much spilling of wisdom in a discussion of the kind where no one can see any plan but his own as possible, we agreed to make another day of it: Windsor on that night (Wednesday) and Marlow on Thursday. Well, we got to Windsor about eight, and beautiful it was coming into; and with all drawbacks even when one saw it next morning seemed a wonderful place: so we only made 17 miles this day. We all slept in the inn on the waterside: that was Wednesday.

Thursday, Dick took us up to Eton; and again in spite of drawbacks it is yet a glorious place. Once more the morning was grey and even threatening rain (wind N.N.E), but very soon cleared up again into the brightest of days: a very pleasant morning we had, and dined just above Bray Lock; cook was I, and shut up in the Ark to do the job, appearing like the high-priest at the critical moment pot in hand, — but O the wasps about that osier bed! We got quite used to them at last and by dint of care did not swallow any with our food, nor were stung.

There was a regatta at Maidenhead and both banks crowded with spectators, so that we had to drop the tow-rope before our time, and as the Ark forged slowly along towards the Berkshire side with your servant steering on her roof, and De Morgan labouring at the sculls, you may think that we were chaffed a little. After Maidenhead you go under Cliefden woods, much admired by the world in general; I confess to thinking them rather artificial; also eyeing Mr. Dick with reference to their owner I couldn't help thinking of Mr. Twemlow and Lord Snigsworthy.[1] But at Cookham Lock how beautiful it was: you get out of the Snigsworthy woods there; the hills fall back from the river, which is very wide there, and you are in the real country, with cows and sheep and farm-houses, the work-a-day world again and not a lacquey's paradise: the country too has plenty of character there, and may even be called beautiful: it was beautiful enough that evening at any rate: the sun had set as we cleared Cookham Lock, and we went facing the west, which was cloudless and golden, till it got quite dark: by that same dark we had to get through the Marlow Lock, with no little trouble, as we had to skirt a huge weir which roared so that we couldn't hear each other speak, and so to our night's lodging: Crom and I in the Ark close to the roaring weir, Dick and De M. in the inn (a noisy one) and the ladies up town, over the bridge. We took them there, and as we left the little house, looked up the street, and saw the streamers of the Northern Lights flickering all across that part of the sky, just as I saw them in '71 (and not since) in the harbour of Thorshaven: it was very mysterious and almost frightening to see them over the summer leafage so unexpectedly in a place I at least had not seen by daylight.

So to bed we went, and again in the morning (Friday) a grey day that cleared presently into a very hot one: and once more the river all new to me, and very beautiful: at Hurley Lock we had to wait for a big steamer that plies regularly between Kingston and Oxford with passengers: as I stood up in the lock afterwards I had the surprise of seeing a long barn-like building two Gothic arches and then a Norman church fitting on to it and joined into a quadrangle by other long roofs: this was Lady Place: once a monastery, then a Jacobean house, and now there is but a farm-house, somewhat gammoned, there: we all went ashore and spent an hour there in great enjoyment, for 'tis a lovely place: there is a huge dove-cot there with carefully moulded buttresses of the 15th century: the church has been miserably gammoned, but kept its old outline.

I played the cook again a little short of Henley; and we went on again in a burning afternoon through a river fuller and fuller of character as we got higher up: stuck in the mud for 20 minutes at Wargrave: past Shiplake, which is certainly one of the most beautiful parts of the Thames, and so to Sonning for the night: a village prepensely picturesque and somewhat stuffy that hot night, but really pretty, with a nice inn where Crom was at home, having spent some time there when Boyce was painting on the river: but we scattered all over the village and Crom and I slept in the Ark. We started earlier on Saturday, as we had to get to Wallingford, a longer run than heretofore. We had got well used to the Ark by now, and there was Janey lying down and working quite at home: very hot and waspy it was at dinner, on the bank between Pang-bourne and Goring, but when we were well past the last place the after-noon got much clouded over for the first time since our start: but now out of the over-rated half picturesque reach of Streatley and Goring here we were on the Thames that is the Thames, amidst the down-like coun-try and all Cockneydom left far behind, and it *was* jolly.

We got to stuffy grubby little Wallingford rather early, and got lodg-ing in a riverside pothouse partly and partly in the town. Here it rather tickled me that, an hour or so being to spare before supper, the girls proposed and did a row upon the water as a novel pastime. That was Saturday: well, Sunday morning it had rained in the night, and the look of the dull grey almost drizzling morning made me expect a regular wet day; but it was only dull and cool all day, and we had a very pleasant day of it, and I cooked 'em their dinner just above Culham Lock; we got out at Dorchester to look the Dykes[2] which Sir J. Lubbock has tried to get into the schedule of his bill and failed;[3] so that the dykes have been partly ploughed over to their hurt: then a bit higher I recognized the place where we stopped for victuals years ago when the Faulkners were with us: and so we got to Oxford a little after nightfall: the banks of the river near the town have been spoilt somewhat since my time; for I have been there but thrice since I was an undergraduate. Well, at Oxford we left the Ark: and Janey the next day (Monday) went on by rail to Kelmscott: while we got up early and by dint of great exertions started from Medley Lock at 9 a.m., with Bossom and another man to tow us as far as New Bridge, where we sent them off, and muddled ourselves home somehow, dining at a lovely place about a mile above New Bridge, where I have stopped twice before for that end. One thing was very pleasant: they were hay-making on the flat flood-washed spits of ground and islets all about Tadpole; and the hay was gathered on punts and the like; odd stuff to look at, mostly sedge, but they told us it was the best stuff for milk.

Night fell on us long before we got to Radcot, and we fastened a lantern to the prow of our boat, after we had with much difficulty got our boats through Radcot Bridge. Charles was waiting for us with a lantern at our bridge by the corner at 10 p.m., and presently the ancient house had me in its arms again: J. had lighted up all brilliantly, and sweet it all looked you may be sure.

TEXT: Mackail, II, 10-14. Published: Henderson, *Letters*, 134-38.

[1] In *Our Mutual Friend*, Mr. Twemlow is the poor relation of Lord Snigsworthy.

² The Dyke Hills, on the Oxfordshire side of the Thames.

³ Sir John Lubbock, first Baron Avebury (1834–1913), banker, scientist, author, and Liberal M.P. for Maidstone, 1870–1874, and for London University 1880–1900. In 1873 he had introduced a bill for the preservation of ancient monuments, which was eventually passed in 1882.

642 • To Mary Frances Andrews Crane

Kelmscott
Lechlade
[August 23, 1880]

Dear Mrs. Crane[1]

The stuff my shirts are made of is *cotton*: I daresay we could get it for you if you wanted it. On the other hand if you want flannel dyed to that shade, or as near to it as wool would be to cotton, we can do that for you at Merton if you will send us the stuff. Only sometimes we cannot do things as quick as they are wanted: but I would do my best in the matter with great pleasure.

I am
Yours very truly
William Morris

MS: Harvard. Published: Walter Crane, *An Artist's Reminiscences* (Macmillan, 1907), 215.

¹ Mary Frances Andrews (d.1915) married Walter Crane in 1871. She became known for her embroideries, which were designed by her husband and often on view at the Arts and Crafts Exhibition Society.

643 • To Georgiana Burne-Jones

Kelmscott House
Upper Mall, Hammersmith
[August 24, 1880]

You may imagine that coming back to this beastly congregation of smoke-dried swindlers and their slaves (whom one hopes one day to make their rebels) under the present circumstances does not make me much more in love with London, though I must admit to feeling this morning a touch of the 'all by oneself' independence which you wot of as a thing I like. I found by the way De Morgan a complete sympathizer on the subject of London: however let that pass, since in London I am and must be. The few days we passed at Kelmscott made a fine time of it for me; our mornings were grey and dull, though we had several fine afternoons and two lovely evenings. Thursday we went to Fairford in the afternoon, and I was pleased to see the glass and the handsome church once more. Though the country that way is not remarkable,

every turn of the road and every by-way set me a-longing to go afoot
through the country, never stopping for a day; after all a fine harvest
time is the crown of the year in England; there is so much to look at.
On the Friday we went to Inglesham and above the Round House, on
what might be called the upperest Thames, for half a mile, to look at
Inglesham church, a lovely little building about like Kelmscott in size
and style, but handsomer and with more old things left in it. Well, we
parted on Sunday morning rather melancholy, but had a beautiful voy-
age to Medley Lock; such an evening, and the best of it at Godstow,
where the moon began to show red over Wolvercot.

So here I am again on the lower Thames, finding it grimy; I have just
been busy over my carpeteers; all going pretty well. The 'Orchard'
being finished is a fair success as manufacture[1] — lies flat on the whole
— and as a work of art has points about it, but I can better it next time.

. . .

TEXT: Mackail, II, 14-15. Published: Henderson, *Letters*, 138.

[1] The figures in the "Orchard" carpet were copied from the roof of Jesus College Chapel.
Morris considered the carpet one of his best, and sent it to the Arts and Crafts Exhibition
of 1891. See P. Thompson, p. 102; and Crow, p. 78.

644 • TO JANE MORRIS   Kelmscott House,
                                             Upper Mall, Hammersmith
                                             August 24 [1880]

Dearest Janey

We got to Oxford on Sunday evening by a little after 8; having pur-
posely loitered by the way a good bit & taken it, I may say Grosvener-
ically easily all the journey: it cleared about 1 & was a fine sunny after-
noon & a lovely evening: Dick lay abed so late on Monday morning
that he got no breakfast before starting; but we all got safe to London:
I found Wardle at Queen Sq: & did a hard days work, getting here at
the usual time: a box of grice[1] came for me to Queen Sq: so I sent them
off to you at once.

On Thursday night I go to Rounton[2] & shall get back on Friday
night, so that I shall manage to be with you again on Saturday, I hope,
starting by the 2.15 train but am not sure; I will try to let you know.

On Ellis I will call this morning. I have just walked down what De
M. called a fair substitute for a garden: well, it *does* look a thought
dingy.

Matthews has brought in a few plums, there are some good ones
amongst them, but they are not many, I suppose the servants had better

stew them & eat them: item I ate a ripe pear last night, pretty to look at but not over good: I will see if I can muster a basket-full of fruit of some sort for you.

Breakfast is over, & I have been carpeteering: the Orchard,[3] spread out on the drawing-room floor, though not perfect as a piece of manufacture is not amiss; as a work of art I am a *little* dissappointed with it: if I do it again it shall have a wider border I think; otherwise I will somewhat alter the colour. The 4 × 4 is out and much improved by the alterations The 3 yellow bordered pots are not so flat as they should be: I fear the worsted warp is to blame for this: I shall use cotton in future, & perhaps dye it blue roughly: the Polly is barking & singing out Annie[?] till I don't quite know what I am writing.

Kiss my babes for me & tell them to be always as good-tempered as Mr. Dick, Uncle Crom, & Mr. De Morgan & then they will do.

I shall be so glad to get back to you.

Your loving
W.M.

MS: BL, Add. MSS. 45338. Extract published: *CW*, 13, xxvi; Henderson, *Letters*, 139.

[1] Young pigs or pork.

[2] Rounton Grange, built for Sir Isaac Lowthian Bell. The house was designed by Philip Webb and decorated by Morris and Burne-Jones. See letter no. 416, n. 1.

[3] See letter no. 643, n. 1.

645 • TO JANE MORRIS
26, Queen Square,
Bloomsbury, London
Thursday
[August 26, 1880?][1]

Dearest Janey

I find they are not ready for me at Rounton; so I shall have to go next week, & must leave Kelmscott by the first train on Thursday: that is a nuisance. howsoever I can gain a day this side; so I will come by the last train *tomorrow* (Friday) ⟨will you please let Mr. Spi —⟩ no you needn't, I will write to Spires[2] myself. So I shall be with you a little after 10 (p.m.) on Friday.

Ellis — I called on him yesterday & he and Miss Lily[3] will come down on Monday; I imagine by the dinner time train i.e. ½ past 5.

All well — myself in a hurry — Edgar expecting twins or some such mess.

De M. & Dick dissappeared at the station & I haven't seen them since.
Love to babes.

Your loving
W.M.

MS. BL, Add. MSS. 45338.

[1] In the original, a date, August 5, is written in by another hand. The plans and events described in this letter, however, would seem to date it following letter no. 644.

[2] Possibly Richard Phené Spiers (1838-1916), a draftsman and painter in watercolors, and one of the first English architects with a Beaux-Arts training. He was an instructor at the Royal Academy School of Architecture from 1870-1906. His works include additions to houses, restorations of churches, and a few new buildings. Some of his most valuable work in architectural research is contained in *Architecture East and West* (collected papers, 1905).

[3] Ellis's daughter.

646 • To Richard Phené Spiers[?]

26, Queen Square,
Bloomsbury, London
August 26, 1880

Dear Sir[1]

I thank you very much for your letter & tracings: I saw the building last year, & was much struck by its historical & artistic value, & called our Committee's attention to it: they have made enquiries, but like you, were not able to find out who is the owner or whom to address   it is of course most important to ⟨be able to⟩ get at this information, but meantime it seems to me it might be well to call attention to the subject in the press: ⟨I have⟩ If you could sent a short notice stating the facts to the Editor of the Athenaeum before next Wednesday he would certainly print it next week,[2] which would be something: I have asked a member of our Committee who I think has some connection with the illustrated papers to go down & view the place & see if he can do anything: I have sent him your letter & tracings, so if he goes there he will no doubt see you if you are still in Salisbury. We have some good correspondents in that town, but the matter seems rather swaddled up in mystery.

It would be indeed a disgrace to Salisbury if they couldn't manage to keep one of their most interesting buildings standing: I remember both the Bridge & the buildings by St. Thomas' well: they are just the sort of buildings whose destruction is desolating so many of our English towns, and of which the ordinary, what I should call 'Academical' Archeologist takes no notice. Oxford is a most miserable example of this. You would do the cause great service if you could anywise find out to whom we could address remonstrance in these cases at Salisbury; but you know what a hard matter it is dealing with buildings that are called 'private property'.[3]

Again thanking you

I am
Dear Sir
Yours truly
William Morris

MS: Doheny.

[1] In his letter to Jane Morris (letter no. 645) which I have conjecturally dated August 26, 1880, Morris says that he will write to "Spires" the same day. See letter no. 645 and n. 2.

[2] *The Athenaeum*, September 11, 1880, printed (p. 345) an article discussing Audley House, Salisbury, an early fifteenth-century building. More recently it had been used as a workhouse, and The City Corporation planned to sell it to the Dean and Chapter of Salisbury Cathedral, whose intention was to raze it and build a grammar school on the site.

[3] In the Annual Report of the S.P.A.B., 1880, Morris wrote (p. 10) that the Society had intervened and saved the building. Repairs were being supervised by a local architect, "who . . . promised to carry out the views of the Society as to the manner in which the necessary repairs should be made."

647 • To Henry Wallis
                                Manor House
                                Kelmscott
                                August 29 [1880]

My dear Wallis

As to the Report of S.P.A.B. I imagine that they have already been sent to all members:[1] I will however write to Marks by this post[2] & suggest withholding them for a while from foreign ones: *but* you must remember 1st that the Society cannot be answerable for *all* its members words, & 2nd that there is no official connection between it & the St. M's Comm[3] as is made obvious by Street being Vice-Chairman of the latter: I admit I was very vexed at that old ass flitting the rubbish he did at the meeting; and I did not imagine that Marks ⟨had⟩ would have sent out the report without revision — he had no business to. The only cure for all this is to assure people of the fact that the S[t.] M[arks] C[ommittee] has no connection with S.P.A.B.

As to Street, you needn't trouble yourself about that: the whole quarrel was at its height before he joined the Committee, & I may add that it was he himself that gave it its somewhat acid turn, for entre nous, though not an ill-tempered man, he dearly loves a row.

For the rest he would restore every building in England if he could, and to our minds with the necessary result of ruining them, clever ar-

[588]

chitect & able man as he is: therefore though I would be as civil to him as I could, it seems to me impossible for the S.P.A.B. to leave him alone without giving up its principles: neither will he leave us alone for the matter of that. besides, I think well enough of him to believe that he is quite in earnest about St. Marks, & would not prejudice it for sake of private pique.

As to the French Prospectus[4] — all right; there can't be much the matter with it: when I sent it for revision I didn't know that it had been struck off.

I sympathise with your revision troubles; since I have done some Icelandic, not much, or I should not now be alive to write this.

I shall be at Queen Sq: next *Thursday* from noon till 5 pm, & should be glad to see you if you were in the way: after that I am away for a week again

Yours very truly
William Morris

MS: BL, Add. MSS. 38831.

[1] This letter refers to the report of the annual meeting of the S.P.A.B. on June 24, 1880. The chairman, Stanley Leighton, noted that in the restoration of Owestry Church, G. E. Street (the architect) had covered over 170 burial stones; had the S.P.A.B. been in existence at the time, "this sacrilege might have been prevented." Morris then reported, followed by Lord Talbot de Malahide, who discussed St. Mark's and said he was pessimistic about the chances of the S.P.A.B.'s influencing the Italian government.

[2] Newman Marks was Secretary of the S.P.A.B. at this time. See next letter.

[3] The St. Mark's Committee, which was an international one, was formed on May 31, 1880 at a meeting of the Society of Arts. A circular, written by G. E. Street, was published in November 1880 with a list of signatures.

[4] The S.P.A.B. Annual Report, 1880, noted that "a Society having a similar aim to this has been set on foot in France, under the auspices of M. Guillon, an Hon. Member of this Society." It seems likely that Morris was commenting on a prospectus for this new association.

648 · To Newman Marks

Manor House
Kelmscott, Lechlade
[August 29, 1880?]

Dear Mr. Marks

I have noted the 'report' of speeches, & I think (if not sent) it might be as well not to send to *foreign* members till St M. Committee is a little established; or say till after our SPAB Committee has met.

Yours truly
W Morris

MS: Huntington.

649 • To Henry Wallis

Kelmscott House
Nr. Lechlade
[August 30-September 1, 1880]

My dear Wallis

I return a clean copy of my french friends amended prospectus:[1] you will see he had chopped it about very much: I have confidence in his judgment, & he is a literary man; but as for myself, I dont know enough French for my opinion to be of value in the matter.

Yours very truly
William Morris

ms: BL, Add. mss. 38831.

[1] See letter no. 647, n. 4.

650 • To Aglaia Ionides Coronio

Kelmscott
Thursday
[early September 1880?]

Dear Aglaia

Thank you very much about the Kermes; I can make use of it, & shall be glad to have it for this time, I have given orders about claiming & paying for it.

I am not coming up to town till Monday; almost any afternoon that week I could call in on you: which shall it be?

Yours affectionately
William Morris

ms: Berger Coll.

651 • To Jane Morris

26, Queen Square,
Bloomsbury, London
Monday
[September 20, 1880]

Dearest Janey

I am sorry to say that you won't see me till Thursday: however when you do see me I shall be in good company, as I believe De M. & his mother[1] are coming with me & also Mr. & Mrs. Richmond: this will bring up our company to what it was when we first got here: I could sleep in the cottage or preferably in the little garret if it could be got ready for me: under these circumstances of larks I suppose you will not object to staying over till the Monday or Tuesday.

All goes well as far as I know: I am glad to have a day or two of work here, as St. James' job begins to press.[2]

They are pulling down Linden House, so we shall soon know the worst of all that.

A box of grice came, so I have risked sending them on to you.

Best love to the girls; I hope they were not angry at my not waking them. What a waterspout of a morning it was! I was none the worse for it. The weather is cold but deliciously clear today. I hope you are much better. Edgar is sending on worsteds & silks.

Your loving W.M.

P.S. I shall come by the 2.15 train: to *prevent mistakes* I shall get to Kelmscott by about 5½ P.M.

MS: BL, Add. MSS. 45338.

¹ Sophia De Morgan. See letter no. 477.

² Morris and Company were called in to redecorate various parts of St. James's Palace on separate occasions between 1866 and 1882. The first involved the decoration of the Armoury and Tapestry Rooms and was probably begun by the end of September 1866 and completed by the middle of January, 1867. Philip Webb was responsible for the general scheme, though Morris had a hand in every stage of design and execution. In November 1879, A. B. Freeman-Mitford, the Secretary of the Board of Works, commissioned Morris and Co. to provide four Axminster carpets for the two State rooms previously decorated. By March 1880 these had been installed. In July 1880, Mitford wrote to the firm saying that he was directed to ask that a member of the firm meet with Ponsonby Fane and himself to discuss redecoration of the approaches in the State Apartments. Morris went himself and met with Mitford in the Lord Chamberlain's office on July 15, 1880. On August 20, Morris and Co. submitted plans to redo the Visitors' Entrance, the Grand Staircase, the Garden Entrance, the Queen's Staircase, and the Ambassadors' Staircase. The tender for this work was accepted on July 29, 1881, redecoration began in September, and by March 11, 1882 the work seems to have been completed. At about the same time, the firm furnished new curtains for the Throne Room, the Ante Room, and the Blue Room. See Charles Mitchell, "William Morris at St. James's Palace," *The Architectural Review* (January 1947), pp. 37-39. See also Henderson, *Life*, p. 215, and Clark, p. 15.

652 • FROM A LETTER TO GEORGIANA BURNE-JONES Kelmscott
[September 27, 1880]

I can't pretend not to feel being out of this house and its surroundings as a great loss. I have more than ever at my heart the importance for people of living in beautiful places; I mean the sort of beauty which would be attainable by all, if people could but begin to long for it. I do most earnestly desire that something more startling could be done than mere constant private grumbling and occasional public speaking to lift the standard of revolt against the sordidness which people are so stupid as to think necessary.

TEXT: Mackail, II, 15-16. Published: Henderson, *Letters*, 139.

653 • FROM A LETTER TO FREDERICK STARTRIDGE ELLIS [October 1880][1]

If the modern books are unsaleable, perhaps you would let me take them out after your valuation, as I have no idea what they are worth to sell (though beastly dear to buy), and though I hate them and should be glad to be rid of them as far as pleasure is concerned, they are of some use to me professionally — though by the way I am not a professional man, but a tradesman.

TEXT: Mackail, II, 87.

[1] Mackail (II, 87) dates this letter October 1882, explaining that it referred to Morris's sale of "the greater part of his valuable library, in order to devote the proceeds to the furtherance of Socialism." However, the letter was probably written in October 1880. On October 6, 1880, Ellis's partner, David White, wrote to Morris: "I have gone over the books received from you yesterday & value them at £130." He went on to mention several titles which had been on a list provided by Morris, but had not been delivered. These titles included books which Mackail says were named in the letter from which he took the extract given here. See Paul Needham, *William Morris and the Art of the Book* (New York: The Pierpont Morgan Library, 1976), p. 26. The letter from David White to Morris, quoted by Needham, is in the F. S. Ellis Archive in the Library of the University of California at Los Angeles.

654 • TO WILLIAM RALSTON SHEDDEN-RALSTON 26, Queen Square,
Bloomsbury, London
Friday [October 8, 1880?]

Dear Ralston[1]

I shall be delighted to see you and Mr. Tourgenief[2] here on Saturday, and will take you and him at your words as to matters of eating and drinking.

Yrs very truly
William Morris

MS: McMinn Papers.

[1] William Ralston Shedden-Ralston (1828-1889), Russian scholar, and translator and friend of Turgenev. From 1853 to 1875, he was assistant in the printed book department of the British Museum. Ralston was active in behalf of the St. Mark's Committee. On August 16, 1880, he sent Henry Wallis the names of several Russians who he thought

would be interested in the St. Mark's Committee. He included Turgenev's name and his address, in Paris.

² On September 12, 1880, Turgenev wrote, from Bougival, to Henry Wallis: "I accept readily the proposition to join the Comm: for the preservation of St. Mark's Church — and consider it an honour that my name should be added to the list of celebrated names, wh: belong to the members of the Comm:

I will be in London in the beginning of October — and would be very glad to make your personal acquaintance. Perhaps you would have the kindness to indicate to me the means of forwarding the aims of the committee in my native country." It seems likely that Wallis, in response to this strong expression of interest, suggested to Ralston and Turgenev that they might meet Morris and that Ralston undertook to write to him.

---

655 • To Edward Williams Byron Nicholson
26, Queen Square,
Bloomsbury, London
November 15, 1880

Dear Mr. Nicholson

Would you kindly give me the actual date of my lecture to come,[1] as it has slipped my memory.

Yours truly,
William Morris

MS: McMinn Papers.

¹ "The Prospects of Architecture in Civilization." It was delivered on March 10, 1881. See letters no. 639, n. 1 and no. 640.

---

656 • To Newman Marks
26, Queen Square,
Bloomsbury, London
November 29, 1880

Dear Mr. Marks

I enclose a copy of the draft letter to M. Gerome:[1] I have arranged that there shall be a *special* committee meeting to receive it at 4½ p.m. *next* Thursday before the Restoration Committee: will you please send out notices to likely members & don't forget Mr. Poole[2] & Mr. Wallis. I have just had Mr. Tupper[3] here complaining of the sticking in the mud of the foreign prospectuses. I thought they were all done.

Of course we can do nothing in the Cairo matter till the General Committee has received our draft so a meeting is necessary.

Mr. Poole will bring the necessary lists with him[4]

Yrs truly
William Morris

MS: Berger Coll.

¹ Jean-Léon Gérôme (1824-1904), French painter and sculptor, and professor at École des Beaux-Arts. Gérôme had proposed establishing a society for the preservation of ancient Egyptian monuments. See *The Times*, Nov. 27, 1880, p. 10.

² Reginald Stuart Poole (1832-1895), an archeologist and orientalist who lectured extensively on Egypt. He was also a keeper in the British Museum.

³ See letter no. 427, n. 1.

⁴ The S.P.A.B. had agreed that its members be signatories to Gérôme's proposal.

657 · RECIPIENT UNKNOWN [November 29? 1880]

Dear Sir[1]

You will doubtless not have forgotten that about a year and a half ago all cultivated Europe was alarmed by a report that the reckless so called restorations which have already seriously injured the artistic & historical interest of St. Marks at Venice were to be wound up by a complete rebuilding of the west front: this report was met by the Italian government putting forward what was practically an official statement that no such rebuilding was now thought of, since it was admitted that the former restorations were disastrous, and that all restorations had been put a stop to, at all events, till the whole matter should be reconsidered.[2] This statement seemed very satisfactory in itself, but within the limits pointed out by it, much doubtful work might still be done to St. Marks: and moreover, whatever might have been the recent conclusions of the Ministry of Public Instruction, those who had followed the lamentable history of the restoration of St. Marks could not doubt that there was a strong party at Venice which would try to upset these conclusions, & was prepared to deal with the building in the most reckless way. Under these circumstances, the committee, whose prospectus I enclose, was formed to strengthen the hands of those in Italy who were advocating a cautious and reasonable treatment of St. Marks, and as you will see by the names adjoined, it has been found possible to give it a thoroughly International Character.[3] The Committee wishes especially to strengthen itself by the association of men known to have devoted their lives to the study of history, and knowing with what great success you have drawn lessons for us from architectural works, and how entirely reckless restoration destroys the value of these on the historical as well as on the artistic side, cannot doubt that you sympathize with its aims, and has therefore bidden me to ask to join it & help those who are trying to preserve what is still left us of one of the most important of historical buildings.

I may add that the Italian papers report the appointment of a new commission for the repair of St. Marks, and (confidentially) that as far as we know anything of the names of the commissioners, it seems to be made up of men who take the side of destruction not preservation, and that Count Zorzi[4] who of all Italians loves St. Marks both wisely & well, has been left out of it; which seems ominous of fresh restorations like the fatal ones of the N & S sides of the Ch & of the pavement of the N. aisle.[5]

MS: Berger Coll.

[1] It seems likely that this letter was addressed to a foreign, not English, architectural historian.

[2] In *The Times*, November 27, 1879, an article by its correspondent in Rome indicated (p. 5) that a report had been sent by the Ministry of Public Information to the Minister of Foreign Affairs to be transmitted to the Italian Ambassador, General Menabrea, in London. The report asserted that the meetings in England were in fact held after the Italian Government had decided to review its policies concerning restoration.

[3] The International Committee was formed on May 31, 1880, and a circular written by G. E. Street was published in November 1880, with a list of signatures.

[4] Count Alvise Pietro Zorzi (1846-1922), a friend of Ruskin, wrote extensively on Venice and St. Mark's. He was also a member of the S.P.A.B. See *The Times*, November 22, 1879; and *The Architect*, 22 (November 22, 1879), p. 5.

[5] The draft of this letter is unsigned, but the handwriting is Morris's.

658 • To Charles Edward Mathews

26, Queen Square,
Bloomsbury, London
December 6, 1880

Dear Sir[1]

I thank you very much for your kind invitation for the banquet of the Alpine Club, & am much flattered by it, but I am obliged to refrain from dining out, because I [am] always somewhat on the verge of gout on the one hand, & on the other I really have not time to indulge myself with a fit of that leisure which is called gout: so I have to be very wary.

I am
Dear Sir
Yours very truly
William Morris

C. E. Mathews Eqre.

MS: Rosenwater Coll.

[1] Charles Edward Mathews (1834-1905) was an alpine climber and writer who helped form the Alpine Club in 1857. A resident of Birmingham, he was a close friend of Joseph Chamberlain.

659 • Three Letters to Aglaia Ionides Coronio

a.
Kelmscott House,
Upper Mall, Hammersmith
Tuesday
December 14 [1880?]

My dear Aglaia

I was away on Friday so I didn't get your letter till yesterday & was so driven that I had not time to answer it at once:

I am afraid I have missed seeing you, as I suppose you are at Herne Bay:[1] otherwise I could come in on Friday: I would have called before, but was not sure you were in town and was very busy for a chance call:

Yours affectionately
William Morris

MSS: Berger Coll.
  [1] On the coast of Kent, near Margate.

b.
Kelmscott House,
Upper Mall, Hammersmith
Tuesday
[December 21, 1880?]

My dear Aglaia

I was thinking of calling tomorrow afternoon, Wednesday: if inconvenient please write to Queen Sq: what beautiful weather!

Yours affectionately
William Morris

c.
26, Queen Square,
Bloomsbury, London
December 30, 1880

My dear Aglaia

I find that I have unluckily to go to a St Mark's meeting tomorrow & fear I shall hardly get to you before 6. I will look in however if I possibly can: I cannot help this as the meeting is important.

Yours affectionately
William Morris

INDEX OF CORRESPONDENTS

SUBJECT INDEX

silk (cont.)
301, 328, 348, 353, 363, 365-67, 369,
383-84, 388-90, 395-97, 402-404, 408,
471, 474. See also filoselle; floss; organ-
zine; tusseh
Simcox, G. A., 118n, 119n
Simon, John, 503n
Skáldskaparmál (Treatise on Poetic Dic-
tion), 243n
Skaþtar Jokul, 200
Skarphedinn, 344
"Skylark, The" (Shelley), 11
Slade Professorship of Art, W. B. Rich-
mond recommended for, 505-506, 506n
Sleigh, John, 298 and n, 315n
Smart, D. G., 262n
Smith, Edwin, 54n
Smith, Frank, 370n
Smith, Robert, 235n, 370n
Smith, Robert Payne (Dean of Canter-
bury), 373-76, 375n, 376n
Snakehead pattern, 288n, 334, 358
Snorri the Priest, 153, 154n
soap, effect of, 266, 267, 269, 283, 284,
315, 316, 389, 395-96
Social Democratic Federation, xli, 10n
Socialism, xxvii, xxix-xxx, xliv-xlviii,
455n; art and, xlv-xlvii; Edward Burne-
Jones and, 10n; Georgiana Burne-Jones
and, xli; mechanism of social change to-
ward, xlv-xlvii; Jane Morris and, xxxii-
xxxiii; May Morris and, xxxiv; state,
xlv, xlvi; as vision of the future, xlv-
xlvi, xlix
Socialist League, 401n, 577n
Society of Antiquaries of London, 493
Society for the Protection of Ancient
Buildings (S.P.A.B.; familiarly known
as "Anti-Scrape"), xxvii, xxxvii, xxxix,
45n, 77n, 352n, 356-58, 357n, 365-66n,
374n, 380-81, 412n, 413, 417n, 445 and
n, 490, 493n, 497, 506n, 512, 523, 525,
566n; Annual Report of (1880), 588 and
n, 589n; The Athenaeum and, 363n, 523;
Baptistery at Ravenna and, 570-72,
573n; Canterbury Cathedral restoration
and, 375n, 376, 379-81; Thomas Carlyle
and, 361 and n; Collegiate Church of
Southwell Minster and, 479-81, 490-92;
Coventry Patmore and, 391n; De Mor-

gan and, 361n; first resolution of (1879),
514; Manifesto of, 359, 359-60n, 366,
545n; Rossetti and, 359, 360n; Ruskin
invited to annual meeting of (1880),
569-70, 570n; Ruskin's Seven Lamps of
Architecture quoted by, 368n, 383; St.
Alban's Abbey and Cathedral and, 493,
495-96; St. Germain's Church (Isle of
Man) and, 507-508; St. Mark's restora-
tion and, 526n, 530n, 538, 539n, 544-
45, 588, 589 and n, 592n, 593 and n;
Salisbury Cathedral and, 587, 588n;
structural repairs to ancient buildings
and, 510; Tewkesbury minster and, 361;
George Wardle and, 357-58, 365n;
T. E. Wardle and, 363, 368n; Water Gate
of York House and, 510-11; P. S. Webb
and, 357, 359
Soðlasmiðus, Jón (Jón Jónsson; John Sad-
dlesmith), 170, 171n, 207, 223, 245
Solomon, Simeon, portrait of Edward
Burne-Jones by, 27 (illus.)
"Some Hints of House Decoration" (lec-
ture), 579n
Songs in a Cornfield (Christina Rossetti),
74n
sonnets, 573, 574
Sonning, 582
Sorcerer, The (Gilbert and Sullivan), 418,
420
Sotheby's Sales Catalogue of Morris's li-
brary (1898), 321n
South Kensington Museum, 46 and n, 51,
105n, 110n, 116n; India Museum collec-
tion at, 256n
Southwell Cathedral (Minster), 514, 523,
524n; Collegiate Church of, 479-81,
481n, 490-92
Sparling, H. Halliday, xxxv, 62n, 165n
Spartali, Marie, 116n
Spectator, The, 29n, 52, 113n, 119n, 423n
speeches: "Address to the English Liber-
als," 428n, 431n; "The Art of the Peo-
ple," 509n; Cambridge School of Art
(1878), 440n, 449n, 450, 451; at January
16, 1878, meeting, 435, 436n; "Opening
of the Dardanelles," 433n. See also lec-
tures
Spencer, Herbert, 433n
Spiers, Richard Phené, 586, 587n, 588n

THE COLLECTED LETTERS OF

WILLIAM MORRIS

COMPOSED IN LINOTRON BEMBO AND
PRINTED ON WARREN'S 1854 BY
PRINCETON UNIVERSITY PRESS

BOUND IN HOLLISTON ROXITE BY
SHORT RUN BINDERY

ENDPAPER DESIGN AFTER THE BRUGES WALLPAPER
CREATED BY WILLIAM MORRIS IN 1887

DESIGNED BY LAURY A. EGAN